Intellectual Property Taxation

Carolina Academic Press
Law Casebook Series
Advisory Board

Gary J. Simson, Chairman
Cornell Law School

Raj K. Bhala
University of Kansas School of Law

John C. Coffee, Jr.
Columbia University School of Law

Randall Coyne
University of Oklahoma Law Center

John S. Dzienkowski
University of Texas School of Law

Paul Finkelman
University of Tulsa College of Law

Robert M. Jarvis
Shepard Broad Law Center
Nova Southeastern University

Vincent R. Johnson
St. Mary's University School of Law

Michael A. Olivas
University of Houston Law Center

Kenneth Port
William Mitchell College of Law

Michael P. Scharf
Case Western Reserve University Law School

Peter M. Shane
H. J. Heinz III School of Public Policy and Management
Carnegie Mellon University

Emily L. Sherwin
University of San Diego School of Law

John F. Sutton, Jr.
Emeritus, University of Texas School of Law

David B. Wexler
University of Arizona College of Law

Intellectual Property Taxation

Problems and Materials

Jeffrey A. Maine

Xuan-Thao Nguyen

CAROLINA ACADEMIC PRESS
Durham, North Carolina

Copyright © 2004
Jeffrey A. Maine and
Xuan-Thao N. Nguyen
All Rights Reserved

ISBN 0-89089-431-0
LCCN 2003106098

CAROLINA ACADEMIC PRESS
700 Kent Street
Durham, North Carolina 27701
Telephone (919) 489-7486
Fax (919) 493-5668
www.cap-press.com

Printed in the United States of America

Contents

Chapter 1.	**Introduction**	3
	Case Example	4
Chapter 2.	**Overview of Intellectual Property**	7
	I. Assignment for Chapter 2	7
	II. Problems for Chapter 2	7
	III. Overview	8
	A. Patents	8
	Types of Patents	12
	B. Trade Secrets	13
	C. Copyrights	15
	D. Trademarks, Trade Names, and Trade Dress	16
	E. Domain Names	18
	F. Computer Software	19
	IV. Materials	20
	Diamond v. Chakrabarty	20
	Feist Publications, Inc. v. Rural Telephone Service Co.	22
	Community for Creative Non-Violence v. Reid	24
	Holtzbrinck Publishing Holdings v. Vyne Communications	26
	Data General Corp. v. Grumman Systems Support Corp.	32
	Two Pesos, Inc. v. Taco Cabana, Inc.	39
	Interstellar Starship Services, Ltd. v. Tchou	41
Chapter 3.	**Overview of Federal Income Taxation**	51
	I. Assignment for Chapter 3	51
	II. Problems for Chapter 3	51
	III. Overview	53
	A. Structure of the Federal Income Tax System	54
	1. Gross Income	54
	2. Deductions	57
	3. Tax Rates	60
	4. Tax Credits	64
	B. Researching Federal Tax Law	64
	1. The Internal Revenue Code	64
	2. Treasury Regulations	65
	3. IRS Rulings and Procedures	66
	(a) Revenue Rulings	66

(b) Private Letter Rulings	66
(c) Revenue Procedures	67
4. Case Law	67
5. Legislative History	68
IV. Materials	68
Commissioner v. Groetzinger	68
Welch v. Helvering	72
Commissioner v. Lincoln Savings & Loan Ass'n	74
INDOPCO, Inc. v. Commissioner	79
Waterman v. Mackenzie	84
Burnet v. Logan	85
Williams v. McGowan	87
Raytheon Production Corp. v. Commissioner	89

Chapter 4. Taxation of Intellectual Property Development

I. Assignment for Chapter 4	91
II. Problems for Chapter 4	91
III. Overview	93
A. Deductibility Under § 162—Ordinary and Necessary Business Expenses	93
1. The "Expense" Requirement	94
(a) Section 263(a): Capital Expenditures	94
(b) Section 263A: Direct and Indirect Expenditures Incurred to Produce Tangible Property	96
2. The "Ordinary and Necessary" Requirement	97
3. The "In Carrying on a Trade or Business" Requirement	97
B. Deductibility Under § 174—Research and Experimental Expenditures	99
1. Research and Experimental Expenditures	99
2. Disqualified Expenditures	100
3. "In Connection with a Trade or Business" Requirement	101
4. Reasonableness of Expenditures	103
5. The Election to Expense or Amortize	103
(a) Current Expense Method	103
(b) Deferred Expense (Amortization) Method	103
C. Alternative Minimum Tax Considerations	104
D. Amortization of Capitalized Intellectual Property Development Costs	105
E. The § 41 Research and Development Credit	106
1. "Qualified Research" Defined	106
(a) Discovery Test	106
(b) Process of Experimentation	107
2. Activities Excluded from "Qualified Research"	108
(a) Research After Commercial Production	108
(b) Internal-Use Computer Software	109
IV. Materials	110
RJR Nabisco, Inc. v. Commissioner	110
Action on Decision	116
Technical Advice Memorandum 9643003	117
I.R.S. Notice 88-62	121
Vitale v. Commissioner	126
Field Service Advice 200125019	135

Snow v. Commissioner	141
Green v. Commissioner	143
Revenue Procedure 2000-50	148

Chapter 5. Taxation of Intellectual Property Acquisitions — 151
- I. Assignment for Chapter 5 — 151
- II. Problems for Chapter 5 — 151
- III. Overview — 153
  - A. Purchase Costs — 153
    - 1. Amortization Under § 197 — 154
      - (a) General Rule — 154
      - (b) Exceptions for Certain Intellectual Property — 154
      - (c) Computing the § 197 Deduction — 156
    - 2. Amortization Under § 167 — 157
      - (a) General Rule — 157
      - (b) Computing the § 167 Deduction — 157
  - B. Licensing of Intellectual Property — 160
    - 1. Licenses Acquired as Part of a Trade or Business — 160
    - 2. Licenses Not Acquired As Part of a Trade or Business — 161
  - C. Income from Holding Intellectual Property — 161
- IV. Materials — 162
  - Revenue Ruling 71-177 — 162
  - Revenue Ruling 60-358 — 163
  - Revenue Ruling 79-285 — 164
  - *Greene v. Commissioner* — 167
  - *Associated Patentees, Inc. v. Commissioner* — 171
  - Revenue Ruling 67-136 — 175
  - Private Letter Ruling 200137013 — 176

Chapter 6. Taxation of Intellectual Property Transfers — 181
- I. Assignment for Chapter 6 — 181
- II. Problems for Chapter 6 — 181
- III. Overview — 183
  - A. Sales of Intellectual Property — 185
    - 1. General Characterization Provisions — 186
      - (a) The Sale or Exchange Requirement — 187
      - (b) The Definition of Capital Asset — 187
      - (c) Holding Period — 189
    - 2. Special Characterization Provisions — 189
      - (a) Section 1231: Quasi-Capital Assets — 189
      - (b) Section 1235: Transfers of All Substantial Rights to Patents — 190
      - (c) Sections 1239 and 707(b) Ordinary Income — 193
      - (d) Section 1245 Recapture — 194
      - (e) Section 1253 Transfers — 195
    - 3. Contingent Payment Sales — 195
  - B. Licenses of Intellectual Property — 197
  - C. Transfers to Business Entities — 197
  - D. Transfers to Charitable Organizations — 199

CONTENTS

IV. Materials	200
Watson v. Commissioner	200
Revenue Ruling 60-226	202
Stern v. United States	203
Levy v. Commissioner	208
Chilton v. Commissioner	210
Kueneman v. Commissioner	217
E.I. du Pont de Nemours & Co. v. United States	224
Revenue Ruling 78-328	228
Newton Insert Co. v. Commissioner	229
Stokely USA, Inc. v. Commissioner	236
Chapter 7. IP Holding Companies and R&D Limited Partnerships	**243**
I. Assignment for Chapter 7	243
II. Problems for Chapter 7	243
III. Overview	244
A. Intellectual Property (IP) Holding Companies	245
1. Formation of IP Holding Companies	246
(a) Tax Treatment of Parent Company	246
(b) Tax Treatment of IP Holding Company	247
2. Transfer-License Back Intellectual Property Arrangements	247
(a) Tax Treatment of IP Holding Company	248
(b) Tax Treatment of the Parent Company	249
3. Dividend Distributions to Parent Company	251
4. Liquidations of IP Holding Companies into Parent Companies	252
(a) Tax Treatment of the Parent Company	252
(b) Tax Treatment of the IP Holding Company	252
B. Research and Development (R&D) Limited Partnerships	253
1. Formation of R&D Limited Partnerships	255
(a) Partner-Level Consequences	255
(b) Partnership-Level Consequences	256
2. Operation of R&D Limited Partnerships	256
(a) Basic Structure of Partnership Taxation	256
(b) Non-Liquidating Distributions of Cash and Property to Partners	257
3. Liquidation of R&D Limited Partnerships	258
IV. Materials	258
Delaware State Statute (Del. Code Ann. tit. 30, § 1902)	258
Vermont State Statute (Vt. Stat. Ann. tit. 32, § 5837)	259
Massachusetts State Statute (M.G.L.A. 62C, § 3A)	259
Geoffrey, Inc. v. South Carolina Tax Commission	260
Acme Royalty Co. v. Director of Revenue	264
SYL v. Comptroller of the Treasury	271
Syms Corp. v. Commissioner of Revenue	275
In re Sherwin-Williams Co.	279
Sherwin-Williams C. v. Commissioner	283
Department of Taxes, State of Vermont	290
Harris v. Commissioner	292
Scoggins v. Commissioner	298

CONTENTS

Chapter 8. Taxation of Intellectual Property Litigation	305
I. Assignment for Chapter 8	305
II. Problems for Chapter 8	305
III. Overview	307
A. Tax Treatment of Intellectual Property Litigation Costs	307
1. Litigation Costs in Patent and Copyright Cases	308
2. Litigation Costs in Trademark Cases	309
(a) Litigation Costs Incurred in Trademark Infringement Cases	309
(b) Litigation Costs Incurred in Unfair Competition Claims	309
B. Tax Treatment of Damage Awards and Settlement Proceeds in Intellectual Property Suits	310
1. Damage Awards or Settlement Proceeds in Patent/Copyright Cases	310
2. Damage Awards/Settlement Proceeds in Trademark Cases	311
3. Tax Treatment of Awards of Attorneys' Fees and Costs	311
C. Tax Treatment of Payments of Acquiring Intellectual Property Liability	312
IV. Materials	312
Safety Tube Corp. v. Commissioner	312
Urquhart v. Commissioner	314
Danskin, Inc. v. Commissioner	317
Georator Corp. v. United States	318
Rust-Oleum Corp. v. United States	320
Big Four Industries, Inc. v. Commissioner	325
Mathey v. Commissioner	326
Inco Electroenergy Corp. v. Commissioner	329
Illinois Tool Works v. Commissioner	334
Field Service Advisory 199925012	339
Chapter 9. Taxation of International IP Transactions and Cost Sharing Arrangements	345
I. Assignment for Chapter 9	345
II. Problems for Chapter 9	345
III. Overview	347
A. Outbound Transactions	348
1. General Taxing Rules	348
(a) Foreign Business Operations Conducted Directly by U.S. Persons	348
(b) Foreign Business Operations Conducted Indirectly	348
2. The Foreign Tax Credit	350
B. Inbound Transactions	351
1. General Taxing Rules	351
2. Taxation of Business Income	351
(a) In General	351
(b) Treaty Exceptions	352
3. Taxation of Non-Business Income from U.S. Sources	353
(a) "Fixed or Determinable, Annual or Periodical" Income	353
(b) Treaty Exceptions	353
C. Source Rules	354
1. Income Source Rules	354
(a) Personal Services	354

(b) Royalties	354
(c) Sales	355
(d) Infringement Awards	356
2. Deduction Allocation and Apportionment Rules	356
(a) In General	356
(b) Research and Development Expenditures	356
D. The Role of Treaties	357
1. In General	357
2. The Relationship Between Treaties and the Code	357
E. Section 367(d): Transfers to Foreign Corporations	357
F. Section 482: International IP Transactions Between Related Parties	358
G. Cost Sharing Arrangements	359
1. Two or More Participants	360
(a) Reasonably Anticipated Benefits Requirement	360
(b) Accounting Requirements	361
(c) Administrative Requirements	361
2. Method for Calculating Each Participant's Share of Intellectual Property Development Costs	361
(a) Share of Intellectual Property Development Costs	361
(b) Share of Reasonably Anticipated Benefits	362
3. Periodic Adjustments	362
4. Documentation Requirements	363
5. Buy-in and Buy-out Payments for Intellectual Property Transfers	363
IV. Materials	364
Excerpt from The Joint Committee on Taxation, Description and Analysis of Present-Law Rules Relating to International Taxation (JCX-40-99), June 28, 1999	364
Boulez v. Commissioner	367
Revenue Ruling 68-443	372
Revenue Ruling 72-232	373
Revenue Ruling 80-362	374
SDI Netherlands B.V. v. Commissioner	375
International Multifoods Corp. v. Commissioner	380
Revenue Ruling 64-206	386
DHL v. Commissioner	388
Field Service Advice 200011021	398
Seagate Technology, Inc. v. Commissioner	409
Chapter 10. Internet/E-Commerce Taxation	**415**
I. Assignment for Chapter 10	415
II. Problems for Chapter 10	415
III. Overview	416
A. The Internet Nondiscrimination Act and The Internet Tax Freedom Act	417
1. No New Tax on Internet Service Access	417
2. No Multiple Taxes on Electronic Commerce Transactions	417
3. No Discriminatory Taxes on Electronic Commerce Transactions	418
B. State Taxation on Internet Sales	418
1. Substantial Nexus Standard—Offline Environment	419
2. Substantial Nexus—Internet Implications	419

3. States' Sales Taxes on Electronic Commerce Transactions	420
IV. Materials	421
Internet Tax Freedom Act, 47 U.S.C. § 151	421
Quill v. North Dakota	425
NEW YORK ADVISORY OPINION, TSB-A-02(7)(S)	433
Wal-Mart Stores, Inc. v. City of Mobile	437
Andersen Consulting, LLP v. Comm'r of Revenue Services	439
NEW YORK ADVISORY OPINION, TSB-A-02(13)(S)	442
NEW YORK ADVISORY OPINION, TSB-A-02(3)(C)	444
NEW YORK ADVISORY OPINION, Pet. No. 5000510A	448
Charts of State Taxation of Online Transactions	
Chart A: Sales of Goods & Information	452
Chart B: Pre-packaged and Custom Software	462
Table of Cases	471
Table of Statutes and Administrative Material	479
Index	489

Acknowledgments

We wish to thank the students whom we have had the pleasure of teaching using these materials and Professors Mary LaFrance, Annette Nellen, David Andrade and other professors who adopted this book in their IP tax courses before it was in final form.

We are particularly indebted to Professor David Cameron of Northwestern University School of Law who provided perceptive comments and concrete suggestions to earlier versions of this book. Professor David Cameron and Professor Philip Postlewaite are pioneers in the field of taxation of intangible property, paving the way for new books and scholarship in IP taxation. We could not have completed the book without the contribution from Professor Anna Teller whose research and editorial assistance was invaluable. We thank Mr. Bruce Muck, Head Research Services at SMU Underwood Law Library for his research assistance.

We wish to express our gratitude to Professor Richard Gershon and Professor Jim Hambleton for providing us tremendous encouragement and support throughout the project. We also wish to thank Joy Gallagher for her patience and endless hours of revising the manuscript through its numerous drafts, keeping us organized, and putting up with our handwriting while incorporating changes. We thank Nancy Eagan for assisting us in the later revision of the book.

In addition to all of those students who labored on the book, special thanks are due to: Michelle Carlson, Jennifer Di Fonso, Cindy Fuqua, Robert Jemerson, Christina Jenkins, Stephen Jones, Kimberly Latham, and Mari Stewart.

Professor Maine would like to thank his mentors Professor Richard Gershon, Professor John (Jack) Miller, and Professor Meade Emory, whose constant support and guidance have led him into a fulfilling professional life. Professor Maine dedicates this book to his family and close friends who constantly remind him that there is more to life than IP tax.

Professor Nguyen also would like to thank Professor Danielle Jones-Conway, Professor Lateef Mtima and Professor Benjamin Davis for their suggestions and support. Professor Nguyen thanks her mentors Professor Hope Lewis, Professor David Hall, Professor John Flynn, Dean and Professor Gilbert Holmes, Maxim H. Waldbaum, Esq., and Lora A. Moffatt, Esq. for their guidance. Professor Nguyen dedicates this book to her soul mate and partner, Erik Darwin Hille and her son Khai-Leif Nguyen-Hille.

Finally, we extend our appreciation to Professors Martin Burke and Michael Friel for inspiring us to adopt their pedagogical approach. Writing this book was a joy for us. We could not believe that combining intellectual property and taxation for the first casebook was a stimulating, challenging, and satisfying experience. We hope that you will enjoy this book.

Intellectual Property Taxation

Chapter 1

Introduction

This casebook provides interdisciplinary coverage of two exciting areas of the law: intellectual property and taxation. Intellectual property has become enormously important in recent years. Valuable business assets are increasingly in the form of intangible assets such as patents, trade secrets, copyrights, trademarks, trade names, and computer software. Moreover, with the arrival of global, e-commerce transactions on the Internet, new forms of intellectual property, such as domain names and web contents, have emerged. Major transactions involving these old and new forms of intellectual property have different tax consequences depending on the form of intellectual property involved. It is important for students of both intellectual property law and tax law to have a strong understanding of the unique tax treatment of intellectual property transactions, such as intellectual property creation, development, acquisition, sales and licenses, as well as the complex tax treatment of litigation expenses and damage awards and settlements.

A separate course on intellectual property taxation is necessary for several reasons. For starters, although there are general tax principles equally applicable to most types of intellectual property, there are special, mutually exclusive tax rules governing different forms of intellectual property. As students soon learn, applying general and special tax provisions to intellectual property transactions is not always easy. This is due in part to the expansion of intellectual property as eluded to above. For example, tax rules do not exist that specifically govern the tax treatment of domain names and web sites. This is also due to the expansion of rights for certain forms of intellectual property. For example, the tax treatment of computer software can be tricky due to the fact that software may be protected as a patent, as a copyright, or as a trade secret.

Another reason a separate course on intellectual property taxation is necessary is that the roles of intellectual property lawyers and tax practitioners have changed due to the expansion of intellectual property. Intellectual property lawyers, for instance, are no longer the lonely prosecutors in the back office. Intellectual property lawyers now serve as advisors to their clients' businesses and must be prepared to answer such questions as: (1) should a client's intellectual property be transferred to an intellectual property holding company; (2) how should a client's intellectual property assignment be structured so as to ensure preferential tax treatment; (3) what is the proper tax treatment of damage awards and settlement proceeds received by a client in intellectual property litigation; and (4) is a client required to collect state sales tax for the distribution of on-line contents, such as digital music and photographic images? With a thorough understanding of the tax treatment of these and other significant transactions, intellectual property lawyers will no longer have to summarily pass the client's inquiry to tax lawyers who often turn around and ask the intellectual property lawyers what the difference is between a copyright and a trademark!

Tax practitioners must also be prepared to handle intellectual property taxation matters, which is a difficult task if they lack an understanding of the different forms of intellectual property and how each is developed, acquired, or licensed. While students may have received some exposure to tax, they may not know the special tax rules that specifically relate to intellectual property. Moreover, most introductory tax courses are limited to federal tax issues and not state and international tax issues. As students will learn, state tax issues often dictate whether and where a client should form an IP holding company or where it should have its website hosted. A separate course in intellectual property taxation can devote sufficient time to the complexities and risks of forming research and development limited partnerships and IP holding companies. Sufficient attention can also be devoted to issues such as whether the presence of a website on a computer server establishes substantial nexus for state taxing authorities to require Internet vendors to collect sales taxes.

For the reasons above, this book was created to provide comprehensive coverage of intellectual property taxation issues. This book adopts the problem method in addressing intellectual property taxation, and covers both general and special tax principles governing different forms of intellectual property. This book presents ten chapters, each of which is devoted to the taxation of a major IP transaction such as intellectual property research and development, acquisitions, sales and licenses, and judgment awards and settlements. Separate chapters are devoted to taxation of Internet transactions, international transfers, and the formation and operation of IP holding companies and R&D partnerships. Each chapter contains a set of relevant problems, a summary of the black letter law, and excerpts of important cases and administrative pronouncements.

Chapter 2 provides a comprehensive overview of the different forms of intellectual property, both the "old" and the "new" intellectual property, summarizing the scope and terms of protection for each form. Similarly, Chapter 3 provides an overview of federal income taxation to ensure the student has the proper foundation for studying intellectual property taxation. Chapter 4 analyzes the tax treatment of research and development expenditures for self-created forms of intellectual property, whereas Chapter 5 explores the tax treatment of intellectual property acquisition (purchase and license) costs. Chapter 6 discusses the tax implications from the transfer of different forms of intellectual property, demonstrating how intellectual property assignments should be structured to receive preferential tax treatment.

Chapter 7 analyzes IP holding companies and R&D limited partnerships. Chapter 8 provides an in-depth analysis of the tax treatment of intellectual property litigation expenses as well as the taxability of damage awards and settlement proceeds received in litigation. Chapter 9 reviews special tax considerations of foreign-related intellectual property transfers (both outbound and inbound transactions), and discusses cost sharing arrangements for intellectual property (one of the hottest and most controversial areas in the international tax area). Chapter 10 explores Internet and e-commerce taxation, and provides comprehensive coverage of state sales taxation of intangible goods, software, and information (web contents).

Case Example

Consider the issues raised below. You do not need to research to find the correct answer. Instead, think about each issue and other factors that may impact NewCo's tax liability.

NewCo is a large chemical company incorporated in Delaware with research and development facilities in the United States and overseas. NewCo hires numerous scientists and assistants to develop new chemical products. NewCo prosecutes some patent applications in-house, but farms out the majority of the prosecution work along with other intellectual property related projects to a law firm at a discounted rate. NewCo is very eager to develop its intellectual property portfolio and is aggressive in its intellectual property development and protection program. What will be the tax treatment for the costs incurred by NewCo in developing its patents, trade secrets, copyrights, trademarks, and goodwill associated with various trademarked chemical products? Will these different forms of intellectual property be treated the same for tax purposes?

If NewCo decides to expand its market share and acquire intellectual property assets from a competitor, what are the tax issues related to the acquisition of all the intellectual property assets? If NewCo decides only to acquire the competitor's most valuable trademarks and associated goodwill, what will be tax consequences of such acquisition? Is the tax treatment of a separate trademark acquisition the same as for an acquisition of a group of intellectual property assets acquired together with the competitor's ongoing trade or business?

If NewCo wishes to transfer all or some of its intellectual property to affiliates overseas, what would be the major tax issues? If NewCo decides instead to transfer some of its inventions to a third party, how should the assignment be structured and drafted to achieve advantageous tax results? What if NewCo wants to divide its exclusive rights in a copyright and transfer only one of the five exclusive rights to a competitor. Such transfer is allowed under copyright law, but is it also allowed under tax law? What tax treatment results if one of the intellectual property transfers is subject to a geographical limitation or field of use restriction? Would the tax results of each assignment differ depending on the form of payments (lump sum versus contingent fees)?

NewCo contemplates forming an intellectual property (IP) holding company after hearing rumors about the benefits of the IP holding company model. What are the benefits and risks associated with the formation of an IP holding company? In which state should NewCo form the IP holding company? What activities will the IP holding company be allowed to engage in without losing tax benefits?

To protect its intellectual property assets, NewCo has an aggressive enforcement program. What if NewCo discovers that one of its licensees has breached a patent agreement and claimed that it owns the licensing patent at issue, and NewCo wants to initiate a suit against the licensee to resolve the ownership of the patent in dispute? How should it treat the costs incurred in the suit for federal tax purposes? If it is determined that the licensee also uses a trademark very similar to NewCo's without permission, and NewCo wants to assert both trademark infringement and unfair competition claims against the licensee, how should it treat the litigation costs in each claim? If NewCo settles the case and receives a large sum from the licensee, what is the tax treatment for the sum received? If two years ago NewCo assumed the risk of intellectual property litigation involving a patent purchased by NewCo from a competitor, what is the proper tax treatment for the assumption of the risk?

NewCo obtains a license to use certain intellectual property from a foreign company for NewCo's products sold in that country. What is the tax treatment of the income generated from the sales of such products in the foreign country? In the United States? And what is the tax treatment of the royalties paid by NewCo to the foreign licensor? On the other hand, if NewCo decides to license out its intellectual property rights to one of NewCo's many foreign subsidiaries, what is the tax treatment for the payments received by NewCo under its license with foreign subsidiaries? If NewCo decides to sell a franchise operation in the far East together with trademarks and goodwill, what is the proper tax treatment for the sale?

NewCo decides to venture into the software industry and create a start-up company, NewCo Online (NCO), to sell software and related services online. NCO selects a memorable domain name, builds a terrific website structure, and creates web contents in-house. What is the proper tax treatment for costs of purchasing a domain name, building a website structure, and developing web contents? Some contents are copyrightable and other contents are not copyrightable. Is the tax treatment for one type of content the same for the other types of contents? Must NCO collect state sale taxes for all fifty states since NCO is selling its products and services to consumers in all fifty states? Worldwide? Does NCO have substantial nexus in each state's taxing jurisdiction?

Chapter 2

Overview of Intellectual Property

I. Assignment for Chapter 2

Read: Overview

Materials: *Diamond v. Chakrabarty*
Feist Publications, Inc. v. Rural Telephone Service Co.
Community for Creative Non-Violence v. Reid
Holtzbrinck Publishing v. Vyne Communications
Data General Corp. v. Grumman Systems Support Corp.
Two Pesos v. Taco Cabana, Inc.
Interstellar Starship Services, Ltd. v. Tchou

Complete the Problems.

II. Problems for Chapter 2

1. JoJoBa is in the business of manufacturing body lotion. The company sends a research team to the Arizona desert to investigate a special cactus extraction. The researchers are successful in identifying the cactus and collecting a creamy liquid substance. JoJoBa submits a patent application for the creamy liquid substance. Will JoJoBa be entitled to patent protection?

2. Data Generator spends significant resources to gather financial information and license the financial database to various brokerage firms. Data Generator wants to obtain copyright registration for its database. Will Data Generator be successful in its copyright registration attempt?

3. SoftCo is a computer software company based in Redmond, Washington. The company spends an estimated amount of $500 million on software research and development. What protection is available for computer software programs? If both copyright and patent protection are available for some of SoftCo's computer software programs, which protection should SoftCo select?

4. SoftCo has been very successful in the software industry because it possesses important trade secrets and know-how relating to software and software business.

Discuss how SoftCo maintains trade secret protection. Why does SoftCo want trade secret protection for some software technologies and patent protection for others?

5. SoftCo develops many operating and users manuals accompanying the software packages distributed to consumers worldwide. SoftCo wants to know whether copyright protection is available for such manuals. What is the term of protection for such manuals? SoftCo hires a known technical artist to provide illustrations and special charts to be included in the manuals. Does SoftCo own the copyright in the illustrations and charts?

6. SoftCo decides to select the trademark MacroSoft for its latest computer software after it has conducted several focus groups. Further, SoftCo hires a website design firm to create a website for the launch of the new software. To direct potential Internet consumers to the website, SoftCo inserts repetition of the word "macrosoft" in the metatags. MacroSoft seems to be a good trademark, but it looks too much like the MicroSoft trademark owned by the other known company that is also located in Redmond, Washington. MicroSoft threatens to sue SoftCo for trademark infringement and unfair competition. Explain how SoftCo should defend its action.

7. Further to Problem 6, what protection, if any, is available for SoftCo's website? Who owns the website?

8. SoftCo decides to register its tradename "SoftCo" as a domain name in the top level domain .com. How should SoftCo obtain such domain name? What protection, if any, is available for the domain name, softco.com?

III. Overview

Intellectual property is becoming an increasingly valuable business asset. Patents, copyrights, trademarks, trade secrets, domain names, and web content are the currency of many businesses in today's economy. The creation, development, acquisitions, sales and licensing of intellectual property have significant tax consequences. It is necessary for practitioners of intellectual property and tax law to have a comprehensive understanding of intellectual property taxation.

A. Patents

Article I, Section 8 of the United States Constitution authorizes Congress to grant exclusive rights for a limited time to inventors for their discoveries. U.S. CONST. art. I, §8. Not all discoveries or inventions will receive patent protection. Patent law only protects inventions that can satisfy five statutory requirements: the invention falls within patentable subject matter; it has utility; it is novel; it is nonobvious; and its disclosure enables others to make and use the invention.

Process, machine, manufacture, and composition of matter are the types of inventions considered for patent protection. The Supreme Court in *Diamond v. Chakrabarty*, included below, interpreted the scope of patentable subject matter to include human-made bacterium. The decision opened the door of patent protection for other human creation such as genetically engineered mice, sheep, and human DNA sequences. In

1998, during the explosive growth of the Internet, the Court of Appeals for the Federal Circuit expanded the scope of patentable subject matter to include methods of doing business that do not rely on anything tangible. *State Street Bank & Trust Co. v. Signature Fin. Group, Inc.*, 149 F.3d 1368 (Fed. Cir. 1998). The *State Street* court declared that the transformation of data, representing discrete dollar amounts, by a machine through a series of mathematical calculations into a final share price, constitutes a practical application of a mathematical algorithm, formula, or calculation, because it produces a "useful, concrete and tangible result." 149 F.3d at 1373. Computer implemented operations that produce a practical application of a mathematical algorithm constitute statutory subject matter even though there is no transformation of subject matter outside the computer.

Subsequently, the Federal Circuit affirmed its previous holding, observing that patent law must adapt to new and innovative concepts, while remaining true to basic principles. *AT&T Corp. v. Excel Communications, Inc.*, 172 F.3d 1352, 1354 (Fed. Cir. 1999). The Federal Circuit held in *AT & T* that a computer-related method claim without physical representation did not disqualify the algorithm from statutory patentable subject matter. In that case the method claim of "generating a message record for an interexchange call" and recording the call for billing purposes is patentable subject matter because the method yields a concrete, tangible, and useful result. *AT&T Corp.*, 172 F.3d at 1354.

The second statutory requirement is utility. In other words, an invention must be useful. This requirement is easily satisfied through a showing that the invention works in an experimental setting. There is no need to establish utility through actual use in the factory or the field. This low threshold is raised to a higher standard when the invention is pharmaceutical related.

Novelty, the third requirement, determines whether the inventor is the first to make the invention as claimed. Under the novelty test, if the claimed invention was known or used by others in the United States, or patented or described in a printed publication in the United States or a foreign country before the invention date, such invention is disqualified from becoming a patent. Obviously, the inventor's own conduct is not included as a bar under the test. However, the inventor's own conduct, such as a failure to file a patent application within one year of invention disclosure at a conference, in a scientific publication, or during an offer to the invention, will bar the inventor from obtaining patent protection. Moreover, if a third party stole the invention and sold it to others over one year prior to the date the inventor applies for patent protection, such sale will bar the inventor from obtaining patent protection for the invention. *Evans Cooling Systems, Inc. v. General Motors Corp.*, 125 F.3d 1448, 1454 (Fed. Cir. 1997).

The nonobviousness requirement represents the most important condition of patentability. It measures, through a combination of references, whether the claimed invention is obvious to those of ordinary skill in the field of the invention. *See, e.g., Karsten Mfg. Corp. v. Cleveland Golf Co.*, 242 F.3d 1376, 1385 (Fed Cir. 2001) ("In holding an invention obvious in view of a combination of references, there must be some suggestions, motivations, or teaching in the prior art that would have led a person of ordinary skill in the art to select the references and combine them in a way that would produce the claimed invention."); *C.R. Bard Inc. v. M3 Sys., Inc.*, 157 F.3d 1340, 1352 (Fed. Cir. 1998) (stating that a showing of a suggestion, teaching, a motivation to combine the prior art references is an "essential evidentiary component of an obviousness holding"). Specifically, the inquiry determines the scope and content of the prior art, the differences between the claimed invention at issue and the prior art, and the level of ordinary skill in the pertinent art. *See Graham v. John Deere Co.*, 383 U.S. 1, 17 (1966). In other words, the claimed invention will be disqualified and not entitled to patent protection if it contains an insignificant advancement in the field of the invention. 35 U.S.C. §103(a) ("A patent may not be obtained though the invention is not identically disclosed or described as set forth in section 102 of this title, if the differences between the subject matter sought to be patented and the prior art are such that the subject matter as a whole would have been obvious at the time the invention was made to a person having ordinary skill in the art to which said subject matter pertains.").

Enablement, the last patentability requirement, requires that the specification of the patent adequately disclose the claimed invention so as to enable a persona skilled in the art to use and make the invention at the time the patent application was filed without undue experimentation. *See* 35 U.S.C. §103(a) ("A patent may not be obtained though the invention is not identically disclosed or described as set forth in section 102 of this title, if the differences between the subject matter sought to be patented and the prior art are such that the subject matter as a whole would have been obvious at the time the invention was made to a person having ordinary skill in the art to which said subject matter pertains.").

A patent specification complies with the requirement even if a reasonable amount of routine experimentation is required in order to use or make the invention, as long as such experimentation is not undue. *Enzo Biochem Inc. v. Calgene, Inc.*, 188 F.3d 1362,1371 (Fed. Cir. 1999). Specifications providing little guidance as the make and use of the claimed invention may amount to "no more than a plan or invitation to practice" the claimed invention. *See, e.g., Enzo Biochem*, 188 F3d at 1374; *In re Vaeck*, 947 F.2d 488, 496 & n.23 (Fed. Cir. 1991) (concluding the teachings set forth in the specifications failed to provide any thing more than a plan or invitation for those skill in the art to experiment practicing antisense in eukaryotic cells.")

A way to comply with the enablement requirement is to include a disclosure of operative embodiments in the specification. *See, e.g., In re Swartz*, 232 F.3d 862 (Fed. Cir. 2000) (affirming the Board of Patent Appeals and Interferences's decision that application failed to meet the enablement requirement because the specification contained no disclosure of any operative embodiment); *In re Wands*, 858 F.2d 731, 737 (Fed. Cir. 1988)(considering factors for enablement such as (1) the quantity of experimentation necessary; (2) the amount of direction or guidance presented, (3) the presence or absence of working examples, (4) the nature of the invention, (5) the state of the prior art, (6) the relative skill of those in the art, (7) the predictability or unpredictability of the art, and (8) the breadth of the claims).

The enablement requirement serves to preclude the patent owners from later claiming that their patent includes an invention that they did not possess at the time of the filing of the patent application. *In re Karl Ziegler*, 992 F.2d 1197, 1200 (Fed. Cir. 1993) (holding the applicant could not claim benefit of its earlier-filed German application's filing date because the German application failed to disclose teaching that would satisfy the "how to use" prong of the enable requirement). Omission of minor details, however, does not cause a specification to fail to meet the enablement requirement. *Genetech, Inc. v. Novo Nordisk, A/S*, 108 F.2d 1361, 1366 (Fed. Cir. 1986).

An invention that meets all five statutory requirements will be granted a patent through a formal process conducted by the United States Patent and Trademark Office ("PTO"). The process is commonly referred as "patent prosecution." The patent application and all communications between the PTO and the applicant or owner and her patent agents or attorneys are kept in confidence during the first 18 months of the prosecution period. During that period of time, the patent application file history is not available to the public. It becomes available to the public when the application is published 18 months after it is filed, regardless of whether the patent has already been issued. An "opt out" procedure is available if the inventor files a request, certifying that he or she will not file a foreign application. The application will not be published at the expiration of the 18 month period. Contrary to prior law which allowed damages to accrue upon issuance of patent, damages now accrue upon patent publication. 35 U.S.C. §271. Indeed, a patent now includes the right to obtain reasonable royalty from any person who, during the publication period (the date from the patent publication to the date the patent is issued), infringes the invention as claimed in the published patent application.

To keep a patent in force after it has been issued by the PTO, maintenance fees must be paid at 3 ½ years, 7 ½ years, and 11 ½ years after the issuance date. If the owner of a patent fails to pay the maintenance fees before the date the fee is due or within a grace period of six months thereafter, the patent will enter the public domain. No maintenance fee is required for a design or plant patent in force.

A patent confers upon the holder the right to exclude others from making, using, selling, offering for sale, or importing the patented invention for a term of twenty (20) years from the date of application. The right conferred in a patent is seen as a negative right because it does not affirmatively grant a right to do anything and a patented invention may be a later-developed invention and itself be covered by a broad, preexisting patent.

Patent applications must only be filed or authorized to be filed by the inventor(s). Inventors who are the first to conceive, but last to reduce the invention to practice with reasonable due diligence, will have priority over the inventor who conceived later yet reduced to practice early. Because the patent system favors early disclosure of innovation, courts limit inactivity in reduction to practice to "hardship" cases. To establish actual reduction to practice, an inventor must demonstrate that the invention is suitable for its intended purpose.

To show actual reduction to practice, an inventor must demonstrate that the invention is suitable for its intended purpose. *Mahurkar v. C.R. Bard, Inc.*, 79 F.3d 1572, 1578 (Fed. Cir. 1996); *Scott v. Finney*, 34 F.3d 1058, 1061 (Fed. Cir. 1994). Depending on the level of complexity of the invention, this showing may require test results. Less complicated inventions do not demand stringent testing. Indeed, as noted by the Federal Circuit, some inventions are simple and their purposes are obvious that their complete construction is sufficient to demonstrate workability. *King Instrument Corp. v. Otari Corp.*, 767 F.2d 853, 861 (Fed. Cir. 1985), *cert. denied*, 475 U.S. 1016 (1986).

Due to research, academic, or business reasons, some inventors must disclose their invention before having an opportunity to file a patent application. Those inventors may take advantage of the "provisional application" to obtain an early priority date. The filing of a provisional application does not begin the twenty year patent term. The patent term will begin when the full, complete application is filed. Inventors have up to twelve months from the date of filing the provisional application to file the complete application.

Most inventors today are employees of a business entity. Consistent with the presumption that the inventor owns his or her invention, an individual owns the patent rights even though the invention was conceived and/or reduced to practice during the course of employment. *Hapgood v. Hewitt*, 119 U.S. 226, 233–34 (1886). Nevertheless, under principles of equity and fairness, the law recognizes that employers may have an interest in an employee's invention. Indeed, under the doctrine of shop right, an employer may obtain a license to use the employee's invention where the employer has contributed to the development of the invention. The employer may use the employee's invention without liability for infringement. The employer may transfer the shop right as part of a transfer of the business, but may not separately assign or license the shop right to others. Moreover, contract law allows individuals to freely structure their employment relationships. An employee may be asked by his or her employer to consent by contract to assign all rights in invention to the employer. Even without an express assignment, employers may still claim ownership in an employee's invention where the employer specifically hires or directs the employee to develop inventive work. Essentially, the employee has received full compensation for his or her invention as the invention purpose is within the scope of employment.

The owner of a patented invention can choose to sell a patent by assigning all rights in the patent, including all the statutory rights and protection under the law to the new owners. Such assignment must be recorded with the Patent and Trademark Office within three months of the transfer. The assignment will be void as against any subsequent purchaser or mortgagee if the assignment was not recorded prior to such purchase or mortgage. The owner, instead of selling the patent, may license the patent to others.

In the event that there is more than one owner of a patent, each co-owner of the patent is free to make, use, offer to sell, or sell the patent without the consent of the other co-owners. These rights encompass the right to license the patent to third party without regard to the wishes of any other co-owner. Absent an agreement to the contrary, the co-owner can exploit its rights in a patent on whatever condition the co-owner chooses. Further, each co-owner may do so without accounting to the other co-owners. In addition, a co-owner of a patented invention may litigate against the other co-owners and their licensees for patent infringement. Essentially, the grant of a license by one co-owner cannot deprive the other co-owner of the right to sue for accrued damages for past infringement against the co-owner's licensee before the date of the license.

The owner(s) of a patent can initiate an infringement action in federal district court against others for making, using, selling, or offering to sell the patented invention or its "equivalents."

Types of Patents

There are three categories of patents: utility patents, design patents, and plant patents. Utility patents cover machine, manufacture, process, and composition of matter. Patent lawyers further subdivide utility patents into product patents (machine, manufacture and composition of matter) and process patents. Utility patents enjoy a twenty year term of protection if the patent applications were filed after June 8, 1995. Existing utility patents and those patent applications that were filed prior to June 8, 1995, enjoy a greater term of seventeen years from the date of issuance or twenty years from the date of application.

Business method patents are process patents, and are sometimes known as "Internet patents" because many of the patents cover various methods of doing various types of business online. For example, Amazon.com's one-click patent provides customers online shopping convenience without entering their shipping and billing information every time they purchase, and Priceline.com's reverse auction patent allows online customers to offer their own price for airline tickets, hotel accommodations, and cruises.

Design patents cover new and ornamental designs for articles of manufacture. The term of protection for design patents is 14 years. There is no fee for maintaining a design patent. Plant patents cover asexually reproducing plants that are new and distinctive. Like design patents, there is no maintenance fee for plant patents.

B. Trade Secrets

Historically, trade secrets have enjoyed protection under common law. In 1979, the National Conference of Commissioners on Uniform State Laws began to promulgate a model state trade secrets statute, the Uniform Trade Secrets Act (UTSA). At least forty states have enacted various trade secret statutes based on the UTSA.

Pursuant to the UTSA, a trade secret is defined as "information, including a formula, pattern, compilation, program, device, method, technique, or process that (i) derives independent economic value, actual or potential, from not being generally known to, and not being readily ascertainable by proper means by, other persons who can obtain economic value from its disclosure or use, and (ii) is the subject of efforts that are reasonable under the circumstances to maintain its secrecy." *See* UNIF. TRADE SECRETS ACT § 1(4), 14 U.L.A. 438 (1990).

Under the Act, a trade secret must be the type of information or knowledge that is entitled to protection under trade secret law. The information or knowledge must not be generally known to or readily ascertained by proper means by others. The information or knowledge possesses and generates economic value to the owner. The owner must keep the information or knowledge secret through reasonable efforts. Such information or knowledge is qualified as trade secret and enjoys protection under trade secret law.

The law treats trade secrets as property because it has many characteristics of more tangible forms of property. A trade secret is assignable; this is significant because it provides individuals with a strong incentive to innovate. Indeed, trade secret law encourages invention in areas where patent law does not. Under patent law, inventors have the right to exclude others from making, using, and selling the patented invention for twenty years in exchange for full disclosure of the invention. Under trade secret law, inventors receive protection for their invention as long as the invention is not of general industry knowledge and is kept secret from the public through reasonable efforts. Consequently, it prompts innovators to proceed with the discovery and exploitation of his or her invention, even though the invention does not receive patent protection. Further, the invention qualified for trade secret protection is not required to meet the more stringent statutory patentability requirements.

Know-how is often used interchangeably with trade secret. Indeed, the Service uses the term "know-how" to refer to "a secret process, formula or other secret information" in connection with the transfer of such information and recognizes the legal protection against the authorized disclosure of "know-how." Rev. Rul. 55-17, 1955-1 C.B. 388, *modified by* Rev. Rul. 64-56, 1964-1 (part 1) C.B. 133, *amplified by* Rev. Rul. 71-564, 1971 C.B. 179 (stating that know how "is not materially different from the right to use...secret processes or formulae"). For tax purposes, the transfer of secret information is viewed as transfer of property. However, the transfer of incidental personal services as part of the transfer of secret information is referred as "show-how" and has different tax treatment.

Trade secret protection aims to prevent misappropriation of trade secrets by improper means. Examples of improper means are theft, bribery, misrepresentation, breach or inducement of a breach of a duty to maintain secrecy, or espionage through electronic or other means.

Misappropriation includes (i) acquisition of a trade secret of another by a person who knows or has reason to know that the trade secret was acquired by improper means; or (ii) disclosure or use of a trade secret of another without express or implied consent by a person who

(A) used improper means to acquire knowledge of the trade secret;

(B) or at the time of disclosure or use, knew or had reason to know that his knowledge of the trade secret was

  I. derived from or through a person who had utilized improper means to acquire it;

  II. acquired under circumstances giving rise to a duty to maintain its secrecy or limit its use; or

  III. derived from or through a person who owed a duty to the person seeking relief to maintain its secrecy or limit its use; or

(C) before a material change of his or her position, knew or had reason to know that it was a trade secret and that knowledge of it had been acquired by accident or mistake.

UNIF. TRADE SECRETS ACT § 1(2), 14 U.L.A. 438 (1990).

To prove a trade secret misappropriation claim, the plaintiff must first establish that the information involved qualifies as a trade secret in accordance with the definition for trade secret. Secondly, the plaintiff must demonstrate that the defendant misappropriated the trade secret. Lastly, the plaintiff must establish that it took reasonable measures under the circumstances to prevent its disclosure. A prevailing plaintiff can obtain injunctive relief, compensatory damages, and exemplary damages for willful and malicious misappropriation of trade secrets.

Essentially, in many states, where a person acquires a trade secret by improper means, *i.e.* theft, bribery, misrepresentation, breach or inducement of a breach of a duty to maintain secrecy, or espionage, or discloses or uses the trade secret of another without express or implied consent, is liable for misappropriation of trade secrets. For example, to prevail under the Oklahoma Trade Secrets Act, the plaintiff must prove (1) the existence of a trade secret; (2) misappropriation of this secret by the defendants; and (3) use of the secret by the defendants to the detriment of the plaintiff. Okla. Stat. Ann. tit. 78 § 86 (2002). *See Micro Consulting, Inc. v. Zubeldia*, 813 F. Supp. 1514, 1534 (W.D. Okla. 1990). Under Texas law, a trade secret owner who prevails in a trade secret theft action is entitled to recover actual damages, court costs, attorney fees, and punitive damages that do not exceed one thousand dollars. Texas Civ. Prac. & Rem. Code Ann. §134.005 (2003). Texas also imposes criminal liability against defendants in certain trade secret theft cases. Under Texas law, a person commits a third degree felony if he or she knowingly steals the trade secret, copies an article representing a trade secret, communicates, or transmits a trade secret. Tex. Penal Code Ann. § 31.05 (2003).

There is no specific term of protection for trade secret. The protection is available as long as confidential proprietary information is kept in secrecy. The protection ceases to exist when the trade secret is disclosed. The loss of trade secret protection upon disclosure prevents a trade secret owner from publishing the information in academic, research, or business forums and from filing for patent protection. Patent law requires the owner to fully disclose the invention to enable those persons with ordinary skill in the field of the invention to make it in exchange for twenty years of patent protection. Obtaining patent protection is too costly to a trade secret owner; it destroys the secrecy of the information. Since both patent and trade secret protection cannot protect the same invention simultaneously, a decision to either seek protection under trade secret or patent law is made at the early stage of the invention.

Further, there is no protection for a trade secret against reverse engineering. For example, the formula for Chanel 5 perfume is a trade secret. A chemist may purchase a bottle of the perfume at a Saks Fifth Avenue store and analyze its content to produce a solution that is similar to Chanel 5. Such reverse engineering conduct is lawful.

Other examples of trade secrets include the specifications of the projector for IMAX pictures, the information contained in object code form in a computer program, a hotel's closely-guarded information about its prices, discounts, and occupancy levels, a company's particular zinc recovery process unknown to and guarded from disclosure to the industry, and a shipping company's guarded information about how to design containers.

C. Copyrights

A work of authorship such as a song, poem, book, computer software, sound recording, painting, architectural plan, or movie is entitled to copyright protection if it is fixed in a tangible medium, independently created by the author, and contains a modicum of creativity. Copyright law extends protection to works of authorship in eight broad categories such as (1) literary works; (2) musical works, including any accompanying words; (3) dramatic works, including any accompanying music; (4) pantomimes and choreographic works; (5) pictorial, graphic, and sculptural works; (6) motion pictures and other audiovisual works; (7) sound recordings; and (8) architectural works. 17 U.S.C. § 102 (2000). *Feist Publications v. Rural Telephone Service*, included below, is a good example of how the United States Supreme Court addresses the extent of copyright protection.

Copyright ownership vests initially in the author or authors of the work. As a general rule, the author is the party who actually creates the work that is original, fixed in a tangible medium of expression, and contains a minimum level of creativity. Copyright ownership vests in the employer under the works made for hire doctrine. *Community for Creative Non-Violence v. Reid*, included below, addresses the works made for hire doctrine. Queries: many companies hire third parties to create websites, so who is the copyright owner of the websites? Do companies have a nonexclusive, irrevocable license to use the websites? *Holtzbrinck Publishing v. Vyne Communications*, excerpted below, attempted to address such issues.

The United States Constitution explicitly grants Congress the power to provide protection to authors for their "writings" for a limited time. U.S. CONST. art. I, § 8, cl. 8. Over the years, the Copyright Act has lengthened the term of copyrights. Currently, a work of authorship enjoys a term of the life of the author and seventy years thereafter. For works created under the works made for hire doctrine, the term is ninety-five years after publication or one hundred twenty years after creation.

Ownership of a valid copyright confers five exclusive rights: the right to make copies of the work; the right to prepare derivative works; the right to distribute copies of the work; the right to perform the work publicly; and the right to display the work publicly. Any violation of the exclusive rights committed by others without permission of the copyright owner constitutes a basis for copyright infringement action.

It is not uncommon to have more than one author of a work. A joint work is "a work prepared by two or more authors with the intention that their contributions be merged into inseparable or interdependent parts of a unitary whole." 17 U.S.C. § 101 (2000). The authors of a joint work are co-owners of the copyright in the work. In other words, each co-author enjoys undivided ownership in the copyrighted work, and can independently exploit the exclusive rights, but must provide an accounting of profits to the other co-author.

Ownership of a copyright, or of any of the exclusive rights under a copyright, is distinct from ownership of any material object in which the work is embodied. For example, ownership of the copyright in a movie is distinct from the physical ownership of a videotape of the movie. Indeed, the transfer of the physical ownership of the videotape does not of itself convey any exclusive rights in the copyrighted movie embodied in the videotape.

The division and transfer of a copyright can only be executed in writing and signed by the copyright owner. The copyright owner may transfer a copyright in whole or in part by transferring any of the exclusive rights to others separately. The new owner of a particular exclusive right is entitled, to the extent of that right, to all of the protection and remedies accorded to the copyright owner under the law. For example, the owner of the copyright in a book may divide the five exclusive rights to five new owners, each owning a separate exclusive right. The copyright owner can choose to license to others the right to prepare a derivative work, and to make copies of the book and sell them to others. In addition, the copyright owner has the exclusive right in the public performance of the copyright, such as reading the book to the public.

Copyright protection is limited by the doctrine of fair use. Fair use of a copyrighted work includes reproduction for purposes of criticism, comment, news reporting, teaching, scholarship, or research. Such use does not constitute copyright infringement. To determine whether the use made of a work is a fair use, the factors that must be considered include: (1) the purpose and character of the use, including whether such use is of a commercial nature or is for nonprofit educational purposes; (2) the nature of the copyrighted work; (3) the amount and substantiality of the portion used in relation to the copyrighted work as a whole; and (4) the effect of the use upon the potential market for or value of the copyrighted work.

The owner of a registered copyright can bring an action against infringers of any of the five exclusive statutory rights. A successful plaintiff may be entitled to injunctive relief, actual damages and profits or statutory damages, attorneys' fees, and costs.

D. Trademarks, Trade Names, and Trade Dress

Trademarks. Generally, a trademark is a word, phrase, logo, device, or design that functions as a source identifier of the goods or services on which the trademark is affixed. A trademark also distinguishes its associated goods or services from those of others. To be qualified as a protectable trademark under the federal Lanham Act, a trademark either is inherently distinctive or has acquired distinctiveness through use in commerce.

In 1976, Judge Henry Friendly's decision in *Abercrombie & Fitch Co. v. Hunting World, Inc.*, 537 F.2d 4 (2d Cir. 1976), formulated a trademark scale based on distinctiveness and it became the authoritative instrument to measure trademarks. The *Abercrombie & Fitch* decision employed a distinctiveness spectrum and dictates that a trademark will be treated as inherently distinctive if it is "arbitrary," "fanciful," or "suggestive" in relation to the goods bearing the trademark. However, a descriptive trademark is entitled to legal protection only if it acquires secondary meaning. A generic trademark is not protected under the law.

Trade Names. A trade name is generally the name of a company or business. Trade names are not entitled to the protection afforded to trademarks because trade names do not serve to identify the source of the goods and distinguish the goods from those of others. Trade names only identify the overall business of a company. Only those trade names that have been used in the same manner as trademarks in commerce will be entitled to protection under trademark law. Further, a trade name is not federally registerable under the Lanham Act, but registerable under state laws. Nevertheless, the Lanham Act and common law provides protection to trade names against unfair competition.

Trade Dress. Trade dress is broadly defined as the total image and overall appearance of a product or service. Trade dress may include features such as size, shape, color or color combinations, textures, graphics, or even particular sales techniques. Trade dress has been held to include the appearance of a video game console, the overall look of greeting cards, the layout and appearance of a mail order catalogue, and the overall look of sales brochures and reminder letters sent by auto repair shops to customers. A trade dress that is the packaging of a product, or a product configuration or design is entitled to protection under the Lanham Act if it if inherently distinctive or has acquired secondary meaning. In addition, a protectable trade dress must be nonfunctional. Functionality is a judicially-created doctrine to balance the right of the owner of a trade dress with the right of a competitor who needs to use elements of the trade dress for effective competition. The functionality limitation on trade dress prevents a perpetual patent grant for a trade dress. Protectable trade dress enjoys similar protection afforded to trademarks.

Two Pesos, Inc. v. Taco Cabana, Inc., included below, provides a good summary of trademark law and addresses the requirement for trade dress protection.

The owner of a trademark does not really "own" the trademark, but instead has the right to enjoin others from using a similar trademark that is likely to cause consumer confusion. Both common law and federal trademark statutes exist side by side to protect trademarks. Section 43(a) of the Lanham Act enjoins unauthorized use of a trademark that is likely to cause consumer confusion as to source. Section 32 of the Lanham Act enjoins unauthorized use of registered trademarks. Common law unfair competition, palming off, and deceptive trade and business practices are state claims usually asserted along with the federal Lanham Act claims.

The 1995 Federal Trademark Dilution Act protects famous trademarks from dilutive use by junior trademarks. *See* 15 U.S.C. §§ 1125(c), 1127. The 1999 Anticybersquatting Consumer Protection Act allows trademark owners to bring action against unauthorized registration, use, or traffic of domain names that are similar, identical or dilutive to the protected trademarks. *See* 15 U.S.C. § 1125(d)(1)(A). Further, trademark owners can opt for an inexpensive means through ICANN's Uniform Dispute Resolution Procedures to enjoin unauthorized and bad faith registration of their trademarks as domain names.

A trademark owner has the right to exploit her trademark as a corporate asset in commercial transactions. She can sell the trademark by assigning it together with its attached goodwill, license the trademark in different fields of use, or use the trademark as security in corporate financing schemes. Some trademarks have become extremely important corporate assets. For example, the trademark "Marlboro" has been valued at $65 billion and the trademark "Coca Cola" has been valued at $24 billion.

Since trademark right is based on use, abandonment of a trademark occurs when the owner stops using the trademark in commerce. Under federal trademark law, abandonment is presumed if non-use of the trademark is three years. Token uses of a trademark for purpose of reserving trademark right does not prevent a finding of abandonment. In addition, abandonment of a trademark could occur if the owner failed to police the trademark so it becomes the generic name for the product or service with which it is used.

The owner of a trademark can bring an action against unauthorized use of a trademark under trademark infringement and/or unfair competition claims. A successful plaintiff may be entitled to injunctive relief, actual damages and profits, attorney's fees, and costs. In some instances, a successful plaintiff may petition the court to cancel a trademark registration.

E. Domain Names

In general, a company seeking to establish its presence in cyberspace first reserves its Internet Protocol ("IP") Address for its websites. Because the IP Address is difficult for users to remember when trying to reach a particular website, "domain name combinations" were introduced. The company, as a potential domain name registrant, may enlist the registration services provided by numerous registrars on the Internet to acquire a second-level domain name in a particular top-level domain name. A second-level domain name is the word that appears on the left side of the dot (.). It is usually a trademark, trade name, or the name of the company, institution, product, or service. For example, in the domain name "microsoft.com," the word microsoft is the second-level domain name. A top-level domain generally describes the nature of the company and it is the word that appears on the right side of the dot (.) (*e.g.*, ".com" (commercial), ".org" (organization), ".gov" (government)).

Generally, a potential registrant may enlist the registration services of numerous registrars on the Internet to acquire a second-level domain name in a particular top-level domain. Registrars neither own nor license domain names. A registrar is an entity that processes the information submitted by potential registrants, and then assigns domain names that have not been previously registered by others to the potential registrants. Registrants can register domain names for a fixed period of time (one, two, five, or ten years) and later renew the domain name registrations before they expire.

Every domain name has a technical purpose on the Web. The domain name serves as an address and Internet surfers who know the domain name will be connected to the corresponding website once the domain name is typed into a web browser. Additionally, the user can enter the domain name as a search engine keyword. The search engine will look for keywords in places such as domain names, actual web page text, and metatags. The search engine performs a search and generates a list of sites relating to the entered keyword. *Interstellar Starship Services, Ltd. v. Tchou*, included below, addresses the clash between trademarks and domain names.

Some domain names are entitled to protection under trademark law if they are arbitrary, fanciful, or suggestive words or phrases, or they are descriptive words that have acquired secondary meaning. A sticky point arises where a domain name is a generic word. Many generic domain names are highly valued in the open market. For example, sex.com was valued at $250 million; business.com at $7.5 million; and loan.com at $3.0 million. *See* Xuan-Thao Nguyen, *Cyberproperty and Juridical Dissonance, The Trouble With Domain Name Classification*, 10 GEORGE MASON L. R. 183 (2001). Under trademark law, generic words are not protected. If trademark law is extended to protect domain names, generic domain names obviously will not be protected. What protection is available for valuable generic domain names?

F. Computer Software

The rapid growth in microcomputers in the 1980's has greatly influenced the software industry, moving from mostly customized computer programs to computer application packages. Software companies, large and small, derive substantial revenue from the manufacture and license of computer application packages for general and daily business and home use purposes. As the network economy has been expanding, the focus has also been shifted to more software for networked computers. Some of such software are also known as "web applications."

Computer technology poses challenges to current intellectual property doctrines. It is not readily discernable to classify a computer program as a copyright, trade dress, trade secret, or patentable invention. Computer programs are seen as products of a mixture of machine, writing, and total concept and feel. Trade secret, patent, copyright, and trade dress laws, together, provide legal protection for computer programs.

Copyright law has traditionally served as the source of legal protection for computer programs. Under copyright, the owner of the copyright in a computer program has the exclusive right to make copies. Unauthorized reproduction of a copyrighted computer program may constitute copyright infringement. With regard to protection for *parts* of a computer program, software copyright law establishes that literal, exact, direct copying of the computer program code infringes the owner's copyright in the code. In this type of copyright infringement, the infringer copies the entire *text* of the computer program. In recent years, computer software owners attempted to extend copyright law to the overall structure of the program, *i.e.*, sequence, organization, menu command hierarchy, and the total look and feel of the program (the non-literal elements of program codes). The scope of copyright protection for software has been diminished over the years. Courts are reluctant to extend copyright protection to all the elements of software. As a result, software owners search for alternative legal protection such as the proposed Uniform Computer Information Transactions Act that allows them to maximize their commercial transactions through licensing of software.

In addition to copyright law, patent protection has been extended to computer software. For years, patent protection was not available for computer software. The focus then was whether software invention consisting of the use of mathematical algorithm could be patented. The Supreme Court and the Federal Circuit slowly changed that inquiry in a series of cases. *See Diamond v. Diehr*, 450 U.S. 175 (1981) (differentiating a claim that is purely a mathematical formula from claims that utilize those formulae); *In re* Alappat, 33 F.3d 1526 (Fed. Cir. 1994) (en banc) (stating that "certain types of mathematical subject matter, standing alone, represent nothing more than abstract ideas until reduced to some type of practical application, and, thus, subject matter is not in and of itself entitled to patent protection"). Recently the Federal Circuit has put to rest any speculation that a computer program is not patentable subject matter. *See State Street Bank & Trust Co. v. Signature Financial Group, Inc.*, 149 F.3d 1368 (Fed. Cir. 1998) (allowing a computer software patent for a method of doing business that yields useful, discrete, and concrete result).

In addition to copyright and patent law, trade secret law has been extended to protect computer programs. In *Data General Corp. v. Grumman Systems Support Corp.*, the court extended trade secret protection to the information contained in object code form in a computer program. *Data General* is excerpted below. What other legal protection is available for the software created by the plaintiff in *Data General*?

Also, trade dress may serve as a potential source of protection for the total concept and feel of a computer program, particularly, the graphic user interfaces. *See* Lauren Fisher Kellner, Note, *Trade Dress Protection for Computer User Interface "Look and Feel,"* 61 U. CHI. L. REV. 1011 (1994). *See also* Xuan-Thao Nguyen, *Should It Be a Free for All? The Challenge of Extending Trade Dress Protection to the Look and Feel of Web Sites*, 49 AMERICAN UNIV. L. REV. 1233 (2000).

IV. Materials

Diamond v. Chakrabarty
Supreme Court of the United States
447 U.S. 303 (1980)

We granted certiorari to determine whether a live, human-made micro-organism is patentable subject matter under 35 U.S.C. § 101.

The Constitution grants Congress broad power to legislate to "promote the Progress of Science and useful Arts, by securing for limited Times to Authors and Inventors the exclusive Right to their respective Writings and Discoveries." Art. I, § 8, cl. 8. The patent laws promote this progress by offering inventors exclusive rights for a limited period as an incentive for their inventiveness and research efforts. *Kewanee Oil Co. v. Bicron Corp.*, 416 U.S. 470, 480-481 (1974); *Universal Oil Co. v. Globe Co.*, 322 U.S. 471 (1944). The authority of Congress is exercised in the hope that "[t]he productive effort thereby fostered will have a positive effect on society through the introduction of new products and processes of manufacture into the economy, and the emanations by way of increased employment and better lives for our citizens." *Kewanee*, 416 U.S., at 480.

The question before us in this case is a narrow one of statutory interpretation requiring us to construe 35 U.S.C. § 101, which provides: "Whoever invents or discovers any new and useful process, machine, manufacture, or composition of matter, or any new and useful improvement thereof, may obtain a patent therefor, subject to the conditions and requirements of this title." Specifically, we must determine whether respondent's micro-organism constitutes a "manufacture" or "composition of matter" within the meaning of the statute.[1]

III

In cases of statutory construction we begin, of course, with the language of the statute. Guided by these canons of construction, this Court has read the term "manufacture" in § 101 in accordance with its dictionary definition to mean "the production of articles for use from raw or prepared materials by giving to these materials new forms, qualities, properties, or combinations, whether by hand-labor or by machinery." *American Fruit Growers, Inc. v. Brogdex Co.*, 283 U.S. 1, 11 (1931). Similarly, "composition of matter" has been construed consistent with its common usage to include "all compositions of two or more substances and...all composite articles, whether they be the results of chemical union, or of mechanical mixture, or whether they be gases, fluids, powders or solids." *Shell Development Co. v. Watson*, 149 F.Supp. 279, 280 (D.C.1957). In choosing such expansive terms as "manufacture" and "composition of matter," modified by the comprehensive "any," Congress plainly contemplated that the patent laws would be given wide scope.

The relevant legislative history also supports a broad construction. The Patent Act of 1793, authored by Thomas Jefferson, defined statutory subject matter as "any new and useful art, machine, manufacture, or composition of matter, or any new or useful improvement [thereof]." Act of Feb. 21, 1793, § 1, 1 Stat. 319. The Act embodied Jefferson's philosophy that "ingenuity should receive a liberal encouragement." 5 Writings of Thomas Jefferson 75–76 (Washington ed. 1871). Subsequent patent statutes in 1836, 1870, and 1874 employed this same broad language. In 1952, when the patent laws were recodified, Congress replaced the word "art" with "process," but otherwise left Jefferson's language intact. The Committee Reports accompanying the 1952 Act inform us that Congress intended statutory subject matter to "include anything under the sun that is made by man." S. Rep. No.1979, 82d Cong., 2d Sess., 5 (1952).

This is not to suggest that § 101 has no limits or that it embraces every discovery. The laws of nature, physical phenomena, and abstract ideas have been held not patentable. Thus, a new mineral discovered in the earth or a new plant found in the wild is not patentable subject matter. Likewise, Einstein could not patent his celebrated law that $E=mc2$; nor could Newton have patented the law of gravity. Such discoveries are "manifestations of...nature, free to all men and reserved exclusively to none." *Funk, supra,* 333 U.S., at 130.

Judged in this light, respondent's micro-organism plainly qualifies as patentable subject matter. His claim is not to a hitherto unknown natural phenomenon, but to a nonnaturally occurring manufacture or composition of matter—a product of human ingenuity "having a distinctive name, character [and] use." *Hartranft v. Wiegmann*, 121 U.S. 609, 615 (1887). [T]he patentee has produced a new bacterium with markedly different characteristics from any found in nature and one having the potential for significant utility. His discovery is not nature's handiwork, but his own; accordingly it is patentable subject matter under § 101.

Accordingly, the judgment of the Court of Customs and Patent Appeals is *Affirmed.*

---

1. This case does not involve the other "conditions and requirements" of the patent laws, such as novelty and nonobviousness. 35 U.S.C. §§ 102, 103.

Feist Publications, Inc. v. Rural Telephone Service Co.
Supreme Court of the United States
499 U.S. 340 (1991)

This case requires us to clarify the extent of copyright protection available to telephone directory white pages.

This case concerns the interaction of two well-established propositions. The first is that facts are not copyrightable; the other, that compilations of facts generally are.

There is an undeniable tension between these two propositions. Many compilations consist of nothing but raw data — *i.e.*, wholly factual information not accompanied by any original written expression. On what basis may one claim a copyright in such a work? Common sense tells us that 100 uncopyrightable facts do not magically change their status when gathered together in one place. Yet copyright law seems to contemplate that compilations that consist exclusively of facts are potentially within its scope.

The key to resolving the tension lies in understanding why facts are not copyrightable. The *sine qua non* of copyright is originality. To qualify for copyright protection, a work must be original to the author. See *Harper & Row*, 471 U.S. at 547–549. Original, as the term is used in copyright, means only that the work was independently created by the author (as opposed to copied from other works), and that it possesses at least some minimal degree of creativity. To be sure, the requisite level of creativity is extremely low; even a slight amount will suffice. The vast majority of works make the grade quite easily, as they possess some creative spark, "no matter how crude, humble or obvious" it might be. *Id.* Originality does not signify novelty; a work may be original even though it closely resembles other works so long as the similarity is fortuitous, not the result of copying. To illustrate, assume that two poets, each ignorant of the other, compose identical poems. Neither work is novel, yet both are original and, hence, copyrightable. See *Sheldon v. Metro-Goldwyn Pictures Corp.*, 81 F.2d 49, 54 (CA2 1936).

Originality is a constitutional requirement. The source of Congress' power to enact copyright laws is Article I, §8, cl. 8, of the Constitution, which authorizes Congress to "secur[e] for limited Times to Authors...the exclusive Right to their respective Writings." In two decisions from the late 19th century — *The Trade-Mark Cases*, 100 U.S. 82 (1879); and *Burrow-Giles Lithographic Co. v. Sarony*, 111 U.S. 53 (1884) — this Court defined the crucial terms "authors" and "writings." In so doing, the Court made it unmistakably clear that these terms presuppose a degree of originality.

Factual compilations, on the other hand, may possess the requisite originality. The compilation author typically chooses which facts to include, in what order to place them, and how to arrange the collected data so that they may be used effectively by readers. These choices as to selection and arrangement, so long as they are made independently by the compiler and entail a minimal degree of creativity, are sufficiently original that Congress may protect such compilations through the copyright laws. Thus, even a directory that contains absolutely no protectable written expression, only facts, meets the constitutional minimum for copyright protection if it features an original selection or arrangement.

This protection is subject to an important limitation. The mere fact that a work is copyrighted does not mean that every element of the work may be protected. Originality remains the *sine qua non* of copyright; accordingly, copyright protection may extend only to those components of a work that are original to the author. Thus, if the compilation author clothes facts with an original collocation of words, he or she may be able to claim a copyright in this written expression. Others may copy the underlying facts from the publication, but not the precise words used to present them. Where the compilation author adds no written expression but rather lets the facts speak for themselves, the expressive element is more elusive. The only conceivable expression is the manner in which the compiler has selected and arranged the facts. Thus, if the selection and arrangement are original, these elements of the work are eligible for copyright protection.

This inevitably means that the copyright in a factual compilation is thin. Notwithstanding a valid copyright, a subsequent compiler remains free to use the facts contained in another's publication to aid in preparing a competing work, so long as the competing work does not feature the same selection and arrangement.

It may seem unfair that much of the fruit of the compiler's labor may be used by others without compensation. As Justice Brennan has correctly observed, however, this is not "some unforeseen byproduct of a statutory scheme." *Harper & Row*, 471 U.S., at 589 (dissenting opinion). It is, rather, "the essence of copyright," *ibid.*, and a constitutional requirement. The primary objective of copyright is not to reward the labor of authors, but "[t]o promote the Progress of Science and useful Arts." Art. I, §8, cl. 8. To this end, copyright assures authors the right to their original expression, but encourages others to build freely upon the ideas and information conveyed by a work. This principle, known as the idea/expression or fact/expression dichotomy, applies to all works of authorship. As applied to a factual compilation, assuming the absence of original written expression, only the compiler's selection and arrangement may be protected; the raw facts may be copied at will. This result is neither unfair nor unfortunate. It is the means by which copyright advances the progress of science and art.

This, then, resolves the doctrinal tension: Copyright treats facts and factual compilations in a wholly consistent manner. Facts, whether alone or as part of a compilation, are not original and therefore may not be copyrighted. A factual compilation is eligible for copyright if it features an original selection or arrangement of facts, but the copyright is limited to the particular selection or arrangement. In no event may copyright extend to the facts themselves.

There is no doubt that Feist took from the white pages of Rural's directory a substantial amount of factual information. At a minimum, Feist copied the names, towns, and telephone numbers of 1,309 of Rural's subscribers. Not all copying, however, is copyright infringement. To establish infringement, two elements must be proven: (1) ownership of a valid copyright, and (2) copying of constituent elements of the work that are original. See *Harper & Row*, 471 U.S., at 548. The first element is not at issue here; Feist appears to concede that Rural's directory, considered as a whole, is subject to a valid copyright because it contains some foreword text, as well as original material in its yellow pages advertisements.

The question is whether Rural has proved the second element. In other words, did Feist, by taking 1,309 names, towns, and telephone numbers from Rural's white pages, copy anything that was "original" to Rural? Certainly, the raw data does not satisfy the originality requirement. Rural may have been the first to discover and report the names, towns, and telephone numbers of its subscribers, but this data does not "'ow[e] its origin'" to Rural. *Burrow-Giles*, 111 U.S., at 58. Rather, these bits of information are uncopyrightable facts; they existed before Rural reported them and would have continued to exist if Rural had never published a telephone directory. The originality requirement "rule[s] out protecting...names, addresses, and telephone numbers of which the plaintiff by no stretch of the imagination could be called the author." Patterson & Joyce 776.

The question that remains is whether Rural selected, coordinated, or arranged these uncopyrightable facts in an original way. As mentioned, originality is not a stringent standard; it does not require that facts be presented in an innovative or surprising way. It is equally true, however, that the selection and arrangement of facts cannot be so mechanical or routine as to require no creativity whatsoever. The standard of originality is low, but it does exist.

The selection, coordination, and arrangement of Rural's white pages do not satisfy the minimum constitutional standards for copyright protection. As mentioned at the outset, Rural's white pages are entirely typical. Persons desiring telephone service in Rural's service area fill out an application and Rural issues them a telephone number. In preparing its white pages, Rural simply takes the data provided by its subscribers and lists it alphabetically by surname. The end product is a garden-variety white pages directory, devoid of even the slightest trace of creativity.

Nor can Rural claim originality in its coordination and arrangement of facts. The white pages do nothing more than list Rural's subscribers in alphabetical order. This arrangement may, technically speaking, owe its origin to Rural; no one disputes that Rural undertook the task of alphabetizing the names itself. But there is nothing remotely creative about arranging names alphabetically in a white pages directory. It is an age-old practice, firmly rooted in tradition and so commonplace that it has come to be expected as a matter of course. It is not only unoriginal, it is practically inevitable. This time-honored tradition does not possess the minimal creative spark required by the Copyright Act and the Constitution.

We conclude that the names, towns, and telephone numbers copied by Feist were not original to Rural and therefore were not protected by the copyright in Rural's combined white and yellow pages directory.

The judgment of the Court of Appeals is *Reversed*.

Community for Creative Non-Violence v. Reid
Supreme Court of the United States
490 U.S. 730 (1989)

In this case, an artist and the organization that hired him to produce a sculpture contest the ownership of the copyright in that work. To resolve this dispute, we must construe the "work made for hire" provisions of the Copyright Act of 1976 (Act or 1976 Act), 17 U.S.C. §§ 101 and 201(b), and in particular, the provision in § 101, which defines as a "work made for hire" a "work prepared by an employee within the scope of his or her employment" (hereinafter § 101(1)).

A

The Copyright Act of 1976 provides that copyright ownership "vests initially in the author or authors of the work." 17 U.S.C. § 201(a). As a general rule, the author is the party who actually creates the work, that is, the person who translates an idea into a fixed, tangible expression entitled to copyright protection. § 102. The Act carves out an important exception, however, for "works made for hire." If the work is for hire, "the employer or other person for whom the work was prepared is considered the author" and owns the copyright, unless there is a written agreement to the contrary. § 201(b). Classifying a work as "made for hire" determines not only the initial ownership of its copyright, but also the copyright's duration, § 302(c), and the owners' renewal rights, § 304(a), termination rights, § 203(a), and right to import certain goods bearing the copyright, § 601(b)(1). See 1 M. Nimmer & D. Nimmer, Nimmer on Copyright § 5.03[A], pp. 5–10 (1988). The contours of the work for hire doctrine therefore carry profound significance for freelance creators — including artists, writers, photographers, designers, composers, and computer programmers — and for the publishing, advertising, music, and other industries which commission their works.

Section 101 of the 1976 Act provides that a work is "for hire" under two sets of circumstances:

(1) a work prepared by an employee within the scope of his or her employment; or

(2) a work specially ordered or commissioned for use as a contribution to a collective work, as a part of a motion picture or other audiovisual work, as a translation, as a supplementary work, as a compilation, as an instructional text, as a test, as answer material for a test, or as an atlas, if the parties expressly agree in a written instrument signed by them that the work shall be considered a work made for hire.

Petitioners do not claim that the statute satisfies the terms of § 101(2). Quite clearly, it does not. Sculpture does not fit within any of the nine categories of "specially ordered or commissioned" works enumerated in that subsection, and no written agreement between the parties establishes "Third World America" as a work for hire.

The dispositive inquiry in this case therefore is whether "Third World America" is "a work prepared by an employee within the scope of his or her employment" under § 101(1). The Act does not define these terms.

The starting point for our interpretation of a statute is always its language. The Act nowhere defines the terms "employee" or "scope of employment." It is, however, well established that "[w]here Congress uses terms that have accumulated settled meaning under...the common law, a court must infer, unless the statute otherwise dictates, that Congress means to incorporate the established meaning of these terms." *NLRB v. Amax Coal Co.,* 453 U.S. 322, 329 (1981). In the past, when Congress has used the term "employee" without defining it, we have concluded that Congress intended to describe the conventional master-servant relationship as understood by common-law agency doctrine. Nothing in the text of the work for hire provisions indicates that Congress used the words "employee" and "employment" to describe anything other than the conventional relation of employer and employee.

B

We turn, finally, to an application of § 101 to Reid's production of "Third World America." In determining whether a hired party is an employee under the general common law of agency, we consider the hiring party's right to control the manner and means by which the product is accomplished. Among the other factors relevant to this inquiry are the skill required; the source of the instrumentalities and tools; the location of the work; the duration of the relationship between the parties; whether the hiring party has the right to assign additional projects to the hired party; the extent of the hired party's discretion over when and how long to work; the method of payment; the hired party's role in hiring and paying assistants; whether the work is part of the regular business of the hiring party; whether the hiring party is in business; the provision of employee benefits; and the tax treatment of the hired party. See Restatement § 220(2) (setting forth a nonexhaustive list of factors relevant to determining whether a hired party is an employee). No one of these factors is determinative.

Examining the circumstances of this case in light of these factors, we agree with the Court of Appeals that Reid was not an employee of CCNV but an independent contractor. True, CCNV members directed enough of Reid's work to ensure that he produced a sculpture that met their specifications. 652 F.Supp., at 1456. But the extent of control the hiring party exercises over the details of the product is not dispositive. Indeed, all the other circumstances weigh heavily against finding an employment relationship. Reid is a sculptor, a skilled occupation. Reid supplied his own tools. He worked in his own studio in Baltimore, making daily supervision of his activities from Washington practicably impossible. Reid was retained for less than two months, a relatively short period of time. During and after this time, CCNV had no right to assign additional projects to Reid. Apart from the deadline for completing the sculpture, Reid had absolute freedom to decide when and how long to work. CCNV paid Reid $15,000, a sum dependent on "completion of a specific job, a method by which independent contractors are often compensated." *Holt v. Winpisinger*, 811 F.2d 1532, 1540 (U.S.App.D.C.1987). Reid had total discretion in hiring and paying assistants. "Creating sculptures was hardly 'regular business' for CCNV." 846 F.2d, at 1494, n. 11. Indeed, CCNV is not a business at all. Finally, CCNV did not pay payroll or Social Security taxes, provide any employee benefits, or contribute to unemployment insurance or workers' compensation funds.

Because Reid was an independent contractor, whether "Third World America" is a work for hire depends on whether it satisfies the terms of § 101(2). This, petitioners concede it cannot do. Thus, CCNV is not the author of "Third World America" by virtue of the work for hire provisions of the Act. However, as the Court of Appeals made clear, CCNV nevertheless may be a joint author of the sculpture if, on remand, the District Court determines that CCNV and Reid prepared the work "with the intention that their contributions be merged into inseparable or interdependent parts of a unitary whole." 17 U.S.C. § 101. In that case, CCNV and Reid would be co-owners of the copyright in the work. See § 201(a).

For the aforestated reasons, we affirm the judgment of the Court of Appeals for the District of Columbia Circuit.

Holtzbrinck Publishing Holdings v. Vyne Communications

U.S. District Court
2000 WL 502860 (S.D.N.Y. April 26, 2000)

MEMORANDUM & ORDER

This action involves a dispute over the ownership of the copyright in the Scientific American website, as well as the parties' respective rights to use the programs and files comprising the website.

FACTUAL BACKGROUND

The plaintiff, Holtzbrinck Publishing Holdings, L.P. ("HPH" or "Holtzbrinck") is a New York limited partnership, and the parent of Scientific American, Inc. ("SA" or "Scientific American"), which publishes *Scientific American* Magazine. Holtzbrinck Electronic Publishing ("HEP"), a division of HPH, coordinates the electronic publishing activities of HPH, Scientific American and W.H. Freeman ("Freeman"), a college textbook publisher and a wholly owned subsidiary of Scientific American. Martin Paul ("Paul") is HEP's Managing Director.

The defendant, Vyne Communications Co., Inc. ("Vyne") is a New York corporation, founded by Jason Kuffer ("Kuffer"), a graphic designer, with Alan Hall ("Hall") as its sole incorporator and one of two shareholders. Vyne is in the business of creating sites on the World Wide Web for third parties, using content provided by the third parties.

Starting in 1995, Holtzbrinck considered developing websites for some of its U.S. publishing units, including Scientific American and Freeman. That same year, it retained Vyne to develop and maintain a website for Freeman. Pursuant to an oral agreement Vyne created files, code, graphics, and design for the website, and maintained the site up until its transfer to Freeman in March 1996. At the time Vyne transferred all files to Freeman's computer, it never claimed any interest in, or ownership of, any part of the website, including the programming, code, or script files created by Vyne in its development of the website.

On a separate project, Holtzbrinck also retained Vyne to assist them in identifying the hardware and software they would need to develop in order to host various websites, including the Freeman and SA websites. Vyne conducted and completed this analysis by May 1996.

In late 1995, Holtzbrinck negotiated with Vyne to create another website, this time for Scientific American (the "SA website"), and service the site until it could also be transferred in-house. Alan Hall, on behalf of Vyne, and Martin Paul, on behalf of HEP, discussed an arrangement whereby Vyne would develop, host, and update the website for a sum of $65,000, to be paid in monthly installments of $5,000. Also, for an additional sum of $1,000 per month, Vyne agreed to host the SA website on Vyne's server until it could be transferred in-house. Scientific American was to provide the editorial materials and Vyne would conduct the necessary programming. Vyne allegedly only agreed to produce two articles from the magazine per month, plus a news section which primarily consisted of approximately seven small articles, and three more articles to be displayed under separate sections.

Vyne commenced work on the SA website in January 1996 and launched the site four months later, hosting it on its own computer. At the time of the launch, plaintiff noticed that the web pages did not contain a copyright notice for Scientific American. After notifying Vyne, Vyne placed Scientific American's copyright notice on the website.

The SA website became more complex after its launch, as additional features were added to the site. Both Vyne and Holtzbrinck discussed the need for reducing their oral agreement to a written contract. In early June, Hall (for Vyne), Paul (for HEP), and Mark Budwig (plaintiff's counsel) met to discuss the drafting of an agreement. On June 12, 1996, Hall sent Budwig a draft contract (the "Hall Draft"). The proposal described, *inter alia*, the scope of the work to be done by Vyne, and a statement about the ownership of the work product.

The draft contained an ownership provision stating that "Scientific American is the sole owner of the existing WWW site and any changes or additions to it that occur in the future. This consists of all HTML files...all unique graphics...all forms and other CGI code...and all content provided by Scientific American or developed for Scientific American by Vyne or its employees." Paul Aff'd, Exh. D. Furthermore, the Hall Draft indicated that upon completion of the contract, Vyne would deliver all files to HPH, and install them for HPH in working order. This draft was never signed.

By July 1996, Holtzbrinck began assembling the hardware and software necessary to host the SA website internally. Paul then asked Shara Zoll, an SA employee who was given a password by Vyne which permitted her access to the website, to arrange for the transfer of the website files to Holtzbrinck's computers to conduct a test. After some initial difficulty downloading certain files, Vyne delivered some files to Holtzbrinck on disk.

In late July, Hall and Budwig resumed their contract discussions. In August, 1996, Budwig forwarded a revised contract to Holtzbrinck ("Budwig Draft"). The draft reiterated that Holtzbrinck would own all the work done by Vyne in creation of the site, including the HTML files, the CGI code, and other software.[2]

Though the draft remained unsigned, HEP and Vyne continued to perform in accordance with their initial understandings until November 1996, at which point Vyne sought to renegotiate its compensation for the work it was doing in updating the website. Also at that point, Vyne claimed that it owned all the coding, programming, and graphics for the SA website, and allegedly threatened to shut down the site unless additional fees were paid. Not only did Vyne claim ownership of the site, but also the right to deny Holtzbrinck use of the site.

On November 15, 1996, after discussions between the parties stalled, Holtzbrinck downloaded the files from Vyne's computer to its own server using the password that Vyne originally gave to Holtzbrinck. The password provided Holtzbrinck the ability to access the Scientific American website stored on Vyne's computer.

The following month, Vyne filed a certificate of copyright registration for the website, entitled "Scientific American: Working Knowledge Custom Written Software for the *Scientific American* Magazine Internet Web Site." Thereafter, Vyne accused Scientific American of copyright infringement.

HPH commenced this action on February 28, 1997, seeking a declaration as to its rights in the programs and files which comprise the Scientific American website, and that as a result of those rights, either as copyright owner or licensee, it did not infringe on Vyne's rights. Vyne asserted counterclaims for copyright infringement, trespass, misappropriation of trade secrets, and other torts.

In its motion for partial summary judgment, plaintiff now seeks a declaration that Vyne granted Holtzbrinck, at a minimum, a nonexclusive license in the programs and files created by Vyne for the Scientific American website, and therefore did not violate the copyright claimed by Vyne. Vyne, on the other hand, argues that it never granted Holtzbrinck a license to use the website files, and that Holtzbrinck infringed on its copyright. Defendant also seeks summary judgment dismissing all other claims raised by the plaintiff.

---

2. The draft also contained a Work for Hire provision, stating that "[t]he parties intend the Work Product, as herein defined, to be a work made for hire under the Copyright Act, and Vyne acknowledges HEP as the sole owner of the copyright and all other intangible rights therein." Website Services Agreement (Budwig Draft), Paul Aff'd, Exh. G.

DISCUSSION

As a result of the rapid growth of the Internet, many companies are creating websites to benefit their businesses, and are hiring website designers to construct the sites for them. Some of these arrangements, however, are made without either a copyright ownership or licensing clause. The resulting problem is evidenced by this case, where a relationship falters and both parties fight over the ownership of the website, and the right to use the files comprising the site. Because of the sparse case law on the subject, this case presents novel issues in the area of copyright law and its application to a website.

Assuming for the purposes of plaintiff's motion that the parties' writings failed to satisfy the requirements of the Copyright Act vesting ownership of the website and its files with HPH, the undisputed writings and conduct of the parties compel a finding that, for the website programs and files for which HPH paid consideration, it possesses a nonexclusive license. As a result, HPH cannot be said to have violated the copyright that Vyne may possess in those files. To the extent that Vyne exceeded the scope of the parties' initial work agreement, and Holtzbrinck did not compensate Vyne for that extra work, Holtzbrinck's implied license is revocable for that extra work. Because material questions of fact still remain about the complete scope of Vyne's work, and because it is not clear if, and by how much, Vyne exceeded the scope of its initial agreement, and what consideration was in fact paid, I cannot conclude whether, and to what extent, Holtzbrinck's license is partially revocable. For this reason, summary judgment is partially denied.

Plaintiff's Nonexclusive License in the SA Website

No triable issues exist as to Holtzbrinck's possession of an irrevocable nonexclusive license to use the programs and files comprising the SA website, for which it paid due consideration. To the extent that Vyne exceeded the scope of its initial work agreement, however, and Holtzbrinck did not pay consideration for that work, Holtzbrinck's license would be partially revocable.

A. The License is Implied by Law

A nonexclusive license is a creation fashioned by the courts for when parties intend to transfer a copyright, but fail to do so in writing. Such a license can be granted orally or implied from the conduct of the parties. Nonexclusive licenses do not constitute transfer of ownership rights and do not come within the purview of copyright law. Rather, they simply permit the use of a copyrighted work in a particular manner. An implied nonexclusive license is granted when (i) a person (the licensee) requests the creation of a work; (ii) the creator (the licensor) makes that particular work and delivers it to the licensee; and (iii) the licensor intends that the licensee copy and distribute his work.

These factors are readily met here. Vyne's undisputed admissions and conduct throughout the course of it's work with Holtzbrinck demonstrates that it granted Holtzbrinck an implied, nonexclusive license in the programs and files comprising the SA website. First, Holtzbrinck, as licensee, requested that Vyne create a website for *Scientific American* Magazine. This came several months after Vyne created and transferred to Holtzbrinck a website for W.H. Freeman. Clearly, Holtzbrinck and Vyne were familiar with each other, and with their respective intentions.

Second, Vyne agreed to do the programming and coding to create a website specifically for Holtzbrinck. In fact, Vyne was paid approximately $105,000 for the development of the programming files needed for the website and its updating, and was paid

$1,000 per month to host the website on its computer. The work product was delivered when the site was launched, and Holtzbrinck used the site.

Third, the codes and files were intended for Holtzbrinck's use for the website. Otherwise, the code would serve no function for Holtzbrinck. If a license is not implied to permit HPH's use of the work, Vyne's work would be worthless to Holtzbrinck, for the code was created to display the magazine's content on the website. *See Design Options, Inc. v. Bellepointe, Inc.*, 940 F.Supp. 86, 92 (S.D.N.Y.1996). Holtzbrinck would have no reason to pay Vyne for the code unless it used it for the website. In fact, Defendant's copyright registration title clearly indicates that the code was intended for use for the SA website.[3]

As similarly reasoned by the Ninth Circuit in one of the few cases in this area, to hold that Vyne did not convey a license to use the code on the website would mean that its contribution was of minimal value, a conclusion that cannot be squared with the fact that Holtzbrinck paid Vyne a substantial amount of money for its work. *See Effects*, 908 F.2d at 559. Holtzbrinck would not pay good consideration to have a website created and not be able to use it.

Moreover, when the parties sought to memorialize their discussions, the documents drafted by both Holtzbrinck and Vyne expressly referenced Holtzbrinck's ownership of the website and all intellectual property contained in the site.[4] In fact, in two separate writings, Hall acknowledged that Holtzbrinck owned the website and all of the programs and files comprising the website. In his affidavit, Hall admitted to his understanding that Holtzbrinck would own the website files.

Aside from these manifest representations, Vyne also gave Holtzbrinck password access to the website, placed a copyright notice on the website indicating that Scientific American was the copyright owner without reserving any similar notice of Vyne's claim to any ownership rights, and transferred files to Holtzbrinck in July 1996 in anticipation of the eventual transfer of the entire website to the Holtzbrinck server. Clearly, Vyne intended for Holtzbrinck to use the files, if not to own them.

The record clearly shows that Vyne was not only aware of Holtzbrinck's intentions to own the site, but acted in accordance with those intentions from the inception of its relationship with Holtzbrinck, generally, and Scientific American, in particular. Its history and course of dealing with Holtzbrinck leads to a conclusion that Vyne conducted itself in a manner commensurate with granting Holtzbrinck a nonexclusive implied license.

An implied license is revocable, however, absent consideration. If there is proper consideration, the license remains irrevocable. *See I.A.E., Inc. v. Shaver*, 74 F.3d 768, 772 (7th Cir.1996). It is undisputed that Holtzbrinck paid Vyne in excess of $60,000 for work performed in creating the website. For that work product, Holtzbrinck's implied license remains irrevocable. If Vyne exceeded the scope of its original agreement and produced work for which it was not adequately compensated,

---

3. The Certificate of Copyright Registration was entitled: "Scientific American: Working Knowledge Custom Written Software for the *Scientific American* Magazine Internet Web Site."

4. Vyne's draft contract defines the website ownership as follows: "Scientific American is the sole owner of the existing WWW side and any changes or additions to it that occur in the future. This consists of all HTML files that comprise the visual entity that can be viewed on the World Wide Web, all unique graphics such as so-called navbars, all forms and other CGI code that are functional elements of the site, and all content provided by Scientific American or developed for Scientific American by Vyne or its employees." (Hall Draft), Paul Aff'd, Exh. D.

Holtzbrinck's license to use that work product would be revocable. The extent of Holtzbrinck's consideration is not clear, and not possible for determination on summary judgment.

It is possible that Vyne exceeded the scope of the parties' original agreement when it published the entire September 1996 issue of Scientific American on the website. It is not clear, however, whether Holtzbrinck paid Vyne additional consideration for that extra work product, or whether the parties intended it to be covered within the scope of their original agreement.

Also, it is not clear whether, when Holtzbrinck transferred files from Vyne's computer to its own using Shara Zoll's password, it transferred files that were outside the scope of the original work agreement, and were not paid for. To the extent that it did, Holtzbrinck does not have the right to continue to use those files as a licensee. The record does not indicate which files were transferred or what the full scope of Vyne's work was, so I cannot determine if Vyne's work exceeded the scope of the parties' understandings, and if Holtzbrinck's license should be revoked for the use of those files.

Defendant's Counterclaim: Copyright Infringement

"A copyright owner who grants a nonexclusive license to use his copyrighted material waives his right to sue the licensee for copyright infringement." *Graham,* 144 F.3d at 236.

Because I find that the defendant granted Holtzbrinck an implied, nonexclusive license in the programs comprising the website, defendant cannot now sue for copyright infringement. To the extent, however, that Holtzbrinck has not paid consideration for work done beyond the scope of the parties' understanding, Holtzbrinck's license for that work is revocable. As such, Vyne may have a recognizable copyright infringement action so long as it is the true copyright owner for that work. Accordingly, summary judgment for Defendant's counterclaim is denied.

Defendant's Summary Judgment Motion

Vyne also... seeks summary judgment on plaintiff's fifth claim for relief, arguing that as true owner of the copyright, their Certification of Copyright Registration is valid. Finally, defendant seeks to dismiss plaintiff's sixth claim asking the defendant to destroy all copies of the website files in its possession. Defendant now seeks a declaration that it is entitled to have as many copies of the files as it wishes. This final analysis, however, turns on whether the defendant is the true copyright owner.

Defendant's motion for partial summary judgment is denied because material issues of fact remain. Here, material issues of fact exist concerning the ownership of the copyright, including (i) whether the parties intended Vyne's work to be a work for hire; (ii) whether the parties intended to create a joint work; and (iii) the extent of Vyne's ownership in its contributions. So long as questions still remain on these issues, defendant cannot be declared the copyright owner of the SA website, and must be denied summary judgment. All claims will be addressed together, as the same issues of fact apply to each one.

There is no dispute that defendant created the custom-written software for the SA website, and that defendant is in the first instance the owner of the copyright in the program code. *See* 17 U.S.C. § 201 (copyright vests initially in the author). Therefore, to the extent that Vyne owned any preliminary copyright in the website, the copyright was never transferred to Holtzbrinck, as the transfer of a copyright must be in writing to satisfy the Statute of Frauds. *See* 17 U.S.C. § 204.

The record isn't developed enough, however, to indicate whether the parties intended that Vyne's work on the SA website be considered a "Work for Hire," or whether the parties intended that their joint contributions to the website be considered a "Joint Work." Thus, I cannot conclude that Vyne is the owner of the copyright, even though it is clear that no transfer of ownership occurred.

Data General Corp. v. Grumman Systems Support Corp.

U.S. District Court
825 F. Supp. 340 (D. Mass. 1993)

Following a vigorously litigated trial spanning more than nine weeks, the jury returned a verdict against defendant Grumman Systems Support Corporation. The jury awarded Data General $27,417,000 on its federal copyright infringement claim and $27,417,000 on its state law misappropriation of trade secrets claim. Finding Grumman's misappropriation of trade secrets to be willful, I increased the trade secrets award by $9,000,000. This court entered judgment, in the form submitted by Data General, on January 29, 1993.

[C]ontested post trial motions are now pending. I have summarized the facts of this case in prior opinions and will not repeat them here except as is relevant to issues under discussion.

Defendant's Motion For Judgment As A Matter Of Law

Pursuant to Fed.R.Civ.P. 50(b), Grumman urges this court to enter judgment for the defendant as a matter of law, contending that Data General failed to prove the content of its copyright, the validity of its copyright registrations, the infringement of the registered copyright, the identity of the alleged trade secrets, the wrongful misappropriation of such trade secrets, and the adequacy of the protection of such trade secrets. Alternatively, Grumman moves for a new trial under Fed.R.Civ.P. 59(a).

A. The Copyright Claim

To prevail on its claim of copyright infringement, Data General was required to prove (1) that it is the owner of a work protected by the Copyright Act, and (2) that Grumman copied that work without authorization. E.g., *Motta v. Weiser, Inc.*, 768 F.2d 481, 483 (1st Cir.), *cert. denied*, 474 U.S. 1033 (1985). In addition, as a prerequisite to suit, Data General was required to prove that it duly registered its copyright claim with the Copyright Office. 17 U.S.C.A. §411(a). Despite Grumman's best efforts to obscure the forest by focusing on the trees, the jury properly concluded, based on ample evidence, that Grumman infringed Data General's copyright in MV/ADEX.

1. Copying a protected work

Grumman argues that it is entitled to judgment in its favor because Data General failed to prove that the MV/ADEX computer programs admittedly copied and used by Grumman were the same works in which Data General held copyrights. More specifically, Grumman asserts that Data General was required to prove that the *object code* programs copied by Grumman are the same as the *source code* programs registered with the Copyright Office.[5] Since Data General did not produce the source code for any version of MV/ADEX, it is argued that Data General could not prove that Grumman's admitted use of the object code programs infringed the source code programs registered with the Copyright Office. As I explained in my October 9, 1992 ruling, Grumman's argument is flawed.

Contrary to Grumman's understanding, the materials deposited with the Copyright Office do not define the substantive protection extended to the registered work. Indeed, the Copyright Act expressly provides that copyright "registration is not a condition of copyright protection," and may be obtained at any time during the subsistence of the copyright. 17 U.S.C.A. §408(a). Since copyright protection exists without regard to copyright registration, it follows that the deposit that accompanies a registration cannot by itself define the copyrighted work. In this case, the source code deposits that were made with the Copyright Office were merely symbols, rather than definitions, of the protected work. See *Midway Mfg. Co. v. Arctic Int'l, Inc.*, 211 U.S.P.Q. 1152, 1158 (N.D.Ill.1981) ("It is the work that cannot be copied or incorporated and not the specific tangible expression on file in the Copyright Office."). Thus, Data General held copyrights on the various versions of the computer program MV/ADEX, not the source code version of MV/ADEX.

Similarly, Grumman misconceives as three separate programs the registered computer program, source code version of that program, and object code version of that program. Though Grumman has admittedly used MV/ADEX in its object code form, it claims there was no proof that it infringed the "registered source code program." The Copyright Office, however, "considers source code and object code as two representations of the same computer program. For registration, purposes, the claim is in the *computer program* rather than in any particular representation of the program." Copyright Office, Compendium II of Copyright Office Practices §321.03 (1984) (emphasis in original); *e.g., Apple Computer, Inc. v. Franklin Computer Corp.*, 714 F.2d 1240, 1249 (3rd Cir.1983), *cert. dismissed,* 464 U.S. 1033 (1984). Accordingly, while Data General had the burden of proving that Grumman copied MV/ADEX in one of its protected forms, Data General could meet that burden by showing infringement of either the source code or the object code version of MV/ADEX.

At trial, Data General introduced the master object code program for each version of MV/ADEX and Mr. Gove, Data General's expert, testified that he compared each major revision of the MV/ADEX tapes used by Grumman to the master object code programs and found them to be identical in all material respects. In addition, the jury heard testimony that Grumman service employees regularly used MV/ADEX object code tapes on service calls, Grumman employees stored the various versions of MV/ADEX in computer libraries so that additional copies could be made to replace worn-out versions, and Grumman had an informal network to distribute recently appropriated copies of MV/ADEX. Grumman employees referred to these programs as "MV/ADEX," usually identifying the specific revision to which they

---

5. Generally, a computer program is written by a programmer using "source code," a computer language that uses a combination of words, symbols, and numbers that are meaningful to a trained programmer. The source code is then compiled by a computer into "object code," a binary machine language appearing as a series of 0's and 1's that is unintelligible to even a trained human observer. A computer runs a program using object code.

were referring or requesting. Moreover, hundreds of tapes labeled as MV/ADEX that were recovered from Grumman were introduced into evidence. Grumman's contention that it is entitled to judgment because Data General failed to prove infringement is frivolous. The jury was clearly entitled to find that Grumman infringed Data General's copyrights.

Grumman also argues that without an analysis of the MV/ADEX source code, Data General could not prove that Grumman copied protectable elements of MV/ADEX. Defendant contends that the expression, originality, modular composition, and functionality of MV/ADEX must be examined to determine which elements are copyrightable and whether those elements were copied by Grumman. In many cases, such an analysis is critical to determining whether the defendant actually infringed the plaintiff's copyright. For example, in a recent, erudite opinion by Judge Walker, the Second Circuit Court of Appeals engaged in a detailed, three-step analysis of the copyrighted work's code, structure, and function to determine whether the infringing program was substantially similar to the protected work. *Computer Assoc. Int'l, Inc. v. Altai, Inc.*, 982 F.2d 693, 701-715 (2nd Cir.1992). *Computer Assoc.*, however, addressed an issue not raised by Data General's copyright claim.

A plaintiff may show unauthorized copying of an copyrighted work in one of two ways: (1) by submitting evidence that the defendant directly copied the work or (2) by showing the defendant had access to plaintiff's copyrighted work and that defendant's work is substantially similar to the plaintiff's copyrighted work. *Computer Assoc.*, 982 F.2d at 701; *Eckes v. Card Prices Update*, 736 F.2d 859, 863 (2nd Cir.1984). *Computer Assoc.* involved two allegedly infringing computer programs, one which was admittedly directly copied from the plaintiff's copyrighted work and one which contained none of the literal elements of the copyrighted work, but was alleged to be substantially similar. *Id.* at 700–01. The district court found that the first program, which directly incorporated approximately 30% of the source code of plaintiff's copyrighted work, infringed the plaintiff's copyright; a finding which the defendant did not pursue on appeal. *Id.* at 702. The appeal addressed the question of whether the second version of the defendant's program, which did not incorporate any of the literal elements of the plaintiff's copyrighted work, infringed the copyrighted work. *Id.* at 710–12. Though the second program did not directly copy any of the copyrighted work's source or object code, the plaintiff claimed the defendant's program infringed the non-literal elements of the plaintiff's program by utilizing a substantially similar structure and operating system. The appeal and the court's thorough analysis of the program's structure and code was aimed at determining substantial similarity of the copyrighted and infringing work, in the absence of direct copying.

Data General's copyright claim is similar to the first infringement claim in *Computer Assoc.* Data General proved infringement of its copyright through the most direct method: by showing that Grumman repeatedly copied 100% of the object code of Data General's MV/ADEX copyrights. It is only in the absence of such direct evidence that a plaintiff must resort to proving infringement by showing a defendant's access to the copyrighted work and substantial similarity of the infringing program. While the three-step analysis used in *Computer Assoc.* may be highly relevant to cases which lack direct evidence of copying, it is not applicable here. Unlike *Computer Assoc.* there was no evidence to suggest that Grumman independently created the object code tapes; no evidence that Grumman incorporated only a portion of the MV/ADEX object code into a larger, original program; and no evidence that Grumman rewrote the object code tapes or somehow enhanced the software.

Nor was an analysis of the source code necessary to determine the validity of Data General's copyrights in MV/ADEX. The copyright registration is prima facie evidence of the validity of the copyright. 17 U.S.C.A. §410(c). Grumman never produced sufficient evidence to rebut the validity of the copyrights. *Dynamic Solutions, Inc. v. Planning & Control, Inc.*, 646 F.Supp. 1329, 1337 (S.D.N.Y.1986) (a registration certificate relieves plaintiff of proving the many facts necessary to show ownership and validity of a copyright unless the defendant effectively challenges the presumption and shifts the burden of so doing to the plaintiff). To the contrary, the evidence demonstrated that Data General authored the program and that MV/ADEX constituted an original expression of a copyrightable work. The originality and nonobviousness of MV/ADEX can be inferred from the inability of competitors to replicate its operation. Forcing Data General to produce the source code would have added nothing to the trial, but would have placed an undue burden on Data General and risked serious trial delay and juror confusion.

2. Copyright registration

The jury found that Data General had validly registered each revision of MV/ADEX. Grumman asserts that this finding should be rejected as a matter of law because of errors contained in the copyright registration.

To register a claim of copyright, the Copyright Office requires an applicant to submit a completed application form, the statutory fee, and an appropriate deposit of the copyrighted work. 17 U.S.C.A. §408(a); Compendium II of Copyright Office Practices §603. In the case of a computer program that contains trade secret material, such as MV/ADEX, the Copyright Office permits the deposit to take the form of a symbolic filing: the first and last ten pages of the source code. 37 C.F.R. §202.20(c)(2)(vii)(A)(2) (1992). Data General filed registration applications with the Copyright Office for each revision of MV/ADEX.

The errors in the registration first came to light during trial.... There was absolutely no evidence that Data General knowingly misrepresented the deposits to the Copyright Office, obtained any benefit by making these errors, or acted with bad faith, either at the time of making the deposits or during trial. To the contrary, the evidence showed that Data General made several innocent, inadvertent errors in its copyright deposits and promptly informed this court as soon as those errors became known. There is no evidence that Data General realized the errors at any point before the issue emerged during trial. Grumman's claim that the deposit errors invalidate the copyright registrations is unsupported by the facts and unwarranted by law: Only the "knowing failure to advise the Copyright Office of facts which might have occasioned a rejection of the application constitute[s] reason for holding the registration invalid and thus incapable of supporting an infringement action... or denying enforcement on the ground of unclean hands...." *Eckes,* 736 F.2d at 861–62.

In *Dynamic Solutions,* the plaintiff filed copyright registrations which identified two software programs as being created in 1983 and 1984, respectively. The plaintiff, however, deposited versions of the software that existed at the time of filing in 1986 and made other unspecified errors in the deposits. *Dynamic Solutions,* 646 F.Supp. at 1341 n.18. The 1983 and 1984 versions no longer existed, could not be reproduced, and the plaintiff could not identify how the programs had changed during the intervening period of time. *Id.* at 1341. The court explained that "[e]rrors on the registration application do not affect plaintiff's right to sue for infringement unless they are knowing and might have caused the Copyright Office to reject the application." *Id.*

The evidence wholly supports the jury's finding that Data General validly registered each revision of MV/ADEX.

B. Misappropriation of Trade Secrets

To prevail on its claim that Grumman misappropriated Data General's trade secrets in MV/ADEX, Data General was required to show that (1) MV/ADEX is a trade secret; (2) Data General took reasonable steps to preserve the secrecy of MV/ADEX; and (3) Grumman used improper means, in breach of a confidential relationship, to acquire and use the trade secret. The evidence produced at trial amply supports the jury's verdict in Data General's favor.

1. *MV/ADEX as a trade secret*

Grumman argues that it is entitled to judgment because Data General failed to identify the specific secret which was misappropriated by Grumman. Though the jury heard extensive testimony as to the function, effectiveness, and use of MV/ADEX, Grumman complains that Data General never produced the precise secret as embodied in the software's source code. Grumman initially offered no case law to support its argument. However, in its supplemental brief, Grumman relies on a recently decided opinion of the Ninth Circuit Court of Appeals, *MAI Sys. Corp. v. Peak Computer, Inc.*, 991 F.2d 511 (9th Cir.1993), for the proposition that a plaintiff must specifically identify the trade secrets which were purportedly misappropriated. Grumman asserts that without producing the source code and without identifying specific lines or sections of the source code, Data General could not prevail on its trade secret claim as a matter of law.

MAI shares some commonalities with the case before me. A computer manufacturer, who also serviced the computers it sold, sued an independent computer maintenance company for, among other things, copyright infringement and misappropriation of trade secrets. *MAI*, 991 F.2d at 513–514. The plaintiff's trade secret claim alleged infringement of its customer data base, field information bulletins, and software. The district court granted summary judgment in plaintiff's favor on all three trade secret grounds, though the plaintiff's brief addressed neither the software nor the field information bulletins. *Id.* at 520. The only evidence establishing that the software contained trade secrets was a conclusory statement that the diagnostic software "contain[s] valuable trade secrets." *Id.* at 523. The court of appeals reversed the award of summary judgment because the plaintiff failed to satisfactorily identify the purported trade secret. *Id.* at 522–523. "[A] plaintiff who seeks relief for misappropriation of trade secrets must identify the trade secrets and carry the burden of showing that they exist." *Id.* at 522.

Though *MAI* shares some similarities to the case before me, the facts of the two cases and their procedural histories are quite distinct. *MAI* arose under California law, was decided by the district court's *sua sponte* award of summary judgment in the *plaintiff's* favor, based on an unsupported assertion that a trade secret existed. In this case, a jury found in the plaintiff's favor after a nine-week trial which involved extensive testimony concerning the misappropriated trade secret.

To the extent *MAI* is relevant to our case, it supports the verdict. Grumman contends that as applied to this case, *MAI's* "specific identification" requires Data General to point to individual trade secrets in the MV/ADEX source code. *MAI*, however, does not go so far. The court was unwilling to allow a plaintiff to prevail on summary judgment by baldly asserting the existence of some undefined trade secret. To that end, the *MAI* court demanded that the plaintiff describe the subject matter of the trade secret with sufficient particularity to separate it from matters of public knowledge, to permit the defendant to ascertain the boundaries of the secret, and to give the defendant notice of the issues to be met at trial—this was the holding of the two California cases upon which *MAI* relied to reach its result. *Diodes, Inc. v. Franzen,* 260 Cal.App.2d 244, 67 Cal.Rptr. 19, 24 (1968); *Universal Analytics, Inc. v. MacNeal-Schwendler Corp.,* 707 F.Supp. 1170, 1177 (C.D.Cal.1989), *aff'd,* 914 F.2d 1256 (9th Cir.1990). Moreover, one of the cases relied on by *MAI* expressly rejected the detailed identification requirement that Grumman argues *MAI* establishes. In *Diodes,* the court explained, "One who seeks to protect his trade secrets from wrongful use or disclosure does not have to spell out the details of the trade secret to avoid a demurrer to a complaint. To so require would mean that the complainant would have to destroy the very thing for which he sought protection by making public the secret itself." *Diodes,* 67 Cal.Rptr. at 24. I cannot believe that the Ninth Circuit intended to overrule a case, *sub silentio,* upon which it expressly relied.

Under the governing law of this case, Massachusetts law, "[a] trade secret may consist of any formula, pattern, device or compilation of information which is used in one's business, and which [provides] an opportunity to obtain an advantage over competitors who do not know or use it.... The subject matter of a trade secret must be secret. Matters of public knowledge or of general knowledge in an industry cannot be appropriated by one as his secret." *J.T. Healy,* 260 N.E.2d at 729 (quoting Restatement of Torts §757, comment b.) The existence of a trade secret depends on the facts of each case. *Jet Spray Cooler, Inc. v. Crampton,* 361 Mass. 835, 282 N.E.2d 921, 925 (1972). Here, the jury was instructed to consider a number of factors, including the nature of the information and the conduct of the parties, and concluded that MV/ADEX was a trade secret—a conclusion well-supported by the evidence.

Several witnesses, including two Grumman witnesses, testified that MV/ADEX contained trade secrets. This evidence was corroborated by testimony about the design, function, and use of MV/ADEX. The evidence showed that MV/ADEX was unique, effective, and conferred a competitive advantage to Data General in the computer service business. Data General's expert witness, Mr. Gove, explained that Data General developed numerous original programs for use in MV/ADEX and testified in some detail as to the more important functions and capabilities of those programs. In addition to this direct evidence, the jury was entitled to infer that MV/ADEX contained trade secrets because Grumman was unable to create functionally comparable diagnostic software. As discussed more fully below, there was no evidence to indicate that MV/ADEX was a matter of public knowledge. Data General took reasonable steps to preserve, and in fact did preserve, the secrecy of MV/ADEX. With the exception of those who lawfully licensed or unlawfully misappropriated MV/ADEX, Data General enjoyed the exclusive use of MV/ADEX. Even those who obtained MV/ADEX and were able to *use* MV/ADEX were unable to discover its trade secrets because MV/ADEX was distributed only in its object code form, which is essentially unintelligible to humans. An infringer may be liable for misappropriating trade secrets when it loads and runs a computer program in its object code form, even if the infringer never understands exactly how the program works. *Trandes Corp. v. Guy F. Atkinson Co.,* 798 F.Supp. 284, 288 (D.Md.1992).

2. Reasonable steps to preserve secrecy

A plaintiff enforcing a trade secret must take reasonable and proper steps to preserve its secrecy. *USM,* 393 N.E.2d at 899–902; *CVD,* 769 F.2d at 851–52. Heroic measures, however, are not required. *Id.* Whether reasonable steps have been taken depends on the circumstances of each case, including the nature of the information sought to be protected and the conduct of the parties. *USM,* 393 N.E.2d at 902. Grumman argues that it is entitled to judgment because Data General failed to establish that it took reasonable steps to preserve the secrecy of its trade secret. Grumman's argument is contrary to the weight of the evidence.

Data General required employees to sign confidentiality agreements which prohibited the unauthorized disclosure of confidential or proprietary information; completed termination checklists, which specifically covered software, when an employee left the company; distributed a company brochure detailing the company's policy on protecting confidential and proprietary information, including software; deployed security guards; required visitors to sign in when visiting and prohibited unescorted visits; restricted employee access to the area in which MV/ADEX was developed; labeled MV/ADEX tapes as "property of Data General," displayed a copyright notice on the exterior of MV/ADEX tapes and on the first display screen of the program itself; did not distribute MV/ADEX source code outside of Data General; and required customers to sign an agreement which, among other things, prohibited unauthorized disclosure to third parties. Grumman cites evidence to the contrary, focusing on perceived shortcomings in the safeguards and instances where Data General's procedures were not followed. The jury heard all testimony, weighed the evidence, and apparently rejected Grumman's evidence as unpersuasive, as they were free to do. The jury properly concluded that Data General took reasonable steps to preserve the secrecy of the information embodied in the MV/ADEX programs.

3. Grumman's misappropriation

Grumman argues that Data General failed to prove that Grumman knowingly misappropriated MV/ADEX and goes so far as to make the remarkable statement that "there is no evidence that [Grumman] knowingly took anything in breach of a duty." The jury, for good reason, differed with Grumman's view of the evidence. Grumman admits that it took copies of MV/ADEX from customer sites and obtained copies from used MV machines on which MV/ADEX resided, but claims that Data General never proved the wrongful acquisition of any one of the hundreds of tapes in Grumman's possession. Grumman's argument is either totally contrary to the evidence or is based on a misunderstanding of the law. Grumman also asserts that the jury erred in rejecting Grumman's "good faith" defense, which alleged that it had a good faith belief that it had a license to use Data General diagnostics.

Though a defendant must "have notice of both the fact that the information claimed to be a trade secret is in fact secret and the fact that disclosure by the third person is a breach of duty before one is subject to liability for the use or disclosure of the trade secret," the requisite notice may be found where the defendant knew *or should have known* that the proffered information is the trade secret of another. *Curtiss-Wright Corp.*, 407 N.E.2d at 323–24. "Studious ignorance" will not insulate a defendant from liability. *Id.* at 324. Moreover, courts have noted that the defendant's knowledge "often must be proved by the weight of credible circumstantial evidence." *Id.* In this case, there was credible evidence from which the jury could infer that Grumman obtained MV/ADEX by taking property known to belong to another or by knowingly participating in the breach of an express or implied confidentiality agreement by, for example, a former employee or customer of Data General.

After this court issued a preliminary injunction enjoining further use of MV/ADEX by Grumman, the defendant returned more than 200 copies of MV/ADEX. Though Data General never proved how Grumman acquired all the tapes, neither could Grumman explain how it came into possession of so many tapes. It was undisputed that Grumman never purchased a copy of MV/ADEX from Data General. On the facts of this case, the unexplained possession of Data General's MV/ADEX tapes is more than suspicious. The tapes were labeled as "property of Data General" and, when run on a computer, displayed a copyright notice identifying Data General as its owner. For some tapes, a Grumman label had been pasted on top of the original Data General label. At the same time Grumman was collecting MV/ADEX tapes from unidentified sources, it was unsuccessful in its attempts to acquire MV/ADEX openly and directly from Data General under a licensing agreement. Moreover, Grumman admitted that it knew confidentiality agreements were widely used in the business to restrict disclosure of proprietary information by customers and former employees. In fact, an internal Grumman memorandum from 1987, which was reviewed by top Grumman officials, stated that use of MV/ADEX diagnostics was illegal unless purchased from Data General. A proper inference is that Grumman was acting with either studied ignorance or actual knowledge of the source of so many copies of a competitor's valuable software program.

Some of the tapes turned in by Grumman were pre-release versions of MV/ADEX. Pre-release versions of MV/ADEX were not sold, distributed, or permitted to leave Data General facilities. The jury could infer that Grumman's possession of these tapes demonstrated that it knew the tapes were taken directly from Data General or were being provided to Grumman by former Data General employees in violation of their employment agreements. This is consistent with Grumman's admission that it came to learn that George Tasso, a former employee of Data General, brought a copy of MV/ADEX when he came to work for Grumman.

As for Grumman's proffered "good faith" defense, further discussion is unnecessary. The purported defense was not based on compelling facts and, in face of inconsistent evidence, the jury was free to reject Grumman's claim of good faith as incredible.

Grumman's Motion For Judgment As A Matter Of Law [is] denied.

Two Pesos, Inc. v. Taco Cabana, Inc.
Supreme Court of the United States
505 U.S. 763 (1992)

We granted certiorari to resolve the conflict among the Courts of Appeals on the question whether trade dress that is inherently distinctive is protectible under §43(a) without a showing that it has acquired secondary meaning.

II

The Lanham Act was intended to make "actionable the deceptive and misleading use of marks" and "to protect persons engaged in...commerce against unfair competition." §45, 15 U.S.C. §1127. Section 43(a) "prohibits a broader range of practices than does §32," which applies to registered marks, *Inwood Laboratories, Inc. v. Ives Laboratories, Inc.*, 456 U.S. 844, 858 (1982), but it is common ground that §43(a) protects qualifying unregistered trademarks and that the general principles qualifying a mark for registration under §2 of the Lanham Act are for the most part applicable in determining whether an unregistered mark is entitled to protection under §43(a).

A trademark is defined in 15 U.S.C. §1127 as including "any word, name, symbol, or device or any combination thereof" used by any person "to identify and distinguish his or her goods, including a unique product, from those manufactured or sold by others and to indicate the source of the goods, even if that source is unknown." In order to be registered, a mark must be capable of distinguishing the applicant's goods from those of others. §1052. Marks are often classified in categories of generally increasing distinctiveness; following the classic formulation set out by Judge Friendly, they may be (1) generic; (2) descriptive; (3) suggestive; (4) arbitrary; or (5) fanciful. See *Abercrombie & Fitch Co. v. Hunting World, Inc.*, 537 F.2d 4, 9 (CA2 1976). The Court of Appeals followed this classification and petitioner accepts it. Brief for Petitioner 11-15. The latter three categories of marks, because their intrinsic nature serves to identify a particular source of a product, are deemed inherently distinctive and are entitled to protection. In contrast, generic marks—those that "refe[r] to the genus of which the particular product is a species," are not registrable as trademarks. *Park 'N Fly, Inc. v. Dollar Park & Fly, Inc.*, 469 U.S. 189, 194 (1985).

Marks which are merely descriptive of a product are not inherently distinctive. When used to describe a product, they do not inherently identify a particular source, and hence cannot be protected. However, descriptive marks may acquire the distinctiveness which will allow them to be protected under the Act. Section 2 of the Lanham Act provides that a descriptive mark that otherwise could not be registered under the Act may be registered if it "has become distinctive of the applicant's goods in commerce." §§2(e), (f), 15 U.S.C. §§1052(e), (f). See *Park 'N Fly, supra*, at 194, 196. This acquired distinctiveness is generally called "secondary meaning." *Kellogg Co. v. National Biscuit Co.*, 305 U.S. 111, 118 (1938). The concept of secondary meaning has been applied to actions under §43(a).

The general rule regarding distinctiveness is clear: An identifying mark is distinctive and capable of being protected if it *either* (1) is inherently distinctive *or* (2) has acquired distinctiveness through secondary meaning. Restatement (Third) of Unfair Competition §13, pp. 37–38, and Comment *a* (Tent. Draft No. 2, Mar. 23, 1990). It is also clear that eligibility for protection under §43(a) depends on nonfunctionality. It is, of course, also undisputed that liability under §43(a) requires proof of the likelihood of confusion.

It would be a different matter if there were textual basis in §43(a) for treating inherently distinctive verbal or symbolic trademarks differently from inherently distinctive trade dress. But there is none. The section does not mention trademarks or trade dress, whether they be called generic, descriptive, suggestive, arbitrary, fanciful, or functional. Nor does the concept of secondary meaning appear in the text of §43(a). Where secondary meaning does appear in the statute, 15 U.S.C. §1052 (1982 ed.), it is a requirement that applies only to merely descriptive marks and not to inherently distinctive ones. We see no basis for requiring secondary meaning for inherently distinctive trade dress protection under §43(a) but not for other distinctive words, symbols, or devices capable of identifying a producer's product.

Engrafting onto §43(a) a requirement of secondary meaning for inherently distinctive trade dress also would undermine the purposes of the Lanham Act. Protection of trade dress, no less than of trademarks, serves the Act's purpose to "secure to the owner of the mark the goodwill of his business and to protect the ability of consumers to distinguish among competing producers. National protection of trademarks is desirable, Congress concluded, because trademarks foster competition and the maintenance of quality by securing to the producer the benefits of good reputation." *Park 'N Fly*, 469 U.S., at 198. By making more difficult the identification of a producer with its product, a secondary meaning requirement for a nondescriptive trade dress would hinder improving or maintaining the producer's competitive position.

Suggestions that under the Fifth Circuit's law, the initial user of any shape or design would cut off competition from products of like design and shape are not persuasive. Only nonfunctional, distinctive trade dress is protected under §43(a). The Fifth Circuit holds that a design is legally functional, and thus unprotectible, if it is one of a limited number of equally efficient options available to competitors and free competition would be unduly hindered by according the design trademark protection. See *Sicilia Di R. Biebow & Co. v. Cox*, 732 F.2d 417, 426 (1984). This serves to assure that competition will not be stifled by the exhaustion of a limited number of trade dresses.

On the other hand, adding a secondary meaning requirement could have anticompetitive effects, creating particular burdens on the startup of small companies. It would present special difficulties for a business, such as respondent, that seeks to start a new product in a limited area and then expand into new markets. Denying protection for inherently distinctive nonfunctional trade dress until after secondary meaning has been established would allow a competitor, which has not adopted a distinctive trade dress of its own, to appropriate the originator's dress in other markets and to deter the originator from expanding into and competing in these areas.

As noted above, petitioner concedes that protecting an inherently distinctive trade dress from its inception may be critical to new entrants to the market and that withholding protection until secondary meaning has been established would be contrary to the goals of the Lanham Act. Petitioner specifically suggests, however, that the solution is to dispense with the requirement of secondary meaning for a reasonable, but brief, period at the outset of the use of a trade dress. Reply Brief for Petitioner 11-12. If §43(a) does not require secondary meaning at the outset of a business' adoption of trade dress, there is no basis in the statute to support the suggestion that such a requirement comes into being after some unspecified time.

III

We agree with the Court of Appeals that proof of secondary meaning is not required to prevail on a claim under §43(a) of the Lanham Act where the trade dress at issue is inherently distinctive, and accordingly the judgment of that court is affirmed.

Interstellar Starship Services, Ltd. v. Tchou

Court of Appeals, Ninth Circuit
304 F.3d 936 (9th Cir. 2002)

TROTT, Circuit Judge.

Epix, Inc. ("Epix") sued Interstellar Starship Services ("ISS") and its president Michael Tchou ("Tchou") in district court alleging that their use of the *www.epix.com* domain name infringed Epix's registered EPIX trademark.

BACKGROUND

Epix manufactures and sells a wide variety of electronic imaging hardware and software products and provides consulting services associated with these products. Epix markets its products to sophisticated consumers, mainly universities, research laboratories, and photography enthusiasts. It advertises in a variety of trade magazines and sells its products through distributors and on the Internet at *www.epixinc.com*. Its products retail for $395 to $2000.

Epix first used the trademark EPIX in 1984, and registered that mark in 1990 with the Patent and Trademark Office ("PTO") for use with "printed circuit boards and computer programs for image acquisition, processing, display, and transmission." The EPIX trademark acquired incontestable status in December 1996. Epix registered its EPIX mark with the State of Oregon on June 17, 1997.

Tchou is an electrical engineer, with a background in electronic imaging, who has worked for Lattice Corporation and more recently, Intel. Tchou is also the sole founder, officer, director, shareholder and employee of ISS. In 1995, as president of ISS, Tchou registered the domain name *www.epix.com* with Network Solutions. Tchou testified that he registered the domain name epix.com because the catchy name connoted electronic ("e") pictures ("pix").

Since its launch, however, ISS's website has not grown to epic proportions. Instead, it has been used mainly to promote the Clinton Street Cabaret, a Portland theater troupe that performs *The Rocky Horror Picture Show*. The website contains numerous digital pictures of the actors and the playhouse, as well as information related to the performance and history of *Rocky Horror*. Several webpages display identification badges that ISS made for members of the Clinton Street Cabaret and a splinter acting group, Sibling Rivalry. A question and answer page provides peculiar information touting Tchou's badge-making abilities.

Initially, the website included uncommonly detailed information about how Tchou transferred the digital pictures onto the Internet and how he touched them up before posting. This information suggested that Tchou prepared the photographs using "proprietary epix.com pixel manipulation (bitt-widdling) tools." In addition, a beta version of the website allegedly hyperlinked to a webpage containing autobiographical information about Tchou. That page purportedly bally-hooed Tchou's technical experience with computer hardware, software, and graphics and also permitted visitors to read about ISS and its consulting services.

The present dispute first erupted when Epix unsuccessfully attempted to register the *www.epix.com* domain name that ISS was already using. Epix demanded that Network Solutions cancel ISS's epix.com registration. When informed by Network Solutions of Epix's demand, ISS filed for a declaratory judgment of non-infringement. Epix counterclaimed, alleging federal unfair competition and trademark infringement, as well as Oregon trademark infringement and dilution. Once Epix counterclaimed, or at some point thereabouts, ISS stripped its site of everything except the Clinton Street Cabaret information.

In the first go-round of this contest, the district court granted summary judgment in favor of ISS, finding no likelihood of confusion between ISS's use of epix.com to support the Clinton Street Cabaret and Epix's business use of the mark EPIX. *Interstellar Starship Servs. v. Epix Inc.*, 983 F.Supp. 1331, 1336–37 (D.Or.1997). Epix appealed. We held that although the district court "undertook a well-reasoned analysis of the appropriate law," there remained contested issues of material fact concerning whether ISS and Tchou infringed Epix's registration of the EPIX mark by using the epix.com website. *Interstellar I*, 184 F.3d at 1111.

On remand, Epix amended its complaint to include a claim of cyber-squatting pursuant to the newly enacted Anticyber-squatting Consumer Protection Act ("ACPA"), 15 U.S.C. § 1125(d) (1999).

DISCUSSION

I. INITIAL INTEREST CONFUSION

The core element of trademark infringement is whether the similarity of the marks is likely to confuse customers about the source of the products. In this case, Epix argues that ISS's and Tchou's use of epix.com causes a likelihood of initial interest confusion among consumers. *See Brookfield*, 174 F.3d at 1062 (applying initial interest confusion to a domain name case); *Mobil Oil Corp. v. Pegasus Petroleum Corp.*, 818 F.2d 254, 260 (2d Cir.1987) (recognizing the possibility of initial interest confusion). Initial interest confusion occurs when the defendant uses the plaintiff's trademark "in a manner calculated 'to capture initial consumer attention, even though no actual sale is finally completed as a result of the confusion.'" *Brookfield*, 174 F.3d at 1062 (quoting *Dr. Seuss Enters. v. Penguin Books*, 109 F.3d 1394, 1405 (9th Cir.1997)); *see also Interstellar I*, 184 F.3d at 1110 ("We recognize a brand of confusion called 'initial interest' confusion, which permits a finding of a likelihood of confusion although the consumer quickly becomes aware of the source's actual identity and no purchase is made as a result of the confusion."). This Court has explained initial interest confusion using the following example:

> [Initial interest confusion] is much like posting a sign with another's trademark in front of one's store. Suppose [Blockbuster Video] puts up a billboard on a highway reading—"West Coast Video: 2 miles ahead at Exit 7"—where West Coast is really located at Exit 8 but Blockbuster is located at Exit 7. Customers looking for West Coast's store will pull off at Exit 7 and drive around looking for it. Unable to locate West Coast, but seeing the Blockbuster store right by the highway entrance, they may simply rent there. Even consumers who prefer West Coast may find it not worth the trouble to continue searching for West Coast since there is a Blockbuster right there. Customers are not confused in the narrow sense: they are fully aware that they are purchasing from Blockbuster and they have no reason to believe that Blockbuster is related to, or in any way sponsored by, West Coast. Nevertheless, the fact that there is only initial consumer confusion does not alter the fact that Blockbuster would be misappropriating West Coast's acquired goodwill.

Brookfield, 174 F.3d at 1064.

Epix contends that ISS's use of www.epix.com initially confuses consumers who expect to find Epix at that web address. In the end, however, this dispute arises because while many brick and mortar companies can peacefully coexist using the EPIX mark, there can be only one owner and user of *www.epix.com*. The epix.com domain name is likely quite valuable. The price tags on other well-recognized domain names are astounding. Reports indicate that sex.com retailed for $250 million, business.com for $7.5 million, broad-band.com for $6 million, loans.com for $3 million, and flu.com for $1.4 million (*reports omitted*).

To evaluate the likelihood of confusion, including initial interest confusion, the so-called *Sleekcraft* factors provide non-exhaustive guidance. *AMF Inc. v. Sleekcraft Boats*, 599 F.2d 341, 346 (9th Cir.1979); *see also Checkpoint Sys., Inc. v. Check Point Software Techs., Inc.*, 269 F.3d 270, 297 (3d Cir.2001) (applying similar factors to initial interest confusion). Those factorsare: (1) the similarity of the marks; (2) the relatedness or proximity of the two companies' products or services; (3) the strength of the registered mark; (4) the marketing channels used; (5) the degree of care likely to be exercised by the purchaser in selecting goods; (6) the accused infringers' intent in selecting its mark;

(7) evidence of actual confusion; and (8) the likelihood of expansion in product lines. *Sleekcraft*, 599 F.2d at 346. This eight factor test is pliant, and the relative import of each factor is case specific. *Brookfield*, 174 F.3d at 1054.

We have held that "in the context of the Web," the three most important *Sleekcraft* factors in evaluating a likelihood of confusion are (1) the similarity of the marks, (2) the relatedness of the goods or services, and (3) the parties' simultaneous use of the Web as a marketing channel. *GoTo.Com*, 202 F.3d at 1205. When this "controlling troika," *id.* at 1205, or internet trinity, "suggests confusion is...likely," *id.* at 1207, the other factors must "weigh strongly" against a likelihood of confusion to avoid the finding of infringement. *Brookfield*, 174 F.3d at 1058. If the internet trinity does not clearly indicate a likelihood of consumer confusion, a district court can conclude the infringement analysis only by balancing all the *Sleekcraft* factors within the unique context of each case.

Epix contends the district court erred as a matter of law in evaluating its claim of initial interest confusion. It argues that the district court erroneously considered all of the *Sleekcraft* factors, rather than just the internet trinity. We disagree.

To the district court's credit, it waded through volumes of evidence and around acrimonious litigants. In making its findings of fact, the district court fastidiously evaluated complex and conflicting testimony. Analyzing the internet trinity, the district court found that the parties' marks (EPIX and epix.com, respectively) were indistinguishable. As for the relatedness of the products, the district court determined that ISS's primary purpose—the promotion of the Clinton Street Cabaret—did not compete with Epix's electronic imaging products, although ISS's incidental purpose—digital image processing and computer-related services—appeared, "at least superficially," the same as services offered by Epix. Finally, the district court determined that both parties maintained an Internet presence, but marketed to a different consumer base. This examination of the "controlling troika" did not clearly indicate that consumer confusion was likely. Thus, the district court appropriately concluded the analysis by balancing all the remaining *Sleekcraft* factors within the unique context of this case.

Considering the remaining *Sleekcraft* factors, the district court determined that Epix's trademark was relatively weak,[1] and that Epix's customers exercised a high degree of care purchasing expensive electronic imaging equipment. Weighing the conflicting evidence, the district court questioned Tchou's veracity, but in the end, found that Tchou adopted epix.com in good faith without knowledge of Epix's mark. Finally, the district court found no evidence of actual confusion and no likelihood that either company would "bridge the gap" to the other company's products or services. The district

---

1. According to the classic test originally formulated by Judge Friendly in *Abercrombie & Fitch Co. v. Hunting World, Inc.*, 537 F.2d 4, 9 (2d Cir.1976), trademarks may be measured on a distinctiveness scale. "Fanciful" trademarks are nondictionary words (e.g. EXXON or KODAK); "arbitrary" trademarks are common words used in uncommon or unexpected ways (e.g. AMAZON for an on-line bookstore); "suggestive" trademarks require imagination, thought, or perception to link the trademark with the goods (e.g. ROACH MOTEL for insect traps); and "descriptive" trademarks merely describe the goods (e.g.YELLOW PAGES). "Generic" marks refer to the "genus of which the particular product is a species." *Id.* at 9. In general, fanciful, arbitrary, and suggestive marks receive automatic protection because of their inherent distinctiveness, whereas descriptive marks are protected only upon proof of distinctiveness acquired in commerce. Generic marks are not entitled to protection. *TCPIP Holding Co. v. Haar Communications, Inc.*, 244 F.3d 88, 93 (2d Cir.2001) ("Generic marks are...totally lacking in distinctive quality [and] are not entitled to any protection....").

court did not err in employing this comprehensive likelihood of confusion analysis, and its factual findings were not clearly erroneous.

What Epix really wants from us, it seems, is a holding that, as a matter of law, *any* use of epix.com by ISS creates initial interest confusion with the EPIX mark and that Epix is therefore entitled to ownership of *www.epix.com*. Contrary to Epix's contentions and, as a matter of law, all uses of www.epix.com do *not* generate initial interest confusion with the EPIX mark. In a similar case, the First Circuit rejected Epix's basic contention. It held that use of the domain name *www.clue.com* for computer services did not infringe Hasbro's trademark on the board game Clue. *Hasbro Inc. v. Clue Computing, Inc.*, 232 F.3d 1, 2 (1st Cir.2000). The *Clue* court found no initial interest confusion because the companies' products were disparate, and there was no evidence of actual confusion. *Id.*

A series of examples further demonstrate why every use of epix.com does not infringe Epix's trademark EPIX for electronic imaging equipment.

If an apple grower adopts a famous trademark, like *www.DRSEUSS.com*, as a domain name, initial interest confusion probably results, even if that business's goods differ significantly from those of Dr. Seuss. Marks of renown, like DR. SEUSS, describe the source of only one company's products, and the apple grower's adoption of the www.DRSEUSS.com domain name inevitably trades on the favorable cachet associated with that company, its works, and its reputation. Actionable initial interest confusion probably results even if every consumer realizes that DRSEUSS.com is owned by an apple grower, and no consumer ever consummates a Winesap, Delicious, or Granny Smith purchase thinking that Dr. Seuss grows apples or endorses, sponsors, or licenses his name to the apple grower.

In some circumstances, however, the apple grower might adopt a famous trademark without causing initial interest confusion. For example, an apple grower in Washington might register *www.apple.com* to promote his business. Although APPLE is a famous registered trademark of Apple Computer, Inc., many other companies also use the term APPLE to describe a variety of products. Indeed, the apple distributor probably does not infringe Apple Computer's mark because APPLE is also a common noun, used by many companies, and the goods offered by these two companies differ significantly. *See Hasbro*, 232 F.3d at 2 (noting very little similarity between Hasbro's board game CLUE and the products and services of Clue Computing); *Brookfield*, 174 F.3d at 1056 (suggesting Schlumberger Ltd (a large oil drilling company) might advertise at *www.moviebuff.com* without infringing the MOVIEBUFF trademark on movie database software because Schlumberger's oil products differ greatly from software).

If, however, the apple grower adopted the *www.apple.com* domain name, and then competed directly with Apple Computer by selling computers, initial interest confusion probably would result. *See Brookfield*, 174 F.3d at 1056 (finding a likelihood of confusion where a company adopted a competitor's trademark as a domain name and offered similar goods under that name). In that circumstance, the apple grower would have acted in a way which traded on the goodwill of Apple Computer's trademark while preventing Apple Computer from using the APPLE trademark itself. This conduct would be actionable because confusion would inevitably result from the apple grower's actions. For example, a consumer might read about the apple grower's computers on *www.apple.com*, where she expected to find computers sold by Apple Computer, and decide to buy one, thereby permitting the apple grower to capitalize on the goodwill of Apple Computer's APPLE trademark—even if the consumer is never confused about the apple grower's lack of connection with Apple Computer. *See Interstellar I*, 184 F.3d at 1111 (defining initial interest confusion in these terms).

The different legal outcomes envisioned by these examples are predicted by the *Sleekcraft* factors. Consumers expect that owners of famous, fanciful trademarks will own the corresponding domain name, like *www.XEROX.com* or *www.KODAK.com.*, for no other companies identify themselves or their products using those marks. Indeed, confusion would abound if anyone other than Xerox owned *www.xerox.com*. Consumers, however, would not be shocked to find an apple grower at *www.apple.com* (although Apple Computer actually owns that domain name), or United Van Lines at www.united.com (although United Airlines happens to own that domain name). Although a consumer might incorrectly guess that United Van Lines would be found at www.united.com, *see Brookfield* 174 F.3d at 1044-45 ("Web users often assume as a rule of thumb that the domain name of a particular company will be company name followed by ".com." "), such an erroneous guess does not generally amount to a likelihood of initial interest confusion.[2]

As the examples demonstrate, actionable initial interest confusion on the Internet is determined, in large part, by the relatedness of the goods offered and the level of care exercised by the consumer. *See Checkpoint Sys.*, 269 F.3d at 296-97 ("Product relatedness and level of care exercised by consumers are relevant factors in determining initial interest confusion."). If a rogue company adopts as its domain name a protected trademark and proceeds to sell goods similar to those offered by the trademark owner, it necessarily free rides on the trademark owner's goodwill, and that rogue company benefits from increasing initial interest confusion as consumers exercise lower levels of care in making their purchasing decisions. Of course, the remainder of the *Sleekcraft* factors complete the case-by-case inquiry necessary to evaluate initial interest confusion on the Internet.

Applying these principles to our case, we find that it most resembles the example of the apple grower registering *www.apple.com* to sell apples. Like Apple Computer (or Hasbro), Epix has no exclusive claim to its trademark. Indeed, the record reflects that at least eight companies have registered the EPIX mark or a close variation with the PTO, and use the term in connection with on a variety of goods, including men's and women's clothing and medical imaging agents. On the Internet, the use of the EPIX mark is even more wide-spread. In addition to the brick and mortar companies using the EPIX mark in cyberspace, an Internet service provider, the Eastern Pennsylvania Internet Exchange and a Canadian emergency preparedness information exchange use EPIX to describe themselves. EPIX is also the word used in common Internet parlance to denote electronic pictures. Tchou has even suggested that EPIX is used so often on

---

2. We note that much has been written about the role and reliability of search engines in the context of Internet trademark infringement and initial interest confusion. In the recent past, "[w]hen a keyword [wa]s entered, the search engine processe[d] it through a self-created index of web sites to generate a (sometimes long) list relating to the entered keyword." *Brookfield*, 174 F.3d at 1045. Each search engine used its own algorithm, based on the domain name, website text, and the metatags, to arrange the results in a proprietary sequence. *Id.* Now, those search engine algorithms incorporate corporate dollars into their formulae. Firms can pay the search engines in return for primary placement among the search results. For example, enter "whitehouse" as the keyword at: *www.overture.com.* and note the dollar amount entered beside each search result.

Accordingly, we find largely irrelevant what results when a given term is input into a search engine. Our initial interest confusion analysis does not depend on a given business's payment or lack thereof to the various search engines.

the Internet to describe electronic pictures that it may have become a generic term. *See Abercrombie & Fitch,* 537 F.2d at 9 (describing how a trademark might shift classifications).

Furthermore, ISS's "products"—the Clinton Street Cabaret and *The Rocky Horror Picture Show*—are extraordinarily different from Epix's digital imaging products. As is obvious by comparing Epix's and ISS's websites, electronic imaging equipment is not *The Rocky Horror Picture Show,* and there is no immediate connection between the products. Upon arriving at ISS's epix.com website, the consumer would not think that Epix licensed, sponsored, or owned the ISS website. *Brookfield,* 174 F.3d at 1057. She would simply come to the inevitable and correct conclusion that more than one company uses the EPIX name and that Epix operates its website at a different address. Indeed, any consumer looking for Epix, who mistakenly guessed that it could be found at *www.epix.com,* would realize in one hot second that she was in the wrong place and either guess again or resort to a search engine to locate the Epix site at *www.epixinc.com.*

We note that although the misdirected consumer might enjoy ISS's digital photography momentarily, ISS could not financially capitalize on that misdirected consumer even if it so desired. Overall, the ISS website had little to do with commerce. The website contained no contact information for ISS or Tchou, and it was otherwise unable to interface with users. Indeed, Epix adduced no evidence that ISS or Tchou ever sold any product or service through its website. Under these circumstances, we discern no likelihood of consumer initial interest confusion.

The district court's additional findings of fact round out the *Sleekcraft* analysis and confirm our conclusion. Epix's mark was weak, even in the field of digital imaging equipment. Moreover, Tchou adopted the name epix.com in good faith because it connoted electronic pictures and no evidence indicated that he sought to trade on the goodwill of Epix or that either company intended to bridge the gap into the other's product line. These findings were not clearly erroneous and they support our conclusion that there was no likelihood of confusion in this case.

II. CYBERSQUATTING

Cybersquatting is the Internet version of a land grab. Cybersquatters register well-known brand names as Internet domain names in order to force the rightful owners of the marks to pay for the right to engage in electronic commerce under their own name. *See Virtual Works, Inc. v. Volkswagen of America Inc.,* 238 F.3d 264, 267 (4th Cir.2001). Congress enacted the ACPA because cybersquatting "threatened 'the continued growth and vitality of the Internet as a platform' for 'communication, electronic commerce, education, entertainment, and countless yet-to-be-determined uses.'" *Id.* (quoting S.Rep. No. 106-140, at 8 (1999)).

A cybersquatter is liable under the ACPA to the owner of a protected mark if the cybersquatter has:

(i) a *bad faith intent* to profit from that mark; and

(ii) registers, traffics in, or uses a domain name that—

(I) in the case of mark that is distinctive..., is identical or confusingly similar to that mark that is distinctive.

(II) in the case of a famous mark..., is identical or confusingly similar to or dilutive of that mark.

See 15 U.S.C. § 1125(d)(1)(A) (emphasis added). A finding of "bad faith" is an essential prerequisite to finding an ACPA violation. Congress enumerated a list of nine factors to consider "in determining whether a person has a bad faith intent." *Id.* Congress did not mean these factors to be an exclusive list; instead, "the most important grounds for finding bad faith are 'the unique circumstances of the case, which do not fit neatly into the specific factors enumerated by Congress.'" *Virtual Works,* 238 F.3d at 271 (4th Cir.2001) (quoting *Sporty's Farm LLC v. Sportsman's Market, Inc.,* 202 F.3d 489, 495 (2d Cir.2000)). In addition, the ACPA contains a safe harbor provision: Bad faith "shall not be found in any case in which the court determines that the person believed and had a reasonable grounds to believe that the use of the domain name was fair use or otherwise lawful." 15 U.S.C. § 1125(d)(1)(B)(ii).

In this case, the district court expressly determined only whether ISS violated the ACPA by registering the domain name *www.epix.cc*—a domain name which Epix now owns and which is not at issue on appeal. The district court did not consider Epix's ACPA claim as it related to ISS's use of the *www.epix.com*.

The district court found, however, that Tchou and ISS adopted the *www.epix.com* domain name in good faith. In particular, it determined that Tchou adopted the domain name epix.com as a descriptive term to connote electronic pictures. Evidencing his good faith, Tchou performed a web search on "epix" before registering epix.com, but did not find Epix because it was not yet on the Internet. Furthermore, Tchou engaged in a bona fide use of his website. To transform his website into a "widely known internet portal site," Tchou continuously used the domain name and invested money on hardware and software as well as significant amounts of time on the development of a viable business plan.

The district court rejected Epix's farfetched idea that Tchou registered epix.com in an effort to assist his employer and Epix competitor, Intel. The district court did not, however, comment on Epix's other purported evidence of bad faith—ISS's offer to sell Epix the epix.com domain name for $25,000. While offers to sell a contested domain name may in certain circumstances be probative evidence of bad faith, *see Panavision Int'l L.P. v. Toeppen,* 141 F.3d 1316, 1323 (9th Cir.1998), here, the offer to sell came from ISS's attorney in the context of settlement negotiations after the commencement of litigation; Tchou was not even present. Epix never established before the district court that the settlement offer was made to extort Epix or for any reason other than to settle the case. Rather, the evidence suggests that ISS offered to sell its investment in hardware, software, and time in an operational website devoted to the Clinton Street Cabaret.

The district court's finding that Tchou adopted *www.epix.com* in good faith was not clearly erroneous considering the "unique circumstances" of this case. Without a finding of bad faith, Epix's cybersquatting claim necessarily fails.

III. OREGON TRADEMARK DILUTION

Under Oregon law, if a trademark is distinctive, it is protected against dilution. *See* Or.Rev.Stat. § 647.107. A distinctive trademark must have "favorable associational value in the minds of consumers." *Wedgwood Homes, Inc. v. Lund,* 294 Or. 493, 659 P.2d 377, 380 (1983). Distinctiveness may be developed by "long use, consistent superior quality instilling customer satisfaction, or extensive advertising." *Id.* Here, although Epix registered its EPIX mark in Oregon once this litigation began, Epix produced no evidence that its EPIX mark had favorable associational value in Oregon, or that Epix had even sold any product to an Oregonian. As Epix was unable to prove its EPIX trademark was distinctive in Oregon, the district court correctly found its dilution claim failed as a matter of law.

IV. SCOPE OF THE INJUNCTION

A. Forced Transfer of www.epix.com.

The district court found that ISS's "past use of epix.com to promote Tchou's digital image processing services and other computer-related services did infringe on Epix's trademark." To prevent future infringement of Epix's EPIX mark, the district court enjoined ISS and Tchou from marketing electronic imaging services, using gray wallpaper, and using the EPIX.COM logo without an appropriate disclaimer. Unsatisfied with this injunction, Epix contends that, as a matter of law, once the district court found that ISS's past use of epix.com infringed the EPIX trademark, Epix was entitled to ownership of the offending domain name.

Despite its continued representations to the contrary, Epix points us to no case which holds that a finding of trademark infringement *requires* the forced transfer of the infringing property. The best Epix offers is a few cases which preliminarily enjoined the infringer from using an infringing domain name. See *TCPIP Holding*, 244 F.3d at 103; *Brookfield*, 174 F.3d at 1066–67. In *Brookfield*, for example, we preliminarily enjoined West Coast from using the domain name movie-buff.com in direct competition with Brookfield, the owner of the federally registered trademark MOVIEBUFF. 174 F.3d at 1066–67. Despite our findings that West Coast likely infringed Brookfield's MOVIEBUFF mark by using the *www.moviebuff.com* website, we did not order the offending domain nametransferred to Brookfield. *Id.*

Indeed, even if a district court finds infringement, it retains the discretion to fashion any remedy which alleviates that confusion. *Sleekcraft*, 599 F.2d at 355. Certainly, it is not required to enjoin the infringer from all uses of the contested mark. In *Sleekcraft*, for example, the defendant was operating in the same industry (recreational boats) and using substantially the same mark as the plaintiff. 599 F.2d at 346. Instead of completely enjoining the defendant's use of its mark, we fashioned a limited injunction requiring the defendant to place a distinctive logo on all aspects of its business so that consumers could differentiate between the two boat manufacturers. *Id.* at 355. This type of limited injunction "balance[d] the conflicting interests both parties have in the unimpaired continuation of their trademark use." *Id.* at 354.

In fact, only upon proving the rigorous elements of cyber-squatting under the ACPA have plaintiffs successfully forced the transfer of an infringing domain name. See *Sporty's Farm*, 202 F.3d at 495 (forcing cybersquatter to relinquish all rights to sportys.com domain name); *Virtual Works*, 238 F.3d at 271 (requiring Virtual Works to turn over vw.com domain name to Volkswagen). The ACPA specifically authorizes this remedy. *See* 15 U.S.C. § 1125(d)(1)(C). Even in egregious cases of cybersquatting, however, the district court retains discretion to fashion appropriate relief, and it need not force the transfer of the offending domain name. See *N. Light Tech., Inc. v. N. Lights Club*, 236 F.3d 57, 60 (1st Cir.2001) (requiring cybersquatter at www.northernlights.com to post a picture of the aurora borealis as well as links to its own webpages and the webpages of the trademark owner, but allowing it to maintain ownership of the domain name).

In this case, the district court did not abuse its discretion by allowing ISS to retain possession of the epix.com domain name. A forced transfer of the domain name was not available by statute because Epix did not prove that ISS violated the ACPA. Nor did Epix prove that ISS acted in bad faith to infringe Epix's trademark.

Although the district court did find that ISS's references to "bit-twiddling or pixel manipulation, use of gray wallpaper, and use of the EPIX.COM logo, taken together, create an impermissible likelihood of consumers affiliating epix.com with [Epix]'s registered mark," it found these past infringing uses were minimal and incidental to the primary purpose of ISS's website. Most importantly, the district court determined that ISS predominantly used the website benignly to promote the Clinton Street Cabaret and its performance of *Rocky Horror*.

We think the injunction crafted by the district court appears particularly proper. EPIX is used by many companies to identify a variety of goods and services, including medical imaging agents and men's and women's clothing. Moreover, the term "epix" appears ubiquitously on the Internet as shorthand for electronic pictures, and the value of epix.com is derived from this descriptive force, not from the goodwill and built by Epix. In these circumstances, nothing gives Epix any more right to epix.com than any other user of the EPIX mark.

Thus, we hold that the district court committed no legal error or abuse of discretion in refusing to transfer the domain name to Epix. To the contrary, the district court's injunction appropriately resolved this case. It ensured no future infringement of the EPIX mark by ISS or Tchou, while permitting Tchou to retain his property and reap the benefits of his investment.

The district court's decision is AFFIRMED.

Chapter 3

Overview of Federal Income Taxation

I. Assignment for Chapter 3

Read: Internal Revenue Code: §§ 61(a); 162(a); 165(a)–(c); 167(a)–(c)(1), (f)(1), (g), (h)(2); 183(a)–(d); 197(a), (f)(7); 262(a); 263(a); 263A(a); 453(a)–(d); 1001(a)–(d); 1011(a); 1012; 1016(a)(1)–(2); 1060(a)–(c); 1211; 1212(a)(1), (b)(1); 1221(a)(1)–(3); 1222; 1231(a)(1)–(3), (b)(1); 1245(a)(1), (a)(3). Skim §§ 1(a)–(f), (h), (i)(2); 11(a)–(b); 41.

Treasury Regulations: §§ 1.61-6(a); 1.167(a)-3, -14; 1.167(b)-1; 1.183-1(b), -2(a)–(b); 1.263(a)-1(b), -2(a); 15A.453-1(c)(1) (and merely skim -1(c)(2)(i)(A), -1(c)(3)(i), -1(c)(4); -1(d)(2)(i), (iii)); 1.1001-2(a)(1); 1.1060-1(c); 1.1221-1(c)(1); 1.1245-3(b). Skim Prop. Treas. Reg. §§ 1.167(a)-3; 1.263(a)-4.

Overview

Materials: *Commissioner v. Groetzinger*
Welch v. Helvering
Commissioner v. Lincoln Savings & Loan Ass'n
INDOPCO, Inc. v. Commissioner
Waterman v. Mackenzie
Burnet v. Logan
Williams v. McGowan
Raytheon Production Corp. v. Commissioner

Complete the problems.

II. Problems for Chapter 3

1. Two years before Rick became eligible to retire from the Treasury Department, he began writing outside of his full-time job with the hope of making writing his second career. During that period, he completed a manuscript for a fictional piece entitled "The One That Got Away" and a collection of short stories called "The Tales

of an Angler." In order to develop characters for the book and stories, he interviewed several fishing guides each weekend and kept a journal describing numerous fishing trips with the guides. Rick did not seek expert advice on how to start or maintain a business as a fiction writer, but he did perform writing-based tasks at the Treasury Department. He did not keep a separate checking account or a well-organized set of books, although he did keep bills or receipts for expenses he incurred to research his books. Last year, Knowles Publishing agreed to publish "The One That Got Away." Before its release, Rick played an active role in all stages of publication (reviewing galley proofs, adding additional chapters, participating in the book's promotion). Although Rick has ceased his efforts to market "The Tales of an Angler," because Knowles told him there was no market for short stories, he has begun research on another book. Prior to this year, Rick's writing activities produced no income. This year, Rick has $2,500 in gross royalties from his writing activity, and expenses of $7,000. Is Rick in the "trade or business" of being an author? Why does it matter?

2. Assuming that Rick in Problem 1 is deemed to be engaged in a "trade or business," discuss whether each of the following expenses should be deductible as "ordinary and necessary" under §162: (1) $50 in long-distance telephone calls to fishing guides and potential publishers; (2) $200 for supplies, such as reams of paper, pens, files, and folders; (3) $350 for books, magazines, and trade publications; (4) $1,400 in cash payments to professional fishing guides; (5) $2,000 in travel expenses; and (6) $3,000 for office expenses, representing 1/5 of taxpayer's household expenses which consist of insurance, mortgage interest, and utilities.

3. Discuss whether each expenditure below is currently deductible as an expense under §162 or constitutes a nondeductible capital expenditure.

   a. The cost of purchasing a patent by a patent vendor.

   b. The costs incurred by an author in researching, preparing, and writing a manuscript, and costs incurred by a publisher to produce and develop the book.

   c. The costs of creating copyrightable advertising materials, such as television commercials and web-based advertising materials.

   d. The costs of registering a trademark, trade name, or domain name.

   e. Software development costs incurred in connection with programming a new computer.

   f. The costs incurred by an on-line company to build its website and costs of licensing contents for the website.

   g. Legal fees incurred in a patent infringement suit.

   h. Litigation costs incurred in defending a trademark registration in a cancellation proceeding.

4. Which of the following types of acquired intellectual property used in a trade or business are eligible for amortization under §167, provided they are not subject to fifteen-year amortization under §197: (1) patents, (2) trade secrets and know how, (3) copyrights, (4) computer software, and (5) generic domain names?

5. Walter, the inventor of a hydraulically operated fire extinguisher, plans to convey to American Fire Company the patented device in exchange for a percentage of the gross receipts realized by American Fire from the sale of the product. What rights

must Walter transfer in order for the assignment to be considered a sale, as opposed to a license, for tax purposes? Why is the "license" versus "sale" distinction critical in determining the proper tax treatment of an intellectual property transfer?

6. Assuming the transfer in Problem 5 is treated as a "sale" for tax purposes, how should Walter account for the gain (*i.e.*, determine the proper amount and timing of gain) considering the fact that the selling price is contingent on future sales by American Fire Company?

7. Determine which of the following types of intellectual property are capital assets:

   a. Patents held by professional inventors.

   b. Self-created trade secrets and know-how used in trade or business.

   c. Musical compositions held by composers.

   d. Trademarks, trade names, and domain names.

   e. Self-developed computer software, which is copyrightable but which is protected under the patent laws.

8. John will sell an existing dry cleaning business which John has operated as a sole proprietor for the last 10 years. Comet Cleaners agrees to pay John $500,000 for the following tangible and intangible assets: (1) accounts receivable, (2) a patent obtained by John on a special dry cleaning chemical, (3) computer accounting software previously purchased by John, (4) the domain name "drycleaning.com", (5) building, and (6) land. In general, how will the tax consequences of the sale be determined? Will the Service respect the agreement between John and Comet Cleaners that allocates the purchase price among these assets and the business's goodwill? What if the agreement is silent as to allocations of the purchase price?

9. Exide, Inc. brought a successful patent infringement suit against Energizer Company for infringing on the Exide's patent for long-lasting batteries, and received a damage award for patent infringement of $500,000. Exide also brought opposition proceedings against Exxon Corporation for its use of the trademark EXXON in connection with battery products, afterwhich Exxon paid Exide $5 million to settle the trademark dispute. What factors should be considered in determining the proper tax treatment of the damage awards and settlement proceeds?

III. Overview

To better understand intellectual property taxation, it is important to understand the overall design of the federal income tax system. This chapter presents an overview of the structure of the federal income tax law and the formula by which a taxpayer's income tax liability is computed. This overview will provide a useful context in which to study intellectual property transactions that have major tax consequences. This chapter presents basic tax concepts that most introductory tax courses cover and that apply to many intellectual property transactions. (Later chapters present special tax rules that specifically deal with intellectual property related issues.) This chapter also summarizes various sources of tax law used by practitioners to resolve any intellectual property tax issue.

A. Structure of the Federal Income Tax System

A taxpayer's federal income tax liability for any given year is determined by applying the appropriate tax rates to the appropriate tax base. The tax base for all taxpayers (individuals, corporations, estates, and trusts) is "taxable income," which is defined loosely as "gross income" minus allowable "deductions." Once the applicable tax rates are applied to the taxpayer's taxable income, certain statutory tax "credits" may be available and subtracted directly from the tax due. Each of the components necessary to determine a taxpayer's federal income tax liability is described below.

1. Gross Income

The starting point for determining a taxpayer's tax liability is determining what is included in gross income. The Code defines gross income broadly as "all income from whatever source derived," and then lists fifteen specific types of receipts that are included within the definition. I.R.C. §61(a). This list is extensive and includes common types of income. For example, the list includes compensation for services, gross income derived from business, gains derived from dealings in property, interest, rent, and royalties. Although extensive, the list is not exhaustive as one would expect. That is why the list is preceded and supplemented by a catch-all clause that includes non-listed items that can properly be defined as "income." In *Commissioner v. Glenshaw Glass Co.*, 348 U.S. 426 (1955), the Supreme Court defined income broadly as "undeniable accessions to wealth, clearly realized." Realization is a fundamental tax concept in that the federal income tax is not imposed on income or gains until they have been realized in some way. For example, increases in the value of intellectual property are not taken into account for tax purposes when they accrue, but only when they are realized by a taxable event (such as a sale or an exclusive license that may be treated as a sale).

Despite the foregoing, gross income does *not* include all "accessions to wealth," to use the *Glenshaw Glass* phrase. The Code contains, for various policy reasons, a number of provisions that exclude particular kinds of receipts from the tax base. For example, the Code specifically excludes from gross income certain gifts and inheritances, compensation for certain injuries, income from discharge of certain indebtedness, and certain fringe benefits provided by an employer. *See, e.g.*, I.R.C. §§ 102, 104, 108, 132.

This course book addresses various intellectual property transactions that produce reportable income, the two most noticeable transactions being licenses and sales. If intellectual property is transferred under a "license," payments received in full—whether lump sum or contingent on exploitation of the intellectual property—are royalties included in gross income under §61(a)(6). If intellectual property is transferred in a "sale," as opposed to a license, the transferor may have a "gain derived from dealing in property," included in gross income under §61(a)(3). Although both licenses and sales produce income, the tax treatment of each differs in material respects. Because of what is at stake, there has been much litigation over whether a particular transaction is treated as a sale or license. Although not a tax case, *Waterman v. Mackenzie*, included below, is the classic exposition of the sale-versus-license distinction.

If an intellectual property assignment is treated as a sale, as opposed to a license, the transfer must determine the amount of gain realized on the transaction. The amount of gain is the "amount realized" from the sale minus the "adjusted basis" for the intellectual property sold. *See* Treas. Reg. § 1.61-6(a) (referring to I.R.C. § 1001).

The "amount realized" from the sale of intellectual property is the sum of any money received plus the fair market value of property (other than money) received in the transaction. I.R.C. § 1001(b). Amount realized also includes the amount of liabilities from which the transferor is discharged as a result of the sale. *See Crane v. Commissioner*, 331 U.S. 1 (1947), *aff'g* 153 F.2d 504 (2d Cir. 1945). The "adjusted basis" of the property sold depends on how the transferor acquired the intellectual property (*e.g.*, self-created, purchased, or gifted) and whether the transferor took any cost-recovery deductions (*e.g.*, depreciation or amortization allowances) with respect to the transferred property. If intellectual property is purchased, its initial basis is the amount paid plus any amount borrowed to pay the purchase price. I.R.C. § 1012. [If the contract calls for fixed installment payments, the entire amount of these payments are included in basis at the time of purchase. If the contract calls for contingent payments, however, the basis is increased only as the contingent amounts are paid.] After initial "basis" is determined, adjustments are later made as a consequence of subsequent events to arrive at "adjusted basis." Basis is adjusted upward for improvements to the property and adjusted downward for cost-recovery deductions (*e.g.*, depreciation or amortization deductions) taken with respect to the property. I.R.C. § 1016.

To illustrate, consider the following simple example: Beth purchased a patent in Year 1 for $10,000. In purchasing the patent, she used $2,000 of her own funds and borrowed the other $8,000 of the purchase price from a bank. Beth began depreciating the patent over its expected useful life under § 167 (discussed below in more detail), and claimed a total of $4,000 in depreciation allowances in Years 1, 2, and 3. In Year 3, Beth sold the patent for $15,000. The purchaser paid Beth $10,000 in cash and assumed the balance of $5,000 that Beth still owed on the loan. What is the amount of gain, if any, that Beth realized on the sale of the patent? The amount of gain from the sale of the patent is the excess of the amount realized therefrom over the patent's adjusted basis. I.R.C. § 1001(a). The amount realized from the sale is $15,000, the amount of money received ($10,000) plus the relief of debt ($5,000). I.R.C. § 1001(b); Treas. Reg. § 1.1001-2. The adjusted basis of the patent sold is $6,000, the initial cost basis of the patent ($10,000, which includes the debt incurred), adjusted downward for the depreciation deductions taken ($4,000). I.R.C. §§ 1012, 1016. Accordingly, the gain realized on the sale of the patent is $9,000 ($15,000 minus $6,000).

Once a taxpayer has calculated the gain "realized" on a sale, the taxpayer must determine whether the gain is "recognized" (*i.e.*, reportable on the current year's tax return). As a general rule, the entire gain realized on a sale of property is recognized for tax purposes unless an exception is provided in the Code. The Code provides a number of exceptions from the general rule requiring recognition of gain. For example, the Code provides that no gain is recognized on the sale of property to a spouse or former spouse incident to divorce. I.R.C. § 1041. Similarly, no gain is generally recognized on the transfer of property to a business entity in exchange for an ownership interest in that entity. I.R.C. §§ 351, 721. These "nonrecognition" provisions, which are narrowly defined, generally permit taxpayers to defer (but not permanently exclude) the reporting of gain to a later year.

A taxpayer typically recognizes gain at the time of the sale. However, intellectual property is often sold on a deferred payment basis (*e.g.*, payments are contingent on use, productivity, or disposition of the intellectual property). When intellectual property is sold on a contingent use basis, it is difficult to determine the total selling price (amount realized) in the year of sale and, hence, the proper amount and timing of gain from the sale. Should gain be spread out as payments are received? Should gain be reported only after the seller has recovered tax free the property's basis? The Supreme

Court, in *Burnet v. Logan*, included in the materials, permitted "open transaction reporting," under which no gain is reported until the seller has first recovered his or her remaining basis in the property. Open transaction reporting is of limited applicability today because contingent payment sales are now governed by the installment reporting rules of § 453 and the regulations thereunder. I.R.C. § 453; Treas. Reg. § 15A.453-1(c)(1)–(4).

Section 453 provides that "income" from an "installment sale" is to reported under the "installment method." I.R.C. § 453(a). An "installment sale" occurs when at least one payment of the total purchase price is to be received after the close of the taxable year in which the sale occurs. I.R.C. § 453(b)(1). As can be seen, this definition is broad and includes all intellectual property sales made on a contingent basis. If § 453 applies, the transferor's gain is generally included in income only as payments are received from the transferee regardless of whether the transferor reports on the cash method or accrual method. In other words, the gain is spread over the life of the payments. The percentage of each payment that must be reported as income (*i.e.*, the income portion of any payment) is determined by multiplying the amount of each payment by a fraction. The numerator is the gross profit realized on the sale or to be realized when payment is completed and the denominator is the total contract or aggregate selling price. I.R.C. § 453(c). This ratio of gross profit to total contract price is known as the gross profit ratio.

Determining the gross profit ratio would seem impossible in the case of contingent payment sales, since gross profit (numerator) or total contract price (denominator) cannot be readily determined in the year of sale when payments are contingent on use, productivity, or disposition of the intellectual property. Nevertheless, the regulations deal with contingent payment sales, and provide necessary guidance. What if the sale is subject to a "stated maximum selling price"? *See* Treas. Reg. § 15A.453-1(c)(2)(i). What if a maximum selling price is not known, but a maximum period of time over which payments may be received is known? *See* Treas. Reg. § 15A.453-1(c)(3)(i). What if there is no maximum selling price or fixed period over which payments may be received? *See* Treas. Reg. § 15A.453-1(c)(4).

A taxpayer may elect out of the installment method, and report gain on the sale in accordance with his or her usual method of accounting. I.R.C. § 453(d). Why would a taxpayer want to accelerate income and therefore exercise his or her option to elect out of § 453? If the taxpayer elects out of installment reporting, gain or loss will be calculated under normal rules, with the contingent payment obligation being valued at its fair market value. Treas. Reg. § 15A.453-1(d)(2)(i). The regulations provide, however, that the contingent payment obligation shall never be valued at less than the fair market value of the intellectual property sold. In the "rare and extraordinary case" in which the fair market value of the obligation cannot be determined, "open transaction" treatment will apply. Treas. Reg. § 15A.453-1(d)(2)(iii). Review *Burnett v. Logan*, included below, which applied open transaction reporting.

Intellectual property is also often sold with a group of assets that constitutes a trade or business. In *Williams v. McGowan*, included below, the Supreme Court required that the sale of a business be analyzed as a sale of its component parts. Accordingly, a separate gain or loss determination must be made with respect to each asset (tangible and intangible) sold. What was the Service's concern in *Williams v. McGowan*? How is the total sales price of a business allocated among the assets transferred? *See* I.R.C. § 1060; Treas. Reg. § 1.1060-1(c).

In addition to sales and licenses, intellectual property litigation, such as patent or copyright infringement cases, may also produce reportable income. Damage awards and settlement proceeds received in intellectual property suits will either be included in income to the recipient or will constitute a non-taxable return of capital. *Raytheon Production Corp. v. Commissioner*, included in this Chapter, is the most-cited case on the proper tax treatment of compensatory damages arising in commerce. What approach does *Raytheon Production Corp.* establish?

2. Deductions

Once gross income has been determined, a taxpayer may subtract certain outlays and expenditures paid or incurred during the year to arrive at taxable income, the tax base on which the tax rates are applied. I.R.C. § 63. Not all expenditures are deductible from gross income in arriving at taxable income, as deductions are a matter of legislative grace. See *INDOPCO, Inc. v. Commissioner*, included in the materials. In other words, to determine whether an expenditure or property loss is deductible, one must find a specific Code provision authorizing the deduction.

There are a number of Code provisions authorizing an immediate deduction usually for the types of expenditures that have been made in order to produce income. As one would expect, there is a general Code provision that allows a current deduction for general trade or business expenses. I.R.C. § 162. The Code also provides a deduction for losses sustained during the year and not compensated by insurance or otherwise (*e.g.*, losses on intellectual property sales and losses on the worthlessness of intellectual property). I.R.C. § 165.

Unlike gross income, which is defined broadly, deductions are narrowly defined and are subject to numerous limitations. For example, the Code provision authorizing a deduction for business expenses limits deductibility only to those expenses that are (1) ordinary and necessary and (2) paid or incurred in carrying on an ongoing business. I.R.C. § 162(a). [In *Welch v. Helvering*, included in this Chapter, the Supreme Court considered the meaning of the terms ordinary and necessary.] Although there is a Code provision that authorizes a deduction for losses sustained during the year, the provision goes on to limit deductions, in the case of individuals, to three types of losses: (1) trade or business losses, (2) investment losses, and (3) casualty losses. I.R.C. § 165(c). The Code further limits the deductibility of losses that are characterized as "capital" losses. In the case of corporations, for example, capital losses are deductible only to the extent of the corporation's capital gains. I.R.C. § 1211. If a corporation has no capital gains for a year, then any losses characterized as "capital" losses may be not be deductible in the current year.

There are a number of *overriding* Code provisions that prevent the current deductibility of otherwise allowable expenditures and losses. Thus, what may seem to be a deductible expense or loss under one provision may be classified as a non-deductible expenditure under another overriding provision. A major overriding provision addressed in this book is one that disallows the immediate deduction of costs that are considered "capital expenditures." See I.R.C. § 263(a) (providing for nondeductibility of capital expenditures). *See also* I.R.C. § 263A(a) (requiring a taxpayer to capitalize all direct and indirect expenditures incurred to produce certain personal property).

Under § 263(a), capital expenditures are those expenditures that "add to the value, or substantially prolong the useful life" of property, or "adapt property to a new or different use." Treas. Reg. § 1.263(a)-1(b). The Regulations list examples of capital expenditures, including the cost of acquiring property "having a useful life substantially beyond the taxable year." Treas. Reg. § 1.263(a)-2(a). The reason such costs are not currently deductible is that the resulting property is not consumed or used within the year, but rather persists and contributes to income over a period of years. If the costs incurred to create or acquire such property were deductible in full in the current year, there would be a mismatching of income and the expenses that produced that income. In other words, income would be understated in the year of creation or acquisition and overstated in later years. This problem is avoided by prohibiting the immediate deduction of capital expenditures.

Distinguishing deductible expenses from nondeductible capital expenditures is not always easy. In *Commissioner v. Lincoln Savings & Loan Ass'n*, included below, the Supreme Court concluded that an expenditure that serves to create or enhance a separate and distinct asset must be capitalized. The Supreme Court noted: "[T]he presence of an ensuing benefit that may have some future aspect is not controlling; many expenses concededly deductible have prospective effect beyond the tax year. What is important and controlling, we feel, is that the...payment serves to create or enhance for Lincoln what is essentially a separate and distinct additional asset and that, as an inevitable consequence, the payment is capital in nature and not an expense." 403 U.S. 345, 354 (1971). In 1992, in *INDOPCO, Inc. v. Commissioner*, also included below, the Supreme Court minimized the importance of the separate-and-distinct asset test of *Lincoln Savings* and expanded the test for capitalization. In *INDOPCO*, the Supreme Court held that, although the separate-and-distinct asset standard is a sufficient condition for capitalization, it is not a necessary condition and that an expenditure that gives rise to future benefits, whether or not the expenditure gives rise to a separate and distinct asset, may require capitalization. The Supreme Court noted: "Although the mere presence of an incidental future benefit...may warrant capitalization, a taxpayer's realization of benefits beyond the year in which the expenditure is incurred is undeniably important in determining whether the appropriate tax treatment is immediate deduction or capitalization." 503 U.S. 79, 87 (1992).

The "significant future benefit" approach adopted in *INDOPCO* has created much controversy and confusion because it seemingly requires the capitalization of many costs that, although producing benefits in current and future years, were previously thought to be currently deductible. In the aftermath of the Supreme Court's decision in *INDOPCO*, the Service issued numerous administrative pronouncements on how *INDOPCO* affects that treatment of different types of expenditures that give rise to future benefits. *See, e.g.*, Rev. Rul. 92-80, 1992-2 C.B. 57 (ruling that *INDOPCO* does not affect the treatment of advertising costs as business expenses even though advertising often yields future benefits). In December 2002, the Service issued proposed regulations under §263 that provide comprehensive rules for capitalization of intangible assets. Surprisingly, the proposed regulations would effectively repeal the significant future benefit standard of *INDOPCO* and revive the separate-and-distinct asset test of *Lincoln Savings*. Read carefully Prop. Treas. Reg. §1.263(a)-4(b). The reason given for using a separate-and-distinct asset standard, as stated in the preamble, is that "[a] 'significant future benefit' standard...does not provide the certainty and clarity necessary for compliance with, and sound administration of, the law. Consequently, the IRS and Treasury Department believe that simply restating the significant future benefit test, without more, would lead to continued uncertainty on the part of taxpayers and continued controversy between taxpayers and the IRS." Preamble, 67 Fed. Reg. at 77702. Do the proposed regulations replace *INDOPCO's* presumption of capitalization with a presumption of favored deduction?

If the costs of creating or acquiring intellectual property are not deductible when paid or incurred (*e.g.*, if the costs must be capitalized), such costs are added to the taxpayer's basis of the intellectual property with respect to which the expenditures are incurred. Although not immediately deductible, these capitalized costs may nevertheless be eligible to be deducted over time through an appropriate depreciation or amortization allowance under another Code provision or administrative pronouncement.

Depreciation is an accounting device that allocates the capitalized cost of an asset to the various periods which are benefitted by that asset. In other words, depreciation allows a taxpayer to recover (deduct) the capitalized costs of assets over a certain time period (a period that usually correlates with the asset's production of income). As an asset is being consumed or depleted, and deprecation (cost recovery) deductions are taken, the asset's adjusted basis is reduced to reflect the distribution of its costs over the accounting periods affected. I.R.C. § 1016(a)(2). Not all property is depreciable under § 167, the principal depreciation provision in the Code. To be eligible for depreciation, property must be (1) "subject to wear and tear, decay or decline from natural causes, exhaustion, or obsolescence," and (2) "used in the trade or business" or "held for the production of income." I.R.C. § 167(a).

With respect to eligible tangible property, § 168 provides a set of arbitrary rules for determining appropriate depreciation allowances. I.R.C. §§ 167(b), 168(a). For example, computers are depreciated using an accelerated depreciation method over an arbitrary five-year recovery period. I.R.C. § 168(b)(1) (providing a default rule that the applicable depreciation method is the 200-percent declining balance method); § 168(c), (e)(3)(B)(iv), (i)(2) (providing five-year recovery period for computers). In contrast to the specific provisions of § 168 applicable to tangible property, the Code contains less detailed provisions applicable to intangible property. Section 197, enacted in 1993, permits a taxpayer to amortize the capitalized costs of certain forms of intangible property ratably over a bright-line, fifteen year period. I.R.C. §§ 167(h)(2),197(a). Intangible property not covered by section 197, however, is governed by the less-detailed provision of § 167. Section 167 generally permits a taxpayer to depreciate the capitalized costs of intangible property over the intangible property's useful life provided the useful life can be reasonably estimated. See Treas. Reg. §§ 1.167(a)-3; -14. But see I.R.C. 167(f)(1), (g).

Personal expenses, such as those paid in carrying on personal hobbies, are generally not deductible. I.R.C. §§ 183(a), 262. Indeed, many deduction provisions require the existence of a trade or business or activity engaged in for profit. See, e.g., I.R.C. §§ 162(a) (requiring an existing "trade or business"); 165(c) (limiting losses to those incurred in a "trade or business" or "transaction entered into for profit"); 167 (requiring property to be used in a "trade or business" or "held for the production of income"); 197 (requiring intangible property be held in connection with the conduct of a "trade or business or an activity described in section 212"). Surprisingly, neither the Code nor the Treasury Regulations define the term "trade or business." The Supreme Court in *Commissioner v. Groetzinger*, included below, considered the meaning of "trade or business." According to the Court, what is the requisite scope of activities and/or requisite profit motive? As noted by *Groetzinger*, an activity will not qualify as a trade or business if it is "[a] sporadic activity, a hobby, or an amusement diversion." Treasury Regulations under § 183 provide nine relevant factors that should be taken into account in determining whether or not an activity is engaged in for profit. Read Treas. Reg. § 1.183-2(b). Although the regulations set out and illustrate the nine "relevant factors" that "should normally be taken into account," no one factor, nor even a majority of them, is controlling and other factors may be relevant. *Id.* What is the proper treatment of hobby expenditures? See I.R.C. § 183(b); Treas. Reg. § 1.183-1(b). How must a taxpayer substantiate his or her expenses? See I.R.C. § 274(d); Treas. Reg. § 1.274-5T(c)(1).

This course book addresses various intellectual property transactions that give rise to deductions. Chapter 4 addresses the deductibility of intellectual property creation costs. As noted in that chapter, some intellectual property creation costs are deductible in full at the time of expenditure; some development costs are permitted to be deducted only over a prescribed time period; and some development costs are not deductible at all, and can be recovered only upon the eventual transfer of the developed intellectual property (in the form of an offset of the selling price). Chapter 5 addresses the proper tax treatment of intellectual property purchases and licenses. Costs of purchasing intellectual property are generally not currently deductible but rather must be capitalized. Nevertheless, the capitalized costs of purchasing intellectual property may be recovered over a certain time period through an appropriate depreciation or amortization allowance. In contrast to purchase costs, payments made under a license for the use of intellectual property are either currently deductible or are capitalized and amortized over a 15-year period. Hence, taxpayers may not be able to avoid fifteen-year amortization and obtain current deductions by licensing intellectual property rather than purchasing such property. Chapter 8 addresses the deductibility of intellectual property litigation costs.

3. Tax Rates

Section 1 of the Code provides the schedule of tax rates that applies to individuals (single individuals, surviving spouses, married spouses filing jointly, etc.), as well to estates and trusts. I.R.C. §1. Section 11 provides a different rate schedule that applies to subchapter C corporations, which—like estates and trusts—are treated as separate tax-paying entities. I.R.C. §11. Partnerships and limited liability companies are not usually subject to an entity tax as these business forms are generally treated as pass-through entities for federal income tax purposes. In other words, items of income and deductions of a partnership flow through to the owners (partners) to be reported on their individual tax returns and taxed using the schedule of rates found in §1 (in the case of individual partners) or §11 (in the case of corporate partners).

As can be seen from skimming §§1 and 11, the schedule of tax rates is progressive or graduated, which means that as income increases a taxpayer's tax liability also increases, but at a greater rate. The rate of tax at each bracket level is called the marginal rate of tax. Presently, there are five rate brackets for individuals. Until recently, the highest marginal rate of tax for individuals was 39.6%. The Economic Growth and Tax Relief Reconciliation Act of 2001 ("2001 EGTRRA"), which became law in June 2001, reduced the top rate of tax on ordinary income from 39.6% to 35% over a six-year period. Under the 2001 EGTRRA, the highest marginal rate of tax on ordinary income for individuals was to be reduced as follows: For years 2001-2003, the top rate was to be reduced to 38.6%; for years 2004-2005, the top rate was to be reduced to 37.6%; and for 2006 and later, the top rate was to be reduced to 35%. In 2003, Congress passed significant tax cuts by accelerating the rate reductions in the regular income tax rates that were scheduled to be phased in under the 2001 EGTRRA. Specifically, the Jobs and Growth Tax Relief Reconciliation Act of 2003 ("2003 JGTRRA") reduced the tax rate bracket for ordinary income to 35% for 2003 and later years. As noted above, this was the top rate scheduled for 2006 under the 2001 EGTRRA. Now, for 2003 and thereafter, the regular income tax rates above 15% are 25%, 28%, 33%, and 35%.

Some property transactions result in "capital" gains, which are not subject to the rate structure above, but instead are taxed at much lower rates. A gain is either capital or ordinary, depending on a number of factors, including the nature of the property, the taxpayer's holding period for the property, and whether the taxpayer disposed of the property in a sale or exchange transaction. *See* I.R.C. §§ 1221, 1222, 1231. Individuals generally prefer gains to be classified as capital gains rather than ordinary income because certain capital gains are subject to reduced tax rates. Before 2003, the maximum rate at which most long-term capital gains were taxed was 20%, much higher than the top rate of tax on ordinary income. The 2003 JGTRRA reduced the 20% long-term capital gains rate to 15% (effective for sales after May 5, 2003). Even though the 2003 JGTRRA also reduced the top rate of tax on ordinary income to 35%, there is still a significant rate differential and premium placed on deriving capital gains rather than ordinary income.

[margin note: lower?]

The Code contains general provisions governing the character of gains for most property transactions, including intellectual property transactions. The Code also contains special provisions that apply specifically to certain intellectual property transfers. Section 1235 (dealing with certain transfers of patents and rights therein) and § 1253 (dealing with transfers of trademarks and trade names) are considered in Chapter 6.

Under the Code's general characterization provisions, the capital gain preference only comes into play if a taxpayer has a "net capital gain" for the year, which is only possible if the taxpayer has a "net long-term capital gain" during the year. I.R.C. §§ 1(h), 1222(11). Net short-term capital gains, unlike net long-term capital gains, are not included in the term "net capital gain" and are taxed as ordinary income. A long-term capital gain is defined as gain (1) from the sale or exchange (2) of a capital asset (3) held for more than a year. I.R.C. § 1222(3). The presence of each of these three factors is necessary before a recognized gain can receive preferential tax treatment.

First, a taxpayer's interest in property must be terminated in a special way (a "sale or exchange") in order to qualify for capital gain treatment. The "sale or exchange" requirement is not met for transfers that constitute licenses under general tax principles. Likewise, the sale or exchange requirement is not satisfied if property is abandoned or if property is stolen or destroyed in a casualty transaction and the taxpayer is reimbursed by insurance or otherwise.

Second, a transaction must involve a "capital asset" in order to qualify for capital gain treatment. The term "capital asset" is defined as all property held by the taxpayer (whether or not connected with a trade or business), subject to certain exceptions. I.R.C. § 1221. The first type of property specifically excluded from the definition of capital asset is stock-in-trade, inventory, and property held by the taxpayer primarily for sale to customers in the ordinary course of a trade or business. I.R.C. § 1221(a)(1). [A professional inventor may run afoul with this exception because a professional inventor may be considered to hold his or her inventions as inventory or property primarily held for sale to customers in the ordinary course of his or her trade or business.] The second type of property excluded from the definition of capital asset is depreciable property used in the taxpayer's trade or business. I.R.C. § 1221(a)(2). [This exclusion is quite broad because many forms of intellectual property are subject to the allowance for depreciation under § 167, and many other forms of intellectual property are considered "section 197 intangible" assets, which are treated as property subject to the allowance for depreciation under § 167. I.R.C. § 197(f)(7).] The third type of property excluded from the definition of capital asset is a copyright, a literary, musical, or artistic composition, or similar property held by the creator (taxpayer whose personal efforts created the property) or a taxpayer with a basis carried over from the creator. I.R.C.

§ 1221(a)(3); Treas. Reg. § 1.1221-1(c)(1). [The exclusion has the effect of putting non-professional writers, authors, and photographers on parity with professional writers, authors, and photographers who are subject to the inventory exclusion discussed above.]

Third, the tax treatment of a capital gain depends on the property's holding period. As discussed above, only long-term capital gains are accorded preferential tax treatment. A long-term capital gain requires a holding period of more than one year. I.R.C. § 1222(3). In certain circumstances, a taxpayer can tack on to his or her actual holding period (1) the period during which another taxpayer held the same property or (2) the period during which he or she held other similar property. I.R.C. § 1223. For example, in the case of property received by gift, the donor's previous holding period in the gifted property is tacked on to the taxpayer's actual holding period of the same property. I.R.C. § 1223(2).

Long-term capital gain consequences require a sale or exchange of a capital asset held for longer than a year. If a transaction does not constitute a sale or exchange or if a transaction does not involve a capital asset, the transaction will give rise to ordinary income unless a special characterization provision applies.

Section 1231 is a special characterization provision that operates on certain transactions that are not already characterized under the characterization provisions discussed above. It is a pro-taxpayer provision in that property excluded from the definition of capital asset (*i.e.*, depreciable trade or business property) may be accorded capital asset status. Likewise, dispositions that do not rise to the level of "sale or exchange" (*i.e.*, thefts and casualties of property) may be accorded sale or exchange status.

Section 1231 applies to only two types of transactions. The first transaction to which § 1231 applies is "the sale or exchange of property used in the trade or business." I.R.C. § 1231(a)(3)(A)(i). The term "property used in the trade or business" means depreciable or real property used in the trade or business that has been held more than one year, and specifically excludes (1) inventory or property held primarily for sale to customers in the ordinary course of trade or business and (2) copyrightable works if held by the creator or a taxpayer with a basis carried over from the creator. I.R.C. § 1231(b)(1)(A)–(C). It should be clear that by referring to depreciable trade or business property, § 1231 embraces property that is not considered a capital asset under § 1221(a)(2). The second transaction to which § 1231 applies is the involuntary or compulsory conversion of (1) depreciable property used in a trade or business held for more than one year or (2) capital assets held for more than one year in connection with a trade or business or a transaction entered for profit. I.R.C. § 1231(a)(3)(A)(ii). As a result, if property is not disposed of through a sale or exchange (*e.g.*, involuntary casualty transaction), capital gain or loss treatment may nevertheless be available.

The operation of section 1231 requires a taxpayer to place in an imaginary basket all "section 1231 gains" and "section 1231 losses" that occur during the year and to net those gains and losses to determine their character. If the taxpayer's "section 1231 gains" exceed "section 1231 losses," all gains and losses are treated as long term capital gains and losses. I.R.C. § 1231(a)(1). On the other hand, if the taxpayer's "section 1231 losses" equal or exceed "section 1231 gains," then all such gains and losses are ordinary. I.R.C. § 1231(a)(2). This treatment gives the taxpayer the best of both worlds. Gains may be characterized as capital gains and losses may remain characterized as ordinary losses. [NOTE: A special rule provides that gains and losses from involuntary conversions are not subject to § 1231 if the total involuntary losses exceed the involuntary gains. I.R.C. § 1231(a)(4)(C). This too is a pro-taxpayer rule, permitting casualty losses to remain characterized as ordinary losses, while permitting §1231 gains in the same year to be characterized as capital gains.]

In sum, §1231 may add to the characterization issue in the event property is excluded from the definition of capital asset under §1221 or the intellectual property is not disposed of in a sale or exchange transaction. For example, a purchased copyright used in a trade or business is excluded from the definition of capital asset under §1221(a)(2). But for §1231, any gain on the disposition of the copyright would necessarily be ordinary gain. Under §1231, however, gain on the sale of the copyright may be long-term capital gain. In other words, §1231 supplies one element in this example (capital asset element) for capital gain treatment.

Section 1245 is another special characterization provision that may impact the character of gain on dispositions of "section 1245 property." ["Section 1245 property" is defined as depreciable personal property, which includes both tangible and intangible personal property. I.R.C. §1245(a)(3); Treas. Reg. §1.1245-3(b).] Section 1245 provides that gain recognized on the disposition of "section 1245 property" shall be reported as ordinary income to the extent of any depreciation or amortization deductions taken with respect to the property. I.R.C. §1245(a). In other words, any part of the gain that is attributable to depreciation or amortization deductions previously attributable to the transferred property must be recaptured as ordinary income. Any gain in excess of the amount treated as ordinary income under §1245 (*i.e.*, gain that reflects appreciation in the property's value) may be entitled to capital gain treatment under the general or special characterization provisions discussed above. Review I.R.C. §§1221, 1222, 1231.

Consider the following example. Taxpayer acquires depreciable intellectual property (*e.g.*, a separately acquired patent) in Year 1 for $10,000. Taxpayer begins depreciating the patent over its expected useful life under §167. The Taxpayer claimed a total of $4,000 in depreciation allowances in Years 1, 2, and 3, and reduced the adjusted basis in the patent accordingly to $6,000. In Year 3, Taxpayer sells the patent for $15,000, which results in a realized gain of $9,000 ($15,000 amount realized minus $6,000 adjusted basis). Although the patent increased in value by only $5,000, Taxpayer realized $9,000 of gain. This was due to the fact that the taxpayer took ordinary depreciation deductions with respect to the property even though the property was increasing in value. Under §1245, $4,000 of the $9,000 gain will have to be recaptured as ordinary income whereas $5,000 of the gain may be entitled to capital gains treatment under general or special characterization provisions. In short, §1245 assures that gain attributable to depreciation is taxed as ordinary income and that gain attributable to true economic appreciation in value is taxed as capital gains. [Query: Is §1245 recapture relevant to those transferors who would have to report ordinary income anyway? Consider the sale of a copyrightable work by the creator.]

[Recall from *Williams v. McGowan*, included below, that the sale of a trade or business must be analyzed as a sale of its component parts. Accordingly the amount and character of gain or loss—ordinary or capital—must be made with respect to each asset (tangible and intangible) sold. The seller and buyer usually allocate the total sales price of the business in accordance with the fair market value of the business assets transferred. *See* I.R.C. §1060; Treas. Reg. §1.1060-1(c).]

Although this chapter focuses mainly on fundamental aspects of the federal income tax system, taxpayers should also be aware of the "alternative minimum tax" when computing their tax liabilities. The alternative minimum tax was enacted to serve one overriding objective: "to ensure that no taxpayer with substantial economic income can avoid significant tax liability by using exclusions, deductions, and credits." *See* H. Rep. No. 99-426, 99th Cong. 1st Sess., 305–06; *see also* Sen. Rep. 99-313, 99th Cong. 2nd Sess., 518–19. In general, taxpayers must generally pay the regular federal income tax (using the rate tables set forth above) or the "tentative minimum tax," whichever is greater. A taxpayer may have to worry about the alternative minimum tax if the taxpayer has taken certain deductions that are treated as tax preference items. Skim I.R.C. §§ 56–58.

4. Tax Credits

Once the applicable tax rates are applied to the taxpayer's taxable income, certain statutory credits may be available which are subtracted directly from the tax due. *See* I.R.C. §§ 21–53. Tax credits, unlike deductions, have the same dollar value for all taxpayers because they are a dollar-for-dollar reduction of the tax liability. For example, a dollar credit would save a dollar in taxes, whereas a dollar deduction would save the taxpayer only 33 cents assuming the taxpayer's tax rate was 33 percent. Chapter 4 discusses the § 41 credit for research and development activities.

B. Researching Federal Tax Law

1. The Internal Revenue Code

The primary source of federal tax law is the Internal Revenue Code (the "Code"), which can be found at Title 26 of the United States Code. Although the Code has developed a bad reputation for being overly complex and incomprehensible, one will find, upon closer look, that the Code is structured in an orderly, logical manner. The Code is divided into nine subtitles, each of which is subdivided into smaller units. Subtitle A of the Code, for example, includes all the income tax provisions. Subtitle B contains all the gift and estate tax provisions; Subtitle C contains all the employment tax provisions; and Subtitle F includes all the procedure and administration rules. This course book will mostly address provisions in subtitle A since it is concerned with the federal *income* tax consequences of intellectual property transactions.

Subtitle A of the Code is divided into chapters, which are then subdivided into subchapters. Subchapter A of Chapter 1 (§§ 1–59A) contains all the provisions necessary to compute a taxpayer's actual tax liability (*e.g.*, the applicable tax rates and the research and development credit). Subchapter B (§§ 61–291) contains all the provisions necessary to determine "taxable income," which is the tax base on which the applicable rates of subchapter A are applied. For example, subchapter B describes what receipts, benefits, and accessions to wealth are included in gross income (*e.g.*, royalties from intellectual property licenses and gains from intellectual property sales). Subchapter B also describes what payments, expenditures, and outlays are deductible from gross income in arriving at taxable income (*e.g.*, intellectual property development costs, and depreciation and amortization allowances for otherwise capitalized expenditures). Subchapter P (§§ 1201 *et. seq.*) contains all the capital gains and loss provisions for intellectual property transactions. Special tax rules for business entities and their owners can be found in three other subchapters. Subchapter C (§§ 301–85) contains special provisions governing C corporations and their shareholders; subchapter K (§§ 701–61) contains rules governing partnerships and their partners; subchapter S (§§ 1361–78) contains rules governing S corporations and their shareholders. Subchapters are divided into smaller units. Specifically, subchapters are divided into "parts"; parts are sometimes divided into "subparts"; and subparts are subdivided into "sections." The "section" is the basic unit in the Code. Sections are numbered sequentially, with breaks in sequence to provide room for new Code provisions to be added.

When researching the tax Code, one should remember several important points. First, Code headings are not authoritative and can often be misleading. For example, § 1235 is titled "Sale or Exchange of Patents." One might jump to the conclusion that § 1235 applies only to *patents*. Interestingly, however, upon further research, one would discover that trade secrets and know-how may also qualify for § 1235 treatment in a couple of situations. Alternatively, one might jump to the conclusion that § 1235 applies to *any sale* of a patent. Upon further reading of the statute, however, it becomes clear that § 1235 applies only when "all substantial rights" in a patent are transferred by certain statutorily defined holders to unrelated parties. The lesson is that it is important to be careful of the limitations of various provisions. With respect to deductions, exceptions often swallow the general rule.

Second, when researching a particular Code provision, one should always make sure to use the version of the Code effective for the year(s) in issue. For example, the special fifteen-year amortization rule of § 197 applies only to certain forms of intellectual property acquired after August 10, 1993. Section 167(g), which describes rules for using the income-forecast method of depreciation, applies only to certain forms of intellectual property placed in service after September 13, 1995. Although it is important to read the Code itself for effective dates and transition rules, it is often necessary to check the underlying legislative acts for such information. For example, because section 197 states that it applies only to § 197 intangibles acquired after "the date of enactment of this section," it is necessary to check the actual act for the section's effective date. *See* I.R.C. § 197(c)(1)(A).

Third, it is important when reading a particular Code provision to understand the scope of the provision. Some Code provisions apply to the entire Code, while others apply only to certain portions of the Code. For example, some income tax provisions start out with the following language: "For purposes of this subtitle...." (indicating that the provision applies broadly to Subtitle A of Title 26 of the U.S.C., which encompasses all the income tax provisions of the Internal Revenue Code). *See, e.g.*, I.R.C. § 1221 (stating: "For purposes of this subtitle, the term 'capital asset' means...."). Other Code sections begin with: "For purposes of this section...." (indicating that the provision is more limited and affects only the particular section at issue, a much smaller unit). *See, e.g.*, I.R.C. § 41(d) (stating: "For purposes of this section—the term 'qualified research' means....").

2. *Treasury Regulations*

Treasury regulations are the most important administrative interpretations of the Code, and should be part of any tax research. Congress has granted general authority to the Treasury Department to promulgate regulations interpreting and giving meaning to the Code. I.R.C. § 7805(a). As a result, regulations have the force and effect of law and will be upheld by a court unless they are clearly contrary to congressional intent. Treasury regulations, which are promulgated under the Administrative Procedures Act, are first issued as "proposed" regulations, published for taxpayer comment in the Federal Register. After the comment period has expired and revisions made, regulations are published in final form as Treasury Decisions in the Code of Federal Regulations. Unlike final regulations, proposed regulations issued in the Federal Register are not authoritative and, hence, should always be cited as such. Although not authoritative, however, proposed regulations are relevant in tax research since the Treasury has authority to apply final regulations retroactively to the date they first appeared as proposed in the Federal Register. Regulations are numbered the same way as the Code sections to which they relate, but preceded by a numerical prefix which indicates the type of tax (income, estate, gift) involved. For example, the term "research or experimental expenditures" as used in § 174 is defined in the regulations under § 174 at the following cite: Treas. Reg. § 1.174-2(a). The numerical prefix of "1" indicates that section 174 is an income tax provision.

It should be noted that there may be Code sections for which no regulations exist as Congress enacts new statutes quite frequently and it sometimes takes years for regulations to be promulgated. Worse yet, there may be regulations that fail to reflect the current law as Congress amends Code provisions quite frequently and the Treasury sometimes does not react promptly with appropriate regulatory revisions.

3. IRS Rulings and Procedures

The Internal Revenue Service issues interpretative pronouncements (rulings) that indicate the Service's position regarding the application of tax law to a certain set of facts. There are two types of rulings: (1) revenue rulings and (2) private letter rulings. The Service also issues statements of its internal practices and procedures. These are known as revenue procedures.

(a) Revenue Rulings

Revenue rulings are official interpretations that are published by the Service for information and guidance to taxpayers. They may arise from various sources. For example, a revenue ruling may indicate the Service's position regarding the application of tax law (from the Service's point of view) to a particular factual situation. A revenue ruling may represent the Service's position on issues arising in the audit of taxpayers' returns; a revenue ruling may also represent the Service's position on issues that have been decided by various courts. Unlike regulations, discussed above, revenue rulings are not published in proposed form for taxpayer comment and are not approved by the Treasury Department. Accordingly, revenue rulings are not as authoritative as regulations. Nevertheless, a revenue ruling can be relied upon by any taxpayer whose circumstances are substantially the same as those described in the ruling. It is important to remember that a revenue ruling's conclusion is limited in scope to the pivotal facts stated in the ruling. Revenue rulings are published weekly in the Internal Revenue Bulletin and consolidated semi-annually in the Cumulative Bulletin, both of which are official publications of the Service.

(b) Private Letter Rulings

Private letter rulings represent taxpayer-specific guidance from the Service. Specifically, a taxpayer may request advice from the Service on the position that the Service would take with respect to a proposed transaction, and the Service in turn may issue a letter ruling indicating its position regarding the application of tax law (from the Service's point of view) to the specific transaction the taxpayer has presented. Unlike revenue rulings, private letter rulings are taxpayer-specific guidance, and cannot be relied upon by other taxpayers or cited as authority. In other words, the Service is not bound by letter rulings in its dealing with other taxpayers. The Code mandates that the Service release private letter rulings, with identifying details redacted. They are published by commercial services.

(c) Revenue Procedures

Like revenue rulings, discussed above, revenue procedures are published initially in the Internal Revenue Bulletin and later consolidated in the Cumulative Bulletin. They are basically statements of the Service regarding IRS practices and procedures. These can prove very useful in structuring a transaction. For example, in Revenue Procedure 97-50, discussed in Chapter 4, the Service indicated that it would not challenge the immediate deductibility of costs paid or incurred to ensure computer systems were year 2000 (Y2K) compliant.

4. Case Law

Three trial courts have original jurisdiction for tax cases: (1) the U.S. District Court; (2) the U.S. Claims Court; and (3) the U.S. Tax Court. The first two courts (district court and claims court) are known as "refund tribunals" since the only way to litigate in those forums is to first pay the asserted tax deficiency and then commence a refund action. More specifically, to litigate in the district court or claims court, a taxpayer must pay the asserted tax deficiency and then file an administrative claim for refund. Upon denial of that claim, the taxpayer may then sue for a refund.

The United States Tax Court is unique in that it is the only forum in which a taxpayer may litigate a disputed tax claim without having to first pay the asserted deficiency. In other words, if the Service asserts a deficiency, the taxpayer may refuse to pay and then petition the Tax Court for a redetermination of the deficiency. I.R.C. § 6213. Although the Tax Court is based in Washington D.C., the court tries cases in several locations throughout the United States. See Tax Court Rules, App. IV, for current locations. The Tax Court has nineteen judges appointed by the President and about twenty special trial judges and retired Tax Court judges who assist with smaller tax cases. The Chief Judge assigns each case to be heard to one member on the court. The judge deciding the case submits a proposed opinion to the Chief Judge, who then decides whether the decision should become the ruling of the court or whether the case should be reviewed by the entire court (typically a case that presents issues of first importance). If a proposed opinion is not to be reviewed by the entire court, the Chief Judge designates the opinion as either (1) a regular decision or (2) a memorandum opinion. Regular opinions involve significant or novel legal issues and are regarded by the Tax Court in its subsequent decisions as binding precedent. They are officially published in the Tax Court Reports (T.C.) and unofficially published by commercial sources, such as the CCH Tax Court Reporter. Memorandum opinions are generally factual or apply established law to the facts of that case. They are unofficially published by commercial services, such as CCH and RIA. In most Tax Court cases in which the Service loses, the Service will either acquiesce or nonacquiesce in the decision. A notice of acquiescence indicates that the Service accepts the decision of the court, whereas a notice of nonacquiescence indicates that the Service may continue to challenge other taxpayers with respect to the issue(s) presented in the case. As an example, the IRS did not acquiesce to the Tax Court's decision in *Nabisco, Inc. v. Commissioner*, a case included in Chapter 4. Action on Dec. 1999-012 (Oct. 4, 1999).

In sum, if the Service issues a notice of deficiency, the taxpayer can litigate the matter (1) by paying the tax, filing an administrative claim for refund, and then filing suit for a refund in either the district court or the claims court; or (2) by filing a petition with the Tax Court for a redetermination of the proposed deficiency. There are several factors a taxpayer should consider in deciding which forum to choose. Some factors to consider include: (1) whether the taxpayer has funds to pay the asserted deficiency, which is necessary to litigate in one of the refund tribunals; (2) whether the taxpayer wants a jury trial, which is available only in the district court; (3) the level of discovery required in each trial court; (4) the expertise of the Tax Court judges; and (5) the prior decisions of each of the three possible trial courts and the appellate courts to which an appeal can be taken. *See Golsen v. Commissioner*, 54 T.C. 742 (1970) (holding the Tax Court will follow a court of appeals decision on point from the circuit in which the taxpayer resides).

Appeals from each of the three trial courts varies. Federal district court decisions may be appealed to the federal court of appeals for the circuit embracing the district court. Decisions of the claims court may be appealed to the court of appeals for the federal circuit in Washington, D.C. Tax Court decisions may be appealed to the appropriate federal circuit in which the taxpayer resides.

5. Legislative History

Legislative history is very helpful in understanding Code provisions, particularly newer Code provisions for which there are no regulations, rulings, or developed case law. For example, if regulations are not available for a recently enacted section, one should consult legislative history to ascertain congressional intent. The process used to enact tax legislation generally parallels that used for other federal laws. A bill is usually introduced and then referred to the appropriate committee: the House Ways and Means Committee or the Senate Finance Committee. Each of these may ignore a tax bill by failing to consider it or may substantially rewrite a tax bill. They also may hold hearings as well as issue a committee report if a bill is reported out of committee. Committee reports are the most important part of the legislative history. Committee reports contain important information, such as a statement of the bill's purpose, a statement of the reasons why a bill should be enacted, a statement of changes the bill would make to existing law, and committee amendments to the bill. If the House and Senate versions of a bill differ, a conference committee made up of House and Senate members meets to resolve these differences. This committee generates a third committee report which explains the resolution of the interhouse differences. When an agreement is reached, the bill goes back to each house for passage in the newly agreed form.

IV. Materials

Commissioner v. Groetzinger
Supreme Court of the United States
480 U.S. 23 (1987)

BLACKMUN, J., delivered the opinion of the Court.

The issue in this case is whether a full-time gambler who makes wagers solely for his own account is engaged in a "trade or business," within the meaning of §§ 162(a) and 62(1) of the Internal Revenue Code of 1954, as amended. The tax year with which we here are concerned is the calendar year 1978; technically, then, we look to the Code as it read at that time.

Respondent Robert P. Groetzinger had worked for 20 years in sales and market research for an Illinois manufacturer when his position was terminated in February 1978. During the remainder of that year, respondent busied himself with parimutuel wagering, primarily on greyhound races. He gambled at tracks in Florida and Colorado. He went to the track 6 days a week for 48 weeks in 1978. He spent a substantial amount of time studying racing forms, programs, and other materials. He devoted from 60 to 80 hours each week to these gambling-related endeavors. He never placed bets on behalf of any other person, or sold tips, or collected commissions for placing bets, or functioned as a bookmaker. He gambled solely for his own account. He had no other profession or type of employment.

Respondent kept a detailed accounting of his wagers and every day noted his winnings and losses in a record book. In 1978, he had gross winnings of $70,000, but he bet $72,032; he thus realized a net gambling loss for the year of $2,032.

Upon audit, the Commissioner of Internal Revenue determined that respondent's $70,000 in gambling winnings were to be included in his gross income and that, pursuant to § 165(d) of the Code, a deduction was to be allowed for his gambling losses to the extent of these gambling gains. But the Commissioner further determined that, under the law as it was in 1978, a portion of respondent's $70,000 gambling-loss deduction was an item of tax preference and operated to subject him to the minimum tax under § 56(a) of the Code. At that time, under statutory provisions in effect from 1976 until 1982, "items of tax preference" were lessened by certain deductions, but not by deductions not "attributable to a trade or business carried on by the taxpayer." § 57(a)(1) and (b)(1)(A), and § 62(1). This statutory scheme was amended by the Tax Equity and Fiscal Responsibility Act of 1982. For tax years after 1982, gambling-loss deductions explicitly are excluded from the minimum tax base.

The phrase "trade or business" has been in § 162(a) and in that section's predecessors for many years. Indeed, the phrase is common in the Code, for it appears in over 50 sections and 800 subsections and in hundreds of places in proposed and final income tax regulations. The slightly longer phrases, "carrying on a trade or business" and "engaging in a trade or business," themselves are used no less than 60 times in the Code. The concept thus has a well-known and almost constant presence on our tax-law terrain. Despite this, the Code has never contained a definition of the words "trade or business" for general application, and no regulation has been issued expounding its meaning for all purposes. Neither has a broadly applicable authoritative judicial definition emerged. Our task in this case is to ascertain the meaning of the phrase as it appears in the sections of the Code with which we are here concerned.

In one of its early tax cases, *Flint v. Stone Tracy Co.*, 220 U.S. 107 (1911), the Court was concerned with the Corporation Tax imposed by the Tariff Act of 1909 and the status of being engaged in business. It said: " 'Business' is a very comprehensive term and embraces everything about which a person can be employed." It embraced the Bouvier Dictionary definition: "That which occupies the time, attention and labor of men for the purpose of a livelihood or profit." And Justice Frankfurter has observed that "we assume that Congress uses common words in their popular meaning, as used in the common speech of men." Frankfurter, Some Reflections on the Reading of Statutes, 47 Colum.L.Rev. 527, 536 (1947).

With these general comments as significant background, we turn to pertinent cases decided here. *Snyder v. Commissioner*, 295 U.S. 134 (1935), had to do with margin trading and capital gains, and held, in that context, that an investor, seeking merely to increase his holdings, was not engaged in a trade or business. Justice Brandeis, in his opinion for the Court, noted that the Board of Tax Appeals theretofore had ruled that a taxpayer who devoted the major portion of his time to transactions on the stock exchange for the purpose of making a livelihood could treat losses incurred as having been sustained in the course of a trade or business. He went on to observe that no facts were adduced in *Snyder* to show that the taxpayer "might properly be characterized as a 'trader on an exchange who makes a living in buying and selling securities.'" These observations, thus, are dicta, but, by their use, the Court appears to have drawn a distinction between an active trader and an investor.

In *Deputy v. Du Pont*, 308 U.S. 488 (1940), the Court was concerned with what were "ordinary and necessary" expenses of a taxpayer's trade or business. In ascertaining whether carrying charges on short sales of stock were deductible as ordinary and necessary expenses of the taxpayer's business, the Court *assumed* that the activities of the taxpayer in conserving and enhancing his estate constituted a trade or business, but nevertheless disallowed the claimed deductions because they were not "ordinary" or "necessary." Justice Frankfurter, in a concurring opinion, did not join the majority. He took the position that whether the taxpayer's activities constituted a trade or business was "open for determination," and observed: "'carrying on any trade or business,' involves holding one's self out to others as engaged in the selling of goods or services. This the taxpayer did not do."

Next came *Higgins v. Commissioner*, 312 U.S. 212 (1941). There the Court, in a bare and brief unanimous opinion, ruled that salaries and other expenses incident to looking after one's own investments in bonds and stocks were not deductible as expenses paid or incurred in carrying on a trade or business. While surely cutting back on *Flint*'s broad approach, the Court seemed to do little more than announce that since 1918 "the present form [of the statute] was fixed and has so continued"; that "[n]o regulation has ever been promulgated which interprets the meaning of 'carrying on a business'"; that the comprehensive definition of "business" in *Flint* was "not controlling in this dissimilar inquiry"; that the facts in each case must be examined; that not all expenses of every business transaction are deductible; and that "[n]o matter how large the estate or how continuous or extended the work required may be, such facts are not sufficient as a matter of law to permit the courts to reverse the decision of the Board." The opinion, therefore—although devoid of analysis and not setting forth what elements, if any, in addition to profit motive and regularity, were required to render an activity a trade or business—must stand for the propositions that full-time market activity in managing and preserving one's own estate is not embraced within the phrase "carrying on a business," and that salaries and other expenses incident to the operation are not deductible as having been paid or incurred in a trade or business. See also *United States v. Gilmore*, 372 U.S. 39, 44-45 (1963); *Whipple v. Commissioner*, 373 U.S. 193 (1963). The Court in that case did not even cite *Du Pont* and thus paid no heed whatsoever to the content of Justice Frankfurter's pronouncement in his concurring opinion. Adoption of the Frankfurter gloss obviously would have disposed of the case in the Commissioner's favor handily and automatically, but that easy route was not followed.

Less than three months later, the Court considered the issue of the deductibility, as business expenses, of estate and trust fees. In unanimous opinions issued the same day and written by Justice Black, the Court ruled that the efforts of an estate or trust in asset conservation and maintenance did not constitute a trade or business. *City Bank Farmers Trust Co. v. Helvering*, 313 U.S. 121 (1941); *United States v. Pyne*, 313 U.S. 127 (1941). The *Higgins* case was deemed to be relevant and controlling. Again, no mention was made of the Frankfurter concurrence in *Du Pont*. Yet Justices Reed and Frankfurter were on the Court.

Snow v. Commissioner, 416 U.S. 500 (1974), concerned a taxpayer who had advanced capital to a partnership formed to develop an invention. On audit of his 1966 return, a claimed deduction under § 174(a)(1) of the 1954 Code for his pro rata share of the partnership's operating loss was disallowed. The Tax Court and the Sixth Circuit upheld that disallowance. This Court reversed. Justice Douglas, writing for the eight Justices who participated, observed: "Section 174 was enacted in 1954 to dilute some of the conception of 'ordinary and necessary' business expenses under § 162(a) adumbrated by Mr. Justice Frankfurter in a concurring opinion in *Deputy v. Du Pont*...where he said that the section in question...'involves holding one's self out to others as engaged in the selling of goods or services.'" He went on to state that § 162(a) "is more narrowly written than is § 174."

From these observations and decisions, we conclude (1) that, to be sure, the statutory words are broad and comprehensive (*Flint*); (2) that, however, expenses incident to caring for one's own investments, even though that endeavor is full time, are not deductible as paid or incurred in carrying on a trade or business (*Higgins; City Bank; Pyne*); (3) that the opposite conclusion may follow for an active trader (*Snyder*); (4) that Justice Frankfurter's attempted gloss upon the decision in *Du Pont* was not adopted by the Court in that case; (5) that the Court, indeed, later characterized it as an "adumbration" (*Snow*); and (6) that the Frankfurter observation, specifically or by implication, never has been accepted as law by a majority opinion of the Court, and more than once has been totally ignored. We must regard the Frankfurter gloss merely as a two-Justice pronouncement in a passing moment and, while entitled to respect, as never having achieved the status of a Court ruling. One also must acknowledge that *Higgins*, with its stress on examining the facts in each case, affords no readily helpful standard, in the usual sense, with which to decide the present case and others similar to it. The Court's cases, thus, give us results, but little general guidance.

If a taxpayer, as Groetzinger is stipulated to have done in 1978, devotes his full-time activity to gambling, and it is his intended livelihood source, it would seem that basic concepts of fairness (if there be much of that in the income tax law) demand that his activity be regarded as a trade or business just as any other readily accepted activity, such as being a retail store proprietor or, to come closer categorically, as being a casino operator or as being an active trader on the exchanges.

It is argued, however, that a full-time gambler is not offering goods or his services, within the line of demarcation that Justice Frankfurter would have drawn in *Du Pont*. Respondent replies that he indeed is supplying goods and services, not only to himself but, as well, to the gambling market; thus, he says, he comes within the Frankfurter test even if that were to be imposed as the proper measure. "It takes two to gamble." Surely, one who clearly satisfies the Frankfurter adumbration usually is in a trade or business. But does it necessarily follow that one who does not satisfy the Frankfurter adumbration is not in a trade or business? One might well feel that a full-time gambler ought to qualify as much as a full-time trader, as Justice Brandeis in *Snyder* implied and as courts have held. The Commissioner, indeed, accepts the trader result. In any event, while the offering of goods and services usually would qualify the activity as a trade or business, this factor, it seems to us, is not an absolute prerequisite.

We are not satisfied that the Frankfurter gloss would add any helpful dimension to the resolution of cases such as this one, or that it provides a "sensible test," as the Commissioner urges. It might assist now and then, when the answer is obvious and positive, but it surely is capable of breeding litigation over the meaning of "goods," the meaning of "services," or the meaning of "holding one's self out." And we suspect that—apart from gambling—almost every activity would satisfy the gloss. A test that everyone passes is not a test at all. We therefore now formally reject the Frankfurter gloss which the Court has never adopted anyway.

Of course, not every income-producing and profit-making endeavor constitutes a trade or business. We accept the fact that to be engaged in a trade or business, the taxpayer must be involved in the activity with continuity and regularity and that the taxpayer's primary purpose for engaging in the activity must be for income or profit. A sporadic activity, a hobby, or an amusement diversion does not qualify.

We would defer, instead, to the Code's normal focus on what we regard as a common-sense concept of what is a trade or business. Otherwise, as here, in the context of a minimum tax, it is not too extreme to say that the taxpayer is being taxed on his gambling losses, a result distinctly out of line with the Code's focus on income.

We do not overrule or cut back on the Court's holding in *Higgins* when we conclude that if one's gambling activity is pursued full time, in good faith, and with regularity, to the production of income for a livelihood, and is not a mere hobby, it is a trade or business within the meaning of the statutes with which we are here concerned. Respondent Groetzinger satisfied that test in 1978. Constant and large-scale effort on his part was made. Skill was required and was applied. He did what he did for a livelihood, though with a less-than-successful result. This was not a hobby or a passing fancy or an occasional bet for amusement.

We therefore adhere to the general position of the *Higgins* Court, taken 46 years ago, that resolution of this issue "requires an examination of the facts in each case." This may be thought by some to be a less-than-satisfactory solution, for facts vary. But the difficulty rests in the Code's wide utilization in various contexts of the term "trade or business," in the absence of an all-purpose definition by statute or regulation, and in our concern that an attempt judicially to formulate and impose a test for all situations would be counterproductive, unhelpful, and even somewhat precarious for the overall integrity of the Code. We leave repair or revision, if any be needed, which we doubt, to the Congress where we feel, at this late date, the ultimate responsibility rests.

The judgment of the Court of Appeals is AFFIRMED.

Welch v. Helvering
Supreme Court of the United States
290 U.S. 111 (1933)

MR. JUSTICE CARDOZO delivered the opinion of the Court.

The question to be determined is whether payments by a taxpayer, who is in business as a commission agent, are allowable deductions in the computation of his income if made to the creditors of a bankrupt corporation in an endeavor to strengthen his own standing and credit.

In 1922 petitioner was the secretary of the E. L. Welch Company, a Minnesota corporation, engaged in the grain business. The company was adjudged an involuntary bankrupt, and had a discharge from its debts. Thereafter the petitioner made a contract with the Kellogg Company to purchase grain for it on a commission. In order to re-establish his relations with customers whom he had known when acting for the Welch Company and to solidify his credit and standing, he decided to pay the debts of the Welch business so far as he was able. In fulfillment of that resolve, he made payments of substantial amounts during five successive years. The Commissioner ruled that these payments were not deductible from income as ordinary and necessary expenses, but were rather in the nature of capital expenditures, an outlay for the development of reputation and good will. The Board of Tax Appeals sustained the action of the Commissioner, and the Court of Appeals for the Eighth Circuit affirmed. The case is here on certiorari.

"In computing net income there shall be allowed as deductions...all the ordinary and necessary expenses paid or incurred during the taxable year in carrying on any trade or business." [I.R.C. § 162(a)]

We may assume that the payments to creditors of the Welch Company were necessary for the development of the petitioner's business, at least in the sense that they were appropriate and helpful. He certainly thought they were, and we should be slow to override his judgment. But the problem is not solved when the payments are characterized as necessary. Many necessary payments are charges upon capital. There is need to determine whether they are both necessary and ordinary. Now, what is ordinary, though there must always be a strain of constancy within it, is none the less a variable affected by time and place and circumstance. Ordinary in this context does not mean that the payments must be habitual or normal in the sense that the same taxpayer will have to make them often. A lawsuit affecting the safety of a business may happen once in a lifetime. The counsel fees may be so heavy that repetition is unlikely. None the less, the expense is an ordinary one because we know from experience that payments for such a purpose, whether the amount is large or small, are the common and accepted means of defense against attack. The situation is unique in the life of the individual affected, but not in the life of the group, the community, of which he is a part. At such times there are norms of conduct that help to stabilize our judgment, and make it certain and objective. The instance is not erratic, but is brought within a known type.

The line of demarcation is now visible between the case that is here and the one supposed for illustration. We try to classify this act as ordinary or the opposite, and the norms of conduct fail us. No longer can we have recourse to any fund of business experience, to any known business practice. Men do at times pay the debts of others without legal obligation or the lighter obligation imposed by the usages of trade or by neighborly amendities, but they do not do so ordinarily, not even though the result might be to heighten their reputation for generosity and opulence. Indeed, if language is to be read in its natural and common meaning, we should have to say that payment in such circumstances, instead of being ordinary is in a high degree extraordinary. There is nothing ordinary in the stimulus evoking it, and none in the response. Here, indeed, as so often in other branches of the law, the decisive distinctions are those of degree and not of kind. One struggles in vain for any verbal formula that will supply a ready touchstone. The standard set up by the statute is not a rule of law; it is rather a way of life. Life in all its fullness must supply the answer to the riddle.

The Commissioner of Internal Revenue resorted to that standard in assessing the petitioner's income, and found that the payments in controversy came closer to capital outlays than to ordinary and necessary expenses in the operation of a business. His ruling has the support of a presumption of correctness, and the petitioner has the burden of proving it to be wrong. Unless we can say from facts within our knowledge that these are ordinary and necessary expenses according to the ways of conduct and the forms of speech prevailing in the business world, the tax must be confirmed. But nothing told us by this record or within the sphere of our judicial notice permits us to give that extension to what is ordinary and necessary. Indeed, to do so would open the door to many bizarre analogies. One man has a family name that is clouded by thefts committed by an ancestor. To add to this own standing he repays the stolen money, wiping off, it may be, his income for the year. The payments figure in his tax return as ordinary expenses. Another man conceives the notion that he will be able to practice his vocation with greater ease and profit if he has an opportunity to enrich his culture. Forthwith the price of his education becomes an expense of the business, reducing the income subject to taxation. There is little difference between these expenses and those in controversy here. Reputation and learning are akin to capital assets, like the good will of an old partnership. For many, they are the only tools with which to hew a pathway to success. The money spent in acquiring them is well and wisely spent. It is not an ordinary expense of the operation of a business.

The decree should be AFFIRMED.

Commissioner v. Lincoln Savings & Loan Ass'n
Supreme Court of the United States
403 U.S. 345 (1971)

MR. JUSTICE BLACKMUN delivered the opinion of the Court.

This case presents the question whether the "additional premium" paid in 1963 by a state-chartered savings and loan association to the Federal Savings and Loan Insurance Corporation under the compulsion of §404(d) of the National Housing Act is deductible by the association, for income tax purposes, as an ordinary and necessary business expense under §162(a) of the Internal Revenue Code.

The Commissioner of Internal Revenue determined a deficiency of $461,454.38 in the 1963 cash basis federal income tax of Lincoln Savings and Loan Association. Nearly all the deficiency was attributable to the disallowance of a deduction claimed for Lincoln's payment of $882,636.86 made pursuant to §404(d). Lincoln sought redetermination in the Tax Court. Judge Raum, in a decision reviewed by the court without dissent, upheld the deficiency. 51 T.C. 82 (1968). On appeal the Ninth Circuit reversed, one judge dissenting. 422 F.2d 90 (1970). Because of the importance of the issue for the savings and loan industry and for the Government, we granted certiorari. 400 U.S. 901, (1970).

I.

The pertinent facts are not in dispute. Lincoln is a California savings and loan association organized in 1925 and is licensed under state law. It is subject to the California Financial Code, and is also subject to the regulations of the State's Savings and Loan Commissioner.

In 1936 Lincoln applied for membership in the Federal Home Loan Bank of San Francisco (then of Los Angeles). That application was granted and Lincoln has remained a member of the Bank since that time. The San Francisco Bank is one of 12 regional ones established and supervised by the Federal Home Loan Bank Board under the Federal Home Loan Bank Act of 1932. These banks provide liquidity and funds for mortgage lending by making advances to member institutions as needed to meet unusual or heavy withdrawal and credit demands. Each member must purchase capital stock in its bank in an amount equal to 1% of its outstanding "aggregate unpaid loan principal" and maintain that percentage.

In June 1938 Lincoln became, and still is, an institution insured by the Federal Savings and Loan Insurance Corporation (FSLIC), a corporation created by § 402 of the National Housing Act, and under the direction of the Federal Home Loan Bank Board. By statute FSLIC has the duty to insure the accounts of all federal savings and loan associations; it also may insure the accounts of qualified state-chartered associations such as Lincoln.

Each institution so insured was originally required, by § 404(a) of the Act, to pay FSLIC an annual insurance premium measured by the total amount of its accounts plus creditor obligations [annual premium was at the rate of 1/12 of 1% of that total]. The statute provided that these premiums were to continue annually until FSLIC's reserve for losses amounted to 5% of the insured accounts plus creditor obligations of all its insured institutions, and at such intervals thereafter as were necessary to maintain the reserve at that level.

This pattern was changed, however, effective January 1, 1962, by the Act of September 8, 1961. Section 404(a) now requires FSLIC to establish two reserves, namely, a Primary Reserve "which shall be the general reserve," and a Secondary Reserve. The requirement for the annual premium of 1/12 of 1% is continued, but the level of the general reserve was lowered from 5% to 2% of the total of accounts plus creditor obligations. The 1961 Act, moreover, added subsection (d) to § 404. This required that the insured institution pay FSLIC, with respect to any calendar year, an "additional premium in the nature of a prepayment with respect to future premiums of such institution under subsection (b)." This "additional premium" was, and still is, 2% of the net increase in the total of the institution's insured accounts, less any amount the institution is required to expend in purchasing stock in the Federal Home Loan Bank. The additional premium is to be credited to the Secondary Reserve.

As noted, FSLIC's statutorily prescribed Primary Reserve is its general reserve. It is credited annually with the Corporation's net income; this net thus represents retained earnings. The § 404(b)(1) premium payments, that is, the 1/12 of 1% required of each insured institution, constitute a major item in FSLIC's gross income. To the extent these premium payments exceed the corporation's expenses and insurance losses for the year, they flow as part of FSLIC's net to the Primary Reserve. The insured institutions have no property interest in the funds constituting the Primary Reserve.

The Secondary Reserve subsists separately and possesses different characteristics. It, of course, receives the 2% "additional premium," to the extent such is payable, required by § 404(d) from each insured institution. FSLIC must also credit the Secondary Reserve annually with a "return" on the Secondary Reserve's "outstanding balances...at a rate equal to the average annual rate of return to the Corporation during the year...on the investments held by the Corporation in obligations of, or guaranteed as to principal and interest by, the United States." In contrast with the Primary Reserve, the Secondary Reserve is "available...only for losses of the Corporation" and then "only to such extent as other accounts of the Corporation which are available therefor are insufficient for such losses."

Each insured institution has a pro rata share in the Secondary Reserve. Section 404(e) states that this is not assignable or transferable except as FSLIC, by regulation or otherwise, provides "in cases of merger or consolidation, transfer of bulk assets...and similar transactions." An insured institution may obtain a cash refund of its pro rata share if its status as an insured is terminated, or if a receiver or other legal custodian is appointed for purposes of liquidation, or if the Corporation determines that the institution has gone into liquidation.

Following any December 31 on which the aggregate of the Primary Reserve and the Secondary Reserve equals or exceeds 2% of the total of all insured accounts plus creditor obligations of all the insured institutions (and the Primary Reserve alone does not equal or exceed such 2%), the additional premiums required by §404(d) are suspended. When this takes place, the pro rata share of each insured institution in the Secondary Reserve is used, to the extent available, to discharge the institution's obligation to pay its regular, or basic, premium required for that year under §404(b)(1). Thereafter, if the aggregate of the two reserves decreases to less than 1 3/4%, the obligation to pay the additional premium under §404(d) resumes and the pro rata share in the Secondary Reserve is no longer used to pay the §404(b)(1) regular premium. Whenever, following any December 31, the Primary Reserve alone equals or exceeds such 2%, the Corporation shall pay in cash to each insured institution its pro rata share of the Secondary Reserve and shall not thereafter accept further §404(d) prepayments.

FSLIC maintains a separate account for each insured institution's share of the Secondary Reserve. It submits to the institution annually a statement disclosing that share and the interest credited to it. Under regulations issued by the California Savings and Loan Commissioner and by the Federal Home Loan Bank Board, Lincoln reports its interest in FSLIC's Secondary Reserve as an asset on its balance sheet and treats the interest earned on its pro rata share of the Secondary Reserve as income.

FSLIC annually sends Lincoln an "Insurance Premium Notice" for the basic premium due under §404(b)(1). It also sends Lincoln annually a "Notice of Insurance Premium Prepayments" for the amount, if any, due under §404(d). For 1963 the former was $135,760.52 and the latter was $882,636.86. Each was paid by Lincoln.

On its 1963 federal income tax return Lincoln deducted both its §404(b)(1) payment and its §404(d) payment as ordinary and necessary business expenses under §162(a) of the Code. The Commissioner allowed the former, but disallowed the latter.

The Tax Court held that the §404(d) payment was a nondeductible capital expenditure and was not an ordinary and necessary business expense, and that the payment was deductible only when used from the Secondary Reserve to pay §404(b)(1) premiums or to meet actual losses of FSLIC. As noted above, the Ninth Circuit reversed by a divided panel.

II.

To qualify as an allowable deduction under §162(a) of the Code, an item must (1) be "paid or incurred during the taxable year," (2) be for "carrying on any trade or business," (3) be an "expense," (4) be a "necessary" expense, and (5) be an "ordinary" expense. This Court has considered these several requirements, or one or more of them, in a number of cases. See, for example, *Welch v. Helvering*, 290 U.S. 111 (1933); *Deputy v. du Pont*, 308 U.S. 488 (1940); *Commissioner v. Tellier*, 383 U.S. 687 (1966).

In *Welch* Mr. Justice Cardozo emphasized the difference between the "ordinary" and the "necessary" and the need for satisfying both in order to achieve the deduction. It is in that case where his well-known, but elusive, suggestion for the answer appears:

"The standard set up by the statute is not a rule of law; it is rather a way of life. Life in all its fullness must supply the answer to the riddle."

In *du Pont* Mr. Justice Douglas stressed the accepted rule of the "popular or received import" of a statute's words, and further emphasized that "[o]rdinary has the connotation of normal, usual, or customary," and that each case "turns on its special facts." In *Tellier* Mr. Justice Stewart also emphasized the double requirement of "ordinary" and "necessary" and said:

> "Our decisions have consistently construed the term 'necessary' as imposing only the minimal requirement that the expense be 'appropriate and helpful' for 'the development of the [taxpayer's] business'.... The principal function of the term 'ordinary' in § 162(a) is to clarify the distinction, often difficult, between those expenses that are currently deductible and those that are in the nature of capital expenditures, which, if deductible at all, must be amortized over the useful life of the asset."

So much for generalities. Here clearly, as to its § 404(d) "additional premium" payment in 1963, Lincoln satisfied three of the five listed requirements. The payment was made during the taxable year. It was made in carrying on a trade or business. And it was a "necessary" payment, for it was compelled by the provisions of the National Housing Act. The Government so concedes. The focus, therefore, and our only concern here, is whether the payment was an expense and an ordinary one within the meaning of § 162(a) of the Code.

Lincoln's argument essentially is that its § 404(d) payment was really no different from its § 404(b)(1) payment for both were premiums for insurance of its depositors' accounts and creditor obligations; that all similarly situated insured savings and loan associations (there were 4,419 on December 31, 1963) paid the § 404(d) premium; and that the possibility of a future benefit from the expenditure does not serve to make it capital in nature as distinguished from an expense.

We feel that the very recital of the facts and of the structure and operation of FSLIC's reserves, in Part I of this opinion, itself provides an answer adverse to Lincoln's argument. It is not enough, in order that an expenditure qualify as an income tax deduction, that it merely be one paid by all similarly insured associations, or that it serves to fortify FSLIC's insurance purpose and operation. Further, the presence of an ensuing benefit that may have some future aspect is not controlling; many expenses concededly deductible have prospective effect beyond the taxable year.

What is important and controlling, we feel, is that the § 404(d) payment serves to create or enhance for Lincoln what is essentially a separate and distinct additional asset and that, as an inevitable consequence, the payment is capital in nature and not an expense, let alone an ordinary expense, deductible under § 162(a) in the absence of other factors not established here. We note the following:

A. The § 404(d) payment to FSLIC, when made, is subject to positive and rigid continuing controls. The payment must flow into the Secondary Reserve. That reserve is primarily available only for stated and circumscribed purposes, namely, the payment of losses and then only to the extent all other assets of FSLIC are insufficient to cover those losses. The Secondary Reserve thus has complete seniority with respect to demands upon FSLIC. It is the asset last called upon.

B. The insured institution has a distinct and recognized property interest in the Secondary Reserve. This is revealed by: (1) The recognition, in § 404(e), of transferability of the institution's pro rata share therein. This transferability is limited and restricted, to be sure, but it exists for approved situations of merger, consolidation, and the like. (2) The prospective refund, and in cash at that, of the institution's pro rata share upon termination of its insured status, or upon receivership or liquidation, or when the Primary Reserve alone reaches the suspension level. (3) The use of the institution's pro rata share to pay its basic premium under §404(b)(1) when the suspension level is reached by the aggregate of the Primary and Secondary Reserves. (4) FSLIC's maintenance of a separate account for each insured institution's share in the Secondary Reserve. (5) The statutorily required annual credit from FSLIC's earnings to the institution's share of the Secondary Reserve. The share thus is an income-producing entity and the income inures to the benefit of the insured institution.

C. Although compulsory accounting rules do not control tax consequences, there is significance in the fact that all concerned here have recognized the presence and the significance of this property interest in the Secondary Reserve. FSLIC submits annual statements to its insured institutions showing payments and credits to their respective shares. Lincoln, albeit by federal and state requirements, shows that interest as an asset on its balance sheet and the credit as income. And Lincoln's parent corporation, First Lincoln Financial Corporation, although not subject to such regulation, has done the same in its financial statements.

D. The nature of the adjustments effected by the 1961 Act is of some import. Due primarily to the rapid growth of insured institutions in the years preceding the passage of that Act, the ratio of FSLIC's reserves to potential liability had declined. By the Act Congress reduced the requirement for Federal Home Loan Bank stock and at the same time channeled new funds to FSLIC's Secondary Reserve. The §404(d) payment and the reduction in the FHLB stock purchase requirement were effectuated together. Certainly the FHLB stock is an asset and its acquisition is capital in nature. The complementary §404(d) payment is directed to a fund. Each is a device designed to achieve a particular and common result, namely, the providing of protection to the insured institution and to its depositors by way, in the one case, of liquidity and availability of loan funds and, in the other, by way of segregated amounts available to offset possible losses. Each is more permanent than temporary. Each partakes more of the character of an asset than of an expense. And the two are made complementary by the very provisions of §404(d).

We do not regard as contrarily persuasive, or as imposing an expense characteristic on the §404(d) payments, six features emphasized by Lincoln or by the Court of Appeals:

A. The possibility that Lincoln's share of the Secondary Reserve would be consumed by FSLIC's losses and thus would never be refunded to Lincoln. The Tax Court pointed out that this hazard exists with any routine investment in a bank or an insurance company and yet its presence does not make that investment an expense rather than a capital undertaking.

B. The general unlikelihood, as a practical matter, of Lincoln's recovery of its pro rata share of the Secondary Reserve. It is suggested that liquidation will not take place because in this day corporate activity is assumed to be a continuing process and not limited in duration. It is further pointed out that termination of FSLIC insurance is a business impossibility for it would result in mass withdrawal of depositors' accounts and in institutional suicide. It may well be true that liquidation is unlikely and that termination of insurance would be an undesirable business decision. The same may usually be said, however, of a manufacturing corporation's investment in plant and equipment or in patents or in many other assets basic to its business and function.

C. The claimed identity of purpose of the §404(b)(1) and §404(d) payments, namely, the providing of insurance for depositors' accounts. The former, however, is only annual in phase and operation. It provides insurance for the year. When the year passes, the insurance ceases. The latter, however, provides a fund available for losses not only in the current year, but in the future. It is a fund capable under certain circumstances of finding its way back to the coffers of the insured institutions. The ultimate purpose of the two payments may have much in common, but the route and the life of each differ from those of the other.

D. The compulsory character of the payment imposed both by the governing statute and the economic facts of life. Lincoln concedes, however, "Compulsion, whether legal or economic, should have no bearing upon the question whether a payment is an expense or a capital expenditure."

E. The annual accounting concept of the income tax. This factor is relevant when the year of deduction is in issue. It has less consequence in the determination of whether an item is or is not an ordinary expense. As to this, the mere maturing of liability is not enough.

F. The suggestion that the §404(d) payment is not included in the list of nondeductible capital expenditures specified by §263 of the Code. It is clear from the very language of §§ 162(a) and 263 that the two sections together are not all inclusive, and that §263 does not provide a complete list of nondeductible expenditures.

III.

Lincoln's pro rata share of the Secondary Reserve, of course, is not without its tax aspects. If its share is used to pay losses or if, when the suspension level is reached, it is devoted to the payment of Lincoln's §404(b)(1) premium, a deduction at that time for the amount so used would appear to be in order. Indeed, the Internal Revenue Service has so ruled. Rev. Rul. 66-49, 1966-1 C.B. 36, 37. Cf. Treas. Reg. §1.162-13.

We emphasize that just as compulsory accounting is not controlling tax wise, so the statutory labels of "prepayment" and "additional premium" contained in §404(d) are not controlling. We also emphasize that the fact that a payment is imposed compulsorily upon a taxpayer does not in and of itself make that payment an ordinary and necessary expense within the meaning of §162(a) of the Code.

We therefore conclude that Lincoln's §404(d) payment made in 1963 is not deductible under §162(a).

The judgment of the Court of Appeals is reversed.

INDOPCO, Inc. v. Commissioner

Supreme Court of the United States
503 U.S. 79 (1992)

JUSTICE BLACKMUN delivered the opinion of the Court.

In this case we must decide whether certain professional expenses incurred by a target corporation in the course of a friendly takeover are deductible by that corporation as "ordinary and necessary" business expenses under § 162(a) of the Internal Revenue Code.

Most of the relevant facts are stipulated. Petitioner INDOPCO, Inc., formerly named National Starch and Chemical Corporation and hereinafter referred to as National Starch, is a Delaware corporation that manufactures and sells adhesives, starches, and specialty chemical products. In October 1977, representatives of Unilever United States, Inc., also a Delaware corporation (Unilever), expressed interest in acquiring National Starch, which was one of its suppliers, through a friendly transaction. National Starch at the time had outstanding over 6,563,000 common shares held by approximately 3,700 shareholders. The stock was listed on the New York Stock Exchange. Frank and Anna Greenwall were the corporation's largest shareholders and owned approximately 14.5% of the common. The Greenwalls, getting along in years and concerned about their estate plans, indicated that they would transfer their shares to Unilever only if a transaction tax free for them could be arranged.

In November 1977, National Starch's directors were formally advised of Unilever's interest and the proposed transaction. At that time, Debevoise, Plimpton, Lyons & Gates, National Starch's counsel, told the directors that under Delaware law they had a fiduciary duty to ensure that the proposed transaction would be fair to the shareholders. National Starch thereupon engaged the investment banking firm of Morgan Stanley & Co., Inc., to evaluate its shares, to render a fairness opinion, and generally to assist in the event of the emergence of a hostile tender offer.

Although Unilever originally had suggested a price between $65 and $70 per share, negotiations resulted in a final offer of $73.50 per share, a figure Morgan Stanley found to be fair. Following approval by National Starch's board and the issuance of a favorable private ruling from the Internal Revenue Service that the transaction would be tax free under § 351 for those National Starch shareholders who exchanged their stock for Holding preferred, the transaction was consummated in August 1978.

Morgan Stanley charged National Starch a fee of $2,200,000, along with $7,586 for out-of-pocket expenses and $18,000 for legal fees. The Debevoise firm charged National Starch $490,000, along with $15,069 for out-of-pocket expenses. National Starch also incurred expenses aggregating $150,962 for miscellaneous items—such as accounting, printing, proxy solicitation, and Securities and Exchange Commission fees—in connection with the transaction. No issue is raised as to the propriety or reasonableness of these charges.

On its federal income tax return for its short taxable year ended August 15, 1978, National Starch claimed a deduction for the $2,225,586 paid to Morgan Stanley, but did not deduct the $505,069 paid to Debevoise or the other expenses. Upon audit, the Commissioner of Internal Revenue disallowed the claimed deduction and issued a notice of deficiency. Petitioner sought redetermination in the United States Tax Court, asserting, however, not only the right to deduct the investment banking fees and expenses but, as well, the legal and miscellaneous expenses incurred.

The Tax Court, in an unreviewed decision, ruled that the expenditures were capital in nature and therefore not deductible under § 162(a) in the 1978 return as "ordinary and necessary expenses." *National Starch & Chemical Corp. v. Commissioner*, 93 T.C. 67 (1989). The court based its holding primarily on the long-term benefits that accrued to National Starch from the Unilever acquisition. *Id.*, at 75. The United States Court of

Appeals for the Third Circuit affirmed, upholding the Tax Court's findings that "both Unilever's enormous resources and the possibility of synergy arising from the transaction served the long-term betterment of National Starch." *National Starch and Chemical Corp. v. Commissioner,* 918 F.2d 426, 432–33 (3d Cir. 1990). In so doing, the Court of Appeals rejected National Starch's contention that, because the disputed expenses did not "create or enhance...a separate and distinct additional asset," see *Commissioner v. Lincoln Savings & Loan Assn.,* 403 U.S. 345, 354 (1971), they could not be capitalized and therefore were deductible under § 162(a). 918 F.2d, at 428–31. We granted certiorari to resolve a perceived conflict on the issue among the Courts of Appeals. 500 U.S. 914 (1991).

Section 162(a) of the Internal Revenue Code allows the deduction of "all the ordinary and necessary expenses paid or incurred during the taxable year in carrying on any trade or business." 26 U.S.C. § 162(a). In contrast, § 263 of the Code allows no deduction for a capital expenditure—an "amount paid out for new buildings or for permanent improvements or betterments made to increase the value of any property or estate." § 263(a)(1). The primary effect of characterizing a payment as either a business expense or a capital expenditure concerns the timing of the taxpayer's cost recovery: While business expenses are currently deductible, a capital expenditure usually is amortized and depreciated over the life of the relevant asset, or, where no specific asset or useful life can be ascertained, is deducted upon dissolution of the enterprise. Through provisions such as these, the Code endeavors to match expenses with the revenues of the taxable period to which they are properly attributable, thereby resulting in a more accurate calculation of net income for tax purposes.

In exploring the relationship between deductions and capital expenditures, this Court has noted the "familiar rule" that "an income tax deduction is a matter of legislative grace and that the burden of clearly showing the right to the claimed deduction is on the taxpayer." The notion that deductions are exceptions to the norm of capitalization finds support in various aspects of the Code. Deductions are specifically enumerated and thus are subject to disallowance in favor of capitalization. See §§ 161 and 261. Nondeductible capital expenditures, by contrast, are not exhaustively enumerated in the Code; rather than providing a "complete list of nondeductible expenditures," *Lincoln Savings,* 403 U.S., at 358, § 263 serves as a general means of distinguishing capital expenditures from current expenses. See *Commissioner v. Idaho Power Co.,* 418 U.S., at 16. For these reasons, deductions are strictly construed and allowed only "as there is a clear provision therefor."

The Court also has examined the interrelationship between the Code's business expense and capital expenditure provisions. In so doing, it has had occasion to parse § 162(a) and explore certain of its requirements. For example, in *Lincoln Savings,* we determined that, to qualify for deduction under § 162(a), "an item must (1) be 'paid or incurred during the taxable year,' (2) be for 'carrying on any trade or business,' (3) be an 'expense,' (4) be a 'necessary' expense, and (5) be an 'ordinary' expense." 403 U.S., at 352. See also *Commissioner v. Tellier,* 383 U.S. 687, 689 (1966) (the term "necessary" imposes "only the minimal requirement that the expense be 'appropriate and helpful' for 'the development of the [taxpayer's] business,'" quoting *Welch v. Helvering,* 290 U.S. 111, 113); *Deputy v. Du Pont,* 308 U.S., at 495 (to qualify as "ordinary," the expense must relate to a transaction "of common or frequent occurrence in the type of business involved"). The Court has recognized, however, that the "decisive distinctions" between current expenses and capital expenditures "are those of degree and not of kind," *Welch v. Helvering,* 290 U.S., at 114, and that because each case "turns on its special facts," *Deputy v. Du Pont,* 308 U.S., at 496, the cases sometimes appear difficult to harmonize. See *Welch v. Helvering,* 290 U.S., at 116.

National Starch contends that the decision in *Lincoln Savings* changed these familiar backdrops and announced an exclusive test for identifying capital expenditures, a test in which "creation or enhancement of an asset" is a prerequisite to capitalization, and deductibility under § 162(a) is the rule rather than the exception. We do not agree, for we conclude that National Starch has overread *Lincoln Savings*.

In *Lincoln Savings*, we were asked to decide whether certain premiums, required by federal statute to be paid by a savings and loan association to the Federal Savings and Loan Insurance Corporation (FSLIC), were ordinary and necessary expenses under § 162(a), as Lincoln Savings argued and the Court of Appeals had held, or capital expenditures under § 263, as the Commissioner contended. We found that the "additional" premiums, the purpose of which was to provide FSLIC with a secondary reserve fund in which each insured institution retained a pro rata interest recoverable in certain situations, "serv[e] to create or enhance for Lincoln what is essentially a separate and distinct additional asset." 403 U.S., at 354. "[A]s an inevitable consequence," we concluded, "the payment is capital in nature and not an expense, let alone an ordinary expense, deductible under § 162(a)." *Ibid.*

Lincoln Savings stands for the simple proposition that a taxpayer's expenditure that "serves to create or enhance...a separate and distinct" asset should be capitalized under § 263. It by no means follows, however, that *only* expenditures that create or enhance separate and distinct assets are to be capitalized under § 263. We had no occasion in *Lincoln Savings* to consider the tax treatment of expenditures that, unlike the additional premiums at issue there, did not create or enhance a specific asset, and thus the case cannot be read to preclude capitalization in other circumstances. In short, *Lincoln Savings* holds that the creation of a separate and distinct asset well may be a sufficient, but not a necessary, condition to classification as a capital expenditure. See *General Bancshares Corp. v. Commissioner*, 326 F.2d 712, 716 (CA8) (although expenditures may not "resul[t] in the acquisition or increase of a corporate asset,...these expenditures are not, because of that fact, deductible as ordinary and necessary business expenses"), cert. denied, 379 U.S. 832 (1964).

Nor does our statement in *Lincoln Savings*, 403 U.S., at 354, that "the presence of an ensuing benefit that may have some future aspect is not controlling" prohibit reliance on future benefit as a means of distinguishing an ordinary business expense from a capital expenditure. Although the mere presence of an incidental future benefit—"*some* future aspect"—may not warrant capitalization, a taxpayer's realization of benefits beyond the year in which the expenditure is incurred is undeniably important in determining whether the appropriate tax treatment is immediate deduction or capitalization. See *United States v. Mississippi Chemical Corp.*, 405 U.S. 298, 310 (1972) (expense that "is of value in more than one taxable year" is a nondeductible capital expenditure); *Central Texas Savings & Loan Assn. v. United States*, 731 F.2d 1181, 1183 (CA5 1984) ("While the period of the benefits may not be controlling in all cases, it nonetheless remains a prominent, if not predominant, characteristic of a capital item"). Indeed, the text of the Code's capitalization provision, § 263(a)(1), which refers to "permanent improvements or betterments," itself envisions an inquiry into the duration and extent of the benefits realized by the taxpayer.

In applying the foregoing principles to the specific expenditures at issue in this case, we conclude that National Starch has not demonstrated that the investment banking, legal, and other costs it incurred in connection with Unilever's acquisition of its shares are deductible as ordinary and necessary business expenses under § 162(a).

Although petitioner attempts to dismiss the benefits that accrued to National Starch from the Unilever acquisition as "entirely speculative" or "merely incidental," Brief for

Petitioner 39-40, the Tax Court's and the Court of Appeals' findings that the transaction produced significant benefits to National Starch that extended beyond the tax year in question are amply supported by the record. For example, in commenting on the merger with Unilever, National Starch's 1978 "Progress Report" observed that the company would "benefit greatly from the availability of Unilever's enormous resources, especially in the area of basic technology." App. 43. See also *id.*, at 46 (Unilever "provides new opportunities and resources"). Morgan Stanley's report to the National Starch board concerning the fairness to shareholders of a possible business combination with Unilever noted that National Starch management "feels that some synergy may exist with the Unilever organization given a) the nature of the Unilever chemical, paper, plastics and packaging operations...and b) the strong consumer products orientation of Unilever United States, Inc." *Id.*, at 77–78.

In addition to these anticipated resource-related benefits, National Starch obtained benefits through its transformation from a publicly held, freestanding corporation into a wholly owned subsidiary of Unilever. The Court of Appeals noted that National Starch management viewed the transaction as " 'swapping approximately 3500 shareholders for one.'" 918 F.2d, at 427; see also App. 223. Following Unilever's acquisition of National Starch's outstanding shares, National Starch was no longer subject to what even it terms the "substantial" shareholder-relations expenses a publicly traded corporation incurs, including reporting and disclosure obligations, proxy battles, and derivative suits. The acquisition also allowed National Starch, in the interests of administrative convenience and simplicity, to eliminate previously authorized but unissued shares of preferred and to reduce the total number of authorized shares of common from 8,000,000 to 1,000. See 93 T.C., at 74.

Courts long have recognized that expenses such as these, " 'incurred for the purpose of changing the corporate structure for the benefit of future operations are not ordinary and necessary business expenses.'" *General Bancshares Corp. v. Commissioner*, 326 F.2d, at 715 (quoting *Farmers Union Corp. v. Commissioner*, 300 F.2d 197, 200 (CA9), cert. denied, 371 U.S. 861 (1962)). See also B. Bittker & J. Eustice, Federal Income Taxation of Corporations and Shareholders, pp. 5-33 to 5-36 (5th ed. 1987) (describing "well-established rule" that expenses incurred in reorganizing or restructuring corporate entity are not deductible under § 162(a)). Deductions for professional expenses thus have been disallowed in a wide variety of cases concerning changes in corporate structure. Although support for these decisions can be found in the specific terms of § 162(a), which require that deductible expenses be "ordinary and necessary" and incurred "in carrying on any trade or business," courts more frequently have characterized an expenditure as capital in nature because "the purpose for which the expenditure is made has to do with the corporation's operations and betterment, sometimes with a continuing capital asset, for the duration of its existence or for the indefinite future or for a time somewhat longer than the current taxable year." *General Bancshares Corp. v. Commissioner*, 326 F.2d, at 715. See also *Mills Estate, Inc. v. Commissioner*, 206 F.2d 244, 246 (CA2 1953). The rationale behind these decisions applies equally to the professional charges at issue in this case.

The expenses that National Starch incurred in Unilever's friendly takeover do not qualify for deduction as "ordinary and necessary" business expenses under § 162(a). The fact that the expenditures do not create or enhance a separate and distinct additional asset is not controlling; the acquisition-related expenses bear the indicia of capital expenditures and are to be treated as such.

The judgment of the Court of Appeals is AFFIRMED.

Waterman v. Mackenzie

Supreme Court of the United States
138 U.S. 252 (1891)

[This case involved the following instruments: (1) An assignment, made February 13, 1884, and recorded March 27, 1884, from Lewis E. Waterman, the plaintiff, to Sarah E. Waterman, his wife, of a whole patent and invention; (2) A "license agreement," made between Mr. and Mrs. Waterman on November 20, 1884, and never recorded, by which she granted to him "the sole and exclusive right and license to manufacture and sell fountain penholders, containing the said patented improvement throughout the United States," and he agreed to pay her "the sum of twenty-five cents as a license fee upon every fountain penholder so manufactured by him."]

Mr. Justice Gray, after stating the facts as above, delivered the opinion of the court.

Every patent issued under the laws of the United States for an invention or discovery contains "a grant to the patentee, his heirs and assigns, for the term of seventeen years, of the exclusive right to make, use, and vend the invention or discovery throughout the United States and the territories thereof." The monopoly thus granted is one entire thing, and cannot be divided into parts, except as authorized by those laws. The patentee or his assigns may, by instrument in writing, assign, grant, and convey, either 1st the whole patent, comprising the exclusive right to make, use, and vend the invention throughout the United States; or 2d an undivided part or share of that exclusive right; or 3d the exclusive right under the patent within and throughout a specified part of the United States. A transfer of either of these three kinds of interests is an assignment, properly speaking, and vests in the assignee a title in so much of the patent itself, with a right to sue infringers; in the second case, jointly with the assignor; in the first and third cases, in the name of the assignee alone. Any assignment or transfer, short of one of these, is a mere license, giving the licensee no title in the patent, and no right to sue at law in his own name for an infringement. In equity, as at law, when the transfer amounts to a license only, the title remains in the owner of the patent; and suit must be brought in his name, and never in the name of the licensee alone unless that is necessary to prevent an absolute failure of justice, as where the patentee is the infringer, and cannot sue himself. Any rights of the licensee must be enforced through or in the name of the owner of the patent, and perhaps, if necessary to protect the rights of all parties, joining the licensee with him as a plaintiff.

Whether a transfer of a particular right or interest under a patent is an assignment or a license does not depend upon the name by which it calls itself, but upon the legal effect of its provisions. For instance, a grant of an exclusive right to make, use, and vend two patented machines within a certain district is an assignment, and gives the grantee the right to sue in his own name for an infringement within the district, because the right, although limited to making, using, and vending two machines, excludes all other persons, even the patentee, from making, using, or vending like machines within the district. On the other hand, the grant of an exclusive right under the patent within a certain district, which does not include the right to make, and the right to use, and the right to sell, is not a grant of a title in the whole patent-right within the district, and is therefore only a license. Such, for instance, is a grant of "the full and exclusive right to make and vend" within a certain district, reserving to the grantor the right to make within the district, to be sold outside of it. So is a grant of "the exclusive right to make and use," but not to sell, patented machines within a certain district. So is an instrument granting "the sole right and privilege of manufacturing and selling" patented articles, and not expressly authorizing their use, because, though this might carry by implication the right to use articles made under the patent by the licensee, it certainly would not authorize him to use such articles made by others. An assignment of the entire patent, or of an undivided part thereof, or of the exclusive right under the patent for a limited territory, may be either absolute or by way of mortgage, and liable to be defeated by non-performance of a condition subsequent, as clearly appears in the provision of the statute, that "an assignment, grant, or conveyance shall be void as against any subsequent purchaser or mortgagee for a valuable consideration without notice, unless it is recorded in the Patent Office within three months from the date thereof."

Before proceeding to consider the nature and effect of the various instruments given in evidence at the hearing in the circuit court, it is fit to observe that (as was assumed in the argument for the plaintiff) by the law of the state of New York, where all the instruments were made and all the parties to them resided, husband and wife are authorized to make conveyances and contracts of and concerning personal property to and with each other, in the same manner and to the same effect as if they were strangers.

By the deed of assignment of February 13, 1884, the plaintiff assigned to Mrs. Waterman the entire patent right. That assignment vested in her the whole title in the patent, and the exclusive right to sue, either at law or in equity, for its subsequent infringement.

The next instrument in order of date is the "license agreement" between them of November 20, 1884, by which she granted to him "the sole and exclusive right and license to manufacture and sell fountain penholders containing the said patented improvement throughout the United States." This did not include the right to use such penholders, at least if manufactured by third persons, and was therefore a mere license, and not an assignment of any title, and did not give the licensee the right to sue alone, at law or in equity, for an infringement of the patent.

Burnet v. Logan
Supreme Court of the United States
283 U.S. 404 (1931)

MR. JUSTICE MCREYNOLDS delivered the opinion of the Court.

Prior to March, 1913, and until March 11, 1916, respondent, Mrs. Logan, owned 250 of the 4,000 capital shares issued by the Andrews & Hitchcock Iron Company. It held 12 per cent. of the stock of the Mahoning Ore & Steel Company, an operating concern. In 1895 the latter corporation procured a lease for 97 years upon the "Mahoning" mine and since then has regularly taken therefrom large, but varying, quantities of iron ore-in 1913, 1,515,428 tons; in 1914, 1,212,287 tons; in 1915, 2,311,940 tons; in 1919, 1,217,167 tons; in 1921, 303,020 tons; in 1923, 3,029,865 tons. The lease contract did not require production of either maximum or minimum tonnage or any definite payments. Through an agreement of stockholders (steel manufacturers), the Mahoning Company is obligated to apportion extracted ore among them according to their holdings.

On March 11, 1916, the owners of all the shares in Andrews & Hitchcock Company sold them to Youngstown Sheet & Tube Company, which thus acquired, among other things, 12 per cent. of the Mahoning Company's stock and the right to receive the same percentage of ore thereafter taken from the leased mine.

For the shares so acquired, the Youngstown Company paid the holders $2,200,000 in money, and agreed to pay annually thereafter for distribution among them 60 cents for each ton of ore apportioned to it. Of this cash Mrs. Logan received 250/4000ths— $137,500; and she became entitled to the same fraction of any annual payment thereafter made by the purchaser under the terms of sale.

Mrs. Logan's mother had long owned 1100 shares of the Andrews & Hitchcock Company. She died in 1917, leaving to the daughter one-half of her interest in payments thereafter made by the Youngstown Company. This bequest was appraised for federal estate tax purposes at $277,164.50.

During 1917, 1918, 1919 and 1920 the Youngstown Company paid large sums under the agreement. Out of these respondent received on account of her 250 shares $9,900 in 1917; $11,250 in 1918; $8,995.50 in 1919; $5,444.30 in 1920—$35,589.80. By reason of the interest from her mother's estate, she received $19,790.10 in 1919, and $11,977.49 in 1920.

Reports of income for 1918, 1919, and 1920 were made by Mrs. Logan upon the basis of cash receipts and disbursements. They included no part of what she had obtained from annual payments by the Youngstown Company. She maintains that until the total amount actually received by her from the sale of her shares equals their value on March 1, 1913, no taxable income will arise from the transaction. Also that, until she actually receives by reason of the right bequeathed to her a sum equal to its appraised value, there will be no taxable income therefrom.

On March 1, 1913, the value of the 250 shares then held by Mrs. Logan *exceeded* $173,089.80—the total of all sums actually received by her prior to 1921 from their sale ($137,500 cash in 1916, plus four annual payments amounting to $35,589.80). That value also exceeded original cost of the shares. The amount received on the interest devised by her mother was less than its valuation for estate taxation; also less than the value when acquired by Mrs. Logan.

The Commissioner ruled that the obligation of the Youngstown Company to pay 60 cents per ton has a fair market value of $1,942,111.46 on March 11, 1916; that this value should be treated as so much cash, and the sale of the stock regarded as a closed transaction with no profit in 1916. He also used this valuation as the basis for apportioning subsequent annual receipts between income and return of capital. His calculations, based upon estimates and assumptions, are too intricate for brief statement. He made deficiency assessments according to the view just stated, and the Board of Tax Appeals approved the result.

The Circuit Court of Appeals held that, in the circumstances, it was impossible to determine with fair certainty the market value of the agreement by the Youngstown Company to pay 60 cents per ton. Also that respondent was entitled to the return of her capital—the value of 250 shares on March 1, 1913, and the assessed value of the interest derived from her mother—before she could be charged with any taxable income. As this had not in fact been returned, there was no taxable income.

We agree with the result reached by the Circuit Court of Appeals.

The 1916 transaction was a sale of stock—not an exchange of property. We are not dealing with royalties or deductions from gross income because of depletion of mining property. Nor does the situation demand that an effort be made to place according to the best available data some approximate value upon the contract for future payments. This probably was necessary in order to assess the mother's estate. As annual payments on account of extracted ore come in, they can be readily apportioned first as return of capital and later as profit. The liability for income tax ultimately can be fairly determined without resort to mere estimates, assumptions, and speculation. When the profit, if any, is actually realized, the taxpayer will be required to respond. The consideration for the sale was $2,200,000.00 in cash and the promise of future money payments wholly contingent upon facts and circumstances not possible to foretell with anything like fair certainty. The promise was in no proper sense equivalent to cash. It had no ascertainable fair market value. The transaction was not a closed one. Respondent might never recoup her capital investment from payments only conditionally promised. Prior to 1921, all receipts from the sale of her shares amounted to less than their value on March 1, 1913. She properly demanded the return of her capital investment before assessment of any taxable profit based on conjecture.

"In order to determine whether there has been gain or loss, and the amount of the gain if any, we must withdraw from the gross proceeds an amount sufficient to restore the capital value that existed at the commencement of the period under consideration." *Doyle v. Mitchell Bros. Co.*, 247 U. S. 179, 184, 185. Ordinarily, at least, a taxpayer may not deduct from gross receipts a supposed loss which in fact is represented by his outstanding note. And, conversely, a promise to pay indeterminate sums of money in not necessarily taxable income. "Generally speaking, the income tax law is concerned only with realized losses, as with realized gains."

From her mother's estate, Mrs. Logan obtained the right to share in possible proceeds of a contract thereafter to pay indefinite sums. The value of this was assumed to be $277,164.50, and its transfer was so taxed. Some valuation—speculative or otherwise—was necessary in order to close the estate. It may never yield as much, it may yield more. If a sum equal to the value thus ascertained had been invested in an annuity contract, payments thereunder would have been free from income tax until the owner had recouped his capital investment. We think a like rule should be applied here. The statute definitely excepts bequests from receipts which go to make up taxable income.

The judgments below are AFFIRMED.

Williams v. McGowan
Circuit Court of Appeals, Second Circuit
152 F.2d 570 (2d Cir. 1945)

L. HAND, CIRCUIT JUDGE.

This is an appeal from a judgment dismissing the complaint in an action by a taxpayer to recover income taxes paid for the year 1940.

Williams, the taxpayer, and one, Reynolds, had for many years been engaged in the hardware business in the City of Corning, New York. On the 20th of January, 1926, they formed a partnership, of which Williams was entitled to two-thirds of the profits, and Reynolds, one-third. They agreed that on February 1, 1925, the capital invested in the business had been $118,082.05, of which Reynolds had a credit of $29,029.03, and Williams, the balance—$89,053.02. At the end of every business year, on February 1st, Reynolds was to pay to Williams interest upon the amount of the difference between his share of the capital and one-third of the total as shown by the inventory; and upon withdrawal of one party the other was to have the privilege of buying the other's interest as it appeared on the books. The business was carried on through the firm's fiscal year, ending January 31, 1940, in accordance with this agreement, and thereafter until Reynolds' death on July 18th of that year. Williams settled with Reynolds' executrix on September 6th in an agreement by which he promised to pay her $12,187.90, and to assume all liabilities of the business; and he did pay her $2,187.98 in cash at once, and $10,000 on the 10th of the following October. On September 17th of the same year, Williams sold the business as a whole to the Corning Building Company for $63,926.28—its agreed value as of February 1, 1940—"plus an amount to be computed by multiplying the gross sales of the business from the first day of February, 1940 to the 28th day of September, 1940," by an agreed fraction. This value was made up of cash of about $8,100, receivables of about $7,000, fixtures of about $800, and a merchandise inventory of about $49,000, less some $1,000 for bills payable. To this was added about $6,000 credited to Williams for profits under the language just quoted, making a total of nearly $70,000. Upon this sale Williams suffered a loss upon his original two-thirds of the business but he made a small gain upon the one-third which he had bought from Reynolds' executrix; and in his income tax return he entered both as items of "ordinary income," and not as transactions in "capital assets." This the Commissioner disallowed and recomputed the tax accordingly; Williams paid the deficiency and sued to recover it in this action. The only question is whether the business was "capital assets" under § 117(a)(1) of the Internal Revenue Code [the predecessor of § 1221].

It has been held that a partner's interest in a going firm is for tax purposes to be regarded as a "capital asset." Stilgenbaur v. United States, 9 Cir., 115 F.2d 283; Commissioner v. Shapiro, 6 Cir., 125 F.2d 532. We too accepted the doctrine in McClellan v. Commissioner, 2 Cir., 117 F.2d 988, although we had held the opposite in Helvering v. Smith, 2 Cir., 90 F.2d 590, 591, where the partnership articles had provided that a retiring partner should receive as his share only his percentage of the sums "actually collected" and "of all earnings * * * for services performed." Such a payment, we thought, was income; and we expressly repudiated the notion that the Uniform Partnership Act had, generally speaking, changed the firm into a juristic entity. See also Doyle v. Commissioner, 4 Cir., 102 F.2d 86. If a partner's interest in a going firm is "capital assets" perhaps a dead partner's interest is the same. New York Partnership Law §§ 61, 62(4), Consol. Laws N.Y. c. 39. We need not say. When Williams bought out Reynolds' interest, he became the sole owner of the business, the firm had ended upon any theory, and the situation for tax purposes was no other than if Reynolds had never been a partner at all, except that to the extent of one-third of the "amount realized" on Williams' sale to the Corning Company, his "basis" was different. The judge thought that, because upon that sale both parties fixed the price at the liquidation value of the business while Reynolds was alive, "plus" its estimated earnings thereafter, it was as though Williams had sold his interest in the firm during its existence. But the method by which the parties agreed upon the price was irrelevant to the computation of Williams' income. The Treasury, if that served its interest, need not heed any fiction which the parties found it convenient to adopt; nor need Williams do the same in his dealings with the Treasury. We have to decide only whether upon the sale of a going business it is to be comminuted into its fragments, and these are to be separately matched against the definition in § 117(a)(1), or whether the whole business is to be treated as if it were a single piece of property.

Our law has been sparing in the creation of juristic entities; it has never, for example, taken over the Roman "universitas facti";[1] and indeed for many years it fumbled uncer-

---

1. "By universitas facti is meant a number of things of the same kind which are regarded as a whole; e.g. a herd, a stock of wares." Mackeldey, Roman Law § 162.

tainly with the concept of a corporation. One might have supposed that partnership would have been an especially promising field in which to raise up an entity, particularly since merchants have always kept their accounts upon that basis. Yet there too our law resisted at the price of great continuing confusion; and, even when it might be thought that a statute admitted, if it did not demand, recognition of the firm as an entity, the old concepts prevailed. Francis v. McNeal, 228 U.S. 695. And so, even though we might agree that under the influence of the Uniform Partnership Act a partner's interest in the firm should be treated as indivisible, and for that reason a "capital asset" within § 117(a)(1), we should be chary about extending further so exotic a jural concept. Be that as it may, in this instance the section itself furnishes the answer. It starts in the broadest way by declaring that all "property" is "capital assets," and then makes three exceptions. The first is "stock in trade * * * or other property of a kind which would properly be included in the inventory"; next comes "property held * * * primarily for sale to customers"; and finally, property "used in the trade or business of a character which is subject to * * * allowance for depreciation." In the face of this language, although it may be true that a "stock in trade," taken by itself, should be treated as a "universitas facti," by no possibility can a whole business be so treated; and the same is true as to any property within the other exceptions. Congress plainly did mean to comminute the elements of a business; plainly it did not regard the whole as "capital assets."

As has already appeared, Williams transferred to the Corning Company "cash," "receivables," "fixtures" and a "merchandise inventory." "Fixtures" are not capital because they are subject to a depreciation allowance; the inventory, as we have just seen, is expressly excluded. So far as appears, no allowance was made for "good-will"; but, even if there had been, we held in Haberle Crystal Springs Brewing Company v. Clarke, Collector, 2 Cir., 30 F.2d 219, that "good-will" was a depreciable intangible. It is true that the Supreme Court reversed that judgment—280 U.S. 384—but it based its decision only upon the fact that there could be no allowance for the depreciation of "good-will" in a brewery, a business condemned by the Eighteenth Amendment. There can of course be no gain or loss in the transfer of cash; and, although Williams does appear to have made a gain of $1,072.71 upon the "receivables," the point has not been argued that they are not subject to a depreciation allowance. That we leave open for decision by the district court, if the parties cannot agree. The gain or loss upon every other item should be computed as an item in ordinary income.

Judgment Reversed.

Raytheon Production Corp. v. Commissioner
Circuit Court of Appeals, First Circuit
144 F.2d 110 (1st Cir. 1944)

Mahoney, Circuit Judge.

This case presents the question whether an amount received by the taxpayer in compromise settlement of a suit for damages under the Federal Anti-Trust Laws is a nontaxable return of capital or income. On December 14, 1931, the petitioner caused its predecessor, Raytheon, to bring suit against R.C.A. in the District Court of Massachusetts alleging that the plaintiff had by 1926 created and then possessed a large and valuable good will in interstate commerce in rectifying tubes for radios and had a large and profitable established business therein; that the defendant conspired to destroy the business of the plaintiff and others by a monopoly of such business; and that by the early part of 1938 the tube business of the plaintiff and its property and good will h ad been totally destroyed at a time when it had a present value in excess of $3,000,000. [R.C.A. agreed to pay the petitioner $410,000 in settlement of the law suit under the federal anti-trust laws.]

Damages recovered in an antitrust action are not necessarily nontaxable as a return of capital. As in other types of tort damage suits, recoveries which represent reimbursement for lost profits are income. The reasoning is that since the profits would be taxable income, the proceeds of litigation which are their substitute are taxable in like manner. Damages for violation of the anti-trust acts are treated as income where they represent compensation for loss of profits.

The test is not whether the action was one in tort or contract but rather the question to be asked is "In lieu of what were the damages awarded?" Where the suit is not to recover lost profits but is for injury to good will, the recovery represents a return of capital and, with certain limitations to be set forth below, is not taxable. Care must certainly be taken in such cases to avoid taxing recoveries for injuries to good will or loss of capital.

Upon examination of Raytheon's declaration in its anti-trust suit we find nothing to indicate that the suit was for the recovery of lost profits. The allegations were that the illegal conduct of R.C.A. "completely destroyed the profitable interstate and foreign commerce of the plaintiff and thereby, by the early part of 1928, the said tube business of the plaintiff and the property good will of the plaintiff therein had been totally destroyed at a time when it then had a present value in excess of three million dollars and thereby the plaintiff was then inured in its business and property in a sum in excess of three million dollars." This was not the sort of antitrust suit where the plaintiff's business still exists and where the injury was merely for loss of profits. The allegations and evidence as to the amount of profits were necessary in order to establish the value of the good will and business since that is derived by a capitalization of profits. A somewhat similar idea was expressed in *Farmers' & Merchants' Bank v. Commissioner*, 59 F.2d at 913. "Profits were one of the chief indications of the worth of the business; but the usual earnings before the injury, as compared with those afterward, were only an evidential factor in determining actual loss and not an independent basis for recovery." Since the suit was to recover damages for the destruction of the business and good will, the recovery represents a return of capital. Nor does the fact that the suit ended in a compromise settlement change the nature of the recovery; "the determining factor is the nature of the basic claim from which the compromised amount was realized."

But, to say that the recovery represents a return of capital in that it takes the place of the business good will is not to conclude that it may not contain a taxable benefit. Although the inured party may not be deriving a profit as a result of the damage suit itself, the conversion thereby of his property into cash is a realization of any gain made over the cost or other basis of the good will prior to the illegal interference. Thus A buys Blackacre for $5,000. It appreciates in value to $50,000. B tortiously destroys it by fire. A sues and recovers $50,000 tort damages from B. Although no gain was derived by A from the suit, his prior gain due to the appreciation in value of Blackacre is realized when it is turned into cash by the money damages.

Compensation for the loss of Raytheon's good will in excess of its cost is gross income.

Chapter 4

Taxation of Intellectual Property Development

I. Assignment for Chapter 4

Read: Internal Revenue Code: §§ 41(d), 162(a); 174; 183; 212; 263(a); 263A(a), (b)(1), (c)(2), (h). Skim I.R.C. §§ 56(b)(2); 59(e)(1), (e)(2)(B), (e)(6); 167(a), (c), (f), (g), (h)(2); 197(a)–(e)(4).

Treasury Regulations: §§ 1.41-4; 1.174-1, -2, -3, -4; 1.183-2(a), -2(b); 1.263(a)-1(b), -2(a); 1.263A-1(e)(2), -1(e)(3), -2(a)(2). Skim Treas. Reg. §§ 1.167(a)-1; 1.167(a)-3; 1.167(b)-1(a); 1.197-2(a)(3), -2(b)(10), -2(c)(7), -2(d)(2); 1.197-2(b)(1), -2(c)(7), -2(d)(2), -2(f). Review Prop. Reg. § 1.41-4; Prop. Reg. § 1.167(a)-3; Prop. Reg. § 1.263(a)-4.

Materials: Overview
RJR Nabisco, Inc. v. Commissioner
Technical Advice Memorandum 9643003
I.R.S. Notice 88-62
Vitale v. Commissioner
Field Service Advice 200125019
Snow v. Commissioner
Green v. Commissioner
Revenue Procedure 2000-50

Complete the problems.

II. Problems for Chapter 4

1. Peeyew, Inc., a perfume manufacturing company, decides to create a new perfume to sell to teenage girls. Discuss the deductibility of the following expenses incurred by Peeyew during the current year:

    (a) $150,000 to conduct consumer surveys to determine the preference of potential customers.

    (b) $50,000 to acquire a new machine to be used in connection with research and experimentation activities.

(c) $100,000 to actually develop the basic scent.

(d) $25,000 to determine whether the perfume causes an allergic reaction.

(e) $35,000 to develop alternative perfumes with different scents and colors.

(f) $50,000 to initially market the perfume.

(g) $35,000 in attorney's fees in the prosecution of a patent application.

2. In Year 1, calendar-year Taxpayer spends $60,000 to develop a process for which he seeks patent protection. On July 1, Year 3, Taxpayer first realizes benefits from the marketing of products resulting from this process and submits a patent application. On July 1, Year 5, the Patent Office issues a patent protecting his process.

   a. If Taxpayer wishes to deduct in full the $60,000 research or experimental expenditures under § 174(a), what is the proper taxable year of deduction? How is an election to use the "current expense method" made? What if Taxpayer fails to currently deduct the expenditures in the proper year?

   b. If Taxpayer wishes to treat the $60,000 as deferred expenses amortized ratably over 60 months under § 174(b), what is the proper amount of deduction, if any, in years Years 1–5? How is an election to use the "deferred expense method" made?

   c. After the initial election is made, can Taxpayer later change methods? How?

3. XYZ, Inc., a company that publishes general reference books, decides to publish textbooks for use in high schools. XYZ incurs expenses to develop the theme and topic of each textbook, obtain manuscripts from authors, edit the textbooks, and obtain illustrations. What is the general tax treatment of XYZ's expenditures? Will the individual authors generally be entitled to deduct fully their expenses in preparing and writing the manuscripts?

4. Chris is a full-time editor for a local publishing company. For the past three years, Chris has also been a choreographer for a dance company that has performed in a number of places and has received local and national media attention. She travels with the dance group on weekends, keeps detailed records of her traveling expenses, and consults with experts in the dance industry to further her choreography. This year, Chris spent $300 to create a dance score and $1,500 to create and produce an instructional video tape of her choreography. Are these amounts deductible?

5. Duesenberg, Inc. of Delaware is a U.S. manufacturer of automobiles. In the current year, the company paid $50,000 to its lawyers for their services and expenses in registering the name "Duesenberg" as a trademark in thirty-five foreign counties. How is the fee treated for tax purposes? If Duesenberg later paid $25,000 in advertising campaign expenditures and $20,000 in advertising execution expenditures to build the goodwill in the trademark rights, how would such costs be treated for tax purposes?

6. Last year, ABC Corporation purchased a new computer that was installed this year. The installation of the new computer required the development by the corporation of an entirely new set of software for use with it. Software costs in the amount of $50,000 were incurred by the corporation this year in connection with programming the new computer. Are the in-house software development costs deductible? Would it make a difference if ABC paid $50,000 to a third party to develop the software?

7. Internet Co. incurred substantial costs to develop its presence online. In the current year, the company spent $50,000 to build the structure of its new website, $25,000 to create photographic images and digital music for the website (content which is registered with the Copyright office), and $100,000 to develop an online catalog for customers and data files (including customer lists and client files). How should these costs be treated for tax purposes?

8. ACE, Inc. is engaged in the business of designing, manufacturing, and selling power tools. ACE delivers its tools in the same manner and time as its competitors. To improve customer service, ACE undertakes to develop computer software that will monitor the progress of the manufacture and delivery of ACE's tools to enable ACE's customers to track their tool orders from origination to delivery. In addition, at the request of a customer, ACE will be able to intercept and return or reroute packages prior to delivery. At the time ACE undertakes its software development activities, ACE is uncertain whether it can develop the real-time communication software necessary to achieve its objective. None of ACE's competitors have a comparable tracking system. ACE commits substantial resources to the development of the system and, because of technical risk, ACE cannot determine if it will recover its investment within a reasonable period. Is the software eligible for the section 41 research credit?

III. Overview

Most taxpayers prefer to deduct intellectual property creation costs in full at the time of expenditure, rather than recover those costs over time or on the eventual transfer of the developed property. Courts generally view deductions as a matter of legislative grace. Therefore, to determine whether costs incurred in intellectual property creation are currently deductible, taxpayers must find a specific Code provision authorizing the deduction. Two Code sections—§ 162 and § 174—provide the basis for current deductibility of intellectual property creation costs. As you study these provisions, consider which has fewer restrictions on deductibility of intellectual property creation costs.

Intellectual property creation costs may fail to qualify under either § 162 or § 174. In such case, the taxpayer must determine whether the expenditures are nevertheless deductible over a period of time through an applicable amortization allowance under another applicable Code provision or administrative pronouncement.

As you study this Chapter, outline the proper tax treatment of development costs for each of the following types of intellectual property: patents, trade secrets and know-how, copyrights, trademarks and trade names, computer software, domain names, and websites.

A. Deductibility Under § 162 — Ordinary and Necessary Business Expenses

Section 162 is the most comprehensive section in the Code concerning business deductions. It allows a taxpayer to deduct "ordinary and necessary expenses paid or incurred during the taxable year in carrying on any trade or business." I.R.C. § 162(a). Section 162 establishes several significant requirements for the deduction of intellectual property creations costs associated with a business. First, the creation cost must be an "expense" as opposed to a nondeductible capital expenditure. Second, the expense must be "ordinary and necessary." Third, the expense must be paid or incurred "in carrying on a trade or business." As you study each of these requirements below, think about which requirements restrict the application of § 162 and force taxpayers to seek current deductibility under § 174.

1. The "Expense" Requirement

What may seem to be a deductible expense under § 162 may be classified as a nondeductible expenditure under another overriding provision. For example, § 263(a) disallows the immediate deduction of costs that are considered "capital expenditures." Further, § 263A requires the capitalization of all direct and indirect costs incurred to produce certain property. Both of these overriding Code provisions, which prevent the current deductibility of otherwise allowable expenses, are discussed below.

(a) Section 263(a): Capital Expenditures

The Code disallows the immediate deduction of "capital expenditures." I.R.C. § 263(a). Distinguishing immediately deductible business "expenses" from nondeductible "capital expenditures" can be difficult. Treasury Regulations under § 263 of the Code describe capital expenditures as those that "add to the value, or substantially prolong the useful life" of property, or "adapt property to a new or different use." Treas. Reg. § 1.263(a)-1(b). The Regulations list examples of capital expenditures, including the cost of acquiring property "having a useful life substantially beyond the taxable year." Treas. Reg. § 1.263(a)-2(a).

Impact of INDOPCO. In *INDOPCO, Inc. v. Commissioner*, a case included in Chapter 3, the United States Supreme Court exacerbated the problem of distinguishing between an expense and a capital expenditure by expanding the test for capitalization. Although the case did not involve an expenditure relating to an intellectual property transaction, the Supreme Court used broad language to emphasize that any expenditure producing benefits beyond the current taxable year may require capitalization. By creating a broad "future benefits" standard, the Supreme Court required the capitalization of costs that were previously deductible. Because most intellectual property creation costs yield benefits extending beyond the current taxable year, such costs would seem to be considered capital expenditures under *INDOPCO* and, hence, not deductible under § 162. In the aftermath of the Supreme Court's decision in *INDOPCO*, the Service issued numerous administrative rulings on how *INDOPCO* affects the treatment of different types of expenditures that give rise to long-term future benefits.

Post-INDOPCO Rulings. In Revenue Ruling 92-80, the Service ruled that *INDOPCO* "[would] not affect the treatment of advertising costs as business expenses which are generally deductible under section 162(a) of the Code." Rev. Rul. 92-80, 1992-C.B. 57. Revenue Ruling 92-80 was applied by the Tax Court in a trade dress and copyright development case, *Nabisco, Inc. v. Commissioner*, which follows this Overview. What was the Service's response to the court's decision? See the Service's 1999 Action on Decision, which follows the case.

In another post-*INDOPCO* Service pronouncement, the Service allowed immediate deductibility of costs paid or incurred to ensure computer systems were year 2000 (Y2K) compliant. *See* Rev. Proc. 97-50, 1997-2 C.B. 525. Such costs, including those to convert existing software, to develop new software to replace existing software, or to develop software tools to assist in converting existing software, would seem to give rise to future benefits within the meaning of *INDOPCO* and, hence, would require capitalization. Nevertheless, the Service relied on a pre-*INDOPCO* Service pronouncement, Revenue Procedure 69-21, 1969-2 C.B. 303, to allow immediate deductibility of such costs. Costs to correct Y2K problems were viewed as similar to the costs to develop computer software, which were currently deductible under Revenue Procedure 69-21. It should be noted that Revenue Procedure 69-21 has been replaced by Revenue Procedure 2000-50, which is included in the materials.

Proposed Regulations Under Section 263. In December 2002, the Service issued proposed regulations under § 263 that provide comprehensive rules for capitalization of amounts paid to create or enhance intangible assets. *See* 67 Fed. Reg. 77701 (Dec. 19, 2002), corrected by 68 Fed. Reg. 4969 (Jan. 31, 2003). Surprisingly, the proposed regulations effectively repeal the significant future benefit standard of *INDOPCO* and adopt a separate-and-distinct asset standard. Under the proposed regulations, a taxpayer is required to capitalize amounts paid to create or enhance an intangible asset. The term "intangible asset" is defined as: (1) certain rights, privileges, or benefits that are created or originated by the taxpayer; (2) separate and distinct intangible assets; and (3) future benefits as identified in subsequent published guidance. Prop. Treas. Reg. § 1.263(a)-4(b)(2). Below is a summary of the proposed regulations.

Subject to an important exception noted below, the proposed regulations require taxpayers to capitalize amounts paid to another party to create or enhance with that party certain identified intangibles. Specifically identified are certain rights obtained from a governmental agency. For example, a taxpayer must capitalize amounts paid to a governmental agency to obtain or renew a trademark, trade name, copyright, license, permit, franchise, or other similar right granted by that governmental agency. *Id.* § 1.263(a)-4(d)(1), -4(d)(5). The preamble to the proposed regulations notes that this general rule is directed at the initial fee paid to a governmental agency. The preamble also notes that this rule does not affect the treatment of expenditures under other provisions of the Code. For example, an amount paid to a government agency to obtain a patent from that agency is not required to be capitalized under the proposed regulations if the amount is deductible under § 174. *See* 67 Fed. Reg. at 77703.

The proposed regulations under section 263 also require capitalization of amounts paid to create or enhance separate and distinct intangible assets. A "separate and distinct intangible asset" means (1) a property interest of ascertainable and measurable value in money's worth (2) that is subject to protection under applicable state or federal law, and (3) the possession and control of which is intrinsically capable of being sold, transferred, or pledged (ignoring any restrictions imposed on assignability). Whether an amount serves to create or enhance a separate and distinct asset is made as of the tax year in which the amount is paid and not later using hindsight. Prop. Treas. Reg. § 1.263(a)-4(b)(2)–(3).

The proposed regulations recognize that there may be expenditures that are not identified in the above categories (created intangible assets and separate and distinct intangible assets), but for which capitalization is nonetheless appropriate. As a result, the proposed regulations require capitalization of non-listed expenditures if those expenditure serve to produce future benefits that the Service and Treasury identify in subsequent future, published guidance as significant enough to warrant capitalization. *Id.* § 1.263(a)-4(b)(2)(i)(D), (ii).

The proposed regulations under § 263 adopt an exception, termed the "12-month rule," applicable to most self-created intangibles. Under this 12-month rule, a taxpayer is not required to capitalize amounts that provide benefits of a relatively brief duration. Specifically, the proposed regulations provide that a taxpayer is not required to capitalize amounts paid to create or enhance an intangible asset if the amounts do not create or enhance any right or benefit for the taxpayer that extends beyond the earlier of 12 months after the first date on which the taxpayer realizes the right or benefit, or the end of the taxable year following the taxable year in which the payment is made. Id. § 1.263(a)-4(f)(1)(i). Amounts paid to create rights or benefits that do extend beyond the prescribed 12-month period must be capitalized in full. The proposed regulations provide rules for determining whether renewal periods should be taken into account in determining whether rights that are renewable fall within the scope of the 12-month rule. Under the proposed regulations, renewal periods are to be taken into account if based on all of the facts and circumstances in existence during the taxable year in which the right is created, the facts indicate a reasonable expectancy of renewal. The proposed regulations list the following factors as significant in determining whether there exists a reasonable expectancy of renewal: (1) renewal history; (2) economics of the transaction; (3) likelihood of renewal by other party; and (4) terms of renewal. Id. § 1.263(a)-4(f)(5).

The proposed regulations require the capitalization of transaction costs that "facilitate" the taxpayer's creation or enhancement of an intangible asset (defined, again, as created or enhanced intangibles, separate and distinct intangibles, and future benefits as identified in future published guidance from the Service). Id. § 1.263(a)-4(e)(1)(i). This rule recognizes that capitalization is required not only for the cost of creating an intangible itself, but also for the ancillary expenditures incurred in creating the intangible asset. The proposed regulations adopt two simplifying conventions application to transaction costs (i.e., rules of administrative convenience). First, a taxpayer is not required to capitalize employee compensation and overhead costs related to the creation or enhancement of an intangible asset. Second, de minimis transaction costs (costs that do not exceed $5,000, as determined on a transaction-by-transaction basis) are not required to be capitalized. Id. § 1.263(a)-4(e)(3).

The proposed regulations amend § 1.167(a)-3 to provide a 15-year safe harbor amortization period for certain created or enhance intangibles that do not have readily ascertainable useful lives. Prop. Treas. Reg. § 1.167(a)-3(b). For example, amounts paid to create trade secrets would be eligible for the safe harbor amortization provision since trade secrets and know how possess indeterminable useful lives. The safe harbor amortization does not apply if amortization periods are already prescribed under existing law. For example, § 167(f)(1) already prescribes a special 36-month amortization period for certain computer software, and section 197 already prescribes a 15-year amortization period for self-created trademarks and trade names. Moreover, the safe harbor amortization does not apply to created intangibles that have readily ascertainable useful lives on which amortization can be based (e.g., self-created patents and copyrights).

(b) Section 263A: Direct and Indirect Expenditures Incurred to Produce Tangible Property

Section 263A requires the capitalization of certain direct and indirect costs attributable to tangible personal property produced by a taxpayer. I.R.C. § 263A(a). Although § 263A mentions "tangible personal property," the phrase actually applies to several types of intellectual property that are considered intangible property. See I.R.C. § 263A(b); Treas. Reg. § 1.263A-2(a)(2)(ii). If § 263A applies, what types of expenditures must be capitalized? See I.R.C. § 263A(a)(2)(A); Treas. Reg. § 1.263A-1(e)(2)–(3), -2(a)(2)(ii)(B)(2).

Section 263A(h) provides an important exemption from the uniform capitalization requirements of §263A in the case of certain writers, photographers, and artists. Section 263A(h), which was added to the Code in 1988, provides that "qualified creative expenses" are not required to be capitalized. What is a "qualified creative expense?" Review I.R.C. §263A(h)(2)–(3), and then read Tech. Adv. Mem. 9643003, included below, which addresses whether costs incurred by a musician in producing a rough-cut "demo" tape constitute qualified creative expenses under §263A(h). Is the exemption provision of §263A(h) broad or narrow?

If the exemption provision of §263A(h) applies, qualified creative expenses are not subject to the uniform capitalization rules of §263A, and may be deductible if the elements of §162 are satisfied. If the exemption provision does not apply, then the uniform capitalization rules will apply and all expenses of producing the intellectual property must be capitalized. If costs of producing intellectual property must be capitalized (*i.e.*, §263A(h) is not applicable, or, even if applicable, the elements of §162 are not met), such costs may be eligible to be deducted over time through two options. The first possibility is that an election may be available under I.R.S. Notice 88-62, an administrative pronouncement included in the materials. Review Tech. Adv. Mem. 9643003. Would an election under Notice 88-62 be available for the musician? If an election is not available under I.R.S. Notice 88-62, the taxpayer may nevertheless be able to amortize capitalized creation costs under §167. *See* I.R.C. §167(a); Treas. Reg. §1.167(a)-3.

2. The "Ordinary and Necessary" Requirement

Even if it is determined that an expense to create intellectual property is not subject to capitalization rules, as described above, the expense must still be both "ordinary and necessary" to be deductible under §162. I.R.C. §162(a). In *Welch v. Helvering*, a case included in Chapter 3, the Supreme Court concluded that "ordinary" does not mean an expense need be habitual or normal in the sense that the same taxpayer will need to pay the expense often. To be ordinary, the expense must be customary or expected in the life of the business. The Supreme Court further described the scope of ordinary in *Deputy v. du Pont*, 308 U.S. 488 (1940), a decision subsequent to *Welch*:

> Ordinary has the connotation of normal, usual or customary. To be sure, an expense may be ordinary though it happen but once in the taxpayer's life.... Yet the transaction which gives rise to it must be of common or frequent occurrence in the type of business involved.... One of the extremely relevant circumstances is the nature and scope of the particular business out of which the expense in question accrued.... It is the kind of transaction out of which the obligation arose and its normalcy in the particular business which are crucial and controlling.

The term "necessary," for purposes of §162, was interpreted by the Court in *Welch* to mean "appropriate and helpful." The Court noted that it would be slow to override a taxpayer's business judgment regarding the necessity of expenses.

3. The "In Carrying on a Trade or Business" Requirement

Section 162 requires that deductible expenses be incurred "in carrying on" a taxpayer's "trade or business." I.R.C. §162(a). Thus, in order to qualify for a §162 deduction, two conditions must be satisfied. First, the taxpayer must have a *trade or business*; and second, the payments must be *in carrying on* that trade or business.

Neither the Code nor the Treasury Regulations define the term "trade or business." Courts considering the meaning of the term have generally concluded that to be engaged in a trade or business, (1) "the taxpayer must be involved in the activity with continuity and regularity," and (2) "the taxpayer's primary purpose for engaging in the activity must be for income or profit." Review *Commissioner v. Groetzinger*, a case included in Chapter 3. Whether a taxpayer has engaged in the requisite scope of activities and has demonstrated the requisite profit motive are questions to be determined by an examination of all the facts in each case.

To be engaged in a trade or business, a taxpayer does not necessarily have to hold himself out to others as offering goods or services. The taxpayer, however, must pursue an activity with sufficient continuity and regularity. Although a business does not need to realize immediate profit, it must be entered into and carried on in good faith for the purpose of making a profit. Mere wishful thinking that an activity will generate profits, without any specific plans to realize profits, will not demonstrate the requisite profit motive. This was the case in *Outten v. Commissioner*, 47 T.C.M. (CCH) 1120 (1984), where the taxpayer sought to deduct costs of researching and promoting his discovery of a nuclear fusion process. The Tax Court denied the deductions finding that no income was ever likely to be generated from the discovery.

Losses in early years, standing alone, do not prevent an operation from being a trade or business within the meaning of §162. This is important because, in most instances, experimental activity yields little, if any, return during the developmental stages, although the potential of producing significant income exists. This common scenario existed in the cases of *Bailey v. Commissioner*, 22 T.C.M. (CCH) 1255 (1963), *Maximoff v. Commissioner*, 53 T.C.M. (CCH) 423 (1987), and *Gestrich v. Commissioner*, 74 T.C. 525 (1980), *aff'd*, 681 F.2d 805 (3d Cir. 1982). In each case, the taxpayer's intellectual property development activity failed to generate any income. Nevertheless, the Tax Court, in each case, found that the taxpayers reasonably expected to realize profits from their activities eventually and allowed §162 deductions for the costs attributable to the activities.

An activity will not qualify as a trade or business under §162 if it is "[a] sporadic activity, a hobby, or an amusement diversion." See *Groetzinger*, included in Chapter 3. Although expenses incurred in a hobby activity (an activity not engaged in for profit) are not deductible under §162, they are allowed under §183 to the extent the hobby activities generate income. I.R.C. §183(a), (b). Treasury Regulations under §183 provide nine relevant factors that should be taken into account in determining whether or not an activity is engaged in for profit. Read carefully Treas. Reg. §1.183-2(a)-(b) and I.R.C. §183(d). Numerous cases have applied these nine factors in intellectual property development activities. For example, in *Dickie v. Commissioner*, 77 T.C.M. (CCH) 1916 (1999), the Tax Court held that the taxpayer's activity as a musician was not an activity engaged in for profit within the meaning of §183 because the taxpayer conducted his music activity in a nonbusiness-like manner, made no reasonable efforts to gain recognition as a musician playing music for hire, and did not have any consultation with experts in the music industry in an effort to further his music career. The Tax Court concluded that petitioner's music activity was only a hobby. Compare the Tax Court's decision in *Dickie* with the Tax Court's decision *Vitale v. Commissioner*, a recent case included in the materials.

The deduction under §162 is available for ordinary and necessary expenses paid or incurred by the taxpayer "in carrying on" a trade or business. I.R.C. §162(a). The purpose of the "in carrying on" requirement is to differentiate between expenses that are associated with the operation of an actual, existing business (*i.e.*, ordinary and necessary business expenses) and those expenses associated with the development of a new business (*i.e.*, start-up or pre-opening expenses). The result is that § 162 permits current deductions only for those costs paid or incurred in connection with an active, ongoing business and denies current deductibility for startup or pre-opening costs incurred prior to the beginning of actual business operations. Whether a venture has crossed the line from start-up to active trade or business depends on whether the business has begun to function as a going concern and engaged in those activities for which it was organized. This determination is a "question of fact that depends on the circumstances of each case." *See Lamont v. United States*, 80 A.F.T.R.2d 97-7320 (Fed. Cl. 1997). The "in carrying on" limitation generally makes it difficult for most individuals and small start-up business enterprises to currently deduct pre-operational research and development expenses under § 162. As a general rule, only larger entities with ongoing research programs or an existing product line are going to be able to meet the "in carrying on" requirement.

B. Deductibility Under § 174 — Research and Experimental Expenditures

Under the special rules of § 174, certain expenditures incurred in developing intellectual property may be deductible even though such expenditures would otherwise be subject to the capitalization rules discussed above. *See* I.R.C. § 263(a)(1)(B) (providing that the capitalization rules under § 263(a) do not apply to research or experimental expenditures deductible under § 174); § 263A(c)(2) (providing that the uniform capitalization rules of § 263A do not apply to amounts deductible under § 174). Section 174 provides a taxpayer with two options for deducting research or experimental expenditures paid or incurred during the taxable year in connection with a trade or business. Under the first option, a taxpayer may choose to treat research or experimental expenditures as "expenses which are not chargeable to capital account." I.R.C. § 174(a). This means that a taxpayer may currently deduct, in full, all research or experimental expenditures incurred during the taxable year. Under the second option, a taxpayer may elect to defer research or experimental expenditures and deduct them ratably over a period of not less than five years. I.R.C. § 174(b). These options, of course, are only available for costs qualifying as "research or experimental expenditures" and for costs paid or incurred "in connection with" a trade or business, and only if the amount of such costs are "reasonable under the circumstances." I.R.C. § 174(a)(1), (b)(1), (e).

1. Research and Experimental Expenditures

Research or experimental expenditures are broadly defined as "expenditures incurred in connection with the taxpayer's trade or business which represent research and development costs in the *experimental or laboratory sense*," and generally include "all costs incident to the development or improvement of a product." Treas. Reg. § 1.174-2(a)(1). How do the regulations define a "product" for these purposes? *See* Treas. Reg. § 1.174-2(a)(2). Should proper focus be on the nature of the product being developed or on the nature of the activity to which the expenditure relates? *See* Treas. Reg. § 1.174-2(a)(1).

The regulations expand on the definition of research and experimental expenditures by clarifying that expenditures are incurred in the "experimental or laboratory" sense if they are incurred in "activities intended to discover information that would eliminate *uncertainty* concerning the development or improvement of a product." Treas. Reg. § 1.174-2(a)(1). If (1) the capability or method for developing or improving the product, or (2) the appropriate design of the product, are not established by the information available to the taxpayer, then "uncertainty" exists. *Id.* Under this uncertainty test, the information available to a taxpayer does not have to be information reasonably available. Rather, the focus should be on information that is actually available and on procedures actually involved as opposed to procedures generally in the nature of research activities. 59 Fed. Reg. 50,159, 50,160 (Oct. 1994).

The regulations under § 174 specifically provide that the costs of obtaining a patent are research and experimental expenditures. Treas. Reg. § 1.174-2(a)(1). Such costs include not only expenses incurred in creating patentable technology, but also attorney's fees in the prosecution of patent applications. *Id.* Research and experimental expenditures generally do not include costs incurred in creating property that is subject to copyright protection, because of the limitation under § 174 of costs in the experimental or laboratory sense. Also, many computer software development costs also fail to qualify as § 174 research and experimental expenditures. Because costs incurred in the development of computer software are not experimental or investigative in a laboratory sense, they will fail to satisfy the uncertainty test under section 174. However, as noted in Revenue Procedure 2000-50, included in the materials, the Service treats certain costs incurred in the development of computer software as currently deductible or deferred expenses analogous to the manner in which research or experimental expenditures are treated under § 174.

Read Field Service Advice 200125019, included in the materials, which dealt with development expenditures for footwear. Given that § 174 applies only to research and development costs in the "experimental or laboratory sense," are you surprised at the outcome?

2. *Disqualified Expenditures*

Certain expenditures incurred in the development of intellectual property are specifically excluded from the definition of research and experimental expenditures and will not qualify for § 174 treatment.

Quality Control Testing. Expenditures incurred for ordinary quality control testing or inspection do not constitute research or experimental expenditures. Treas. Reg. § 1.174-2(a)(3)(i). For this purpose, quality control testing includes "testing or inspection to determine whether particular units of materials or products conform to specified parameters." Treas. Reg. § 1.174-2(a)(4). While quality control includes validation testing to ensure a product design meets its intended objectives, it does not include testing to determine the appropriateness of the design of a product. *Id.*

Efficiency Surveys, Management Studies, and Consumer Surveys. Business management expenses such as efficiency surveys, management surveys, and consumer surveys do not qualify as research or experimental expenditures. Treas. Reg. § 1.174-2(a)(3)(ii)–(iv).

Advertising or Promotion. Advertising and promotion costs associated with the development of intellectual property do not constitute deductible research and experimental expenditures under § 174. Treas. Reg. § 1.174-2(a)(3)(v). Section 174 does not apply under the theory that such expenses do not relate to the actual development of a new product. However, as discussed above, the Service ruled in Revenue Ruling 92-80,

1992 C.B. 57, that ordinary business advertising may be deductible under §162 if the taxpayer incurs such costs in the operation of an existing business, notwithstanding the fact that they often produce benefits that continue well beyond the year.

Acquisition of Another's Patent, Model, Production, or Process. Costs of acquiring (purchasing) a patent, model, production, or process of another do not constitute research or experimental expenditures. Treas. Reg. §1.174-2(a)(3)(vii). The treatment of such acquisition costs are dealt with in Chapter 5.

Research in Connection with Literary, Historical, or Similar Projects. Expenditures for research in connection with literary, historical, or similar projects do not qualify as research and experimental expenditures under §174. Treas. Reg. §1.174-2(a)(3)(vii). Rather, such expenditures are subject to the cost capitalization rules of §263A, discussed above. Remember that an important, but limited, exception to the uniform capitalization rule is provided in §263A(h). Amortization options for otherwise capitalized costs of research in connection with literary or similar projects are provided in I.R.S. Notice 88-62, which is included below, and in §167, which is discussed in Chapter 5.

Land and Depreciable and Depletable Property in Connection with Research and Experimentation—General Rule. Section 174 does not apply to amounts spent to acquire or improve land or depreciable or depletable property even if the taxpayer uses the property or improvement in connection with its research and experimentation activities. I.R.C. §174(c). However, any depreciation or depletion allowances with respect to depreciable or depletable property that is used by a taxpayer in connection with research and experimentation are considered as research and experimental expenditures for purposes of §174 (to the extent that the property or improvements are used in connection with research or experimentation). *Id.*; Treas. Reg. §1.174-2(b)(1). Why would this be significant as the depreciation or depletion allowance provisions would permit a current deduction anyway?

Although §174 does not apply to amounts spent to acquire or improve land and depreciable/depletable property in connection with research, §174 *may* apply to amounts paid to another party even though these amounts represent expenditures for the acquisition or improvement of land and depreciable property. Specifically, amounts paid by a taxpayer to another person (such as a research institute, foundation, engineering company, or similar contractor) that represent expenditures for the acquisition or improvement of land or depreciable property used in connection with research performed on the taxpayer's behalf may qualify as §174 research and experimental expenditures *so long as* the taxpayer does not obtain ownership of the land or depreciable property. Treas. Reg. §1.174-2(a)(8)–(9).

For the deductibility of research and experimental expenditures that result, as an end product, in the creation of depreciable property to be used in a taxpayer's trade or business, see Treas. Reg. §1.174-2(b)(2), -2(b)(4), -4(a)(2), -4(a)(4).

For the deductibility of research and experimental expenditures incurred in connection with the construction or manufacture of depreciable property by another, see Treas. Reg. §1.174-2(b)(3) (providing deductibility under §174(a) "only if made upon the taxpayer's order and at his risk"). Is a deduction allowed if the taxpayer purchases a product from another under a performance guarantee?

3. *"In Connection with a Trade or Business" Requirement*

To qualify as a research or experimental expenditure under §174, an expenditure must not only represent a cost in the experimental or laboratory sense, but must also be incurred "in connection with" the taxpayer's trade or business. I.R.C. § 174. Prior to 1974, the Service and the courts took the position that in order to qualify for § 174 treatment, a taxpayer must have already engaged in a trade or business. In *Snow v. Commissioner*, included below, however, the United States Supreme Court rejected this narrow approach and held that pre-operational research or experimental expenditures could qualify for the § 174 deduction. In light of *Snow*, compare the "in connection with" requirement of § 174 with the "in carrying on" requirement under § 162.

Although a taxpayer need not be currently conducting a business in order for research or experimental expenditures to meet the "in connection with a trade or business" requirement under § 174, the taxpayer must, however, demonstrate a realistic prospect of entering into a trade or business that will exploit the technology under development. In making this determination, the taxpayer must demonstrate both an objective intent to enter into the trade or business and the capability to do so. *Kantor v. Commissioner*, 998 F.2d 1514 (9th Cir. 1993). Review *Green v. Commissioner*, a case presented in the materials. Why did the Tax Court disallow § 174 deductions to the taxpayer?

The trade or business issue most often arises in situations where an entity contracts out the performance of research and development. The § 174 trade or business requirement is usually met where the taxpayer contracts out its research and experimental activities, but then engages or clearly intends to engage in substantial subsequent production or marketing activities with respect to the results of such research. In the wake of *Green v. Commissioner*, however, the § 174 trade or business requirement is not satisfied if a taxpayer that contracts out research and development activities engages in less than substantial subsequent production or marketing activities. Would the outcome in *Green* have been different if the partnership had engaged in necessary in-house research activities or retained the right to subsequently produce and market the products resulting from the research? Research and development partnerships are considered in Chapter 7.

The § 174 trade or business issue also arises in cases where a taxpayer conducts research "in house" but intends to exploit the resulting product through sale or license. For example, a taxpayer may conduct research in house, but may intend to transfer all rights thereto in exchange for royalties derived by the licensee from the production and marketing of the resulting inventions. As a general rule, the receipt of royalties alone does not constitute a trade or business. Courts have held, however, that in-house research activities and the exploitation of the resulting inventions by sale or license may constitute a trade or business. *See Avery v. Commissioner*, 47 B.T.A. 538 (1942); *Louw v. Commissioner*, 30 T.C.M. (CCH) 1421 (1971).

The § 174 trade or business issue may also arise when individuals' inventive activities look like hobby activities as opposed to trade or business activities. As discussed above in connection with the discussion of § 162, an activity does not qualify as a trade or business activity if it is "[a] sporadic activity, a hobby, or an amusement diversion." *Groetzinger*, included in Chapter 3. The regulations set out and illustrate nine relevant factors that should normally be taken into account in determining whether an inventive activity constitutes a hobby. Treas Reg. § 1.183-2(b). As discussed above, expenses incurred in a hobby activity (an activity not engaged in for profit) are generally allowed under § 183 only if and to the extent that the hobby activity generates income. I.R.C. § 183(a), (b).

4. Reasonableness of Expenditures

Research and experimental expenditures are eligible for immediate deduction or deferral and amortization under § 174 only to the extent that the amount of the expenditure is reasonable under the circumstances. I.R.C. § 174(e). The amount of an expenditure is considered reasonable if the amount would ordinarily be paid for similar activities conducted by similar enterprises under like circumstances. Why do you suppose Congress has imposed a reasonableness limitation on research or experimental expenditures? Is there a requirement that research activities themselves be of a reasonable type or nature?

5. The Election to Expense or Amortize

Section 174 provides two methods for treating research and experimental expenditures. A taxpayer may choose to currently deduct such expenditures paid or incurred during the taxable year. I.R.C. § 174(a). Alternatively, a taxpayer may elect to treat these expenditures as deferred expenses amortized ratably over a period of not less than 60 months. I.R.C. § 174(b). If neither approach is taken, then the expenditures must be capitalized. Treas. Reg. § 1.174-1.

(a) Current Expense Method

Without the consent of the Service, a taxpayer may elect to treat § 174 expenditures as currently deductible for the first taxable year in which such expenditures are paid or incurred. I.R.C. § 174(a)(2)(A); Treas. Reg. § 1.174-3(b)(1); Rev. Rul. 58-74, 1958-1 C.B. 148. The election is made by actually taking a deduction for research or experimental expenditures on the tax return for the year in which the research and experimental expenditures are paid or incurred and by attaching an election statement to the return. Treas. Reg. § 1.174-2(b)(1); Rev. Rul. 58-356, 1958-2 C.B. 104; Rev. Rul. 76-324, 1976-2 C.B. 77. The election applies to all of the taxpayer's research and experimental expenditures incurred within that taxable year. The current expense method applies to all subsequent years, unless the Service approves a change to the deferred expense method. Any requested change may relate to some or all of the expenditures. A change must relate, however, to all expenditures with respect to a particular project. I.R.C. § 174(a)(3); Treas. Reg. § 1.174-3(a), (b). Permission can be obtained through a signed application to the IRS which includes certain information. Treas. Reg. § 1.174-3(b)(1). The Service has provided a simplified procedure for obtaining automatic consent to change methods of treating § 174 expenditures. *See* Revenue Procedure 99-49, 1999-2 C.B. 725 (providing a cut-off method that applies to all § 174 expenditures for a particular project or projects during the year of change and subsequent years).

(b) Deferred Expense (Amortization) Method

If a taxpayer chooses not to deduct currently qualified research and experimental expenditures, it may elect to treat the expenditures as deferred expenses amortized ratably over a period of not less than sixty months as selected by the taxpayer. I.R.C. § 174(b); Treas. Reg. § 1.174-4(a)(1). The sixty-month period (or other period) over which research and experimental expenditures can be amortized begins with the month in which the taxpayer first realizes benefits from the expenditures. I.R.C. § 174(b)(1);

Treas. Reg. §1.174-4(a)(3). Hence, a taxpayer who is developing a product must postpone deductions under the deferred expense method until the taxpayer markets the product and starts receiving income. This is problematic for many intellectual property creation processes that take several years to develop a specific product. If different projects are commenced at the same time, the taxpayer may select different amortization periods for each product. Treas. Reg. §1.174-4(a)(3).

The deferred expense method is not available for expenditures that give rise to property that has a determinable useful life. Treas. Reg. §1.174-4(a)(2). Expenditures with respect to such property must be depreciated over the determinable useful life of that property. *Id.* This twist presents a problem because uncertainty almost always exists whether research and experimental expenditures will give rise to property—much less property with a determinable useful life (*e.g.*, patents). The regulations fortunately provide that a taxpayer can elect the deferred expense method and begin to amortize research and experimental expenditures under that method until it is determined that a determinable useful life exits. Once it is determined that a determinable useful life exists, any remaining deferred expenses must be amortized over the determinable useful life. Treas. Reg. §1.174-4(a)(4).

The election to amortize research and experimental expenditures ratably over a sixty-month period (or other period) must be made no later than the due date, including extensions, for filing the tax return for the first taxable year for which the election is made. I.R.C. §174(b)(2); Treas. Reg. §1.174-4(b)(1). The election does not necessarily have to apply to all research and experimental expenditures incurred during the year, but can apply with respect to certain projects. Once an election is made to amortize, the method and the amortization period chosen must be followed in computing taxable income for the first year in which the election is made and all subsequent years covered within the scope of the election, unless the Service approves a change to a different method or period with respect to some or all of the expenditures. I.R.C. §174(b)(2); Treas. Reg. §1.174-4(b)(2), -4(a)(5) Thus, a taxpayer who wishes to change from treating expenditures as deferred expenses under §174(b) to current expenses under §174(a) may do so only with the Service's permission, which can be obtained through a signed application with certain required information. Treas. Reg. §1.174-3(b). *See* Rev. Proc. 99-49, 1999-2 C.B. 725 (providing a simplified procedure for obtaining automatic consent to change the treatment of §174 expenditures).

If neither approach under §174 is taken (*i.e.*, current expense method or the deferred expense method), then the taxpayer must capitalize all research and experimental expenditures. As noted below, however, the capitalized costs of self-created intangibles may be deducted over a period of time under another Code section (*i.e.*, §§197 or 167).

C. Alternative Minimum Tax Considerations

If §174(a) performs the basis for deductibility of research and experimental expenses, the excess of deductions taken over the amount that would be deductible if such costs were amortized ratably over ten years is treated a tax preference item for purposes of determining the alternative minimum tax. I.R.C. §56(b)(2). This tax preference item would have the effect of increasing "alternative minimum taxable income" and, hence, the alternative minimum tax. I.R.C. §55(b)(2) (defining alternative minimum taxable income). It should be noted that § 174(a) deductions are not a tax preference item for taxpayers who materially participate in an activity within the meaning of § 469(h). I.R.C. § 56(b)(2)(D).

To avoid an alternative minimum taxable income adjustment, noncorporate taxpayers have another amortization option. Under section 59(e), taxpayers may elect to capitalize and amortize research and experimental expenditures ratably over 10 years beginning with the year in which they are incurred. I.R.C. § 59(e)(1), (2). If the ten-year write-off election of § 59(e) is made, the amortization deductions are not treated as items of tax preference for purposes of the alternative minimum tax (*i.e.*, no adjustment is made to alternative minimum taxable income). I.R.C. § 59(e)(6). Query: Would an election under § 59(e) ever provide a faster recovery of research and experimental expenditures than an election under § 174(b)? *See* I.R.C. § 174(b)(1) (noting amortization under §174(b) does not begin until the taxpayer first realizes benefits); Treas. Reg. § 1.174-4(a)(2) (noting amortization under § 174(b) stops once expenditures result in depreciable property, and depreciation continues under § 167).

D. Amortization of Capitalized Intellectual Property Development Costs

If neither § 162 nor § 174 apply to intellectual property creation costs, then the costs must be capitalized. Nevertheless, the capitalized costs of creating intellectual property may be recovered through an amortization deduction under another section. Section 197 permits a taxpayer to amortize over fifteen years a limited number of self-created intangibles. Section 167 permits a taxpayer to amortize/depreciate certain self-created intangibles over their determinable useful lives or under the income forecast method.

Section 197 allows an amortization deduction for the capitalized costs of any "amortizable section 197 intangible." I.R.C. § 197(a); Treas. Reg. § 1.197-2(a)(3) (providing that § 197 does not apply to amounts that are otherwise deductible under §§ 162 or 174). The amortization deduction is determined by amortizing the capitalized costs ratably over a fifteen-year period. Although many *purchased* intangible assets are considered "section 197 intangibles," most *self-created* intangible assets are specifically excluded from the definition of § 197 intangibles. I.R.C. § 197(c)(2); Treas. Reg. § 1.197-2(d)(2).

There is one important exception to the exclusion for self-created intangibles. Section 197 does apply to self-created trademarks and trade names. I.R.C. § 197(d)(1)(F); Treas. Reg. § 1.197-2(b)(10). As a result, taxpayers must amortize over fifteen years the capitalized costs incurred in connection with the development or registration of a trademark or trade name. All other intellectual property creation costs (*e.g.*, costs incurred in developing patents, trade secrets and know how, copyrightable works, and computer software) are not eligible for the fifteen-year amortization treatment of § 197. I.R.C. § 197(e)(3)–(4); Treas. Reg. § 1.197-2(c)(7).

If § 197 does not apply, such costs may nevertheless be recovered over the useful life of the property under § 167 or over another period pursuant to a relevant administrative pronouncement. For example, costs incurred to create certain works subject to copyright protection may be recovered under the three-year safe harbor of I.R.S. Notice 88-62, provided in the materials, or the longer useful life of the property under § 167 in the event such costs are not currently deductible under §§ 263A(h) and 162.

A more detailed discussion regarding §§ 197 and 167 is provided in Chapter 5.

E. The § 41 Research and Development Credit

The research credit, found in § 41 of the Code, has been modified and extended many times since its creation in 1981, and has generated a great deal of controversy over the last few years, particularly in the area of computer software development. In its current form, the research credit is actually made up of two components (two credits), and equals (1) 20% of the excess (if any) of the "qualified research expenses" for the taxable year over a "base amount" plus (2) 20% of the "basic research payments." I.R.C. § 41(a)(1)–(2).

To fully understand the research credit, one must look to the Treasury regulations under § 41. In January 2001, the Treasury issued a set of final regulations relating to the computation of the research credit and the definition of qualified research. 66 Fed. Reg. 280 (2001). Shortly thereafter, however, the Treasury and IRS announced that these final regulations were suspended for further review and comment. Notice 2001-19, 2001-10 I.R.B. 784. On December 14, 2001, the Treasury issued a new set of proposed regulations. 66 Fed. Reg. 66362 (2001). According to the Preamble, taxpayers may rely on the proposed regulations until the date final regulations are published in the Federal Register.

Below is a summary of qualified research activities under § 41, including a review of the prior suspended regulations, as well as modifications made by the current proposed regulations. Computation methods are beyond the scope of the Chapter. Merely skim I.R.C. §§ 41(b) (defining "qualified research expenses"); 41(c) (providing basic method and elective alternative incremental method for computing credit).

1. "Qualified Research" Defined

The term "qualified research" is defined in § 41(d) of the Code as research: (1) with respect to which expenditures may be treated as expenses under section 174; (2) that is undertaken for the purpose of discovering information that is technological in nature, and the application of which is intended to be useful in the development of a new or improved business component of the taxpayer; and (3) substantially all of the activities of which constitute elements of a process of experimentation that relates to a new or improved function, performance, reliability, or quality.

(a) Discovery Test

Under § 41(d), qualified research must be undertaken for the purpose of discovering information which is technological in nature. I.R.C. § 41(d)(1)(B)(i). The suspended regulations expanded on this requirement by providing that "research is undertaken for the purpose of discovering information only if it is undertaken to obtain knowledge that exceeds, expands, or refines the common knowledge of skilled professionals in a particular field of science or engineering." Treas. Reg. § 1.41-4(a)(3)(i). The proposed regulations eliminate this requirement that qualified research be undertaken to "obtain knowledge that exceeds, expands, or refines the common knowledge of skilled professionals in a particular field of science of engineering" Instead, the proposed regulations repeat the requirement from Treas. Reg. §1.174-2(a)(1) by stating that research is undertaken for the purpose of discovering information if it is intended to eliminate uncertainty concerning the development or improvement of a business component. As stated in the Preamble, "there should be no 'discovery' requirement in the research credit regulations separate and apart from that already required under §1.174-2(a)(1)." 66 Fed. Reg. 66363.

The suspended regulations expanded on the definition of "technological in nature." The suspended regulations provided that information is technological in nature if the process of experimentation used to discover such information fundamentally relies on principles of the physical or biological sciences, engineering, or computer science. The suspended regulations provided that a taxpayer may employ existing technologies and rely on existing scientific principles of the physical or biological sciences, engineering, or computer science to satisfy the technological in nature test. The suspended regulations clarified that research need not be successful in order to qualify for the credit. Treas. Reg. §1.41-4(a)(3)–(4). As with the suspended regulations, the proposed regulations permit the use of existing technologies and the reliance on existing scientific principles. The proposed regulations also provide that a taxpayer need not succeed in research efforts in order to qualify for the credit. Prop. Treas. Reg. §1.41-4(a)(3)–(4).

The suspended regulations provided a patent safe harbor, under which the issuance of a patent is conclusive evidence that a taxpayer has obtained knowledge that exceeds, expands, or refines the common knowledge of skilled professionals in the relevant field of science or engineering. Treas. Reg. §1.41-4(a)(3)(iv). The proposed regulations retain the patent safe harbor. Prop. Treas. Reg. §1.41-4(a)(3)(iii).

(b) Process of Experimentation

Along with the requirements discussed above, §41(d) provides that qualified research means research substantially all of the activities of which constitute elements of a process of experimentation related to a new or improved function, performance, or reliability or quality. I.R.C. §41(d)(1)(C). The suspended regulations provided that a process of experimentation is a process to evaluate more than one alternative designed to achieve a result where the capability or method of achieving that result is uncertain at the outset. The suspended regulations also provided that a process of experimentation does not include the evaluation of alternatives to establish the appropriate design of a business component when the capability and method for developing or improving the business component are not uncertain. For illustrative purposes, a four-step process of experimentation was provided in the suspended regulations. See Treas. Reg. §1.41-4(a)(5). As can be seen, the process of experimentation required by section 41(d) and the suspended regulations differed from research and development in the experimental or laboratory sense required by §1.174-2(a)(1).

Under the proposed regulations, the requirements for a process of experimentation under §41 continue to be more stringent than the requirements for research and development in the experimental or laboratory sense under Treasury regulations §1.174-2(a)(1). In contrast to the suspended regulations, however, the proposed regulations provide that activities to establish the appropriate design of a business component may qualify for the credit. Accordingly, the proposed regulations provide that a process of experimentation is a process designed to evaluate one or more alternatives to achieve a result where the capability or method of achieving that result, or the appropriate design of that result, is uncertain as of the beginning of the taxpayer's research activities. Prop. Treas. Reg. § 1.41-4(a)(5).

Under the proposed regulations, the process of experimentation test is a facts and circumstances determination. The proposed regulations include a list of several factors that are indicative of a process of experimentation: (1) the taxpayer tests and analyzes numerous alternative hypotheses to develop a new or improved business component; (2) the taxpayer engages in extensive, comprehensive, intricate, or complex scientific or laboratory testing; or (3) the taxpayer evaluates numerous or complex specifications related to the function, performance, reliability, or quality of a new or improved business component. Prop. Treas. Reg. § 1.41-4(a)(5)(iv).

The proposed regulations clearly provide that a taxpayer's activities do not constitute elements of a process of experimentation where the capability and method of achieving, and the appropriate design of, the desired new or improved business component are "readily discernible and applicable as of the beginning of the taxpayer's research activities" so that true experimentation in the scientific or laboratory sense would not have to be undertaken to test, analyze, and chose among viable alternatives. A process of experimentation does not include any activities to select among several alternatives that are readily discernible and applicable. Prop. Treas. Reg. § 1.41-4(a)(5)(ii).

The suspended regulations provided that the "substantially all" requirement under § 41(d)(1)(C) is satisfied only if 80 percent or more of the research activities, measured on a cost or other consistent reasonable basis, constitute elements of a process of experimentation that relates to a new or improved function, performance, reliability or quality of a business component. Treas. Reg. § 1.41-4(a)(6). The proposed regulations apply the same substantially all rule. Prop. Treas. Reg. § 1.41-4(a)(6).

2. Activities Excluded from "Qualified Research"

Section 41(d)(4) excludes several types of research activities from the term "qualified research," including: (1) any research conducted after the beginning of commercial production of the business component; and (2) certain computer software which is developed by (or for the benefit of) the taxpayer primarily for internal use.

(a) Research After Commercial Production

Activities conducted after the beginning of commercial production of a business component are not qualified research. I.R.C. § 41(d)(4)(A). The suspended regulations provides that activities are deemed to occur after the beginning of commercial production of a business component if such activities are conducted after the component is developed and is ready for commercial sale or use, or meets the basic functional and economic requirements of the taxpayer for the component's sale or use. The suspended regulations provided that the following activities shall be deemed to occur after the beginning of commercial production of a business component: (1) pre-production planning for a finished business component; (2) tooling-up for production; (3) trial production runs; (4) trouble shooting involving detecting faults in production equipment or processes; (5) accumulating data relating to production processes; and (6) debugging flaws in a business component. Treas. Reg. § 1.41-4(c)(2). The proposed regulations contain these rules. Prop. Treas. Reg. § 1.41-4(c)(2).

(b) Internal-Use Computer Software

Internal-Use Software Defined. Section 41(d)(4)(E) provides that, except to the extent provided by regulations, research with respect to "computer software which is developed by (or for the benefit of) the taxpayer primarily for internal use by the taxpayer" (internal-use software) is excluded from the definition of qualified research. I.R.C. §41(d)(4)(E). The suspended regulations provided a definition of internal-use software. Under the suspended regulations, "[s]oftware is developed primarily for the taxpayer's internal use if the software is to be used internally, for example, in general administrative functions of the taxpayer (such as, payroll, bookkeeping, or personnel management) or in providing non-computer services (such as accounting, consulting, or banking services)." Non-computer services are services offered by a taxpayer to customers who conduct business with the taxpayer primarily to obtain a service other than a computer service, even if such other service is enabled, supported, or facilitated by computer or software technology. The suspended regulations contained an exception, which provided that internal-use software does not include software if, at the time the research was undertaken, (1) the software is designed to provide customers a new feature with respect to a noncomputer service, (2) the taxpayer reasonably anticipated that customers would choose to obtain the noncomputer service from the taxpayer because of those new features, and (3) those new features were not available from any of the taxpayer's competitors. Treas. Reg. §1.41-4(c)(6).

The proposed regulations clarify the definition of internal-use software contained in the suspended regulations. The proposed regulations provide that unless software is developed primarily to be commercially sold, leased, licensed, or otherwise marketed for separately stated consideration to an unrelated third party, computer software is presumed developed by (or for the benefit of) the taxpayer primarily for the taxpayer's internal use." As did the suspended regulations, the proposed regulations exclude from the definition of internal-use software computer software and hardware developed as a single product. Moreover, the proposed regulations actually expand the computer software/hardware rule to include purchasers of combined software/hardware products (purchasers that develop their own software to operate the package or modify the imbedded software). Specifically, internal-use software does not include a new or improved package of computer software and hardware developed together by the taxpayer as a single product (or to the costs to modify an acquired computer software and hardware package), of which the software is an integral part, that is used directly by the taxpayer in providing services in its trade or business to customers. Prop. Treas. Reg. §1.41-4(c)(6).

High Threshold of Innovation Test. The suspended regulations provided that the development of internal-use software constitutes qualified research only if the research satisfies the general requirements for credit eligibility under §41 (including that the research not be otherwise excluded), and an additional, three-part high threshold of innovation test. Under the suspended regulations, computer software satisfies the high threshold of innovation test only if the taxpayer can establish that: (1) the software is innovative in that the software is intended to result in a reduction of cost, improvement in speed, or other improvement, that is substantial and economically significant; (2) the software development involves significant economic risk in that the taxpayer commits substantial resources to the development and there is a substantial uncertainty, because of technical risk, that such resources would be recovered within a reasonable period; and (3) the software is not commercially available for use by the taxpayer. Treas. Reg §1.41-4(c)(6)(vi). Under the proposed regulations, the second and third prongs of the high-threshold of innovation test remain unchanged. The third prong, however, is modified by providing that software is innovative only if the software is intended to be unique or novel and is intended to differ in a significant and inventive way from prior software implementations or methods. Prop. Treas. Reg. § 1.41-4(c)(6)(vi).

Software Not Required To Satisfy the High Threshold of Innovation Test. The suspended regulations contained five categories of software excluded from the high threshold of innovation test: (1) software used in conducting qualified research; (2) software used in a production process; (3) software used as part of a package of hardware and software developed concurrently; and (4) software used in providing computer services to customers; and (5) software used to deliver non-computer services to customers with features that are not yet offered by a taxpayer's competitors. Treas. Reg. § 1.41-4(c)(6). The proposed regulations retain the first four exclusions from the high threshold of innovation test, but eliminate the fifth exclusion for software used to deliver non-computer services. According to the Preamble, the Treasury and the IRS believed that software targeted by this fifth exclusion would generally be credit eligible without the rule. 66 Fed. Reg. 66365.

Effective Date of Internal-Use Software Rules. The Preamble to the proposed regulations state that the proposed revisions to the internal-use software rules are effective retroactive to December 31, 1985. The Preamble notes, however, that taxpayers may continue to rely on the suspended regulations until the proposed regulations are finalized. 66 Fed. Reg. 66366.

IV. Materials

RJR Nabisco, Inc. v. Commissioner
T.C. Memo. 1998-252

HALPERN, JUDGE:

A. *Issue*

We must determine whether the litigated expenses are currently deductible business expenses. Respondent determined that they are capital expenditures and, therefore, not currently deductible. The litigated expenses include expenditures relating to the graphic design of cigarette packaging materials (cartons, soft-packs, and crush-proof boxes) and cigarette papers, tips, and other components of the cigarette product, as well as a relatively small amount of expenditures relating to package design (the physical construction of the package itself).

B. *Arguments of the Parties*

Petitioner starts with the premise that expenditures for ordinary business advertising (to sell a product or service or for institutional or "goodwill" advertising that keeps the taxpayer's name before the public) are deductible under section 162(a) and argues that the litigated expenses give rise to a benefit that is indistinguishable from the benefit derived from ordinary business advertising. Consequently, petitioner argues, the litigated expenses are also deductible under section 162(a). Petitioner also argues that, like expenditures for ordinary business advertising, the litigated expenses represent a recurring, day-to-day business expense, deductible under section 162(a) for that reason alone. In the alternative, petitioner argues that the litigated expenses are deductible under section 174.

Respondent agrees that the litigated expenses are similar to some expenditures for ordinary business advertising, but he argues that not all expenditures for ordinary business advertising are deductible under section 162(a). Respondent distinguishes between the costs of developing advertising campaigns (advertising campaign expenditures) and the costs of executing those campaigns by way of, for instance, the production of television commercials (advertising execution expenditures). Respondent argues that advertising execution expenditures generally give rise to expenses deductible under section 162 (deductible business expenses) but that advertising campaign expenditures do not. Respondent sees a "decisive difference" between advertising campaign expenditures and advertising execution expenditures in that the former give rise only to long-term benefits while the latter give rise principally to short-term benefits. Respondent analogizes the litigated expenses to advertising campaign expenses and argues that the litigated expenses provide an intangible benefit to Reynolds over the economic lives of the brands to which they attach. Consequently, respondent concludes that the litigated expenses must be capitalized and are not currently deductible business expenses. Respondent also argues that the litigated expenses are neither recurring, day-to-day expenditures nor are they deductible under section 174.

C. *Tax Rules Governing Advertising Expenditures*

1. *Introduction*

Petitioner's principal claim is that "graphic design and advertising activities are indistinguishable in any way that would justify their inconsistent tax treatment". Petitioner supports its claim that graphic design and advertising are indistinguishable by analyzing and comparing the functions of those activities. Respondent attempts to counter petitioner's functional analysis with a functional analysis of his own, candidly conceding, however, that his disagreement with petitioner "is only a matter of degree". Neither party argues that the term "advertising" is a term of art for Federal income tax purposes. Indeed, respondent implicitly concedes that the rules with respect to advertising govern the deductibility of the litigated expenses, although, under respondent's interpretation of those rules, the litigated expenses are not deductible business expenses because they are capital expenses. Moreover, respondent called as an expert witness Mukesh Bajaj, Ph.D., senior associate, Business Valuation Services, Inc. Dr. Bajaj was accepted by the Court as an expert in corporate finance and business valuation, and his written report was received into evidence as his expert testimony. Dr. Bajaj testified that there is an accepted textbook definition of advertising. On cross-examination, he conceded that cigarette package graphic designs qualify as advertising under that definition. On brief, respondent agrees that cigarette pack graphic designs fit the textbook definition of advertising. We are, thus, satisfied that, on the evidence before us, petitioner has proven that the litigated expenses are advertising expenditures, and we so find.

2. *Deductible Business Expenses*

Section 162(a) allows as a deduction "all the ordinary and necessary expenses paid or incurred during the taxable year in carrying on any trade or business". Generally, no deduction is allowed for any capital expenditure. Compare sec. 179 with sec. 263(a)(1). The Supreme Court has held that a taxpayer's expenditure that "serves to create or enhance * * * a separate and distinct" asset must be capitalized. *Commissioner v. Lincoln*

Sav. & Loan Association, 403 U.S. 345, 354 (1971). Subsequently, the Court held that, although the separate-or-distinct-asset standard is a sufficient condition for capitalization, it is not a necessary condition and that an expenditure that gives rise to more than incidental future benefits, whether or not the expenditure gives rise to a separate and distinct asset, may require capitalization. *INDOPCO, Inc. v. Commissioner,* 503 U.S. 79, 87 (1992). "Although the mere presence of an incidental future benefit—'some future aspect'—may not warrant capitalization, a taxpayer's realization of benefits beyond the year in which the expenditure is incurred is undeniably important in determining whether the appropriate tax treatment is immediate deduction or capitalization." *Id.* (emphasis added). We have characterized the inquiry as to whether an expenditure may be deducted under section 162(a) or must be capitalized as "an inquiry into the proper time to give tax effect to the expenditure." *A.E. Staley Manufacturing Co. v. Commissioner,* 105 T.C. 166, 193, revd. and remanded 119 F.3d 482 (7th Cir. 1997). In *A.E. Staley Manufacturing Co.,* we stated that the inquiry is "fact specific", and we described the general nature of the inquiry as follows: "Assuming that the expenditure is ordinary and necessary in the operation of the taxpayer's business, the answer to the question of whether the expenditure is a deduction allowable as a business expense must be determined from the nature of the expenditure itself which in turn depends on the extent and permanence of the work accomplished by the expenditure." *Id.* at 193–194 (quoting 6 Mertens, Law of Federal Income Taxation, sec, 25.37, at 118 (1992 rev.).

3. *Ordinary Business Advertising*

"Advertising" is commonly defined as: "The activity of attracting public attention to a product or business, as by paid announcements in print or on the air." The American Heritage Dictionary of the English Language 26 (3d ed. 1992). A business may advertise principally to attract customers, and there is no doubt that such advertising may contribute to the goodwill enjoyed by the business. "Goodwill", the Supreme Court stated, "is the expectancy of continued patronage". *Newark Morning Ledger Co. v. United States,* 507 U.S. 546, 555–556 (1993) ("the shorthand description of good-will as the expectancy of continued patronage * * * provides a useful label with which to identify the total of all the imponderable qualities that attract customers to the business" (internal quotation marks and citations omitted)). Thus, if an expenditure for ordinary business advertising gives rise to goodwill, then, at least in theory, the proper time to give tax effect to the expenditure may be a period running beyond the taxable year of expenditure. Nevertheless, the regulations interpreting section 162 include "advertising and other selling expenses" among the class of deductible business expenses: "Business expenses deductible from gross income include the ordinary and necessary expenditures directly connected with or pertaining to the taxpayer's trade or business * * * Among the items included in business expenses are * * * advertising and other selling expenses." Section 1.162-1(a), Income Tax Regs. The regulations do not further describe the nature of those advertising and selling expenses (hereafter, without distinction, advertising expenses) that are deductible business expenses, although section 1.162-20(a)(2), Income Tax Regs., provides that expenditures for institutional or "goodwill" advertising that keeps the taxpayer's name before the public are generally deductible business expenses "provided the expenditures are related to the patronage the taxpayer might reasonably expect in the future." The regulations, thus, suggest that expenditures for ordinary business advertising are not subject to the usual inquiry when it comes to the question of the proper time to give tax effect to such an expenditure.

Sections 1.162-1(a) and 20(a)(2), Income Tax Regs., however predates *INDOPCO, Inc. v. Commissioner, supra* at 87, in which the Supreme Court concluded that significant future benefits were "undeniably important" in making the capitalization inquiry. Subsequently, the Commissioner ruled that *INDOPCO, Inc.* does not affect the treatment of advertising expenditures under section 162(a). In pertinent part, Rev. Rul. 92-80, 1992-2 C.B. 57, provides:

> The *Indopco* decision does not affect the treatment of advertising costs under section 162(a) of the Code. These costs are generally deductible under that section even though advertising may have some future effect on business activities, as in the case of institutional or goodwill advertising. See section 1.162-1(a) and section 1.162-20(a)(2) of the regulations. Only in the unusual circumstance where advertising is directed towards obtaining future benefits significantly beyond those traditionally associated with ordinary product advertising or with institutional or goodwill advertising, must the costs of that advertising be capitalized.

Although Rev. Rul. 92-80, *supra,* may raise some question of just what benefits are traditionally associated with ordinary product advertising or with institutional or goodwill advertising, there is no doubt that such traditional benefits include not only patronage but also the expectancy of patronage (i.e., "goodwill"). Compare sec. 1.162-1(a), Income Tax Regs. (deductible business expenses include "advertising and other selling expenses"), with sec. 1.162-20(a)(2), Income Tax Regs. (same as to institutional or goodwill advertising "provided the expenditures are related to the patronage the taxpayer might reasonably expect in the future"). Thus, even if advertising is directed solely at future patronage or goodwill (i.e., ordinary business advertising), Rev. Rul. 92-80, *supra,* indicates that normally the costs are deductible.

The unusual treatment of expenditures for ordinary business advertising manifest in Rev. Rul. 92-80, *supra,* is longstanding. Its genesis is in efforts by taxpayers in the early years of income taxation to capitalize the costs of large-scale advertising campaigns and to amortize the capitalized amounts over a period of years, efforts that were consistently opposed by the Commissioner on the ground that allocating advertising expenditures between current expenses and capital outlays was not feasible. Although the courts did not entirely foreclose the propriety of capitalizing some advertising expenditures, taxpayers found it difficult to prove an appropriate allocation between current and long-term benefits. In time, this insistence on evidence hardened into a rule of law that capitalization is proper only if the taxpayer can establish "that the future benefits can be determined precisely and are not of indefinite duration."

Although the case law admits the possibility of allocation between the short- and long-term benefits of advertising expenditures and, thus, would provide a basis for the Commissioner to insist that a taxpayer prove the portion of his advertising expenditures allocable to current benefits, the authorities previously cited, section 1.162-20(a)(2), Income Tax Regs., and Rev. Rul. 92-80, *supra,* establish that the Secretary and the Commissioner, respectively, have eschewed that approach with respect to ordinary business advertising, even if long-term benefits (e.g., goodwill) are the taxpayer's primary objective.

The result, as a practical matter, is that, notwithstanding certain long-term benefits, expenditures for ordinary business advertising are ordinary business expenses if the taxpayer can show a sufficient connection between the expenditure and the taxpayer's business. Generally, expenditures for billboards, signs, and other tangible assets associated with advertising remain subject to the usual rules with respect to capitalization. See, e.g., *Best Lock Corp. v. Commissioner,* 31 T.C. 1217, 1235 (1959) ("The amounts paid in

1951 and 1952 to produce * * * [a sales catalog] were capital items contributing to earning income for several years in the future and not ordinary and necessary expenses of doing business in 1951 and 1952."); *Alabama Coca-Cola Bottling Co. v. Commissioner*, T.C. Memo. 1969-123 (costs of signs, clocks, and scoreboards, having a useful life of 5 years not deductible business expense). But see *E.H. Sheldon & Co. v. Commissioner*, 214 F.2d 655, 659 (6th Cir. 1954) (expenditures to produce sales catalog likely to be used for several years deductible business expense).

D. *Advertising Campaign Expenditures*

Respondent would have us distinguish between the creation of an advertising campaign and the execution of that campaign: "A marketing [advertising] campaign does not sell anything. It prescribes a long-term intangible marketing concept, its imagery, its theme, and its slogan and/or message. That marketing concept is then portrayed in advertisements with ever-changing art work to maintain customer interest in the campaign." Respondent argues that advertising campaign expenditures are not deductible business expenses because: "The cost of developing a successful marketing campaign is expected to generate benefits for future indefinite business operations." To respondent, advertising campaign expenditures are distinguishable from advertising execution expenditures on the basis that the former are solely long-term oriented, and that is a "decisive difference" foreclosing an immediate deduction.

It is clear, however, that to distinguish advertising campaign expenditures from advertising execution expenditures solely on the basis of the taxpayer's expectations regarding the duration of the expected benefits is insufficient to require capitalization of an advertising expenditure. See sec. 1.162-1(a), 20(a)(2) (providing for the general deductibility of "goodwill" advertising). So long as all of the benefits resulting from advertising campaign expenditures are among the traditional benefits associated with ordinary business advertising, the regulations, as interpreted by respondent's own ruling, Rev. Rul. 92-80, 1992-2 C.B. 57, preclude capitalization.

Nevertheless, respondent argues that advertising campaign expenditures (and, likewise, the litigated expenses) create intangible assets and benefits that are not among the benefits traditionally associated with ordinary business advertising (e.g., goodwill). Respondent describes those benefits of advertising campaign expenditures as certain "legal rights and economic interests" of a long-term nature. Respondent identifies the pertinent legal rights as the Federal statutory rights and common-law trademark rights that attach to "trade dress", a term that the courts have used to describe, "essentially * * * [the] total image and overall appearance" of a product. Respondent identifies the economic interests that are benefitted by the litigated expenses as the various brands of cigarettes to which the litigated expenses pertain. Respondent adopts the term "brand equity" to define the economic value inherent in a successful brand. Dr. Bajaj testified as to the major elements of brand equity: (1) brand name awareness, (2) brand loyalty, (3) perceived quality, and (4) brand association. He describes those elements as follows:

> Brand name awareness comes from advertising, as well as from previous use or from word or mouth. Brand loyalty is primarily a result of being satisfied with the product from prior use. Perceived quality has two main elements: (1) a user understands the product and has an opinion on its quality, [and] (2) advertising and package design can create a "personality" for the product. For example, Mercedes cars are considered luxurious, while Volvo cars are considered safe. * * * Finally, brand associations can be about imagery created through advertising or other means.

Dr. Bajaj is of the opinion that the litigated expenses "created intangible assets that are inseparable from brand equity and goodwill".

Petitioner does not dispute that (1) advertising campaign expenditures (or expenditures for graphic design) may contribute to trade dress or (2) trade dress is protected by law. Petitioner points out, however, that trade dress is in fact also a product of ordinary business advertising, including what respondent labels as advertising executions. See *id.* ("A product's image may be created by words, symbols, collections of colors and designs, or *advertising materials or techniques*" (internal quotation marks omitted; emphasis added.)). Petitioner argues that, in *Philip Morris, Inc. v. Star Tobacco Corp., supra,* the image and overall appearance of the Marlboro brand that Philip Morris sought to protect by its trade dress infringement action was, in substantial part, its advertising executions:

> The trade dress Philip Morris seeks to protect consists of specific manifestations of a Western motif: the picture of a cowboy on a cigarette pack; figures of cowboys who have come over time to be known as the "Marlboro Man"; and those evocative stretches of the Western landscape, not to be found on any map or ordinance survey, called "Marlboro Country."

Id. at 385. Petitioner points out that the parties have stipulated that, with respect to Philip Morris' "Come to Marlboro Country" campaign: "The campaign is characterized by a masculine cowboy image in a rugged western setting. The *individual executions* show the cowboy in various settings—roping a steer, riding a horse into the sunset, etc." Petitioner further cites other trade dress cases holding that a variety of other marketing materials and techniques are subject to trade dress protection. We agree with petitioner's analysis and conclude that *both* advertising campaign expenditures *and* advertising execution expenditures account for at least some of the value of the typical trade dress. Since advertising execution expenditures are ordinary business expenses, we conclude that the long-term benefit associated with trade dress is a benefit traditionally associated with ordinary business advertising. It therefore cannot serve as a basis to require the capitalization of the litigated expenses.

In connection with his discussion of trade dress, respondent refers to the copyright and trademark protection available to the various elements making up trade dress. The parties have stipulated, however, that Reynolds placed notices of copyright on its advertising executions, and exhibits in evidence establish that other companies did the same. Thus, we conclude that copyright protection afforded to copyrightable advertising materials is a traditional benefit associated with ordinary business advertising, and, for that reason, it cannot serve as the basis for requiring the capitalization of the litigated expenses.

With respect to trademark protection, the parties have stipulated that none of the litigated expenses were incurred in connection with the purchase, creation, acquisition, protection, expansion, registration, or defense of a trademark or trade name.

As to the economic interests of Reynolds benefitted by the litigated expenses, petitioner agrees with respondent's expert, Dr. Bajaj, that the litigated expenses created intangible assets that are inseparable from brand equity and goodwill. Indeed, petitioner argues: "[T]he record uniformly shows that *successful* graphic designs, together with *successful* advertising and other marketing activities, combine to build an *overall* brand value or equity—the marketing terms for goodwill." Petitioner argues that, nevertheless, the litigated expenses are deductible. We agree. We think that "brand equity", as described by Dr. Bajaj, represents "goodwill", as we understand that term (i.e., "the expectancy of continued patronage"). That being the case, and goodwill clearly being a traditional benefit associated with ordinary business advertising, we must conclude that the litigated expenses are not capital expenditures simply because they contribute to brand equity.

E. *Conclusion*

We have found that the litigated expenses are advertising expenditures. Respondent classifies the litigated expenses as advertising campaign expenditures and would have us distinguish between such expenditures and advertising execution expenditures on the basis that the latter give rise principally to short-term benefits while the former give rise only to long-term benefits. The experience of our predecessor, the Board of Tax Appeals, and other courts in an earlier era lead us to doubt the sharpness of that distinction. Moreover, no case distinguishes between advertising execution and campaign expenditures, and the long-term, short-term distinction respondent would draw is incompatible with section 1.162-1(a) and 20(a)(2), Income Tax Regs., and Rev. Rul. 92-80, 1992-2 C.B. 57. Respondent's distinction will not hold; the litigated expenses are advertising expenditures that are ordinary business expenses.

Action on Decision
RJR Nabisco, Inc., v. Commissioner
AOD 1999-012 (1999)

We disagree with the rationale of the Tax Court. Rev. Rul. 92-80 should not be read as a concession that package design costs are advertising and, therefore, deductible. In Rev. Rul. 89-23, 1989-1 C.B. 85, modified in Rev. Proc. 98-39, 1998-26 I.R.B. 36, the Service concluded that package design costs are capital expenditures and that package designs have an indeterminate useful life. Rev. Rul. 89-23 states that advertising costs are distinguishable from package design costs (as defined in the ruling) and are deductible either because they are of a recurring nature or because their benefit does not extend beyond the tax year. See Davee v. United States, 444 F.2d 551 (Ct. Cl. 1971). The ruling also states, however, that package design costs are capital expenditures because they more closely resemble nonrecurring promotional or advertising costs that result in benefits which extend beyond the year in which the costs are incurred. See Alabama Coca-Cola Bottling Co. v. Commissioner, T.C. Memo. 1969-123; Cleveland Electric Illuminating Co. v. United States, 7 Cl. Ct. 220 (1985).

The Tax Court characterized graphic design and advertising campaign costs as advertising costs and, based on that characterization, concluded that the costs were deductible under Rev. Rul. 92-80. We believe the Tax Court erred by finding that the Service had conceded the deductibility of advertising costs in Rev. Rul. 92-80 and in not considering Rev. Rul. 89-23. The Service has expressly determined that package design costs are essentially different from deductible advertising costs. We disagree with the opinion and do not acquiesce. We will continue to litigate the treatment of package design costs where appropriate.

Recommendation: Nonacquiescence

Technical Advice Memorandum 9643003
October 25, 1996

Issue

Are production and engineering costs incurred to produce a sound recording "qualified creative expenses" that are excepted from the general rule of §263A?

Facts

Taxpayer, who uses the cash receipts and disbursements method of accounting and files returns on a calendar year, is both employed and self-employed as a A. For his Year 1 tax return, Taxpayer filed a Form 1040, U.S. Individual Income Tax Return, with an attached Schedule C (Form 1040), Profit or Loss From Business (Sole Proprietorship) for his self-employment income. In that same year, Taxpayer composed and recorded several songs on a rough-cut "demo" tape hoping that he would find a record company to produce and distribute his music. The production of the tape required Taxpayer to rent a recording studio, and to hire musicians and a recording engineer. The production costs totaled Amount 1, and the sound engineering costs, Amount 2.

Taxpayer deducted the costs of producing the demo tape as a current expense on his return for Year 1, the year the costs were paid. During an examination of Taxpayer's Year 1 return, the examining agent disallowed these deductions, arguing that the demo tape is a sound recording, sound recordings are tangible personal property, and §263A of the Internal Revenue Code and the regulations thereunder require taxpayers to capitalize the costs of producing tangible personal property.

Taxpayer disagrees with the position of the examining agent. Taxpayer correctly notes that §263A(h) excepts the creative expenses incurred by a writer from capitalization, and "writer" is defined to mean an individual whose personal efforts may reasonably be expected to create a literary manuscript, a musical composition (including any accompanying words), or a dance score. Taxpayer argues that he is a writer that has created a musical composition, his musical composition is recorded on the demo tape, and, therefore, the costs he incurred to produce the demo tape are within the exception provided by the Code for the creative expenses of writers.

Furthermore, Taxpayer argues that the examining agent's position does not reflect the reality of the modern process of creating popular music; many composers of popular music can neither read nor write music, and, therefore, "write" their compositions in a recording studio by recording them on magnetic tape. The taxpayer proposes that the Code should be interpreted to accord him the same treatment it allows a free-lance writer who uses an electric word processor to record his literary creations on a floppy disk. That is, the taxpayer should be allowed a current deduction for the recording costs in the year they were paid.

Taxpayer submitted this request for technical advice to resolve what he perceives to be a lack of uniformity in the treatment of creative expenses incurred by free-lance authors using word processors to record their writings and songwriters composing and recording their works on audio tape.

The examining agent did not request, and we do not express, an opinion of whether the costs incurred by Taxpayer in producing the demo tape were costs incurred in an activity not engaged in for profit under §183.

Law

Section 263A(a) provides in the case of any property to which § 263A applies, the direct costs of the property, and such property's proper share of part or all of those indirect costs that are allocable to such property, shall be included in inventory costs in the case of property which is inventory in the hands of the taxpayer, and shall be capitalized in the case of any other property.

Section 263A(b)(1) provides that § 263A applies to real or tangible personal property produced by the taxpayer.

Section 263A(b) (flush language) additionally provides that for the purposes of § 263A(b)(1), the term "tangible personal property" shall include a film, sound recording, video tape, book, or similar property.

Section 263A(h)(1) provides an exception from the general rule of § 263A for any qualified creative expense.

Section 263A(h)(2) provides the term "qualified creative expense" means any expense which is paid or incurred by an individual in the trade or business of such individual (other than as an employee) of being a writer, photographer, or artist, and which without regard to § 263A would be allowable as a deduction for the taxable year.

Section 263A(h)(2) (flush language), however, provides the term "qualified creative expense" does not include any expense related to printing, photographic plates, motion picture films, video tapes, or similar items.

Section 263A(h)(3)(A) provides the term "writer" means any individual if the personal efforts of such individual create (or may reasonably be expected to create) a literary manuscript, musical composition (including any accompanying words), or a dance score.

Section 263A(h)(3)(C) provides the term "artist" means any individual if the personal efforts of such individual create (or may reasonably be expected to create) a picture, painting, sculpture, statue, etching, drawing, cartoon, graphic design, or original print edition.

Section 1.263A-1(c)(3) of the Income Tax Regulations provides that "capitalize" means, in the case of property that is inventory in the hands of a taxpayer, to include in inventory costs and, in the case of other property, to charge to a capital account or basis.

Section 1.263A-2(a) provides § 263A applies to real property and tangible personal property produced by the taxpayer for use in its trade or business or for sale to its customers.

Section 1.263A-2(a)(1)(i) provides that "produce" includes construct, build, install, manufacture, develop, improve, create, raise, or grow.

Section 1.263A-2(a)(2)(i) provides, in general, § 263A applies to the costs of producing tangible personal property, and not to the costs of producing intangible property.

Section 1.263A-2(a)(2)(ii) provides, for the purposes of determining whether a taxpayer producing intellectual or creative property is producing tangible personal property or intangible property, the term tangible personal property includes films, sound recordings, video tapes, books, and other similar property embodying words, ideas, concepts, images, or sounds by the creator thereof.

Section 1.263A-2(a)(2)(ii)(A)(2) lists sound recordings as an example of tangible personal property and defines "sound recording" as a work that results from the fixation of a series of musical, spoken, or other sounds, regardless of the nature of the material objects, such as discs, tapes, or other phonorecordings, in which such sounds are embodied.

Analysis

Section 263A, enacted in the Tax Reform Act of 1986 (Pub.L. No. 99-514), provides uniform capitalization rules that govern the treatment of costs incurred in the production of property or the acquisition of property for resale.

Section 263A(b) provides that tangible personal property produced by a taxpayer is subject to capitalization. Moreover, this section provides, for the purposes of the uniform capitalization rules, the term "tangible personal property" shall include a film, sound recording, video tape, or similar property. See also 2 H.R.Conf.Rep. No. 841, 99th Cong., 2d Sess. II-308 (1986), 1986-3 (Vol. 4) C.B. 302, 308 n. 1 (Conference Report) ("[T]angible property includes films, sound recordings, video tapes, books, and other similar property embodying words, ideas, concepts, images, or sounds, by the creator thereof.").

A "sound recording" is defined as a work that results from the fixation of a series of musical, spoken, or other sounds, regardless of the nature of the material objects, such as discs, tapes, or other phonorecordings, in which such sounds are embodied. § 1.263A-2(a)(2)(ii)(A)(2).

Thus, the demo tape is a sound recording, is tangible personal property, and is subject to capitalization unless otherwise excepted by the Code.

The Miscellaneous Revenue Act of 1988 (Pub.L. No. 100-647, the "1988 Act") provided an exemption from the capitalization provisions of § 263A for "qualified creative expenses" incurred by free-lance authors, photographers, and artists in the trade or business of being a writer, author, photographer or artist. See § 263A(h). The exemption is retroactive and effective as if included in the Tax Reform Act of 1986. The exemption does not apply to "any expense that is related to printing, photographic plates, motion picture films, video tapes, or similar items." H.R.Conf.Rep. No. 1104, 100th Cong., 2d Sess. II-145 (1988), 1988-3 C.B. 473, 635 (Conference Report); § 263A(h) (flush language).

To be within the "qualified creative expense" exception from § 263A, the expense must meet three requirements: (1) the individual or qualified corporation must have paid or incurred the expense while in the trade or business (other than as an employee) of being a writer, photographer, or artist (as defined in § 263A(h)(3)), (2) the expense must be allowable as a deduction, without regard to § 263A, for the taxable year, and (3) the expense must not be related to printing, photographic plates, motion picture films, video tapes, or similar items ("excluded items").

Our analysis is limited to determining whether the expense of producing the demo tape is included in the term "qualified creative expense," or if it is excluded because it is an expense related to an excluded item.

The expense of recording a musical composition on magnetic tape is not specifically listed in either § 263A(h)(3)(A), the paragraph that defines "writer," or as an excluded cost in the flush language of § 263A(h)(2). The paragraph that defines "writer," however, does except the expense of creating a musical composition, and the demo tape is a recording of Taxpayer's musical composition.

Section 263A(h)(2) provides exception for any expense that meets certain qualifications; the § 263A(h)(2) flush language excludes from the exception the expenses related to certain types of items. Section 263A(h)(3)(A) defines who is a "writer." In defining who is a writer, the paragraph also defines the creative property to which the expense must relate to be excepted from capitalization. The paragraph does not provide that every creative expense of a writer is exempt from capitalization. Together, the flush language and the paragraph limit the forms a writer's creation may take and still be excepted from capitalization.

For example, paragraphs (2) and (3) of subsection (h) provide the expense of a literary manuscript created by a free-lance writer is a qualified creative expense excepted from capitalization, but the flush language provides the term "qualified creative expense" does not include the expenses related to a motion picture film. Thus, if the free-lance writer created a literary manuscript, and then created a motion picture film to express his literary manuscript, the expense of the motion picture film would not be a qualified creative expense because a motion picture film is an excluded item. Similarly, if a writer creates a musical composition, and then creates a sound recording of the musical composition, if the expense of the sound recording is an expense related to a "similar item" (an item that is similar to an excluded item specifically identified in the flush language), the cost of producing the sound recording is not a qualified creative expense.

The plain meaning of § 263A(h)(3)(A) is to define a "writer" as a person who creates by writing. Thus, the exception for qualified creative expenses is limited to written creations. This is true even if the creation is a musical composition; the excepted medium for communicating the musical composition is a writing, not a sound recording. The demo tape produced by Taxpayer is an expression of his musical composition, however, it is not a writing that fits within the narrow exception to the general rule.

Furthermore, the demo tape is a "similar item," and the cost of producing the tape is expressly excluded from the definition of a qualified creative expense. Motion picture films and video tapes are specifically identified as examples of both tangible personal property and items that are not qualified creative expenses. A sound recording is specifically identified only as an example of tangible personal property. It is reasonable, however, to conclude that if in one subsection a sound recording is property similar to a film and a video tape, it is an item similar to a motion picture film and a video tape in another subsection of the same section. Thus, our conclusion is based on the similarity of the items specifically identified in the § 263A(h)(2) flush language as excluded from the term "qualified creative expenses" to the property specifically identified in § 263A(b) as tangible personal property, and the provision in each subsection for "similar property" or "similar items."

Moreover, Notice 89-67, 1989-1 C.B. 723, in its discussion of the amendments to § 263A made by the Technical and Miscellaneous Revenue Act of 1988, states "[t]he exemption [for qualified creative expenses] under section 6026(a) of the 1988 Act does not apply to any expense that is related to printing, photographic plates, motion picture films, sound recordings, video tapes, or similar items." Notice 89-67, 1989-1 C.B. at 724 (emphasis added).

Conclusion

Production and engineering costs incurred to produce a sound recording are not § 263A(h) "qualified creative expenses," and therefore the costs of producing a sound recording are not exempt from the general rule of § 263A.

I.R.S. Notice 88-62
1988-1 C.B. 548

APPLICATION OF UNIFORM CAPITALIZATION RULES TO AUTHORS AND OTHER PRODUCERS OF "CREATIVE PROPERTIES"

This notice provides guidance to certain authors, photographers, artists, and other similarly situated persons regarding the uniform capitalization rules under section 263A of the Internal Revenue Code.

I. Background.

Section 263A of the Code, enacted in the Tax Reform Act of 1986 (Pub. L. 99-514, the "1986 Act"), provides uniform capitalization rules that govern the treatment of costs incurred in the production of property or the acquisition of property for resale. Section 263A was enacted, in part, to prevent the inappropriate mismatching of income and expense that resulted from the current deduction of the costs of producing or acquiring property.

Section 263A(b) of the Code generally provides that the uniform capitalization rules apply to the "production" (including the development or improvement) of real or tangible personal property produced by the taxpayer. Moreover, this section provides that, for purposes of the uniform capitalization rules, the term "tangible personal property" shall include a film, sound recording, video tape, book, or similar property.... Based on section 263A(b) and its accompanying legislative history, section 1.263A-1T(a)(5)(iii) of the regulations provides, for example, that section 263A requires the capitalization by authors of the costs of researching, preparing and writing literary works. Similar rules apply to the production of other properties enumerated as tangible properties in section 263A(b).

For example, costs required to be capitalized under section 263A by authors and other similar persons consist of the costs of creating, researching, writing and preparing the literary works and other properties being produced, including costs of travel undertaken for business purposes (e.g., research); depreciation, rent and repairs on equipment and facilities used in producing the properties; all labor and compensation costs (including pension costs, where applicable) of any persons involved in the production activity; office overhead; interest (where required under section 263A(f)); and any other direct or indirect costs relating to the production of such properties as described in 1.263A-1T(b)(2) of the regulations.

Taxpayers are required to allocate and capitalize costs to the particular properties being produced, and to recover such costs under other applicable provisions of the Code. *See, e.g.,* section 167 (depreciation); Rev. Rul. 60-358, 1960-2 C.B. 68, *Siegel v. Commissioner*, 78 T.C. 659 (1982) (income forecast method); section 1.61-3(a) of the regulations (cost of goods sold).

II. Authority and Need for Safe Harbor.

The Internal Revenue Service has received numerous inquiries from authors, photographers and other persons expressing concern regarding the application of the uniform capitalization rules to their businesses. These concerns have focused both on the allocation and capitalization of costs under section 263A, as well as the amortization or recovery of these capitalized costs under other sections of the Code.

The legislative history of section 263A indicates that Congress was aware of the possible administrative complexities resulting from the application of the uniform capitalization rules to businesses. In response to this concern, Congress granted the Treasury Department authority under section 263A to "adopt other simplifying methods and assumptions where, in the judgment of the Secretary of the Treasury, the costs and other burdens of literal compliance may outweigh the benefits." S. Rep. 99-313, 99th Cong., 2d Sess. 141-42 (1986).

Moreover, in the preamble to temporary regulations under section 263A, published in the Federal Register on March 30, 1987 (52 FR 10057, T.D. 8131), the Internal Revenue Service generally solicited comments and suggestions regarding the use of simplified methods in complying with the uniform capitalization rules under section 263A. In response to this request for comments, the Internal Revenue Service has received numerous suggestions from taxpayers asking that additional simplified methods be provided for individual authors, photographers, and other taxpayers creating various types of property.

III. Elective Safe Harbor—In General.

Based on the foregoing, this notice provides an elective three-year "safe harbor" for certain authors and other taxpayers with respect to their capitalization of costs under section 263A and the recovery or amortization of such costs under other sections of the Code.

Under the three-year safe harbor provided herein, taxpayers shall aggregate and capitalize all "qualified creative costs" incurred during each taxable year and shall amortize and deduct 50 percent of such aggregate costs in the year they are incurred, 25 percent of such costs in the year following the year in which they are incurred, and the final 25 percent of such costs in the second year following the year in which they are incurred.

The three-year safe harbor provided in this notice substantially reduces the administrative complexities of complying with the uniform capitalization rules by eliminating the necessity to amortize the capitalized costs under the income forecast method for taxpayers otherwise required to use such method. (The income forecast method requires the taxpayer to estimate the future expected income to be received from the property in issue, in addition to only allowing the taxpayer to amortize the property's capitalized costs for the periods during which the taxpayer recognizes income from such property).

Moreover, the three-year safe harbor provided here eliminates any need for the taxpayer to allocate total costs incurred in the taxpayer's trade or business between (i) costs that are required to be capitalized under section 263A and costs that are permitted to be expensed; and (ii) costs incurred with respect to separate properties produced by the taxpayer (e.g., various manuscripts being created by an author). It is anticipated that the 50 percent portion of total aggregate qualified creative costs deducted in the year such costs are incurred under the safe harbor, reasonably approximates the amounts of both otherwise deductible costs incurred during that taxable year and the amortization of costs required to be capitalized under section 263A for that year.

IV. Properties Covered By Safe Harbor.

This three-year safe harbor is available only for the qualified creative costs paid or incurred ("incurred") in producing "creative properties" defined as films, sound recordings, video tapes, books (including, for example, articles and poems), photographs, plays and other dramatic works, musical and dance compositions (including accompanying words), graphic and pictorial compositions, fine art paintings and sculptures, and other similar fine art products (but not including jewelry).

No other properties other than those defined herein as creative properties are eligible for this safe harbor. For example, section 263A is itself applicable, in part, to the production of a film, sound recording, video tape, book or "similar property." The term "similar property" in section 263A is not limited to properties which are defined as creative properties in this notice. Thus, the term "similar property" in section 263A may include specific types of properties other than, and in addition to, the properties defined herein as being eligible for the three-year safe harbor. Similarly, certain properties (*e.g.*, paintings and sculptures) defined as creative properties for purposes of this notice are tangible properties and hence subject to the capitalization rules of section 263A without reference to the provisions of section 263A(b) providing that certain enumerated properties shall be treated as tangible for purposes of the uniform capitalization rules.

Taxpayers electing to use the three-year safe harbor in accounting for the costs of producing any creative property to which this three-year safe harbor applies shall be deemed to have also elected to use the three-year safe harbor in accounting for the production of any other creative property to which the safe harbor applies. Thus, for example, a taxpayer producing both books and films who elects to use the three-year safe harbor in accounting for the production of the books must also use the three-year safe harbor with respect to the production of the films.

V. Qualified Creative Costs—In General.

The three-year safe harbor provided herein only applies to "qualified creative costs" which are defined as certain costs incurred by a self-employed individual (except as provided in section VIII herein), in the production of creative properties where the personal efforts of such individual predominantly create such properties. Qualified creative costs do not include the costs paid or incurred by a person in his capacity as an employee, nor do they include costs incurred by an individual in producing creative properties where the personal efforts of such individual do not predominantly create such properties (*e.g.*, where the properties are predominantly created by persons other than the individual such as employees or independent contractors).

With respect to any properties predominantly created by employees of the individual or by independent contractors hired by the individual, the provisions of this safe harbor are not available in accounting for the costs of producing such properties under section 263A. (Qualified creative costs do, however, include amounts paid by an individual to employees or independent contractors assisting in the production of the creative properties, if the personal efforts of such individual predominantly create such properties.)

Moreover, except as provided in section VIII herein, qualified creative costs do not include costs incurred by any person other than an individual. For example, except as provided in section VIII, qualified creative costs do not include costs incurred by a partnership, trust, or corporation.

For purposes of the three-year safe harbor, qualified creative costs consist of all costs incurred by the taxpayer in the trade or business or activity conducted for profit (collectively, "trade or business") of producing creative properties that would be otherwise deductible under the Internal Revenue Code of 1986, excluding the provisions of section 263A. Thus, qualified creative costs consist of: (i) all costs required to be capitalized under section 263A and the regulations thereunder with respect to the production of creative properties ("section 263A costs"); and (ii) all other costs incurred and otherwise deductible by the taxpayer in the trade or business of producing creative properties.

VI. Qualified Creative Costs — Examples.

Qualified creative costs eligible for this safe harbor would generally include, for example, depreciation deductions taken with respect to a computer or automobile (*i.e.*, equipment and facilities) used to produce creative properties, since these costs are required to be capitalized under section 263A as a cost of producing such properties. In contrast, qualified creative costs would not include the costs of purchasing a computer or an automobile that will be used to produce creative properties because, although such purchase costs are capitalized (*see, e.g.*, section 263), they are not capitalized under section 263A as costs of producing creative properties. Moreover, such costs are not otherwise deductible by the taxpayer.

Qualified creative costs also include all other costs incurred by the taxpayer that would be otherwise deductible in the trade or business of producing creative properties. Thus, such costs include the costs of marketing, selling, advertising and distributing creative properties undertaken by an individual in the trade or business of producing creative properties. For example, costs incurred by a taxpayer in promoting or selling a finished manuscript or photograph would be qualified creative costs and thus would be subject to the provisions of this three-year safe harbor. In addition, qualified creative costs include all office overhead (*e.g.*, general and administrative costs), and all otherwise deductible interest expense incurred in the trade or business of producing creative properties, regardless of whether such costs would be required to be capitalized under section 263A.

Moreover, qualified creative costs include the costs of producing properties that are sold (or otherwise disposed of, in their entirety) by the taxpayer in the same taxable year that such costs are incurred. For example, costs incurred by a taxpayer in writing an article (or producing a photograph) that the taxpayer sells in its entirety to a magazine in the same year that the costs are incurred would be qualified creative costs and thus would be subject to this three-year safe harbor.

Similarly, costs incurred by a taxpayer in a hobby are not qualified creative costs eligible for this safe harbor because (i) such costs are not section 263A costs; and (ii) qualified creative costs only consist of costs incurred in a trade or business or an activity conducted for profit.

VII. Mechanics of Three-Year Safe Harbor.

Assume, for example, that a photographer elects to use the three-year safe harbor beginning in 1987 when the taxpayer incurs a total of $16,000 in qualified creative costs consisting of all the taxpayer's section 263A costs, and all other costs incurred that year in the photography business that would be otherwise deductible by the taxpayer. Under the three-year safe harbor, the photographer would capitalize $16,000 of costs in 1987 and would expense $8,000 of these costs in 1987, and $4,000 of these costs in each of 1988 and 1989. In addition, assume that the photographer incurs a total of $20,000 in qualified creative costs in 1988. The photographer would capitalize $20,000 of costs in 1988 and would expense $10,000 of these costs in 1988, and $5,000 of these costs in each of 1989 and 1990.

VIII. Availability of Safe-Harbor to Certain Entities.

The three-year safe harbor may be used with respect to a corporation or partnership engaged in the trade or business of producing creative properties (an "eligible corporation" or "eligible partnership"), but only if the requirements of this section VIII are met. A corporation or partnership may use the three-year safe harbor if substantially all of such entity is owned by one "qualified employee owner", as defined herein. For purposes of this provision, ownership by any members of such qualified employee owner's family, as defined in section 267(c)(4) of the Code, shall be treated as ownership by the qualified employee owner.

A qualified employee owner shall be deemed to own substantially all of a corporation if such individual owns at least 95 percent (by value) of the stock of such corporation. Similarly, a qualified employee owner shall be deemed to own substantially all of a partnership if such individual has an interest in partnership profits and capital of at least 95 percent.

A qualified employee owner is an individual employed by an eligible corporation or eligible partnership where the personal efforts of such qualified employee owner produce creative properties for such corporation or partnership. Moreover, "qualified creative costs" eligible for this safe harbor only include costs incurred in the production of creative properties where the personal efforts of the qualified employee owner predominantly create such properties. Qualified creative costs do not include any of the costs of creating properties where the personal efforts of the qualified employee owner do not predominantly create such properties (*e.g.*, where the properties are predominantly created by persons other than the qualified employee owner such as other employees or independent contractors). With respect to any properties predominantly created by persons other than the qualified employee owner, the provisions of this safe harbor are not available in accounting for the costs of producing such properties under section 263A.

Any corporation or partnership meeting the requirements of this section VIII may use the three-year safe harbor provided in this notice in accounting for qualified creative costs, subject to all the requirements, conditions and procedures of this notice applicable to individuals electing such safe harbor (except where expressly noted).

IX. Election to Use Three-Year Safe Harbor

Taxpayers may automatically elect to use the three-year safe harbor by determining and reporting their taxable income under such safe harbor on a timely filed (with regard to extensions) Federal income tax return for the first taxable year to which the provisions of section 263A apply to the particular taxpayer's production of creative properties.

Taxpayers automatically electing to use the three-year safe harbor on a Federal income tax return shall note such election of the safe harbor by typing or legibly printing the following statement at the top of page 1 of Schedule C (Form 1040): "Three-Year Safe Harbor Adopted Under the Provisions of Notice 88-62." With respect to corporations and partnerships automatically electing to use the three-year safe harbor, such statement shall be provided on the top of Schedule A, Form 1120, or Schedule A, Form 1065, respectively.

Except as otherwise provided in this notice, taxpayers may not elect the use of the three-year safe harbor for any taxable year, unless consent to such change in method of accounting is obtained from the Commissioner. Moreover, taxpayers electing to use this three-year safe harbor may not discontinue such use unless consent to such change in method of accounting is obtained from the Commissioner.

Vitale v. Commissioner
T.C. Memo. 1999-131

FAY, JUDGE:

Respondent determined deficiencies in petitioner's 1993 and 1994 Federal income taxes in the respective amounts of $4,256 and $6,702.

The issues for decision are: (1) Whether petitioner was in the trade or business of being an author during the years in issue; if so, (2) whether expenses that petitioner incurred are deductible as ordinary and necessary under section 162 and whether he has adequately substantiated under section 274(d) his travel expenses.

FINDINGS OF FACT

Some of the facts have been stipulated and are so found. The stipulation of facts and second stipulation of facts, together with the exhibits attached thereto and exhibits offered at trial, are incorporated herein by this reference. Petitioner resided in Arlington, Virginia, when he filed his petition.

Petitioner holds a bachelor's degree in marketing and advertising from the University of Maryland. Towards completion of that degree, he earned more than 24 credit hours of study in English, journalism, and speech. Petitioner worked 40 hours per week for the U.S. Department of the Treasury (hereinafter Treasury) as a budget analyst until January 1997, when he retired after more than 35 years of service. He had been employed at a GS-12 pay grade. As part of his job, he was required to "write budget justifications, procedures, and other written material by applying professional level writing ability to create high quality written work." In an office staffed mostly by accountants, petitioner was often the one delegated to perform writing-based tasks, such as contributing to the Federal Managers' Financial Integrity Act report, in which agencies evaluate their internal control and accounting systems. At some point during his employment, petitioner also served as editor of an in-house newsletter of the Treasury.

In 1992, approximately 2 years before petitioner became eligible to retire, he began writing outside of his full-time job. At trial, petitioner testified that he was "fearful of the concept of retirement" and began writing in 1992 with the hope of making it his second career. The first book-length manuscript he began writing was a fictional piece titled "Lightning at Dawn". Later that same year, petitioner wrote a collection of short stories called "Boys and Girls Together". Before marketing these manuscripts for publication, petitioner had an idea for another book—a story about the experiences of two men who travel cross-country to patronize a legal brothel in Nevada. In early 1993, petitioner wrote an 18,000-word draft of this basic story line, which he submitted for copyright protection in June.[4] In order to authenticate the story and develop characters for the book, petitioner visited numerous legal brothels in Nevada by acting as a customer for prostitutes.

In a journal describing his experiences at the brothels, petitioner recorded the brothels he visited, the dates (and sometimes the hours) of his visits, the prostitutes he met, and the amount of cash he paid each one. For each entry, petitioner wrote about his visit with the prostitute and about the happenings at brothels in general. For example,

---

4. Petitioner's two previous works, "Lightning at Dawn" and "Boys and Girls Together", were also copyrighted in 1993.

he described the manner in which he selected her, the house rules of the brothel, the manner in which he negotiated a price for her time, their dialogue, and the type of clothing worn by her. He also included personal information on the prostitute, including her age, physical characteristics, city or State of residence, religious background, ethnicity, level of education, and the name and age of her offspring, if any. The journal indicates that, at some point during these meetings, petitioner told the prostitutes that he was writing a book about Nevada's legal brothels and that he wished to use them as characters in his book. The journal shows that, during 1993, petitioner spent, on average, 3 days per month (except during the months of February, May, and December) meeting with prostitutes at the brothels.

Using the material that he gathered during these meetings (hereinafter sometimes referred to as interviews), petitioner produced a manuscript called "Searchlight, Nevada" which he submitted for publication. On October 13, 1993, petitioner entered into an agreement for its publication with Northwest Publishing, Inc. (Northwest). In pertinent part, the agreement provided that,

(1) Petitioner was to pay Northwest $4,375 to publish 10,000 copies of his book;

(2) of the 10,000 copies printed, Northwest would (a) give 100 free copies to petitioner; (b) give away 200 copies to major bookstores and book reviewers; (c) sell 2,500 copies through its "test market program"; and (d) sell the remaining books in the retail marketplace;

(3) petitioner would be paid 40% of the retail amount of each book sold through the test market program, and a royalty equal to 15% of the retail price of any remaining books sold to bookstores and wholesalers;

(4) Northwest was to pay royalties on January 31 and July 31 of each year, along with interest penalties for late payments;

(5) Northwest was to do a certain amount of sales promotion, advertising, and publicity; and

(6) Northwest was to have exclusive rights to the book.

Representatives of Northwest had told petitioner that his book would probably earn him at least $20,000 in royalties.

"Searchlight, Nevada" was published by Northwest and released in December 1995 at a retail price of $7.95. The book is 131 pages long and has an international standard book number. It was available for immediate purchase at Barnes & Noble Booksellers in Boynton Beach, Florida, and Falls Church, Virginia, and at Super Crown Books, store # 106. The book could also be purchased by special order at Borders Books and Music in Baileys Crossroads, Virginia.

Prior to the book's being released, petitioner played an active role in all stages of its publication. In 1994, after reviewing the first galley proofs, petitioner inquired about adding two additional chapters to the novel. Then by letter dated February 27, 1995, petitioner made detailed suggestions for the book's cover design and attached pictures of how he thought the characters on the cover should look. Petitioner closed the letter with the following words:

> Any additional assistance I can provide will be done gladly. I realize that the cover design is as important as the story on the inside. It doesn't matter if the story is good if we fail to motivate the reader into purchasing [sic] the book.

* * *

> Perhaps with our joint venture on "Searchlight, Nevada" we can add a hot seller to * * * [Northwest's] catalog. I'd like us to sell over 100,000 copies.

Petitioner also actively participated in the promotion of his book. He provided Northwest's public relations department with mailing lists and telephone numbers of bookstores, newspapers, magazines, and radio and motion picture companies. Petitioner, on his own, mailed about 60 complimentary copies of his book, along with individualized letters, to bookstores, newspapers, magazines, and hotels. He worked with a marketing expert at Northwest to get his book stocked by distributors, and to set up book signings at major bookstores. When petitioner was unhappy with the contents of his press release, he rewrote it and sent his changes to Northwest. Moreover, when petitioner became dissatisfied with Northwest's marketing efforts, he wrote a letter demanding that the publishing company comply with the terms of its agreement.

By letter dated January 22, 1996, Northwest's account executive informed petitioner that 6,800 copies of his book had been ordered and shipped, and that another 2,500 copies had been ordered by the Books By Millions chain. The letter also stated that Northwest's royalty statements would be mailed in approximately 3 weeks. On his 1996 Federal income tax return, petitioner reported $2,600 in gross royalties from his writing activity.

In late 1993, after petitioner had signed an agreement with Northwest to have "Searchlight, Nevada" published, he began research on another book, "Nevada Nights, San Joaquin Dawn". He wanted to document the difficulties that women face in their attempt to break free from a life of prostitution, because, as "the story's never been done before to any degree of authenticity", he thought it commercially viable. After discovering that the rooms at the brothels were equipped with listening devices, he began meeting the women at other locations on "out calls," which he paid for by personal credit card. In 1994, during the months of January, February, April, May, June, and July, petitioner spent anywhere from 1 to 6 days per month in Nevada on out calls with prostitutes. He successfully encouraged 10 prostitutes to leave their profession. As of the trial date, petitioner had not yet completed "Nevada Nights, San Joaquin Dawn".

Some time after a contract had been signed for the publication of "Searchlight, Nevada", petitioner submitted another manuscript to Northwest for consideration; i.e., "Lightning at Dawn", which was about 450 pages in length. He was under the impression that Northwest required a joint venture payment for first novels only, and that, if Northwest agreed to publish "Lightning at Dawn", he would have to pay nothing. Petitioner also attempted to market "Boys and Girls Together", but he ceased his efforts when he was told that there was no need or market for short stories at that time.

On May 1, 1996, 4 months after "Searchlight, Nevada" had been on the market, Northwest filed for bankruptcy protection. The corporation had been the subject of a continuing investigation by State authorities. On November 8, 1996, petitioner filed a proof of claim with the U.S. Bankruptcy Court for the District of Utah in the amount of $17,854 for unpaid royalties and breach of contract.

After securing the return of his rights in "Searchlight, Nevada", petitioner began soliciting other publishing houses to have his book published a second time. Petitioner received several responses, including a request by the president of Regnery Publishing, Inc., and an invitation by the editor-in-chief of Farrar, Straus & Giroux, Inc., to submit his manuscript for review. He also began to send letters to literary agents soliciting their interest in his book. At the time of trial, petitioner had since rewritten parts of "Searchlight, Nevada" and had sent his revised manuscript to Paladin Press of Boulder, Colorado, at its request. Petitioner also received a letter from Neal Sperling, a Hollywood script agent, requesting that he submit a plot summary of his book for consideration as a made-for-television movie or feature film. Petitioner is presently a member of Washington Independent Writers, The Authors Guild, Poets and Writers, and Writers Market Book Club. During the years in issue, petitioner spent approximately 25–35 hours per week on his writing activity.

Apart from that activity, petitioner reported the following income on his Federal income tax returns:

	1993	1994
Wages	$53,076	$54,243
Dividend income	6,111	4,847
State/local tax refund	174	999
Capital gain (loss)	(3,000)	(3,000)
Total	56,361	57,089

In 1993, petitioner began treating his writing activity as a trade or business. From that year on, he began filing a Schedule C (Profit or Loss From Business), in which he listed his principal business or profession as author.

For the years in issue, petitioner reported no income from his writing activity but claimed the following as deductible expenses on his Schedules C:

	1993	1994
Advertising	—	$100
Commissions and fees	$40	80
Office expense	420	600
Supplies	150	—
Travel	4,230	9,195
Meals and entertainment	2,520	786
Utilities	—	657
Other expenses	7,830	12,099
Total	15,190	23,517

For 1993, the item denominated "other expenses" consists of a $4,350 joint venture payment to Northwest and $3,480 in cash payments to prostitutes. For 1994, other expenses consist of the following: $2,349 for the purchase of a computer, supplies, and furniture; $480 for mailing expenses; $313 for membership dues; $5,660 for credit card expenses on out calls; $1,295 for tuition and books; $500 for sponsoring a race car team; and $1,502 for miscellaneous other expenses.

Petitioner's travel and meal deductions include expenditures for airfares, rental car expenses, food, and lodging in connection with his travels to Nevada. For the years in issue, the record contains documentary evidence of petitioner's travel and meal expenses; i.e., airline tickets and travel schedules, and hotel, restaurant, rental car, and credit card receipts.

With respect to petitioner's interviews, he characterized the amounts he paid to the prostitutes as business related depending upon whether information gleaned from the interviews was used in his books. Petitioner has personal credit card receipts for 1994 supporting the expenditures he incurred to interview prostitutes away from the brothels. Petitioner does not have receipts of his cash expenditures in 1993 for the interviews that took place at the brothels. Nor does petitioner have records supporting his deductions for advertising, commissions and fees, office expenses, supplies, utilities, or those expenses comprising "other expenses" for 1994 (with the exception of the interviews).

Around the time of the parties' preparation of a stipulation of facts, petitioner prepared a five-page reconstruction of his expenditures, using information reflected on airline tickets and itineraries, hotel and rental car bills, credit card receipts, and petitioner's own memory. This included summary statements for 1993 and 1994, a flight log, and a log of his interviews.

In the notice of deficiency, respondent disallowed under sections 162 and 183 all of the expenses claimed on petitioner's Schedules C for the years in issue because "it has not been shown that * * * [petitioner] either started a trade or business or entered into an activity for profit. * * * [Nor has he] established that any amount was for an ordinary and necessary business expense".

OPINION

Section 162(a) generally allows a deduction for all ordinary and necessary business expenses paid or incurred during the taxable year in carrying on any trade or business. To be engaged in a trade or business within the meaning of section 162, "the taxpayer must be involved in the activity with continuity and regularity and * * * the taxpayer's primary purpose for engaging in the activity must be for income or profit." *Commissioner v. Groetzinger*, 480 U.S. 23, 35 (1987).

We are satisfied that petitioner's writing activity was conducted with continuity and regularity during the years in issue. Nevertheless, in order for an activity to be considered a trade or business within the meaning of section 162, a taxpayer must conduct the activity with the requisite profit motive or intent. See *id.*

Petitioner argues that he engaged in his writing activity with the intent to make a profit and that his Schedule C expenses for tax years 1993 and 1994 were ordinary and necessary to his endeavor as an author. Respondent does not dispute that amounts were in fact expended, but rather contests their deductibility. Respondent maintains petitioner was not engaged in the trade or business of being an author, and, accordingly, expenses incurred for the writing (and publication of one) of his books are not business expenses deductible under section 162(a). Rather, he argues, they are deductible only to the extent of the income derived from the activity under section 183.[12] Alternatively, if the activity is found to have been entered into for profit, respondent asserts that the claimed expenses were not properly deductible as ordinary and necessary under section 162 and that certain expenses were not adequately substantiated under section 274(d). At trial, respondent conceded that, with respect to section 274(d), the only element of substantiation lacking in this case is business purpose.

Petitioner bears the burden of proving by a preponderance of the evidence that he was engaged in writing for profit. Rule 142(a). The test of whether a taxpayer engaged in an activity for profit is whether he entered into, or continued, the activity with an actual and honest objective of making a profit. Although the taxpayer's expectation of

---

12. Sec. 183 was enacted to codify the distinction between a business and a hobby and to prohibit a taxpayer from obtaining a loss from an activity considered to be a hobby which was then used to offset other income. See S. Rept. 91-552, at 104 (1969), 1969-3 C. B. 423, 490.

profit need not be reasonable, it must be bona fide, as determined from all the surrounding facts and circumstances. Thus, whether the requisite profit motive exists is a factual question that must be determined upon the record, with more weight given to objective facts than to petitioner's statement of intent.

The Treasury regulations list nine factors as an aid in making the profit objective determination. They include: (1) The manner in which the taxpayer carried on the activity; (2) the expertise of the taxpayer or his advisers; (3) the time and effort expended by the taxpayer in carrying on the activity; (4) the expectation that the assets used in the activity may appreciate in value; (5) the success of the taxpayer in carrying on other similar or dissimilar activities; (6) the taxpayer's history of income or loss with respect to the activity; (7) the amount of occasional profits that are earned; (8) the financial status of the taxpayer; and (9) whether elements of personal pleasure or recreation are involved. No one factor is conclusive, and we do not reach our decision herein by merely counting the factors that support each party's position. See sec. 1.183-2(b), Income Tax Regs. Moreover, certain factors are given more weight than others because they are more meaningfully applied to the facts in this case. Respondent concedes that the fourth element, the expectation that assets used in the activity may appreciate in value, is inapplicable to the present case.

Taking into account the above factors and considering the record as a whole, we conclude that, during the years in issue, petitioner had a bona fide intention to derive a profit from his writing activity. In addition to petitioner's testimony, which we found to be credible and forthright, the evidence in the record shows an intent and effort by petitioner to engage in and continue in the writing field with the purpose of producing income and a livelihood.

We first look to the manner in which petitioner carried on the activity. Petitioner managed some aspects of this activity in a businesslike fashion. He kept bills, receipts, and schedules for his traveling expenses, and he kept a contemporaneous journal to substantiate cash expenditures that he incurred to interview prostitutes at the brothels, for which receipts were not available. Petitioner was able to use his records, including credit card statements, to compile logs for 1993 and 1994, showing his travel dates, the dates, times, and places of his interviews, the names of the prostitutes he interviewed, the per hour charges he negotiated, and his method of payment. While petitioner may not have kept a separate checking account or a well-organized set of books, he did attempt to keep an accurate account of the expenses he incurred to research his books. The record also indicates that, after signing a contract for the publication of "Searchlight, Nevada", petitioner made concerted efforts to promote his book. He took steps to gain maximum personal benefit from Northwest by working closely with its public relations department to ensure that his book was widely advertised and readily available in bookstores. Petitioner then supplemented Northwest's efforts by adopting various methods of his own, while, at the same time, remaining active as an author by writing other manuscripts. Furthermore, when Northwest filed for bankruptcy protection, petitioner did not abandon his writing activity; rather, he sought the return of his rights in "Searchlight, Nevada", and began an extensive search for a new publisher. He had rewritten and revised his manuscript, in an effort to make it more salable to the public, and thus, more attractive to prospective publishers. As an alternative marketing technique, petitioner also made attempts to engage a literary agent. In sum, although petitioner could have been more organized in keeping track of his expenditures, his efforts to make a financial success of his writing activity show a profit objective.

The fact that petitioner did not seek expert advice on how to start or maintain a business as a fiction writer does weigh against his argument that he carried on the activity in a businesslike manner. While petitioner had writing skills, it appears that they were mainly in the technical field of budget analysis. However, it is important to consider that petitioner used his writing skills extensively in his job at Treasury, where he worked for more than 30 years. Moreover, by virtue of his job assignments and performance rating, petitioner was led to believe that writing was his strong point. Although his success at Treasury is not a reasonable predictor of his success as a fiction writer, his prior writing experience is not unrelated to his anticipated performance as a writer in another field. We also note that petitioner has a bachelor's degree in marketing and advertising, which suggests that he has more than a basic familiarity with the business side of his writing activity. It is apparent from the record that petitioner took great interest in the commercial aspects of his endeavor.

The third factor in the regulations focuses on the time and effort expended by the taxpayer in carrying on the activity. There is little question that, during the years at issue, petitioner spent numerous hours per week on his writing activity; i.e., doing research, writing manuscripts, soliciting publishers, and conferring in the early stages of publication. Respondent emphasizes that petitioner worked 40 hours per week as a budget analyst and suggests that his writing activity could not rise to the level of a trade or business because he also had a full-time job. We disagree with respondent. Petitioner's employment at Treasury does not preclude the possibility that his writing activity constituted a separate trade or business. We have recognized that a taxpayer may engage in more than one trade or business at any one time. It is also well settled that the term "trade or business" includes the arts. Furthermore, as we stated in *Dickson v. Commissioner*, T.C. Memo. 1986-182, "[Taxpayer's] maintaining a full-time job * * * in addition to his profit-seeking activities is a positive factor reflecting his motivation, rather than respondent's attempt at negative inference from the fact that petitioner devoted time to other activities."

The fifth factor, the success of the taxpayer in carrying on other similar or dissimilar activities, does not influence our analysis because petitioner has not previously engaged in a writing activity. We accept petitioner's testimony at trial that he was best known at Treasury for his writing ability and that he was often called upon to perform writing-based tasks. This may have contributed to petitioner's belief that he could make money as an author. Moreover, we are convinced that petitioner viewed his agreement with Northwest as offering a real potential for generating profit.

The next two factors, the taxpayer's history of income or losses with respect to the activity and the amount of occasional profits, if any, which are earned, are examined in tandem. Respondent argues that petitioner's continuous record of losses from his activity is persuasive evidence that he was not engaged in this activity for profit. Petitioner argues that, while his efforts as an author have not proved profitable up to this time, his hard work will be rewarded with substantial income when his search for a new publisher proves successful.

It is undisputed that petitioner did report a loss in each year of operation. However, there are two important facts in this case which should be considered with respect to these losses.

First, section 1.183-2(b)(6), Income Tax Regs., states that losses incurred during the startup phase of a business are not necessarily indicative of a lack of profit motive. Because petitioner did not begin treating his writing activity as a trade or business until 1993, the tax years in issue mark the initial stages of his activity. A significant amount of petitioner's total deductions for 1993 and 1994 were travel expenses, which he incurred to collect material for his books. Now that such material has been amassed and incorporated in the manuscripts, petitioner, as a published author, expects his writing activity to be profitable. To remedy the unforeseeable circumstance of his publisher's going bankrupt, petitioner has demonstrated that he has ideas and plans for future publications which would enable him to recoup not only his expenses, but also to make a profit.

Second, these losses should be viewed in the context of the nature of petitioner's activity. Works of fiction are difficult to write and to market. We are persuaded by petitioner's statement that first-time authors are not normally offered cash advances. It is not surprising then, that, for the first 2 years of his writing activity, petitioner sustained losses. This field appears to pay large amounts of money to those who succeed in it and "an opportunity to earn a substantial ultimate profit in a highly speculative venture is ordinarily sufficient to indicate that the activity is engaged in for profit even though losses or only occasional small profits are actually generated." Sec. 1.183-2(b)(7), Income Tax Regs. Likewise, we are not inclined to give much weight to the seventh factor, the amount of occasional profits, if any, that are earned, because only the first 2 years of petitioner's writing activity are in issue.

Respondent argues that the next factor, the financial status of the taxpayer, negates petitioner's profit motive because his independent sources of income are such that the writing activity generated tax benefits for him. We disagree with respondent. We do not believe that petitioner's income was so high as to make tax savings his primary objective. We also do not find it unlikely that petitioner, aware of his upcoming retirement and of the change in his pre and postretirement income, would choose to embark on something new. No doubt the fact that he began his writing activity during his preretirement years contributed to his ability to try his hand at it. Nothing in the record, however, indicates that writing then became a hobby for him. Rather, we find it clear from his testimony and from the objective evidence that petitioner was a writer who desired success and who intended to make a profit from his work.

The last factor looks to elements of personal pleasure or recreation. It is obvious that petitioner enjoyed writing and derived personal satisfaction in helping prostitutes seek a new way of life. Nevertheless, "the fact that the taxpayer derives personal pleasure from engaging in the activity is not sufficient to cause the activity to be classified as not engaged in for profit if the activity is in fact engaged in for profit as evidenced by other factors". Sec. 1.183-2(b)(9), Income Tax Regs.

Petitioner has succeeded in proving that he engaged in his writing activity with a profit objective. There are admittedly some factors in this case which indicate the absence of a profit motive: Petitioner has a history of losses, he did not seek any expert advice, and, arguably, there is a recreational element in his writing. These factors, however, are outweighed by the facts demonstrating that petitioner did engage in writing for profit. And though his writing venture may have been speculative and his expectation of profit unreasonable, that alone does not preclude us from finding that petitioner was in the trade or business of being an author during the years before us.

Respondent next asserts that, for 1993 and 1994, petitioner's claimed expenses were not ordinary and necessary business expenses.[15] Section 162(a) allows a deduction for

---

15. Respondent makes no claim that these amounts, if otherwise allowable, must be capitalized rather than deducted currently.

all ordinary and necessary expenses incurred in carrying on a trade or business. Whether an expense is deductible under section 162 is ultimately a question of fact. An ordinary and necessary expense is one which is appropriate or helpful to the taxpayer's business and which results from an activity which is a common and accepted practice. No deduction, however, is allowed for personal, living, or family expenses, even if related to one's occupation. See sec. 262.

Deductions are strictly a matter of legislative grace, and petitioner bears the burden of providing supporting evidence to substantiate the claimed deductions. See Rule 142(a); INDOPCO, Inc. v. Commissioner, 503 U.S. 79, 84 (1992). A taxpayer must keep sufficient records to establish their amount. See sec. 6001. Except in the case of expenses subject to section 274, if the taxpayer's records are inadequate or there are no records, the Tax Court may still allow a deduction based on a reasonable estimate, see Cohan v. Commissioner, 39 F.2d 540, 543-544 (2d Cir. 1930), provided the taxpayer establishes that he is entitled to some deduction, see Williams v. United States, 245 F.2d 559, 560 (5th Cir. 1957); Vanicek v. Commissioner, 85 T.C. 731, 743 (1985). In making an estimate, the Court may bear heavily against the taxpayer "whose inexactitude is of his own making". Cohan v. Commissioner, supra at 544.

On his Schedules C for the years in issue, petitioner claimed deductions for advertising, commissions and fees, office expense, supplies, and utilities. Petitioner presented no proof, such as bills, receipts, or canceled checks, or offered any testimony to establish that he incurred these expenses. The record does show, however, that, during 1993 and 1994, petitioner completed one manuscript and submitted it for publication. The Court is satisfied that petitioner incurred office expenses in this respect.[16] Applying Cohan v. Commissioner, supra, and "bearing heavily" against petitioner, we allow an office expense deduction of $400 for each of the years in question. Petitioner is not entitled to deductions for advertising, commissions and fees, supplies, and utilities for 1993 and 1994.

Petitioner claimed "other expenses" not included above in the amounts of $7,830 and $12,099, respectively, for 1993 and 1994. The amount for 1993 consists of a joint venture payment to Northwest and cash payments to prostitutes at Nevada's legal brothels. Petitioner produced a canceled check reflecting his payment to Northwest and a contemporaneous journal supporting his deductions for amounts paid to prostitutes to research his book. The amount for 1994 consists of a variety of expenses, for which petitioner has provided no documentary or testimonial evidence, with the exception of his expenses to interview prostitutes on out calls, which he substantiated by personal credit card receipts.

We allow petitioner to deduct the joint venture payment of $4,350 for 1993. However, no deduction is allowed for the interview expenses. We find that the expenditures incurred by petitioner to visit prostitutes are so personal in nature as to preclude their deductibility. In evaluating whether certain expenses are personal or qualify as business expenses under section 162, the Court has found that some expenses are so "inherently personal" that they almost invariably are held to come within the ambit of section 262.[17] Fred W. Amend Co. v. Commissioner, supra. All the other items constituting "other expenses" for 1993 and 1994 are disallowed for lack of substantiation.

---

16. Sec. 280A limits the deductibility of expenses of a home office; respondent, however, did not raise the applicability of that section. We, therefore, do not consider it.

17. Sec. 262 provides that "no deduction shall be allowed for personal, living, or family expenses."

Respondent next asks us to find that petitioner has not adequately substantiated under section 274(d) his travel expenses. Section 274(d) overrides the *Cohan* doctrine with respect to expenses of travel away from home (including meals and lodging). See *Sanford v. Commissioner*, 50 T.C. 823, 827-828 (1968), affd. per curiam 412 F.2d 201 (2d Cir. 1969); sec. 1.274-5T(a), Temporary Income Tax Regs., 50 Fed.Reg. 46014 (Nov. 6, 1985). A taxpayer must substantiate the amount, time, place, and business purpose of the expenditures, using adequate records or sufficient evidence corroborating his own statement. See sec. 1.274-5T(c)(1), Temporary Income Tax Regs., 50 Fed. Reg. 46016 (Nov. 6, 1985).

Respondent conceded at trial that petitioner substantiated the amount, time, and place, but not the business purpose, of his travel expenses. In view of our holding that petitioner's interview expenses are nondeductible personal expenses, we find that his trips to Nevada served a dual purpose. This dual purpose warrants an allocation of travel expenses between business and nonbusiness use. While the evidence in this case does not permit an exact allocation, there is a basis for some allowance—if necessary, by drawing upon petitioner's own method of allocating his interview expenses. Petitioner characterized the money he paid to prostitutes as business related if he incorporated the material from the interviews in his book. According to petitioner's figures, approximately three fifth's of the total amount that he paid for interviews was deducted as business expenses. Although the Court disallows any part of these interview expenses, we find that petitioner's allocation might well apply in determining the portion of his travel expenses attributable to business. Accordingly, for 1993 and 1994, we allow petitioner to deduct three fifths of his claimed travel expenses (including meals and lodging) under section 274(d). We sustain respondent's disallowance of the claimed deductions to the extent of two fifths thereof.

Field Service Advice 200125019
June 22, 2001

ISSUE

Whether expenditures incurred by Taxpayer's design and prototype department relating to the design, development, modification, and improvement of athletic footwear constitute "research and experimental expenditures" under I.R.C. § 174.

CONCLUSION

Expenditures incurred by Taxpayer's design and prototype department relating to the design, development, modification, and improvement of athletic footwear constitute "research and experimental expenditures" under section 174 only if such expenditures are attributable to activities intended to eliminate uncertainty concerning the development or improvement of the footwear products and if such expenditures are not otherwise excludable under section 174.

FACTS

Taxpayer is in the trade or business of designing, developing, selling, and distributing athletic footwear products. Taxpayer's design and prototype department (design department) is engaged in all activities related to the design, development, modification, and improvement of Taxpayer's footwear products.

Taxpayer's product development and/or improvement cycle begins with the design phase during which each member of Taxpayer's design department attempts to conceptualize and design either a new footwear product or an improvement to an existing footwear product. Each design department member produces drawings containing ideas or concepts of what product or improvement might appeal to a particular market segment. Because trends in athletic footwear change frequently, Taxpayer is never certain of what might appeal to the current market.

The design department members then draft and evaluate detailed technical "blue print" design drawings of footwear components, including "cut-away" views illustrating how each of the product's components fit together. The design department will discard the majority of drawings while approximately ten percent of the drawings will be redrafted and reevaluated until certain design concepts are identified as potential designs for the coming year's product line. Design department activities include tasks related to nonfunctional aspects of the product, such as evaluating colors or positioning insignia, or more complex tasks related to functional aspects of the product, such as designing a new footwear component (e.g., a tread pattern or lace hook), or improving the functionality of an existing footwear component (e.g., an improved tread or a more water-resistant boot). Design department activities may also include developing a new footwear product, which would include activities related to both functional and nonfunctional aspects of the product.

As soon as the design department arrives at a tentative agreement on the designs for the coming year's product line, the proposed designs are reviewed and evaluated by Taxpayer's management. For those designs approved by Taxpayer's management, the design department determines the necessary components for manufacturing, as well as the appropriate methods of manufacturing, each product. Upon final approval of the component and/or footwear product design, the design department evaluates the appropriate manufacturing process for that new design. Once these various design elements are finalized and approved, Taxpayer then asks a foreign manufacturer to construct prototype pairs of the footwear design. Taxpayer does not manufacture either the components used in the construction of the footwear or the footwear itself. As part of the design process, however, the design department frequently constructs a rough prototype of a proposed product or product component while experimenting with different design features. The rough prototypes are constructed from various scrap materials including discarded prototype models and returned merchandise.

When the prototype pairs of footwear are constructed by the foreign manufacturer, they are returned to Taxpayer where the design department inspects them for inherent design flaws. Such design flaws may be functional (i.e., generally relating to the product's purpose, action or performance) or non-functional (i.e., generally relating to color or style). Once Taxpayer approves the design, the prototypes are marketed to Taxpayer's customers. When and if the prototypes are successfully marketed, Taxpayer submits an order to its foreign manufacturer for further production of the product.

Taxpayer performs no internal testing to determine how the footwear will hold up to sustained use and instead relies upon the ultimate consumer to test its product. Thus, design flaws that are not identified upon inspection during the design evaluation process become apparent only when the consumer has purchased, used, and returned the product to the store where it was purchased. If a product has a correctable problem, members of the design department evaluate and attempt to eliminate the problem. The design department addresses diverse problems, ranging from the color of the shoe, the placement of the insignia, the overall design of the tread, or the design of the entire footwear product.

Taxpayer has claimed all costs incurred by the design department for the x, y, and z taxable years as research or experimental expenditures under § 174. Taxpayer's accounting for the costs incurred by the design department does not delineate the nature of the costs incurred.

LAW

Prior to 1954, the tax laws authorized no specific treatment for research and experimental expenditures. In order to provide guidance to taxpayers on the proper accounting treatment of research and experimental expenditures, as well as to encourage taxpayers to carry on research and experimentation, Congress enacted section 174, effective for expenses incurred after December 31, 1953.

Section 174 generally provides that research and experimental expenditures paid or incurred during the taxable year in connection with a taxpayer's trade or business may, at the taxpayer's election, be deducted currently rather than capitalized. Section 174(c) generally provides that section 174 will not apply to any expenditure for the acquisition or improvement of land, or for the acquisition or improvement of property to be used in connection with the research or experimentation and of a character which is subject to the allowance for depreciation under section 167.

Treas. Reg. § 1.174-2(a)(1) provides, in relevant part, that the term "research or experimental expenditures" means expenditures incurred in connection with the taxpayer's trade or business which represent research and development costs in the experimental or laboratory sense. The term generally includes all such costs incident to the development or improvement of a product. Further, expenditures represent research and development costs in the experimental or laboratory sense if they are for activities intended to discover information that would eliminate uncertainty concerning the development or improvement of a product. Uncertainty exists if the information available to the taxpayer does not establish the capability or method for developing or improving the product or the appropriate design of the product. Whether expenditures qualify as research or experimental expenditures depends on the nature of the activity to which the expenditures relate, not the nature of the product or improvement being developed or the level of technological advancement the product or improvement represents.

Treas. Reg. § 1.174-2(a)(2) provides that the term "product" includes any pilot model, process, formula, invention, technique, patent, or similar property, and includes products to be used by the taxpayer in its trade or business as well as products to be held for sale, lease, or license.

Treas. Reg. § 1.174-2(a)(3) provides that the term "research or experimental expenditures" does not include expenditures for—

(i) The ordinary testing or inspection of materials or products for quality control (quality control testing);

(ii) Efficiency surveys;

(iii) Management studies;

(iv) Consumer surveys;

(v) Advertising or promotions;

(vi) The acquisition of another's patent, model, production or process; or

(vii) Research in connection with literary, historical, or similar projects.

Treas. Reg. § 1.174-2(a)(4) provides that for purposes of Treas. Reg. § 1.174-2(a)(3)(i), testing or inspection to determine whether particular units of materials or products conform to specified parameters is quality control testing. However, quality control testing does not include testing to determine if the design of the product is appropriate.

Treas. Reg. § 1.174-2(b) contains rules relating to certain expenditures with respect to land and other property. Treas. Reg. § 1.174-2(b)(1) provides that expenditures by the taxpayer for the acquisition or improvement of land, or for the acquisition or improvement of property which is subject to an allowance for depreciation under section 167, are not deductible under section 174, irrespective of the fact that the property or improvements may be used by the taxpayer in connection with research or experimentation. However, allowances for depreciation of property are considered as research or experimental expenditures, for purposes of section 174, to the extent that the property to which the allowances relate is used in connection with research or experimentation. If any part of the cost of acquisition or improvement of depreciable property is attributable to research or experimentation (whether made by the taxpayer or another), see Treas. Reg. § 1.174-2(b)(2), (3), and (4).

Treas. Reg. § 1.174-2(b)(2) provides, in relevant part, that expenditures for research or experimentation which result, as an end product of the research or experimentation, in depreciable property to be used in the taxpayer's trade or business may, subject to the limitations of Treas. Reg. § 1.174-2(b)(4), be allowable as a current expense deduction under section 174(a).

Treas. Reg. § 1.174-2(b)(3) provides, in relevant part, that if expenditures for research or experimentation are incurred in connection with the construction or manufacture of depreciable property by another, they are deductible under section 174(a) only if made upon the taxpayer's order and at his risk. No deduction will be allowed (i) if the taxpayer purchases another's product under a performance guarantee (whether express, implied, or imposed by local law) unless the guarantee is limited, to engineering specifications or otherwise, in such a way that economic utility is not taken into account; or (ii) for any part of the purchase price of a product in regular production. However, see Treas. Reg. § 1.174-2(b)(4).

Treas. Reg. § 1.174-2(b)(4) provides, in relevant part, that the deductions referred to in Treas. Reg. § 1.174-2(b)(2) for expenditures in connection with the acquisition or production of depreciable property to be used in the taxpayer's trade or business are limited to amounts expended for research or experimentation. Thus, amounts expended for research or experimentation do not include the costs of the component materials of the depreciable property, the costs of labor or other elements involved in its construction and installation, or costs attributable to the acquisition or improvement of the property. See Ekman v. Commissioner, 184 F.3d 522 (6th Cir. 1999), aff'g T.C. Memo. 1997-318 (holding that the cost incurred for the purchase of a used car engine is not deductible under section 174 because the engine is of a character subject to an allowance for depreciation).

ANALYSIS

The issue in this request for Field Service Advice is whether expenditures attributable to Taxpayer's design, development, sale, and distribution of athletic footwear are research or experimental expenditures under section 174. The materials accompanying the incoming request do not state whether Taxpayer's accounting for the costs incurred by the design department include expenses attributable to property that is subject to an allowance for depreciation. Inasmuch as we have been advised that Taxpayer has classified all costs of the design department as section 174 expenses, we believe we should address this issue briefly.

Treas. Reg. § 1.174-2(b)(1) generally provides that expenditures by the taxpayer for the acquisition or improvement of property which is subject to an allowance for depreciation under section 167, are not deductible under section 174, irrespective of the fact that the property or improvements may be used by the taxpayer in connection with research or experimentation. Treas. Reg. § 1.174-2(b)(2) provides, in relevant part, that expenditures for research or experimentation which result, as an end product of the research or experimentation, in depreciable property to be used in the taxpayer's trade or business may, subject to the limitations of Treas. Reg. § 1.174-2(b)(4), be allowable as a current expense deduction under section 174(a).

These rules describe two types of expenses: (1) expenses incurred for activities intended to discover information that would eliminate uncertainty concerning the development or improvement of a product; and (2) expenses attributable to the component material, labor or other elements involved in the construction and installation of a product. The former type of expense, to the extent it can be traced to activities intended to discover information that would eliminate uncertainty concerning the development or improvement of a product, are deductible for purposes of section 174. The latter type of expense, to the extent it represents costs for the construction of a depreciable asset, is not deductible. See Rev. Rul. 73-275, 1973-1 C.B. 134 (holding that costs attributable to the development and design of an automated manufacturing system, as distinguished from costs attributable to the production of the manufacturing system, are deductible under section 174). Therefore, if the facts of this case suggest that the rough prototypes produced by Taxpayer's design department for use in Taxpayer's trade or business are property of a character subject to the allowance for depreciation, then the cost of the component materials to produce these prototypes are not deductible under section 174.

Treas. Reg. § 1.174-2(b)(3) generally provides that if expenditures for research or experimentation are incurred in connection with the construction or manufacture of depreciable property by another, they are deductible under section 174(a) only if made upon the taxpayer's order and at his risk. The materials accompanying the incoming request for Field Service Advice contain no information concerning Taxpayer's contractual arrangement with the foreign manufacturer. If it is determined that the prototypes are depreciable property, however, then the contract(s) should be examined to determine which party bears the risk of loss.

Assuming that some, if not all, of the costs incurred by Taxpayer's design department do not include expenses attributable to property that is subject to an allowance for depreciation, then we must consider other bases for disallowance under section 174. As noted above, neither the Code nor the regulations provide an explicit definition of the term "research or experimental expenditures." Existing case law is likewise unhelpful and generally predates the 1994 amendments to the regulations at Treas. Reg. § 1.174-2. See, e.g., Mayrath v. Commissioner, 41 T.C. 582 (1964), aff'd on other grounds, 357 F.2d 209 (5th Cir. 1966) (holding that the regulatory definition of research or experimental expenditures was reasonable and consistent with Congress' intent to limit deductions to those expenditures of an investigative nature expended in developing the concept of a product); Kollsman Instrument Corp. v. Commissioner, T.C. Memo. 1986-66, aff'd on other grounds, 870 F.2d 89 (2d Cir. 1989) (denying section 174 treatment because the contracts in question did not require the taxpayer to invent, develop the concept of, or design any product); Agro Science Co. v. Commissioner, T.C. Memo. 1989-687, aff'd but opinion withdrawn, 927 F.2d 213 (5th Cir. 1991) (finding that research requires an element of experimentation rather than simply a repetition of what has already been done); Crouch v. Commissioner, T.C. Memo. 1990-309 (finding that the amounts expended by petitioner were paid to research, write, publish and promote an ordinary literary work and thus were not research costs in the experimental or laboratory sense); TSR, Inc. v. Commissioner, 96 T.C. 903 (1991) (examining, for section 44 research credit purposes, such terms as "laboratory" and "experimental" under section 174).

At best, we are able to discern from this line of cases, together with the statute and regulations, that the term "research or experimental" encompasses the notion that scientific research and development includes an attempt to develop or improve a product, or develop or improve upon a technique or procedure. The 1994 amendments support the notion that scientific research is distinguishable from research of other types in that the amendments provide that expenditures represent research and development costs in the experimental or laboratory sense if the expenditures are for activities intended to discover information that would eliminate uncertainty concerning the development or improvement of a pilot model, process, formula, invention, technique, patent, or similar property. See Treas. Reg. §1.174-2(a)(2). See also H.R. Rep. No. 83-1337, at 28 (1954); S. Rep. No. 83-1622, at 33 (1954).

In delineating the scope of the term "research or experimental," the 1994 amendments clarify that uncertainty exists if the information available to the taxpayer does not establish the capability or method for developing or improving the product. Treas. Reg. §1.174-2(a)(1). However, the term "uncertainty" must be limited to technological or scientific uncertainty in that a taxpayer must be uncertain as to whether it will be able to develop or improve its product in the scientific or laboratory sense. Put differently, the taxpayer must be uncertain as to whether it will be able to achieve its product development objective through its research activities. Conversely, uncertainty attributable to business or market concerns is not determinative of the existence of research and experimentation for purposes of section 174.

The section 174 regulations provide several exclusions from the definition of research or experimental expenditures. For example, the term does not include expenditures such as those for the ordinary testing or inspection of materials or products for quality control, or those for efficiency surveys, management studies, consumer surveys, advertising, or promotions. Treas. Reg. §1.174-2(a)(3). Significantly, these exclusions are related to activities that generally occur after the research is completed in that the purpose of such activities is to evaluate and disseminate the results of the research. For example, once a product, such as a shoe, is developed, the existence of this shoe must be promoted and advertised. Advertising in this respect is the publication or announcement to the public of the availability of a new or improved product. The fact that these excluded activities tend to occur after the research is completed is further supported by the clarification in the 1994 amendments to the exclusion for quality control testing. Treas. Reg. §1.174-2(a)(4) provides that the exclusion for quality control testing does not apply to testing to determine whether the design of the product is appropriate. If a taxpayer finds that the design of its product is inappropriate, then the research is not completed and the taxpayer must resume its research activities.

In reviewing the materials accompanying the request for Field Service Advice, we note that a distinction appears to be drawn between the functional and nonfunctional aspects of the footwear product. Prior to the finalization of the 1994 amendments to the section 174 regulations, this distinction was relevant. The section 174 regulations proposed in 1989 provided six exclusions in addition to the exclusions contained in the 1957 regulations. In relevant part, the 1989 proposed regulations excluded costs incurred in connection with activities not directed at the functional aspects of a product including expenses relating to style, taste, cosmetic, or seasonal design factors. See 1989 Prop. Treas. Reg. § 1.174-2(a)(3)(v). The 1994 amendments, while retaining the exclusions contained in the final 1957 regulations, did not retain the six additional exclusions proposed in 1989. Therefore, expenditures for any of these six activities qualify as research or experimental expenditures if they fall within the general definition of the term "research or experimental expenditure" and are not covered by one of the existing exclusions. See Explanation of Provisions to the 1993 proposed regulations, 58 Fed. Reg. 15820.

In this case, the fact that Taxpayer's activities are with respect to the development or improvement of any nonfunctional aspects of the footwear product is, by itself, not a supportable basis for disallowance under section 174. Rather, the costs incurred must represent research and development costs in the experimental or laboratory sense and must be attributable to activities intended to eliminate uncertainty concerning the development of the product.

Snow v. Commissioner
Supreme Court of the United States
416 U.S. 500 (1974)

MR. JUSTICE DOUGLAS delivered the opinion of the Court.

Section 174 (a)(1) of the Internal Revenue Code allows a taxpayer to take as a deduction "experimental expenditures which are paid or incurred by him during the taxable year in connection with his trade or business as expenses which are not chargeable to capital account." Petitioner Edwin A. Snow (hereafter petitioner) was disallowed as a deduction his distributive share of the net operating loss of a partnership, Burns Investment Company, for the taxable year 1966. The United States Tax Court sustained the Commissioner, 58 T.C. 585. The Court of Appeals for the Sixth Circuit affirmed, 482 F. 2d 1029 (1973). The case is here on a writ of certiorari because of an apparent conflict between that court and the Fourth Circuit in *Cleveland v. Commissioner*, 297 F. 2d 169 (1961).

Petitioner was a limited partner in Burns, having contributed $10,000 for a four-percent interest in Burns. The general partner was one Trott who had previously formed two other limited partnerships, one called Echo, to develop a telephone answering device and the other Courier, to develop an electronic tape recorder. Petitioner had become a limited partner in each of these other partnerships.

Burns was formed to develop "a special purpose incinerator for the consumer and industrial markets." Trott was the inventor and had conceived of this idea in 1964 and between then and had made a number of prototypes. His patent counsel had told him in 1965 that several features of the burner were in his view patentable but in 1966 advised him that the incinerator as a whole had not been sufficiently "reduced to practice" in order to develop it into a marketable product. At that point Trott formed Burns, petitioner putting up part of the capital. Thereafter various models of the burner were built and tested. During 1966 Burns reported no sales of the incinerator or any other product but expectations were high; and Trott was giving about one-third of his time to the project, an outside engineering firm doing the shopwork.[2] Trott obtained a patent on the incinerator in 1970, and it is currently being produced and marketed under the name Trash-Away.

Section 174 was enacted in 1954 to dilute some of the conception of "ordinary and necessary" business expenses under § 162 (a) (then § 23 (a)(1) of the Internal Revenue Code of 1939) adumbrated by Mr. Justice Frankfurter in a concurring opinion in *Deputy v. DuPont*, 308 U.S. 488, 499 (1940), where he said that the section in question (old § 23 (a)) "involves holding one's self out to others as engaged in the selling of goods or services." The words "trade or business" appear, however, in about 60 different sections of the 1954 Act. Those other sections are not helpful here because Congress wrote into § 174 (a)(1) "in connection with," and § 162 (a) is more narrowly written than is § 174, allowing "a deduction" of "ordinary and necessary expenses paid or incurred...in carrying on any trade or business." That and other sections are not helpful here.

The legislative history makes fairly clear the reasons. Established firms with ongoing business had continuous programs of research quite unlike small or pioneering business enterprises.[5] Mr. Reed of New York, Chairman of the House Committee on Ways and Means, made the point even more explicit when he addressed the House on the bill:[6]

> "Present law contains no statutory provision dealing expressly with the deduction of these expenses. The result has been confusion and uncertainty. Very often, under present law small businesses which are developing new products and do not have established research departments are not allowed to deduct these expenses despite the fact that their large and well-established competitors can obtain the deduction.... This provision will greatly stimulate the search for new products and new inventions upon which the future economic and military strength of our Nation depends. *It will be particularly valuable to small and growing businesses.*" (Emphasis added.)

Congress may at times in its wisdom discriminate taxwise between various kinds of business, between old and oncoming business and the like. But we would defeat the congressional purpose somewhat to equalize the tax benefits of the ongoing companies

---

2. Treasury Regulation § 1.174-2(a)(2) provides: "The provisions of this section apply not only to costs paid or incurred by the taxpayer for research or experimentation undertaken directly by him but also to expenditures paid or incurred for research or experimentation carried on in his behalf by another person or organization (such as...[an] engineering company, or similar contractor)...."

5. Hearings on H.R. 8300 before the Senate Committee on Finance, 83d Cong., 2d Sess., pt. 1, p. 105.

6. 100 Cong. Rec. 3425 (1954).

and those that are upcoming and about to reach the market by perpetuating the discrimination created below and urged upon us here.

We read § 174 as did the Court of Appeals for the Fourth Circuit in *Cleveland* "to encourage expenditure for research and experimentation." That incentive is embedded in § 174 because of "in connection with," making irrelevant whether petitioners were rich or poor.

We are invited to explore the treatment of "hobby-losses" under § 183. But that is far afield of the present inquiry for it is clear that in this case under § 174 the profit motive was the sole drive of the venture.

Reversed.

Green v. Commissioner
83 T.C. 667 (1984)

SIMPSON, JUDGE:

[P was a limited partner in a partnership formed to acquire, develop, and license four unpatented inventions. The partnership executed, on the same day, an acquisition agreement, a research and development agreement, and an exclusive license agreement with respect to each of the four inventions. Under the acquisition agreements, the partnership acquired all of the rights in the inventions from the inventors thereof. Under the research and development agreements, the partnership agreed to pay N $650,000 over 3 years to develop the inventions into commercially exploitable products. Under the license agreements, the partnership granted N an exclusive worldwide license to make, use, and sell the four inventions and any improvements thereto for the duration of their patent lives in return for the payment by N of royalties based upon future sales of the developed products. The partnership claimed depreciation deductions with respect to the inventions and a deduction under sec. 174 (a), I.R.C. 1954, of $650,000 for the obligation under the research and development agreements.]

LaSala was organized as an Illinois limited partnership on December 29, 1977. It was reorganized and expanded on December 19, 1979, for the stated purpose of acquiring four inventions for investment and income-producing purposes and to thereafter patent, improve, maintain, and exploit the inventions. Tower Hill Co., Inc. (Tower Hill), an Illinois corporation organized on November 30, 1979, became the general partner of LaSala in the reorganization. LaSala's general partner, Tower Hill, had the sole and exclusive power to operate and manage the business of the partnership. Tower Hill had no previous experience in the acquisition and exploitation of inventions as its position as general partner of LaSala was its first corporate undertaking.

On or about December 24, 1979, LaSala entered into four sets of agreements, each set concerning one of four inventions acquired by the partnership. Each set included three separate agreements: (1) an acquisition agreement, (2) a research and development agreement (R&D agreement), and (3) an exclusive license agreement (license agreement). The sets of agreements are virtually identical, the principal distinctions being the inventor, the invention, and the amount of the consideration covered by each set of agreements.

Each acquisition agreement was entered into between LaSala and an inventor and, by its terms, conveyed to the partnership all the inventor's right, title, and interest in his invention or inventions, including any patent rights. Of the four inventions thus acquired, none was patented as of December 24, 1979, although at least one had a patent application pending.

On the same day as it entered into the acquisition agreements, LaSala entered into four R&D agreements with NPDC. NPDC was a patent development company engaged in activities worldwide. It had been in existence for more than 20 years, and its stock was traded on the American Stock Exchange.

NPDC agreed to provide research and experimental services, systems analysis, and technical documentation "as are reasonably necessary and customary to develop the Product into a commercially viable, marketable product or process." NPDC further agreed to furnish LaSala with quarterly progress reports of functions performed, changes in personnel or subcontractors, and funds expended, and agreed to confer with representatives of LaSala to explain such progress reports. All product development was to be "at the Client's risk," and NPDC expressly disclaimed any warranty to the effect that the invention would be "developed into a commercially viable, marketable product or process of any economic utility." NPDC did represent that it would "extend its best efforts, within the resources * * * provided, to accomplish the objectives stated." The research and development services were to commence immediately upon execution of the agreement and to terminate by October 1, 1981, regardless of whether development had been completed.

The R&D agreements gave LaSala no power to supervise, review, or direct the activities of NPDC with respect to the inventions. LaSala's sole remedy, in the event that NPDC breached an obligation of the agreement, was to terminate the agreement and sue for breach of contract.

During the years 1979 through 1981, LaSala paid a total of $650,000 to NPDC pursuant to the terms of the four R&D agreements: $200,000 was paid in 1979, $225,000 was paid in 1980, and $225,000 was paid in 1981. During the same years, LaSala received no royalties from commercial exploitation of the inventions by NPDC. The research and experimental expenditure deduction of $650,000 in 1979 was calculated by accruing and expensing in such year the fees due NPDC in 1979, 1980, and 1981, under the terms of the four R&D agreements.

At issue were the partnership's claimed deductions for depreciation and research and experimental expenses.

LaSala, having sold its rights in the inventions simultaneously with its acquisition of such rights, neither "used" such rights in a trade or business, nor "held" such rights for the production of income, within the meaning of section 167(a). Consequently, we hold that LaSala was not entitled to any depreciation deduction with respect to such inventions.

The next issue for decision is whether LaSala is entitled to a deduction for research and experimental expenditures for 1979. Section 174(a)(1) states, as a general rule, that "research or experimental expenditures which are paid or incurred by * * * (a taxpayer) during the taxable year in connection with his trade or business," may, at the election of the taxpayer, be treated as expenses not chargeable to capital account and, therefore, may be deducted in the taxable year. The provisions of section 174(a)(1) "apply not only to costs paid or incurred by the taxpayer for research or experimentation undertaken directly by him but also to expenditures paid or incurred for research or experimentation carried on in his behalf by another person or organization (such as a research institute, foundation, engineering company, or similar contractor)." Sec. 1.174-2(a)(2), Income Tax Regs.

The Commissioner asserts that LaSala's expenditure of $650,000 under the R & D agreements was not "in connection with" any trade or business because LaSala was never intended to enter into, nor financially capable of carrying on, an active trade or business. Additionally, he asserts that the research payments were not expended "in * * * (LaSala's) behalf" because LaSala had divested itself of ownership of the inventions. The petitioners contend that, even if a sale of the inventions occurred in December 1979, LaSala's role with regard to the development of the inventions was sufficient under *Snow v. Commissioner*, 416 U.S. 500 (1974), and *Cleveland v. Commissioner*, 297 F.2d 169 (4th Cir. 1961), to qualify as being "in connection with" a trade or business, and further that LaSala's interest in future royalties is sufficient in itself to mean that NPDC conducted the development activities on LaSala's behalf.

Prior to the Supreme Court's decision in *Snow*, this Court had taken the position that expenditures for research and experimentation had to be made in connection with an existing business to which such research and experimentation was proximately related in order to be deductible under section 174(a)(1). *Best Universal Lock Co. v. Commissioner*, 45 T.C. 1 (1965); *Koons v. Commissioner*, 35 T.C. 1092 (1961). Research expenditures by a taxpayer not currently engaged in a trade or business were held to be nondeductible, pre-operating expenses. *Koons v. Commissioner, supra.*

In *Snow v. Commissioner*, 416 U.S. 500 (1974), revg. 482 F.2d 1029 (6th Cir. 1973), affg. 58 T.C. 585 (1972), Mr. Snow was an executive with Proctor & Gamble Co. In 1966, he contributed $10,000 for a 4-percent interest in Burns Investment Co. (Burns), a limited partnership formed to develop an unpatented trash-burning device. Mr. Trott was the general partner of the partnership and the inventor of the trash burner. Mr. Trott conveyed all his rights in the invention to the partnership. During 1966, Burns had no manufacturing plant or office. Development of the burner began in that year and was conducted by a company owned by Mr. Trott on behalf of the partnership. No patent was applied for until 1968, and Burns made no effort to market or sell the device in 1966. The Tax Court held that the taxpayer was not entitled to deduct a distributive share of his partnership's research expenses in 1966 because the partnership was not then engaged in a trade or business and the research was not related to the taxpayer's own trade or business.

In determining that the partnership's research expenditures in *Snow* were not made "in connection with a trade or business," we applied the facts and circumstances test of section 162, as announced in *Higgins v. Commissioner*, 312 U.S. 212 (1941). However, one factor was given particular weight, and that was the fact that the partnership had made no sales of any product either before or during 1966. We cited with approval the concurring opinion of Justice Frankfurter in *Deputy v. du Pont*, 308 U.S. 488, 499 (1940), wherein he maintained that carrying on any trade or business (for purposes of the predecessor of section 162) "involves holding one's self out to others as engaged in the selling of goods or services." The Sixth Circuit affirmed our conclusion that the partnership's expenditures were pre-operating expenses and therefore nondeductive under section 174.

The Supreme Court reversed and stated that the meaning of the phrase "in connection with a trade or business" used in section 174 should not be limited by other restrictive definitions of "trade or business" which had been suggested for other sections of the Code. The Court specifically disclaimed the restrictive test of a trade or business advanced by Justice Frankfurter in *Deputy v. du Pont, supra*, as inappropriate to the purpose of section 174. Section 174 is intended to encourage research and experimentation by "small or pioneering business enterprises," as well as by established, on-going businesses. A trade or business test under section 174 which depended upon the existence of production or sales of the invention "would defeat the congressional purpose somewhat to equalize the tax benefits of the ongoing companies and those that are upcoming and about to reach the market." Therefore, the Court held that the partnership was entitled to a deduction under section 174 even though it had not had any sales.

Although the Supreme Court established in *Snow* that the taxpayer need not currently be producing or selling any product in order to obtain a deduction for research expenses, it did not eliminate the "trade or business" requirement of section 174 altogether. For section 174 to apply, the taxpayer must still be engaged in a trade or business *at some time*, and we must still determine, through an examination of the facts of each case, whether the taxpayer's activities in connection with a product are sufficiently substantial and regular to constitute a trade or business for purposes of such section.

The existence of a profit motive is an important factor because it distinguishes between an enterprise carried on in good faith as a trade or business and an enterprise merely carried on as a hobby. However, the Commissioner's concession that LaSala's activities were profit-motivated establishes only the first step in our inquiry; we still must decide whether those activities were such as to constitute a trade or business.

The fact that LaSala carried on its investment activity through a partnership form establishes little. At common law, a partnership is generally defined as an association of two or more persons to carry on, as co-owners, a business for profit (see Uniform Partnership Act sec. 6), but the Internal Revenue Code's definition of partnership for tax purposes is substantially broader. See secs. 761, 7701(a)(2); sec. 301.7701-3, Proced. and Admin. Regs. In numerous cases, arrangements treated as partnerships for tax purposes were found not to be engaged in a trade or business. See, e.g., *Mitchell v. Commissioner*, 47 T.C. 120 (1966); *Cohen v. Commissioner*, 39 T.C. 886 (1963).

An examination of LaSala's limited activity reveals that it functioned only as a vehicle for injecting risk capital into the development and commercialization of the four inventions. Its activities never surpassed those of an investor. It was not the up-and-coming *business* which section 174 is intended to promote.

LaSala's activities in 1979, the year for which the section 174 deduction is claimed, were very limited. Reorganized in December 1979 by the substitution of all new partners, LaSala had no history as a trade or business. Its general partner, Tower Hill, likewise had no business history as it had been incorporated just the month before. On December 24, 1979, the partnership executed the acquisition and license agreements which effected the simultaneous purchase and sale of the four inventions in which it was formed to invest. Under the terms of the acquisition agreements, LaSala was obligated to the inventor-sellers to exercise the rights that it acquired and to promote the use and sale of the inventions. LaSala satisfied this obligation by engaging NPDC to develop the inventions into commercially viable products, and by assigning to NPDC all its rights in the underlying inventions subject to the rights of the inventors.

In the years that followed, LaSala's activities were purely ministerial. It maintained a partnership bank account and each year deposited into it the yearly installments due from its limited partners under the terms of the promissory notes by which each partner acquired his interest in the partnership. From the account, LaSala paid the annual recourse installments due the inventors under the acquisition agreements, Tower Hill's management fee, and legal and accounting fees. Employees of Tower Hill also met with representatives of NPDC to discuss the progress of NPDC's development work, but LaSala itself did not conduct any research or experimentation. If the inventions were eventually marketed by NPDC, LaSala would have to collect royalties due under the license agreements and thereafter make further payments to the inventors and distribute any profits left over to its partners. However, LaSala itself would never be able to produce or market the inventions because of the exclusiveness of NPDC's license.

The management of investments is not a trade or business, irrespective of the extent of the investments or the amount of time required to perform the managerial functions. A taxpayer who holds securities for long-term appreciation and who seeks current income from dividends and interest paid on such securities, rather than from frequent short-term trades, is an investor

LaSala's "royalty" interest in the development and commercialization of the four inventions was analogous to that of an investor in securities. After the transactions of December 24, 1979, LaSala had no ownership interest in the inventions and no control over their actual development, production, or marketing. However, LaSala retained an investor-like interest in such development and commercialization because the purchase price under the license agreements was contingent upon future sales by NPDC. Any proceeds from the sale to NPDC would necessarily be received over the long term, if at all, because of the time required for development.

Furthermore, while this Court has held that the exploitation of inventions through regular licenses and sales may constitute a business (*Avery v. Commissioner*, 47 B.T.A. 538 (1942)), there is no indication in the present case that LaSala intended to buy and sell inventions for profit on a regular basis. Under the terms of its amended limited partnership agreement and according to statements contained in the private offering memorandum distributed to prospective limited partners, the four inventions bought and sold by LaSala in December 1979 were the only inventions in which LaSala would invest. Although there were four inventions, they were acquired and sold in a single, prearranged transaction and therefore may be treated as a single entity. A partnership or joint venture organized to dispose of a single property in an isolated sale, without making substantial improvements to the property between its acquisition and sale, is not in the business of selling property of such kind or character.

The petitioners contend that LaSala retained the right to control the research and development of the inventions and that the extent to which LaSala exercised such right is a material issue of fact requiring a trial. The petitioners maintain that LaSala's activities pursuant to such right were in fact sufficiently substantial and continuous to qualify as a trade or business. However, we have already determined that the R & D agreements gave LaSala no right to control NPDC's research activities. That LaSala may in fact have taken an active role in directing the research does not place LaSala in a trade or business. Such activity would be no greater than that of certain shareholders who do not, by devoting their time and energies to a corporation, engage in a trade or business. *Whipple v. Commissioner*, 373 U.S. 193 (1963). As the Supreme Court in *Whipple* observed: "Though such activities may produce income, profit or gain (to the shareholder) in the form of dividends or enhancement in the value of an investment, this return is distinctive to the process of investing and is generated by the successful operation of the corporation's business as distinguished from the trade or business of the taxpayer himself." 373 U.S. at 202. Likewise, in the present case, any income generated by the eventual marketing of the developed inventions, although perhaps redounding to LaSala's benefit, would arise from the business of NPDC, the owner of all rights in the inventions. We therefore conclude that the extent of LaSala's supervision (if any) is not material to the issue before us.

Finally, the petitioners rely on *Cleveland v. Commissioner*, 297 F.2d 169 (4th Cir. 1961), revg. in part and affg. in part 34 T.C. 517 (1960). In *Cleveland*, the investor-taxpayer, until 1956, made loans to an inventor to finance the inventor's research and development activities. The Fourth Circuit found that, in such year, the relationship between Mr. Cleveland and the inventor changed from that of creditor-debtor to become that of equal participants in a joint venture. The joint venture owned the inventions developed by the inventor. The inventor's extensive research activities, conducted on behalf of the joint venture, were therefore attributed to the joint venture. Mr. Cleveland, himself, provided the necessary funds to the venture, negotiated transfers to users of the venture's inventions, and prepared any necessary legal documents. The court found that after the formation of the joint venture, Mr. Cleveland was "engaging with * * * (the inventor) in the trade or business of promoting the commercial development of the invention in which Cleveland was the owner of a participating one-half interest." Therefore, the court upheld a deduction for Mr. Cleveland's contributions for research made after the formation of the joint venture, but not for the loans made before.

The present case is distinguishable from *Cleveland* because LaSala, unlike the joint venture in *Cleveland*, had sold to NPDC all its rights to any product that might result from the research, and after the sale, LaSala, unlike the joint venture in *Cleveland*, was not engaged in the business of developing the product. LaSala would never be able to utilize such product in a trade or business. Compare also *Snow v. Commissioner, supra*. Furthermore, the court in *Cleveland* did not hold that the act of financing research in itself constitutes the trade or business of promoting an invention. The combined activities of both participants in the joint venture formed the basis for the court's finding of a trade or business. See *Cleveland v. Commissioner*, 297 F.2d at 171–172.

Because of our determination that LaSala's research expenditures were not incurred in connection with a trade or business, it is unnecessary for us to determine whether such research was conducted on LaSala's behalf within the meaning of section 1.174-2(a)(2), Income Tax Regs. We hold that the petitioners are not entitled to deduct any partnership losses attributable to the section 174 deduction claimed in 1979, and we will grant the Commissioner's motion for partial summary judgment.

Revenue Procedure 2000-50
2000-1 C.B. 601

Section 1. Purpose

This revenue procedure provides guidelines on the treatment of the costs of computer software.

Section 2. Definition

For the purpose of this revenue procedure, "computer software" is any program or routine (that is, any sequence of machine-readable code) that is designed to cause a computer to perform a desired function or set of functions, and the documentation required to describe and maintain that program or routine. It includes all forms and media in which the software is contained, whether written, magnetic, or otherwise. Computer programs of all classes, for example, operating systems, executive systems, monitors, compilers and translators, assembly routines, and utility programs as well as application programs, are included. Computer software also includes any incidental and ancillary rights that are necessary to effect the acquisition of the title to, the ownership of, or the right to use the computer software, and that are used only in connection with that specific computer software. Computer software does not include any data or information base described in § 1.197-2(b)(4) of the Income Tax Regulations (for example, data files, customer lists, or client files) unless the data base or item is in the public domain and is incidental to a computer program. Nor does it include any cost of procedures that are external to the computer's operation.

Section 3. Background

.01 In the preamble to the final regulations issued January 25, 2000, under §§ 167(f) and 197 of the Internal Revenue Code (T.D. 8865, 2000-7 I.R.B. 589), the Internal Revenue Service advised taxpayers that they may not rely on the procedures in Rev. Proc. 69-21, 1969-2 C.B. 303, to the extent the procedures are inconsistent with § 167(f) or § 197, or the final regulations thereunder.

.02 Except as otherwise expressly provided, §§ 446(e) and 1.446-1(e) provide that a taxpayer must obtain the consent of the Commissioner of Internal Revenue before changing a method of accounting for federal income tax purposes. Section 1.446-1(e)(3)(ii) authorizes the Commissioner to prescribe administrative procedures setting forth the limitations, terms, and conditions deemed necessary to permit a taxpayer to obtain consent to change a method of accounting.

Section 4. Scope

This revenue procedure applies to all costs of computer software as defined in section 2 of this revenue procedure. This revenue procedure does not apply to any computer software that is subject to amortization as an "amortizable section 197 intangible" as defined in § 197(c) and the regulations thereunder, or to costs that a taxpayer has treated as a research and experimentation expenditure under § 174.

Section 5. Costs of Developing Computer Software

.01 The costs of developing computer software (whether or not the particular software is patented or copyrighted) in many respects so closely resemble the kind of research and experimental expenditures that fall within the purview of § 174 as to warrant similar accounting treatment. Accordingly, the Service will not disturb a taxpayer's treatment of costs paid or incurred in developing software for any particular project, either for the taxpayer's own use or to be held by the taxpayer for sale or lease to others, where:

(1) All of the costs properly attributable to the development of software by the taxpayer are consistently treated as current expenses and deducted in full in accordance with rules similar to those applicable under § 174(a); or

(2) All of the costs properly attributable to the development of software by the taxpayer are consistently treated as capital expenditures that are recoverable through deductions for ratable amortization, in accordance with rules similar to those provided by § 174(b) and the regulations thereunder, over a period of 60 months from the date of completion of the development or, in accordance with rules provided in § 167(f)(1) and the regulations thereunder, over 36 months from the date the software is placed in service.

....

Section 8. Application

.01 A change in a taxpayer's treatment of costs paid or incurred to develop...computer software to a method described in section 5 of this revenue procedure is a change in method of accounting to which §§ 446 and 481 apply. However, a change in useful life under the method described in section 5.01(2) of this revenue procedure is not a change in method of accounting. Section 1.446-1(e)(2)(ii)(b).

.02 A taxpayer that wants to change the taxpayer's method of accounting under this revenue procedure must follow the automatic change in method of accounting provisions in Rev. Proc. 99-49, 1999-2 C.B. 725 (or its successor), with the following modifications:

(1) In order to assist the Service in processing changes in method of accounting under this section and to ensure proper handling, section 6.02(3)(a) of Rev. Proc. 99-49 is modified to require that a Form 3115, Application for Change in Accounting Method, filed under this section include the statement: "Automatic Change Filed Under Section 8.01 of Rev. Proc. 2000-50." This statement must be legibly printed or typed at the top of any Form 3115 filed under this revenue procedure.

(2) If a taxpayer is changing to the method described in section 5.01(2) of this revenue procedure, the taxpayer must attach a statement to the Form 3115 stating whether the taxpayer is choosing the 60-month period from the date of completion of the development of the software, or the 36-month period from the placed-in-service date of the software.

.03 For taxable years ending on or after December 1, 2000, the Service will not disturb the taxpayer's treatment of costs of computer software that are handled in accordance with the practices described in this revenue procedure.

Chapter 5

Taxation of Intellectual Property Acquisitions

I. Assignment for Chapter 5

Read: Internal Revenue Code: §§ 167(a)–(c), (f), (g); 179(a), (b)(3), (d)(1)(A); 197(a), (b), (c)(1), (d)(1), (e)(1), (e)(3), (e)(4), (f)(4)(C); 1060(c); 1253(d). Skim §§ 162(a); 168(b)(1), (c), (e)(3)(B)(iv), (i)(2); 212; 338; 541; 542(a)(1)–(2); 543(a)(1), (a)(4), (d); 545(a); 547; 561(a); 1012; 1235(a)(1).

Treasury Regulations: §§ 1.167 (a)-1(b), -3, -14; 1.167(b)-1(a); 1.197-2(a), -2(b)(5), (10)-(11); -2(c)(4)–(5), (7); -2(e)(1)–(2), (5); -2(f)(1)–(2); -2(f)(3)(ii)–(iii); -2(g)(7); 1.263(a)-2(a); 1.1060-1(b)(1)–(2); 1.1060-1(c). Skim Prop. Treas. Reg. §§ 1.167(n)–1 through -7; § 1.263(a)-4(c).

Materials: Overview
Revenue Ruling 71-177
Revenue Ruling 60-358
Revenue Ruling 79-285
Greene v. Commissioner
Associated Patentees, Inc. v. Commissioner
Revenue Ruling 67-136
Private Letter Ruling 200137013

Complete the problems.

II. Problems for Chapter 5

1. Best Cleaners, Inc. will purchase all the assets of an existing dry cleaning business from Comet Cleaners, Inc., including the following intangible assets:

   (a) A patent obtained by Comet on a dry cleaning chemical that does not dissolve buttons.

   (b) Comet's website including all the copyrighted contents.

   (c) Off-the-shelf computer software previously used by Comet under the terms of a non-exclusive license from a software developer. The software was developed by the software developer for use by dry cleaning businesses to maintain accounting systems and is marketed directly to ultimate users.

(d) The domain name "drycleaning.com" that is registered by Comet. The remaining duration for the domain name registration is two years.

The agreement between Best and Comet allocates the purchase price to the above items in the amount of their respective fair market values. Explain in general the tax consequences to Best Cleaners of the purchase of these assets.

2. Your client Orvis Company is considering acquiring all of the tangible and intangible assets of Trout Illustrated, Inc., which publishes a monthly fishing magazine. The purchase price will be $500,000 in cash and 5% of each magazine copy sold.

   (a) Will Orvis be entitled to deduct the annual contingent payments made to Trout, assuming the contingent payments are specifically identified in the purchase agreement as the consideration for the transfer of Trout's trademark?

   (b) What if the purchase price is $500,000 in cash and an installment note for $100,000? The note, which is specifically identified in the purchase agreement as the consideration for Trout's trademark, requires Orvis to pay 50 cents for each magazine copy sold up to a maximum of $10,000 per year until the total payments equal $100,000.

3. Hessaco, Inc., a calendar-year taxpayer, purchases from its competitor a secret technique on how to refine crude oil on March 10, Year 1, and immediately begins applying the technique in its refinery business. Hessaco agrees to pay its competition an initial payment of $1.8 million on March 10, Year 1 and contingent payments in later years pursuant to an agreed-upon formula. What is the proper tax treatment of the initial $1.8 million payment? What is the proper tax treatment of a $850,000 contingent payment made on January 1, Year 2? What is the proper tax treatment of a $150,000 contingent payment made on January 1, Year 17?

4. On January 1, Year 1, PappaJoes, Inc., a local pizzeria, purchased from a young inventor a patent for tofu-filled pizza crust for $80,000, and immediately began using the patented technique. PappaJoes estimated that the patented pizza would produce $120,000 of income during its 8-year useful life, after which it would have no salvage value. The patent, which was not acquired as part of the acquisition of a trade or business and which had a remaining legal life of 18 years, actually produced $60,000 of income within the first taxable year, $30,000 of income in the second year, and only $1,200 of income in the third year. Is the patent amortizable under § 197? If not, is the patent depreciable under § 167? Assuming § 167 applies, what are the proper deductions for Years 1–3 under the straight-line method and income-forecast method?

5. Dreamworks, a cash-basis limited partnership, was formed with the intent of purchasing and exploiting a documentary movie entitled the "The Life of Donny Osmond." In Year 1, Dreamworks purchased the movie from Universal Films for a total of $1 million, consisting of $150,000 cash contributed by the limited partners/investors and a nonrecourse note obtained by the partnership in the amount of $850,000 secured only by the movie. Dreamworks turned over the function of distributing the film to a distributor who undertook to advertise and promote the movie in return for a percentage of the gross film rentals. Under the distribution agreement, gross film rentals were to be split equally after the distributor was reimbursed for distribution expenses. The pitiful results were as follows:

(a) In Year 1, gross film rentals equaled the distributor's distribution expenses. Thus, Dreamworks received no payments for exploitation of the movie.

(b) In Year 2, gross film rentals totaled $50,000 and the distributor's distribution expenses totaled $22,000. Thus, Dreamworks received $14,000 for exploitation of the film.

(c) In Year 3, Dreamworks received no payments for exploitation of the movie, but "anticipated" net receipts of $10,000 at the beginning of Year 4 based on rentals in Year 3.

Explain whether Dreamworks will be entitled to any deductions in Years 1–3 under the income-forecast method of depreciation.

6. Genius, a professional inventor, granted to Larry the exclusive right to make, use, and sell certain products that utilize the processes claimed in one of Genius's patents. As consideration for the transfer, Larry agreed to pay Genius royalty fees equal to 7% of net sales.

(a) Is Larry entitled to deduct each year's payment to Genius?

(b) What if Genius, instead of transferring the "exclusive right to make, use, and sell," decided to license the patented technology and accompanying know-how, subject to a field of use restriction, for a term of 18 years (two years less than the remaining life of the patent), and Larry agreed to pay Genius 3% of net sales. Would Larry be entitled to deduct each year's payment to Genius?

7. Becky purchases all of the assets of an existing trade or business from Sam. One of the assets acquired is a customized computer installed with various software.

(a) Discuss in general the tax treatment of the software acquisition assuming the cost of the software was not separately stated. Would the result be the same if the computer was acquired separately (not as part of the acquisition of a trade or business)?

(b) What if, six months later, Becky decided to purchase a new package of software for $5,000 from Microsoft?

III. Overview

Intellectual property may be acquired by purchase or license. Moreover, intellectual property may be acquired in a transaction involving the acquisition of a trade or business or may be acquired separately or together with a group of assets that do not constitute a trade or business. As consideration, transferees may make up-front principal payments, installment payments of a fixed amount, payments contingent on exploitation of the intellectual property, or any combination. The deductibility of these acquisition costs varies, depending on the specific type of intellectual property involved and the manner in which the intellectual property was acquired.

A. Purchase Costs

Unlike costs paid or incurred in developing intellectual property, which may be fully deductible in the year paid or incurred, costs of purchasing intellectual property "having a useful life substantially beyond the year" are generally not currently deductible but rather must be capitalized. Treas. Reg. § 1.263(a)-2(a). In December 2002, the Service issued proposed regulations under section 263 that reflect well-established law requiring capitalization of amounts paid to acquire intangible assets. 67 Fed. Reg. 77701 (Dec. 19, 2002). See Prop. Treas. Reg. §1.263(a)-4. The proposed regulations list examples of intangible assets that must be capitalized if the intangible is acquired from another person (e.g., patents, copyrights, trademarks, trade names, and computer software). See Prop. Treas. Reg. § 1.263(a)-4(c)(1).

Although not immediately recoverable (i.e., deductible), the capitalized costs of purchasing intellectual property may be recovered over a certain time period through an amortization allowance to effectuate a fairer allocation of costs to the period in which the taxpayer realizes income. The acquisition costs of several types of intellectual property must be amortized over a fifteen-year period under § 197. The acquisition costs of intellectual property that is excluded from fifteen-year amortization under § 197 may generally be amortized over the intellectual property's useful life or some other statutory recovery period under the rules of § 167.

1. Amortization Under § 197
(a) General Rule

Section 197 allows an amortization deduction for the capitalized costs of an "amortizable section 197 intangible" and prohibits any other depreciation or amortization with respect to that property. I.R.C. § 197(a), (b). An "amortizable section 197 intangible" is any "section 197 intangible" acquired after August 10, 1993 and held in connection with the conduct of a trade or business or an activity described in §212. I.R.C. § 197(c)(1). Subject to important exceptions noted below, a "section 197 intangible" generally includes any patent, copyright, formula, process, design, pattern, know-how, format, package design, computer software, or interest in a film, sound recording, video tape, book, or other similar property. I.R.C. § 197(d)(1)(C). Treas. Reg. § 1.197-2(b)(5). See I.R.C. § 197(e)(3)(B); Treas. Reg. § 1.197-2(c)(4)(iv) (defining computer software for purposes of § 197). A "section 197 intangible" also includes any trademark or trade name. I.R.C. § 197(d)(1)(F). Treas. Reg. § 1.197-2(b)(10). Although the definition of "section 197 intangible" appears broad enough to encompass most forms of intellectual property, there are several important exceptions. As you consider these exceptions below, ask yourself whether a taxpayer would prefer to fall within an exception to § 197? If so, why?

(b) Exceptions for Certain Intellectual Property

Several exceptions in § 197 apply to intellectual property that is *not* acquired in a transaction (or series of related transactions) involving the acquisition of assets constituting a trade or business or substantial portion thereof. Read § 197(e)(4) and § 1.197-2(c) carefully and note which forms of separately acquired intellectual property are excluded from fifteen-year amortization under § 197 and which forms of intellectual property are subject to fifteen-year amortization under § 197 regardless of whether acquired as part of a trade or business or separately.

Determining whether or not intellectual property was acquired in a transaction involving the acquisition of assets constituting a trade or business or substantial portion thereof is not always easy. For purposes of § 197, an asset or group of assets constitutes a trade or business or a substantial portion thereof if their use would constitute a trade or business under § 1060. Treas. Reg. § 1.197-2(e)(1). *See* Treas. Reg. § 1.1060-1(b)(2)(i)(A)–(B). In some circumstances, the acquisition of a single asset may be treated as the acquisition of a trade or business or a substantial portion thereof. For example, the regulations provide that the acquisition of a trademark or trade name constitutes the acquisition of a trade or business or a substantial portion thereof. Treas. Reg. § 1.197-2(e)(2)(i). Doesn't this make sense considering the nature of trademarks and trade names? There are certain circumstances, however, in which the single acquisition of a trademark or trade name is not to be construed as the acquisition of a trade or business. Read carefully Treas. Reg. § 1.197-2(e)(2)(ii)(A)–(C).

What if a taxpayer buys a corporation's stock rather than the corporation's intellectual property assets that constitute a trade or business? Are the costs of acquiring stock of a corporation with substantial intellectual property assets that constitute a trade or business amortizable under § 197? The answer would appear "no" because the Code provides that stock in a corporation is not a "section 197 intangible." I.R.C. § 197(e)(1). However, if the requirements of § 338 are satisfied and if a proper election is made under § 338, a "qualified stock purchase" will be treated as a transaction involving the acquisition of assets constituting a trade or business (deemed asset purchase) if the direct acquisition of the assets of the corporation would have been treated as the acquisition of assets constituting a trade or business. Treas. Reg. § 1.197-2(e)(5). Note the quid pro quo for obtaining a cost basis in the underlying assets and fifteen-year amortization. *See* I.R.C. § 338.

Exception for Readily Available Software and Bundled Software. With respect to computer software, there are additional exceptions in § 197 (in addition to the exception for separately acquired software). A § 197 intangible does not include any interest in computer software that (1) is (or has been) readily available to the general public on similar terms, (2) is subject to a nonexclusive license, and (3) has not been substantially modified. Treas. Reg. § 1.197-2(c)(4). Can this exception for publicly available software be met if the software is not available through a system of retail distribution? Note that computer software will not be considered to have been substantially modified if the cost of all modifications to the version of the software that is readily available to the general public does not exceed the greater of $2,000 or 25% of the price at which the unmodified version of the software is readily available to the general public. *Id.* Are costs incurred to install the computer software considered? What about costs for customization?

Section 197 does not apply to the cost of an interest in computer software where such cost is included, without being separately stated, in the cost of the hardware or other tangible property and is consistently treated as part of the cost of the hardware or other tangible property. Treas. Reg. § 1.197-2(g)(7). Under Revenue Ruling 71-177, included in the materials, the software is included in the hardware's basis and recovered under § 168, which provides depreciation rules for tangible personal property, such as computers. Under § 168, computers are depreciated using an accelerated depreciation method (as opposed to the straight-line method) over an arbitrary five-year recovery period (as opposed to the computer's useful life). I.R.C. § 168(b)(1), (c), (e)(3)(B)(iv), (i)(2).

Exception for Rights of Fixed Duration or Amount. Excluded from the scope of § 197 is any right under a contract (not acquired in a transaction involving the acquisition of a trade or business or a substantial portion thereof) that (1) has a fixed duration of less than fifteen years, or (2) is fixed as to amount and without regard to § 197 would be recoverable under a method similar to the unit-of-production method. I.R.C. § 197(e)(4)(D).

Exception for Contingent Payments for Trademarks and Trade Names. A special rule applies to certain contingent payments for trademarks and trade names. Under § 1253(d)(1), contingent serial payments made by a transferee of a trademark or trade name are not subject to fifteen-year amortization under § 197, but rather are currently deductible under § 162 if several requirements are satisfied. Read I.R.C. § 1253(d)(1) carefully for the elements and review the general requirements for a § 162 trade or business deduction. In most instances, the special rule of § 1253(d)(1) does not apply to payments made pursuant to sales. Why? (As explained below, the special rule applies mainly to payments pursuant to licenses.) If the special rule of § 1253(d)(1) does not apply, then what is the proper tax treatment of contingent payments for trademarks and trade names?

(c) Computing the § 197 Deduction

The amount of the § 197 amortization deduction is determined by amortizing the adjusted basis of the acquired intellectual property ratably over a fifteen-year period irrespective of the intellectual property's useful life. I.R.C. § 197(a); Treas. Reg. § 1.197-2(a)(1). Estimated salvage value is disregarded, so the entire adjusted basis may be recovered through the fifteen-year amortization. Treas. Reg. § 1.197-2(f)(1)(ii). The fifteen-year period begins on the first day of the month in which the intellectual property is acquired and held in connection with either a trade or business (within the meaning of § 162) or an activity conducted for profit (within the meaning of § 212). Because § 197 applies only to acquired intellectual property held in connection with a trade or business or activity conducted for profit, the fifteen-year period cannot begin before the first day of the month in which the conduct of the trade or business or investment activity begins. I.R.C. § 197(c)(1); Treas. Reg. § 1.197-2(f)(1)(i).

To illustrate the fifteen-year amortization rule, assume ABC Corporation, a calendar year taxpayer, acquires intellectual property that is a § 197 intangible for $180,000 on March 10, 2003, and immediately begins using the intellectual property in its trade or business. Because the intellectual property is a § 197 intangible, ABC Corporation must amortize ratably the $180,000 purchase cost over 180 months (15 years x 12 months), or at $1,000 per month. Thus, ABC's amortization deduction in 2003 is $10,000 (10 months @ $1,000 per month). ABC Corporation's amortization deduction in years 2004–2017 will be $12,000 (12 months @ $1,000 per month). The corporation's amortization deduction in the year 2018 will be $2,000 so the entire purchase price is recovered.

Determining Adjusted Basis in Acquired Intellectual Property. The amount amortizable over fifteen years is the taxpayer's adjusted basis in the acquired intellectual property. If intellectual property is purchased, its basis is the amount paid plus any money borrowed to pay the purchase price. I.R.C. § 1012. Included in basis is not only the amount paid for the intellectual property, but also the capitalized acquisition costs (*e.g.*, accounting and legal fees). If intellectual property is acquired as part of the acquisition of an ongoing trade or business, it is important to determine how much of the total purchase price is allocable to the intellectual property. The Code provides allocation rules in the case of certain trade or business acquisitions. For example, in the case of intellectual property acquired in an "applicable asset acquisition" under § 1060, the basis shall be determined under the rules of that section (the "residual method"). *See* I.R.C. § 1060(c); Treas. Reg. § 1.1060-1(b)(1)-(2). In the case of intellectual property deemed to have been acquired as the result of a "qualified stock purchase" within the meaning of § 338, the basis shall be determined under the rules of that section. *See* I.R.C. § 338.

Treatment of Contingent Payments. If the purchase contract calls for fixed installment payments, the entire amount of these payments should also be included in the basis at the time of purchase and amortized over fifteen years. However, if the contract calls for contingent payments—that do not qualify as contingent serial payments as described above—the basis is increased only as the contingent amounts are paid. Read Treas. Reg. § 1.197-2(f)(2)(i)-(ii). What if a contingent payment—that is not a contingent serial payment—is made during the fifteen-year amortization period? What if a contingent payment—that is not a contingent serial payment—is made after the expiration of the fifteen-year period?

2. Amortization Under § 167

(a) General Rule

As discussed in Chapter 4 and this Chapter, § 197 does not apply to a number of different types of intellectual property. If § 197 does not apply to self-created or acquired intellectual property (*e.g.*, patents, copyrights, and certain computer software acquired separately), amortization continues to be governed by pre-section 197 law, and capitalized purchase (or creation) costs may nevertheless be recovered through amortization deductions under § 167. *See* Treas. Reg. § 1.167(a)-14 (providing rules for the amortization of intellectual property not covered by § 197). To be eligible to amortize the capitalized costs of acquiring (or creating) intellectual property under § 167, several requirements must be met: (1) the intellectual property must not be covered by § 197; (2) the intellectual property must have an ascertainable useful life (and, of course, an ascertainable cost basis); and (3) the taxpayer must be engaged in either a trade or business or an activity conducted for profit. I.R.C. § 167(a).

As to the first requirement, which purchased intellectual property assets fall within the exception to the definition of the term "section 197 intangible," and thus may be eligible for amortization under § 167 provided the other requirements are met? Review I.R.C. § 197(e); Treas. Reg. § 1.197-2(c), discussed above. As to the second requirement, which forms of intellectual property excluded from § 197 amortization have determinable, useful lives (*i.e.*, which intellectual property assets are "known from experience or other factors to be of use in the trade or business or in the production of income for only a limited period, the length of which may be estimated with reasonable accuracy")? See Treas. Reg. § 1.167(a)-3, discussed in Chapters 3 and 4. As to the third requirement, what is the test for determining whether a taxpayer is engaged in a trade or business or an activity conducted for profit? Review Chapters 3 and 4 for the standards and relevant factors that should be taken into accounting in determining whether or not an activity is a hobby.

(b) Computing the § 167 Deduction

There are different methods of amortizing the capitalized costs of purchasing (or creating) eligible intellectual property under § 167. The regulations provide that amortization must be determined in accordance with a "reasonably consistent plan." Common methods are the straight-line method and the income-forecast method, both of which are discussed below. Some methods are generally not available. Read Revenue Ruling 79-285, included in the materials, below.

(i) Straight-line Method

The simplest method is the straight-line method, under which capitalized costs of acquiring (or creating) eligible property (less salvage value) are deducted ratably over the period the taxpayer expects the property to be useful in his or her trade or business. Recall from Chapter 2 the statutory recovery periods for separately acquired patents and copyrights. Do the purchase costs for such assets necessarily have to be amortized over such long recovery periods? Hint: See the regulatory definition of useful life in Treas. Reg. §1.167(a)-1(b). Does this regulatory definition of useful life permit a faster or slower recovery of the costs of acquiring eligible patents and copyrightable works?

With respect to computer software not covered by §197, the period over which software may reasonably be expected to be useful to the taxpayer in her trade or business is irrelevant. This is because the Code provides very favorable treatment for computer software in a set of arbitrary recovery rules. The cost of any computer software that is not subject to §197 and that is not taken into account as part of the cost of computer hardware (non-bundled software) is amortized ratably over a 36-month recovery period beginning on the first day of the month the computer software is placed in service. I.R.C. §167(f). The cost of any computer software that is taken into account as part of the cost of computer hardware or other tangible property (bundled software) is depreciated over the appropriate recovery period of the related hardware. See Rev. Rul. 71-177, which follows this Overview.

(ii) Income-Forecast Method

Although the regulations contemplate use of the straight-line method, they permit a taxpayer to amortize eligible intellectual property using a method other than the straight-line method if the alternative method provides a more reasonable allowance. Treas. Reg. §1.167(b)-1(a). A permitted alternative amortization method for eligible intellectual property acquisition (or creation) costs is the "income-forecast" method. Under the income-forecast method, capitalized costs of acquiring (or creating) eligible intellectual property are recovered as income is earned from exploitation of the property. More specifically, a taxpayer determines the amortization deduction each year by multiplying the taxpayer's basis in (usually cost of) eligible intellectual property by an amortization fraction. The numerator of the fraction is the income from the asset for the taxable year. The denominator is the forecasted or estimated total income to be earned in connection with the asset during its useful life. Review Revenue Procedure 60-358, included below, which illustrates the mechanics of the income-forecast method. Note that this Revenue Procedure was amplified by Revenue Procedure 79-285, also included below.

Although the income-forecast method has been a permissible method for certain properties since the early 1960s, Congress enacted §167(g) in 1996 to ensure that, for certain properties, the allowances for depreciation appropriately match the basis of an income-forecast property with the income derived therefrom. Small Business Job Protection Act of 1996, P.L. 104-188, 1604 (Aug. 20, 1996). In 1997, Congress amended §167(g) to place limitations on the type of property that could be depreciated using the income-forecast method. Taxpayer Relief Act of 1997, P.L. 105-34, 1086 (Aug. 5, 1997). In May 2002, the IRS and Treasury Department issued proposed regulations relating to the income-forecast method of depreciation under §167(g) to reflect changes to the law made in 1996 and 1997. 67 Fed. Reg. 38025 (May 31, 2002). The proposed regulations can be found in Prop. Treas. Reg. §§ 1.167(n)-1 through § 1.167(n)-7. Read § 167(g), which limits the types of property for which the income-forecast method may be used. Why is the income-forecast method appropriate for the properties listed in § 167(g)?

As noted above, the depreciation allowance for an income-forecast property for a given taxable year is computed by multiplying the depreciable basis of the property by a fraction, the numerator of which is current year income and the denominator of which is forecasted total income. Consider the following example:

> In 2003, Fran purchases and places in service income forecast property with a depreciable basis of $100, and estimates that forecasted total income from the property will be $200. In 2003, current year income is $80. The depreciation allowance for 2003 is $40, computed by multiplying the depreciable basis of the property of $100 by the fraction obtained by dividing current year income of $80 by forecasted total income of $200.

Under the proposed regulations to § 263, taxpayers must evaluate the accuracy of their income forecasts annually. If information is discovered in a later taxable year that indicates that forecasted total income is inaccurate, a taxpayer must compute "revised forecasted total income" for the taxable year. Prop. Treas. Reg. § 1.167(n)-3(c). If revised forecasted total income differs from forecasted total income, a taxpayer may determine the depreciation allowance using a revised computation. Id. § 1.167(n)-4(b)(1). Under the revised computation, the unrecovered depreciable basis of the income-forecast property is multiple by a fraction, the numerator of which is current year income and the denominator of which is obtained by subtracting from revised forecasted total income the amounts of current year income from prior taxable years. Id. Assume the facts in the above example.

> In the second year, 2004, Fran's current year income is $40. In addition, Fran computes revised forecasted total income to be $176. The depreciation allowance for 2004 computed under the revised computation is $25, computed by multiplying the unrecovered depreciable basis of $60 by the fraction obtained by dividing current year income of $40 by $96 (revised forecasted total income of $176 less current year income from prior taxable years of $80).

Under the proposed regulations, a taxpayer is required to use the revised computation if forecasted total income in the immediately preceding taxable year is either less than 90% or greater than 110% of revised forecasted total income for the taxable year. Id. § 1.167(n)-4(b)(2). Under the proposed regulations, would Fran in the above example be *required* to compute her depreciation allowance using the revised computation described above?

Under the Code, a taxpayer may deduct as a depreciation allowance the remaining depreciable basis of income-forecast property in the tenth taxable year following the taxable year the income-forecast property is placed in service. I.R.C. § 167(g)(1)(C). What happens if the income-forecast property ceases to generate income before the end of the tenth year following the taxable year that the property is placed in service? See Prop. Treas. Reg. § 1.167(n)-4(d)(1)(i), (3). What if additional amounts are paid or incurred with respect to income-forecast property after final depreciation has been taken? See id. § 1.167(n)-4(d)(2), (4).

The income-forecast method generally permits a taxpayer to recover intellectual property acquisition (or creation) costs more quickly than the straight-line method would allow. As illustrated by *Greene v. Commissioner*, included in the materials, the income-forecast method is not without its drawbacks. Does the income-forecast method require use of net income or gross income in the amortization fraction? Is any amortization deduction allowed under the income-forecast method for a year in which no income is earned? If not, can a taxpayer who uses the income-forecast method wish to switch to the straight-line method or some other allowable method to get a deduction for that year?

(iii) Treatment of Contingent Payments
(The Variable Contingent Payment Method)

Another alternative (and popular) method for the amortization of intellectual property that is not subject to § 197 is the variable contingent payment method. The variable contingent payment method is perhaps the most important method for amortizing intellectual property that is not subject to § 197 but that is purchased for contingent payments. Under the variable contingent payment method, a taxpayer who purchases intellectual property (that is not subject to § 197) for contingent payments (*e.g.*, payments computed by reference to income from the use of the intellectual property) adds such payments to the basis of the intellectual property in the taxable year paid but then amortizes the full amount paid in that year. In other words, the amortization deduction each year equals the amount of the royalty paid or incurred each year. The Tax Court sanctioned use of this method in *Associated Patentees, Inc. v. Commissioner*, a case included in this Chapter. The IRS later agreed to follow the *Associated Patentees* decision in Revenue Ruling 67-136, also included in the materials. What is the rationale behind permitting an immediate deduction for each year's payment? Is the treatment of contingent payments for intellectual property that is not subject to § 197 (*e.g.*, separately acquired patents) more generous than the treatment of contingent payments for intellectual property that is subject to § 197 (*e.g.*, patents acquired with a trade or business)?

B. Licensing of Intellectual Property

So far, consideration has been given to the tax consequences of purchasing intellectual property. Intellectual property, however, may also be acquired by license. What are the tax consequences of licensing rather than purchasing such property? Can a taxpayer avoid § 197 treatment (*i.e.*, fifteen-year amortization) and obtain current deductions by licensing intellectual property rather than purchasing such property?

1. Licenses Acquired as Part of a Trade or Business

A contract for the use of a § 197 intangible *is itself a § 197 intangible*. Treas. Reg. § 1.197-2(b)(11). Section 197 intangibles include many forms of intellectual property acquired in a transaction involving the acquisition of a trade or business. Thus, with the exceptions noted below, payments made under a contract for the use of intellectual property that is a § 197 intangible and that is acquired as part of the acquisition of a trade or business must be capitalized, even if such payments would be deductible under normal tax principles without regard to § 197. Treas. Reg. § 1.197-2(f)(3)(ii)(A). Initial payments under such a license are capitalized and amortized over a fifteen-year period. Later payments made under such a license are capitalized and amortized over the remaining fifteen-year period.

A broad exception exists for certain licenses acquired as part of the purchase of a trade or business, under which payments may be currently deductible. Specifically, payments made for the use of any information base, patent, copyright, formula, process, design, pattern, know-how, format, package design, certain computer software, interest in a film, sound recording, video tape, book, or other similar property do not have to be capitalized even though acquired as part of the acquisition of a trade or business, provided the taxpayer establishes that (1) the transfer of the right is not, under the principles of § 1235, a transfer of all substantial rights to such property or of an undivided interest in all substantial rights to such property; and (2) the right was transferred for an arm's-length consideration. Treas. Reg. § 1.197-2(f)(3)(ii)(B)(1)–(2).

Another exception exists for contingent payments for trademarks and trade names. As discussed above, contingent payments under a trademark or trade name are currently deductible provided they qualify as contingent serial payments under section 1253. I.R.C. § 1253(d)(1). What is the proper tax treatment of license payments that fail to qualify as contingent serial payments?

2. Licenses Not Acquired as Part of a Trade or Business

Payments made under a contract for the use of intellectual property and that is not acquired as part of the acquisition of a trade or business may be deducted under normal tax principles (§ 162) over the license term. It should be noted that licenses not acquired as part of a purchase of a trade or business will be closely scrutinized to determine whether the arrangement is really a sale under the principles of § 1235. Treas. Reg. § 1.197-2(f)(3)(iii). Private Letter Ruling 200137013, included in the materials, provides an example of how the IRS applies the principles of § 1235 to determine whether or not license payments are currently deductible.

It should be noted that certain rights of fixed duration or amount under a contract not acquired in a transaction involving the acquisition of a trade or business are excluded from the scope of § 197. See I.R.C. § 197(e)(4)(D). The amount of the deduction for a right of fixed duration or amount under such a contract depends on whether the rights are (1) to a fixed amount or (2) to an unspecified amount, over a fixed duration of less than fifteen years. See Treas. Reg. § 1.167(a)-14(c)(2)–(3) for rules determining the amount of the deduction in either case.

C. Income from Holding Intellectual Property

After a taxpayer acquires intellectual property, the taxpayer is taxed on any income generated by that property. See I.R.C. § 61(a)(6) (including in gross income royalties derived from the licensing of property). Many individual taxpayers prefer not to operate their business as a sole proprietorship, but instead choose to operate through a business form of statutory creation. A variety of state-law business forms are available that provide limited liability protection to owners of intellectual property. Unincorporated business entities, such as limited partnerships and limited liability companies, generally are not separate taxable entities for federal income tax purposes, but rather are treated as pass-through entities. Items of income and deductions are determined at the entity level, but then flow through to the individual owners and are reported on their individual returns. Corporations, however, generally are separate tax entities that have to pay tax on their taxable income. *See* I.R.C. § 11 (tax rates applicable to C corporations). Shareholders pay a second level of tax when the corporation's income is distributed. I.R.C. § 61(a)(7).

A corporation holding intellectual property might also be subject to a personal holding company tax. The personal holding company tax is a penalty tax that is imposed on certain closely held corporations that have a substantial amount of undistributed passive income. The tax is equal to the highest tax rate under § 1(c) times the "undistributed personal holding company income" of every "personal holding company." I.R.C. § 541.

The Code provides that any corporation is a personal holding company if it meets two mechanical tests, one relating to the character of income earned during the year (passive income test) and the second relating to the number of stockholders (the stock ownership test). Under these tests, a corporation is deemed to be a personal holding company if (1) at least 60% of the corporation's adjusted ordinary gross income (operating income minus operating deductions) for the taxable year is personal holding company income (interest, dividends, royalties, etc.); and (2) at any time during the last half of the taxable year, more than 50% in value of the corporation's outstanding stock is owned, directly or indirectly, by or for not more than 5 individuals. I.R.C. § 542(a)(1)–(2).

The tax is imposed on undistributed personal holding income. I.R.C. §§ 545(a), 561(a), 547. Personal holding company income is "passive"-type income and generally includes royalties derived from the licensing of intellectual property. I.R.C. § 543(a)(1) (general royalty provisions). The Code deals specifically with certain copyright royalties. I.R.C. § 543(a)(4) (special royalty provision for certain copyrights). Generally, copyright royalties are considered personal holding company income, unless such royalties constitute 50% or more of the corporation's ordinary gross income and if certain other personal holding company income does not exceed 10% of the corporation's ordinary gross income. The Code goes on to state that the term "copyright royalties" means compensation, however designated, for the use of, or the right to use, copyrights in works protected by copyright issued under title 17 of the United States Code. Because computer software may now obtain copyright protection under title 17 without formal application, this special rule seemingly impacts royalties derived from the licensing of computer software. An exception is made, however, for corporations that engage almost exclusively in the licensing of computer software. Under § 543(d), corporations actively engaged in the development and licensing of software will not be treated as receiving personal holding company income. I.R.C. § 543(d).

The personal holding company tax is designed to prevent corporations from accumulating passive-type earnings for the purpose of tax avoidance. How could a corporation avoid the penalty tax?

IV. Materials

Revenue Ruling 71-177
1971-1 C. B. 5

During 1968, a taxpayer purchased a new computer. The cost of the software provided with the computer was not separately stated. In accordance with his consistent practice, the taxpayer capitalized the entire cost of the computer, including the cost of the software provided with it, and deducted depreciation thereon based upon a useful life in excess of four years.

Held, the cost of the computer, in the instant case, includes the cost of the software provided with it for purposes of the depreciation allowed under section 167 of the Internal Revenue Code of 1954 and the investment credit allowed under section 38 of the Code.

Revenue Ruling 60-358
1960-2 C.B. 68

It has come to the attention of the Internal Revenue Service that the methods of computing depreciation described in [former] section 167(b) of the Code are in most cases inadequate when applied to television films, resulting in a distortion of income on the returns filed by taxpayers deriving income from such films. This distortion is caused by a strikingly uneven flow of income, earned by groups of programs within the series, resulting from contract restrictions, methods of distribution and audience appeal of the programs. If the film series is a success, additional income will be forthcoming from reruns over a period of years, depending upon its popularity; whereas, unsuccessful film series may produce little or no income after the initial exhibition. Thus the usefulness of such assets in the taxpayer's trade or business is measurable over the income it produces and cannot be adequately measured by the passage of time alone. Therefore, in order to avoid distortion, depreciation must follow the "flow of income."

Some producers of television films have used the so-called "cost recovery" method in reporting their income. By use of this method, no taxable income is reported until the income from the films exceeds the cost thereof. However, such "cost recovery" method is not acceptable for Federal income tax purposes.

After an extensive study and consideration of the matter, the Service has concluded that the so-called "income forecast" method is readily adaptable in computing depreciation of the cost of television films without producing any serious distortion of income. This method requires the application of a fraction, the numerator of which is the income from the films for the taxable year, and the denominator of which is the forecasted or estimated total income to be derived from the films during their useful life, including estimated income from foreign exhibition or other exploitation of such films. The term "income" for purposes of computing this fraction means income from the films less the expense of distributing the films, not including depreciation. This fraction is multiplied by the cost of films which produced income during the taxable year, after appropriate adjustment for estimated salvage value. The "income forecast" method may be illustrated as follows:

> *Example*: Certain television films which produced income within the first taxable year cost 800x dollars, after appropriate adjustment for estimated salvage value. The income therefrom for the first taxable year was 600x dollars; second year 150x dollars; and third year, 300x dollars. Total estimated income to be derived from the films 1200x dollars.
>
> 600x dollars/1200x dollars x 800x dollars=400x dollars (first year's depreciation)

150x dollars/1200x dollars x 800x dollars=100x dollars (second year's depreciation)

300x dollars/1200x dollars x 800x dollars=200x dollars (third year's depreciation)

If the estimated income from the television films should be less than the cost thereof, thus resulting in a loss, the use of the "income forecast" method for computing depreciation will reflect such loss in the proper taxable years based on the amount of income from the films derived in each taxable year.

If in subsequent years it is found that the income forecast was substantially overestimated or underestimated by reason of circumstances occurring in such subsequent years, an adjustment of the income forecast for such subsequent years may be made. In such case, the formula for computing depreciation would be as follows: income for the taxable year divided by the revised estimated income (the current year's income and estimated future income), multiplied by the unrecovered depreciable film cost remaining as of the beginning of the taxable year.

The total forecast or estimated income to be derived from the films should be based on the conditions known to exist at the end of the period for which the return is made. This estimate can be revised upward or downward, as explained above, at the end of subsequent taxable periods based on additional information which became available after the last prior estimate.

Accordingly, it is the position of the Service that the "income forecast" method described above constitutes an acceptable method for computing a reasonable allowance for depreciation of the cost of television films under section 167(a) of the Code.

In applying the above methods of depreciation, television films shall not be depreciated below a reasonable salvage value, such value being the amount which it is estimated will be realizable upon sale or other disposition of such films when they are no longer useful in the taxpayer's business or in the production of his income. The time when such films are no longer useful in the taxpayer's business, etc., may vary according to his policy with respect to the use thereof. If the taxpayer's policy is to dispose of the films after the initial showing, the salvage value may represent a relatively large proportion of the original cost of such films. However, if the taxpayer customarily uses the films after the initial showing for reruns, syndication, foreign exhibition, or other exploitation thereof, the salvage value may represent a relatively small proportion of the original cost. If there is a redetermination of the "income forecast," as explained above, salvage value may be redetermined based upon the known facts at the time of such redetermination of the "income forecast."

The principle of "income forecast" as set forth in this Revenue Ruling is limited in its application to television films, taped shows for reproduction and other property of a similar character.

Revenue Ruling 79-285
1979-2 C. B. 91

ISSUES

Does use of a "sliding scale" method of computing depreciation for a book manuscript result in a reasonable allowance for depreciation under section 167(a) of the Internal Revenue Code...under circumstances described below?

When is a book manuscript placed in service for purposes of section 1.167(a)-10(b) of the Income Tax Regulations?

FACTS

On January 1, 1975, A, an individual, purchased all rights to a book manuscript for the sum of 200x dollars and entered into an agreement with P, a publisher, to print, publish, and sell the book. The first copies of the regular trade edition were published and sold during October 1975.

Under terms of the publishing contract, A will receive specified royalties on sales of the book, and a share of the proceeds from the sale or licensing of other publication rights by the publisher. In April and October of each year following publication of the book, P will provide A with semi-annual statements showing royalties or other sums accruing to A for the preceding semi-annual periods ending December 31 and June 20 respectively, together with payment of amounts due A for the period covered by the statement.

A reported no income from the book for the taxable year 1975. However, A did claim a depreciation deduction in the amount of 100x dollars computed by use of a "sliding scale" method of depreciation. The schedule attached to the return showed an estimated life for the book of 4 years with depreciation rates of 50 percent for the first year, 25 percent for the second year, 15 percent for the third year, and 10 percent for the fourth year.

LAW

Section 461(a) of the Internal Revenue Code provides that any deduction shall be taken for the taxable year that is proper under the method of accounting used in computing taxable income.

Section 446(b) of the Code provides that if the taxpayer does not use a regular method of accounting, or if the method used by the taxpayer does not clearly reflect income, taxable income will be computed in accordance with a method that, in the opinion of the Secretary, does clearly reflect income.

Section 167(a) of the Code provides that there shall be allowed as a depreciation deduction a reasonable allowance for the exhaustion, wear and tear, and obsolescence of property used in the trade or business or held for the production of income.

Section 1.167(a)-3 of the regulations provides that intangible assets such as copyrights and patents with determinable useful lives may be the subject of a depreciation allowance. Section 1.167(a)-6(a) provides that a patent or copyright may be depreciated over its remaining useful life.

Section 1.167(a)-10(b) of the regulations provides that the period of depreciation for an asset begins when the asset is placed in service and ends when the asset is retired from service. A proportionate part of one year's depreciation is allowable for that part of the first year and last year during which the asset was in service.

Rev. Rul. 60-358, 1960-2 C.B. 68, as amplified by Rev. Rul. 64-273, 1964-2 C.B. 62, recognizes that methods of computing depreciation described in [former] section 167(b) of the Code are in most cases inadequate when applied to motion picture and television films and other property of a similar character, because such methods result in a distortion of income. Rev. Rul. 60-358 states that the usefulness of such assets in the taxpayer's trade or business is measurable over the income it produces and cannot be adequately measured by the passage of time alone. Therefore, in order to avoid distortion of income, depreciation must follow the "flow of income." The Revenue Ruling holds that the income forecast method of depreciation is an acceptable method for computing a reasonable allowance for depreciation of the cost of such property.

Rev. Rul. 78-28, 1978-1 C.B. 61, holds that income reflected in the numerator of the fraction used to compute the depreciation for the taxable year under the income forecast method must reflect the same gross income used to compute taxable income from the property for the same period.

ANALYSIS

In Rev. Rul. 60-358, it is recognized that the usefulness of assets such as movie and television films, and property used to generate a similar uneven flow of income, is measurable over the income it produces, and that the income forecast method of computing depreciation permits recovery of asset costs without producing any serious distortion of income. Books, patents, and sound recordings used to produce income in a manner similar to television and movie films are other property similar in character for purposes of Rev. Rul. 60-358.

Any method other than the straight line and income forecast methods of computing depreciation deductions for intangible assets must clearly reflect income as provided in section 446(b) of the Code. In *KIRO, Inc. v. Commissioner*, 51 T.C. 155 (1968), acq., 1974-2 C.B. 3, the court found that the "sliding scale" method of computing depreciation for television films subject to contract terms limiting their use, and indicating a rate of exhaustion as a function of sequential exposures, resulted in a reasonable depreciation allowance. The sliding scale rate was based largely on the rate of exhaustion indicated by the contract terms. Films not subject to comparable contract terms could not be depreciated by use of the sliding scale method.

In the present case, there is no contract or other pertinent data to support the contention that the depreciation deductions computed by use of the "sliding scale" method are reasonable and clearly reflect income.

Motion picture rights are placed in service when the film is initially released for public exhibition. Manuscript rights having the same characteristics for purposes of depreciation as motion picture film rights, are placed in service when books produced from the manuscript are first released for distribution and sale.

HOLDING

In this case, the sliding scale method of computing depreciation allowances for the book manuscript fails to clearly reflect income as provided in section 446(b) of the Code and is, therefore, not an acceptable method of depreciation for Federal income tax purposes. The income forecast and straight line methods are acceptable methods for computing depreciation allowances for book manuscripts. The same conclusion applies to patents and master recordings.

Rights to manuscripts are placed in service when copies of the book are first released for distribution and sale. Similarly, rights to patents and master recordings are placed in service when products or processes resulting from these rights are first released for distribution and sale, or are used in the trade or business or for the production of income. However, patents are not placed in service prior to the issue date.

EFFECT ON OTHER REVENUE RULINGS

Revenue Ruling 60-358 is amplified.

Greene v. Commissioner
81 T.C. 132 (1983)

SIMPSON, JUDGE:

This matter is before the Court on the parties' cross motions for partial summary judgment pursuant to Rule 121, Tax Court Rules of Practice and Procedure. The sole issue raised by the motions is whether Alpha Film Company (Alpha) is entitled to a depreciation deduction for 1975 under the income forecast method.

The Commissioner determined a deficiency of $9,195.00 in the petitioners' Federal income tax for 1975. The deficiency resulted from the disallowance of the depreciation deduction claimed by Alpha and from certain other adjustments not now before us. The petitioners, Lorne and Nancy Greene, husband and wife, resided in Los Angeles, Calif., at the time they filed their petition with this Court seeking a redetermination of such deficiency. Mr. Greene will sometimes be referred to as the petitioner.

In 1975, the petitioner was a limited partner of Alpha, a New York partnership. Alpha was organized in 1972 for the stated purpose of purchasing the sole and exclusive right to exhibit, distribute, and otherwise exploit the motion picture "Ten Days' Wonder" (the film) in the United States, portions of Canada, and certain other limited areas of the world. The partnership purchased the film from Les Films La Boetie, the French owner of the film, in 1972 for a stated price of $2,250,000.

After purchasing the film, Alpha entered into a distribution agreement with Levitt-Pickman Film Corporation (Levitt-Pickman). The agreement granted Levitt-Pickman "each and every right, license and privilege with reference to the Picture and the exploitation thereof" for a period of 10 years in the territory purchased by Alpha with certain minor exceptions. In return for distributing the film, Levitt-Pickman was to receive a distribution fee of 30 percent of the gross receipts from the theatrical exhibition of the film. Additionally, Levitt-Pickman was to be reimbursed for certain distribution expenses.

The distribution agreement further provided that Levitt-Pickman was to deposit all gross receipts which it received from exhibitors into a bank account to be opened by Alpha, entitled the "Ten Days' Wonder Special Account" (special account). Withdrawals could be made from this account only over the joint signatures of representatives of both Alpha and Levitt-Pickman. Insofar as is relevant, the distribution agreement provided that until the gross receipts exceeded $1,000,000 and the net receipts exceeded $625,000, the gross receipts were to be withdrawn from the account and distributed according to the following order of priority:

(1) To Levitt-Pickman for unrecouped distribution expenses;

(2) Balance, if any, to Levitt-Pickman for distribution fees;

(3) Remaining balance, if any, to Alpha.

Levitt-Pickman began distributing the film in 1972. It premiered in several major cities and, over the next few years, was exhibited in more than 100 motion picture theaters in 76 cities throughout the country. Pursuant to the distribution agreement, Levitt-Pickman deposited in the special account the gross receipts as they were received from the theaters for the exhibition of the film. In 1972, Levitt-Pickman incurred reimbursable distribution expenses of $104,091.83, and by the end of 1973, such expenses totaled $111,578.00.

For 1972 through 1976, Alpha filed returns on a calendar year basis and used the cash method of accounting. On such returns, the following amounts were reported:

Item	1972	1973	1974	1975	1976
Gross receipts	$34,901	$16,006	$2,920	$6,049	$902
Distribution expenses	34,901	16,006	2,920	6,049	902
Other expenses	9,442	—	—	—	—
Depreciation	1,358,458	480,043	51,458	146,653	7,719

Because the gross receipts for 1972 through 1976 totaled $60,778, Levitt-Pickman was reimbursed over such years for only that amount of its distribution expenses.

The depreciation deductions claimed on such returns were computed by use of the income forecast method. On the returns, the calculation of the deductions were set forth as follows:

	1972	1973	1974	1975	1976
Current exhibition receipts:					
Cash	$34,901	$1,397	$1,920	$6,049	$902
Accrued	14,609	4,433	—	—	—
	49,510	5,830	1,920	6,049	902
Total of current and future receipts	74,500	8,330	7,820	6,367	902
Unrecovered basis of film	2,044,331	685,873	205,830	154,372	7,719
Depreciation rate (Ratio of current exhibition receipts to total current and future receipts)	X 66.45%	X 69.99%	X 25%	X 95%	X 100%
Depreciation for year	1,358,458	480,043	51,458	146,653	7,719

On their Federal income tax return for 1975, the petitioners claimed a deduction for a loss attributable to the operation of Alpha. Such loss resulted from the depreciation deduction claimed by Alpha in that year. In his notice of deficiency, the Commissioner determined that Alpha was not entitled to such depreciation and disallowed the deduction claimed by the petitioners.

Section 167(a) of the Internal Revenue Code of 1954 provides that a taxpayer shall be allowed, as a depreciation deduction, a reasonable allowance for the exhaustion of property used in a trade or business. Depreciation is "an accounting device which recognizes that the physical consumption of a capital asset is a true cost, since the asset is being depleted." *Commissioner v. Idaho Power Co.*, 418 U.S. 1, 10 (1974). "[I]t is the primary purpose of depreciation accounting to further the integrity of periodic income statements by making a meaningful allocation of the cost entailed in the use (excluding maintenance expense) of the asset to the periods to which it contributes." *Massey Motors, Inc. v. United States*, 364 U.S. 92, 104 (1960). Because television films typically generate an uneven flow of income, the Commissioner took the position in Rev. Rul. 60-358, 1960-2 C.B. 68, that, in most cases, the time-based methods of depreciation described in [former] section 167(b) are inadequate when applied to such films. The usefulness of a television film in a taxpayer's trade or business is more accurately measured over the stream of income it produces than over the passage of time alone. Consequently, the Commissioner has authorized use of the income forecast method.

In relevant part, Rev. Rul. 60-358 states at pp. 68–69:

> After an extensive study and consideration of the matter, the Service has concluded that the so-called "income forecast" method is readily adaptable in computing depreciation of the cost of television films without producing any serious distortion of income. This method required the application of a fraction, the numerator of which is the income from the films for the taxable year, and the denominator of which is the forecasted or estimated total income to be derived from the films during their useful life, including estimated income from foreign exhibition or other exploitation of such films. The term "income" for purposes of computing this fraction means income from the films less the expense of distributing the films, not including depreciation. This fraction is multiplied by the cost of films which produced income during the taxable year, after appropriate adjustment for estimated salvage value. * * *
>
> If in subsequent years it is found that the income forecast was substantially overestimated or underestimated by reason of circumstances occurring in such subsequent years, an adjustment of the income forecast for such subsequent years may be made.

By Rev. Rul. 64-273, 1964-2 C.B. 62, the Internal Revenue Service also authorized the use of the income forecast method with respect to motion picture films. The application of such method by the Commissioner has been approved by the Court in a series of cases. *Wildman v. Commissioner*, 78 T.C. 943, 950 (1982); *Siegel v. Commissioner*, 78 T.C. 659, 692 (1982); *Schneider v. Commissioner*, 65 T.C. 18, 32-33 (1975).

In most cases involving the distribution of motion picture films, the owner or producer includes in gross income only "net receipts." In the typical distribution agreement, the producer grants a license to the distributor to exploit the film. The distributor then sublicenses or leases the film to theatre owners for exhibition. The gross rentals are received by the distributor and includable in his gross income. The distributor passes over to the producer a net producer's share, which represents the gross rentals less the distributor's fee and distribution expenses, and the producer includes in gross income only the net producer's share. Thus, in applying the income forecast method, a producer under a typical distribution agreement computes his depreciation deduction on a net producer's share, or net income.

In his motion for partial summary judgment, the Commissioner takes the position that the distribution agreement between Alpha and Levitt-Pickman did not substantially differ from the standard distribution agreement, despite the arrangements with respect to the special account. He argues that because the gross receipts from the exhibition of the film were less than the distribution expenses, Alpha had no right to any of such receipts. On the other hand, the petitioners moved for a partial summary judgment in their favor on the grounds that the gross receipts were includable in the gross income of Alpha, and they urge us to hold, as a matter of law, that they are entitled to apply an income forecast method utilizing such gross receipts in the income forecast fraction. If we deny their motion, the petitioners request, in the alternative, that they be given a trial and an opportunity to prove that their method is a reasonable method for computing the allowable depreciation.

When Alpha filed its return for 1972, it had to select a depreciation method for the film. It could have used the straight line method (cf. *Tribune Publishing Co. v. Commissioner*, 52 T.C. 717 (1969), affd. per curiam 451 F.2d 600 (9th Cir. 1971); *Inter-City Television Film Corp. v. Commissioner*, 43 T.C. 270 (1964)), or the income forecast method described in Rev. Rul. 60-358, *supra*. Under the revenue ruling, the numerator and denominator of the income forecast fraction clearly were to consist of actual net income and estimated total net income, respectively. Alpha's professional advisors could not have misunderstood such requirement. Despite that requirement, the partnership elected to use the income forecast method. Now, having failed to compute its depreciation in accordance with the conditions of the revenue ruling, Alpha wishes to use a method different from both that prescribed by the Commissioner and that it actually used.

In *Siegel v. Commissioner, supra*, the partnership kept its books under the cash method of accounting. However, in reporting its gross income and calculating its depreciation deduction under the income forecast method, the partnership included the net producer's share of the film's exhibition rentals and the amount belonging to the distributor for its expenses, even though such amounts were not actually received by the partnership. The Court rejected the taxpayers' argument that "income" for purposes of the numerator of the income forecast fraction is the gross rentals received by the distributor, whether or not such rentals are includable in the gross income of the owner. We observed that the underlying purpose of the income forecast method is to match income with the expenses incurred in the production of such income. Therefore, we held that the taxpayer must have receipts properly reportable as income under its method of accounting in order to be entitled to a depreciation deduction under the income forecast method. Because the partnership had no reportable income in the year in issue, the numerator of the income forecast fraction was zero, and therefore, no depreciation deduction was allowable. 78 T.C. at 693.

Likewise, this Court rejected another attempted variation in the use of the income forecast method in *Wildman v. Commissioner, supra*. The taxpayer in that case conceded that net receipts were to be used in applying the income forecast method but argued that the partnership should be allowed to use the accrual method for computing the net receipts to be used for such purpose even though the partnership used the cash method for reporting its income. The partnership had not actually received any payments from the distributor. Relying on *Siegel*, we held that the partnership was not entitled to a depreciation deduction because it had no reportable income in the year in issue which could be used in the numerator of the income forecast method. 78 T.C. at 951.

In both *Siegel* and *Wildman*, the owners of films elected to compute their depreciation deductions by use of the income forecast method, but in both cases, they sought to vary the method prescribed in Rev. Rul. 60-358. In both cases, the Court rejected the proposed variation and held that no deduction was allowable. In *Wildman*, the owner then sought to change its election and to compute depreciation by use of a different method. The Court also rejected that claim and held that the owner could not change the method chosen by it without the consent of the Commissioner. The Court said:

> petitioners herein chose a clearly acceptable method (income forecast) but simply used such method improperly. Even the case upon which petitioners rely recognized that once a taxpayer selects an acceptable method of depreciation, he may only change that method with the consent of respondent. [78 T.C. at 952.]

Thus, in both *Wildman* and *Siegel*, we held that since the owners of the films had elected to compute depreciation by use of the income forecast method, they had to use the method as prescribed by the Commissioner.

Moreover, the use of the income forecast method as prescribed by the Commissioner has the advantage of assuring similarity of tax treatment for owners of films. If the owner uses a standard distribution agreement, his depreciation deduction is based on the net income received by him. An owner may distribute his own film or may employ an agent, and in such case he will be treated in a like manner if he is required to compute his depreciation on the basis of his net income.

The petitioners have requested an opportunity to prove that their method is reasonable; yet, they neither used a method consistently nor used the method now urged by them. In 1975, Alpha reported actual cash receipts as gross income and used that amount as the numerator of the income forecast fraction. However, in 1972 through 1974, Alpha reported actual cash receipts as gross income but calculated the numerator under an accrual method, adding accrued (but not yet paid) receipts to only those cash receipts earned during the year. Because Alpha reported income under the cash receipts method, it was clearly improper for Alpha to use accrued receipts in computing its income forecast (*Wildman v. Commissioner*, 78 T.C. at 951), and under no view was the method actually used by Alpha acceptable under the law.

After a review of all the arguments, we have concluded that the petitioners have failed to establish that there is any reason for a trial. Because Alpha elected to use the income forecast method, it was required to use that method as prescribed by the Commissioner in the absence of requesting and securing his approval to change its method. Moreover, Alpha never actually used the method urged by it, and its method was clearly improper. Thus, we hold that, as a matter of law, Alpha was required to use net income in the numerator of the income forecast fraction. There is a question as to whether the gross receipts deposited in the special account constituted gross income received by Alpha, but in view of our conclusion that only net income was to be used in the numerator of the income forecast fraction, and in view of the fact that Alpha had no net income in 1975, we need not decide whether the gross receipts constituted gross income of Alpha. Consequently, on the record before us, we can and do hold that Alpha was entitled to no depreciation deduction for 1975, and we will grant the Commissioner's motion for a partial summary judgment.

Associated Patentees, Inc. v. Commissioner
4 T.C. 979, acq. 1959-2 C.B. 3

Memorandum findings of fact and opinion was entered in this proceeding on August 31, 1943. The deficiencies involved arose wholly from the disallowance by respondent of a deduction of $42,209.76 taken by petitioner for the calendar year 1940 as patent royalties paid in that year by it to four individuals. Our conclusion was that this payment was a capital expenditure by petitioner in the acquisition of the patents from those individuals and as such as not deductible. Decision was entered for the respondent.

Thereafter, petitioner filed timely motions to vacate the decision, to reconsider the opinion, and for rehearing or new trial. On October 20, 1943, we entered an order, upon petitioner's motions vacating our decision and opinion theretofore entered, and granted petitioner's motion for rehearing, directing that such rehearing be limited to the question of the depreciation to which petitioner would be entitled in the taxable year in question for exhaustion of its capital investment in view of our holding that the expenditures deducted by petitioner were capital in character. Petitioner, by our order, was permitted to file an amended petition raising the issue as to allowance of depreciation. Such amended petition was duly filed.

The rehearing as directed by our order was held May 8, 1944. Certain evidence was introduced, without objection, bearing upon the question of the value of the patents in question. We make the following findings of fact.

FINDINGS OF FACT

The petitioner is a business corporation organized in 1933 under the laws of the State of New Jersey. Its authorized capital stock consisted of 100 shares of common without par value. All shares were issued. In about 1928 or 1929, Alwyn E. Borton, Frederick Koch, and Walter P. Powers, all inventors and holders of patent rights, together with Cecil Todd, a financier, entered into an oral agreement to pool the patents and inventions on an equal share basis of one-quarter to each. They caused the petitioner to be formed. Each became an officer and director of the corporation. At the first meeting of the directors, held on January 14, 1933, the aforementioned individuals made an offer to sell, assign, and transfer to the petitioner all of their right, title, and interest in and to 20 patents in exchange for the 100 shares of the capital stock of the petitioner. The directors, by resolution, accepted the offer. On January 16, 1933, these individuals executed and delivered to the petitioner a written assignment of 20 patents, designated therein by number, date of issue, and a brief description thereof. Thereupon the petitioner caused to be issued to each of these assignors 25 shares of its capital stock of no par value.

The following instrument was [later] executed by the petitioner and the four individuals:

> WHEREAS, since January 14, 1933, C. Todd, A. E. Borton, F. Koch and W. P. Powers have made certain inventions and have obtained numerous patents, and
>
> WHEREAS, the said C. Todd, A. E. Borton, F. Koch and W. P. Powers are now working on numerous inventions and are applying for and seeking numerous patents, and
>
> WHEREAS, the patents as obtained have been turned over to Associated Patentees, Inc., from time to time without any arrangement being made as to compensation, and
>
> WHEREAS, the understanding was that the parties would arrive at the matter of compensation in due time, and
>
> WHEREAS, Associated Patentees, Inc., have licensed certain patents and invention to others, and are obtaining certain royalties from time to time, and
>
> WHEREAS, almost the entire income of Associated Patentees, Inc., consists of royalties received from licensing others to use these patents and inventions, and
>
> WHEREAS, a verbal arrangement was made earlier this year to the effect that the Associated Patentees, Inc., would pay to each C. Todd, A. E. Borton, F. Koch, and W. P. Powers, 20 percent of all royalties receive for the use of the patents and inventions turned over by them since January 14, 1933, to Associated Patentees, Inc., and
>
> WHEREAS, it is thought wise, because of the volume of business being done, and for other reasons, to reduce the whole arrangement to writing.
>
> NOW THIS CONTRACT WITNESSETH:

THAT in consideration of one dollar, and other good and valuable considerations, the receipt whereof is hereby acknowledged, and in consideration of the use of numerous patents and inventions as listed on attached Schedule A, and in further consideration of the promise on the part of C. Todd, A. E. Borton, F. Koch, and W. P. Powers to keep such patents and inventions current in so far as they can do so, and in further consideration of the promise on the part of C. Todd, A. E. Borton, F. Koch, and W. P. Powers to turn over any inventions they may make to the Associated Patentees, Inc., the Associated Patentees, Inc., this 31st day of December, 1940, agrees to pay to each of the said C. Todd, A. E. Borton, F. Koch, and W. P. Powers, as royalties for the use of the patents and inventions turned over to Associated Patentees, Inc. since January 14, 1933, as shown in Exhibit A attached, an amount of cash equal to twenty (20) per cent of all royalties received by the said Associated Patentees, Inc.; and

Further, the Associated Patentees, Inc. agrees to pay to each of the said C. Todd, A. E. Borton, F. Koch and W. P. Powers as royalties for the use of the patents and inventions turned over to the Associated Patentees, Inc., since January 14, 1933, as shown on Exhibit A attached, and as royalties for the use of patents and inventions to be turned over by the said C. Todd, A. E. Borton, F. Koch, and W. P. Powers, to the Associated Patentees, Inc. in the future, an amount of cash equal to twenty (20) per cent of all royalties that Associated Patentees, Inc., hereafter receives.

This contract shall continue in full force and effect during the entire life of said patents and inventions, including the life of any patents and inventions that may be turned over to the Associated Patentees, Inc., in the future.

ASSOCIATED PATENTEES, INC. By (Signed) A. E. BORTON President C. TODD A. E. BORTON FREDERICK KOCH W. P. POWERS

(Signed) W. P. POWERS

Secretary

Prior to the end of 1940 petitioner paid $42,209.76 to the four individuals in equal amounts. The value of the patents in question was far in excess of $42,209.76, the amount of the payments made by petitioner to the individuals for the calendar year 1940. These payments were capital expenditures in acquisition of legal and equitable title to the patents.

OPINION

LEECH, JUDGE:

Petitioner asks us to find from the evidence introduced upon the rehearing that the patents in question had a cost to it of $3,000,000. This we can not do. That evidence was directed to the question of value, whereas the question we have is one of cost. Moreover, that evidence consists of an opinion based upon such uncertain factors that we do not think it carries weight in determining the value of the patents. We are convinced, however, from the testimony that the patents had great value, largely in excess of the total amounts paid by petitioner in the year 1940, and have so found.

Petitioner acquired the patents from four individuals. The patents had varying lives. The consideration to be paid for the patents was 80 percent of the yearly income received by petitioner from licenses granted by it to use the patents. The four individuals further contracted, in consideration of petitioner's agreement to make these annual payments, to perform services in keeping up the patents, all improvements thereon invented by them to become the property of the petitioner.

Thus the amount of $42,209.76, paid in 1940 by petitioner under the contract, in no sense constitutes the total cost of the patents. This cost includes the future payments which will be made and can not be determined until the expiration of the patents, at which time their value passes out. Of course, it is unquestioned that petitioner is entitled to recover this total cost through reasonable deductions for exhaustion over the period of their lives. The obstacle to computation of depreciation over the term of the lives of the patents in the ordinary way by a proration of total cost is the fact that we have here the first year of the term. It is impossible to determine in this year what the total cost will be, since it will include a percentage of earnings of petitioner in each year of that term. These earnings can not now be determined.

Under these conditions, it is respondent's contention that for the year 1940 there should be allowed as depreciation only a proportionate part of the $42,209.76 paid in that year, the balance of that cost to be prorated over the succeeding years of the lives of the patents, and that in each succeeding year there should be allowed depreciation upon payments made therein based upon the then remaining lives of the patents, petitioner to be allowed this amount plus the amount of depreciation allocated to such succeeding year from prior payments.

It will readily be seen that although this method of computation will give to the petitioner aggregate theoretical deductions for depreciation equaling the total ultimate cost, its practical result will be an entirely inadequate allowance for depreciation at the beginning of the term and excessive allowances for depreciation at the end. Actually, in the later years, the depreciation allowances would largely exceed income from the patents. Under such a method of computation the petitioner might not, in fact, recover its cost from income.

Petitioner's contention is that the cost payment made each year is subject to depreciation in its full amount because it is a cost pertaining to that year alone and measured by income over that period. It is argued that, with an allowance so made, at the close of the lives of the patents the petitioner will have recovered the amount of their cost prorated equitably over their lives.

Section 23(1) [now Section 167(a)] provides for "a reasonable allowance" for depreciation. It provides no specific method for its computation. Respondent's regulations recognize the fact that there is no fixed rule, but that the cost should be apportioned over the useful life in such ratable amount as may reasonably be considered necessary to recover during the remaining useful life of the property the unrecovered cost or other basis. The situation here is unusual. But we think that the method for computing depreciation for which petitioner argues gives it a reasonable, and not more than a reasonable, allowance, whereas the method urged by respondent might deny petitioner the recovery of its cost and would unquestionably result in a distortion of income.

Accordingly, we have found here that petitioner acquired legal and equitable title to the patents in question prior to the tax year. But we now hold that in computing its contested taxes for that year petitioner is entitled to a deduction for exhaustion of the patents equal to the total payments of $42,209.76 made in that year.

Decision will be entered for the petitioner.

Revenue Ruling 67-136
1967-1 C.B. 58

Advice has been requested whether, under the circumstances described below, a taxpayer may deduct as an allowance for depreciation of property under section 167 of the Internal Revenue Code of 1954, an amount which equals the annual payments made on the purchase price of certain patents and patent applications where the invention covered by the patent application is one for which a patent will be issued in the normal course.

The taxpayer, who is engaged in the business of purchasing patents and patent applications and licensing their use to third persons, entered into a contract with an individual who owned certain United States patents and United States patent applications relating to inventions on which a patent will be issued in the normal course. The agreement provided that the seller would convey to the taxpayer all his right, title, and interest in these patents and patent applications.

As consideration for the transfer, the taxpayer agreed to pay to the seller each year a reasonable percentage of all royalties or other consideration which he received from any licenses of the patents and patent applications. The agreement provides for termination of the contract if the taxpayer becomes bankrupt, in which case all rights transferred by the contract will revert to the seller.

Section 167(a) of the Code provides, in part, that as a general rule there shall be allowed as a depreciation deduction a reasonable allowance for the exhaustion, wear and tear (including a reasonable allowance for obsolescence), of property used in the trade or business, or of property held for the production of income.

In accordance with section 1.167(a)-3 of the Income Tax Regulations, if an intangible asset is known from experience or other factors to be of use in the business or in the production of income for only a limited period, the length of which can be estimated with reasonable accuracy, such an intangible asset may be the subject of an allowance for depreciation. Examples are patents and copyrights. An intangible asset, the useful life of which is not limited, is not subject to an allowance for depreciation.

A depreciation deduction is designed, generally, to allow a taxpayer to recover his cost or other basis in assets over the period of their usefulness in his trade or business. Similarly, by the terms of the contract in the instant case, the price of the assets is tied to the benefits the taxpayer derives from them; as the assets produce income their cost or basis increases and their period of usefulness to the taxpayer is proven. The use of the amounts which the taxpayer in this case is contractually obligated to pay on the price as the measure of the allowance for depreciation assures minimum distortion of income. The contrary would be the case if the taxpayer were required to delay recapturing his capital investment in the assets until their total price is established.

Accordingly, since the invention covered by each of the applications is one for which a patent will be issued in the normal course and the purchase price of the patents and patent applications is contractually fixed as a reasonable percentage of the annual earnings from such patents and patent applications over the period of their remaining lives, the taxpayer-purchaser may deduct a sum equal to the payments made during the taxable year on the purchase price of such patents and patent applications as an allowance for depreciation under section 167 of the Code. See *Associated Patentees, Inc. v. Commissioner*, 4 T.C. 979 (1945), acquiescence, C.B. 1959-2, 3.

Private Letter Ruling 200137013

Dear *** :

This letter responds to your letter dated February 6, 2001, submitted on behalf of Taxpayer, requesting a letter ruling under §§ 197 and 1235 of the Internal Revenue Code. Taxpayer represents that the facts are as follows.

FACTS

Taxpayer is a corporation organized and existing under the laws of State. Taxpayer was incorporated in Year 1 ***. Prior to Year 2, ***. In Year 2, ***. ***, Taxpayer (including its subsidiaries) is engaged *** in ***.

In general, Taxpayer and its Group subsidiaries enter into licensing agreements with Licensor (or affiliates of licensor) for the use of applicable trademarks, trade names, and/or technology in manufacturing, marketing, distributing, and selling various products. *** Licensor's technology is ***. Licensor's technology is proprietary to Licensor, and its confidentiality is closely guarded through non-disclosure agreements with employees and suppliers. ***, Licensor provides equipment used by Group in its laboratories. However, the bulk of Group's *** equipment is purchased from ***.

In Date 1, Group purchased the stock of Company and its subsidiaries (Acquired Group). Following the acquisition, an Acquired Group member entered into a technology agreement with Licensor giving it access to Licensor's technology for use in producing and distributing Acquired Group *** products in Country 1. The initial technology agreement between Acquired Group and Licensor was terminated by agreement of the parties. Taxpayer and Licensor wish to enter into a new technology agreement (Technology Agreement) which will provide Taxpayer with continuing and expanded access to Licensor's technology for use in connection with Acquired Group's products.

Under the Technology Agreement, Licensor will grant Taxpayer the right to use the Technology (as defined in the Technology Agreement) on an exclusive basis in the Territory (as defined in the Technology Agreement), subject to the existing rights of certain Licensor affiliates therein; and the exclusive right to import, manufacture, market, distribute, and sell the Licensed Products (as defined in the Technology Agreement) in the Territory.

The Technology Agreement will provide, in part, that the present license is personal to Taxpayer with respect to the manufacturing, marketing, distribution, and selling of the Licensed Products in the Territory. Taxpayer must use it itself and may not, except as specifically provided in the Technology Agreement, transfer the license to a third party in any way, or sub-grant or sub-contract it in whole or part, under penalty of termination. Notwithstanding the foregoing, Taxpayer will have the right, without the consent of Licensor, to grant distribution rights (including the right to grant sub-distribution rights to Taxpayer's affiliates), exclusively or otherwise, to its affiliates, providing each grant (including sub-grants) is made expressly subject to the Technology Agreement and Licensor's rights thereunder.

In consideration of the rights granted under the Technology Agreement and the services to be rendered thereunder, Taxpayer will pay a royalty to Licensor of e percent of net sales of Licensed Products for the right to use the Technology and the technology-related services to be performed. In the event that Taxpayer will sublicense the use of the Technology to third parties other than its affiliates, it will pay a royalty to Licensor of b percent of net sales achieved by the third party sublicensees with Products (as defined under the Technology Agreement) based on the Technology.

The Technology Agreement will continue for a specified period, unless earlier terminated. The Technology Agreement will be renewed for successive periods of b years each, unless either party objects to the renewal by registered letter sent to the other party at least d months prior to the expiration of the current term.

In addition, Taxpayer makes the following representations: 1) The entering into of the Technology Agreement will not be part of a broader transaction that constitutes the acquisition of a trade or business; 2) the Licensed Technology or a substantial portion thereof has significant application in the industry beyond the manufacture of the Licensed Products; 3) ***; 4) none of the intangibles subject to the Technology Agreement are customer-based intangibles; and 5) the Licensed Technology has significant application in areas outside of Country 1.

RULING REQUESTED

Taxpayer requests the Service to rule that the payments made by Taxpayer to Licensor pursuant to the Technology Agreement will not be chargeable to capital account under § 197, and will be currently deductible.

LAW AND ANALYSIS

Section 197(a) provides that a taxpayer shall be entitled to an amortization deduction with respect to any "amortizable section 197 intangible." The amount of the deduction is determined by amortizing the adjusted basis (for purposes of determining gain) of the intangible ratably over a 15-year period beginning with the month in which the intangible was acquired.

Section 197(c) generally defines the term "amortizable section 197 intangible" to mean any § 197 intangible that is acquired by the taxpayer after the date of enactment of § 197, and held in connection with the conduct of a trade or business activity described in § 212.

Section 1.197-2(a)(3) of the Income Tax Regulations provides that § 197 does not apply to amounts that are not chargeable to capital account under § 1.197-2(f)(3) (relating to basis determinations for covenants not to compete and certain contracts for the use of § 197 intangibles) and are otherwise currently deductible.

Section 1.197-2(f)(3)(iii) provides that the transfer of a right or term interest described in § 1.197-2(b)(11) (relating to contracts for the use of, and term interests in, § 197 intangibles) by the owner of the property to which such right or interest relates but not as part of a purchase of a trade or business will be closely scrutinized under the principles of § 1235 for purposes of determining whether the transfer is a sale or exchange and, accordingly whether amounts paid on account of the transfer are chargeable to capital account. If under the principles of § 1235 the transaction is not a sale or exchange, amounts paid on account of the transfer are not chargeable to capital account under § 1.197-2(f)(3).

Section 1235(a) provides that a transfer (other than by gift, inheritance, or devise) of property consisting of all substantial rights to a patent, or an undivided interest therein which includes a part of all such rights, by any holder shall be considered the sale or exchange of a capital asset held for more than 1 year, regardless of whether or not payments in consideration of such transfer are (1) payable periodically over a period generally coterminous with the transferee's use of the patent, or (2) contingent on the productivity, use, or disposition of the property transferred.

Section 1.1235-2(b)(1) defines the term "all substantial right to a patent" to mean all rights (whether of not then held by the grantor) which are of value at the time the rights to the patent (or undivided interest therein) are transferred. The term "substantial rights" does not include a grant of rights to a patent (i) which is limited geographically within the country of issuance; (ii) which is limited in duration by the terms of the agreement to a period less than the remaining life of the patent; (iii) which grants rights to the grantee, in the fields of use within trades or industries, which are less than all the rights covered by the patent, which exist and have value at the time of the grant; or (iv) which grants to the grantee less than all the claims or inventions covered by the patent which exist and have value at the time of the grant. The circumstances of the whole transaction, rather than the particular terminology used in the instrument of transfer, shall be considered in determining whether or not all substantial rights to a patent are transferred in a transaction.

Section 1.1235-2(b)(2) provides that rights which are not considered substantial for purposes of § 1235 may be retained by the holder. Examples of such rights are: (i) The retention by the transferor of legal title for the purposes of securing performance or payment by the transferee in a transaction involving a transfer of an exclusive license to manufacture, use, and sell for the life of the patent; and (ii) The retention by the transferor of rights in the property which are not inconsistent with the passage of ownership, such as the retention of a security interest (such as a vendor's lien), or a reservation in the nature of a condition subsequent (such as a provision for forfeiture on account of nonperformance.)

Section 1.1235-2(b)(3) provides that examples of rights which may or may not be substantial, depending upon the circumstances of the whole transaction in which rights to a patent are transferred, are: (i) The retention by the transferor of an absolute right to prohibit sublicensing or subassignment by the transferee; and (ii) The failure to convey to the transferee the right to use or to sell the patent property. Section 1.1235-2(b)(4) provides that the retention of a right to terminate the transfer at will is the retention of a substantial right for the purposes of § 1235.

The Technology Agreement will be for a stated period with tacit renewal periods, unless either party objects in writing. Under these terms, Licensor will retain the power to terminate the transfer at will after the initial term of the Technology Agreement. Also, by virtue of its retained power to determine the identity of any sublicensee and to dictate as well the terms and conditions of any sublicense, Licensor controls, and indeed may prohibit, sublicensing by Taxpayer. In addition, the rights conveyed by the Technology Agreement are geographically limited. Thus, applying the principles of § 1235 to the Technology Agreement, we conclude that the Technology Agreement will not constitute a transfer by Licensor to Taxpayer of all substantial rights to the property that is the subject of the Technology Agreement.

Accordingly, based on the foregoing analysis and the representations made by Taxpayer, we rule that the amounts paid by Taxpayer to Licensor pursuant to the Technology Agreement will not be chargeable to capital account under § 197, pursuant to § 1.197-2(f)(3)(iii), and will be currently deductible. No opinion is expressed on the correctness of whether the amounts to be paid by Taxpayer to Licensor under the Technology Agreement represent arm's-length consideration.

In accordance with the power of attorney filed with this request, we are sending a copy of this letter ruling to Taxpayer and Taxpayer's second authorized representative.

This ruling is directed only to the taxpayer who requested it. Section 6110(k)(3) of the Code provides that it may not be used or cited as precedent.

Sincerely,

Assistant to the Chief, Branch 5
Office of Associate Chief Counsel, Passthroughs and Special Industries

# Chapter 6

Taxation of Intellectual Property Transfers

I. Assignment for Chapter 6

Read: Internal Revenue Code: §§ 61(a)(7); 197(f)(1), (f)(2), (f)(7); 267(a)(1), (b), (c); 453(a)–(d), (i); 707(b); 1001(a)–(d); 1012; 1016(a)(2); 1211; 1212(a)(1), (b); 1221(a)(1)–(3); 1222; 1223(2); 1231(a), (b)(1)(A)–(C); 1235; 1239; 1245(a)(1)–(3)(A); 1253(a)–(c). Skim §§ 1(h), (i); 167(a), (c); 170(a), (e)(1)(A); 174; 351(a); 358(a); 483(a)–(c)(1), (d)(4); 721; 722; 1274(a)–(c)(1), (c)(3)(C), (c)(3)(E), (d).

Treasury Regulations: §§ 1.167(a)-3; 1.170A-1(c)(1)-(2); 15A.453-1(c)(2)(i), -1(c)(3)(i), -1(c)(4), -1(d)(2)(i), -1(d)(2)(iii); 1.1001-2(a)(1); 1.1221-1(c)(1), -1(c)(3); 1.1235-1(b), -1(c)(2), -2(a)–(d); 1.1239-1(b), -1(c)(5); 1.1245-3(b). Skim § 1.483-1(a)(2)(ii).

Materials: Overview
Watson v. Commissioner
Revenue Ruling 60-226
Stern v. United States
Levy v. Commissioner
Chilton v. Commissioner
Kueneman v. Commissioner
E.I. du Pont de Nemours & Co. v. United States
Revenue Ruling 78-328
Newton Insert Co. v. Commissioner
Stokely USA, Inc. v. Commissioner

Complete the problems.

II. Problems for Chapter 6

1. Ruth is the author of a well-known book "My Sister Eileen," which portrays the adventures of two main characters, the pretty-but-dumb and plain-but-bright sisters. Ruth assigned the radio and television rights in the characters and stories

to Arthur, an independent writer and producer of radio and television programs, who was interested in creating and producing a serial television program utilizing the two main characters. The assignment was for a period to begin upon commencing of production and was to remain in force so long as production was continued. Ruth was to receive a percentage of what Arthur obtained. Does the assignment constitute a "license" or a "sale" for tax purposes? Why does it matter?

2. Assume Arthur in Problem 1 submitted to CBS his ideas for a weekly television program, "My Friend Irma," which was built around the pretty-but-dumb and plain-but-bright theme. In consideration of a payment of $250,000 by CBS, Arthur assigned and conveyed to CBS all of his title and interest in "My Friend Irma," and in the television program conceived and invented by him. What is the proper tax treatment of the assignment, assuming Arthur was not able to obtain copyright protection for either the name or essential features of the television program?

3. Your client, State Street Company, is the developer and owner of a well-known patented software relating to financial investments. Recently, a major competitor of State Street offered a very attractive price for the patented software. Your client is considering selling it, but would like to know the tax consequences of a sale. What is your advice? Would your advice be different if the self-developed software was copyrighted rather than patented? Would your advice be different if your client was an individual rather than a company?

4. Tom was hired by Lockheed Aircraft Corp. as a layout draftsman to design window installations for aircraft being developed. His application for employment contained the following agreement: "In consideration for the wages to be paid to me in the event of my employment, I hereby agree to assign to Lockheed all right, title, and interest in any inventions relating to Lockheed's business that might be made by me during my employment." Subsequently, Lockheed announced to its employees a plan for paying employee-inventors certain percentages of any income received by Lockheed as the result of its sale or licensing of employee inventions to third parties. Although Tom was assigned by Lockheed as a layout draftsman to design window installations and not to design new windshield construction, Tom conceived, invented, and perfected a new and different windshield construction to be used on aircraft. Tom assigned all his rights in the patented invention to Lockheed, which subsequently derived substantial royalties from three licensing agreements covering the invention. This year, Tom received, in addition to his salary, a royalty payment of $50,000 from Lockheed, which was paid out of royalties received by Lockheed pursuant to the above licensing agreements. How should Tom report the payment received under the plan?

5. Lisa, the inventor of an electronic device, applied for a patent and then granted to General Electric, a publicly traded company, the "sole and exclusive right, privilege and license to use, manufacture, produce and sell the invention covered by the patent application for a period of 20 years." What is the proper tax treatment of the assignment, assuming Lisa receives (1) a lump sum payment of $200,000, or (2) a percentage of the gross receipts realized by General Electric from the sale of the product? Would the answer be different if Lisa transferred the patent application to a corporation in which Lisa owned one-third of the outstanding stock? What if the transfer was to a corporation in which Lisa owned 80% of the outstanding stock?

6. Drew is a successful inventor who has been issued over 200 patents during his lifetime. His latest patented invention is an indicator light that permits the testing of

an internal lighting circuit without the removal of a bulb. Drew agreed to transfer to Signal, Inc., an unrelated corporation, the exclusive right for the life of the patent to manufacture, use, and sell the indicator lights throughout the United States east of the Mississippi River in exchange for 10% of the gross selling price on sales made by Signal. How should Drew treat payments received by Signal each year? Would your answer change if Drew reserved (1) the right to act jointly with Signal in resisting infringement of the invention, and (2) the right to terminate the agreement if Signal failed to make and sell 1,000 indicator lights during any six-month period?

7. David is the inventor of a patented leveling device for tables and chairs. In 2003, David entered into an agreement with American Seating Company whereby it was granted the right, for a period of five years, to make, use, and sell the leveling devices but only in the public seating field (furniture for schools, churches, courtrooms, theaters, and hospitals, but not furniture for restaurants and cafeterias) for a royalty of one cent on each device sold. In 2004, David entered into an agreement with Ever-Level, Inc, an unrelated corporation, whereby it was granted the right to make use, and sell leveling devices for the life of the patent, subject to the American Seating license, for a royalty of 7% of sales. Does § 1235 apply, even though non-exclusive rights in the patent are outstanding?

8. Sally sells her restaurant, which is famous for its fruit pies, to Bob for $500,000 in cash. As part of the transaction, Sally transfers to Bob several "section 197 intangible" assets. Sally grants to Bob the right to continue using Sally's name as the name of the restaurant in perpetuity subject to the following three restrictions: (1) the right of Sally to prescribe ingredients that may be used in making the pies for five years, (2) the right of Sally to train all new chefs at the restaurant for five years, and (3) a limitation against using Sally's name on clothing for twenty years. What is the tax treatment of the sale? What if Bob agreed to pay $100,000 in cash and 5% of the gross income of the business for the next 5 years?

9. Assume that Bob, in Problem 8, subsequently sells one of the § 197 intangibles at a loss. What is the proper tax treatment of the loss?

10. Assume that General Electric, in Problem 5, purchased the invention from Lisa for a percentage of the gross receipts realized by General Electric from the sale of the product. Pursuant to the agreement, General Electric paid Lisa $20,000 in Year 1 and $40,000 in Year 2. At the beginning of Year 3, General Electric sold all substantial rights in the patent to an unrelated third party for $300,000. What is the amount of General Electric's gain on the sale? Will any gain be recaptured as ordinary income under § 1245? Does it matter?

III. Overview

A common dispute between taxpayers and the Service is whether intellectual property has been sold or whether intellectual property has only been licensed. The stakes can be great. If an intellectual property transfer is characterized as a sale, then the transferor is permitted to recover basis in the intellectual property transferred and may be eligible for preferential capital gains treatment. If an intellectual property transfer is characterized as a license, then payments received in full, whether lump sum or contingent, are reported in income with no recovery of basis in the transferred property, and are considered royalties taxed as ordinary income and not as capital gains.

Whether a particular transfer or assignment is a sale or license depends on the facts and circumstances of the whole transaction, and not the particular terminology used in the transfer agreement. Review *Waterman v. Mackenzie*, a case included in Chapter 3. As a general rule, a transfer of intellectual property will qualify as a sale, as opposed to a license, if the transferor assigns all substantial rights to the intellectual property (or the rights retained by the transferor are of no substantial value). This means that the transferor must generally transfer the exclusive right to make, use, and sell for the life of the intellectual property in order for the transfer to constitute a sale for tax purposes. In *Watson v. Commissioner*, included below, the Tenth Circuit addressed whether a patent transfer was a sale or a licence for tax purposes. In Revenue Ruling 60-226, also included below, the Service described when a transfer of a copyright will be considered a sale, rather than a license. In Revenue Ruling 64-56, the Service described what needs to be transferred in order for a sale of trade secrets or know-how to exist: "The unqualified transfer in perpetuity of the exclusive right to make, use, and sell an unpatented but secret process within all the territory of a country." Rev. Rul. 64-56, 1964-1 C.B. 144, *amplified by* Rev. Rul. 71-564, 1971-2 C.B. 179.

Transfers that grant the transferee only nonexclusive rights (segregated or limited rights) to intellectual property are generally characterized as licenses rather than sales. For example, transfers with duration limitations (transfers for less than the entire life of the intellectual property) are generally characterized as licenses rather than sales. *See Pickren v. United States*, 378 F.2d 595 (5th Cir. 1967); *Oak Mfg. Co. v. United States*, 301 F.2d 259 (7th Cir. 1962). Transfers that divide the manufacturing of intellectual property between the transferor and transferee, and transfers that grant the right to make and sell, but not the right to "use" intellectual property may also be treated as licenses rather than sales. *See Broderick v. Neale*, 201 F.2d 621 (10th Cir. 1953); *National Bread Wrapping Mach. Co. v. Comm'r*, 30 T.C. 550 (1958).

Although limitations and restrictions may preclude a transfer of intellectual property from being treated as a sale, certain restrictions or limitations do not preclude a finding of a sale for tax purposes. For instance, restrictions that serve to protect the transferor will not prevent the transfer from being treated as a sale, especially if the restrictions do not interfere with the full use of the intellectual property by the transferee. Thus, a transfer may be deemed a sale even though the transferor reserves the right to terminate for failure to make payments or in the event of insolvency or bankruptcy of the transferee. *See Myers v. Comm'r*, 6 T.C. 258 (1946), *acq.* 1958-2 C.B. 3; *Comm'r v. Celanese Corp.*, 140 F.2d 339 (D.C. Cir. 1944). Likewise, a transfer may be deemed a sale despite a restriction that the transferee cannot grant a sublicense without the written consent of the transferor, if the purchase price was paid in installments and the restriction served to protect the parties. *See Rollman v. Comm'r*, 244 F.2d 634 (4th Cir. 1957). Along these same lines, the transferor's retention of the right to sue for infringement will not necessarily preclude a finding of sale if the restriction is viewed as a security device (*e.g.*, if the transfer involves contingent payments based on the transferee's use). *See Watson v. Commissioner*, included in the materials. Transfers of intellectual property rights can be treated as sales rather than licenses, despite the existence of contingent payments. *See* Revenue Ruling 60-226, also included in the materials.

Prior to 1954, common law had established that transfers of intellectual property rights with geographical limitations or field of use restrictions could nevertheless qualify for sale treatment, as long as the entire bundle or rights and privileges within a geographical area or field of use were transferred. For example, the grant of an exclusive right to make, use, and sell intellectual property to only a certain geographical area could be considered a sale, even though the transferor retained those rights with respect to all other geographical areas. *See Watson v. Commissioner*, which follows this Overview. *See also Marco v. Comm'r*, 25 T.C. 544 (1955). Moreover, the grant of the exclusive right to make, use, and sell intellectual property to only a particular industry could be considered a sale, even though the transferor retained those rights with respect to all other industries. *See United States v. Carruthers*, 219 F.2d 21 (9th Cir. 1955); *Rouverol v. Comm'r*, 42 T.C. 186 (1964), nonacq. 1965-2 C.B. 3. In 1954, Congress enacted § 1235 to clarify the tax treatment of certain patent dispositions. As discussed below, § 1235 provides preferential tax treatment when "all substantial rights" in a patent are transferred by certain statutorily defined holders to unrelated parties. Interestingly, the "all substantial rights" test of § 1235 is not satisfied for transfers with geographical and field of use limitations. An important issue discussed below is whether § 1235 has modified pre-section 1235 law for transfers with geographical and field of use limitations or whether transfers with geographical and field of use restrictions can still qualify for "sale" treatment under general tax principles.

A. Sales of Intellectual Property

If an intellectual property transfer is considered a sale, the transferor must determine the amount of gain or loss *realized* on the transaction. The transferor realizes gain if the "amount realized" is greater than the "adjusted basis" of the property. The transferor realizes a loss if the "amount realized" is less than the "adjusted basis" of the property. I.R.C. § 1001(a). The "amount realized" from the sale of intellectual property is the sum of any money received plus the amount of liabilities from which the transferor is discharged as a result of the sale. I.R.C. § 1001(b); Treas. Reg. § 1.1001-2. The "adjusted basis" of the intellectual property is generally its development or acquisition cost, adjusted downward for deductions and amortization allowances with respect to the intellectual property. I.R.C. §§ 1012, 1016.

Once a taxpayer has calculated the gain or loss realized on a sale, the taxpayer must determine whether the gain or loss realized is *recognized* (*i.e.*, reportable on the tax return). As a general rule, the entire gain or loss realized on a sale of intellectual property is recognized for tax purposes, unless an exception is provided in the Code. I.R.C. § 1001(c). The Code provides a number of exceptions from the general rule requiring the recognition of gain or loss upon the sale or other disposition of intellectual property. *See, e.g.*, I.R.C. §§ 351, 721, 1031, 1041. For example, no gain or loss is recognized on the sale of intellectual property to a spouse or former spouse incident to divorce. I.R.C. § 1041.

The Code also contains a few provisions that disallow losses on certain intellectual property transfers in an effort to curb sales for tax avoidance reasons. Section 267(a), for example, denies a deduction for any loss incurred on the sale or exchange of intellectual property "directly or indirectly" between certain related persons. I.R.C. § 267(a). The purpose of the disallowance rule under § 267(a) is to prevent the deduction of artificial losses (*e.g.*, losses through transactions between members of a family and close corporations, when the transferor may still may still have practical control over the property). What relationships trigger the disallowance rule? *See* I.R.C. § 267(b)(1)–(3), (10)–(12), (c)(4), (f). If the seller of intellectual property is denied a loss deduction under § 267(a), the purchaser may receive some relief. *See* I.R.C. § 267(d). For a similar loss disallowance provision, see I.R.C. § 707(b) (denying a deduction for any loss sustained on the sale or exchange of property to a controlled partnership or between controlled partnerships).

Section § 197(f)(1), another disallowance provision, disallows losses on certain sales of intellectual property that have been amortized under the rules of § 197. Specifically, if a taxpayer acquires two or more § 197 intangibles in a single transaction or a series of related transactions, and then subsequently sells one of the § 197 intangibles at a loss, the taxpayer will not be able to recognize the loss. What do you think is the purpose of this disallowance rule? Note that the loss disallowance rule applies only to intellectual property included within the definition of "section 197 intangibles." Review Chapters 4 and 5. What types of self-created and acquired intellectual property are included within the definition? If the disallowance rule of § 197(f)(1) prevents the recognition of loss on the disposition of a § 197 intangible, the loss will be allocated among the remaining § 197 intangibles and increase their basis accordingly. The loss is allocated among the retained section 197 intangibles in the proportion that the basis of each retained asset bears to the total basis of these assets. The increased basis in each retained asset will be amortized over the remaining amortization period. H.R. Conf. Rep. No. 103-213, at 685 (1993), *reprinted in* 1993 U.S.C.C.A.N. 1088 (describing rules for allocating basis increase to retained section 197 intangibles). So, in effect, the taxpayer will still be able to recover costs through amortization deductions; the taxpayer will not, however, be able to accelerate cost recovery deductions by selling one piece of property at a loss and keeping other property that was acquired in the same transaction.

After determining whether gain or loss is realized and recognized, character of the gain or loss must be determined. A gain or loss is either capital or ordinary, depending on a number of factors, including the nature of the property, the taxpayer's holding period for the property, and whether the taxpayer disposed of the property in a sale or exchange transaction. As discussed below, the Code contains general provisions governing the character of gains and losses for most property transactions, as well as specific provisions that apply in the case of certain intellectual property transfers.

As discussed in Chapter 3, individual taxpayers generally prefer gains to be classified as capital gains rather than ordinary income because certain capital gains are subject to reduced tax rates. What is the maximum rate at which long-term capital gains are taxed? What is the top rate of tax on ordinary income? Skim I.R.C. § 1(a)–(d), (h), (i). In contrast to gains, taxpayers prefer losses to be characterized as ordinary losses because of a statutory limitation on capital loss deductions. In the case of corporations, capital losses (both short-term and long-term) can only be used to offset capital gains. In the case of individuals, capital losses (both short-term and long-term) can only be used to offset capital gains plus $3,000 of ordinary income. I.R.C. § 1211. Why is there a limitation on the deductibility of capital losses? What happens to unused capital losses? *See* I.R.C. § 1212. Much of the discussion that follows on the general and special characterization provisions in the Code will focus on the character of gains, rather than losses.

1. *General Characterization Provisions*

The capital gain preference only comes into play if a taxpayer has a "net capital gain" for the year, which is only possible if the taxpayer has a "net long-term capital gain" during the year. I.R.C. §§ 1(h), 1222(11). Net short-term capital gains, unlike "net long-term capital gains," are not included in the term "net capital gain" and are taxed as ordinary income. A long-term capital gain is defined in § 1222 as gain (1) from the sale or exchange (2) of a capital asset (3) held for more than a year. I.R.C. §§ 1222(3). The presence of each of these three factors is necessary before a recognized gain can receive preferential tax treatment.

(a) The Sale or Exchange Requirement

A taxpayer's interest in intellectual property must be terminated in a special way (a "sale or exchange") in order to qualify for capital gain treatment. The "sale or exchange" requirement is usually met if it has been established that an intellectual property transfer constitutes a sale rather than a license. See discussion *supra*. Although Congress intended the words "sale or exchange" to have a broad meaning, the requirement is not always easily satisfied. For example, the sale or exchange requirement is not satisfied if intellectual property is abandoned. Likewise, the sale or exchange requirement is not met if intellectual property is stolen or destroyed in a casualty transaction and the taxpayer is reimbursed by insurance or otherwise. Although an involuntary conversion, such as a theft or casualty, into cash is considered an "other disposition" within the meaning of § 1001(a), it is not considered a "sale or exchange" within the meaning of § 1222. As a result, an involuntary conversion produces ordinary gain or loss unless § 1231, which is discussed below, adds to the characterization issue.

(b) The Definition of Capital Asset

A transaction must involve a capital asset in order to qualify for capital gain treatment. Section 1221 defines the term "capital asset" as all property held by the taxpayer (whether or not connected with a trade or business), subject to certain exceptions noted below.

Inventory and Inventory-Like Property—Section 1221(a)(1). The first type of property specifically excluded from the definition of capital asset is stock-in-trade, inventory, and property held by the taxpayer primarily for sale to customers in the ordinary course of a trade or business. I.R.C. § 1221(a)(1). A professional inventor may run afoul to this exception because a professional inventor may be considered to hold his or her inventions as stock-in-trade, inventory, or property primarily held for sale to customers in the ordinary course of his or her trade or business. What factors should dictate whether a taxpayer is a professional inventor or an amateur? See *Lockhart v. Comm'r*, 258 F.2d 343 (3d Cir. 1958) (finding that 37 inventions over a 19-year period were held primarily for sale to customers in a trade or business); *Rollman v. Comm'r*, 244 F.2d 634 (4th Cir. 1957) (holding that patents were not held for sale to customers in the ordinary course of business); *First Nat'l Bank of Princeton v. United States*, 136 F. Supp. 818 (D.C. N.J. 1955) (holding that patents were capital assets because taxpayer was an amateur inventor).

Depreciable Trade or Business Property—Section 1221(a)(2). The second type of property excluded from the definition of capital asset is depreciable property used in the taxpayer's trade or business. I.R.C. § 1221(a)(2). This exclusion is quite broad for two reasons. First, many forms of intellectual property, such as separately acquired patents, copyrights, and computer software are subject to the allowance for depreciation under § 167. Second, many other forms of intellectual property, such as trademarks and trade names, are considered "section 197 intangible" assets. Review Chapters

4 and 5. The Code provides that §197 intangibles, although amortizable over a prescribed fifteen-year period, are nevertheless treated as property subject to the allowance for depreciation under §167. I.R.C. §197(f)(7).

Some forms of intellectual property, such as self-created trade secrets and know-how, do not fall within the exclusion from the capital asset definition because, even though used in a trade or business, they are not depreciable. Treas. Reg. §1.167(a)-3 (providing that intellectual property, the useful life of which is not limited, is not subject to the allowance for depreciation). Query: Is intellectual property, the costs of which were immediately deductible under §174(a) or deferred and amortized under §174(b), still considered depreciable property and therefore excluded from the definition of capital asset? *See* Rev. Rul. 85-186, 1985-2 C.B. 84.

The exclusion for depreciable trade or business property seems overly broad. This overreaching exclusion, however, is limited by §1231. As discussed below, §1231 is a pro-taxpayer provision that may qualify depreciable intellectual property used in a trade or business for preferential capital gain treatment. More specifically, although depreciable intellectual property used in a trade or business is not a capital asset under §1221, it may nevertheless qualify for capital gain treatment under §1231.

Self-Created Copyrights and Similar Property—Section 1221(a)(3). The definition of capital asset also excludes a copyright, a literary, musical, or artistic composition, or similar property held by the creator (taxpayer whose personal efforts created the property) or a taxpayer with a basis carried over from the creator. I.R.C. §1221(a)(3); Treas. Reg. §1.1221-1(c)(1). This exclusion does not apply to (1) third parties who purchased copyrights; and (2) non-individual creators, such as corporations whose employees or independent contractors created the copyrights. *See* Rev. Rul. 55-706, 1955-2 C.B. 300, *superseded by* Rev. Rul. 62-141, 1962-2 C.B. 181 (applying inventory exclusion, but not copyright exclusion, suggesting that the copyright exclusion does not apply to works-for-hire creations).

Traditional copyrighted works are obviously included within the scope of the copyright exclusion. But, what about abstract ideas, such as cartoon characters, or formats or ideas for television or radio shows, which are not copyrightable per se? In *Stern v. United States*, a case included in the materials, the court addressed whether a character ("Francis" the talking mule) was "similar property" and hence within the scope of §1221(a)(3).

Another question arises whether the copyright exclusion applies when property, such as design patents or computer software, is eligible for both patent and copyright protection. Do you agree with the approach taken by Treas. Reg. §1.1221-1(c)(1)? *Levy v. Commissioner*, also included in the materials, involved computer software in which only copyright protection—and not patent protection—was stressed. Would the outcome have been different if the taxpayer in that case was using the patent laws for protection?

The purpose of treating self-created copyrights as noncapital in the hands of its creator is consistent with taxing wages and salaries as ordinary income. Gains from personal efforts should be taxed as ordinary income just as wages and salaries are taxed as ordinary income. The exclusion has the effect of putting nonprofessional writers, authors, and photographers on parity with professional writers, authors, and photographers who are subject to the inventory exclusion discussed above. One should note that patents are deliberately not included within this exclusion for self-created property and, hence, may be entitled to capital gain treatment.

(c) Holding Period

The tax treatment of a capital gain depends on the property's holding period. As discussed above, only long-term capital gains are accorded preferential tax treatment. A long-term capital gain requires a holding period of more than one year. I.R.C. § 1222(3). In certain circumstances, a taxpayer can tack on to his or her actual holding period (1) the period during which another taxpayer held the same property, or (2) the period during which he or she held other similar property. I.R.C. § 1223. For example, in the case of intellectual property received by gift, the donor's previous holding period in the gifted property is tacked on to the taxpayer's actual holding period of the same property. I.R.C. § 1223(2).

2. Special Characterization Provisions

Long-term capital gain consequences require a sale or exchange of a capital asset held for longer than a year. If a transaction does not constitute a sale or exchange or if a transaction does not involve a capital asset, the transaction will give rise to ordinary income unless a special characterization provision applies. There are several special characterization provisions that may apply to intellectual property transfers. For example, under § 1231, property excluded from the definition of capital asset (trade or business property) may nevertheless be accorded capital asset status, and involuntary conversions that are not considered sales or exchanges may be accorded sale or exchange status. Under § 1235, all three requirements for long-term capital gain treatment (sale/exchange, capital asset, and requisite holding period) are supplied for transactions involving certain dispositions of patent rights.

In other situations, Congress has enacted overriding characterization provisions that require the transferor to recognize ordinary income. For example, § 1239 mandates ordinary income treatment for any gain recognized on the sale or exchange of depreciable property to a related person. Section 1245 mandates that gain on the disposition of certain property be treated as ordinary income to the extent of the depreciation or amortization deductions taken with respect to the property. Section 1253 imposes ordinary income treatment on certain transfers of trademarks and trade names. These special characterization rules are discussed below.

(a) Section 1231: Quasi-Capital Assets

As discussed in Chapter 3, section 1231 is a special characterization provision that operates on certain transactions that are not already characterized under general tax principles. One transaction to which § 1231 applies is "the sale or exchange of property used in the trade or business." I.R.C. § 1231(a)(3)(A)(i). The term "property used in the trade or business" means depreciable or real property used in the trade or business that has been held more than one year, and specifically excludes (1) inventory or property held primarily for sale to customers in the ordinary course of trade or business, and (2) copyrightable works if held by the creator or a taxpayer with a basis carried over from the creator. I.R.C. § 1231(b)(1)(A)–(C). It should be clear that by referring to depreciable trade or business property, § 1231 embraces property that is not considered a capital asset under § 1221(a)(2). [Recall which forms of intellectual property are depreciable under § 167 and, hence, eligible for § 1231 treatment (if used in a trade or business). Remember that intellectual property amortizable under § 197 are also eligible for §1231 treatment because such assets are treated as property subject to the allowance for depreciation under §167. I.R.C. §197(f)(7).]

Review Chapter 3 for the mechanics of §1231. Recall that §1231 is a pro-taxpayer provision in that property excluded from the definition of capital asset (*i.e.*, depreciable trade or business property) may be accorded capital asset status. Likewise, dispositions that do not rise to the level of "sale or exchange" (*i.e.*, thefts and casualties) may be accorded sale or exchange status. Other Code provisions, such as §1235, supply all three elements to clarify the status of certain property transfers.

(b) Section 1235: Transfers of All Substantial Rights to Patents

Section 1235 is a special characterization rule that provides all three requirements for long-term capital gain treatment (sale or exchange, capital asset, and requisite one-year holding period) in connection with the transfer of all the substantial rights to a patent. [As a result, §1235 is usually the starting point for determining the tax treatment of patent transfers.] Specifically, §1235 provides that a transfer of all substantial rights to a patent, or of an undivided interest in all such rights to a patent, by a statutorily defined holder to a person other than a related person constitutes the *sale or exchange of a capital asset held for more than one year.* I.R.C. §1235(a). As can be seen, the sale of patent property may qualify for long-term capital gain treatment even though the transferor is a professional inventor in the business of selling patents to customers in the ordinary course of business (*e.g.*, §1235 supplies the capital asset requirement). Likewise, the sale of patent property may qualify for long-term capital gain treatment even if the sale occurs the moment the patent property is created or if the patent has been held for less than one year (*e.g.*, §1235 supplies the requisite holding period). Further, the sale of a patent may receive preferential capital gain treatment even though the sale includes installment or contingent payments. By assuring certain patent holders that these sales will qualify for long-term capital gain treatment, §1235 has the effect of encouraging research and development that will lead to patentable inventions. [Query: Does §1235 apply to losses as well as gains?]

To benefit from §1235, a transaction must involve the *transfer* by a *holder* of *all substantial rights* to a *patent*. Each of these requirements is discussed below.

Transfer. Section 1235 applies to transfers that result in income to the transferor. As a result, will §1235 apply to transfers by gift, devise, or inheritance? Section 1235 may not apply to transfers of patents that arise out of an employment relationship. *See* Treas. Reg. §1.1235-1(c)(2). Whether payments received by an inventor-employee from his employer are treated as compensation for services rendered by the employee or treated as proceeds derived from the transfer of patent rights is a question of fact. *Id.* In *Chilton v. Commissioner,* a case included in the materials, the Tax Court decided whether payments received by an inventor-employee were for property or for services. Do you agree with the decision in light of the fact that the employment agreement provided that the employee shall "devote his whole time and apply his experience and his inventive ability to the problems, improvements, and developments relating to the company's products"? Would the result necessarily have been different if the employee was obligated to assign any inventions to the employer? *See Beausoleil v. Comm'r,* 66 T.C. 244 (1976); *but see McClain v. Comm'r,* 40 T.C. 841 (1963).

Holder. Section 1235 applies only if the transferor is a statutorily defined "holder" of the patent. The holder of a patent is defined as (1) any individual whose personal efforts created the patent property or (2) any other individual—other than the employer or relative of the inventor—who acquired his interest in the patent property from the original inventor in exchange for money or money's worth prior to the actual reduction to practice of the invention covered by the patent ("financial backer"). I.R.C. § 1235(b). Although corporations, partnerships, trusts, and estates may not be qualified holders, each member of a partnership who is an individual, however, may qualify as a holder as to his pro-rata share of a patent owned by the partnership. See Treas. Reg. § 1.1235-2(d)(2). What if a partnership is not composed solely of individuals?

All Substantial Rights. Section 1235 only applies to a transfer "of all substantial rights" to a patent or an "undivided interest" therein. The term "all substantial rights" refers to all rights (whether or not then held by the grantor) that are of value at the time the rights to the patent (or an undivided interest in it) are transferred. Treas. Reg. § 1.1235-2(b)(1). Therefore, to qualify for the benefits under § 1235, a transferor must typically transfer the entire bundle of rights under a patent (*e.g.*, convey the exclusive right to make, use, and sell the patent in all geographical regions and in all fields of use). Whether or not all substantial rights to a patent are transferred in a transaction depends upon the circumstances surrounding the entire transaction and not the particular terminology used in the transfer instrument. *Id.*

Although the facts and circumstances surrounding a transfer are to be considered, regulations promulgated in 1965 list four transfers that, because they are limited in scope, do not result in a transfer of all substantial rights to qualify for capital gain treatment under § 1235. They are: (1) the grant of a patent that is limited geographically within the country of issuance; (2) the grant of a patent that is limited in duration by the terms of the agreement to a period less than the remaining life of the patent; (3) the grant of a patent that is limited to fields of use within trades or industries, which are less than all the rights covered by the patent, which exist and have value at the time of the grant; and (4) the grant of less than all the claims or inventions covered by the patent that exist and have value at the time of the grant. *Id.* The Tax Court initially held that the 1965 regulations were invalid to the extent of the first and third restrictions (geographical and field of use restrictions) because prior case law allowed "sale" treatment despite geographical and field of use restrictions, and Congress intended for § 1235 to codify existing case law. These Tax Court decisions were subsequently reversed. *See Fawick v. Commissioner*, 436 F.2d 655 (6th Cir. 1971), *rev'g* 52 T.C. 104 (1969); *Mros v. Commissioner*, 493 F.2d 813 (9th Cir. 1974), *rev'g* 30 T.C.M. (CCH) 519 (1971); *Klein v. Commissioner*, 507 F.2d 617 (7th Cir. 1974), *rev'g* 61 TC 332 (1973). The Tax Court later reversed its position in *Kueneman v. Commissioner*, included in this Chapter.

According to the legislative history, the "all substantial rights" test of § 1235 "recognizes the basic criteria of a 'sale' under existing law." S. Rep. No. 83-1622, at 439–40, *reprinted in* 1954 U.S.C.C.A.N. 4621, 5082-83. In light of the above case law upholding the validity of the 1965 regulations, is it correct to say that § 1235 "codifies" prior case law with respect to the "all substantial rights" issue? Although a geographic or field of use restriction will prevent a transfer from qualifying under § 1235, will it, taken alone, prevent a transfer from being characterized as a sale (versus a license)? *E.I. du Pont de Nemours & Co. v. United States*, a case included in the materials, is an important non-section 1235 case decided after the 1965 regulations that allowed capital gain treatment for a transfer having such limitations under general capital gains provisions. *See also Allied Chemical Corp. v. United States*, 370 F.2d 697 (2d Cir. 1967). It would seem that pre-section 1235 law should continue to apply to geographic and field of use restrictions under general capital gains provisions.

In determining whether all substantial rights to a patent are transferred, courts generally look at what the transferor has retained, rather than what he has given up. The regulations provide two examples of rights that may be retained by the holder, because they are not considered "substantial." See Treas. Reg. § 1.1235-2(b)(2)(i)–(ii). The regulations also provide two examples of retained rights that may or may not be substantial depending upon the circumstances of the whole transaction in which rights to a patent are transferred. See Treas. Reg. § 1.1235-2(b)(3). The regulations make clear, however, that the retention of a right to terminate or revoke the transfer at will or negate the transfer is the retention of a substantial right that will negate a § 1235 transfer. Treas. Reg. § 1.1235-2(b)(4). Although the right to terminate the transfer at will is considered substantial, the right to terminate the transfer upon a condition subsequent which is beyond the transferor's control is not a substantial right. For pre-section 1235 cases, see *Myers v. Comm'r*, 6 T.C. 258 (1946), *acq.* 1958-2 C.B. 3 (right to terminate if royalties not paid in a given year); *Comm'r v. Celanese Corp.*, 140 F.2d 339 (D.C. Cir. 1944) (right to terminate upon bankruptcy or receivership of vendee); *First Nat'l Bank of Princeton v. United States*, 136 F. Supp. 818 (D.C. N.J. 1955) (right to terminate if court holds the patent invalid). Although not addressed by the regulations, the retention of the right to sue for infringement and collect damages may negate a § 1235 transfer.

A question may arise whether § 1235 applies to the transfer of all patent rights held by a transferor, even though non-exclusive rights in the patent are outstanding. In other words, does "all substantial rights" mean all rights that ever existed in the patent or does it mean all rights that the seller can transfer at the time of conveyance? See Treas. Reg. § 1.1235-2(b)(1). In *MacDondald v. Commissioner*, 55 T.C. 840 (1971), *acq.* 1973-1 C.B. 2, a case in which § 1235 did not apply, the Tax Court held that the sale of all the rights a taxpayer ever had in a patent, but which rights did not include all existing rights in the patent because the patent was already subject to a nonexclusive license, may qualify for capital gain treatment under general characterization provisions. Revenue Ruling 78-328, included in the materials, addressed a related non-section 1235 situation. Query: Will § 1235 apply to the transfer by a taxpayer to a licensee of his remaining rights to a patent, after having previously transferred substantial rights to another licensee? In *Blake v. Commissioner*, 615 F.2d 731 (6th Cir. 1980), *rev'g* 67 T.C. 7 (1976), the Sixth Circuit held that § 1235 did not apply to a second transfer of bifurcated patent rights, ruling that under § 1235, "all substantial rights" means all rights then in existence, whether or not held by the transferor. What impact, if any, does *Blake* have on Revenue Ruling 78-328?

Patent. Section 1235 applies only to patents and not to other forms of intellectual property, such as copyrights, and trademarks. Although the Code does not define a "patent" for purposes of § 1235, the regulations provide that the term "patent" means a patent granted under the provisions of Title 35 of the United States Code, as well as any foreign patent granting rights generally similar to those under a United States patent. Treas. Reg. § 1.1235-2(a).

The regulations under § 1235 also provide that it is not necessary that the patent or patent application for the invention be in existence if the requirements of § 1235 are otherwise met. *Id.* Thus, § 1235 can apply to patentable technology for which a formal patent application has not yet been made. This is significant because transferors often transfer ownership of perfected but unpatented inventions before the patent or patent application is in existence. In such case, payments received by an inventor may qualify for capital gain treatment under § 1235. It should be noted that trade secrets and know-how may qualify under § 1235 if they are of a patentable nature. Even if they are not patentable, trade secrets and know how may qualify if they are transferred in connection with property that does qualify.

Section 1235 applies only to the transfer of a patent and not the provision of services. In other words, if the transferor receives payment for the patent and for significant or unrelated services, he or she must allocate the payment and separately state that portion accorded long-term capital gain treatment and that portion taxable as ordinary income. Such allocation is not necessary, however, if the services rendered are ancillary to the patent transfer. *See* Rev. Rul. 54-56, 1964-1 C.B. 133.

Related Person. The capital gains benefits of § 1235 are not available when an individual transfers a patent to a "related person." I.R.C. § 1235(d). Who is treated as a related person for purposes of § 1235? Read carefully I.R.C. § 1235(d)(2) and §§ 267(b), 707(b). Are brothers and sisters considered related for purposes of section 1235? What about a holder of a patent and a corporation in which she owns 25% in value of the outstanding stock? Why do you think this limitation was added?

[NOTE: If a transfer does not qualify for capital gain treatment under § 1235, can the transfer still qualify for capital gain treatment under the general characterization rules discussed above? *See* Treas. Reg. § 1.1235-1(b). In *Poole v. Comm'r*, 46 T.C. 392 (1966), the Tax Court held that § 1235 was the exclusive means by which a "holder" could qualify for capital gain treatment. Therefore, the Tax Court denied capital gain treatment for the transfer by a holder not qualifying under § 1235. Later, in Revenue Ruling 69-482, 1969-2 C.B. 164, the Service stated that it would not follow *Poole*. Recently, the Tax Court applied Revenue Ruling 69-482 in permitting capital gain treatment despite the inapplicability of § 1235. *See Cascade Designs, Inc. v. Comm'r*, 79 T.C.M. (CCH) 1542 (2000).

(c) Sections 1239 and 707(b) Ordinary Income

Under § 1239, any gain recognized on the sale or exchange of intellectual property, directly or indirectly, between related parties will be treated as ordinary income if such property is, in the hands of the transferee, subject to the allowance for depreciation provided in § 167. I.R.C. § 1239(a). Section 1239 is a special characterization rule requiring all such gain to be reported as ordinary income; no part of the gain may be characterized as capital gain under general or special characterization provisions, such as § 1235. *See* Rev. Rul. 59-210, 1959-1 C.B. 217. The purpose behind § 1239 is to prevent taxpayers from selling low-basis, high-value depreciable property to a related party, such as a controlled corporation, in order to step up the property's basis for depreciation purposes in the hands of the related transferee at the low cost of a capital gains tax to the transferor.

Section 1239 applies to sales or exchanges between related persons. Read § 1239(b) and (c) for the definition of "related persons." What related party transactions are covered by § 1239? In determining whether a transferor and transferee are related parties, do any constructive stock ownership rules apply?

Section 1239 comes into play only when the property sold is, in the hands of the transferee, subject to the allowance for depreciation provided in § 167. Some forms of intellectual property are clearly depreciable under § 167, whereas other forms of intellectual property are not. Review Chapters 4 and 5 for the types of self-created and acquired intellectual property that are depreciable under § 167. It should be noted that although patent applications are not depreciable, § 1239 specifically provides that patent applications are treated as depreciable for § 1239 purposes. I.R.C. § 1239(e). It should also be noted that intellectual property that is considered a "section 197 intangible" is treated as property subject to the allowance for depreciation under § 167 and thus would fall within § 1239. I.R.C. § 197(f)(7). Review Chapters 4 and 5 for the types of self-created and acquired intellectual property that are considered "section 197 intangibles."

Section 707(b) requires that gain realized and recognized on the sale or exchange of intellectual property to a controlled partnership or between controlled partnerships be treated as ordinary income. Specifically, § 707(b) requires ordinary income treatment on the sale or exchange of intellectual property between a person and a partnership in which the person owns a 50% capital or profits interest. Moreover, § 707(b) requires ordinary income treatment on the sale or exchange of intellectual property between two partnerships, if a person owns a 50% capital or profits interest in both. I.R.C. § 707(b)(2). In determining a taxpayer's ownership interest, the Code imposes certain attribution rules for constructive ownership of partnership interests. I.R.C. § 707(b)(3). Accordingly, a taxpayer may be considered to own, in addition to his direct interest, the partnership interest owned by members of his family or other entities in which he has an interest.

(d) Section 1245 Recapture

As discussed in Chapter 3, section 1245 provides that gain recognized on the disposition of "section 1245 property" shall be reported as ordinary income to the extent of any depreciation or amortization deductions taken with respect to the property. I.R.C. § 1245(a). In other words, any part of the gain that is attributable to depreciation or amortization deductions previously attributable to the transferred property must be recaptured as ordinary income. Any gain in excess of the amount treated as ordinary income under § 1245 (*e.g.*, gain that reflects appreciation in the property's value) may be entitled to capital gain treatment under the general or special characterizations discussed above. Review I.R.C. §§ 1221, 1222, 1231, and 1235. See Chapter 3 for an example.

Section 1245 property is defined as depreciable personal property, which includes both tangible and intangible personal property. I.R.C. § 1245(a)(3); Treas. Reg. § 1.1245-3(b). See *Newton Insert Co. v. Commissioner*, included in the materials, in which the Tax Court clarified that intangible property was not excluded from the provisions of § 1245. Section 1245 property encompasses intellectual property that is subject to the allowance for depreciation or amortization under § 167, as well as intellectual property that is subject to fifteen-year amortization under § 197 (because § 197 intangibles are treated as property subject to the allowance for depreciation under § 167). I.R.C. § 197(f)(7). Does § 1245 encompass intellectual property that has been depreciated in accordance with the method approved in *Associated Patentees, Inc. v. Commissioner*, a case included in Chapter 5? See *Newton Insert Co.*, included below.

Intellectual property that is not depreciable, such as self-created trade secrets and know-how, are not subject to the depreciation recapture rules of § 1245. Also, intellectual property, the creation costs of which were deducted under § 174, are not subject to § 1245 recapture. *See* Rev. Rul. 85-186, 1985-2 C.B. 84. Thus, gain attributable to intellectual property creation costs that were currently deducted under § 174 do not have to be recaptured as ordinary income. However, if creation costs were not currently deducted under § 174, but were capitalized and depreciated under § 167 or amortized under § 197, then gain must be treated as ordinary income to the extent attributable to the depreciation or amortization deductions taken. Because § 174 is an elective provision, do you see any planning opportunities?

(e) Section 1253 Transfers

Prior to 1969, there was much litigation, and considerable diversity of opinion among courts, as to whether the transfer of a franchise, trademark, or trade name constituted a license or a sale. It is quite common for payments made to the transferor of a franchise, trademark, or trade name to be payable over a period of time and to be contingent upon production, sale, or use of products. Historically, some courts concluded that such transactions were licenses and, thus, payments received were taxable as ordinary income. Other courts, however, did not regard the form of payment as controlling and concluded that such payments received were entitled to capital gain treatment. In 1969, Congress enacted § 1253 to resolve the problem of characterizing payments for the transfer of franchises, trademarks, and trade names. See S. Rep. No. 552, reprinted at 1969-3 C.B. 554.

Section 1253 imposes ordinary income treatment on all payments that are *contingent* on the productivity, use, or disposition of a trademark or trade name. I.R.C. § 1253(c). (Note that contingent amounts received or accrued for the transfer of a trademark or trade name constitute ordinary income regardless of whether the transfer is in substance a sale or a license.) Section 1253 also imposes ordinary income treatment on *noncontingent* payments (whether up-front or installment payments) received for the transfer of a trademark or trade name if the transferor retains any significant power, right, or continuing interest with respect to the subject matter of the mark or name. I.R.C. § 1253(a). [It should be clear that § 1253 parallels § 1235 by denying sale treatment whenever the transferor retains any significant power, right, or continuing interest.]

The Code sets forth six potentially significant powers, any one of which, if retained, would require ordinary income treatment. Read I.R.C. § 1253(b)(2). This list of retained powers that may qualify as significant powers is not exhaustive. Rather, consideration is given to all the facts and circumstances existing at the time of a transfer when determining whether an unenumerated power constitutes a significant power. For example, the duration of the relevant restriction is important in determining whether the restriction is significant. In *Stokely USA, Inc. v. Commissioner*, a case included in the materials, how did the Tax Court treat the transferor's five-year right to disapprove a transfer? How did the Tax Court treat the twenty-year restriction preventing the transferee from using the trademark on certain products?

If a transfer is within the scope of § 1253, (*e.g.*, the transferor retains a proscribed power over the trademark or trade name after its sale), then the transferor will realize ordinary income. A question arises whether all payments received in a *sale* should be treated as ordinary income with no basis recovery or whether the transferor should be permitted to recover his or her basis. In other words, does § 1253 transform a transaction that in form and substance is a sale into a license? See *Tomerlin Trust v. Comm'r*, 87 T.C. 876 (1986) (holding characterization of payments under § 1253 was inconclusive in determining whether payments were royalties for purposes of the personal holding company tax, because § 1253 does not determine whether a "sale" has occurred).

3. Contingent Payment Sales

A taxpayer typically recognizes gain or loss at the time of the sale. However, intellectual property is often sold on a deferred payment basis (*i.e.*, payments are contingent on use, productivity, or disposition of the intellectual property). When intellectual property is sold on a contingent use basis, a question arises as to the proper amount and timing of the gain realized and recognized on the sale. For example, should gain be recognized in the year of sale or should the gain be spread out over the life of the payments?

Section 453 provides that "income" from an "installment sale" is to reported under the "installment method." I.R.C. §453(a). An "installment sale" occurs when at least one payment of the total purchase price is to be received after the close of the taxable year in which the sale or other disposition occurs. I.R.C. §453(b)(1). As can be seen, this definition is broad and includes all intellectual property sales made on a contingent basis. If §453 applies, the transferor's gain is included in income only as payments are received from the transferee, regardless of whether the transferor reports on the cash method or accrual method. In other words, the gain is spread over the life of the payments. *But see* I.R.C. §453(i) (requiring a taxpayer to recognize income in the year of sale equal to the amount recaptured as ordinary income under §1245). The percentage of each payment that must be reported as income (*i.e.*, the income portion of any payment) is determined by multiplying the amount of each payment by a fraction. The numerator is the gross profit realized on the sale or to be realized when payment is completed and the denominator is the total contract or aggregate selling price. I.R.C. §453(c). This ratio of gross profit to total contract price is known as the gross profit ratio.

Determining the gross profit ratio would seem impossible in the case of contingent payment sales, because gross profit (numerator) or total contract price (denominator) cannot be readily determined in the year of sale when payments are contingent on use, productivity, or disposition of the intellectual property. Nevertheless, the regulations deal with contingent payment sales, and provide necessary guidance. What if the sale is subject to a "stated maximum selling price"? *See* Treas. Reg. §15A.453-1(c)(2)(i). What if a maximum selling price is not known, but a maximum period of time over which payments may be received is known? *See* Treas. Reg. §15A.453-1(c)(3)(i). What if there is no maximum selling price or fixed period over which payments may be received? *See* Treas. Reg. §15A.453-1(c)(4).

A taxpayer may elect out of the installment method, and report gain on the sale in accordance with his or her usual method of accounting. I.R.C. §453(d). Why would a taxpayer want to accelerate income and therefore exercise his or her option to elect out of §453? If the taxpayer elects out of installment reporting, gain or loss will be calculated under normal rules, with the contingent payment obligation being valued at its fair market value. Treas. Reg. §15A.453-1(d)(2)(i). The regulations provide, however, that the contingent payment obligation shall never be valued at less than the fair market value of the intellectual property sold. In the "rare and extraordinary case" in which the fair market value of the obligation cannot be determined, "open transaction" treatment will apply. Treas. Reg. §15A.453-1(d)(2)(iii). Review *Burnett v. Logan*, a case included in Chapter 3, which applied open transaction reporting.

If intellectual property is sold on a deferred payment basis, the parties must provide for adequate interest on the unpaid balance (adequate interest must be stated and paid annually). If adequate interest is not provided, minimum interest will be imputed by the Code, and a portion of the selling price (each deferred payment) will be recharacterized as interest. With the selling price adjusted accordingly, the seller will have less capital gain and some ordinary interest income; the purchaser will receive less depreciation and have interest expense.

Minimum interest is required under either §1274 (called "OID") or §483 (called "unstated interest"), depending on the size of the contract. If the total payments do not exceed $250,000, then § 1274 is inapplicable and imputed interest will be provided by § 483. I.R.C. § 1274(c)(3)(C). Likewise, if no payment is due under a debt instrument more than six months after the sale, then § 1274 is inapplicable. I.R.C. § 1274(c)(1)(B). Generally, however, it makes little difference, except that if § 1274 applies, minimum interest is included in income even if there are not current payments whereas if § 483 applies, minimum interest is included in income under the taxpayer's normal method of accounting. Treas. Reg. § 1.483-1(a)(2)(ii). Section 1274 generally applies to most intellectual property sold on a contingency basis because, since it cannot be stated that payments will not exceed the $250,000 threshold requirement. Section 483 does not apply if no payment is due more than one year after the sale. I.R.C. § 483(c)(1)(A).

Contingent payments received in a § 1235 transfer are excluded from the interest imputation rules of § 1274 and § 483. I.R.C. §§ 483(d)(4), 1274(c)(3)(E). Transfers by holders to related parties (that are not eligible for § 1235 treatment) are nevertheless transfers described in § 1235 and, as such, are not subject to the interest imputation rules. *See Busse v. Comm'r*, 479 F.2d 1147 (7th Cir. 1973), *aff'g* 58 T.C. 389 (1972), *acq.* 1978-2 C.B.1. [Remember that if a transfer qualifies under both § 1235 and general character provisions, the taxpayer has a choice of qualifying under either. *See* Revenue Ruling 69-482, 1969-2 C.B. 164.]

The minimum interest necessary to avoid the imputation of interest is determined by monthly tables promulgated by the Service and based upon average yields of outstanding U.S. government obligations. I.R.C. § 1274(d).

B. Licenses of Intellectual Property

The tax treatment of nonexclusive licenses (which do not constitute sales) is straightforward. Payments received, whether lump sum or contingent, are royalties taxed as ordinary income and not as capital gains. I.R.C. § 61(a)(7). Because a nonexclusive license cannot be treated as a sale, the licensor is not permitted to recover the unamortized basis in the transferred property, and full amounts received must be reported in income. However, because the licensor is still deemed to own the intellectual property, the licensor may continue to depreciate or amortize the property provided the property qualifies for deprecation or amortization allowances.

C. Transfers to Business Entities

The transfer of intellectual property to a business entity in exchange for an interest in that entity is a realization event within the meaning of § 1001(a). Fortunately, the Code contains non-recognition provisions that apply to transfers of property to corporations and partnerships in exchange for ownership interests. Section 351(a) provides that no gain or loss shall be recognized upon the transfer by one or more persons of property to a corporation solely in exchange for stock in such corporation if, immediately after the exchange, such person or persons are in control of the corporation to which the property was transferred. I.R.C. §§ 351(a), 368(c) (defining control). Section 721 provides that no gain or loss shall be recognized to either the partnership or to any of its partners upon a contribution of property to the partnership in exchange for a partnership interest. I.R.C. § 721. An important issue that arises is whether intellectual property, such as secret processes and know-how created by the services of the transferor, constitute "property" which can be transferred without recognition of gain or loss under these provisions.

In Revenue Ruling 64-56, 1964-1 C.B. 133, the Service ruled that the transfer of all substantial rights in technical know-how (trade secrets) will be treated as a transfer of property for purposes of section 351 of the Code. In explaining the phrase "all substantial rights," the Service adopted an "in perpetuity" requirement: "The unqualified transfer *in perpetuity* of the exclusive right to use a secret process or other similar secret information qualifying as property within all the territory of a country, or the unqualified transfer *in perpetuity* of the exclusive right to make, use and sell an unpatented but secret product within all the territory of a country, will be treated as the transfer of all substantial rights in the property in that country." In Revenue Ruling 71-564, 1971-2 C.B. 179, the Service later explained the phrase "in perpetuity" as used in Revenue Ruling 64-56. The Service began by looking to some of the general tax principles relating to the transfer of patents. As explained earlier in this Chapter, in order for a transfer of patent rights to constitute a sale or exchange for tax purposes, the transfer must generally consist of all substantial rights to the patent, one of which is the right to use the patent for its full life. Because trade secrets are sufficiently akin to patents, the Service applied, by analogy, this principle to the transfer of trade secrets: "Trade secrets, however, have useful periods which may last for an indefinite period of time, that is until they become public knowledge. Once a trade secret becomes public knowledge it is no longer protectible under the applicable law of the country in which the rights have been granted to the transferee. At this point, the property interest in the trade secret ceases. Accordingly, it is held that an unqualified transfer of the exclusive right to use a trade secret until it becomes public knowledge and no longer protectible under the applicable law of the country where the transferee is to operate is a transfer of property for purposes of Revenue Ruling 64-56."

Although an unqualified transfer of the exclusive right to intellectual property constitutes a transfer of property within the meaning of § 351 of the Code, what about a nonexclusive license of intellectual property? In Revenue Ruling 69-156, 1969-1 C.B. 101, the Service addressed whether a grant by a domestic corporation to its foreign subsidiary of the exclusive rights to import, make, use, sell, and sublicense certain patent rights in a chemical compound in the foreign subsidiary's country of operation was a transfer of property within the meaning of § 351. The problem was that in the grant, the foreign subsidiary (transferee) agreed not to prevent the domestic corporation (transferor) and its subsidiaries from also importing, using, and selling the chemical compound in the foreign subsidiary's country of operation. Because, the domestic corporation (transferor) retained for itself and its subsidiaries the substantial rights to import, use, and sell the chemical compound in the foreign subsidiary's country of operation, the Service concluded that the foreign subsidiary did not have all substantial rights in the patent. As a result, the grant of the patent rights did not constitute a transfer of property within the meaning of § 351. Subsequent to the Revenue Ruling 69-156, the Court of Claims in *E.I. DuPont de Nemours & Co. v. United States*, 471 F.2d 1211 (Ct. Cl. 1973), took a different position and held that a non-exclusive license of patents from a domestic corporation to its foreign, wholly-owned subsidiary in exchange for the subsidiary's stock qualified as a transaction in which no gain would be recognized under § 351. The Court held that the non-exclusive license of patents was "property" covered by § 351. Do you agree with the Service or Claims Court?

If a non-recognition provision applies to an intellectual property transfer to a business, the reporting of gain or loss realized is postponed to a later year (*e.g.*, when the property received in the transaction is later sold or disposed of in a taxable transaction).

Gain is preserved by generally giving the taxpayer the same basis in the stock or partnership interest received as he or she had in the intellectual property given up in the transaction. I.R.C. §§ 358, 722. Because a taxpayer's basis in the stock or partnership interest received in a nontaxable transaction is determined by reference to the taxpayer's basis in the intellectual property given up, the taxpayer's previous holding period in the intellectual property contributed to the entity is "tacked" on to the taxpayer's actual holding period of the stock or partnership interest received. I.R.C. § 1223(1). Why is the taxpayer's holding period in the stock or partnership interest relevant?

If the intellectual property contributed to a corporation or partnership in a section 351 or section 721 transaction is a "section 197 intangible," and the transferee receives a carry over basis in the section 197 intangible asset, the transferee corporation/partnership will continue to amortize the intellectual property over the same period as would the transferor shareholder/partner had no transfer occurred. I.R.C. § 197(f)(2)(A); Treas. Reg. § 1.197-2(g)(2)(ii). In other words, the transferee corporation/partnership is not required to amortize the carry over basis over a new fifteen-year recovery period, but instead will amortize the asset ratably over the remainder of the transferor's fifteen-year amortization period.

D. Transfers to Charitable Organizations

Section 170 provides a deduction for any contribution to or for the use of a qualified charity. I.R.C. §§ 170(a) (authorizing the deduction), 170(b) (imposing various ceilings on amount deductible), 170(c) (providing five classifications of qualified charitable organizations). As a general rule, if intellectual property is donated to a charity, the amount of the charitable deduction is the property's fair market value. Treas. Reg. § 1.170A-1(c)(1)–(3). However, if gain on a hypothetical sale of the intellectual property by the donor would be taxed as *ordinary income* or *short-term capital gain*, the amount of the charitable deduction is reduced by the amount of that gain. I.R.C. § 170(e)(1)(A). In other words, to determine whether there should be a reduction in the amount of the contribution, one must determine the character of the gain that would be recognized if the intellectual property were sold by the donor. If the gain on a hypothetical sale would be *long-term capital gain*, no reduction is made and the amount of the contribution is the intellectual property's fair market value. If, however, the gain on a hypothetical sale would be *ordinary income* or *short-term capital gain*, the amount of the contribution would be reduced by the amount of that gain. Note that the related use restriction of § 170(e)(1)(B) does not apply to intangible property. I.R.C. § 170(e)(1)(B).

Review the general and special characterization provisions discussed above. Would an individual donating a *patent* to a charity be entitled to a charitable deduction equal to the full fair market value of the patent? Review I.R.C. § 1235 (providing gain from sale of patent taxed as long-term capital gain). What if the individual donated a trademark? Review I.R.C. § 1253 (providing ordinary income treatment if the transferor retains any significant power, right, or continuing interest with respect to the subject matter of the trademark). What if the individual donated a copyright? Review I.R.C. §§ 1221(a)(3), 1231(b)(1)(C) (excluding self-created copyrights from the definition of capital asset and § 1231 property).

IV. Materials

Watson v. Commissioner
Circuit Court of Appeals, Tenth Circuit
222 F.2d 689 (10th Cir. 1955)

BRATLON, JUDGE:

The crucial question in this case is whether for income tax purposes a contract constituted an assignment of patent rights and therefore the income which the patentee derived therefrom was long-term capital gain, or whether the contract constituted a license and hence the income derived from it was ordinary income.

Orla E. Watson conceived the idea of a cart that could be telescoped horizontally, one into another. The cart was designed particularly for use in grocery stores. Watson made a pencil drawing of the cart, finished two experimental models, tested them successfully, and demonstrated them to others. Watson and Fred E. Taylor entered into a partnership agreement by the terms of which it was agreed that, in consideration of advancements made and to be made by Taylor for use in financing the manufacture and distribution of the carts, Watson would for a term of ten years give Taylor an undivided forty-nine per cent interest in and to the telescope feature. Notwithstanding the language contained in the agreement, it was the intention of the parties that Taylor should receive one-half of the profits derived from the invention but no interest in the patent rights. An application for a patent on the cart was filed and later the patent issued. While the application was pending, Watson—with the consent and assistance of Taylor—entered into an agreement with George Oliver O'Donnell, as trustee for Telescope Carts, Inc., to be thereafter incorporated. The agreement provided among other things that Watson thereby granted to the corporation the exclusive right, license, and privilege to manufacture, distribute, sell, develop, and use the telescope carts for and during the period of the application for letters patent, during the term for which letters patent were issued, and during any extension of such patent or patents. The corporation was organized and O'Donnell assigned to it all of his right, title, and interest in and to the agreement between himself and Watson. During 1950, Watson received from the corporation payment or payments under the contract in the aggregate amount of $78,442.75, out of which he paid Taylor $39,221.38. In their income tax return for the year 1950, Watson and his wife reported as ordinary income $39,221.37 which had been received from the corporation and paid the tax thereon. Within the statutory time, they filed a claim for refund in the amount of $7,450.04 upon the ground that the income received under the contract was part of the purchase price of the invention and therefore was subject to tax as long-term capital gain. The claim was not acted upon within six months after the date of its filing, and this action was filed to recover the asserted refund. In its findings of fact, the court found among other things that Watson held the invention relating to the carts for more than six months prior to the execution of the contract with O'Donnell; that he did not hold the invention primarily for sale to customers in the ordinary course of his trade or business; and that the agreement was a license agreement and did not constitute a sale of the invention. In its conclusions of law, the court concluded that for income tax purposes the contract did not constitute a sale of the invention; and that the income received from the corporation constituted ordinary income, not capital gain. Judgment was entered against the taxpayers, and they appealed.

It is a firmly accepted principle of law that if the patentee conveys by an instrument in writing the exclusive right to make, use, and vend the invention throughout the United States, or an undivided part or share of that exclusive right, or the exclusive right under the patent within a specified area within the United States, the conveyance constitutes an assignment of the patent, complete or partial as the case may be; and that a transfer short of that is not an assignment but a license. *Waterman v. Mackenzie*, 138 U.S. 252. In language too clear for doubt, the agreement into which Watson and O'Donnell entered expressly granted to Telescope Carts, Inc., the exclusive right to make, use, and vend the carts throughout the United States.

The agreement between Watson and O'Donnell was entitled License Agreement, and in it the parties were referred to as licensor and licensee, respectively. But nomenclature of that kind has little if any significance in resolving the question whether the instrument amounted to an assignment or was a license. The calling of the instrument a license agreement, and the denomination of the parties thereto as licensor and licensee, respectively, did not fix, limit, or qualify the scope and effect of the grant. The legal question whether the instrument constituted an effective assignment or was a license must be determined by considering together the several provisions contained in the instrument, not its title or the manner in which reference was made to the parties.

The agreement contained a provision relating to the termination of its exclusive character. The substance of the provision was that, in the event the corporation should after one year from the date of the agreement fail to make and sell 2,500 carts during any six-months period, the licensor should be free to license others to manufacture and sell carts. But that provision concerned itself exclusively with a condition subsequent. It did no more than provide that upon the occurrence of a stated event the grantor was empowered to terminate the exclusive right and title theretofore conveyed. It did not detract from the effectiveness of the agreement as constituting an assignment of the patent rights.

The contract contained a further provision that the rights of the licensee thereunder should not be assigned without the consent of the licensor having been obtained in writing. That precautionary provision was intended to protect the rights of the parties under the contract, not to proscribe, limit, or nullify their intent and purpose to vest immediately in the transferee the right to manufacture, sell, and use the carts throughout the life of the patent, as well as any extension or extensions thereof.

The agreement contained a provision for payment of royalties. That provision merely fixed the compensation to be paid as consideration for the transfer. It did not reserve to Watson any control over the patent or its use. It did not limit or qualify the scope of the grant. And since the agreement contained language vesting in the corporation the exclusive right to manufacture, sell, and use carts throughout the United States, the provision for payment of royalties did not change the nature of the transfer to a license.

The agreement contained two provisions relating to suits for infringement. The substance of one provision was that in the event a suit was filed charging that the manufacture and sale of carts designed by Watson constituted infringement of a prior patent, payment of royalties to Watson should be suspended during the pendency of the action; that in the event it should be judicially determined that such invention did not infringe, payment of the suspended royalties should be paid in a lump-sum; and that in the event it should be determined that the invention did infringe, payment of royalties under the agreement shouldcease. That provision concerned itself solely and exclusively with the question of royalties in the event of a suit or suits charging that the Watson invention infringed. It did not reserve to Watson or vest in him any property or proprietary rights in the invention. The other provision obligated Watson and the corporation to act jointly in resisting infringement of the Watson invention, and fixed the manner in which damages recovered for infringement should be divided between them. Without such a provision, the Telescope Carts, Inc., would have the right to institute and maintain in its own name an action for infringement of the patent and retain all damages recovered. *Waterman v. Mackenzie, supra.* And in the absence of a provision of that nature, Watson would have been under no obligation to institute and maintain alone or in conjunction with the company any action for infringement. The underlying reason for the insertion of that provision must have been that in the prosecution of such an action the presence and aid of the inventor would be of value in protecting the property and proprietary rights of the corporation in the invention and the patent covering it, and would also be of value in safeguarding the financial interest of the patentee in respect to continued payment of royalties. The provision was one designed to protect and safeguard such respective rights and interests. It was not intended to reserve to Watson any property or proprietary right in the invention which was at variance with an assignment to the corporation of the right to manufacture, sell, and use carts throughout the life of the patent.

The contract between Watson and O'Donnell constituted an assignment to the corporation of the invention relating to the collapsible carts. Such assignment amounted to a sale of a capital asset. And inasmuch as Watson held the invention for more than six months prior to the transfer, and did not hold it primarily for sale to customers in the ordinary course of his trade or business, the income which the taxpayers received in the form of royalties from the corporation constituted long-term gain as distinguished from ordinary income.

The judgment is reversed and the cause is remanded with directions to enter judgment for the taxpayers.

Revenue Ruling 60-226
1960-1 C.B. 26

Revenue Ruling 54-409 deals generally with the circumstances under which a grant of a copyright proprietor's right may confer a license or constitute a transfer of property. The Revenue Ruling holds, in pertinent part, that when the proprietor of a copyright grants the exclusive right to exploit the copyrighted work throughout the life of the copyright in a medium of publication or expression for a consideration which is not measured by a percentage of the receipts from the sale, performance, exhibition, or publication of the copyrighted work, is not measured by the number of copies sold, performances given or exhibitions made of the copyrighted work, and is not payable periodically over a period generally coterminous with the grantee's use of the copyrighted work, the consideration is to be treated as the proceeds of a sale of property and not as rentals or royalties.

Mimeograph 6490 held that, effective for taxable years beginning after May 31, 1950, payments received by inventors from the assignment of a patent or the license of the exclusive right to make, use and sell a patented article under an agreement whereby payments are measured by production, sale, or use by the transferee, or are payable periodically over a period generally coterminous with the transferee's use of the patent, constitute ordinary income. Revenue Ruling 55-58 announced that the Internal Revenue Service would continue to apply the rule of Mimeograph 6490 in cases where section 1235 of the Internal Revenue Code of 1954 was not applicable.

By Revenue Ruling 58-353, C.B. 1958-2, 408, the Service revoked Mimeograph 6490 and Revenue Ruling 55-58 and announced acquiescence in the decisions of the Tax Court of the United States in *Edward C. Myers v. Commissioner*, 6 TC 258, *Leonard Coplan et ux. v. Commissioner*, 28 TC 1189, and *Roy J. Champayne v. Commissioner*, 26 TC 634. This action means that the consideration received by the owner of a patent for the assignment of the patent, or the granting of an exclusive license to such patent, may be treated as the proceeds of a sale of property, for Federal income tax purposes, even though the consideration received by the transferor is measured by production, use, or sale of the patented article.

Since the property rights of patents and copyrights are similar in substance, it is concluded that the Service should adopt, in the case of copyrights, the position that is being taken in the case of patents.

Accordingly, it is held that the consideration received by a proprietor of a copyright for a grant transferring the exclusive right to exploit the copyrighted work in a medium of publication throughout the life of the copyright shall be treated as proceeds from a sale of property, regardless of whether the consideration received is measured by a percentage of the receipts from the sale, performance, exhibition, or publication of the copyrighted work, or is measured by the number of copies sold, performances given, or exhibitions made of the copyrighted work, or whether such receipts are payable over a period generally coterminous with the grantee's use of the copyrighted work.

The modification, here announced, of Revenue Ruling 54-409, *supra*, is to the effect that assignments of copyrights will not be denied treatment as sales solely because of the form which purchase price takes. In cases where interests resembling royalties are retained by the copyright proprietor along with other rights in the transferred interest, the transaction may under some conditions fail to have the required characteristics of a sale. See Revenue Ruling 58-353, *supra*.

It should be noted that whether a copyright is a capital asset within the meaning of section 1221 of the Code and when the provisions of section 1302 of the Code with respect to copyrights would apply are separate and distinct questions which are not considered in this ruling.

Revenue Ruling 54-409, *supra*, is modified to the extent that it holds that the consideration received by the proprietor of a copyright for a grant of the exclusive right to exploit the copyrighted work in a medium of publication is to be treated as proceeds from a sale of property only if the consideration received is not measured by the publication, use, or sale of the copyrighted work, and is not payable over a period generally coterminous with the grantee's use of the copyrighted work.

Stern v. United States
United States District Court, E.D. Louisiana, New Orleans Division.
164 F. Supp. 847 (1958)

J. SKELLY WRIGHT, DISTRICT JUDGE:

This case concerns "Francis," the talking mule. Francis is a product of World War II. It was created by a lonely second lieutenant in the Pacific theater of operations who sometimes wondered whether there was anything in the Army lower than a second lieutenant. Francis convinced him there was. Now, seven motion pictures later, that second lieutenant, the taxpayer here, is claiming that the income from "Francis" is entitled to capital gains treatment under the Internal Revenue laws.

In 1933, after attending Harvard University, David Stern, III, was employed as a dramatic critic for the *Philadelphia Record*, a newspaper owned by his father. Beginning four months later, he became successively comptroller of the *Record*, classified advertising salesman, assistant classified manager, classified manager, promotion manager, and general manager. During the time that Stern was learning the business, he continued to serve the *Record* as part-time dramatic critic. In 1938 he became publisher of the *Courier-Post* newspapers in Camden, New Jersey. Throughout the prewar years, when Stern was a newspaper business executive, his hobby was writing. He wrote some stories and articles in his spare time, but he was unable to sell any of them.

In the spring of 1943, Stern enlisted as a private in the United States Army. He was later commissioned as a second lieutenant, and subsequently became co-officer in charge of the Central Pacific Edition of *Stars and Stripes*. While in the Pacific, Stern wrote some imaginary dialogue between a second lieutenant and an old Army mule, some of which he sold to *Esquire* for approximately $200. He also wrote several short stories while in the Army which he sold to magazines for $50 to $250.

After his release from the Army in 1946, Stern returned to Camden as publisher of the *Courier-Post* newspapers. In 1947 Stern's connection with the *Courier-Post* newspapers was terminated. He immediately entered negotiations to purchase a newspaper. While so doing and at the suggestion of a book publisher, he rewrote in book form all of the episodes about the talking mule, Francis. During this period he also wrote a sequel to "Francis," called "Francis Goes to Washington." It, too, was published by Farrar-Strauss, publisher of "Francis." In July 1949 Stern completed negotiations for the purchase of *The New Orleans Item* and took over the controlling interest and active management of the newspaper as its publisher. Since that date, he has devoted virtually his full time to the newspaper business as publisher.

On June 2, 1950 Stern sold to Universal Pictures Co., Inc., all of his "right, title and interest * * * in and to * * * that certain character known as 'Francis' conceived and created by" him, together with all of his rights to the two novels mentioned above and all of his rights to any contracts with respect to the properties conveyed. In consideration of this transfer, Universal agreed to pay him $50,000 plus 5% of the net profits from photoplays based on the character Francis, and 75% of all sums received by Universal under contracts for the use of licensing of the property. Payment of the $50,000 entitled Universal to a "commitment period" of two years within which to make a motion picture. Thereafter, and following release of each picture, Universal was entitled to additional commitment periods by paying a similar fixed consideration of $50,000 as to each picture or period. The contract further provided that "if purchaser shall elect not to pay fixed consideration with respect to any next succeeding commitment period * * * the property shall revert to the seller," all rights in motion pictures produced to remain in Universal. Under this agreement, Universal produced six additional motion pictures in which the character Francis was used. Stern prepared the screen play for the first of these pictures but has had no connection whatever with the writing or production of subsequent pictures except occasionally and incidentally as a consultant. The novel, "Francis Goes to Washington," was not used for screen material.

Plaintiffs have reported as ordinary income for tax purposes all amounts received by them from the sale of the motion picture and publishing rights to the novel "Francis," for preparing a short screen treatment of the book, "Rhubarb," and income received under the agreement for writing screen plays. Only those amounts received from Universal for the character Francis have been treated by plaintiffs as capital gains, accrued during the years received. For the year 1950, the Internal Revenue Service originally accepted plaintiffs' treatment of this income as capital gains from the sale of the character Francis. In considering subsequent years, the Appellate Division of the Internal Revenue reopened the return for the year 1950 and ruled that income from the character Francis was not subject to capital gains treatment for the reason that the contract with Universal was not a sale of the character Francis, that if it were, Francis was property held by the taxpayer primarily for sale to customers in the ordinary course of his business and, further, under the provision of Section 210(a) of the Revenue Act of 1950, amending the provisions of Section 117(a)(1) of the Internal Revenue Code of 1939, 26 U.S.C.A. § 117(a)(1), the character Francis was similar to a copyright, a literary or artistic composition and, therefore, not a capital asset.

Taxpayer has paid the Government the asserted deficiencies in income taxes for the years 1950-53 resulting from the Commissioner's refusal to recognize his treatment of amounts received from Universal Pictures Company pursuant to the contract in suit as a long-term capital gain. Timely claims for refund have been filed and disallowed, after which disallowance this suit was instituted. Taxpayer's position here is the same as it has been since the filing of his original income tax returns. He states that his contract with Universal Pictures Company was a sale of the capital asset, Francis, not in the ordinary course of his business, and, consequently, he is entitled to capital gains treatment of the income received from that sale. The Government here takes the same position taken by the Appellate Division of Internal Revenue Service as well as the Commissioner in his disallowance of the claim for refund.

The question as to whether the taxpayer's contract with Universal Pictures is a sale will be considered first because if it is not a sale, it will be unnecessary to consider the other objections to capital gains treatment of the income made by the Government. It will be noted in the contract that Stern sold all of his interest in the books "Francis," and "Francis Goes to Washington," the character Francis, and all rights and pending contracts concerning them. The agreement makes reference to "the full and complete ownership in the property sold, transferred and granted to (Universal) hereunder." It declares that Stern "hereby sells, transfers and conveys * * * all right, title and interest" in the property to Universal and guarantees "the full benefit of (Universal's) full and complete ownership in the property." Obviously, the draftsmen of this contract intended that it be a sale and called it such. Apparently they were familiar also with the one case, *Cory v. Commissioner of Internal Revenue*, 2 Cir., 230 F.2d 941, which the Government cites as authority for its contention that this agreement is not a sale, because the language of the agreement leaves no doubt that Stern transferred his entire bundle of rights in all the Francis properties, together with rights of future exploitation, to Universal Pictures. Thus this agreement is different from the agreement under consideration in *Cory v. Commissioner, supra*, because there the agreement provided for "a transfer of a part of the cluster of rights" inhering in the taxpayer.

The Government's suggestion, without citation of authority, that the contract in suit is not a sale because it provided for contingent payments of indeterminate sums similar to royalties, and because the property reverted back to Stern if the fixed consideration for any period is not paid, cannot convert this contract of sale into a licensing agreement. Perhaps a sale which provides for contingent payments of indeterminate sums and reversion does violence to the doctrinaire concepts of what a sale should be. But the tax cases interpreting Section 117 of the Code have so long and so consistently held such contracts to be sales that the Internal Revenue Service itself in a recent ruling[1] is now indicating its acquiescence in this classification.

The Government next contends that if the contract in suit is a sale, then the income therefrom is still not entitled to capital gains treatment because it was a sale of "property held by the taxpayer primarily for sale to customers in the ordinary course of his trade or business." Section 117(a)(1)(A), Internal Revenue Code of 1939. The resolution of this question depends on appraisal of the total factual situation. Unquestionably, under Section 117(a) of the Code, a taxpayer may have more than one business. Before any business can come within Section 117(a), however, it must be an "occupational undertaking which required the habitual devotion of time, attention or effort with substantial regularity." The criteria in making this determination are fully set forth in opinions by the Fifth Circuit[2] so it would serve no useful purpose to repeat them here. Those cases do show that a court should not be quick to put a man in business under Section 117(a) simply because he has been successful in earning extra income through a hobby or some other endeavor which takes relatively small part of his time.

Here the taxpayer is a newspaper publisher and has been, with the exclusion of the war years, actively directing newspapers since 1938. Virtually his entire time has been given to that endeavor. As a hobby he has written a few short stories, some of which have been productive of small amounts of income. On two occasions he has written screen plays. He has created the character Francis and written two novels about it. This literary work has taken relatively little of his time. It was more or less a relaxation from his principal employment. Under the circumstances, it can hardly be said that the taxpayer created "Francis" to hold as "property held by the taxpayer primarily for sale to customers in the ordinary course of his trade or business." Section 117(a)(1)(A), I.R.C., 1939.

The Government makes much of the fact that in one of the schedules attached to taxpayer's return, he professes to be a writer. Even if the taxpayer were responsible for this statement, his literary license in this regard should not be allowed to affect the tax treatment accorded his income. Actually, the indication of Stern as a writer was the work of the accountant who prepared the return. It is further noted that the schedule on which the profession appears relates to income and expenses attendant his writing. On the first page of each return in the space provided for "Occupation," the word "Publisher" appears.

Finally, and unfortunately for the taxpayer, the Government's position on the 1950 amendment to the 1939 Code is well taken. That amendment excludes from capital gains treatment income from the sale of "a copyright; a literary, musical, or artistic composition; or similar property" held by "a taxpayer, whose personal efforts created such property." The purpose of this amendment is obvious. It is intended to deny capital gains treatment to income from the sale, by their creator, of literary, musical, or artistic compositions, or similar property. Prior to 1950, various rulings of the Internal Revenue Service had approved capital gains treatment of various literary, musical and artistic compositions, including books and radio programs. Congress determined to eliminate such treatment for such compositions. Hence the amendment.

---

1. I.R.S., TIR-81, 6-27-58 [Rev. Rul. 58-353, 1958-2 C.B. 408].
2. Gamble v. Commissioner of Internal Revenue, 5 Cir., 242 F.2d 586; Smith v. Dunn, 5 Cir., 224 F.2d 353.

The taxpayer contends that the character "Francis" is not covered by the amendment, that it is not subject to copyright, that it is not a literary, musical or artistic composition or similar property. He argues that he has paid his taxes at the regular rates on all his income from his writings. He states that the character "Francis" is an "intellectual conception" and that as such the income from the sale thereof is entitled to capital gains treatment.

The taxpayer cites several cases[9] in support of his position that the character Francis is not subject to being copyrighted. And he spends much time in his brief arguing that the Internal Revenue Service itself has limited the words of the statute "or similar property" to property capable of being copyrighted.[10] It is not necessary for this Court to appraise the taxpayer's citations, his argument on this point, or the counter citations and argument of the Government. It is this Court's view that the character Francis, irrespective of its susceptibility to copyright, is "a literary composition" and as such the income from the sale thereof is not entitled to capital gains treatment. The taxpayer concedes, as he must, that the novel, "Francis," in which the character Francis is the leading figure, is a literary composition, but he argues that Francis, the principal characterization in the book, is not. In this he is mistaken. The character Francis gets its definition and its delineation from the book. The literary description in the book composes the character. How can it be said that the book is a literary composition yet the main character delineated therein is not? A slice of the loaf is still bread. It would be absurd to attribute to Congress the intention, under the 1950 amendment, of covering whole literary compositions but not parts thereof, particularly in view of the catchall, "or similar property," which appears at the end of the amendment.

Without the literary description of Francis, his mannerisms and his manifestations, Francis would cease to exist. In any event, an amorphous Francis could hardly be called "property held by the taxpayer," the sale of which is entitled to capital gains treatment. Section 117(a)(1), I.R.C., 1939. If Francis is, as taxpayer suggests, an "intellectual conception," sans form and substance, existing in the mind alone, it is incapable of ownership and, therefore, of being "property held by the taxpayer." If Francis has sufficient form and substance to be considered property capable of ownership, this is so because of its literary composition.

The taxpayer is entitled to capital gains treatment on the income from the contract in suit for the year 1950 because the 1950 amendment to the Code does not apply to income received during that year. As to subsequent years, however, capital gains treatment of the income from the contract must be denied as proscribed by that amendment.

---

9. Bobbs-Merrill v. Straus, 2 Cir., 147 F. 15, affirmed 210 U.S. 339; Warner Bros. Pictures v. Columbia Broadcasting System, 9 Cir., 216 F.2d 945, 948, certiorari denied 348 U.S. 971; Universal Pictures Co. v. Harold Lloyd Corp., 9 Cir., 162 F.2d 354, 363; Nichols v. Universal Pictures Corp., 2 Cir., 45 F.2d 119, 121; Dymow v. Bolton, 2 Cir., 11 F.2d 690; Chappell & Co. v. Fields, 2 Cir., 210 F. 864; Savage v. Hoffmann, C.C., 159 F. 584; Bloom & Hamlin v. Nixon, D.C., 125 F. 977.

10. The taxpayer refers to that portion of the Treasury Regulations (Treas.Reg. 118, Secs. 39.117(a)-1) which reads as follows:

> "The phrase 'similar property' includes, for example, such property as a theatrical production, a radio program, a newspaper cartoon strip, or any other property eligible for copyright protection (whether under statute or common law)."

Levy v. Commissioner
T.C. Memo. 1992-471

SCOTT, JUDGE:

The issue for decision is whether the sale made by petitioner to Mr. Ernest Johns was the sale of a capital asset or was the sale of a computer program, an asset which is excludable from the definition of capital asset under section 1221(3).

David D. Levy (petitioner) is a computer programmer. From October 1978 to January 1984, petitioner was employed by Fort Howard Paper Co. of Green Bay, Wisconsin. In 1982, Larry Lawler, another computer programmer, joined the company. Petitioner and Mr. Lawler developed a computer software program to monitor and improve the performance of an International Business Machines (IBM) teleprocessing software system known as the Customer Information Control System (CICS). The software could be utilized on any IBM or IBM-compatible mainframe computer capable of executing the CICS system. Petitioner and Mr. Lawler had an agreement with Fort Howard Paper Co. that they would retain their property rights over the computer software program.

In 1983, on a visit to Fort Howard Paper Co., Mr. Ernest Johns saw the product developed by petitioner and Mr. Lawler in operation at Fort Howard Paper Co., and expressed interest in purchasing the computer software program. The program was being operated at Fort Howard Paper Co. on a source code that contained two programs. On January 27, 1984, an agreement of sale was executed whereby petitioner and Mr. Lawler transferred to Mr. Johns "all rights and interest in and to the Systems, including without limitation, all source and object code and manuals and all other related documentation and materials therefor and all enhancements now existing or hereafter made thereto." The agreement called for petitioner and Mr. Lawler to each receive as consideration $1,500 per month for 6 months plus one-third of the net proceeds after expenses incurred by Mr. Johns from any subsequent sale or license of the system. On January 25, 1985, petitioner and Mr. Johns entered into an agreement whereby petitioner granted to Mr. Johns "all rights, title to, and interest in and to the SYSTEM, including without limitation, all source and object code and manuals and all other related documentation and materials therefor and all enhancements now existing or hereafter made thereto." On April 19, 1985, Mr. Johns, through his wholly owned subsidiary corporation, Quantum International Corp., sold the computer software program to Boole & Babbage, Inc., for $850,000. Prior to this sale, Mr. Johns had licensed the system to several companies.

Petitioners on their Federal income tax returns for the years here in issue reported the gain from the sale to Mr. Johns as long-term capital gain. Respondent in the notice of deficiency determined that the gain from the sale was ordinary income and increased petitioners' income as reported accordingly.

OPINION

Section 1221 defines capital assets as all assets held by the taxpayer except those specifically excepted by statute. However, it is well established that the definition of a capital asset is narrowly construed.

The parties in this case recognize that the asset sold by petitioner qualifies as a capital asset unless it falls within the exception for a copyright or similar property. Sec. 1221(3). Petitioner takes the position that the asset he sold to Mr. Johns was "an idea" on which a copyright could not be obtained. Respondent contends that petitioner sold Mr. Johns a computer program on which a copyright could have been obtained.

The parties agree that the Federal copyright law is applicable to computer programs. Petitioner did not seek copyright protection for his product. However, section 1.1221-1(c)(1), Income Tax Regs., expressly includes within the definition of property similar to a copyright, property eligible for copyright protection. The fact that petitioner and Mr. Lawler developed the property together causes the interest of each party to be excluded from the capital asset category if the asset otherwise comes within the definition of similar property under section 1221(3).

We must therefore determine whether the asset held by petitioner was eligible for copyright protection as a computer program under the copyright law. A computer program has been defined since the copyright statute was amended in 1980 in 17 U.S.C. sec. 101, as a "set of statements or instructions to be used directly or indirectly in a computer in order to bring about a certain result." In *Whelan Associates, Inc. v. Jaslow Dental Laboratory, Inc.*, 797 F.2d 1222 (3d Cir.1986), the court elaborated on the definition by holding that a computer program includes not only the literal elements (including object codes and source codes) but also the organization, structure, and sequence.

In the present case petitioner, in conjunction with Larry Lawler, had an idea to monitor and improve the performance of an existing computer network at the Fort Howard Paper Co. known as the CICS. The record shows that the expression of that idea was put in the form of a computer program installed at Fort Howard Paper Co. after several months of development. Petitioner testified that at no time did Fort Howard Paper Co. have any property rights in the computer program developed for the CICS.

The record shows that petitioner owned an asset that included a source code which fit the definition of a program under the copyright law. The program was being used at Fort Howard Paper Co. As a computer program the asset also fit the enumerated exception to capital asset contained in section 1221(3) for copyright or similar property. Petitioner's primary argument is that he did not sell his computer program (i.e., the expression) to Mr. Ernest Johns but rather simply sold the idea underlying the program. The facts in this record do not support petitioner's contention. The agreement of sale signed on January 27, 1984, transferred to Mr. Ernest Johns all rights in and to the system including "without limitation, all source and object code and manuals and all other related documentation and materials therefor and all enhancements now existing or hereafter made." Clearly the program codes were part of the sale.

Petitioner testified that prior to the sale Mr. Johns had seen the computer program in operation at Fort Howard Paper Co. This testimony further supports the conclusion that more than an idea was sold by petitioner to Mr. Johns. We hold that petitioner sold an expression of his idea embodied in the computer program in use at Fort Howard Paper Co. to Mr. Johns. Accordingly, we hold that petitioner sold an asset eligible for copyright protection and, hence, excluded from the definition of a capital asset under section 1221(3).

Petitioner's contention that he did not transfer the computer program in use at Fort Howard Paper Co. to Mr. Johns is based on his claim that he did not physically deliver the codes in use at Fort Howard Paper Co. to Mr. Johns. Petitioner says that he worked further and enhanced the codes before they were physically delivered to Mr. Johns. Under the sales contract the codes were included in the property sold to Mr. Johns. Therefore, Mr. Johns owned the codes whether or not they were physically delivered to him. The fact that petitioner transferred the structure, organization, and sequence of the computer program to Mr. Johns does not cause the asset to fall outside the copyright protection and therefore outside the enumerated exception from the definition of a capital asset. *Whelan Associates, Inc. v. Jaslow Dental Laboratory, Inc., supra.*

Petitioner admits that by the time he and Mr. Johns entered into the contract executed on January 25, 1985, the asset transferred was a computer program but contends that this contract was not a sale of the computer program since Mr. Johns already owned the computer program. The record is not clear as to the reason for the January 25, 1985, contract. However, this record is clear that all rights to the computer program as it then existed including the codes and any enhancement of the program was sold to Mr. Johns on January 27, 1984.

Petitioner contends that he did not seek a copyright on the computer program used at Fort Howard Paper Co. because of his desire to keep the source codes a secret. However, as we have heretofore pointed out, the literal language of section 1.1221-1(c)(1), Income Tax Regs., provides that exception to the definition of a capital asset set forth in section 1221(3) includes those assets eligible for copyright protection whether or not such protection is sought. Using eligibility as the standard, it is irrelevant whether the asset was in fact protected by copyright. Petitioner has the burden of affirmatively proving that respondent's determination of ordinary income treatment for the sale of the computer program is incorrect. Petitioner has failed to meet his burden of proof.

Based on this record, we conclude that petitioner has failed to establish that he is entitled to capital gains treatment on the gain from the sale of the asset he sold to Mr. Johns.

Chilton v. Commissioner
40 T.C. 552 (1963)

SCOTT, JUDGE:

The issue for decision is whether amounts received in the years here involved by Roland Chilton pursuant to contracts with his employers constitute ordinary income as compensation or long-term capital gains from the sale or exchange of patents.

FINDINGS OF FACT

Roland Chilton (hereinafter referred to as petitioner) is an engineer. He was educated in England. Prior to 1918 petitioner had been employed as an engineer successively by the Sunbeam Motor Car Co., D. Napier & Sons, J. B. Ferguson, and Crane Simplex Corp. In 1918 petitioner became employed as chief engineer by the Aeromarine Plane and Motor Co. (hereinafter referred to as Aeromarine). He remained employed by this company until September 1929, when he became employed by Wright Aeronautical Corp. Petitioner's work at Aeromarine consisted primarily of designing and supervising the construction and testing of aircraft engines. During the time petitioner was employed by Aeromarine, he made approximately 50 patentable inventions, although only a relatively small part of his time was devoted to making inventions. An important area of petitioner's inventive activities at Aeromarine was in the field of variable speed transmissions and starter devices, particularly the inertia starter. Petitioner had no specific agreement with Aeromarine in regard to his inventions. Aeromarine claimed that it owned all inventions made by petitioner by virtue of the fact that petitioner was its employee. Before petitioner's employment with Aeromarine was terminated, he had obtained an agreement from Aeromarine to pay royalties to him on the inventions and patents covering the inertia starter.

While petitioner was employed by Aeromarine, he had extensive sales contacts on behalf of that company with the Bureau of Aeronautics of the U.S. Navy Department and particularly with an employee of that bureau who subsequently became vice president of sales and service at Wright Aeronautical Corp. (hereinafter referred to as Wright). It was this officer of Wright who suggested that petitioner be employed by Wright. At that time Wright was having serious operating difficulties with one of its engines, which had failed to meet a test established by the U.S. Navy Department which had been successfully met by Aeromarine.

Early in 1928, Wright entered into negotiations looking toward the employment of petitioner. Wright had a compelling need at that time to strengthen its engineering department and the officers of Wright knew of petitioner's ability and experience as a skilled engineer and troubleshooter. The officers of Wright also knew of petitioner's reputation as an inventor. Wright was primarily interested in acquiring petitioner's services as an engineer and initially submitted to him a contract which simply provided for payment to him of an annual salary of $15,000. Because of petitioner's prior disputes with Aeromarine with respect to that company's obligation to pay royalties for his inventions, petitioner insisted upon a contract with Wright which would make special provision with respect to his inventions. On September 3, 1929, petitioner and Wright entered into a contract which provided in part as follows:

I. The Company shall employ Chilton and Chilton shall enter the employ of the Company.

II. Chilton shall be known under the title of "Consulting Engineer".

III. The Company shall pay Chilton as compensation at the rate of Fifteen thousand dollars ($15,000.00) per year, payable in semi-monthly installments during the term of Chilton's employment.

IV. The term of Chilton's employment shall be from the date of the execution of this contract to the date of its termination as hereinafter provided.

V. The services that Chilton shall render to the Company shall consist in engineering work relating to the improvement of existing types of aircraft engines and other products of the Company or products similar to the products of the Company and to the development of new types and in allied engineering activities. Chilton shall during business hours devote his whole time and apply his experience and his inventive ability to the problems, improvements, and developments relating to the Company's products and products similar to the Company's products, referred to him by the Company.

VI. (A) Chilton shall assign to the Company the entire right, title, and interest in and to all inventions and improvements made by him during his employment by said Company relating to aircraft engines and other products manufactured by the Company or products similar thereto, and all said inventions and improvements shall belong to and be the sole and exclusive property of said Company in and for all countries of the world, and Chilton hereby acknowledges that all said inventions and improvements shall be made for and in the interest and for the account of said Company and he hereby expressly transfers and assigns all said inventions and improvements to said Company in and for all countries of the world.

(B) Chilton shall disclose promptly to the Company all inventions and improvements which he may make relating to or upon aircraft engines and other products manufactured by the Company, or products similar thereto, during the term of this contract.

VII. (A) The Company shall pay for the preparation, filing, and prosecution of all applications for Letters Patent which the Company desires to be filed in its behalf on the inventions or improvements of Chilton.

(B) Chilton shall do all acts and things and execute and deliver all application papers, assignments, and other instruments in writing that may be necessary to secure to and vest in the Company the entire right, title, and interest in and to said inventions and improvements, in and to all applications for Letters Patent covering said inventions and improvements, and in and to all Letters Patent of the United States and of all other countries that may be granted for said inventions and improvements.

VIII. Chilton shall furnish the Company, with such assistance as the Company can give him, complete copies of detailed working drawings covering all inventions and improvements and shall furnish the Company with such information as he may have available with respect to the construction of any products covered by said inventions and improvements.

IX. The Company shall have 90 days after completion of a development test on any invention or improvement to determine whether or not it will accept any such invention or improvement offered to it by Chilton, and unless within said 90 days the Company gives Chilton written notice that it accepts said invention or improvements, Chilton shall be at liberty to file applications on his own behalf and at his own expense on any of such inventions which have not so been accepted by the company.

X. Chilton shall have and retain full rights in and shall be free to file in his own behalf applications for patents on any and all of his inventions not directly relating to aircraft engines or other products of the Company or products similar thereto, and, in addition thereto, Chilton shall have and retain full rights in and to any and all inventions in or directly relating to engine starting devices and shall be at liberty to file in his own behalf applications for patents on said inventions.

XI. As additional compensation, the Company shall pay Chilton:

(a) Two and one-half percent (2 ½%) royalty on the published list price, * * *

XII. The employment of Chilton by the Company may be terminated by either of the parties hereto upon thirty (30) days' notice in writing each to the other, such notice to be by registered mail, addressed to the last known address of the party who receives such notice. Upon the termination of the employment by such written notice, the payment of the compensation herein provided shall terminate. The Company, however, shall continue to make the payments to Chilton in accordance with subdivisions (a) and (b) of paragraph XI hereof, said payments to continue with respect to each invention or improvement during the life of the Letters Patent granted thereon.

XIII. The Company shall keep complete books of account and records respecting the manufacture and sale of all devices, components, assemblies, or parts hereunder and shall give Chilton or his duly authorized representative the privilege of inspecting or examining the Company's books in his behalf at all reasonable times, not to exceed four such inspections or examinations per year.

XV. Chilton shall assist the Company to prosecute infringers of any of the Letters Patent included within this agreement and also to defend any action instituted against the Company by reason of its manufacture, sale, and/or use of any products in accordance with the provisions of this contract; if as the result of the decision of a court of last resort in any suit brought on a patent assigned by Chilton to the Company, or by the decision of an inferior court from whose decree no appeal is taken within the time provided by law, such patent is declared either invalid or an infringement, or for any reason whatsoever, then the payments by the Company to Chilton with respect to such patent shall cease and terminate and there shall be no further liability on the part of the Company to Chilton thereunder.

XVI. This agreement shall be binding upon the heirs and assigns of Chilton and upon the successors and assigns of the Company.

The contract between petitioner and Wright was terminated on December 31, 1934, at which time petitioner was employed by Reed Propeller Co., Inc. (hereinafter referred to as Reed). Reed and Wright were both subsidiaries of Curtiss-Wright Corp. (hereinafter referred to as Curtiss-Wright). The contract dated December 31, 1934, between petitioner and Reed, insofar as here pertinent, contained provisions identical to those of petitioner's contract of September 3, 1929, with Wright. On December 31, 1934, Wright assigned to Reed all its right, title, and interest in the patents and patent applications in which it had an interest. Petitioner remained employed by Reed under this contract until June 30, 1938, when his employment was terminated, and he simultaneously entered the employ of Wright under a contract dated June 30, 1938, which insofar as here pertinent, contained substantially the same provisions as the September 3, 1929, contract between petitioner and Wright except that paragraph 6(a) thereof provided only:

> 6.(a) CHILTON shall assign to WRIGHT the entire right, title and interest in and to all inventions and improvements made by him during his employment by WRIGHT directly relating to aircraft engines and/or their accessories, and all said inventions and improvements shall belong to and be the sole and exclusive property of WRIGHT in and for all countries of the world.

Reed on June 30, 1938, assigned to Wright all the right, title, and interest it had in patents and patent applications. At no time was petitioner represented by counsel in connection with the preparation or execution of the 1929, 1934, or 1938 contracts.

The 1938 contract between petitioner and Wright was amended several times, primarily to provide for limitation of the amount of royalties which petitioner might be entitled to receive in view of the greatly increased demand for Wright's products caused by war conditions during the period 1941 to 1945. On October 12, 1949, Wright notified petitioner that his employment under the agreement dated June 30, 1938, would terminate on November 15, 1949. Petitioner has not been an employee of Wright, Reed, or Curtiss-Wright since November 15, 1949.

During the period from September 3, 1929, through November 15, 1949, whenever petitioner developed an invention covered by his contract with Wright or Reed, he offered such invention to his employing company. In each instance the company notified petitioner in writing whether or not it was interested in acquiring the invention. Whenever the company indicated its desire to acquire an invention, a formal application for patent and an assignment by petitioner to the company were prepared by the employer's attorneys and executed by petitioner. If petitioner's employing company did not indicate a desire to acquire the invention, no instrument of transfer from petitioner to Wright or Reed was executed.

During petitioner's association with Wright he devoted the major portion of his time to the diagnosis of problems involving the functioning and development of Wright's products in a manner not designed to and in fact not resulting in patentable inventions. Among his duties were giving advice and counsel to layout men, supervising test operations, analyzing and screening inventions submitted by outside inventors, traveling for inspection and other business purposes, serving as a member on Wright's engineering council, handling problems with the U.S. Government, and preparation of service reports. A relatively minor portion of petitioner's time at Wright was spent in inventing. However, petitioner did obtain 91 patents which were assigned to Wright, Reed, or Curtiss-Wright pursuant to these contracts. During this same period petitioner applied for and obtained 27 patents which were not assigned to Wright, Reed, or Curtiss-Wright.

Wright and Reed did not use all the patents assigned to them by petitioner in their manufacture of aircraft engines and accessories.

Subsequent to 1949 the Wright Aeronautical Division of Curtiss-Wright assumed the obligations of Reed and Wright under the contracts of these companies with petitioner. During the taxable years 1954 through 1957 Curtiss-Wright paid to petitioner the following amounts with respect to the patents [$168,851, $71,285, $13,771, $4,883].

During the period that petitioner was associated with Wright or Reed he conducted extensive design and patent activities away from the premises of these corporations and outside his regular employment hours. The office and drafting facilities used by petitioner in his independent research were maintained at his own expense and he paid the compensation of his associates and assistants for the work they performed for him. As a result of this work away from Wright's or Reed's premises petitioner developed a number of patents or inventions, some of which were sold to parties other than Wright or Reed, and some to Wright outside of the contract between petitioner and Wright.

Petitioner at no time owned any stock in Wright and never had more than a nominal interest in any corporation affiliated with Wright.

Wright, on its books and income tax returns, treated the $15,000 a year paid to petitioner from September 3, 1929, through November 15, 1949, as a salary payment, and the remaining payments to petitioner as royalty payments. No deduction was made from the amounts treated as royalty payments for income tax or social security tax and such payments were not included in the base for determination of petitioner's pension rights. During the period of World War II, the Salary Stabilization Unit of the Bureau of Internal Revenue issued a ruling to Wright that the amount paid to petitioner which it designated as royalties did not constitute salary within the meaning of the applicable salary stabilization regulations.

At the time of petitioner's original employment by Wright in 1929, Wright's treasurer and chief engineer received less salary than petitioner, and its factory manager, the same salary as petitioner. This situation generally prevailed until around 1941 when Wright made a general salary adjustment and most of its employees' salaries were increased, the salary of the vice president and general manager going up to $60,000 a year. There was no increase in petitioner's salary (except for a small increase for a period of about a year) from 1929 until the termination of his employment with Wright on November 15, 1949.

Other employees of Wright who made inventions were required to assign such inventions to the company for only a nominal consideration. Most of these employees received salary increases during the period in which petitioner received no such increase.

Petitioner usually received 5-percent royalty on inventions he assigned to parties other than Wright as compared to the 2 ½ percent on inventions assigned to Wright.

On petitioner's income tax returns for the years 1939 to 1953, he reported the payments received from Wright, Reed, or Curtiss-Wright in respect of the inventions made during his employment by Wright and Reed as ordinary income from a business or profession. On his income tax returns for the years 1954, 1955, 1956, and 1957 he reported the payments received from Curtiss-Wright in respect to such inventions as capital gains.

Respondent, in his notice of deficiency, determined that the payments received by petitioner from Curtiss-Wright during the years 1954, 1955, 1956, and 1957, pursuant to his contracts with Reed and Wright, constituted ordinary income and gave the following explanation in each of these years:

> The grounds for this determination are: (1) the amount constitutes compensation for personal services; (2) you have failed to establish that said amount qualifies for treatment as long-term capital gain.

OPINION

Section 1235 of the Internal Revenue Code of 1954 provides that a transfer of property consisting of all substantial rights to a patent by the person whose efforts produced such patent shall be considered the sale or exchange of a capital asset held for more than 6 months, regardless of whether or not payments in consideration of such transfer are contingent on the productivity, use, or disposition of the property transferred and regardless of the taxable year in which such transfer occurred. The amounts received by petitioner during the years here involved were with respect to patents produced by his efforts. Therefore, under section 1235 these amounts are capital gains from the sale or exchange of a capital asset if at any time petitioner made a transfer of all substantial rights to these patents.

It is respondent's position that petitioner never made a transfer of all substantial rights to any of the patents with respect to which the payments during the years in issue were received. Respondent takes the position that petitioner never owned any substantial rights in such patents and therefore his assignment of the patents to Wright or Reed did not transfer to those companies any substantial rights. Respondent contends that under petitioner's contracts with Wright and Reed those companies owned the inventions which petitioner made at all times from the discovery leading to the inventions. In support of his position, respondent relies primarily upon his regulations[2] which provide that payments received by an employee as compensation for services rendered as an employee under an employment contract requiring the employee to transfer to the employer the right to any invention by such employee are not attributable to a transfer to which section 1235 applies, and the case of *Arthur N. Blum*, 11 T.C. 101 (1948), affd. 183 F.2d 281 (C.A. 3, 1950).

Petitioner contends that under the facts here present, he was not employed to invent so as to make his inventions the property of Wright or Reed. Petitioner distinguishes the *Blum* case on the basis of the differences in the facts in that case and the instant case. He

---

2. Income Tax Regs., sec. 1.1235-1(c)(2). *Payments to an employee*. Payments received by an employee as compensation for services rendered as an employee under an employment contract requiring the employee to transfer to the employer the rights to any invention by such employee are not attributable to a transfer to which section 1235 applies. However, whether payments received by an employee from his employer (under an employment contract or otherwise) are attributable to the transfer by the employee of all substantial rights to a patent (or an undivided interest therein) or are compensation for services rendered the employer by the employee is a question of fact. In determining which is the case, consideration shall be given not only to all the facts and circumstances of the employment relationship but also to whether the amount of such payments depends upon the production, sale, or use by, or the value to, the employer of the patent rights transferred by the employee. If it is determined that payments are attributable to the transfer of patent rights, and all other requirements under section 1235 are met, such payments shall be treated as proceeds derived from the sale of a patent.

also contends that the controlling law is different in the instant case since no provisions similar to section 1235 were applicable to the years involved in the *Blum* case.

It is clear from the contracts between petitioner and Reed and Wright that petitioner was obligated to disclose to Wright and Reed all inventions or improvements which he made relating to aircraft engines and their accessories. If within 90 days after completion of development tests, Wright or Reed notified petitioner in writing that it accepted the invention, petitioner was obligated by his contract to execute and deliver all application papers, assignments, and other writings necessary to secure to Reed or Wright the entire right, title, and interest in and to the inventions relating to aircraft engines and their accessories and all letters patent that might be granted for such inventions, developments, or improvements.

Respondent argues that these provisions of the contract made Wright or Reed the equitable owners of any inventions with respect to aircraft engines and their accessories made by petitioner. Respondent states that had petitioner refused to assign any rights in any inventions which he made or applications for patents or patents on such inventions to Wright or Reed, these companies could have obtained such an assignment by an action in equity for specific performance. Petitioner does not contend that Wright and Reed could not under the contracts have enforced specific performance of his agreement to transfer to them his inventions and patents. Petitioner argues that this right created by the contracts did not, itself, constitute the transfer of the patents and that when the transfer occurred the companies acquired "all substantial rights" to the patents. Petitioner relies on a number of cases involving executory contracts to assign patents. The facts in each of these cases differ from those in the instant case but in each case a sale was held to have been made at the time of the assignment of the patent even though prior to such assignment a contract to assign had been executed.

Petitioner further points out that even if an executory contract to assign an invention is construed as transferring all rights to such invention immediately upon the conception of the invention, section 1235 makes the transfer of the invention at that time the sale of a capital asset held for more than 6 months. Respondent's regulations do not state that all payments to an employee who is required to assign his inventions to his employer are compensation for services. These regulations refer to compensation for services rendered "as an employee."

We agree with petitioner that his agreement with Wright and Reed to assign to them the rights to his inventions, standing alone, would not cause section 1235 to be inapplicable to the payments received by him in the years here in issue pursuant to these contracts.

The real question in issue here is whether petitioner was "hired to invent" aircraft engines and accessories or assigned the duties of devoting himself to such specific inventions. If a person is employed by another "to invent" a specific product of specific products, the fruits of the employee's labor, the invention, belongs to his employer. *United States v. Dubilier Condenser Corp.*, 289 U.S. 178 (1933); and *Marshall v. Colgate-Palmolive-Peet Co.*, 175 F.2d 215 (C.A. 3, 1949).

The payment to the employee is for his labor, not for the product, "the invention."[3] The payment is therefore compensation for services and taxable as such.

---

3. In *United States v. Dubilier Condenser Corp.*, 289 U.S. 178, 187, the Court stated:
One employed to make an invention, who succeeds, during his term of service, in accomplishing that task, is bound to assign to his employer any patent obtained. The reason is that he has only produced that which he was employed to invent. His invention is the precise subject of the contract of employment. A term of the agreement necessarily is that

The nature of the relationship between petitioner and his employers must be determined from the contracts between them and the conduct of the parties. If the provisions of the contract were unambiguous, it might be unnecessary to consider other facts. However, these provisions are not clear as to the nature of petitioner's employment. Petitioner agreed to apply his "inventive ability" to his employers' products. However, preceding the sentence referring to petitioner's "inventive ability" is a sentence classifying petitioner's services as "engineering work." There is a similar inconsistency between the reference in the contracts to all petitioner's aircraft engine inventions being the property of Wright or Reed and the provision that if written notice were not given to petitioner within 90 days after the completion of development tests, all rights to the inventions shall belong to petitioner.

Turning to the other evidence, we think it clear that petitioner was not "hired to invent" aircraft engines, improvements thereon, or accessories thereto. Such, in substance, was the testimony of several witnesses. The actions of the parties support this testimony. Wright at the time it hired petitioner had not proposed to have the contract make provision for his inventions. From at least 1939 petitioner on his income tax returns reported the amounts received with respect to the patents assigned to Wright or Reed as income from his business of inventing. When these returns were filed, this income was taxable as ordinary income. There existed no self-serving reason for petitioner to report the payments as income from a business or profession as distinguished from compensation for services. Reed, Wright, and Curtiss-Wright each on their books and records and Federal income tax returns, treated the payments to petitioner with respect to the patents as royalties and not as compensation. These facts and others in the record indicate that none of the parties to these contracts considered the payments with respect to the patents to be compensation to petitioner for services as an employee.

Since the payments petitioner received with respect to the patents in accordance with his contracts with his employers were not compensation for services rendered "as an employee," the amounts were payments to petitioner for transfer to his employers of his inventions and patents. This is the very type of payment which section 1235 states shall be considered as received from the sale or exchange of a capital asset. We sustain petitioner in his contention that the payments he received from Curtiss-Wright during the years here involved are taxable as gain from the sale of a capital asset held for over 6 months.

Kueneman v. Commissioner
68 T.C. 609 (1977)

SIMPSON, JUDGE:

As a result of a concession by the Commissioner, the sole issue for decision is whether the petitioners are entitled to report as long-term capital gains royalty payments received

---

what he is paid to produce belongs to his paymaster. *Standard Parts Co. v. Peck*, 264 U.S. 52. On the other hand, if the employment be general, albeit it cover a field of labor and effort in the performance of which the employee conceived the invention for which he obtained a patent, the contract is not so broadly construed as to require an assignment of the patent. *Hapgood v. Hewitt*, 119 U.S. 226; *Dalzell v. Dueber Watch Case Mfg. Co.*, 149 U.S. 315. * * *

from an exclusive transfer of patent rights within a specified geographical area. That issue turns on whether such a transfer disposed of "all substantial rights" to the patents within the meaning of section 1235(a) of the Internal Revenue Code of 1954.

The petitioners Don Kueneman and John R. Kueneman were the principal inventors of a type of rock-crushing machine for which they obtained patents (the patents) in the 1940's. By agreement dated August 27, 1946, the ownership of such patents was altered so that John R. Kueneman, Don Kueneman, Alma B. Harrell, and Cyril P. Kenville each acquired a specified undivided ownership interest in them. In addition, the agreement provided that John R. Kueneman was authorized to act on behalf of all the owners of the patents in connection with any sale, lease, or other arrangement affecting the patents.

On November 1, 1948, John R. Kueneman entered into a licensing agreement with Pennsylvania Crusher Co. (Crusher), a New York corporation. Under the licensing agreement, Crusher was granted the exclusive right to make, vend, and use the patents throughout Puerto Rico, eastern Canada, and all of the United States east of North Dakota, South Dakota, Nebraska, Kansas, Oklahoma, and Texas during the lives of such patents. In return for the transfer, Cursher agreed to make specified royalty payments to the undivided owners in accordance with their ownership interests in the patents, as set forth in the licensing agreement.

Petitioners	Royalty payments	
	1971	1972
John R. Kueneman	$7,814	$7,910
Don and Irene Kueneman	7,814	7,910
Edmund W. and Ella M. Harrell	2,293	2,322

On their Federal income tax returns for the years in issue, the petitioners treated such royalties as long-term capital gains. In his deficiency notices, the Commissioner determined that such royalty income was ordinary income.

We must decide whether the petitioners are entitled to report the income received from their patent transfers as long-term capital gains or whether it is ordinary income. The petitioners contend they are entitled to capital gain treatment under section 1235 and make no argument for capital gain treatment outside such provision. They argue that their exclusive geographical transfers disposed of "all substantial rights" in such patents within the meaning of section 1235(a). In two prior decisions, *Rodgers v. Commissioner*, 51 T.C. 927 (1969), and *Estate of Klein v. Commissioner*, 61 T.C. 332 (1973), revd. 507 F.2d 617 (7th Cir. 1974), cert. denied 421 U.S. 991 (1975), this Court held that such a transfer automatically meets that statutory requirement and qualifies for capital gain treatment. In so holding, we overturned a Treasury regulation to the contrary.[3] The action of the Seventh Circuit in reversing our decision in *Estate of Klein* clearly calls for a reconsideration of our position with respect to geographically limited

---

3. Sec. 1.1235-2(b)(1), Income Tax Regs.:
 * * * (1) The term "all substantial rights to a patent" means all rights (whether or not then held by the grantor) which are of value at the time the rights to the patent (or an undivided interest therein) are transferred. The term "all substantial rights to a patent" does not include a grant of rights to a patent—
  (i) Which is limited geographically within the country of issuance;
 The circumstances of the whole transaction, rather than the particular terminology used in the instrument of transfer, shall be considered in determining whether or not all substantial rights to a patent are transferred in a transaction.

transfers of patent rights. Moreover, the rationale on which we relied in the *Rodgers* and *Estate of Klein* cases has been rejected by the Ninth and Sixth Circuits. *Mros v. Commissioner*, 493 F.2d 813 (9th Cir. 1974), revg. per curiam a Memorandum Opinion of this Court;[4] *Fawick v. Commissioner*, 436 F.2d 655 (6th Cir. 1971), revg. 52 T.C. 104 (1969). In view of such general criticism of our position, we have carefully reexamined the basis for our decision in *Rodgers*.

Prior to the enactment of section 1235, there was no specific statutory provision prescribing the tax consequences resulting from a transfer of patent rights; instead, taxpayers seeking capital gains for the proceeds of such transfers had to meet the general requirements relating to capital gains contained in section 117 of the Internal Revenue Code of 1939. Thus, it was necessary for a taxpayer to show that the patent rights transferred by him were in his hands a "capital asset"[5] and that he disposed of them in a transaction that qualified as a "sale or exchange." In understanding the approach we took in *Rodgers*, it is helpful to discuss the rationale by which exclusive geographical transfers had qualified as a "sale."

Originally, when the courts were confronted with the necessity of deciding when a transfer of patent rights constituted a "sale" for tax purposes, they turned to Federal patent law for guidance as to the recognized and divisible property interests in a patent. If a patent transfer represented under patent law a disposition of an identifiable and distinct piece of property, then a "sale" could be found; otherwise, the transfer did not amount to a "sale." The patent law already recognized such a distinction with respect to the transfer of patent rights by use of the concepts of "assignment" and "license." For patent law purposes, certain legal consequences flowed from whether one achieved the status of the distinction was merely a licensee. The classic exposition of the distinction between such concepts appears in the Supreme Court's opinion in *Waterman v. MacKenzie*, 138 U.S. 252, 255 (1891), wherein it was said:

> Every patent issued under the laws of the United States for an invention or discovery contains "a grant to the patentee, his heirs and assigns, for the term of seventeen years, of the exclusive right to make, use and vend the invention or discovery throughout the United States and the Territories thereof." The monopoly thus granted is one entire thing, and cannot be divided into parts, except as authorized by those laws. The patentee or his assigns may, by instrument in writing, assign, grant and convey, either 1st, the whole patent, comprising the exclusive right to make, use and vend the invention throughout the United States; or 2d, an undivided part or share of that exclusive right; or 3d, the exclusive right under the patent within and throughout a

---

4. In *Mros v. Commissioner*, 493 F.2d 813 (1974), the Ninth Circuit rejected our position that a transfer of patent rights within a field of use automatically qualifies as a disposition of "all substantial rights" to a patent within the meaning of sec. 1235. See *Rouverol v. Commissioner*, 42 T.C. 186 (1964); *Fawick v. Commissioner*, 52 T.C. 104 (1969), revd. 436 F.2d 655 (6th Cir. 1971). However, since the case before us involves an exclusive geographical patent transfer, a distinct and separate legal question as the Commissioner recognizes, our decision is not governed by *Golsen v. Commissioner*, 54 T.C. 742 (1970), affd. 445 F.2d 985 (10th Cir. 1971), cert. denied 404 U.S. 940 (1971).

5. This issue presented the question of whether any of the exclusions to the definition of capital asset applied. The exclusion most often in issue was whether the patent constituted property held by the taxpayer primarily for sale to customers in the ordinary course of his trade or business. Sec. 117(a)(1), I.R.C. 1939; sec. 1221(1). That question turned on whether the taxpayer was a professional or amateur inventor. Sec. 1235 did away with this requirement so that professional inventors became eligible to receive capital gains upon the "sale or exchange" of their patents. S. Rept. 1622, 83d Cong., 2d Sess. 439 (1954).

specified part of the United States. A transfer of either of these three kinds of interests is an *assignment*, properly speaking, and *vests in the assignee a title in so much of the patent itself*, with a right to sue infringers; in the second case, jointly with the assignor; in the first and third cases, in the name of the assignee alone. *Any assignment or transfer, short of one of these, is a mere license, giving the licensee no title in the patent*, and no right to sue at law in his own name for an infringement. Any rights of the licensee must be enforced through or in the name of the owner of the patent * * * [Emphasis supplied.]

In accordance with the *Waterman* definition of an assignment of patent rights, it was held that, for tax purposes, a "sale" of patent rights occurred upon the transfer of: (1) The whole patent,[7] (2) an undivided interest in the whole patent,[8] or (3) the exclusive right to the patent within a specific geographical area.[9] Thus, exclusive geographical transfers automatically qualified as a "sale" because of *Waterman*.

In *Rodgers v. Commissioner*, 51 T.C. 927 (1969), this Court first had occasion to pass upon the effect of the enactment of section 1235 on an exclusive transfer of patent rights within a geographical area. In that case, the taxpayer was the holder of patents on three varieties of almonds. He made several transfers which together granted all of his rights to such patents within the State of California. California was the only State in which there was commercial production of almonds. We observed that section 1235 did not impose "any further or different impediments to capital gains treatment than were contained in section 117 of the 1939 Code"; and consequently, we concluded that such exclusive geographical patent transfers were to continue to be treated as a "sale," thereby automatically qualifying for capital gain treatment. In support of such conclusion, the Court offered the following rationale for interpreting the all-substantial-rights test:

We read * * * [in sec. 1235] no prohibition on the division of patent into different fields of application or into different geographical areas so long as all substantial rights to the patent so divided are granted. [51 T.C. at 930; emphasis supplied.]

Rodgers was not appealed by the Government, perhaps because the transfers of all patent rights in California, in fact, disposed of all rights of any value. However, the rationale of *Rodgers* has generally been disapproved by other courts. The issue next arose in *Estate of Klein v. Commissioner*, 61 T.C. 332 (1973), in which the owner of a patented process for the production of organic compost granted an exclusive right to manufacture, use, and sell the compost in certain Eastern States of the United States. We followed our decision in *Rodgers* and held that such a transfer of patent rights automatically qualified for capital gain treatment under section 1235. On appeal, our decision was reversed by the Seventh Circuit (507 F.2d 617 (1974)). That court reviewed

---

7. *Watson v. United States*, 222 F.2d 689, 690-691 (10th Cir. 1955); *Commissioner v. Hopkinson*, 126 F.2d 406, 410 (2d Cir. 1942), affg. 42 B.T.A. 580 (1940); *Kronner v. United States*, 110 F.Supp. 730, 735 (Ct. Cl. 1953); *Myers v. Commissioner*, 6 T.C. 258, 263 (1946); *Taylor v. Commissioner*, 16 T.C. 376, 384 (1951); *Ruge v. Commissioner*, 26 T.C. 138, 141 (1956); Reid v. Commissioner, 26 T.C. 622, 632-633 (1956); see *Lamar v. Granger*, 99 F.Supp. 17, 36-37 (W.D.Pa. 1951); cf. *Commissioner v. Celanese Corp.*, 140 F.2d 339, 341-342 (D.C. Cir. 1944), affg. a Memorandum Opinion of this Court.

8. *Dreymann v. Commissioner*, 11 T.C. 153, 159-160 (1948); *Parke, Davis & Co. v. Commissioner*, 31 B.T.A. 427, 430-431(1934); *Lamar v. Granger*, 99 F.Supp. 17, 36-37 (W.D. Pa. 1951).

9. *Marco v. Commissioner*, 25 T.C. 544 (1955); see *Watson v. United States*, 222 F.2d 689, 690 (10th Cir. 1955); *Reid v. Commissioner*, 26 T.C. 622, 632 (1956); cf. *Kimble Glass Co. v. Commissioner*, 9 T.C. 183 (1947).

the circumstances surrounding the enactment of section 1235 and found that one of its purposes was to allow capital gain treatment even though the owner of the patent was compensated by royalties which were contingent or periodic. The court went on to say:

> Section 1235(a) went further, however, to provide, as we have seen, that the transfer of patent rights shall be considered a sale or exchange of a capital asset only if "all substantial rights to a patent, or an undivided interest therein which includes a part of all such rights" are included in the transfer. In Rodgers v. Commissioner, 1969, 51 T.C. 927, the Tax Court took the view that this language of § 1235 was not intended to exclude from capital gains treatment a transfer of patent rights limited geographically, and it followed and applied that decision in the present case. We cannot agree with this conclusion.
>
> * * * we think that the statutory requirement that the "substantial rights" transferred shall be "all" of them, even in the case of the transfer of an undivided interest in them, indicates a Congressional intention that the transfer of a part of the patent rights, divided off from the rest by a limitation on their use or the geographical area of their exercise, shall not be deemed a sale or exchange of a capital asset. * * * [507 F.2d at 620–621.]

In *Fawick v. Commissioner*, 52 T.C. 104 (1969), we were faced with the question of whether a transfer of the exclusive rights to a patent limited to a field of use qualified for capital gain treatment under section 1235. We embraced the *Rodgers'* statement that patent rights can be subdivided before applying the all-substantial-rights test and held that an exclusive transfer of patent rights within a field of use qualified for capital gain treatment under section 1235 irrespective of the value of the retained rights. Cf. *Redler Conveyor Co. v. Commissioner*, 303 F.2d 567, 569 (1st Cir. 1962), affg. a Memorandum Opinion of this Court.

Our decision in *Fawick* was appealed to the Sixth Circuit, and after an extensive review of the authorities and legislative history of section 1235, that court also reversed our holding (436 F.2d 655 (1971)). After reviewing the event leading to the enactment of section 1235, the court said with respect to the reasons for the enactment of the section:

> From this review of the germination of § 1235, we conclude that the section was intended to assure inventors that their license royalties would be afforded capital gain treatment "regardless of whether or not payments in consideration of such transfer are—
>
> '(1) payable periodically over a period generally coterminous with the transferee's use of the patent, or
>
> (2) contingent on the productivity, use, or disposition of the property transferred.'
>
> * * * The 'incentive to inventors to contribute to the welfare of the Nation' resulted when capital gain treatment was provided under § 1235 for 'professional' as well as 'amateur' inventors otherwise qualifying under the statute. Thus, the two-fold purpose of the section * * * does not point to the interpretation * * * that the section was designed to permit capital gain treatment of income from transfers having a field-of-use restriction." [436 F.2d at 661.]

After reviewing the legislative history, the court suggested:

it is our opinion that a two prong inquiry is necessary to determine if a transaction qualifies for special treatment under § 1235. The initial inquiry for determining whether or not there has been a transfer by the holder of "property consisting of all substantial rights to a patent" requires consideration of what the holder has left after the transfer. If he retains any substantial rights to the patent, then he has not transferred the property that comprises all those rights.

If the taxpayer can show that he has no substantial rights in the patent after the transfer, as a second inquiry we must look at what he actually relinquished to the transferee. * * * [436 F.2d at 662.]

In conclusion, the court stated:

we conclude that *Waterman v. Mackenzie*, * * * relied upon by several of the courts in analyzing the issue is not authority for determination of the present issue one way or the other. That case was concerned with whether or not a transfer was of a character that would give the transferee the right to sue and did not involve the tax consequences of the transfer. Section 1235 does not speak in terms of assignments or licenses, but rather, it is concerned with the transfer of all substantial rights to a patent, and whether that transfer falls within the *Waterman* definition of an assignment or not is of no consequence to the operation of the statute. [434 F.2d at 665.]

The issue arose again in connection with a field-of-use limitation in the case of *Mros v. Commissioner*, T.C. Memo. 1971-123. We again followed the rationale of *Rodgers* and held that the transfer qualified for capital gain treatment under section 1235, but our decision was reversed by the Ninth Circuit (493 F.2d 813 (1974)). That Circuit Court approved of the tests suggested by the Sixth Circuit in *Fawick*, and since it found that the transferor retained valuable rights to the patent after the transfer, it held that the transfer limited to a field of use did not qualify for capital gain treatment under section 1235.

Our own review of section 1235 and the circumstances surrounding its enactment also leads us to the conclusion that we should no longer follow the interpretation suggested by *Rodgers*. As the Courts of Appeals have pointed out, it appears that section 1235 was enacted to extend capital gain treatment to professional inventors and to allow all inventors capital gain treatment upon the "sale" of a patent, even though payment for the patent was to be made by royalties, payable periodically or contingent on the use of the patent. See S. Rept. 1622, 83d Cong., 2d Sess. 438-439 (1954). We can surely assume that the framers of section 1235 were familiar with the *Waterman* decision. Yet, they did not make the availability of capital gain treatment turn on whether there was a "sale" within the meaning of *Waterman*; instead, they elected to make capital gain treatment available in two situations: a transfer of all substantial rights in a patent, or a transfer of an undivided interest therein. The legislative history relating to the all-substantial-rights test clearly shows, as the Courts of Appeals have pointed out, that Congress did not intend for that test to be applied after first slicing up a patent into fields of use or into geographical areas; instead, it was to be applied by examining whether a transfer disposed of all substantial rights of the patent owner:

The section does not detail precisely what constitutes the formal components of a sale or exchange of patent rights beyond requiring that all substantial rights evidence by the patent (other than the right to such periodic or contingent payments) should be transferred to the transferee for consideration. * * * *It is the intention of your committee to continue this realistic test, whereby the entire transaction, regardless of formalities, should be examined in its factual context to deter-*

mine whether or not substantially all rights of the owner in the patent property have been released to the transferee, rather than recognizing less relevant verbal touchstones. * * * [S. Rept. 1622, *supra* at 439–440; emphasis supplied.]

Also, the adoption of the *Rodgers* interpretation would lead to results which are capricious or clearly inconsistent with the legislative history. If the patent can be sliced into smaller segments, and the all-substantial-rights test satisfied merely by transferring all substantial rights with respect to that segment, capital gain treatment would be allowed, even though the patent holder retains very substantial rights to the patent. On the other hand, if the patent rights are not sliced in any manner, the patent holder could obtain capital gain only by transferring all substantial rights with respect to the whole patent. Moreover, although section 1235 allows capital gain treatment for the transfer of an undivided interest in all substantial rights to the patent, the adoption of the *Rodgers* interpretation would allow capital gain treatment when there is a transfer of an undivided interest in a field of use or an exclusive geographical area, but the legislative history explicitly indicates that no such restrictive transfer was intended to qualify under that test:

> By "undivided interest" a part of each property right represented by the patent (constituting a fractional share of the whole patent) is meant (and not, for example, a lesser interest such as a right to income, or a license limited geographically, or a license which conveys some, but not all, of the claims or uses covered by the patent). * * * (S. Rept. 1522, *supra* at 439.)

See also H. Rept. 1337, 83d Cong., 2d Sess. A279 (1954).

In addition, in asserting that section 1235 made no change in the test of qualification, the Court in *Rodgers* overlooked the fact that the tests for qualification were in fact changed. The *Waterman* test of a "sale," by which exclusive geographical transfers had been approved, was not carried forward into section 1235. Under the all-substantial-rights test which was adopted by section 1235, an exclusive geographical transfer could not automatically qualify. Whether such a transfer could qualify under the all-substantial-rights test required a detailed factual examination and evaluation of the nature and quantity of the patent rights transferred and retained.[10] Although the Court in *Rodgers* purported to apply the all-substantial-rights test, it made no such factual inquiry, and cited as legal authority for its conclusion *Marco v. Commissioner*, 25 T.C. 544 (1955), a case decided under the *Waterman* sale test. We are now convinced that an exclusive geographical patent transfer does not automatically dispose of all substantial rights in a patent, and we conclude that section 1235 cannot properly be applied without a factual inquiry into the value of the rights transferred and retained. Accordingly, we will no longer follow *Rodgers* and *Estate of Klein* to the extent that they hold to the contrary.

Having so concluded, we now turn to the facts of this case to determine whether there was a transfer of all substantial rights, bearing in mind that the petitioners have the burden of establishing that their disposition satisfied such test. Rule 142(a), Tax Court Rules of Practice and Procedure. The parties have stipulated that the petitioners retained the rights to make, sell, and use the patented rock-crushing machines in the

---

10. In making such statement, we are not passing upon how the rule is to be applied when there is a series of transfers. For example, in *Blake v. Commissioner*, 67 T.C. 7 (1976), we recently held that the all-substantial-rights test can be satisfied by a final transfer in a sequence of field-of-use transfers; and nothing said herein is meant to question that application of the general rule.

western portion of the United States. Nothing of record would allow us to conclude that such rights were not substantial; the petitioners have not so contended, nor have they offered any evidence to support such a contention. Thus, we must conclude that they have failed to establish that the exclusive geographical transfer to Crusher disposed of "all substantial rights" to their patents.[12]

In light of our conclusion that the petitioners have failed to prove their transfers met the statutory test and the general definition of all substantial rights contained in the Treasury regulations, it is unnecessary for us to pass on the validity of section 1.1235-2(b)(1)(i), Income Tax Regs., which may be read to provide that an exclusive geographical patent transfer can never dispose of all substantial rights.

E.I. du Pont de Nemours & Co. v. United States
United States Court of Appeals, Third Circuit
432 F.2d 1052 (3d Cir. 1970)

FULLAM, JUDGE:

The taxpayer was the owner of eight Brazilian patents relating to the manufacture of nylon fibers. All were process patents, but four also covered apparatus used in the manufacture of the fibers and four included claims having applicability to dacron as well.

In January 1954, the taxpayer entered into two related agreements with a French chemical corporation, Societa Rhodiaceta (hereinafter Rhodiaceta) and its Brazilian affiliate, Companhia Brasileira Rhodiaceta (hereinafter CBR), the effect of which was to transfer rights in all of these eight Brazilian patents to CBR, for a consideration of $5,500,000, so that CBR could engage in the manufacture of nylon in Brazil. Of the agreed payment, $4,094,000 was paid during 1954, and in its tax return for that year, the taxpayer included this amount as ordinary income. Thereafter, a timely claim for refund was filed, on the theory that this payment should have been treated as a capital gain. When the refund was refused, the taxpayer brought suit in the court below and recovered judgment in its favor.

It is undisputed that the taxpayer had held that patent rights in question for more than six months prior to the transfer, and had not held them for sale to customers. Accordingly, the only question is whether the transfer constituted a sale of such rights within the meaning of sections 1222 and 1231 of the Code. Neither the Code itself, nor treasury regulations define what constitutes a sale for capital gains purposes.[2]

Patent rights are intangible property rights, the transfer of which may qualify as a sale for capital gain purposes. The precise form and terminology of the transfer are not

---

12. Since the petitioners have not argued for capital gain treatment under any provision other than sec. 1235, we do not reach the issue of whether patent holders, such as the petitioners, may seek capital gain treatment outside sec. 1235 when the consideration received for their patent transfer is royalty payments described in sec. 1235(a). Cf. S. Rept. 1622, *supra* at 441; sec. 1.1235-1(b), Income Tax Regs.

2. Section 1235 of the Code provides for capital gain treatment of certain patent transfers, whether or not they would otherwise qualify under the general capital gain provisions of sections 1201–1231. However, this section does not apply to transfers by corporations. Section 1235 does not, of course, deny capital gain treatment to patent transfers by corporations, if such transfers qualify as sales under the general capital gain provisions. Treasury Regulations 1.1235-1(b) Robert L. Holcomb, 30 T.C. 354, ACQ. 1958-2 CB 6; Revenue Ruling 69-482, IRB 1969-36, page 16.

controlling, so long as it transfers exclusive rights for the full life of the patent. Lockhart v. Commissioner of Internal Revenue, 258 F.2d 343 (3rd Cir. 1958); Merck & Co., Inc. v. Smith, 261 F.2d 162 (3rd Cir. 1958); General Aniline & Film Corp. v. Commissioner of Internal Revenue, 139 F.2d 759 (2d Cir. 1944). As stated by this Court in Merck & Co., Inc. v. Smith, *supra*, at page 164 of 261 F.2d:

> "* * * a transfer of all of the substantial rights in a patent is deemed an assignment and qualifies the transferor for capital gains treatment. A transfer of anything less is called a license with a resultant assessment of the tax at ordinary income rates."

To determine whether the taxpayer did transfer all of the substantial rights in the patents in question, the key question is whether the transferor retained any rights which, in the aggregate, have substantial value. See Allied Chemical Corp. v. United States, 370 F.2d 697 (2d Cir. 1967); Merck & Co., Inc. v. Smith, *supra*; Schmitt v. Commissioner of Internal Revenue, 271 F.2d 301 (9th Cir. 1959).

In the present case, the government contends that the taxpayer retained the following valuable rights in connection with the transfer:

1. The right to import into Brazil nylon lawfully manufactured elsewhere;

2. The right to control any subsequent licensing or assignment of the rights granted Rhodiaceta and CBR with respect to the use of the patented process and apparatus in making nylon;

3. The right to make any use it saw fit (including manufacturing under its own auspices, licensing, sale, etc.) of the patent rights in connection with dacron; and

4. The right to manufacture for sale the apparatus covered by the patent or to license others to manufacture the apparatus for use, in connection with the manufacture of fibers other than nylon (especially dacron).

The District Court carefully analyzed all of the rights retained by the taxpayer, and specifically found that they were of no substantial value. On appeal, the government contends that each of these findings was erroneous, and that, in any event, the District Court erred in treating each right individually and in failing to make a finding that, in the aggregate, the retained rights had substantial value.

In our view, this latter argument represents a too narrow reading of the District Court opinion. After analyzing each of the rights individually, and finding it valueless, the District Court concluded that the taxpayer had not retained substantial rights in the patents, and that the transfer qualified for capital gains treatment. Indeed, at the conclusion of his discussion of the various retained rights, Chief Judge Wright expressly stated:

> "No substantial rights in the eight patents transferred having been retained, the 1954 transactions constituted a sale of those patents, the proceeds of which are entitled to capital gains treatment." (296 F.Supp. 833).

Accordingly, the only issue before this Court is whether the District Court findings are clearly erroneous. We have concluded that the record adequately supports the findings of the District Court.

1. *Right to import.* There was ample evidence in the record to justify the conclusion that the reservation by the taxpayer of the right to import nylon into Brazil, and to license others to do so, preserved nothing of value to the taxpayer. The parties contemplated that the government of Brazil would adhere to its policy of excluding such im-

ports, once a Brazilian company entered the market. Subsequent events have borne out the accuracy of this assumption.

In this connection, we note, but need not pass upon, taxpayer's further argument that this reservation was included in the agreement because it was believed to be required by the provisions of an antitrust decree; hence, the argument goes, the taxpayer lacked the legal capacity to transfer a right to preclude imports, so that this right should be deemed non-existent rather than retained.

Moreover, it is by no means clear that the (theoretical) right to import into Brazil nylon lawfully manufactured in the United States (presumably, under taxpayer's American patents) derogates from the completeness of the transfer of the Brazilian patents. Rather, such rights would seem to be more directly related to the independent American patent rights.

2. Right to sell and sublicense equipment. As noted above, four of the eight patents transferred covered apparatus as well as process. The two 1954 agreements (Article V of the Rhodiaceta agreement and Article III of the CBR agreement) can be read to mean that, while both grantees received the right to make and use, in their own plants, the apparatus and equipment covered by the patents, neither grantee had the right to sell such equipment. The agreements can also be read to mean that while CBR had the right to sublicense others to make, use and sell nylon, it did not have the right to sublicense others to make and use the required equipment. The District Court found that the only limitation, insofar as Rhodiaceta is concerned, was the inability to sell equipment; and that, "* * * the manufacture of equipment for sale to other fiber producers is a function separate and distinct from manufacture of equipment for use in one's own fiber production. Accordingly, the apparatus patents in issue here are divisible along that line." (832).

Insofar as CBR is concerned, the District Court found that, under the foregoing interpretation of the agreements, the taxpayer in effect reserved to itself a veto power over CBR's ability to sublicense production use and sale of nylon. The District Court concluded that this veto power was of no substantial value.

The taxpayer suggested at oral argument in the court below, and reiterates on appeal, that the 1954 agreements are ambiguous on these matters, and that the parties did not intend to impose the above restrictions. No evidence was presented on this point, and the District Court found it unnecessary to choose the correct interpretation of the agreements. We likewise find it unnecessary to consider the taxpayer's alternative argument.

In our view, the District Court was correct in concluding that, assuming the taxpayer retained a veto power over sublicensing, that fact would not mean that the taxpayer failed to transfer substantially all rights in the patents. In Rollman v. Commissioner of Internal Revenue, 244 F.2d 634 (4th Cir. 1957), the transfer documents expressly provided that the grantee could not grant sublicenses under the patents except with the written consent of the transferor. The court held:

> "Such a limitation does not interfere with the full use of the patent by the assignee * * * Moreover, the assignor retains no use of the patent for himself by reason of the limitation since he has granted the exclusive rights to the assignee and cannot grant a sublicense without the purchaser's consent." (At page 640)

The Court of Claims has adopted the same reasoning. Bell Intercontinental Corp. v. United States, 381 F.2d 1004, 1017, 180 Ct.Cl. 1071 (1967).

3. The dacron rights. Four of the eight patents in question are at least theoretically applicable to dacron as well as nylon, but only the nylon rights were transferred. The

District Court found that the retained dacron rights were not of substantial value, and that, in any event, they were severable. The government here challenges both of these findings.

It is apparent that the District Court was persuaded by the testimony presented on behalf of the taxpayer, to the effect that the patents were of extremely minor importance in the manufacture of dacron; that dacron could be manufactured without resort to the processes and equipment covered by these patents; and that use of these patents for dacron in Brazil was foreclosed by the basic Whitfield and Dixon patent, owned by Imperial Chemical Industries, Ltd. In view of this evidence, we certainly cannot say that the District Court's finding of no substantial value was clearly erroneous.

Moreover, we agree with the District Court's conclusion that, for capital gains purposes, the nylon rights, considered independently, were proper subjects for a sale. For such purposes, patent rights are divisible between different industries and different industrial products. Merck & Co., Inc. v. Smith, *supra*; United States v. Carruthers, 219 F.2d 21 (9th Cir. 1955); First National Bank of Princeton v. United States, 136 F.Supp. 818 (D.N.J.1955); Estate of M. J. Laurent, Sr., 34 T.C. 385 (1960) and William S. Rouverol, 42 T.C. 186 (1964). *See also* Thomas L. Fawick, 52 T.C. 104 (1969). These cases are not in conflict with Pope Manufacturing Co. v. Gormully & Jeffery Manufacturing Co. (No. 3) 144 U.S. 248 (1892); E. W. Bliss Co. v. United States, 253 U.S. 187 (1920); Waterman v. Mackenzie, 138 U.S. 252 (1891), or the other cases relied upon by the government, all of which dealt with the presently non-controlling procedural issue of whether the transferee could bring suit in its own name.

For the foregoing reasons, we have concluded that the District Court was correct in deciding that the reservation of dacron rights (including equipment rights, government's contention No. 4 above) did not amount to a reservation of anything having substantial value, derogating from the completeness of the transfer of the nylon rights.

4. *Know-how allocation.* The government's final contention on the patent issue is that some portion of the $5,500,000 purchase price should have been allocated as consideration for the transfer of technical information, which the taxpayer was required to furnish pursuant to the agreements, and which was in fact furnished by permitting representatives of the purchasers to visit the taxpayer's Martinsville, Virginia, plant in 1954. The government argues that the value of this technical information is established in the record at $250,000; alternatively, the government argues that the case should be remanded to the District Court for specific findings as to the proper allocation.

The District Court found that the Martinsville visit was insignificant, and that substantially all of the technical information had already been furnished pursuant to previous arrangements in 1952. There is support in the record for such findings. Moreover, we are satisfied that whatever transfer of technical information occurred in 1954 was incidental to the sale of the patent rights. The suggestion that Rhodiaceta may have obtained some information which would be helpful in its European operations, independently of the Brazilian patents, we regard as too ephemeral for present significance. The government's contention really amounts to an assertion that the taxpayer should have charged Rhodiaceta an additional sum for this information, rather than a contention that the taxpayer actually did receive such income.

The government has apparently abandoned the argument, made in the court below, that a $250,000 "security deposit" received by the taxpayer in connection with the aborted 1952 agreement, and credited in 1954 on account of the 1954 agreements, constituted ordinary income in 1954. In any event, we see no occasion to disturb the lower court's disposition of this contention.

For the foregoing reasons, the Judgment of the District Court, insofar as it concerns the Brazilian patents issue, will be affirmed.

Revenue Ruling 78-328
1978-2 C.B. 215

Advice has been requested whether the sale of all rights to a patent by a corporation that is not a dealer in patents is the sale of property used in its trade or business within the meaning of section 1231 of the Internal Revenue Code of 1954 when the rights transferred are all the then existing rights to the patent except for a non-exclusive, royalty-free license acquired by an unrelated party from the corporation's predecessor transferor.

In 1974 X corporation developed a device and secured a patent on it. In 1975 X assigned to Y corporation a royalty-free, nonexclusive license for the sale or use of the device and sold its remaining rights in the patent to Z corporation. Z used the patent in its manufacturing business. Z depreciated the cost of the patent over its remaining useful life under the provisions of section 1.167(a)-6 of the Income Tax Regulations.

In 1976, more than 6 months after acquiring the patent rights, Z sold all the rights it ever held in the patent (although not all the existing rights) and realized a gain on the sale. Z realized no losses from the sale of other property during 1976. The consideration for this transfer was a lump-sum of 100,000x dollars and certain additional amounts to be paid in the future based on a percentage of gross sales from marketing the device.

The question presented is whether the gain from the transaction is income to Z attributable to the sale of property used in the trade or business within the meaning of section 1231 of the Code.

Although section 1235 of the Code is inapplicable to this case because that section only applies to transfers of patents by individuals, Rev. Rul. 69-482, 1969-2 C.B. 164, states that when holders make transfers of patents that do not meet the requirements for capital gains treatment under section 1235, the tax consequences of such transfers will be determined under other sections of the Code.

Section 1231(a) of the Code provides, in part, that if, during the taxable year, the recognized gains on sales of property used in the trade or business held for more than 6 month (9 months for taxable years beginning in 1977; 1 year for taxable years beginning after 1977), exceed the recognized losses from such sales, such gains and losses shall be considered as gains and losses from sales of capital assets held for more than 6 months (9 months for taxable years beginning in 1977; 1 year for taxable years beginning after 1977).

Section 1231(b) of the Code provides, in part, that the term "property used in the trade or business" means property used in the trade or business of a character that is subject to the allowance for depreciation provided in section 167, and that is held for more than 6 months (9 months for taxable years beginning in 1977; 1 year for taxable years beginning after 1977).

Section 167(a)(1) of the Code provides that there shall be allowed as a depreciation deduction a reasonable allowance for the exhaustion, wear, and tear of property used in the trade or business.

Section 1.167(a)-6 of the regulations provides that the cost or other basis of a patent shall be depreciated over its remaining useful life.

In *MacDonald v. Commissioner*, 55 T.C. 840 (1971), acq., 1973-1 C.B. 2, a case in which section 1235 of the Code did not apply, the United States Tax Court concluded that the sale of all the rights a taxpayer ever held in a patent, but which rights did not include all existing rights in the patent because the patent was already subject to a nonexclusive license, may qualify for capital gains treatment under section 1231.

In *MacDonald*, the court questioned the validity of section 1.1235-2(b) of the regulations. The issue in *MacDonald* was whether the sale of less than all the then existing, substantial rights to a patent was nevertheless the sale of a capital asset within the meaning of sections 1221 or 1231 (as the case may be) of the Code when the taxpayer transferred all the rights the taxpayer had. The Service's acquiescence in *MacDonald* merely indicates that the Service agrees with the court that the sale of the patent in question qualifies for capital gain treatment. No inference should be drawn from the Service's acquiescence in *MacDonald* that the regulations under section 1235 are not controlling for purposes of section 1235. In addition, the Tax Court indicated in *Kueneman v. Commissioner*, 68 T.C. 609 (1977), taxpayer on appeal to 9th Cir., that it will no longer follow the case of *Rodgers v. Commissioner*, 51 T.C. 619 (1977), and *Fawick v. Commissioner*, 52 T.C. 104 (1969), rev'd 436 F.2d 655 (6th Cir. 1971), which were cited in *MacDonald* as the authority for the invalidity of the section 1235 regulations.

In the present case, Z acquired the patent already subject to a license and transferred no interest in the patent prior to its sale. Therefore, Z transferred all the rights it had ever held in the patent.

Consequently, because Z transferred all the rights it had ever held in the patent and because these rights are depreciable property used in Z's business, the sale of the patent rights is considered the sale of property used in the trade or business within the meaning of section 1231(a) of the Code.

Accordingly, except to the extent provided in section 1245 of the Code, the income from the sale of all the rights the taxpayer had in the patent will be treated as long term capital gain.

Newton Insert Co. v. Commissioner
61 T.C. 570 (1974)

SCOTT, JUDGE:

Newton [Insert Co.] entered into an agreement in 1961 with City of Hope, a California nonprofit corporation, whereby City of Hope granted Newton in return for a percentage of sales the exclusive rights to make, use, and sell patented products for the entire life of the patents. Newton entered into an exclusive license agreement in 1966 with Rubert Neuschotz, covering other patents in return for a percentage of annual sales of the products. Petitioner purchased the entire outstanding stock of Newton in 1967, and, upon the liquidation of Newton into it under sec. 332(b), I.R.C. 1954, allocated a portion of the adjusted basis of Newton stock to the 1961 and 1966 agreements pursuant to sec. 334(b)(2).

The sole issue for decision is whether percentage payments made by Newton under [the] 1961 and 1966 licensing agreements represent depreciation of patents acquired thereunder which amounts are subject to recapture under section 1245.

Section 1245 provides that if personal property of a taxpayer of a character subject to depreciation or amortization is disposed of during a taxable year, the excess of (1) the recomputed basis of the property, or (2) in case of a sale, exchange, or involuntary conversion, the amount realized, or (3) in the case of any other disposition, the fair market value of the property over the adjusted basis of the property shall be treated as gain from the sale or exchange of property which is neither a capital asset nor property described in section 1231.

Section 1.1245-3(b), Income Tax Regs., includes within the definition of personal property, intangible personal property. Petitioner does not contest the validity of this regulation but accepts the fact that if Newton owned the patents covered by the 1961 and 1966 agreements so that those patents were intangible personal property subject to depreciation in Newton's hands, they are personal property within the provisions of section 1245.

Petitioner concedes that the 1966 license agreement constituted a sale of the patents covered thereby to Newton and therefore those patents were depreciable assets in Newton's hands, but takes issue with respondent's determination of the amount of this depreciation which is recapturable.

Petitioner contends, however, that the 1961 license agreement was a license and did not amount to a sale of patent rights and therefore Newton acquired no depreciable intangible property under the 1961 agreement but that the payments by Newton to Neuschotz under this agreement were merely for the use of a capital asset and are deductible business expenses. Sec. 162(a)(3).

The 1961 license agreement granted Newton the "exclusive right to make, use and sell the products and to utilize the processes disclosed in the Patents for the full term of the last maturing patent." These terms are identical in impact to the language stated in *Waterman v. MacKenzie*, 138 U.S. 252 (1891), to be necessary to effect a sale of a patent. There, the Supreme Court found that a patent was composed of the "exclusive right to make, use and vend an invention," and "the granting of an exclusive right under the patent * * * which does not include the right to make, and the right to use, and the right to sell, is not the grant of a title in the whole patent * * * and is therefore only a license." However, a transfer of the rights to make, use, and vend amounts to a transfer of all substantial rights to a patent, and has consistently been deemed to be a sale.

The 1961 license agreement unequivocally granted to Newton the three substantial rights necessary to a sale of a patent. City of Hope did not reserve any right which might preclude our finding a sale of the patents.

Examples of substantial rights retained by a transferor include the right to terminate the agreement with or without cause, *Bell Intercontinental Corporation v. United States*, 381 F.2d 1004, 1020-1021 (Ct. Cl. 1967); rights to grant a nonexclusive license to another firm and to compel the transferee to sublicense another, *Allied Chemical Corporation v. United States*, 370 F.2d 697 (C.A. 2, 1967); and the right to prohibit assignment of the agreement without the transferor's written consent. *Oak Manufacturing Co. v. United States*, 301 F.2d 259, 262 (C.A. 7, 1962).

The provisions of the 1961 license agreement clearly did not reserve any such right to City of Hope. The obligation which the agreement imposed on Newton to use its best efforts to promote the sale of products manufactured under the patents and the requirement that Newton utilize appropriate accounting methods and allow City of Hope access to Newton's books of account, were simply provisions included to protect City of Hope's right to compensation under the agreement. Such provisions provide security for the transferor, but do not cause there to be no transfer of ownership.

Petitioner makes some argument that even though there was no retention of a substantial right in the patents by City of Hope, since there was no affirmative statement in the agreement that City of Hope granted Newton the right to sublicense others to utilize the patents, this right was not granted to Newton by the agreement. In our view an unlimited transfer of the exclusive rights to use, manufacture, and sell for the life of the patent would automatically include the right to authorize others to use, manufacture, and sell. Furthermore, even if the agreement could be interpreted as not granting to Newton the right to sublicense, the failure to grant Newton the right to sublicense does not result in the reservation of a substantial right to City of Hope, since City of Hope was foreclosed from granting other licenses by the exclusiveness of Newton's license.

Petitioner further contends that the 1961 license agreement was not a sale because some of the patents later covered by the agreement were not in existence in 1961. However, we have held that it is not significant in determining whether an agreement constitutes a sale of a patent that a patent has not been issued or even applied for at the time that all substantial rights are transferred. *Estate of Milton P. Laurent, Sr.*, 34 T.C. 385 (1960).

Having reviewed the transaction both from the standpoint of what was transferred, as well as what was retained, we find that the broad and unlimited language contained in the 1961 license agreement shows that the parties thereto intended a sale of the patents.

Petitioner contends that if we find from the terms of the agreement that there was a sale, Newton was nevertheless entitled to treat the transaction as a mere license because the amounts paid under the license agreements were contingent and not fixed. This argument of petitioner is without merit. The Court has stated that a taxpayer which was paying a percentage of sales for use of a patent was entitled to deduct the percentage payments either because the sums were ordinary and necessary expenses paid for the use of the invention or because they represented depreciation allowable on the purchased invention. This statement was merely a recognition that it was unnecessary to determine in the particular case whether the amounts are deductible as royalties or as depreciation since the licensee was entitled to a deduction for the amount as a business expense if the agreement between the parties was a mere license or to a deduction of the same amount as depreciation of a capital asset if the agreement was the sale of the invention. This statement in no way indicates that where there has been a sale of the patents, the purchaser has the choice of characterizing the deduction of the percentage payments made as royalties deductible under section 162 or as depreciation deductible under section 167. We have held to the contrary. In *Associated Patentees, Inc.*, 4 T.C. 979 (1945), we held that since a transfer of patents in return for 80 percent of the income generated by their use was found to be a purchase of capital assets with a determinable useful life, the purchaser was entitled to deduct the percentage payments, but only as depreciation of the cost of the patents.

Petitioner's final argument is that the provisions of section 1235 preclude the possibility that the 1961 license agreement could effect a sale of the underlying inventions.

Section 1235, enacted in 1954, deals with the tax treatment of payments received by a "holder" as consideration for this transfer of all substantial rights to a patent, where the payments are contingent upon the productivity of the patent or payable periodically over the period the patent is used by the transferee. Prior to the enactment of section 1235, the Government had contended, generally unsuccessfully, in certain cases that transactions transferring patents for contingent rather than fixed amounts were licenses and not sales, and that transferors of patents on such terms were not entitled to treat the payments which they received as capital gains.

Section 1235 was enacted to clarify the tax treatment of percentage payments to inventors and their financial backers, and to allow persons whose efforts led to the development of valuable inventions capital gains treatment on the sale or assignment of the underlying patents, regardless of the mode of payment involved and whether the inventor was in the business of inventing. The substance of the provisions is that a transfer shall be deemed a sale or exchange of a capital asset held for more than 6 months — and, consequently, result in long-term capital gain — where enumerated conditions are met.

In S. Rept. No. 1622, to accompany H.R. 8300 (Pub. L. No. 591), 83d Cong., 2d Sess., p. 441, the statement is made that:

> It is the intention of your committee that, *if the mode of payment* is as described in subsection (a) (of Sec. 1235) * * * the sale of a patent by any "*holder*" must qualify under the section in order for such "*holder*" to obtain capital gain treatment. [Emphasis supplied.]

In *Myron C. Poole*, 46 T.C. 392 (1966), cited by petitioner, the issue was whether Poole, an inventor, was entitled to capital gains treatment. Poole was a "holder" under section 1235, and he transferred his rights to a patent to an intermediary corporation, which then granted an exclusive license to a corporation controlled by him. Both transfers were for consideration contingent upon production of the inventions under the patent. We found that Poole had made an indirect transfer of all substantial rights to the patent to his controlled corporation, a "related" entity within the meaning of section 1235(d). Accordingly, we held that Poole was not entitled to treat the payments he received as capital gains under section 1235, and the payments which he received from the transfer were taxable to him as ordinary income. Having found that section 1235(a) did not apply to cause the payments Poole received to be capital gains, we held against Poole on his alternative contention that he was entitled to capital gains treatment under other sections of the Code. We explained our conclusion as follows (at pp. 404–405):

> The legislative history with respect to section 1235 explains that a holder's recourse to prior case law is proper only when the transaction is not one described in section 1235(a). In other words, if the payments for a patent are contingent upon productivity, use, or disposition, or if they are payable periodically over a period generally coterminous with the transferee's use of the patent, section 1235 is the holder's exclusive provision for qualifying for capital gains treatment. Moreover, this interpretation of the effect of section 1235 is supported by an analysis of the effect of the provisions of the section. If a holder transfers a patent resulting in the payment of royalties in the manner described in section 1235(a) to a related person, and if we were to hold that such a transfer is entitled to capital gains treatment under another provision of law, we would be nullifying section 1235(d). Since section 1235(d) was included in the law, it must have been done for a purpose — the purpose of denying capital gains treatment to a holder's transfer to related persons when the payments are of the type described in section 1235(a). [Fn. omitted.]

Petitioner contends that the excerpt from the *Poole* case defining the scope of section 1235 should be applied to this case in such a manner as to support the conclusion that Newton had not purchased the patents and was not the owner of the patents. There are factual similarities between the *Poole* case and the instant case. However, it does not follow, as petitioner contends, that the failure of Neuschotz to qualify for capital gains treatment under section 1235 results not only in denying Neuschotz capital gains treatment but also rules out the possibility of the transfer being a sale. If we assume that there was an "indirect transfer" from Neuschotz to Newton so that Neuschotz would be denied capital gains treatment on the payments he received from Newton, it does not follow that the transfer from Neuschotz to Newton was a license and not a sale.

Section 1235 governs when a holder, as defined therein, is entitled to capital gains treatment, but it does not purport to govern with respect to any other party or situation when the transfer of patents for consideration contingent upon productivity amounts to a sale.

The wording of the statute and the legislative history of section 1235 indicate that Congress did not intend to define what constituted a sale of patents, but rather that the purpose behind the enactment of section 1235 was to clarify, and in several cases to extend capital gains treatment to "holders." Section 1235 allows capital gains to professional as well as amateur inventors. It does away with the 6-month holding period required ordinarily for long-term capital gains and it deemphasizes the mode of payment in deciding the effect of a transaction. There is not, however, any indication that Congress was attempting to change existing principles of law which have long determined what is a sale of patents.

The report of the Senate Finance Committee, S. Rept. No. 1622, *supra*, states that the purpose of the legislation was to "give statutory assurance to certain patent holders that the sale of a patent (whether as an 'assignment' or 'exclusive license') shall not be deemed *not* to constitute a 'sale or exchange' for tax purposes solely on account of the mode of payment." This language indicates that Congress was concerned with the position which had been taken by the Government that certain transfers were not sales or exchanges of a patent because of payment being contingent on production. The Senate committee report in no way supports petitioner's position that the transfer of a patent will be characterized as a mere license *solely* on account of the fact that payments made in consideration of such transfer resemble generally payments of royalties or that failure of the holder who transfers the patent to qualify under section 1235 for capital gain treatment of the payments he receives will result in the transfer not being a sale to the assignee of the rights.

The following language, from S. Rept. No. 1622, *supra* at pp. 439–440, indicates that Congress intended that previously developed criteria be used in determining what constitutes a sale:

> The section (1235) does not detail precisely what constitutes the formal components of a sale or exchange of patent rights beyond requiring that all substantial rights evidenced by the patent (other than the right to such periodic or contingent payments) should be transferred to the transferee for consideration. This requirement recognizes the basic criteria of a "sale or exchange" under existing law, with the exception noted relating to contingent payments, which exception is justified in the patent area for "holders" as herein defined. To illustrate, exclusive licenses to manufacture, use, and sell for the life of the patent, are considered to be "sales or exchanges" because, in substan-

tive effect, all "right, title, and interest" in the patent property is transferred (irrespective of the location of legal title or other formalities of language contained in the license agreement). Moreover, the courts have recognized that an exclusive license agreement in some instances may constitute a sale for tax purposes even where the right to "use" the invention has not been conveyed to the licensee, if it is shown that such failure did not represent the retention of a substantial right under the patent by the licensor. It is the intention of your committee to continue this realistic test, whereby the entire transaction, regardless of formalities, should be examined in its factual context to determine whether or not substantially all rights of the owner in the patent property have been released to the transferee, rather than recognizing less relevant verbal touchstones. The word "title" is not employed because the retention of bare legal title in a transaction involving an exclusive license may not represent the retention of a substantial right in the patent property by the transferor. Furthermore, retention by the transferor of rights in the property which are not of the nature of rights evidenced by the patent and which are not inconsistent with the passage of ownership, such as a security interest (e.g., a vendor's lien) or a reservation in the nature of a condition subsequent (e.g., a forfeiture on account of non-performance) are not to be considered as such a retention as will defeat the applicability of this section. On the other hand, a transfer terminable at will by the transferor would not qualify.

In our view there is nothing in the statute, the regulations, or the legislative history of section 1235 which indicates that a transfer described in section 1235(a) cannot be a sale simply by reason of its being made to a related person. We hold that the 1961 agreement constituted a sale to Newton of the patents covered by that agreement.

Having concluded that the 1961 license agreement, as well as the 1966 agreement, constituted a sale of the patents enumerated therein to Newton, amounts paid by Newton annually represent payments of the purchase price of intangible assets. Therefore, Newton was not entitled to deduct the payments made as business expenses but was entitled to deductions for depreciation allowable under section 167. Section 167 provides that "There shall be allowed as a depreciation deduction a reasonable allowance for the exhaustion, wear and tear * * * (1) of property used in the trade or business." In *Associated Patentees, Inc., supra*, we held that where payment is made for purchase of a patent on a yearly percentage of production basis, a depreciation deduction of the total annual payment is allowable so that the purchaser will be able to recover the amount of the cost of the patent prorated equitably over its life. This method takes into consideration the fact that since a patent purchased for percentage payments has no fixed cost, it is impossible to compute the depreciation allowance ratably over its useful life. Thus, permitting the yearly cost payment to be deducted in the year the payment is made provides minimum distortion of income. By this method at the end of the life of the patent, the purchaser will have recovered the total cost of the asset.

Petitioner contends that to apply section 1245 to the purchase of patents where the purchase price is contingent, and not fixed, will pervert the legislative intent of that section. Petitioner points out that the intent of Congress, in enacting a provision to "recapture" depreciation, was aimed at recovering only that amount of depreciation deducted which exceeded the actual decline in value of the respective asset. However, in order to achieve this result, Congress set forth an objective, mathematical formula in section 1245 which was made applicable to depreciable personal property. Intangible personal property was not excluded from the provisions of section 1245, and section

1.1245-3(b)(2), Income Tax Regs., specifically includes in the definition of personal property "intangible" property. There is nothing in section 1245 to indicate that the absence of a fixed cost for patents justifies exempting their disposition from the application of section 1245.

Respondent computed the amount of recapture of depreciation by considering that Newton had no cost of the patents when they were acquired since no payment was due until the patents were used in Newton's production. Considering the basis of the patents to Newton when acquired to be zero, respondent applied precisely the formula set forth in section 1245 to determine the amount of recapture. Since each year the amount petitioner paid under the agreements is considered deductible as depreciation, at the end of each year Newton's adjusted basis in the patents is zero. Petitioner objects to respondent's use of a zero adjusted basis in the recapture computation. Petitioner concedes that the basis of an asset does not include contingent or indefinite amounts payable in the future such as royalties based on future earnings but contends that since the stipulated fair market value of the license agreements takes into consideration future earnings anticipated for the years 1967 through 1972, the basis of the license agreements should likewise be increased at least by the amount of future royalty payments estimated to be due after 1967. In our view contention of petitioner lacks merit. The computation of the fair market value of the patents is an estimate of the price which a willing buyer would pay a willing seller allowing a reasonable length of time to find a knowing and willing buyer, and assuming a knowing and willing seller. It is the value which petitioner agreed to place on the license agreements at the time Newton was liquidated but it does not in any way affect the amount which petitioner will pay for the patents in the following years. Therefore, the fact that the estimate used 5-year earnings projections has no bearing on the 1967 cost basis of the patents.

We also find that respondent's use of a zero basis, aside from literally complying with the statute, reflects accurately the basis of the patents at the time of their disposition. At that time, future payments under the license agreements were contingent, and petitioner could not be certain that it would incur additional royalty costs. Therefore, petitioner cannot increase the basis of the agreements by speculative amounts which may never become due and which certainly Newton had not paid.

The more troublesome problem is whether section 1245 was intended to apply to dispositions of assets which had no fixed cost at the time of purchase. Section 1245 was enacted to correct the situation which arose when a buyer of property had written off its cost too rapidly or had underestimated the property's useful life in computing the annual depreciation allowance. When these circumstances existed, certain inequities arose. The purpose of the provision as reflected in S. Rept. No. 1881, 87th Cong., 2d Sess. (1962), 1692-3 C.B. 801 was:

> Wherever the depreciation deductions reduce the basis of the property faster than the actual decline in its value, then when it is sold there will be a gain. Under present law this gain is taxed as a capital gain, even though the depreciation deductions reduced ordinary income. The taxpayer who has taken excessive depreciation deductions and then sells an asset, therefore, has in effect converted ordinary income into a capital gain.

To correct this, section 1245 requires that a certain amount of the "gain" be treated as ordinary income. This amount in petitioner's case is the lower of (a) the fair market value of the property in excess of its basis, or (b) the full amount of depreciation taken after December 31, 1961. There is no special consideration given to a situation like the one before us, where the asset did not have a fixed cost. At the same time, the statute applies broadly to all personal property which is subject to a depreciation allowance under section 167, and there is no basis in the law for finding an intangible asset such as patents to be exempt from the provisions of section 1245.

As petitioner points out, applying the statutory formula to an asset without a fixed cost may result in recapture of amounts which would not ordinarily have been excessive depreciation. If Newton had continued to use the patents for their full lives, the depreciation allowable to Newton over the lives of the patents would have exactly equaled the cost to Newton of the patents. However, when Newton disposed of the patents to petitioner under the provisions of section 334(b) petitioner received a fixed basis for the patents in an amount of a pro rata part of the $3,750,000 which it paid for the Newton stock which it will be entitled to recover through depreciation proratable over the remaining useful lives of the patents. Since the basis of the patents in petitioner's hands was not determined by their basis in the hands of Newton, section 1245 is applicable by its terms to the disposition of the patents by Newton to petitioner. See sec. 1245(b)(3).

We hold for respondent except to the extent of the concession made by respondent as to the recapture as to the patents covered by the 1961 agreements being limited to $569,500, their fair market value on November 1, 1967, and the recapture as to the patents covered by the 1966 agreement being limited to $100,047.67.

Stokely USA, Inc. v. Commissioner
100 T.C. 439 (1993)

RUWE, JUDGE:

Petitioner is in the business of processing, canning, and marketing canned and frozen vegetables, fruits, tomato products, and juices. Its principal products are canned corn, beans, peas, and beets.

Petitioner and Quaker Oats agreed to the transfer of certain trademarks owned by Quaker Oats. On November 5, 1984, Quaker Oats transferred to the Quaker Oats Foundation (the Foundation), a private foundation controlled by Quaker Oats, the trademarks that it intended to transfer to petitioner. On November 15, 1984, the Foundation and petitioner entered into a trademark transfer agreement pursuant to which, for a lump-sum payment of $1,584,500, the Foundation:

> [transferred], [sold] and [assigned] to * * * [petitioner] * * * THE FOUNDATION'S right, title and interest, both statutory and at common law, in The Trademarks and the registrations thereof, subject to * * * [certain restrictions] * * * including the right to sue for and collect damages for any past infringement * * *.

The trademarks referred to in the agreement were Stokely's, Shellie, Bavarian Style, and the two Stokely's Finest trademarks (the Stokely trademarks). The agreement contained the following restrictions:

> 2.1 [Petitioner] shall not use The Trademarks on * * * [pork and beans, and products containing beans and wieners (such wieners being composed of either beef, pork, chicken or poultry or a combination thereof) for] [20 years].

> 2.4 The FOUNDATION shall have the right to disapprove any assignment of [Petitioner's] right, title and interest in the Trademarks for a period of five years.

The only issue is whether petitioner is entitled to amortize the $1,584,500 payment it made for the purchase of the Stokely trademarks. Section 1253(d)(2)(A) provides for amortization of the cost of a trademark over a 10-year period if, pursuant to section 1253(a), the transfer of the trademark is not treated as a sale or exchange of a capital asset. Section 1253(a) states:

> A transfer of a franchise, trademark, or trade name shall not be treated as a sale or exchange of a capital asset if the transferor retains any significant power, right, or continuing interest with respect to the subject matter of the franchise, trademark, or trade name.

There is no question that the Stokely trademarks were transferred to petitioner. Therefore, whether the transfer of the Stokely trademarks is to be treated as the sale or exchange of a capital asset under section 1253(a) depends upon (1) whether the Foundation retained any "power, right, or continuing interest with respect to the subject matter" of the Stokely trademarks and, if so, (2) whether one or more of these rights was "significant".

1. Did the Transferor Retain Any Power, Right, or Continuing Interest in the Subject Matter of the Trademarks?

Petitioner contends that the Foundation's 5-year right to disapprove any assignment of petitioner's right, title, and interest in the trademarks and the 20-year prohibition on petitioner's use of the trademarks with respect to pork and beans (the pork and beans restriction), represent powers, rights, or continuing interests retained by the Foundation. We agree with petitioner that the Foundation's right to disapprove transfer of the trademarks by petitioner during the first 5 years after the transfer constitutes a retained power, right, or continuing interest with respect to the subject matter of the trademarks. Respondent does not dispute this. Respondent's only argument with respect to this retained power, right, or interest is that it is not "significant" within the meaning of section 1253(a).

Respondent argues, however, that the pork and beans restriction does not constitute a retained power, right, or continuing interest, but rather, merely defines the assets that petitioner purchased. In essence, respondent contends that petitioner simply did not purchase the right to use the Stokely trademarks for pork and beans. According to respondent, petitioner purchased the right to use the Stokely trademarks on everything except pork and beans, and the Foundation retained no right to use the Stokely trademarks. Respondent, therefore, concludes that the pork and beans restriction did not give the Foundation a retained power, right, or continuing interest over what petitioner purchased.

Respondent's analysis begs the question. It is clear that petitioner did not "purchase" the right to use the Stokely trademarks on pork and beans (for 20 years). It is equally clear that the Foundation retained no right to continue to use the specific trademarks that were transferred to petitioner. However, the relevant statutory language of section 1253 refers to neither of these factors. Rather, section 1253(a) refers to a "transfer of a * * * trademark". This reference to the transfer of a trademark contemplates all transfers, including those with substantial restrictions and limited durations.

Section 1253(a) states that such "transfer" "shall not be treated as a sale or exchange of a capital asset if the transferor retains any significant power, right, or continuing interest with respect to the subject matter of the * * * trademark." (Emphasis added.) The subject matter of the Stokely trademarks included the ability to use them in the marketing of food products. Trademarks and trade names represent goodwill. Goodwill is characterized as "the expectancy of continued patronage, for whatever reason." Petitioner purchased the Stokely trademarks with the expectation that potential customers would be more likely to purchase petitioner's products if they were identified by the Stokely trademarks. Stokely trademarks could have been used to market pork and beans. Registration number 277,037 (one of the Stokely's Finest trademarks) expressly includes pork and beans within the products for which the trademark is to be used. The other two transferred trademarks have less detailed usage descriptions, but both could be used for pork and beans products. While petitioner acquired less than the full use of the Stokely trademarks, this was the direct result of the pork and beans restriction, through which the Foundation was able to prevent petitioner from using the trademarks on pork and beans products.

The statute contains examples that show the error of respondent's reliance on the fact that petitioner did not purchase the right to use the trademarks on pork and beans. Section 1253(b)(2) lists several significant retained powers, rights, or continuing interests. One of these is the right of the transferor to disapprove any transfer. Sec. 1253(b)(2)(A). The purchaser of a trademark encumbered by this type of restriction clearly does not "purchase" the unencumbered right to transfer the trademark. Nevertheless, it is clear that this type of restriction was to qualify as a retained power within the meaning of section 1253. Another example is the "right to prescribe the standards of quality of products used or sold". Sec. 1253(b)(2)(C). A transferee subject to such a right clearly does not purchase the right to use a trademark with respect to any product that it wishes. Yet, in this situation, the statute states that the transferor retains a significant power, right, or continuing interest. Sec. 1253(b)(2)(C).

Respondent argues that the pork and beans restriction is not a power, right, or continuing interest retained by the "transferor", since the Foundation itself did not market pork and beans products. In the trademark transfer agreement, petitioner specifically acknowledged that its use of the trademarks for pork and beans products during the 20-year period would result in irreparable injury to the Foundation and that injunctive relief for the Foundation would be appropriate if petitioner violated this restriction. The Foundation is a private entity controlled by Quaker Oats. Quaker Oats' control over the Foundation also indicates that the restriction on petitioner's use of the Stokely trademarks on pork and beans products was a genuine restriction designed to protect Quaker Oats and the Foundation.

Based on the foregoing factors, we find that the pork and beans restriction was a retained power, right, or continuing interest with respect to the subject matter of the Stokely trademarks.

2. Were the Retained Powers, Rights, or Continuing Interests "Significant"?

Petitioner's primary argument is that the Foundation's right to disapprove assignment of the Stokely trademarks for 5 years is, as a matter of law, "significant". Section 1253(b)(2) states:

> The term "significant power, right, or continuing interest" includes, but is not limited to, the following rights with respect to the interest transferred:
>
> > (A) A right to disapprove any assignment of such interest, or any part thereof.
> >
> > (B) A right to terminate at will.

(C) A right to prescribe the standards of quality of products used or sold, or of services furnished, and of the equipment and facilities used to promote such products or services.

(D) A right to require that the transferee sell or advertise only products or services of the transferor.

(E) A right to require that the transferee purchase substantially all of his supplies and equipment from the transferor.

(F) A right to payments contingent on the productivity, use, or disposition of the subject matter of the interest transferred, if such payments constitute a substantial element under the transfer agreement.

The powers, rights, or continuing interests specified in section 1253(b)(2) are deemed significant by the terms of the statute. If a retained power, right, or continuing interest falls within the rights listed in section 1253(b)(2), no further inquiry is necessary. This list, however, is nonexclusive and does not preclude the possibility that other retained powers, rights, or continuing interests may be "significant".

Petitioner contends that the Foundation's right to disapprove assignment of the Stokely trademarks for 5 years is "a right to disapprove any assignment of such interest, or any part thereof" within the meaning of subparagraph (A) of section 1253(b)(2). Respondent counters by pointing out that the Foundation's right to disapprove assignments was limited to the 5-year period following the transfer, whereas petitioner's rights in the transferred trademarks were for an unlimited duration. Respondent therefore argues that the Foundation's disapproval rights did not extend to "any assignment" within the meaning of the statute. In essence, the parties ask us to decide whether the words "any assignment" in the statute mean *all* assignments (suggested by respondent), or *some* assignments (suggested by petitioner).

Respondent argues that "any assignment" means "all assignments" because any other interpretation would mean that every transitory right to disapprove an assignment would be deemed significant regardless of how short (or insignificant) the period during which the disapproval right could be exercised. In response, petitioner contends that if the period during which a transferor retains the right to disapprove an assignment is so short as to be meaningless, the courts could treat such a right as a sham and disregard it.

The parties' arguments present us with a conundrum. Subparagraph (A) refers to "*any* assignment of such interest, or *any* part thereof." (Emphasis added.) The second "any" in subparagraph (A) can only mean "some". It would be arguably inconsistent to interpret the first "any" in a single sentence to mean "all" and the second "any" to mean "some". Yet, if the first "any" means "some", the interpretative problems noted by respondent arise.

The better course, and the one we adopt, is to interpret subparagraph (A) in light of the statute as a whole. Section 1253(b)(2) contains a list of retained rights upon which Congress conferred significance as a matter of law. Once a right falls within one of the specifically enumerated rights in subsection (b)(2), Congress intended that there should be no further inquiry into its significance. However, unless the retained rights listed in subsection (b)(2) are coextensive in duration with the interest transferred, it can readily be seen that any one of them could be objectively insignificant if the time period during which the transferor could exercise such right was restricted. Courts would then be faced with the dilemma of either interpreting the statute in a way that would produce absurd results or making a case-by-case determination of the actual significance of whatever temporal limits had been placed on the retained right. Neither approach is satisfactory or in keeping with the legislative objective of subsection (b)(2). We believe, therefore, that the retained rights enumerated in subsection (b)(2) must be exercisable for a period of time that is coextensive with the duration of the interest that was transferred. This interpretation is consistent with the language in section 1253, the legislative history, and the objective of the statute.

The language of section 1253 makes a literal distinction between the object of a significant retained right referred to in subsection (a) and the object of the specifically described rights in subsection (b)(2). Section 1253(a) refers to retained rights "with respect to the *subject matter* of the franchise, trademark, or trade name." (Emphasis added.) While a transferred interest in a franchise, trademark, or trade name may itself have a specifically limited duration, the "subject matter" of these intangibles, including the goodwill associated with them, would not likely have an ascertainable limit. In contrast, section 1253(b)(2), which lists specifically defined rights, refers to rights retained "with respect to the *interest* transferred". (Emphasis added.) The "interest transferred" can encompass less than the subject matter of a franchise, trademark, or trade name. The "interest transferred" can be, and often is, for a limited period. Thus, the duration of a retained right takes on added importance "with respect to the interest transferred" under subsection (b)(2). Our interpretation of the statute recognizes that importance.

The legislative history of section 1253 also emphasizes the importance of duration in regard to the retained rights enumerated in subsection (b)(2). It states:

> If the transfer agreement includes significant conditions or restrictions which are subject to the transferor's approval on a *continuing* basis, this power to exercise *continuing*, active, operational control over the transferee's business activities is to be considered as a retention by the transferor of a significant power, right, or continuing interest. * * * [S.Rept. 91-552, *supra*, 1969-3 C.B. at 556; emphasis added.]

The legislative history then lists six retained rights (found in section 1253(b)(2)) that, in the view of Congress, meet the above standards without question. *Id.* The focus of the legislative history on *continuing* control supports our interpretation that retained rights listed in subsection (b)(2) must be coextensive with the duration of the interest transferred.

One of the objectives of Congress in enacting section 1253 was to provide a simple, uniform method for determining whether the transfer of a trademark, franchise, or trade name should receive capital gains treatment. *Id.* Courts had previously conducted detailed factual analyses of such transfers to determine the significance of rights retained by the transferor. These factual analyses led to divisions of authority among courts about the significance of many retained rights. *Id.* Subsection (b)(2) was intended to end this diversity. *Id.* If, as suggested by petitioner, the duration of the retained rights listed in subsection (b)(2) need not be coextensive with the duration of the interest transferred, two potential interpretative scenarios follow.

Under the first scenario, a retained right listed in subsection (b)(2) would be deemed significant regardless of its duration. If we were to adopt this approach, a 1-month or 1-week right to disapprove the assignment of a 20-year franchise would, as a matter of law, be considered significant for purposes of section 1253(b)(2). The same problem exists with respect to the other six rights enumerated in section 1253(b)(2). For example, restaurant franchises are typically granted for a limited period. If such a franchise gave the transferor a right to terminate at will that could only be exercised in the first month of a 20-year franchise, such a right would probably be objectively insignificant but would nonetheless automatically qualify as significant if we adopted petitioner's approach. This is clearly not what Congress intended.

Under the second scenario, a retained right listed in subsection (b)(2) might or might not have significance, depending upon an analysis of the facts and circumstances in order to determine whether its duration was adequate. This type of analysis leads directly back to the problems and resulting uncertainty that existed prior to the enactment of section 1253, and therefore, subverts the intent of Congress.

Based on the foregoing analysis, we hold that those powers, rights, or continuing interests retained by a transferor that are enumerated in subsection (b)(2) must be coextensive with the duration of the interest transferred. It follows that the Foundation's 5-year transfer disapproval right is not a significant right within the meaning of section 1253(b)(2).

Petitioner next argues that the 20-year restriction on using the Stokely trademarks on pork and beans products is itself a "significant" retained power, right, or continuing interest. Respondent contends that this restriction is not significant for two reasons. First, respondent asserts that the name "Stokely" is barely visible on Quaker Oats' well-known line of Van Camp's pork and beans products. This, according to respondent, belies the claim that the Stokely trademarks could have been used by petitioner to successfully market pork and beans products. Second, respondent notes that petitioner was not in the business of producing pork and beans products at the time it entered the transaction to acquire the trademarks. From this, respondent argues that the restriction had no significance for petitioner's business or its use of the Stokely trademarks. We disagree.

The restriction clearly had significance for Quaker Oats. The specific reason for its inclusion in the contract was to protect the company's Van Camp's line. Because of the close connection in the public mind between the Van Camp's and Stokely names, Quaker Oats' management believed that the Van Camp's mark would be "seriously diluted", and Quaker Oats' sales of pork and beans products materially and adversely affected, if petitioner were allowed to use the Stokely trademarks for these products. On brief, respondent agrees that the Stokely and Van Camp's names have been associated with one another in the minds of the public. Thus, it is probable that the use of the Stokely trademarks on pork and beans products would have had considerable importance in any effort by petitioner to market such products.

Moreover, petitioner wanted to enter into the market for pork and beans. Petitioner initially approached Quaker Oats regarding the purchase of the Stokely-Van Camp's trademark, but was rejected. Petitioner wanted to use the Stokely trademarks on pork and beans products and would have done so but for the restriction. Despite the restriction, petitioner attempted to sell pork and beans for a short period under another label. Petitioner was forced to abandon its plans for that market due to the lack of a strong brand name. Stokely could have been that name.

In light of these facts, the pork and beans restriction carried undoubted significance for the Foundation, Quaker Oats, and petitioner. The trademark transfer agreement states this clearly:

> [Petitioner] recognizes and acknowledges that such use of The Trademarks before expiration of the applicable time period would result in immediate and irreparable injury to the FOUNDATION, which could not be adequately compensated by payment of money damages, and hence injunctive relief would be

appropriate in favor of the FOUNDATION or its designees to prevent use of The Trademarks in such manner.

Respondent contends that section 1.1253-2(d)(9), Proposed Income Tax Regs., 36 Fed.Reg. 13159 (July 15, 1971), requires a different conclusion. Proposed regulations constitute a body of informed judgment on which courts may draw for guidance, but do not carry the weight of a final regulation. They are considered to be nothing more than respondent's position for purposes of litigation.

Section 1.1253-2(d), Proposed Income Tax Regs., *supra*, lists nine rights that are considered to be "significant". Six of the rights listed in the proposed regulations are identical to those listed in section 1253(b)(2). The right listed in section 1.1253-2(d)(9), Proposed Income Tax Regs., *supra*, is: "Any other right which permits the transferor to exercise continuing, active, and operational control over the transferee's trade or business activities." Respondent argues that active, operational control is the sine qua non of significance. We observe, however, that the proposed regulation itself belies respondent's conclusion. It introduces its list with the caveat that "The term 'significant power, right, or continuing interest' *includes, but is not limited to*, the following rights". See sec. 1.1253-2(d), Proposed Income Tax Regs., *supra*. (Emphasis added.)

Respondent points to the Senate Finance Committee report and its reference to powers, rights, or interests allowing the transferor "active, operational control" and argues that, in contrast to this language, the pork and beans restriction does not grant such control to the Foundation. However, the Senate Finance Committee report also indicates that "any general control of the transferee's activities and operations by the transferor", can be significant. We believe the pork and beans restriction allows the Foundation control of the transferee's activities and operations in that it prevents petitioner from using its trademarks for a significant market that petitioner could have and would have otherwise entered. This constitutes a "significant [condition] or [restriction]".

We recognize that the pork and beans restriction is not coextensive with the duration of petitioner's rights in the trademarks. The restriction lasts for 20 years, whereas petitioner acquired its right, title, and interest in the trademarks in perpetuity. Section 1253(a) provides that a transfer "not be treated as a sale or exchange of a capital asset if the transferor retains any significant power, right, or continuing interest with respect to the *subject matter of the franchise, trademark, or trade name.*" (Emphasis added.) As previously noted, the subject matter of a trademark may be broader than the "interest transferred" referred to in section 1253(b)(2). Section 1253(a) is therefore distinguishable from section 1253(b)(2). Unlike section 1253(b)(2), section 1253(a) contains no specifically enumerated criteria for determining the significance of a retained right. While the duration of a restriction may be an important factor, the ultimate determination of whether a retained right is "significant" for purposes of section 1253(a) must be based on all the facts and circumstances. In the context of petitioner's business, 20 years is a significant period.

We have examined all the facts and circumstances regarding the Stokely trademarks and the pork and beans restriction and conclude that the pork and beans restriction qualifies as a "significant power, right, or continuing interest with respect to the subject matter of the * * * [trademarks]" within the meaning of section 1253(a). As a result, petitioner is entitled to deductions that it claimed under section 1253(d)(2).

Chapter 7

IP Holding Companies and R&D Limited Partnerships

I. Assignment for Chapter 7

Read: Internal Revenue Code: §§ 243; 331; 332(b); 334(b); 337; 351(a); 358(a)(1); 362(a); 482; 1032; 1223(1)-(2). Merely skim: §§ 56(b)(2); 465; 469; 701; 704(a), (b), (d); 705(a); 721; 722; 723; 731(a)(1); 732(a)(1); 733; 741; 742; 751; 752(a), (d).

Treasury Regulations: §§ 1.332-3, -4; 1.351-1(a)(1); 1.482-7. Skim §§ 1.482-1(a)(1), (b)(1), -4(a)-(c)(1), -5, -6; 1.704-1(b)(2); 1.752-2, -3.

Materials: Overview
Delaware State Statute
Vermont State Statute
Massachusetts State Statute
Geoffrey, Inc. v. South Carolina Tax Commission
ACME Royalty Co. v. Director of Revenue
SYL v. Comptroller of the Treasury
Syms Corp. v. Commissioner of Revenue
In re Sherwin-Williams Co.
Sherwin-Williams Co. v. Commissioner of Revenue
Department of Taxes, State of Vermont Ruling 2002-01
Harris v. Commissioner
Scoggins v. Commissioner

Complete the Problems.

II. Problems for Chapter 7

1. MapQuest is a major map company doing business in all fifty states with its headquarters located in Pasadena, California. It owns 5 patents, 50 trademarks, and 5,000 copyright titles. MapQuest wants to form an intellectual property holding company in Delaware to manage the intellectual property assets. MapQuest intends to transfer the intellectual property (with a fair market value of $15 million and an

adjusted basis of $5 million) to the holding company in exchange for 100% of the IP holding company's stock. Please advise MapQuest of the tax consequence of its asset transfer to its IP holding subsidiary.

2. MapQuest wants to know what tax benefits are available under Delaware law for its wholly-owned IP holding company. Also, to avail itself of such tax benefits, what types of business should the IP holding company be allowed to operate? Would your answers be different if the IP holding company is incorporated in Vermont?

3. Assume that MapQuest followed your advice and formed MQIP, a wholly owned subsidiary that holds and manages the intellectual property assets of MapQuest. MQIP is incorporated in Delaware and has an office with two employees in Wilmington, Delaware. The employees oversee the licensing transactions and intellectual property prosecution matters. MQIP licenses the intellectual property to MapQuest and MapQuest's affiliates at a reasonable royalty rate. MapQuest has retail operations in all fifty states. The taxing authorities in the jurisdictions below have recently learned about MQIP existence while they conducted audit of MapQuest. Discuss various tax challenges MapQuest and MQIP may face in the following jurisdictions:

   (a) South Carolina
   (b) Missouri
   (c) Maryland
   (d) New York
   (e) Massachusetts

   You are free to assume additional information that would be useful for your or the taxing authorities' arguments.

4. A state legislator from your home state is concerned about the economic reality of the Intellectual Property Holding Company's tax avoidance scheme, and she requests that you suggest proposed legislation curbing such practices. What would you recommend?

5. Taxpayers, Mr. and Mrs. Smith, are limited partners in Drug-Med, Ltd. The recently formed partnership is considering entering into a research and development agreement with PharmaCo Industries. Under the agreement, Drug-Med will contribute $8 million to PharmaCo, enabling PharmaCo to develop new antiviral medications, specifically for Hepatitis C. PharmaCo will have the exclusive rights to make, sell, and license the new viral Hepatitis medications. Under the agreement, PharmaCo will pay Drug-Med 5% of PharmaCo's revenues from the new medications, as a royalty, until Drug-Med recovers its $2 million; the royalty will then drop to 1%. Byproducts of the research and development (*i.e.*, other antiviral medications that are developed) will belong to Drug-Med, although PharmaCo will be given the right to purchase rights to byproducts for $200,000. The agreement will grant Drug-Med the right to monitor the company's use of money and the receipt of written reports. The Smiths ask you whether they will be entitled to deduct their distributive share of Drug-Med's payment to PharmaCo. What's your answer?

III. Overview

In recent years, intellectual property (IP) holding companies have become popular business tools selected by intellectual property owners for both tax and non-tax benefits. Under the intellectual company model, a parent corporation establishes a wholly owned subsidiary corporation, transfers intellectual property to the newly formed subsidiary corporation in exchange for stock of the subsidiary corporation, and then licenses back the right to use the intellectual property. Research and development (R&D) limited partnerships have also been widely used. These partnerships are financing devices for research undertaken by an R&D company. As long as the R&D research company shares the potential up-side of the developed technology with the partnership, tax benefits may pass through to the investors. This Chapter discusses IP holding companies and R&D limited partnerships. Cost sharing arrangements are discussed in Chapter 9 as they are one of the hottest and most controversial areas in international tax.

A. Intellectual Property (IP) Holding Companies

Corporations with substantial intellectual property assets often establish wholly owned subsidiaries to own and manage their intellectual property holdings. The segregation of intellectual property in separate holding companies provides numerous non-tax benefits. Segregation, for example, permits more efficient management of intellectual property, provides more opportunities for enhancement and exploitation of the assets, allows more accurate measuring and matching of intellectual property expenses and related income for decisionmaking, and insulates the parent company from involvement in litigation concerning the intellectual property. While improving the ability to manage intellectual property, IP holding companies also provide significant tax benefits. In fact, the main benefit of using an IP holding company is an overall reduction in state income taxes.

IP holding companies are typically formed in a state that has favorable state tax laws for IP holding companies, laws that exempt some or all royalty income from intangibles from state taxation. A few states—Delaware, Michigan, and Nevada—are typically considered for the location of IP holding companies. In Delaware, Delaware IP holding companies are exempt from Delaware's state income tax on income earned from the maintenance or management of most forms of intellectual property. *See* Del. Code Ann. tit. 30, § 1902(b)(8), included in the materials. By establishing an IP holding company in one of these states, a business with substantial intellectual property holdings can enjoy significant state tax savings. It should be noted that an IP holding company may lose its tax breaks if it becomes too active or aggressive (*e.g.*, activities cross over from passive management of intellectual property to something more active). Accordingly, an IP holding company must generally limit its activities to managing its assets.

In the typical IP holding company model, a corporate owner of intellectual property that is located in a state with a state income tax ("parent company") forms a wholly owned subsidiary company in one of the few states listed above that does not tax royalty income from intellectual property ("IP holding company"). After the IP holding company is established in a state with favorable tax treatment, the parent company then contributes its intellectual property to the newly formed IP holding company in exchange for all the stock in that subsidiary. At the same time, the IP holding company licenses the right to use the intellectual property back to the parent company in exchange for royalties. Pursuant to licensing agreements executed by the parties, the parent company makes royalty payments to the IP holding company for the right to use the intellectual property. The parent company deducts the royalty payments as ordinary business expenses. The royalty income received by the IP holding company is then typically invested in passive investments (*e.g.*, equity or debt instruments) and then distributed back to the parent company in the form of dividends. In some cases, the IP holding company uses the royalty income to make loans to the parent company at an appropriate interest rate. The parent company then further deducts the interest payments. Federal and state tax consequences of the following transactions must be considered: (1) contribution of intellectual property by the parent company in exchange for stock of the IP holding company; (2) the transfer of royalty payments by the parent company to the IP holding company; and (3) receipt of dividends by the parent company.

1. *Formation of IP Holding Companies*

The contribution of intellectual property by the parent company in exchange for stock of the IP holding company is usually a tax-free transaction for both the parent company and the IP holding company.

(a) *Tax Treatment of Parent Company*

In General. Although the parent company may realize gain (or loss) on the receipt of IP holding company stock (with a fair market value approximating the value of the intellectual property transferred) in exchange for intellectual property with an adjusted basis lower (or higher) than the value of the stock received, the parent company may not have to recognize that gain on formation. Section 351(a) provides that no gain or loss shall be recognized upon the transfer by one or more persons of property to a corporation solely in exchange for stock in such corporation if, immediately after the exchange, such person or persons are in control of the corporation to which the property was transferred. In *Sherwin-Williams (New York)*, excerpted below, the Sherwin-Williams parent corporation transferred $50,000 and its ownership rights in certain trademarks in exchange for shares of SWIMC and DIMC, wholly owned IP holding companies. No gain was recognized by Sherwin-Williams on this exchange pursuant to § 351.

Several requirements must be met before non-recognition treatment is available under § 351. First, "property" must be transferred from the parent company to the IP holding company (*e.g.*, intellectual property transferred must qualify as "property" for purposes of § 351). A transfer of a non-substantial right in intellectual property may qualify as a transfer of "property" for purpose of § 351. See *E.I. duPont de Nemours & Co. v. United States*, 471 F.2d 1211 (Ct. Cl. 1973); Gen. Couns. Mem. 36,922 (Nov. 16, 1976).

Second, the transfer must be "solely in exchange for stock" of the IP holding company. The Code relaxes the "solely in exchange" requirement and permits other property or money (*e.g.*, "boot") to be received. However, if other property or money is received, then gain will be recognized to the extent of the boot received. I.R.C. § 351(b). As a general rule, the assumption of a liability by an IP holding company in a § 351 exchange will neither constitute boot nor prevent the exchange from qualifying under § 351. I.R.C. § 357(a). However, if liabilities assumed by the IP holding company exceed the aggregate adjusted basis of the intellectual property transferred by the parent company, the excess must be reported as gain. I.R.C. § 357(c).

Third, the parent company must be in "control" of the IP holding company immediately after the exchange. To be in control of the IP holding company, the parent company must own stock possessing at least 80 % of the total combined voting power of all classes of stock entitled to vote, and at least 80 % of the total number of shares of all other classes of stock of the IP holding company immediately after the transfer. I.R.C. § 368(c). The phrase "immediately after the exchange" does not necessarily require a simultaneous exchange, but "comprehends a situation where the rights of the parties have been previously defined and the execution of the agreement proceeds with an expedition consistent with orderly procedure." Treas. Reg. § 1.351-1(a)(1).

Stock Basis and Holding Period. If § 351 applies to a contribution of intellectual property to an IP holding company, the reporting of gain or loss realized by the parent company is postponed to a later year (*e.g.,* when the IP holding company stock received in the transaction is later sold or disposed of in a taxable transaction). Gain is preserved by generally giving the parent company the same basis in the IP holding company stock acquired as it had in the intellectual property given up. I.R.C. § 358(a)(1). In other words, the basis in stock received in a § 351 transfer will be determined by reference to the basis of the intellectual property transferred to the IP holding company. Because the parent company's basis in the stock received is determined by reference to the parent company's basis in property given up, the parent company's holding period of the stock received includes the holding period of the intellectual property given up, provided the intellectual property transferred is a capital asset or § 1231 property. I.R.C. § 1223(1).

(b) Tax Treatment of IP Holding Company

When an IP holding company issues stock in exchange for intellectual property with value, it would seem that the company might have reportable gain, because an IP holding company is a separate taxpaying entity. However, an IP holding company does not recognize gain or loss when it issues stock in exchange for intellectual property. I.R.C. § 1032. An IP holding company that receives intellectual property in exchange for its stock in a nontaxable formation steps into the shoes of the parent company. Thus, an IP holding company's basis in any property received in a section 351 exchange is the same as the parent company's basis. I.R.C. § 362(a). Because the contributed intellectual property has a transferred basis to the IP holding company, the parent company's holding period likewise carries over to the holding company. I.R.C. § 1223(2).

2. Transfer-License Back Intellectual Property Arrangements

When a parent company forms an IP holding company, the parties typically execute licensing agreements, under which the IP holding company licenses the right to use the intellectual property back to the parent company in exchange for royalties. Such arrangement can be seen in the cases included in the materials. *See also Crown Cork & Seal, Inc. v. Comptroller of the Treasury,* 1999 WL 322699 (Md. Tax Ct. April 26, 1999).

The transfer-license back arrangement produces significant tax savings at both the federal and state levels. For example, royalty payments paid by a parent corporation to an IP holding company are usually deductible by the parent company. Also, royalty payments received by an IP holding company from a parent company are usually partially or wholly exempt from state taxation provided the IP holding company is formed in a state with favorable tax laws. In addition to these and other benefits, numerous risks associating with the transfer-license back arrangement are discussed below.

(a) Tax Treatment of IP Holding Company

Royalties received by the IP holding company are included in gross income for federal income tax purposes. I.R.C. § 61(a)(7). Of course expenses incurred in the maintenance and management of the company's intellectual property holdings, as well as the collection and distribution of income from such investments, are typically deductible and help offset royalty income for federal tax purposes. I.R.C. § 162.

Although royalties are subject to federal income taxes, they are exempt from state income taxes *if* the IP holding company is incorporated in a state that *does not* tax royalty income from intangibles. Several states such as Delaware and Michigan provide favorable tax treatment as seen in the state statutes and regulations included in the materials.

(i) Risk That Royalties Will Be Subject to Tax by the IP Holding Company's State

An IP holding company must generally limit its activities to managing its intellectual property or will risk losing its non-taxable status. Delaware, for instance, exempts only certain corporations from the state income tax—*e.g.*, corporations whose activities within Delaware are "confined to the maintenance and management of their intangible investments...and the collection and distribution of the income from such investments." *See* Del. Code Ann. tit. 30, § 1902(b)(8), included in the materials. Thus, if an IP holding company becomes too active or aggressive, it risks losing its tax breaks.

(ii) Risk that Royalties Will Be Subject to Tax by Other States

There is always a risk that the parent company's or affiliate's state may view the IP holding company as a tax avoidance sham and determine that royalties received by the IP holding company should be subject to tax in the parent company's or affiliate's state despite their non-taxable status in the IP holding company's state. How did the Supreme Court in South Carolina determine that the IP holding company, organized under the laws of Delaware with its principal offices in that state, was subject to South Carolina taxation on royalties? *See Geoffrey, Inc. v. South Carolina Tax Commission*, included below. Compare the result in that case to *Acme Royalty Co. v. Director of Revenue* and *SYL v. Comptroller of the Treasury*, included below. *See also Kmart Properties, Inc. v. Taxation and Revenue Department*, NM 21140 (Ct. of App. N.M., Nov. 30, 2002); *Secretary of Revenue of North Carolina v. A & F Trademark, Inc.*, No. 381 (N.C. Tax Rev. Bd., May 7, 2002).

Some state courts and taxing authorities have determined that the assessment of an out-of-state affiliate (IP holding company) of a corporate group for state income taxes is constitutionally proper only if there exists a nexus between the activities of the out-of-state affiliate and the taxing state. It has been held that the attribution of a nexus to a foreign corporation (IP holding company) under state law is limited to phantom entities (*i.e.*, no substance). *See SYL, Inc. v. Comptroller of the Treasury*, 1999 Md. Tax LEXIS 3, included in the materials. If the foreign corporation (IP holding company) is not a phantom entity and has no nexus with the taxing state, the IP holding company is not subject to the taxing state's income tax.

To avoid being deemed a sham or phantom corporation, the IP holding company must be an entity of substance. Courts have upheld an IP holding company as non-phantom entity when the company was a viable entity established for valid business purposes, such as the protection of valuable intellectual property rights from hostile takeovers of the parent corporation, maintained an office in the state of incorporation, met all corporate formalities, had separate bank accounts and employees performing services pursuant to employment agreements, and received royalty income from third parties. How did the taxing authorities in *SYL* (Maryland) and *Sherwin-Williams* (New York) determine that the IP holding companies were not phantom entities?

If the IP company is a phantom entity, the parent company's state can require the IP holding company to file tax returns on a combined basis with the parent company in the parent's state, thus subjecting the IP holding company to taxation. How did the taxing authority in *Sherwin-Williams* (New York) arrive at its conclusion regarding whether the IP holding company be subject to New York taxation? Compare *Sherwin-Williams* (New York) to *In re Burnham Corporation*, 1997 N.Y. Tax LEXIS 304. See *Express, Inc. v. State of New York*, 1995 N.Y. Tax LEXIS 495 (1995).

(b) Tax Treatment of the Parent Company

Provided the IP holding company is not deemed a sham, the parent company may generally deduct royalty payments paid to an IP holding company for the use of its intellectual property (*e.g.*, the right to make patented products or to affix a trademark to goods). See *Crown Cork & Seal, Inc. v. Comptroller of the Treasury*, 1999 WL 322699 (Md. Tax Ct. April 26, 1999) (noting the Maryland parent company's federal taxable income was reduced by the amount of the royalties paid to its Delaware IP holding subsidiary). If the transfer-license back transaction is a sham, a state taxing authority may disallow the parent company to deduct royalty payments made to the IP holding subsidiary or require the parent company to file a combined tax report with the IP holding subsidiary.

(i) Risks of Disallowance of Deduction for Royalty Payments

A parent company will not be entitled to a deduction for royalty payments if it is determined that the transfer-license back transaction is a sham and the royalty payments to the IP holding subsidiary are not ordinary and necessary expenses.

Under federal tax law, a deduction for royalty payments is permitted under § 162. Section 162 allows a deduction for all "ordinary and necessary expenses paid or incurred during the taxable year in carrying on any trade or business," including "rentals or other payments required to be made as a condition to the continued use or possession, for purposes of the trade or business, or property to which the taxpayer has not taken or is not taking title or in which he has no equity." I.R.C. § 162(a). Section 162 permits the deduction of royalties for the use of intellectual property provided the payments are for the "continued use or possession" of intellectual property and not to acquire ownership. As can be seen, § 162 establishes several significant requirements for the deduction of royalty payments. The payments must be "ordinary and necessary." They must also be paid or incurred "in carrying on a trade or business."

In *Syms Corp. v. Commissioner of Revenue*, excerpted below, the Massachusetts Supreme Judicial Court held in a case where a parent company transferred trademarks to and licensed back the trademarks from its affiliated Delaware IP Holding company that (1) the transfer and leaseback of the marks was a sham and could be disregarded under the "sham transaction doctrine," and (2) the Massachusetts company's royalty payments were not deductible as ordinary and necessary business expenses where there was no valid business purpose justifying the expense and the IP Delaware holding company added little or no value to the marks. In a subsequent case, *Sherwin-Williams* (Massachusetts), the Court ruled in favor of the taxpayer. How did the Massachusetts high court reach its decisions? What facts influenced the Court's rulings? In 2003, the Massachusetts legislature enacted a new statute. See M.G.L.A. 62C §3A (2003), excerpted below. Did the new statute effectively repeal *Sherwin-Williams*?

(ii) Risk that Royalties Will Be Subject to Transfer Pricing Adjustments

Even if a transfer-license back arrangement is found not to be a sham, the parent company may not be able to deduct the royalty fees in full if royalty payments are artificially high. There is an incentive for companies to set the royalty rate unreasonably high because royalties are deductible by the parent company and therefore reduce the parent company's tax liability. At the same time, royalties received by IP holding companies incorporated in states with favorable tax laws are exempt from state income tax. Unreasonable royalty rates, however, face the risk of being disallowed under both federal and state law.

For both federal and state tax purposes, royalty payments must be at an arm's length rate (*e.g.*, the IP holding company must charge the parent company the same price it would charge unrelated parties). See *In re Sherwin-Williams Co.*, included below, finding that the royalty rates charged by the Delaware IP holding subsidiaries were at arm's length). If the IP holding company fails to charge an arm's length royalty rate, there is a risk that the government will impose pricing adjustments and find that additional tax is due along with related non-deductible penalties and interest. See *Syms Corp. v. Commissioner of Revenue*, also included in the materials below. How did the New York and Massachusetts taxing authorities reach their results?

Section 482 specifically authorizes the Commissioner to reallocate gross income, deductions, credits, or allowances among commonly controlled entities in order to ensure that taxpayers clearly reflect income attributable to related party transactions, and to prevent the avoidance of taxes with respect to such transactions. I.R.C.§ 482; Treas. Reg. § 1.482-1(a)(1). Its purpose is to place a controlled taxpayer on a tax parity with an uncontrolled taxpayer by determining the true taxable income of the controlled taxpayer. Treas. Reg. § 1.482-1(a)(1). In determining the true taxable income of a controlled taxpayer, the standard to be applied is that of a taxpayer dealing at arm's length with an uncontrolled taxpayer. Treas. Reg. § 1.482-1(b)(1). In short, § 482 often presents a trap for the unwary because it permits the Commissioner to determine the taxable income of commonly controlled entities as if they were unrelated entities dealing at arm's length.

Transfers of intellectual property between parent companies and their holding companies are particularly subject to § 482's trap. The Tax Reform Act of 1986 amended § 482 by adding: "In the case of any transfer (or license) of intangible property..., the income with respect to such transfer or license shall be commensurate with the income attributable to the intangible." Intangible property for purposes of § 482 is defined to include most forms of intellectual property, such as (1) patents, inventions, formulae, processes, designs, patterns, or know-how, (2) copyrights and literary, musical, or artistic compositions, (3) trademarks, trade names, or brand names, and (4) methods, programs, systems, procedure, or technical data. Treas. Reg. § 1.482-4(b).

The regulations provide several methods for determining an arm's length price for the transfer or use of intellectual property: (1) the comparable uncontrolled transaction method, (2) the comparable profits method, and (3) the profit split method. Treas. Reg. § 1.482-4(a). The comparable uncontrolled transaction method, which is perhaps the best method for determining an arm's length price, evaluates whether the amount charged for a controlled transfer of intellectual property was arm's length by reference to the amount charged in a comparable uncontrolled transaction. Treas. Reg. § 1.482-4(c)(1). The comparable profits method evaluates whether the amount charged in a controlled transaction is arm's length based on objective measures of profitability derived from uncontrolled taxpayers that engage in similar business activities under similar circumstances. Treas. Reg. § 1.482-5(a). The profit split method evaluates whether the allocation of the combined operating profit or loss attributable to one or more controlled transactions is arm's length by reference to the relative value of each controlled taxpayer's contribution to that combined operating profit or loss. Treas. Reg. § 1.482-6.

As does the federal government, states also apply § 482 principles to require arm's length pricing. State taxing authorities are allowed under state tax law to recompute income in order to properly reflect tax liability or if it is determined that a taxpayer (parent company) has engaged in an arbitrary shift of income.

For example, in *Sherwin-Williams* (Massachusetts), the Massachusetts Supreme Judicial Court noted that General Laws c. 63, § 39A, provides that the Massachusetts commissioner may determine the "net income of a foreign corporation which is a subsidiary of another corporation or closely affiliated therewith by stock ownership" by "eliminating all payments to the parent corporation or affiliated corporations in excess of fair value." The purpose of the statute is to give the commissioner the "authority to make adjustments to correct the effect of less than arm's length transactions," between closely affiliated companies, and thereby address concerns that "tax evasion by means of intercorporate transactions...would depress the...income of corporations subject to taxation in Massachusetts." 778 N.E. 2d 504, 522 (Mass. 2002). The board found that the transfer and license back of the marks in exchange for royalty payments were not arm's-length transactions because Sherwin-Williams controlled the subsidiaries and there was never a question that the marks would be licensed back to Sherwin-Williams because its existence depended on their use. It further found that the royalty payments had no economic purpose because Sherwin-Williams had itself created the obligation by transferring the marks, and the subsidiaries did nothing to add value to them which would justify such payments. Consequently, it concluded that any payments were in excess of fair market value. The Massachusetts Supreme Judicial Court rejected the board's argument. The case is excerpted below.

3. *Dividend Distributions to Parent Company*

Royalty income received by an IP holding company is typically invested in passive investments (*e.g.*, equity or debt instruments or loans back to the parent company) and then distributed back to the parent company in the form of dividends. Dividends received by the parent company are treated favorably for federal income tax purposes. This is because royalties would be subject to three levels of tax for federal tax purposes if parent companies were taxed in full on dividends they received: royalties would be subject to federal tax once when earned by the IP holding company, a second time when received by the parent company, and a third time when distributed by the parent company to its non-corporate shareholders. The Code alleviates this multiple taxation by permitting the parent company to deduct from income 70% of the dividends received from an IP holding company that is a domestic corporation. I.R.C. §243(a)(1). This "dividends received deduction" is increased to 80% if the parent company owns 20% or more of the IP holding company, and increased to 100% if the IP holding company and the parent company are members of an electing consolidated group. I.R.C. §243(a)(3), (b), (c). To qualify for the 100% dividends received deduction, the parent/distributee company must own at least 80% of the stock of the subsidiary/distributing corporation and elect to file consolidated returns. I.R.C. §243. Because corporations have found ways to exploit the dividends received deduction, Congress has enacted several provisions that either limit or eliminate the dividends received deduction. See, e.g., I.R.C. §§246, 246A, 1059.

4. Liquidations of IP Holding Companies into Parent Companies

(a) Tax Treatment of the Parent Company

The liquidation of an IP holding company into its corporate parent is generally non-taxable. Section 332 provides that a parent corporation recognizes no gain or loss on the receipt of property in complete liquidation of its subsidiary corporation. I.R.C. §332 (providing an exception to the general rule of §331 for liquidating distributions). To receive non-recognition, two requirements must be met. First, the parent must own at least 80% of the total voting power of stock of the IP holding company and 80% of the total value of all outstanding stock of the IP holding company from the adoption date of the complete liquidation plan and at all times thereafter until the liquidation is completed. I.R.C. §332(b)(1). The 80% requirement is usually not a problem because most IP holding companies are wholly owed by the parent corporation. Second, the liquidation will qualify for non-recognition treatment only if (1) the IP holding company distributes all of its assets within one taxable year, or (2) if the distributions span more than one taxable year, the plan provides that the IP holding company will distribute all property within three years after the close of the taxable year in which the plan is adopted. I.R.C. §332(b)(2)-(3); Treas. Reg. §1.332-3, -4. In a non-taxable liquidation of an IP holding company, the parent corporation takes a transferred basis in property received from the subsidiary. I.R.C. §334(b)(1).

(b) Tax Treatment of the IP Holding Company

Under §337, a liquidating IP holding company generally does not recognize gain or loss on distributions of property to its parent corporation (an 80% distributee) in a complete liquidation to which §332 applies. I.R.C. §337 (providing exception to the general rule in §336). In this case, the parent corporation takes a carryover basis for the distributed property. I.R.C. §334(b). The non-recognition rules applies only to a liquidating distribution to an 80% distributee.

B. Research and Development (R&D) Limited Partnerships

Following the Supreme Court's decision in *Snow v. Commissioner* (discussed in Chapter 4), but prior to Tax Court's decision in *Green v. Commissioner*, (also discussed in Chapter 4), the research and development (R&D) limited partnership was a popular investment vehicle for raising funds for research and development projects. In short, it was an effective financing device for research undertaken by a research and development company that could not take advantage of the tax benefits under §174. In the R&D limited partnership model, investors would inject risk capital to a limited partnership, which would then provide the necessary financing to a research and development company engaged in an active trade or business. Partnership payments to the research company would be deducted by the partnership under §174(a), and ultimately pass through to the partners to be enjoyed on their individual tax returns. Although the R&D partnership took title in the inventions being developed, it would often license the inventions back to the third party development company or some other party in exchange for royalty payments from exploitation of the inventions. The royalty rate was often set to provide the limited partners with a sufficient return to attract their money. If the R&D limited partnership sold the invention to the research company or another third party, it would recognize capital gains, which (as with the §174 deductions) would pass through to the limited partners/investors. In sum, the R&D limited partnership provided a tax-shelter arrangement for investors: current deductibility under §174 of amounts invested by limited partners as well as preferential capital gains treatment on the disposition of the developed inventions.

As discussed in Chapter 4, to receive a deduction under §174, an expenditure must not only represent a cost in the experimental or laboratory sense, but must also be incurred "in connection with" the taxpayer's trade or business. Prior to 1974, the Service and the courts took the position that in order to qualify for §174 treatment, a taxpayer must have already engaged in a trade or business—something most R&D partnership could not show. In *Snow*, included in Chapter 4, however, the United States Supreme Court rejected this narrow approach and held that pre-operational research or experimental expenditures could qualify for the section 174 deduction. Tax planners interpreted *Snow* as permitting §174 deductions to passive limited partnerships that contracted out research and development projects.

The R&D limited partnership model was widely used until the mid-1980s. In 1984, however, the Tax Court, in *Green*, disallowed §174 deductions to a limited partnership whose activities the court found did not rise to the level of a trade or business. While recognizing that a taxpayer "need not currently be producing or selling any product," the Tax Court held that the taxpayer "must still be engaged in a trade or business *at some time*" in order for research or experimental expenditures to qualify as being incurred in connection with a trade or business. In the wake of *Green*, and other post-*Snow* cases, the relevant inquiry, in the case of an R&D limited partnership seeking deductions under §174, is whether the partnership has any realistic prospect of entering into a trade or business involving the technology under development.

A number of cases have applied the passive investor principle of *Green* and concluded that an entity, such as a limited partnership, was nothing more than an investment vehicle for injecting risk capital into the development and commercialization of inventions (investment vehicle to fund research) and had no realistic possibility of entering a trade or business with respect to the technology being developed. *Harris v. Commissioner*, which follows this Overview, and cases cited therein, are good examples of how courts have had to scrutinize claimed research and development expenditures to distinguish those that are legitimate from those that are merely designed to shelter the income of passive investors. What are some relevant facts and circumstances that govern whether an entity is merely an investment vehicle to fund research or has a realistic prospect of entering into a trade or business with respect to the technology under development?

It is unlikely that the § 174 trade or business requirement would be satisfied if a taxpayer grants the third-party researcher an exclusive license to exploit the technology prior to the commencement of research, or has a mere understanding at the time the research contract is entered into that an exclusive license will be granted. Review *Green v. Commissioner*, included in Chapter 4. *See also Spellman v. Commissioner*, 845 F.2d at 148 (7th Cir. 1988) (denying deduction for research and development expenditures where economic realities insured that partnership would grant a license to the research company).

The existence of an option to acquire the technology developed by the research contractor and the likelihood of its exercise may also be relevant in determining whether an entity is merely an investment vehicle to fund research or has a realistic possibility of exploiting technology in its own trade or business. Courts generally conclude, for example, that taxpayers do not have a realistic prospect of entering into a trade or business with respect to technology under development if the taxpayer grants an option to a research contractor, and that option is exercisable for a nominal sum. In *Diamond v. Commissioner*, 930 F.2d 372 (4th Cir. 1991), the Fourth Circuit denied a § 174 deduction where the taxpayer/partnership granted an option to a research contractor to acquire an exclusive license to the technology at some future time for a relatively nominal amount. Courts also generally conclude that taxpayers do not have a realistic possibility of entering a trade or business in cases where optionees will certainly exercise their rights if the activity appears profitable. *See LDL Research & Development II, Ltd. v. Commissioner*, 124 F.3d 1338 (10th Cir. 1997).

Other factors that may be relevant in determining whether an entity is merely an investment vehicle or has a realistic prospect of entering into a trade or business include the exercise of control by the entity over the person or organization doing the research, the financial ability of the entity to carry on an active trade or business, the business activities of the entity during the relevant years, and the experience of the entity owners. *See Kantor v. Commissioner*, 998 F.2d 1514 (9th Cir. 1993).

Read *Scoggins v. Commissioner*, included in the materials. Are you surprised that the court concluded that the research partnership was entitled to § 174 deductions? Be prepared to compare *Scoggins* with *Harris* and the cases discussed therein.

While *Green* and post-*Snow* cases clearly limited the use of R&D limited partnerships, several congressional enactments also had the effect of limiting the tax shelter benefits of R&D limited partnerships. Now, even if an R&D limited partnership is deemed to be engaged in an active trade or business within the meaning of *Green*, one or more Code provisions, particularly § 469, could restrict the tax benefits of § 174. *See also* I.R.C. §§ 56(b)(2), 465.

Section 469, added in 1986, restricts the current deductibility of "passive losses," including deductions for research and experimentation expenditures. In general, passive losses (§ 174 deductions) may offset passive income without limitation under § 469.

However, excess § 174 deductions from a taxpayer's "passive activities" are disallowed in the current year. Section 174 deductions disallowed by the § 469 limitation are carried forward and treated as losses from passive activities in succeeding years (and may offset passive income in those years). I.R.C. § 469(b). Any § 174 deductions suspended by the operation of § 469 are allowable in full when the taxpayer disposes of his or her investment in the passive activity in a fully taxable transaction. I.R.C. § 469(g). Although partnerships are not subject to the passive activity loss rules, the partners are generally governed by § 469 with respect to passive activity losses passed through to them. I.R.C. § 469(a)(2).

A passive activity is any trade or business or profit seeking activity in which the taxpayer-owner does not materially participate. The term "trade or business" includes any activity involving research or experimentation within the meaning of § 174. I.R.C. § 469(c)(5). Material participation is satisfied only if the taxpayer-owner is involved on a regular, continuous, and substantial basis in the operations of the activity. I.R.C. § 469(h)(1). The Service has promulgated regulations that provide a substantially mechanical set of rules to determine whether the material participation test is satisfied. *See* Treas. Reg. § 1.469-5T(a) (providing seven situations in which the test may be satisfied).

As can be seen, § 469 eliminates section 174 deductions for a great number of individual investors. In short, the passive activity loss rules restrict § 174 deductions (1) to investors who materially participate or (2) to those who do not materially participate who have enough passive income to offset their passive losses. Most individual investors in an R&D limited partnership cannot meet the "material participation" standard. As a general rule, an individual is not generally treated as materially participating in any activity of a limited partnership. I.R.C. § 469(h)(2). The regulations provide several exceptions in which a limited partner may be deemed to materially participate. *See* Treas. Reg. § 1.469-5T(e)(2) (referring to § 1.469-5T(a)(1), (a)(5), (a)(6)). Investors who do not materially participate in an R&D limited partnership can claim § 174 deductions only if they have enough passive income to offset the deduction. Unfortunately, many investors may not be able to generate sufficient passive income to take full advantage of the § 174 deductions.

In light of *Green* and other post-*Snow* cases, and in light of the impact of statutory hurtles, such as § 469, one may wonder whether R&D limited partnerships have any continuing utility. If an R&D limited partnership can demonstrate that it has a realistic prospect of entering into a trade or business involving the technology under development, § 174 deductions should be available to investors who materially participate or to those investors with passive income. To the extent individual investors in an R&D limited partnership have sufficient passive income to absorb research and development deductions, § 469 should not affect the investors. Even if individual investors have insufficient passive income in a particular year, the § 174 deductions will become available when the investor realizes passive income or when the technology developed is sold. Section 469 merely defers research and development deductions.

The following general tax rules apply to the formation, operation, and liquidation of R&D limited partnerships.

1. Formation of R&D Limited Partnerships
(a) Partner-Level Consequences

If an investor contributes money in exchange for a partnership interest, the tax consequences to the investor/partner are straightforward: (1) the partner will have no gain on the contribution; (2) the partner will have a basis in the partnership interest acquired equal to the amount of cash contributed; and (3) the partner's holding period in the partnership interest acquired will begin the day after the exchange. I.R.C. §§ 721, 722.

If an inventor transfers intellectual property (*e.g.*, preliminary technology or existing technological processes) in exchange for a partnership interest, no gain or loss is usually recognized. Section 721 provides that no gain or loss shall be recognized to partners upon a contribution of property to the partnership in exchange for a partnership interest. If § 721 applies to a contribution of property to a partnership, the reporting of gain or loss realized is postponed to a later year (*e.g.*, when the partnership interest received in the transaction is later sold or disposed of in a taxable transaction). Gain is preserved by generally giving the taxpayer the same basis in the property acquired as he or she had in the property given up in the transaction. In other words, the basis in a partnership interest ("outside basis") received in a § 721 non-recognition transaction will be determined by reference to the basis of the intellectual property transferred to the partnership. I.R.C. § 722. A partner's outside basis represents the partner's investment in the partnership, and is later adjusted upward for the partner's share of profits and downwards for the partner's share of loss. I.R.C. § 705. Because a taxpayer's basis in the partnership interest received in a nontaxable transaction is determined by reference to the taxpayer's basis in property given up, the taxpayer's holding period of the partnership interest received includes the holding period of the property given up. I.R.C. § 1223(1). The taxpayer's holding period in the partnership interest will be relevant for purposes of determining the character of any gain or loss upon the eventual taxable disposition of that property.

(b) Partnership-Level Consequences

Consistent with the tax treatment of corporations that issue stock for property, partnerships do not recognize gain or loss when they issue partnership interests in exchange for money or property. I.R.C. § 721. A partnership that receives property in exchange for its partnership interests in a nontaxable formation steps into the shoes of the transferor. Thus, an R&D limited partnership's basis in any intellectual property received in a § 721 exchange is the same as the transferor partner's basis. I.R.C. § 723. Because the contributed property has a transferred basis for the partnership, the transferor's holding period likewise carries over to the partnership. I.R.C. § 1223(2).

2. Operation of R&D Limited Partnerships
(a) Basic Structure of Partnership Taxation

R&D limited partnerships that elect to be classified as partnerships are not subject to the federal income tax. I.R.C. § 701. Instead, each partner reports his or her distributive or allocable share of partnership income, deductions, and other items on his or her individual tax return (*e.g.*, royalty income and § 174 deductions). A partner's distributive or allocable share of partnership items is determined by reference to the partnership agreement. I.R.C. § 704(a). Thus, partners have great flexibility in allocating tax items among themselves. A 50% partner does not necessarily have to report 50% of every kind of income and deduction generated by the partnership business. Rather, a partner's allocable share may be specified item-by-item, so that a partner might be allocated 30% of intellectual property royalties, but 50% of the partnership deductions. As should be expected, there are limitations. An important limitation is that a partner's distributive share reflected in the partnership agreement will not be given effect if it lacks "substantial economic effect." I.R.C. § 704(b); Treas. Reg. § 1.704-1(b)(2).

With respect to a partner's distributive share of deductions (such as § 174 deductions), a variety of additional limitations must be overcome before the tax benefit of those deductions flow through to the partners. An important loss limitation is that a partner's distributive share of partnership losses can be claimed on the partner's individual tax return only to the extent of the partner's adjusted basis in the partnership interest. I.R.C. § 704(d). Losses disallowed under this limitation are not lost forever, but are carried over to future years and taken when the partner's adjusted basis in the partnership interest can absorb them.

A partner's adjusted basis in his partnership interest is known as "outside basis." Outside basis represents the partner's investment in the partnership, and is adjusted upwards for the partner's share of profits and downwards for the partner's share of losses. I.R.C. § 733. An increase in a partner's share of partnership debt is treated as a deemed contribution of money by the partner to the partnership. I.R.C. § 752(a). A constructive contribution of cash to the partnership increases the partner's adjusted basis of his or her partnership interest. I.R.C. §§ 705(a), 722. As a result of including a partner's share of debt in his or her basis, greater opportunity exists for losses to pass through to the partner and for cash distributions to be received tax-free. The regulations under § 752 provide complex rules for determining how partnership debt is allocated among partners. See Treas. Reg. §§ 1.752-2, -3.

(b) Non-Liquidating Distributions of Cash and Property to Partners

No gain or loss is recognized on a distribution of cash (*e.g.*, royalties from exploitation of developed technology), unless the cash distribution exceeds the partner's adjusted basis in his partnership interest (outside basis). I.R.C. § 731(a)(1). A partner must recognize gain to the extent a cash distribution exceeds outside basis. The gain is treated as gain from the sale or exchange of the partnership interest and, thus, is typically capital gain unless § 751 applies. I.R.C. § 741. The partner's outside basis is adjusted downward, but not below zero, by the amount of the distribution. I.R.C. § 733.

In contrast to a distribution of cash, which may cause a partner to have gain, no gain or loss is generally recognized on a distribution of property to a partner by a partnership. I.R.C. § 731(a). The reason for the distinction is that a distribution of property, unlike a distribution of cash, provides an opportunity for deferral of gain. The partner's basis in the distributed property is a transferred basis (the same basis the partnership had in the property). I.R.C. § 732(a)(1). The partner's basis in his partnership interest (outside basis) is reduced by the amount of the transferred basis in the distributed property. I.R.C. § 733. The result is that the partner's pre-distribution outside basis is allocated between the partnership interest and the distributed property. In other words, the partner's overall basis is not changed, but is divided between the partnership interest and the newly acquired property.

A partner who contributes property to a partnership may have gain or loss if that contributed property is distributed to a non-contributing partner. See I.R.C. § 704(c)(1)(B). A partner who contributes appreciated property to a partnership will have gain if the partnership distributes other partnership property to him while the partnership continues to own the contributed property. See I.R.C. § 737.

A partnership recognizes no gain or loss on the distribution of cash or property. I.R.C. § 731(b).

3. Liquidation of R&D Limited Partnerships

A limited partner/investor who wishes to terminate his or her interest in an R&D limited partnership can either sell his or her interest to the remaining partners or to a third party or can liquidate his or her interest in the partnership in exchange for partnership property.

The sale of a limited partnership interest is taxed under the general non-partnership rules governing sales and exchanges of property. I.R.C. § 741. The transferor partner will have gain or loss on the sale of the partnership interest. The amount realized on the sale includes money received, as well as relief of the transferor-partner's share of partnership liabilities. I.R.C. § 752(d). Adjusted basis is the partner's adjusted basis in his partnership interest. The gain or loss is capital gain unless the look-through rules of § 751 apply. Section 751 comes into play if the partnership has ordinary income assets, such as receivables and inventory, and may cause the taxpayer to bifurcate the overall gain or loss between ordinary income and capital gain components. Treas. Reg. § 1.751-1(a). The buying partner takes a cost basis for a partnership interest acquired by purchase, which includes the partner's share of any partnership liabilities. I.R.C. §§ 742, 752(d).

Payments made to a partner in liquidation of the partner's interest are taxed pursuant to the rules of § 736. See I.R.C. § 761(d). Section 736 classifies payments made in liquidation of a partnership interest into two categories: (1) Payments in the first category are liquidating distributions that are attributable to the retiring partner's interest in most partnership property; and (2) Payments in the second category are those attributable to the partner's share of unrealized receivables and payments for unstated goodwill in liquidation of a general partner's interest in a partnership in which capital is not a material income-producing factor. I.R.C. § 736. Payments in the first category, which is the broader category of the two, are taxed under the same rules applicable to operating distributions. No gain or loss is recognized by the partner with respect to cash distributions, unless the cash distribution exceeds the partner's adjusted basis in his partnership interest (outside basis). I.R.C. § 731(a)(1). A partner must recognize gain to the extent a cash distribution exceeds outside basis. The gain is treated as gain from the sale or exchange of the partnership interest and, thus, is typically capital gain unless § 751 applies. See I.R.C. § 741. No gain or loss is recognized on a distribution of property to a partner by a partnership. I.R.C. § 731(a). The partner's basis in the distributed property is generally a transferred basis (the same basis the partnership had in the property). I.R.C. § 732(a)(1).

IV. Materials

Delaware State Statute
Del. Code Ann. tit. 30, § 1902

§ 1902 Imposition of tax on corporations; exemptions.

(a) Every domestic or foreign corporation that is not exempt under subsection (b) of this section shall annually pay a tax of 8.7 percent on its taxable income, computed in accordance with § 1903 of this title, which shall be deemed to be its net income derived from business activities carried on and property located within the State during the income year. Any receiver, referee, trustee, assignee or other fiduciary or any officer or agent appointed by any court who conducts the business of any corporation shall be subject to the tax imposed by this chapter in the same manner and to the same extent as if the business were conducted by the corporation.

(b) The following corporations shall be exempt from taxation under this chapter:

. . . . .

(8) Corporations whose activities within this State are confined to the maintenance and management of their intangible investments or of the intangible investments of corporations or statutory trusts or business trusts registered as investment companies under the Investment Company Act of 1940, as amended (15 U.S.C. 80a-1 et seq.) and the collection and distribution of the income from such investments or from tangible property physically located outside this State. For purposes of this paragraph, "intangible investments" shall include, without limitation, investments in stocks, bonds, notes and other debt obligations (including debt obligations of affiliated corporations), patents, patent applications, trademarks, trade names and similar types of intangible assets;

Vermont State Statute
Vt. Stat. Ann. tit. 32, § 5837

§ 5837 Investment and holding companies

The tax imposed by this subchapter as it applies to corporations whose activities are confined to the maintenance and management of their intangible investments and the collection and distribution of the income from such investments or from tangible property physically located outside this state shall not exceed the $150.00 minimum tax provided by section 5832 of this title. For purposes of this section "intangible investments" shall include without limitation investments in stocks, bonds, notes and other debt obligations (including debt obligations of affiliated corporations), patents, patent applications, copyrights, trademarks, trade names and similar types of intangible assets.

Massachusetts State Statute
M.G.L.A. 62C § 3A (West 2003)

§ 3A. Disallowance of sham transactions and related doctrines; burden on taxpayer to show business purpose and economic substance commensurate with claimed tax benefit.

In applying the laws referred to in section 2, the commissioner may, in his discretion, disallow the asserted tax consequences of a transaction by asserting the application of the sham transaction doctrine or any other related tax doctrine, in which case the taxpayer shall have the burden of demonstrating by clear and convincing evidence as determined by the commissioner that the transaction possessed both: (i) a valid, good-faith business purpose other than tax avoidance; and (ii) economic substance apart from the asserted tax benefit. In all such cases, the taxpayer shall also have the burden of demonstrating by clear and convincing evidence as determined by the commissioner that the asserted nontax business purpose is commensurate with the tax benefit claimed. Nothing in this section shall be construed to limit or negate the commissioner's authority to make tax adjustments as otherwise permitted by law.

(Effective March 5, 2003 for tax years beginning on or after January 1, 2002).

Geoffrey, Inc. v. South Carolina Tax Commission
437 S.E.2d 13 (S.C. 1993)

HARWELL, CHIEF JUSTICE:

Geoffrey, Inc. (Geoffrey), a foreign corporation, appeals from a ruling that requires it to pay South Carolina income tax and business license fees. We affirm.

I. FACTS

Geoffrey is a wholly-owned, second-tier subsidiary of Toys R Us, Inc. (Toys R Us) incorporated in Delaware with its principal offices in that state. It has no employees or offices in South Carolina and owns no tangible property here.

In 1984, Geoffrey became the owner of several valuable trademarks and trade names, including "Toys R Us." Laterthat year, Geoffrey executed a License Agreement (Agreement) that allows Toys R Us to use the "Toys R Us" trade name, as well as other trademarks and trade names, in all states except New York, Texas, Pennsylvania, Massachusetts, and New Jersey. The Agreement further grants Toys R Us a right to use Geoffrey's merchandising skills, techniques, and "know-how" in connection with marketing, promotion, advertising, and sale of products covered by the Agreement.

As consideration for the licenses granted by the Agreement, Geoffrey receives a royalty of one percent "of the net sales by [Toys R Us], or any of its affiliated, associated, or subsidiary companies, of the Licensed Products sold or the Licensed Services rendered under the Licensed Mark." Toys R Us reports the aggregate sales of all stores to Geoffrey in a single figure on a monthly basis. The royalty payment is made annually via wire transfer from a Toys R Us account in Pennsylvania to a Geoffrey account in New York.[1]

Toys R Us began doing business in South Carolina in 1985 and has since then made royalty payments to Geoffrey based on South Carolina sales. In 1986 and 1987, Toys R Us deducted the royalty payments made to Geoffrey from its South Carolina taxable income. The South Carolina Tax Commission (Commission) initially disallowed the deduction, but later took the position that Toys R Us was entitled to the deduction and that Geoffrey was required to pay South Carolina income tax on the royalty income. The Commission also held that Geoffrey was required to pay the South Carolina corporate license fee.

---

1. The net effect of this corporate structure has been the production of "nowhere" income that escapes all state income taxation. *See* Rosen, *Use of a Delaware Holding Company to Save State Income Taxes,* 20 Tax Adviser 180 (1989). One commentator has recognized such income as the "product of a divide and conquer strategy that some members of the corporate world have exercised effectively for decades." Corrigan, *Interstate Corporate Income Taxation—Recent Revolutions and a Modern Response,* 29 Vand.L.Rev. 423, 429 (1976). The strategy's effectiveness is unquestionable. In 1990, Geoffrey, without any full-time employees, had an income of approximately $55 million and paid no income taxes to any state.

Geoffrey paid the taxes under protest and filed this action for a refund, claiming, among other things, that it did not do business in South Carolina and that it did not have a sufficient nexus with South Carolina for its royalty income to be taxable here. The trial judge upheld the Commission's assessment of taxes against Geoffrey. Geoffrey appealed.

II. DISCUSSION

S.C.Code Ann. § 12-7-230 (Supp.1992), pursuant to which both foreign and domestic corporations are taxed, provides:

> [E]xcept as otherwise provided, every foreign corporation transacting, conducting, doing business, or having an income within the jurisdiction of this State, whether or not the corporation is engaged in or the income derived from intrastate, interstate, or foreign commerce, shall make a return and shall pay annually an income tax equivalent to five percent of a proportion of its entire net income, to be determined as provided in this chapter. The term "transacting," "conducting," or "doing business," as used in this section, includes the engaging in or the transacting of any activity in this State for the purpose of financial profit or gain.

Section 12-7-230 levies a tax on the income of foreign corporations "transacting, conducting, doing business, or having an income *within the jurisdiction of this State*," which "includes," but is not limited to, "theengaging in or the transacting of any activity in this State for the purpose of financial profit or gain." We construe this language as extending to the limits of the constitution South Carolina's authority to tax foreign corporations. Here, Geoffrey contends that the Due Process Clause, U.S. Const. amend. XIV, § 1, and the Commerce Clause, U.S. Const. art. I, § 8, cl. 3, prohibit the taxation of its royalty income by South Carolina. We disagree.

A. Due Process

The Due Process Clause requires "some definite link, some minimum connection, between a state and the person, property or transaction it seeks to tax," and that the "income attributed to the state for tax purposes must be rationally related to values connected with the taxing State." *Quill Corp. v. North Dakota*, 504 U.S. 298, 112 S.Ct. 1904, 1909–10 (1992). Geoffrey argues that the Commission has failed to satisfy both of these requirements. We disagree.

The nexus requirement of the Due Process Clause can be satisfied even where the corporation has no physical presence in the taxing state if the corporation has purposefully directed its activity at the state's economic forum. *Quill,* 112 S.Ct. at 1909–10. Geoffrey asserts that it has not purposefully directed its activities toward South Carolina. To support its position, Geoffrey points out that Toys R Us had no South Carolina stores when it entered into the Agreement and urges, therefore, that Toys R Us's subsequent expansion into South Carolina was unilateral activity that cannot create the minimum connection between Geoffrey and South Carolina required by due process.

In our view, Geoffrey has not been unwillingly brought into contact with South Carolina through the unilateral activity of an independent party. Geoffrey's business is the ownership, licensing, and management of trademarks, trade names, and franchises. By electing to license its trademarks and trade names for use by Toys R Us in many states, Geoffrey contemplated and purposefully sought the benefit of economic contact with those states. Geoffrey has been aware of, consented to, and benefitted from Toys R Us's use of Geoffrey's intangibles in South Carolina. Moreover, Geoffrey had the ability to control its contact with South Carolina by prohibiting the use of its intangibles here as it did with other states. We reject Geoffrey's claim that it has not purposefully directed its activities toward South Carolina's economic forum and hold that by licensing intangibles for use in South Carolina and receiving income in exchange for their use, Geoffrey has the "minimum connection" with this State that is required by due process. See *American Dairy Queen Corp. v. Taxation and Revenue Dep't,* 93 N.M. 743, 605 P.2d 251 (1979); *AAMCO Transmissions, Inc. v. Taxation and Revenue Dep't,* 93 N.M. 389, 600 P.2d 841, *cert. denied,* 598 P.2d 1165 (1979).

In addition to our finding that Geoffrey purposefully directed its activities toward South Carolina, we find that the "minimum connection" required by due process also is satisfied by the presence of Geoffrey's intangible property in this State. Geoffrey's Secretary, a certified public accountant, agreed during cross examination that sales by Toys R Us in South Carolina create an account receivable for Geoffrey. In addition, the trial judge found that Geoffrey had a franchise in South Carolina. That the presence of these intangibles is sufficient to sustain a tax is settled law. In *Virginia v. Imperial Coal Sales Co., Inc.,* 293 U.S. 15 (1934), the United States Supreme Court stated:

> It is not the character of the property that makes it subject to such a tax, but the fact that the property has a situs within the state and that the owner should give appropriate support to the government that protects it. That duty is not less when the property is intangible than when it is tangible. Nor are we able to perceive any sound reason for holding that the owner must have real estate or tangible property within the state in order to subject its intangible property within the state to taxation.

Geoffrey asserts that under the doctrine of *mobilia sequuntur personam,* the situs of its intangibles is its corporate headquarters in Delaware, not South Carolina. However, in *Mobil Oil Corp. v. Comm'r of Taxes of Vermont,* 445 U.S. 425 (1980), the United States Supreme Court rejected the view that the constitution requires taxation of intangibles by allocation to a *single* situs, finding no adequate justification for preferring that rule over taxation by apportionment. The High Court concluded that:

> [a]lthough a fictionalized situs of intangible property sometimes has been invoked to avoid multiple taxation of ownership, there is nothing talismanic about the concepts of "business situs" or "commercial domicile" that automatically renders those concepts applicable when taxation of income from intangibles is at issue. The Court has observed that the maxim *mobilia sequuntur personam,* upon which these fictions of situs are based, "states a rule without disclosing the reasons for it." The Court has also recognized that "the reason for a single place of taxation no longer obtains" when the taxpayer's activities with respect to the intangible property involve relations with more than one jurisdiction. Even for property or franchise taxes, apportionment of intangible values is not unknown. Moreover, cases upholding allocation to a single situs for property tax purposes have distinguished income tax situations where the apportionment principle prevails. (Citations omitted).

Id. at 445. *See also Wheeling Steel Corp. v. Fox,* 298 U.S. 193 (1936) (intangibles may acquire a situs for taxation other than at the domicile of the owner if they have become integral parts of some local business); *Southern Express Co. v. Spigener,* 118 S.C. 413, 110 S.E. 403 (1920) (the situs of intangible property is within this State if the right afforded by it is exercised here); Dexter, *Taxation of Income from Intangibles of Multistate-Multinational Corporations,* 29 Vand.L.Rev. 401 (1976); J. Hellerstein & W. Hellerstein, *State Taxation,* Para. 9.08-.09 (2d ed. 1992). We reject Geoffrey's claim that its intangible assets are located exclusively in Delaware. Accordingly, we find that Geoffrey's purposeful direction of activity toward South Carolina as well as its possessing intangible property here provide a definite link between South Carolina and the income derived by Geoffrey from the use of its trademarks and trade names in this State.

We also find that the second prong of *Quill* test has been met. Contrary to Geoffrey's assertion, South Carolina has conferred benefits upon Geoffrey to which the challenged tax is rationally related. As the United States Supreme Court recognized in *Curry v. McCanless,* 307 U.S. 357, 365–66 (1939):

> Very different considerations, both theoretical and practical, apply to the taxation of intangibles, that is, rights which are not related to physical things. Such rights are but relationships between persons, natural or corporate, which the law recognizes by attaching to them certain sanctions enforceable in courts. The power of government over them and the protection which it gives them cannot be exerted through control of a physical thing. *They can be made effective only through control over and protection afforded to those persons whose relationships are the origin of the rights....* Obviously, as sources of actual or potential wealth—which is an appropriate measure of any tax imposed on ownership or its exercise—*they cannot be dissociated from the persons from whose relationships they are derived.* (Citations omitted). (Emphasis added).

The real source of Geoffrey's income is not a paper agreement, but South Carolina's Toys R Us customers. *Cf. Avco Financial Services Consumer Discount Co. v. Director, Division of Taxation,* 100 N.J. 27, 494 A.2d 788 (1985). By providing an orderly society in which Toys R Us conducts business, South Carolina has made it possible for Geoffrey to earn income pursuant to the royalty agreement. *See, e.g., Allied-Signal v. Comm'r of Finance,* 580 N.Y.S.2d 696, 588 N.E.2d 731 (1991) (benefits afforded to an in-state corporation inure to non-resident shareholders). That Geoffrey has received protection, benefits, and opportunities from South Carolina is manifested by the fact that it earns income in this state. *Accord AAMCO,* 93 N.M. at 393, 600 P.2d at 845 (quoting *Besser Co. v. Bureau of Revenue,* 74 N.M. 377, 394 P.2d 141 (1964)). That the tax is rationally related to these protections, benefits, and opportunities is evidenced by the fact that the State seeks to tax only that portion of Geoffrey's income generated within its borders. Based on the foregoing reasons, we hold that the Due Process Clause does not prohibit South Carolina's taxation of Geoffrey's royalty income.

B. Commerce Clause

A tax will survive challenge under the Commerce Clause so long as it 1) is applied to an activity with a substantial nexus with the taxing state, 2) is fairly apportioned, 3) does not discriminate against interstate commerce, and 4) is fairly related to the services provided by the State. *Complete Auto Transit, Inc. v. Brady,* 430 U.S. 274, 279 (1977). Relying on *Nat'l Bellas Hess, Inc. v. Dep't of Revenue of Ill.,* 386 U.S. 753 (1967), Geoffrey contends that it does not have a substantial nexus with South Carolina because it is not physically present in this state. In our view, Geoffrey's reliance on the physical presence requirement of *Bellas Hess* is misplaced.[2]

It is well settled that the taxpayer need not have a tangible, physical presence in a state for income to be taxable there. The presence of intangible property alone is suffi-

---

2. The U.S. Supreme Court recently revisited the physical presence requirement of *Bellas Hess* and, while reaffirming its vitality as to *sales and use taxes,* noted that the physical presence requirement had not been extended to other types of taxes. *Quill,* 112 S.Ct. at 1914.

cient to establish nexus. *American Dairy Queen*, 93 N.M. at 747, 605 P.2d at 255. *See also Int'l Harvester Co. v. Wisconsin Dep't of Taxation*, 322 U.S. 435, 441–442 (1944) (a state may tax such part of the income of a non-resident as is fairly attributable either to property located in the state or to events or transactions which, occurring there, are within the protection of the state and entitled to the numerous other benefits which its confers); J. Hellerstein & W. Hellerstein, *supra*, at 6.08 (any corporation that regularly exploits the markets of a state should be subject to its jurisdiction to impose an income tax even though not physically present). A taxpayer who is domiciled in one state but carries on business in another is subject to taxation measured by the value of the intangibles used in his business. *Curry*, 307 U.S. at 368. We hold that by licensing intangibles for use in this State and deriving income from their use here, Geoffrey has a "substantial nexus" with South Carolina.

Geoffrey finally contends that even if it is subject to South Carolina income tax, all of its royalty income would be allocated or apportioned to Delaware pursuant to S.C.Code Ann. §§ 12-7-1120(5) or 12-7-1140 (1977 and Supp.1992). These statutes are inapplicable to the income received by Geoffrey. Section 12-7-1120(5) allocates gains or losses from the sale of intangible personal property not connected with the business of the taxpayer, other than any intangible personal property held for sale to customers in the regular course of business. Section 12-7-1140 apportions the income of taxpayers whose principal business in this State is (a) manufacturing or any form of collecting, buying, assembling or processing goods and materials within this State, or (b) selling, distributing or dealing in tangible personal property within this State.

In conclusion, we hold that the taxation of Geoffrey's royalty income pursuant to section 12-7-230 is not prohibited by the Due Process Clause or the Commerce Clause of the United States Constitution. Our finding that Geoffrey may be taxed pursuant to section 12-7-230 settles the question whether Geoffrey must pay the corporate license fee. All corporations subject to section 12-7-230 are required to do so. *See* S.C.Code Ann. §§ 12-19-20, 12-19-70 (1977 & Supp.1992). The order of the trial judge is affirmed.

Acme Royalty Co. v. Director of Revenue
96 S.W.3d 72 (Missouri 2003)

WHITE, JUDGE:

The Director of Revenue assessed Acme Royalty Company ("ARC" or "Acme") and Brick Investment Company ("BIC"), collectively ("Appellants"), for income derived from the licensing of trademarks and trade names to a related corporation for the annual tax periods from 1992–96. Similarly, the Director assessed Gore Enterprise Holdings, Inc. ("Gore") for income derived from royalties received from a related company as a result of patents held by Gore for the tax periods from 1993–95. Acme, BIC and Gore each challenged the assessment.

The Administrative Hearing Commission ("AHC") ruled against the taxpayers, finding that they were subject to Missouri income tax. The taxpayers seek review, and the cases are consolidated for opinion.[3] Review of this case will necessarily involve the con-

---

3. Although the specific factual situation in each case is different, the legal question to be decided is identical. The Acme case will be the focus of this consolidated opinion, and there will be no separate discussion of the facts as they relate to Gore Holdings.

struction of the revenue laws of this state. As such this Court has exclusive jurisdiction. The decision of the AHC is reversed and remanded.

II.

Acme Royalty Company and Brick Investment Company are separate though related entities that have exclusive licensing contracts with Acme Brick Company ("ABC"), which is also a related company. ABC conducts a portion of its business in Missouri. ABC was formed in 1891, and since that time its principal business has been the manufacturing and distribution of clay bricks and other related building products. In 1968, ABC merged with Justin Boot Company, forming First Worth Company, which in turn became Justin Industries Inc. ("Justin"). Justin undertook a complete corporate reorganization in December 1991, separately incorporating its Acme brick company division under the name ABC. Justin transferred all of the assets of its brick company division to ABC; in exchange, Justin received all of the stock in ABC. Acme was also a result of Justin's reorganization. Similar to the creation of ABC, Justin transferred all of its trademarks[4] to Acme in exchange for all of the stock in Acme. Acme and ABC were incorporated in the state of Delaware.

Acme subsequently entered into an exclusive licensing agreement with ABC that assigned the exclusive use of the trademarks owned by Acme to ABC. The agreement, which became effective January 1, 1992, provided that ABC would pay royalties to Acme for the use of the trademarks owned by that company. The amount of the royalty payment to ARC was to be equal to a percentage of the net sales of the licensed merchandise during each contract year.

In December 1993, Acme Royalty Company Limited Partnership ("ARCLP") was formed. Acme attained a 99% limited partnership interest in ARCLP in exchange for the contribution of its trademarks. Brick Investment Company was formed for the purpose of becoming the general partner in ARCLP. BIC transferred to ARCLP the cash equivalent of one-percent of the value of the trademarks contributed by Acme in exchange for a one percent general partnership interest in ARCLP. As general partner, BIC was responsible for the day-to-day operations of ARCLP. ARCLP has held the Trademarks since its formation in 1994.

Since their formation, Acme and BIC have collectively received over $34 million in royalty payments. As a result of an audit of Missouri taxpayer ABC, the Director learned of the existence of Acme and BIC. The Director determined that Appellants were subject to Missouri income tax on their royalty income, attributing ABC's sales in Missouri to the Appellants as income from wholly within Missouri.

Pursuant to the audit of ABC, the Director issued notices of deficiency to the Appellants, assessing Missouri income tax based on Acme's receipt of royalties from ABC and on ARCLP's receipt of the royalties after its formation. Appellants protested the notices of deficiency. The Director upheld the assessments, and in its findings of fact and conclusions of law, the AHC agreed with the Director, upholding the assessments.

III.

The dispositive point of this appeal is the exclusive licensing agreement between ARC and ABC, the payments that resulted, and whether those payments constitute sales in

---

4. The trademarks in question are: "Acme"; "Acme Brick"; "Acme Brick and Design"; "Acme Brick. The Best Thing to Have Around your House"; "Acme Everset"; "Everlast"; "Acmeseal 85"; and "Thinwall Fences".

the State of Missouri attributable to the Appellants. This Court finds that Appellants had no Missouri source income because they had no sales in Missouri.

Section 143.431.1 states "The taxable income of a corporation...shall be so much of its federal taxable income...as is derived from sources within Missouri as provided in section 143.451." Section 143.451 begins with a restatement of the rule that "Missouri taxable income of a corporation shall include all income derived form sources within this state." The section then goes on to explain the allocation of income derived partially within and partially outside the state, but fails to give a further definition of the phrase "derived from sources within this state." Accordingly, this Court looks to its prior decisions to determine whether the Appellant's income in question is Missouri source income.

The basic requirement for there to be Missouri source income is that there is some activity by the *taxpayer* in Missouri that justifies imposing the tax. Although corporate activities can be immeasurably diverse, for multi-state income tax purposes they fall into three succinct categories: property, payroll and sales. While Appellants are "related" to ABC, a Delaware corporation that conducts business and pays taxes in Missouri, they are separate legal entities, and as such each must have its own property, payroll or sales in Missouri to be taxed in Missouri.

The Director's brief states that having property, payroll or sales is not a requirement for taxation when the transactions are between related companies. In an attempt to distinguish the holding in *Central Cooling & Supply Co. v. Director of Rev.*, 648 S.W.2d 546 (Mo. banc 1983), the Director asserts that the case stands only for the principle that common ownership will not allow a corporation to avoid the tax consequences arising from the creation of separate corporate entities. While the holding in *Central Cooling*, does stand for that principal, it undoubtedly must also stand for the reverse. The corporate subdivision instituted by the Appellants created separate legal entities, and they should be treated as such.

As this Court has previously held, in order for the Appellants to be liable for taxes in Missouri, *they* must have had some activity: property, payroll, or sales, in the State of Missouri. ARC is a Delaware corporation; all of its offices, board meetings and employees are located or held in Delaware. Appellant BIC is also a Delaware corporation; it holds its board meetings in Fort Worth, Texas, and pays taxes in that state.

Aside from the current litigation, neither ARC, BIC, nor ARCLP has ever done business, owned property, maintained employees or agents, conducted sales or distributed payroll in Missouri. The licensing agreement between the Appellants and ABC was negotiated and executed entirely outside of the state of Missouri. In addition to the licensing agreement, the Appellants have absolutely no sales—in Missouri or elsewhere—because they sell no products at all. The income the Director attempts to reach is outside the scope of Missouri taxation because the Appellants have no contact, and specifically no sales, within the state.

IV.

The decisions of the AHC are *reversed*, and the cases are *remanded*.

MICHAEL A. WOLFF, Judge, *dissenting*.

The economic reality of these cases is simple. The "taxpayers"—or, in light of the result here, perhaps one should say the tax-evaders—are entities that own intellectual property, i.e., patent and trademark rights. These entities, sited in Delaware, license these rights to related corporations that manufacture products sold in Missouri. One holds patents on "Goretex" fabric for outdoor clothing. The other entity holds trademark rights to "Acme" bricks. Without the participation of these "taxpayers," the Gore clothing would not repel water while "breathing" and the Acme product would be a mere unadorned brick. Thus, these "taxpayers" own the intellectual property essential to the products as they are marketed and sold in Missouri. The income derived from sales in this state is Missouri-source income.

It defies economic reality to hold that income derived from the Missouri market—in which these "taxpayers" participate through their related manufacturing companies—is not taxable here.

Corporate Reorganizations to Avoid Taxes

One of the great achievements of the legal profession in the past two centuries has been the development and creative use of the corporation. The corporate entity as a separate person is a legal fiction essential to the development of the modern capitalistic society. The invention of the modern corporation allows investors to aggregate capital while risking only their investments, not their own personal resources beyond the amounts invested. The fundamental concept is that the investor and the corporation are different "persons" so that a mere investor is not personally responsible for the liabilities of the corporation.

The overarching question in these cases is whether the Missouri tax statute, section 143.451.1, which taxes "all income derived from sources within this state," permits this salutary legal fiction to be used perversely for avoiding legitimate taxes imposed by the state of Missouri.

In both these cases, the corporate reorganization appears to be simply for tax avoidance. It starts with a company that makes something—bricks, clothing products, or whatever. The making of the product involves two things: the intellectual property (patent or trademark) and the physical product itself. Before the corporate reorganizations here, the same company owned both the intellectual property and the means of production. The manufacturing companies made and sold their products but did not pay royalties to themselves.

But what if a "separate" person owns the intellectual property, i.e., the patents or trademarks? If a separate person holds the intellectual property, such as an inventor who holds a patent, the separate person would be entitled to charge royalties to the person making the product, and the royalty payments would be deducted from the manufacturer's taxable income.

But in the case of Gore or Acme, what would be the incentive to create a "separate" person to own the intellectual property? How about a "person" that "lives" in a place where there are no taxes to pay on income?

So, here's the tax avoidance scheme: First, a manufacturing corporation creates a separate person in a state (or foreign country, for that matter) that does not tax that person's income. Second, the manufacturer assigns the patent or trademark to the new person, essentially for free. Third, the manufacturer agrees to pay the new "person" royalties for use of the patent or trademark.

To those of us who are unabashed admirers of the modern corporation, this kind of creativity may seem to be an unremarkable use of the corporate fiction. But here is a kicker: the royalty agreement is structured so that most if not all of the manufacturer's profits—but not one cent in excess of the profits—are paid to the "separate" person.

This new "person"—which received the patent or trademark rights for free—then claims that it has no connection with Missouri and owes Missouri no tax on the income it derived from sales of the products in Missouri.

This certainly is clever, but it is absurd to say that Missouri cannot tax the income derived from economic activity conducted on behalf of these "taxpayers" in this state. The income is, in the words of section 143.451.1, "derived from sources within this state." There is nothing in the record seriously to suggest that this corporate reorganization is for some legitimate purpose other to disguise the fact that this income from the manufacture and sale of the taxpayers' products in Missouri is subject to Missouri taxation.

Facts: The Gore and Acme Corporate Structures

W.L. Gore (Gore) sells its goods, which include "Goretex" and other synthetic materials, in Missouri and other states. Gore is registered to do business in Missouri and files Missouri income tax returns. In 1983, Gore formed "Gore Enterprise Holdings" (Holdings) as a holding company for its patents. Holdings is a Delaware corporation that, for two of three tax periods at issue, had no employees or offices of its own. Holdings' activities, which consisted of collecting royalty payments, were conducted by Gore's employees at Gore's offices. For the third tax period at issue, Holdings rented 120 square feet of space, which held a desk, chair, computer and file cabinet, to house its sole employee, a paralegal.

Gore transferred to Holdings all of its patents in return for Holdings' stock. Holdings then licensed those patents to Gore exclusively in exchange for royalty payments totaling 7.5% of the sales price of all products Gore made in the United States and sold for use in the United States. Seven and one-half percent conveniently amounts to the approximate total of profits Gore historically made on these products. In no event, however, could the royalty payments made by Gore to Holdings exceed Gore's net income.

Acme Brick employed a similar reorganization scheme. Acme Brick formed Acme Royalty Company (Acme Royalty) in 1991 to manage its trademarks.[5] Acme Brick paid Acme Royalty a portion of its sales in exchange for use of the trademarks in connection with its manufacture, sale and distribution of merchandise within Missouri. Like Holdings, Acme Royalty is a Delaware corporation that, during part of the tax period in question, shared approximately 1,100 square feet of office space with 40 other companies and employed one individual who spent two hours monthly on Acme Royalty business. This individual served as officer and director for Acme Royalty, as well as 20 to 30 other companies. Acme Brick paid Missouri income tax but was allowed a deduction for royalties paid to Acme Royalty.

A Tax Avoidance Trend

Using this corporate reorganization, these corporations shifted income taxable in Missouri to Delaware, where income from patents and trademarks is tax-free. The Missouri Director of Revenue aptly describes this recent trend in tax avoidance: "[A] bare corporate change can make income that is taxable today not taxable tomorrow." The result is the creation of so-called "nowhere income"—income that is taxed in no state.

---

5. In 1993, Acme Royalty became a limited partnership in which it contributed all of the trademarks and trade names it owned in exchange for 99% interest in the partnership. Brick Investment Company (BIC) was formed to be the general partner. BIC contributed cash in an amount estimated to be one percent of the value of the trademarks in exchange for one percent general partnership interest.

"Nowhere income," it might be noted, is not just affecting individual states. The *Wall Street Journal* reports that the Internal Revenue Service is also concerned about loss of federal income tax. Companies set up offshore subsidiaries so they can transfer royalties from sales of products made outside the United States to places like Bermuda. Glenn R. Simpson, *A New Twist in Tax Avoidance: Firms Send Best Ideas Abroad*, WALL ST. J., June 24, 2002, at A1. The *Journal* reports that more than two dozen pharmaceutical and computer companies have set up subsidiaries in Bermuda. *Id.* "The transfer of intellectual property—such as trademarks and patents—has become so widespread that it has prompted an aggressive crackdown by the Internal Revenue Service on alleged abuses that one IRS consultant says could eventually involve tax claims in the tens of billions of dollars." *Id.*

By moving their profits to places where such income is not taxable, companies are avoiding taxation in places such as Missouri where those profits were derived. These companies argue that they should be immune from income taxation because they have no connection or nexus to the taxing state.

The Missouri Connection

Missouri taxable income of a corporation "shall include all income derived from sources within this state." Section 143.451.1.

Holdings and Acme Royalty argue that the royalty income is derived from the license agreement, which has no Missouri connection. However, the source of income to Holdings and Acme Royalty is not merely a written license agreement. The two derive income from the use of the intellectual property, which is an essential ingredient in the products sold in Missouri. The products sold in Missouri are just as much a result of the patents and trademarks as they are the result of the physical manufacturing processes. In both cases, Goretex clothing and Acme bricks, the source of income is Missouri's Gore and Acme Brick customers. Gore Enterprise Holdings does not make a cent until Gore makes a sale. Acme Royalty and Acme Brick have the same relationship. Missouri sales produce income for Holdings and Acme Royalty; thus, this income is taxable because it is derived from sources within Missouri—Missouri customers.

The tax avoidance scheme that has been endorsed by the principal opinion here was apparently first detected and snuffed out by the taxing authority and the Supreme Court of South Carolina in *Geoffrey, Inc. v. South Carolina Tax Commission*, 313 S.C. 15, 437 S.E.2d 13 (1993). In *Geoffrey, Inc.*, the well-known toy store, Toys R Us, formed a subsidiary in Delaware named Geoffrey to own its trademarks and trade names. Geoffrey had no offices, employees or tangible property in South Carolina. As in the instant cases, Geoffrey executed a license agreement allowing Toys R Us to use its trademarks and trade name. In return, Geoffrey received a royalty of one percent of Toys R Us' net sales. In 1990, Geoffrey had no full-time employees and had an approximate income of $55 million, paying no income tax to any state.

In finding that Geoffrey's royalty income was subject to South Carolina income tax, the court found that "[t]he real source of Geoffrey's income is not a paper agreement, but South Carolina's Toys R Us customers." *Id.* at 18. This Court should apply the *Geoffrey* principle here. The real source of income for Holdings and Acme Royalty is Missouri's Gore and Acme Brick customers—a relationship that is made possible in part by Missouri's business infrastructure and legal protections. "By providing an orderly society in which Toys R Us conducts business, South Carolina has made it possible for Geoffrey to earn income pursuant to the royalty agreement," the South Carolina court aptly concluded. "That Geoffrey has received protection, benefits, and opportunities from South Carolina is manifested by the fact that it earns income in this state." *Id.*

Missouri's Director of Revenue seeks to tax only that portion of income generated within Missouri's borders. As in South Carolina, this coincides with the notion that assessment of tax is rationally related to the protections the state provides. Missouri, like South Carolina, provides a place that allows these companies to produce their only form of income.

The "taxpayers," Holdings and Acme Royalty, derive economic benefit from the protection of the Missouri marketplace. Their intellectual properties, the patent and trademark rights, are part of the products that are sold. Or put another way, the manufacturing companies are the vehicle through which the "taxpayers" get money from Missouri for their properties. Missouri not only creates a marketplace for these products, including their licenses, but also affords legal protections to these "taxpayers." For instance, if a company were to sell "Goretex" products or "Acme" bricks in Missouri without licenses from these "taxpayers," there is no doubt that these "taxpayers" could use Missouri courts to enforce their rights to the intellectual property.

Missouri offers a market to these companies for making money from their licenses through their related manufacturing companies. Missouri, accordingly, is due tax from income that is derived within its borders from its citizens.

Doing Business in Missouri

Section 143.441.1(1) defines a corporation subject to Missouri taxation to include "... every corporation, association, joint stock company, and joint stock association, licensed to do business in this state, or doing business in this state, and not organized, authorized, or existing under the laws of this state...." Both Holdings and Acme Royalty argue that they did nothing in Missouri and that the director's focus is instead on the conduct of Gore and Acme Brick.

However, a taxpayer need not have a tangible, physical presence within a state for income to be taxable there. It is not necessary for Holdings and Acme Royalty to be the actual "seller" of the goods for Missouri to tax the income they receive from the sales. It is enough that the transactions, from which Holdings and Acme Royalty receive income, occur in Missouri and, thus, are subject to state regulation and protection. The controlling principle is set forth in *Int'l Harvester Co. v. Wisconsin Dep't of Taxation*, 322 U.S. 435, 441–42 (1944), where the United States Supreme Court said: "A state may tax such part of the income of a non-resident as is fairly attributable either to property located in the state or to events or transactions which, occurring there, are subject to state regulation and which are within the protection of the state and entitled to the numerous other benefits which it confers."

For these reasons, I would find, as did the South Carolina Supreme Court, that this "nowhere" income is properly taxable somewhere. And one of those places is the State of Missouri.[6]

---

6. A simple alternative would seem to be available, though the director of revenue did not pursue it in these cases. Even if Gore Enterprise Holdings and Acme Royalty are not subject to Missouri tax, as the principal opinion holds, the director does have tax returns from W.L. Gore and Acme Brick, which paid their profits as royalty fees to these supposedly untouchable holding companies. Perhaps the director should disallow the deduction of such royalty payments by W.L. Gore and Acme Brick and tax their Missouri income accordingly. That appears to be authorized by section

This is not a case where Gore, for example, is paying royalties to inventors who created and patented their product materials. Holdings created nothing. Gore created Holdings to shield Gore's profits from taxation. The same is true of the trademark rights held by Acme Royalty. These profits, derived from sales to Missouri customers but siphoned off to related companies through royalty agreements, are subject to the state's tax.

The modern corporation is an invention that lawyers can rightly be proud of. But the result reached here by the principal opinion rewards this invention inappropriately. The legal fiction of the corporation should not override economic reality.

The bottom line, economic reality is simple: These companies earn money in Missouri. Under section 143.451.1, they should pay taxes here.

SYL v. Comptroller of the Treasury
1999 WL 322666 (Md. Tax Ct. Apr. 26, 1999)

SYL, Inc. (hereinafter "Petitioner"), appeals an assessment issued by the Comptroller of the Treasury (hereinafter "Respondent") for Maryland income tax for the tax years 1986 through 1993. Taxes assessed totaled $326,685 for the eight years, plus penalties and interest, for total assessments of $637,362.

Petitioner was formed in December, 1986 as a subsidiary of Syms, a corporation engaged in the retail of off-price men's, women's, and children's retail clothing with its principal place of business in New Jersey. Syms has retail operations in Maryland. Evidence indicates that Petitioner was formed to hold and manage intangible asset such as trademarks, service marks, and trade names of its parent, Syms. The intangible assets transferred to Petitioner produced certain benefits to the corporate family, among them being the reduction of Maryland income tax liability of its parent, Syms. Petitioner and Syms executed a licensing agreement whereby the "marks", now owned by Petitioner, were licensed to Syms for a fee. This fee paid to Petitioner reduced the Maryland taxable income of Syms and increased income to Petitioner. However, Delaware law does not tax Petitioner's licensing income. Since Maryland law requires each entity of an affiliated group to file their tax returns separately, the money paid to Petitioner from Syms was never taxed by Maryland.

An audit by Respondent claimed a basis for finding that the licensing fees paid to Petitioner were taxable. An assessment was issued, which was affirmed by the Respondent's hearing officer.

The central issue for this Court involves whether Maryland statute or case law permits the imposition of tax on the income of an out-of-state affiliate of a Maryland parent corporation. The issue is identical to that addressed in *MCIIT v. Comptroller*, Mary-

---

143.451.7, which allows deduction "for expenses in determining Missouri taxable income as were incurred...to produce such income...." The director also has statutory authority to prescribe regulations to adjust, assess or compute the tax liability of affiliated corporations "in such manner as clearly to reflect the Missouri taxable income derived from sources within this state and in order to prevent avoidance of such tax liability." Section 143.431.3(5). By either route, where related corporations are using the deduction for royalty payments to remove income earned in Missouri from the amount to be taxed, the director should disallow the deduction. That would ensure that these companies that produce income from Missouri pay the taxes they owe to this state.

land Tax Court No. C-96-0028-01 (1999) and it is to that decision that most of our analysis will refer. The major difference between this case and *MCIIT* is that the entity involved here is a holding company, not an operating corporation.

Similar to *MCIIT*, Petitioner asserts that a sufficient nexus does not exist between itself and Maryland to subject Petitioner to Maryland income tax. Respondent relies on Maryland case law for support of its assessment.

I. Nexus.

The nexus arguments were fully addressed in *MCIIT*, supra. The parties presented the same statutory and case law as support of their positions as in the instant appeal. The *MCIIT* analysis provided:

> Maryland imposes a tax on the taxable income of a corporation defined as "its Maryland modified income as allocated to the State..." § 10-301 of the Tax- General Article of the Annotated Code of Maryland. Maryland modified income of a corporation is its federal taxable income, adjusted by the Maryland additions and subtractions, § 10-304 through 10-308. The computation of the tax requires the corporation to allocate Maryland modified income "derived from or reasonably attributable to its trade or business in this State," § 10-402(a). If the entity earns its income from in and out of the State, that income derived from instate business activities must be allocated to Maryland, § 10- 402(a)(1) & (2). If the corporation is unitary, then a 3-factor apportionment formula is applied to its income in order to determine Maryland taxable income of that corporation, § 10-402(c). Under subsection (d) of § 10-402, the Respondent may alter the allocation and apportionment of a corporation's income "to reflect clearly the income allocable to Maryland." Each corporate member of an affiliated group, even if unitary, is required to file a separate tax return to the Respondent, § 10-811.

The parties both agree that Petitioner is a part of a unitary group of entities. Accordingly, relying on precedent established in two Maryland Court decisions, *Comptroller of the Treasury v. Armco Export Sales Corp.*, 82 Md.App. 429 (1990) and *Comptroller of the Treasury v. Atlantic Supply Co.*, 294 Md. 213 (1982), the Respondent asserted nexus over Petitioner based on the in-state activity of an affiliate. Respondent first determined that Petitioner lacked "substantial economic substance," labeling Petitioner as a "phantom" corporation. As such, Respondent determined that the cases cited permit the attribution of "nexus and apportionment factors of the company or companies actually engaging in any real activity to the phantom company," Notice of Final Determination (Petitioner's Exhibit # 63).

For the following reasons, we conclude that Petitioner is an entity of substance and not a "phantom."

In the instant case, the evidence clearly indicates that Petitioner is not just a book entry corporation. Petitioner maintains an office in Delaware. That office contains office furniture and corporate and financial records are kept there. Mail is received at the Delaware office location. It has its own bank account and has an employee. Legal counsel was retained by Petitioner for purposes of protecting its "marks." The requisites for corporate existence were met; i.e. the drafting of by-laws, the election of a board of directors and corporate officers, the holding of regular and annual meetings, the recording of corporate minutes, and the ratification of dividends.

Respondent claims that Petitioner "was little more than a corporate vehicle designed to reduce state income taxes," (Respondent's Memorandum, p. 40), and points to the minimal expenses, the one employee, the mere formality of the corporate existence of Petitioner, and the timing of inter-entity transactions as support that Petitioner was creating the "illusion of substance," (Resp's Memorandum, p. 31). In short, Respondent assessed on the basis that the Petitioner was a sham entity for the sole purpose to avoid Maryland taxes.

Even if that were true, *Armco* and *Atlantic Supply* only apply to entities with no substance whatsoever. In addition, it is well settled that tax avoidance (rather than tax evasion) is a legitimate business purpose. If Petitioner was legally created with a tax avoidance purpose, absent authority and in a separate return environment, the Respondent cannot tax it. However, the evidence presented leads to the conclusion that Petitioner was established for non-tax reasons, among them:

- To hold and manage intangible assets in a separate corporation;
- To protect the transferred intangibles from the claims of Syms' creditors and from liabilities of Syms;
- To incorporate in a favorable corporate jurisdiction;
- To avert hostile take-overs; and
- To protect and enhance the value of Syms' name and its borrowing and business acquisition ability.

These facts easily distinguish the Petitioner from the phantom taxpayers in *Armco* and *Atlantic Supply*. Nexus cannot be attributed to it for Maryland taxation purposes.

Similar to *MCIIT*, the issue then turns to whether nexus can be directly found in Petitioner's activities. The Court finds the analysis provided in that case is applicable to the present facts:

> The limits on the taxing powers of a state are found in the Due Process and Commerce Clauses of the Constitution. The Supreme Court reviewed the requirements of both Clauses in *Quill Corp. v. North Dakota*, 504 U.S. 298 (1992).

In *Quill*, the Court reiterated that the "Due Process Clause 'requires some definite link, some minimum connection, between a state and the person, property or transaction it seeks to tax,' and that the 'income attributed to the State for tax purposes must be rationally related to values connected with the taxing State,'" *supra* at p.307, *citations omitted*. Overruling prior holdings, the Court determined that the minimum contacts necessary to establish the jurisdiction to tax does not require actual physical presence in the state, but can be found "if a foreign corporation purposefully avails itself of the benefits of an economic market in the forum State," *supra* at p. 307.

The Supreme Court's analysis of the Commerce Clause begins with the requirements as set forth in its decision in *Complete Auto Transit, Inc. v. Brady*, 430 U.S. 274 (1977). *Complete Auto* provides a four part test which must be satisfied in order for a tax to pass muster against a Commerce Clause challenge. A tax is sustained so long as the tax: "1) is applied to an activity with a substantial nexus with the taxing State, 2) is fairly apportioned, 3) does not discriminate against interstate commerce, and 4) is fairly related to the services provided by the State," *Complete Auto* at p. 279. In discussing the first prong of the test, the Supreme Court held that the "substantial nexus requirement is not, like due process' 'minimum contacts" requirement, a proxy for notice, but rather a means for limiting state burdens on interstate commerce. Accordingly... a corporation may have the 'minimum contacts' with a taxing State as required by the Due Process Clause, and yet lack the 'substantial nexus' with that State as required by the Commerce Clause," *Quill* at p. 313. The Court reaffirmed the "bright-line" test it established in *National Bellas Hess, Inc. v. Department of Revenue*, 386 U.S. 753 (1967), that a taxpayer must have a physical presence in the taxing state in order to satisfy the substantial nexus requirement of the Commerce Clause.

In addressing the stricter "substantial nexus" requirement, Petitioner argues that since it has no physical presence in Maryland, the attempt to tax its income is a Commerce Clause violation pursuant to *Quill*. Respondent contends that the *Quill* Court explicitly noted that the physical presence requirement applies to sales and use taxes only. Reliance is also placed on the *Armco* and *Atlantic Supply* decisions to support the application of an apportioned income tax to a corporation without any physical presence in Maryland.

The Respondent is correct in that the tax the *Quill* Court analyzed was a sales/use tax. The Court did note that "concerning other types of taxes we have not adopted a similar bright-line, physical presence requirement." 504 U.S. at p. 316. However, the Supreme Court also refused to restrict the rule to only sales and use taxes. "Although we have not, in our review of other types of taxes, articulated the same physical presence requirement that *Bellas Hess* established for sales and use taxes, that silence does not imply repudiation of the *Bellas Hess* rule," *supra* at p. 314. This lack of clarity on the parameters of the physical presence test has led to differing interpretations among the States as to what the Commerce Clause requires in relation to income-based taxes.

Absent apparent explicit direction, we hesitate to expand the *Quill* physical presence requirement to taxes other than sales and use. In so doing however, we note that "substantial nexus" with the taxing state is still required in order to pass constitutional muster. In the rulings of *Armco* and *Atlantic Supply*, due to the nature of the corporate phantoms, with no substance and therefore no presence anywhere, the normal nexus rules were ignored and the Courts found that nexus could be attributed based on the in-state presence and activity of an affiliate. The Commerce Clause was satisfied through the substantial nexus (the production and export of goods) of the in-state unitary affiliate.

However, as stated above, the instant case does not present us with a phantom. Petitioner is an entity of substance with a presence somewhere and thus the normal nexus (versus nexus attribution) rules apply. The focus of the substantial nexus requirement is on the entity sought to be taxed, not its in-state affiliate. *MCIIT, supra*, p. 9–11.

Focusing solely on Petitioner, we find that its lack of in-state activity precludes the imposition of the tax. Petitioner is not doing business in Maryland. Its income producing activity all occurs outside of Maryland. Petitioner has no offices, employees, agents or property in Maryland. Its only Maryland contact is an affiliation with an entity with a Maryland presence. This affiliation is hardly enough to satisfy substantial nexus.

Respondent relies on *Armco* and *Atlantic Supply* as support for the application of nexus due to the presence of Syms in Maryland. That reliance has been shown above to be erroneous. Respondent then points to the decision of *Geoffrey, Inc. v. South Carolina Tax Commission*, 313 S.C. 15 (1993) as precedent in the taxing of a Delaware holding company licensing trademarks and trade names to its parent in-state company. The *Geoffrey* Court concluded that the use of intangible property (the "marks") by the in-state affiliate was sufficient to pass the constitutional nexus requirements in order to tax the out-of-state entity.

For two reasons, we disagree with the Respondent's use of the *Geoffrey* decision. First, *Geoffrey* dealt with South Carolina law and its application and therefore is not precedent for Maryland application. Second, as indicated above, we differ in our conclusions as to whether the substantial nexus requirement of the Commerce Clause was met. *Geoffrey* focused on the use of the marks by the in-state affiliate of the unitary group in order to determine the nexus of the foreign corporation. We disagree that that activity constitutes "substantial" nexus.

In addition, the unitary relationship between entities does not automatically establish nexus on all of the corporate entities in the unitary group. As we stated in *MCIIT, supra*:

> The mere presence of an in-state affiliate of a unitary group does not confer nexus on a non-phantom out-of-state affiliate of the same group, *Chesapeake Industries, Inc. v. Comptroller,* 59 Md.App. 370 (1984). In the unitary taxation scheme, the foreign corporation's income and factors may be included in determining the tax liability of the in-state affiliate.

However, without nexus, the foreign corporation does not become subject to the taxing jurisdiction. The Respondent claims that the corporate structure present here allows for the diversion of income away from Maryland through the internal transactions of affiliated entities which have no overall impact on the income of the unitary group. While this may be true, all such transactions are not necessarily abusive and in any event, these are the consequences of requiring affiliated corporations to file and report income separately. The Maryland Courts have addressed the treatment of such transactions when dealing with phantom corporations. With non-phantom corporations, such as Petitioner, the nexus rules as reiterated in *Quill* must still be applied to each affiliate before the State can tax. *MCIIT, supra,* p. 11.

Accordingly, we find that the Respondent has failed to satisfy the substantial nexus requirement of the Commerce Clause and the imposition of income tax on Petitioner's income is unconstitutional.

Syms Corp. v. Commissioner of Revenue
765 N.E.2d 758 (Mass. 2002)

Cordy, Judge:

Syms Corp. (Syms) appeals from a decision of the Appellate Tax Board ("board") affirming the refusal by the Commissioner of Revenue ("commissioner") to abate $291,571 in corporate excise taxes assessed against it for the tax years 1986, 1987, 1989, 1990, and 1991. The assessments resulted from the commissioner's disallowance of deductions Syms had taken for royalty payments it had made to its wholly owned subsidiary, SYL, Inc. (SYL). The royalties were paid to SYL for the use of certain trade names, trademarks, and service marks (marks), which Syms had transferred to SYL in December, 1986.

After an evidentiary hearing, the board found that Syms had not sustained its burden of establishing its entitlement to an abatement, and that the commissioner had properly disallowed the deductions on three alternative grounds: (1) the transfer and leaseback of the marks was a sham and could be disregarded under the "sham transaction doctrine";[7] (2) the royalty payments were not deductible as ordinary and necessary business expenses where there was no valid business purpose justifying the expense and SYL added little or no value to the marks; and (3) G.L. c. 63, §39A, permitted the commissioner to eliminate the royalty payments from the calculation of net income because they were made between affiliated corporations and were in excess of fair value.

On appeal, Syms claims that the board's findings are not supported by the record, that G.L. c. 63, §39A, only permits the elimination of payments between subsidiaries and not from a parent corporation to its subsidiary, and that the disallowance of the deductions violates the due process and commerce clauses of the United States Constitution. Syms also challenges the board's refusal to abate the penalties assessed against it by the commissioner. We conclude that the board's findings are supported by substantial evidence in the record and that the disallowances do not violate the United States Constitution. We need not and therefore do not reach the question of the applicability of G.L. c. 63, §39A, to the payments in this case.

1. *Background.* Syms is a New Jersey corporation engaged in "off-price" retailing, which is the retail sale of brand name clothing at prices lower than those in department stores. It was founded in 1959 by Sy Syms. It operates two stores in the Commonwealth and therefore is subject to Massachusetts corporate excise tax.

Syms used several marks in its business, including the Syms name, a multiple 'S' logo that it placed on its own brands of clothing, and the slogan, "An Educated Consumer is Our Best Customer." Prior to December, 1986, Syms owned these marks.

SYL was incorporated in Delaware on December 4, 1986, as Syms's wholly owned trademark holding company. Its board of directors and officers were Sy Syms, Marcy Syms, Richard Diamond, and Edward Jones, a partner in a Delaware accounting firm. SYL and Syms executed a license agreement on December 18, 1986. SYL, acting as the owner of the marks, granted to Syms the right to use the marks nationally for a royalty equal to four per cent of Syms's annual net sales. The marks were transferred from Syms to SYL the next day, December 19, 1986.

For the calendar year 1986, Syms paid SYL a royalty for the marks that constituted four per cent of its annual net sales from October 1, 1986, until the end of December. The 1986 royalty was approximately $2.8 million. In subsequent years, the royalty amount increased from nearly $10 million in 1987 to $12.7 million in 1991. In each of these years SYL received one annual royalty payment from Syms, which it held in Delaware for a few weeks before paying it back to Syms, with interest (minus expenses) as a tax-free dividend. SYL's only income came from Syms's annual royalty payments, and its expenses amounted to approximately one-tenth of one per cent of its income.

SYL's corporate "office" consisted of an address rented from Jones's Delaware accounting firm, for an annual fee of $1,200. The accounting firm provided this same service to "a couple of hundred" other corporations that used Delaware subsidiary corporations to hold their intangible assets. Jones was not only a partner of the accounting firm, he was SYL's only employee, serving in a part-time capacity for which he was paid $1,200 per year.

The business operations of Syms did not change after the transfer and license-back of the marks. All of the work necessary to maintain and protect the marks continued to be done by the same New York City trademark law firm that had previously per-

---

7. A "sham transaction" in this context means a transaction that in fact occurred in an effort to exploit a feature of the tax laws, not a transaction that did not occur, or did not occur as reported.

formed those services, and Syms (not SYL) continued to pay all the expenses attendant thereto. All efforts to maintain the good will and thus to preserve the value of the marks were undertaken by Syms, and all advertising using the marks was controlled and paid for by Syms or by a wholly owned Syms subsidiary formed solely to do advertising. The choice of which products would be sold under the marks, as well as the quality control of those products, remained the responsibility of the same persons who had done that work before the transfer—Sy Syms himself, and the Syms staff of buyers.

2. *Sham transaction.* Syms does not contest the validity of the "sham transaction doctrine" and the commissioner's authority under that doctrine to disregard, for taxing purposes, transactions that have no economic substance or business purpose other than tax avoidance. It is a doctrine long established in State and Federal tax jurisprudence dating back to the seminal case of *Gregory v. Helvering*, 293 U.S. 465 (1935). It works to prevent taxpayers from claiming the tax benefits of transactions that, although within the language of the tax code, are not the type of transactions the law intended to favor with the benefit. *Horn v. Commissioner of Internal Revenue*, 968 F.2d 1229, 1236–1237 (D.C.Cir.1992). "Usually, transactions that are invalidated by the doctrine are those motivated by nothing other than the taxpayer's desire to secure the attached tax benefit," and are structured to completely avoid economic risk. *Id.* at 1236.

Syms contends that the doctrine does not apply in this case because it had business purposes, other than tax avoidance, for incorporating SYL and then transferring to it and licensing back the marks which it previously owned. It complains that the board ignored the "uncontroverted" evidence of these other business purposes, and based its decision on the record in another case litigated shortly after this one, and on an across-the-board policy of the "disallowance of deductions for all related trademark protection companies."

The question whether or not a transaction is a sham for purposes of the application of the doctrine is, of necessity, primarily a factual one, on which the taxpayer bears the burden of proof in the abatement process. *Koch v. Commissioner of Revenue*, 416 Mass. 540, 556, 624 N.E.2d 91 (1993).

The board found that the transfer and license back transaction had no practical economic effect on Syms other than the creation of tax benefits, and that tax avoidance was the clear motivating factor and its only business purpose. See *Casebeer v. Commissioner of Internal Revenue*, 909 F.2d 1360, 1365 (9th Cir.1990) (taxpayer must show both that transaction was supported by business purpose other than tax avoidance and had economic substance other than creation of tax benefit); *James v. Commissioner of Internal Revenue*, 899 F.2d 905, 908–909 (10th Cir.1990) (consideration of business purpose and economic substance are factors in determining whether transaction had any practical effect other than creation of income tax losses). The board rejected the other business purposes claimed by Syms during the hearing, finding them to be "illusory, not supported by the evidence, or contrary to the weight of the evidence."[8]

---

8. Syms proffered, and the board rejected, almost a dozen non-tax business purposes to support its claim that the transfer and license-back was not intended solely to avoid taxation. For example: Syms's assertion that the transfer would protect the marks from claims of Syms's creditors was rejected by the board, because creditors could reach assets of Syms's wholly owned subsidiary; Syms's claim that the transfer would protect the marks from a hostile takeover was rejected, because Syms could only have achieved that goal by transferring the marks to an independent third party, and with eighty per cent of the stock controlled by the company founder, such a takeover was hypothetical at best; Syms's claim that the transfer would result in better management of the marks was re-

Our review of the record of the proceedings before the board confirms that it rejected the purported business purposes not by ignoring "strong, uncontested, evidence" of their existence, but after carefully examining and weighing the evidence proffered as to each of them. Its detailed findings on these matters are supported by substantial evidence, and Syms's allegation that the board's decision was based on the record of another case is without foundation. While there may be many important business purposes attendant to the transfer and licensing back of intangible assets within corporate families, to be viable for the purposes claimed by Syms, they must be more than theoretical musings, concocted to provide faint cover for the creation of a tax deduction.

3. *Ordinary and necessary expense.* General Laws c. 63, § 1 ("[n]et income"), provides that corporations may take business deductions allowable under the Internal Revenue Code (Code). Underthe Code, only "ordinary and necessary" business expense deductions are allowable. I.R.C. § 162. Deductions are not permitted if the expense was "created solely for the purpose of effectuating a camouflaged assignment of income." *United States v. Estate Preservation Servs.*, 202 F.3d 1093, 1101 (9th Cir.2000). As an alternative ground for the disallowance of Syms's deduction for royalty expense, the board concurred with the commissioner's position that the royalty payments were not an "ordinary and necessary" business expense.

The board found that the value of the marks had been created entirely by Syms, and, even after their transfer and the payment of the royalties, Syms continued to pay the expenses associated with owning them, including the legal expenses incurred in maintaining them. It concluded that, in such circumstances, Syms's royalty payments to SYL for the use of the marks was unnecessary. In effect, Syms was paying twice for their use. The board further reasoned that it was irrelevant that the measure of royalty payments might have been equivalent to what would have been paid in an arm's-length transaction where, as here, the payments were not for services provided by SYL but rather part of a contrived mechanism by which affiliated entities shifted income, tax free, between themselves in a circular transaction for the benefit of Syms.

Syms counters that, having validly transferred the trademarks to SYL in consideration for receipt of SYL stock, it was required to pay royalty fees, and, therefore, they were a necessary business expense. It also argues that there is no requirement that owners add value to assets before allowing their use by another entity, and that the sole test whether the royalty payments are deductible is whether they were made at "arm's length."

These arguments closely mirror those made on the question whether the transfer and license back of the marks constituted a "sham" transaction. The central issue for the court to decide is whether the board's finding that there was no business reason for Syms to incur the expense of millions of dollars in royalties other than to create tax deductions is supported by the record. As we have already concluded, it is. The royalty expense to Syms "resulted not as an ordinary, necessary incident in the conduct of the taxpayer's business, but instead was created solely for the purpose of effectuating a camouflaged assignment of income." *United States v. Estate Preservation Servs., supra* at 1101.

---

jected because Syms retained the same responsibilities for managing and maintaining the marks after the transfer; and Syms's assertion that the formation of the subsidiary would enhance Syms's ability to borrow funds was rejected because creditors would have viewed the two entities as intermingled and would not have offered any different financing arrangements, Syms's founder strenuously opposed borrowing money, and the subsidiary never borrowed any money.

Decision of the Appellate Tax Board affirmed.

In re Sherwin-Williams Co.
2001 N.Y. Tax Lexis 134 (N.Y. Div. Tax. App. 2001)

ISSUE

Whether the Division of Taxation may require petitioner to file its franchise tax report on a combined basis with SWIMC, Inc. and DIMC, Inc., two of its subsidiaries.

FINDINGS OF FACT

Petitioner, incorporated under the laws of Ohio in 1884, has its principal place of business and commercial domicile in Cleveland, Ohio. It is engaged in the manufacture, distribution and sale of coatings, e.g., paints and related products, and is one of the largest manufacturers of paints and varnishes.

Petitioner has always used trademarks, tradenames and service marks (collectively "Marks") in conducting its business. The Marks included the "Sherwin-Williams" brand, registered on April 20, 1948, various "Cover the Earth" logos, the first one registered in 1906, several "Dutch Boy" trademarks, the first one registered on March 5, 1918, "Protecting the American Dream" a common law trademark and "The Look that Gets the Look" slogan, that was filed on March 2, 1990, to name just a few.

[Petitioner formed two corporations...] named SWIMC, Inc. (for Sherwin-Williams Investment Management Company) and DIMC, Inc. (for Dupli-Color Investment Management Company). SWIMC, the wholly-owned subsidiary, would own the non-aerosol Marks. While DIMC, which would be 85% owned by Sherwin-Williams and 15% owned by Dupli-Color Products Company ("Dupli-Color") (a wholly-owned subsidiary of Sherwin-Williams), would own the aerosol marks.

CONCLUSIONS OF LAW

Article 9A of the Tax Law imposes a tax on foreign corporations doing business in New York State (Tax Law §209[1]). In order to properly reflect that tax liability, Tax Law §211(4) gives the Division the discretion to require or permit corporations subject to New York State tax to file combined reports with certain other corporations. The statute requires that the parent own or control substantially all of the stock of the subsidiary. The statute further limits the Division's discretion by providing that: "no combined report covering any corporation not a taxpayer shall be required unless the [Division] deems such a report necessary, because of inter-company transactions...in order properly to reflect the tax liability." Tax Law §211[4].

The Division's regulations provide that the Division may require or allow the filing of a combined report where three conditions are met: (1) a stock ownership test (20 NYCRR 6-2.2[a]); (2) a unitary business test (20 NYCRR 6-2.2 [b]); and (3) a distortion of income test (20 NYCRR 6-2.3). The distortion of income test provides, in part, that the Division: may permit or require a group of taxpayers to file a combined report if reporting on a separate basis distorts the activities, business, income or capital in New York State of the taxpayers. The activities, business, income or capital of a taxpayer will be presumed to be distorted when the taxpayer reports on a separate basis if there are substantial intercorporate transactions among the corporations. 20 NYCRR 6-2.3[a].

The regulation goes on to provide that "[t]he substantial intercorporate transaction requirement may be met where as little as 50 percent of a corporation's receipts or expenses are from one or more qualified activities described in this subdivision" (20 NYCRR 6-2.3[c]).

Pursuant to section 6.2-5(a) of the Division's regulations, a corporation not subject to tax in New York State (i.e., not a taxpayer) will not be permitted or required to file on a combined basis with a New York taxpayer corporation or combined group unless the stock ownership test (20 NYCRR 6-2.2 [a]) and the unitary business test (20 NYCRR 6-2.2[b]) are met and the Division "determines that inclusion is necessary to properly reflect the tax liability of one or more taxpayers included in the group" because of (1) substantial intercorporate transactions or (2) some agreement or arrangement or transaction which causes the business, income, or capital of any taxpayer to be improperly or inaccurately reflected (20 NYCRR 6-2.5[a]).

For purposes of this matter, there is no dispute that the stock ownership and unitary business requirements have been met.... During 1991, SWIMC received almost all of its royalty income from Sherwin-Williams. DIMC received the vast majority of its royalty income from Sherwin-Williams, with the remainder coming from Dupli-Color, a Sherwin-Williams affiliate. Since there are substantial intercorporate transactions between petitioner and SWIMC and DIMC, a presumption of distortion exists in this case.

As explained in *Matter of Silver King Broadcasting of N.J.* (Tax Appeals Tribunal, May 9, 1996),

> there are two scenarios for required or permitted combination—presumption and non-presumption. In the presumption cases, the burden is on the taxpayer to show that the intercorporate transactions which give rise to the presumption are arm's-length in order to prove that reporting on a separate basis is a proper reflection of income.
>
> Where the taxpayer rebuts the presumption of distortion...and in the non-presumption cases, the Division, in order to require combination, must show why it believes that reporting on a separate basis does not properly reflect income (citations omitted).

The Division contends that it has a presumption and a non-presumption basis for requiring petitioner to file a combined report with its subsidiaries, SWIMC and DIMC. The Division's primary argument is that Sherwin-Williams' trademark assignment and license-back transactions with SWIMC and DIMC are distortive by their very nature and, therefore, that it is unnecessary to look to the presumption of distortion created by the substantial intercompany transactions.

.....

Delaware imposes a corporation income tax, but exempts from that tax "[c]orporations whose activities within [Delaware] are confined to the maintenance and management of their intangible assets [including] patents, patent applications, trademarks, trade names and similar type of intangible assets." 30 Del Code Ann § 1902[b][8].

SWIMC and DIMC were incorporated in Delaware on January 31, 1991. Under their articles of incorporation and bylaws, the activities of SWIMC and DIMC are confined to the maintenance and protection of their intangible investments and therefore qualify for exemption from Delaware corporation income tax. Sherwin-Williams assigned trademarks to SWIMC and DIMC in exchange for stock in both corporations. Sherwin-Williams did not recognize any gain on those exchanges pursuant to IRC § 351. SWIMC and DIMC licensed those Marks back to Sherwin-Williams on a non-exclusive basis.

In support of its argument that SWIMC and DIMC served no legitimate business purpose and were formed solely to shield income from state taxes, the Division draws attention to writings which have touted the Delaware trademark corporation as a vehicle to avoid state taxes. The majority of these articles were written after SWIMC and DIMC were formed. I am not persuaded by these articles; taxpayers are free to structure their business affairs as they choose, including the use of any legal corporate structure to minimize state taxes. The assignment of the Marks by petitioner to SWIMC and DIMC and the license back of those Marks to petitioner will not be disregarded for tax purposes if those transactions were effected for legitimate business purposes and were not entered into merely to avoid taxation. *See Frank Lyon Company v. U.S.*, 435 US 561, 577.

Two factors are considered in determining whether transactions between controlled corporations will be respected: (1) whether the transactions were accomplished for a valid business purpose; and (2) whether they had economic substance (*Frank Lyon, supra*). The "business purpose" test looks to the taxpayer's motives for entering into the subject transaction, while the "economic substance" test looks to whether there was "a reasonable possibility of profit…apart from tax benefits" (*Rice's Toyota World, Inc. v. Commissioner*, 752 F2d 89, 94–95). A tax avoidance motivation does not preclude respecting a transaction if that was not the only basis for entering into the transaction (*Frank Lyon, supra; Rice's Toyota World, supra*).

The record is clear in establishing that SWIMC and DIMC were formed for valid business purposes and carried out substantial business in their own names. The credible testimony of Messrs. McDonald, Ivy and Ault and the documents in the record clearly establish that Sherwin-Williams formed SWIMC and DIMC for valid business reasons, among them: to hold and manage the Marks; to increase the protection of the Marks; to license the Marks to both related and unrelated entities; to incorporate in a favorable corporate jurisdiction; to avert hostile takeovers; to maximize the return on the stream of royalty income to SWIMC and DIMC through investment in longer-term investments and to have an additional source of financing through the securitization of the royalty income stream to SWIMC and DIMC. SWIMC and DIMC actively managed and protected their respective Marks. They paid for and filed trademark applications and renewals for their respective Marks. SWIMC and DIMC pursued potential infringers of their respective Marks. As president of SWIMC and DIMC, Dr. Puglisi actively managed and protected the Marks. To assist Dr. Puglisi in the management and protection of the Marks, SWIMC and DIMC employed third-party service providers including Duane, Morris, Wood, Emhardt, Naughton, Moriarty and McNett, and Sherwin-Williams. Each company paid for the services provided by the third-party service providers. Subsequent to 1991, SWIMC and DIMC also employed Stewart & Associates and Wade & Santora as third-party service providers as well. During 1991, SWIMC entered into third-party license agreements. Although third-party license inquiries were made to DIMC, no third-party licenses were entered into by DIMC until November of 1992. On a number of occasions, Dr. Puglisi denied third-party licenses for use of the Marks that he felt would undermine their value. Since 1991, SWIMC and DIMC have entered into a significant number of licensing agreements. Dr. Puglisi invested the royalty income that SWIMC and DIMC received from their license agreements in accordance with their respective investment guidelines. The record clearly shows that the directors of SWIMC and DIMC gave Dr. Puglisi full authority and discretion to choose the appropriate security to maximize investment returns, and that over time the investment returns realized by SWIMC and DIMC have been greater than those achieved by Sherwin-Williams.

As for the modification in the License Agreements with respect to the timing of royalty payments by Sherwin-Williams to SWIMC and DIMC, I do not find that those modifications signify that Sherwin-Williams rather than SWIMC and DIMC was in control. The modification in the time to report quarterly sales figures was not changed significantly. Moreover, the record establishes that Sherwin-Williams usually sent SWIMC and DIMC the quarterly sales production reports within 45 days of the end of each quarter. In addition, petitioner began to send SWIMC and DIMC quarterly estimates of sales. Those quarterly estimates of sales allowed Dr. Puglisi to monitor the quality control under the License Agreements with Sherwin-Williams through sales. The record also establishes that subsequent to 1991, SWIMC and DIMC conducted additional quality control activities. Furthermore, the documentation in the record clearly establishes that, during 1991, both SWIMC and DIMC maintained good corporate form and operated not only through Dr. Puglisi, but through regular board of directors meetings.

As for the Division's assertion that unnamed tax promoters were involved in the creation of SWIMC and DIMC, the record does not support that assertion, nor is there any evidence that petitioner relied on advertising brochures from tax promoters when it made the decision to form SWIMC and DIMC. The articles to which the Division refers and Stewart & Associates' web page are all post-1991, the year in which SWIMC and DIMC were formed. Petitioner does not deny that tax considerations played a role in its decision to create SWIMC and DIMC. However, there were significant business reasons for the creation of SWIMC and DIMC which cannot be ignored (*Frank Lyon, supra*).

In sum, the assignment of the trademarks by Sherwin-Williams to SWIMC and DIMC and the license back of those trademarks to Sherwin-Williams were accomplished for valid business purposes, were characterized by economic substance, and were not motivated solely by tax avoidance.

. . . . .

The Division asserts that the licensing agreements between Sherwin-Williams and SWIMC and DIMC are anomalous. It argues that as a result of the assignment and license-back transaction, SWIMC and DIMC had trademarks, but they did not have core businesses in which they used the trademarks to sell branded products.... Contrary to the Division's contention, the Licensing Agreements between petitioner and SWIMC and DIMC are not anomalous. Trademarks can exist unrelated from a core business. Indeed, Mr. Bromberg, the Division's trademark expert, had first hand experience with a company that owned trademarks, but did not have any ongoing business. Trademarks have increasingly become recognized as property that exists separate from the business. There are no normal or abnormal licensing arrangements, just different types depending upon the needs of the parties.

The License Agreements between Sherwin-Williams and SWIMC and DIMC require Sherwin-Williams to pay royalties for its use of the trademarks. The royalty rates set forth in the License Agreements were determined by American Appraisal Associates ("AAA") when that company determined the fair market value of petitioner's domestic trademarks and trade names. AAA set forth its valuation study in an appraisal report.

The Genetelli arm's length study also supports petitioner's position that the interest rate SWIMC charged Sherwin-Williams was an arm's length rate.

The foregoing Conclusions of Law establish the following: [1]since the royalties, interest rate on the intercompany loan and the charges for intercompany trademark services were at arm's length, petitioner has rebutted the presumption of distortion arising from the existence of a unitary business and substantial intercorporate transactions; [2]the Division has not established the existence of distortion in connection with the royalties, the interest rate or the charges for the intercompany services; and [3]accordingly, the Division may not require petitioner to file a combined corporation franchise tax report with SWIMC and DIMC.

Sherwin-Williams Company v. Commissioner
778 N.E.2d 504 (Mass. 2002)

Cordy, Judge:

The Sherwin-Williams Company (Sherwin-Williams) appealed from a decision of the Appellate Tax Board (board) upholding the denial by the Commissioner of Revenue (commissioner) of its request to abate $59,445.40 in corporate excise taxes assessed for tax year 1991 and we transferred the case to this court on our own motion. The contested assessment was the result of the commissioner's disallowance of approximately $47 million that Sherwin-Williams had deducted from its taxable income for royalty payments to two wholly owned subsidiaries, Sherwin-Williams Investment Management Company, Inc. (SWIMC), and Dupli-Color Investment Management Company, Inc. (DIMC) (collectively referred to as the subsidiaries), for the use of certain trade names, trademarks, and service marks (marks), that Sherwin-Williams had transferred to the subsidiaries and licensed back as part of a corporate reorganization of its intangible assets in January, 1991. The commissioner also disallowed $80,000 that Sherwin-Williams had deducted for interest payments to SWIMC, in connection with a $7 million loan made to it by SWIMC in the fourth quarter of 1991, which was repaid in the first quarter of 1992.

We conclude that the board erred when it found that the transfer and licensing back transactions between Sherwin-Williams and its subsidiaries were without economic substance and therefore a sham. We also conclude that: the payment of royalties and interest to SWIMC and DIMC were properly deductible by Sherwin-Williams because obtaining licenses to use the marks was necessary to the conduct of its business; even assuming G.L. c. 63, §§ 39A, empowers the commissioner to eliminate payments made between a foreign parent corporation and its subsidiaries, it does so only to the extent that such payments are in excess of fair value, and in light of the substantial evidence that the royalties paid by Sherwin-Williams reflected fair value, there is no basis to support the elimination of these payments; and, because the transactions were not a sham, and the loan between SWIMC and Sherwin-Williams was genuine, interest was properly chargeable to Sherwin-Williams when it borrowed the funds and was, accordingly, properly deductible.

Sham transaction. Massachusetts recognizes the "sham transaction doctrine" that gives the commissioner the authority "to disregard, for taxing purposes, transactions that have no economic substance or business purpose other than tax avoidance." Syms

Corp. v. Commissioner of Revenue, 436 Mass. 505, 509–510 (2002) (Syms). The doctrine generally "works to prevent taxpayers from claiming the tax benefits of transactions that, although within the language of the tax code, are not the type of transactions the law intended to favor with the benefit." Id. at 510.

"The question whether or not a transaction is a sham for purposes of the application of the doctrine is, of necessity, primarily a factual one, on which the taxpayer bears the burden of proof in the abatement process." Syms, supra at 511. Our review of the board's factual findings is limited to whether, as a matter of law, the evidence is sufficient to support them. Olympic & York State St. Co. v. Assessors of Boston, 428 Mass. 236, 240 (1998). If supported by sufficient evidence, we will not reverse a decision of the board unless it is based on an incorrect application of the law. Koch v. Commissioner of Revenue, 416 Mass. 540, 555 (1993).

In Syms, we upheld a finding of the board that a transfer and licensing back of trademarks between a parent and its newly formed subsidiary was a sham transaction for taxing purposes. There, the evidence that the transaction was specifically designed as a tax avoidance scheme; royalties were paid to the subsidiary once a year and quickly returned to the parent company as dividends; the subsidiary did not do business other than to act as a conduit for the circular flow of royalty money; and the parent continued to pay all of the expenses of maintaining and defending the trademarks it had transferred to the subsidiary, fully supported the board's findings that the transaction had no practical economic effect other than the creation of a tax benefit and that tax avoidance was its motivating factor and only purpose.

The facts of the present case are substantially different. There is no evidence that the transfer of the marks to the subsidiary corporations and their licensing back to Sherwin-Williams was specifically devised as a tax avoidance scheme. The revenue earned by the subsidiaries, including the proceeds from the royalty payments made by Sherwin-Williams, was not returned to Sherwin-Williams as a dividend but, rather, was retained and invested as part of their ongoing business operations, earning significant additional income. The subsidiaries entered into nonexclusive license agreements not only with Sherwin-Williams, but also with unrelated parties. The subsidiaries assumed and paid the expenses of maintaining and defending their trademark assets. Whether the board properly applied the sham transaction doctrine to these facts requires a more rigorous analysis of the origin and purposes of that doctrine than was necessary in Syms.

We start with two principles first articulated by Judge Learned Hand in Helvering v. Gregory, 69 F.2d 809 (2d Cir.1934), the seminal case establishing the sham transaction doctrine. The first principle is: "Any one may so arrange his affairs that his taxes shall be as low as possible; he is not bound to choose the pattern which will best pay the Treasury; there is not even a patriotic duty to increase one's taxes." Id. at 810. Or, as stated by the United States Supreme Court in its affirmance of Judge Hand's decision: "The legal right of a taxpayer to decrease the amount of what otherwise would be his taxes, or altogether avoid them, by means which the law permits, cannot be doubted." Gregory v. Helvering, 293 U.S. 465, 469 (1935) (Gregory). See Yosha v. Commissioner of Internal Revenue, 861 F.2d 494, 497 (7th Cir.1988) ("There is no rule against taking advantage of opportunities created by [the Legislature or revenue service] for beating taxes"). The second principle is that a transaction "does not lose its [tax] immunity, because it is actuated by a desire to avoid, or, if one chooses, evade, taxation." Helvering v. Gregory, supra at 810. In other words, our tax system is a rule-based system, objective in nature, that places principal importance on what taxpayers do and the economic consequences attached to those actions, not on what may have subjectively motivated them to act in the first place.

Based on these two principles, Sherwin-Williams, on initially going into business, could have organized itself in such a way that its intangible assets (e.g., its marks) were held in a corporation separate from the corporations holding its production facilities and sales operations; the corporation owning the marks could have licensed those marks to its sister corporations; and this arrangement would have been respected by taxing authorities even if the structure were motivated entirely by a desire to minimize Sherwin-Williams's over-all tax burdens. Although motivated by tax considerations, such a structure would not have been an uncommon way of doing business nor an artificial construct whose only possible effect was the avoidance of taxes. Against this backdrop, we decide what an established business enterprise must prove when it undertakes to reorganize itself to effectuate a more efficient tax structure in order that the taxing authorities recognize the reorganization for tax purposes, rather than disregard it as a sham.

[The Supreme Court] decisions suggest that for a business reorganization that results in tax advantages to be respected for taxing purposes, the taxpayer must demonstrate that the reorganization is "real" or "genuine," and not just form without substance. Stated otherwise, the taxpayer must demonstrate that the reorganization results in "a viable business entity," that is one which is "formed for a substantial business purpose or actually engage[s] in substantive business activity." Northern Ind. Pub. Serv. Co. v. Commissioner of Internal Revenue, 115 F.3d 506, 511 (7th Cir.1997).

Sham transaction cases most often involve discrete transactions by businesses or individuals rather than business reorganizations. In determining whether a transaction is real or just form over substance, a number of Federal courts have adopted a "two prong" sham transaction inquiry. Rice's Toyota World, Inc. v. Commissioner of Internal Revenue, 752 F.2d 89 (4th Cir.1985) (Rice's Toyota). The first prong of the inquiry examines whether the transaction has economic substance other than the creation of a tax benefit, which has been labeled the "objective" economic substance test. The second prong examines whether the transaction was motivated by any business purpose other than obtaining a tax benefit, which has been labeled the "subjective" business purpose test. While often using similar language, courts have applied this "two prong" inquiry in different ways. In Rice's Toyota, supra at 91, the court concluded that "[t]o treat a transaction as a sham, the court must find that the taxpayer was motivated by no business purposes other than obtaining tax benefits in entering the transaction, and that the transaction has no economic substance because no reasonable possibility of a profit exists" (emphasis added). According to Rice's Toyota and its progeny, if a taxpayer's transaction satisfies the requirements of either prong of the test it must be respected for taxing purposes. (*citations omitted*).

Other courts have rejected a rigid two-step analysis, opting instead to treat economic substance and business purpose as "more precise factors to consider in the application of [the] traditional sham analysis; that is, whether the transaction had any practical economic effects other than the creation of income tax losses." Sochin v. Commissioner of Internal Revenue, 843 F.2d 351, 354 (9th Cir.), *cert. denied*, 488 U.S. 824 (1988). (*citation omitted*).

We agree with those courts that have concluded that whether a transaction that results in tax benefits is real, such that it ought to be respected for taxing purposes, depends on whether it has had practical economic effects beyond the creation of those tax benefits. In the context of a business reorganization resulting in new corporate entities owning or carrying on a portion of the business previously held or conducted by the taxpayer, this requires inquiry into whether the new entities are "viable," that is, "formed for a substantial business purpose or actually engag[ing] in substantive business activity." Northern Ind. Pub. Serv. v. Commissioner of Internal Revenue, supra at 511. In making this inquiry, consideration of the often interrelated factors of economic substance and business purpose, is appropriate.

We turn now to the questioned transactions in this case. The board found that none of the transactions at issue, however defined, had either economic substance or business purpose other than tax avoidance. The board also found that, even if the transactions had had a business purpose other than tax avoidance, their lack of economic substance was fatal to Sherwin-Williams's claim. We disagree. These transactions (the transfer and license back of property) are a product and intended part of a business reorganization, and their economic substance and business purpose must be assessed not in the narrow confines of the specific transactions between the parent and the subsidiaries, but in the broader context of the operation of the resultant businesses. See Northern Ind. Pub. Serv. Co. v. Commissioner of Internal Revenue, supra at 512 (newly created subsidiary's existence, transactions with parent, and other economic activities all relevant to sham transaction analysis). After applying the proper legal standards to the evidence, we conclude that the reorganization, including the transfer and licensing back of the marks, had economic substance in that it resulted in the creation of viable business entities engaging in substantive business activity.

The evidence of economic substance, or substantive business activity, beyond the creation of tax benefits for Sherwin-Williams, was substantial. Legal title and physical possession of the marks passed from Sherwin-Williams to the subsidiaries, as did the benefits and burdens of owning the marks. The subsidiaries entered into genuine obligations with unrelated third parties for use of the marks. The subsidiaries received royalties, which they invested with unrelated third parties to earn additional income for their businesses. The subsidiaries incurred and paid substantial liabilities to unrelated third parties and Sherwin-Williams to maintain, manage, and defend the marks. In sum, the subsidiaries became viable, ongoing business enterprises within the family of Sherwin-Williams companies, and not businesses in form only, to be "put to death" after exercising the limited function of creating a tax benefit. Gregory v. Helvering, 293 U.S. 465, 470 (1935).

In the face of this substantial evidence, the board rested its finding that the reorganization and consequent transactions were without economic substance, principally on subsidiary findings that after the reorganization (1) Sherwin-Williams owned the stock of, and therefore controlled, the subsidiaries; (2) Sherwin-Williams (and not the subsidiaries) expended the money to advertise the products that carried the marks; and (3) Sherwin-Williams's employees continued to provide the services necessary to maintain the marks. While these subsidiary findings are supported in the record, they do not support the board's ultimate finding that the reorganization was without economic substance or effect and therefore a sham.

The separate corporate identities of Sherwin-Williams and the subsidiaries must be respected for tax purposes (where they conduct equivalent of business activity), see Moline Props. v. Commissioner of Internal Revenue, 319 U.S. 436, 438–439 (1943), regardless of their stock ownership. While transactions that occur between related companies require close scrutiny to ensure that they have substance as well as form (and that they are valued at levels neither artificially inflated nor deflated because of the interrelated nature of their ownership), the fact that Sherwin-Williams owned the stock of the subsidiaries does not mean that the reorganization had no economic substance or effect on its business. It no longer owned the marks. Instead, it owned stock in the companies that do. It no longer had the exclusive right to use the marks. Instead, it had nonexclusive and time-limited licenses to most but not all of them. The new owners of the marks were free, under their amended bylaws, to enter into licensing agreements with companies other than Sherwin-Williams without shareholder approval, and the subsidiaries did so. In addition, Sherwin-Williams relinquished control over monies it previously retained but now paid to the subsidiaries as royalties. These monies were not returned to it as dividends. They were invested (and therefore placed at risk) by the subsidiaries, under their own investment guidelines and with third parties outside of Sherwin-Williams's control. These changes resulted from the reorganization and have legal, practical, and economic effects on Sherwin-Williams regardless of its stock ownership position. More importantly, they are ample evidence of a reorganization that has resulted in the creation of new, viable business enterprises.

Sherwin-Williams incurred advertising expenses to sell its products not to promote or strengthen the marks. While the marks undoubtedly benefited from the advertising and sale of Sherwin-Williams products bearing their names, such benefits are secondary to the principal purpose of the expenditures. Sherwin-Williams properly expended and expensed these advertising costs against its sales. In this regard, the board's finding that Sherwin-Williams and not the subsidiaries incurred the costs of advertising its products is inconsequential to the ultimate question whether the reorganization was real.

Finally, that the subsidiaries contracted with Sherwin-Williams for professional services necessary to maintain the marks bears little relationship to whether the reorganization had economic substance. What is relevant is whether the subsidiaries paid the expenses of running their businesses (with whomever they may have contracted) or whether those expenses continued to be paid by the parent company, as they were in the Syms case. Here, those expenses were paid by the subsidiaries to Sherwin-Williams and, in significantly greater amounts, to other unrelated professionals.

We turn next to the board's assessment of business purpose about which there was a great deal of contested evidence. Applying our limited scope of review to the evidence before the board, we conclude that there was sufficient evidence to support the board's finding that Sherwin-Williams failed to prove that it undertook the reorganization for any of the reasons adopted by its board of directors on January 23, 1991, other than reducing its State tax burden. This finding is of course not conclusive on the ultimate question whether the reorganization was real. Indeed, the board found that, even if the reorganization and the consequent transfer and licensing transactions had been motivated by nontax reasons, or served other business purposes, they would still be a sham because they lacked economic substance beyond the creation of tax benefits.

We embrace the reasoning of courts that have concluded that tax motivation is irrelevant where a business reorganization results in the creation of a viable business entity engaged in substantive business activity rather than in a "bald and mischievous fiction." Moline Props. v. Commissioner of Internal Revenue, supra at 439. (*citation omitted*). Because the record in this case establishes that the reorganization and subsequent transfer and licensing transactions were genuine, creating viable businesses engaged in substantive economic activities apart from the creation of tax benefits for Sherwin-Williams, they cannot be disregarded by the commissioner as a sham regardless of their tax-motivated purpose.

Ordinary and necessary business expenses. General Laws c. 63, §§ 1 ("[n]et income"), provides that corporations may take such deductions as are allowable under the Internal Revenue Code (IRC). See G.L. c. 63, §§ 1. Under the IRC, only "ordinary and necessary" business expenses are allowable deductions. 26 U.S.C. §§ 162 (2000). The determination whether an expenditure satisfies the requirements for deductibility under §§ 162 is a question of fact. See Commissioner of Internal Revenue v. Heininger, 320 U.S. 467, 475 (1943).

To qualify as an allowable deduction under §§ 162, a taxpayer must demonstrate that an expenditure satisfies five requirements: (1) it was paid or incurred during the taxable year, (2) it was used to carry on a trade or business, (3) it was an expense, (4) it was a necessary expense, and (5) it was an ordinary expense. See Commissioner of Internal Revenue v. Lincoln Sav. & Loan Ass'n, 403 U.S. 345, 352 (1971). The issue here is whether the royalty payments for the use of the marks were ordinary and necessary business expenses.

As an alternative ground for the disallowance of Sherwin-Williams's deduction of royalty payments, the board concluded that Sherwin-Williams's payment of royalties to its wholly owned subsidiaries was not deductible as an ordinary and necessary business expense because "the transfer and license-back transactions between Sherwin-Williams and its subsidiaries should have been royalty-free." It based this conclusion on its findings that Sherwin-Williams maintained the value of the marks after the transfer (by way of advertising and services), and that the subsidiaries "had not developed the [m]arks in any way, or built any goodwill, or created anything of value that could be licensed back to the parent."

We disagree with the board's analysis. As noted earlier, advertising costs were incurred for the purpose of selling products not maintaining the value of the marks, and any services provided by Sherwin-Williams to maintain the marks were paid for by the subsidiaries. More fundamentally, however, the board misconstrues the nature of the reorganization. While Sherwin-Williams may have voluntarily conveyed the marks to its newly formed subsidiaries, it received full consideration for the conveyance, i.e., one hundred per cent of their stock. The relevant question is not who created the value in the marks, but who had the right to that value, at the time the royalty payments were made. Once conveyed, Sherwin-Williams had no legal right or claim to the marks absent licensing agreements. Moreover, the subsidiaries were not required to add value to what they had acquired from Sherwin-Williams in order to get fair market royalty rates from it or from the unrelated third-party licensees with whom they did business. If the subsidiaries had used some of their stock (or cash) to acquire marks from another company and in turn licensed them to Sherwin-Williams, there would be no need for them to "add value" in order properly to demand the payment of royalty fees, and none is required in these circumstances. As the commissioner's expert, Professor Alan L. Feld, conceded on cross-examination, "In the corporate world...a company does have the right to make a bona fide complete transfer of a tree...and then whoever owns the tree, they get the fruit."

Because we have concluded that the reorganization of Sherwin-Williams's intangible assets was not a sham, the answer to the question who had the right to the value of the marks, as a matter of law and substance, is the subsidiaries. The deductibility of the royalty payments between Sherwin-Williams and the subsidiaries must therefore be treated as the deductibility of any other expense incurred in a bona fide transaction between related entities.

The payment of the royalties was a necessary expense because Sherwin-Williams had "irrevocably divested itself of all title [to the marks] and had a right to enjoy the property thereafter only upon payment of reasonable rental." Stearns Magnetic Mfg. Co. v. Commissioner of Internal Revenue, 208 F.2d 849, 853 (7th Cir.1954). Once the marks had been transferred to the subsidiaries, the royalty payments were necessary so that Sherwin-Williams could use the marks to advertise and sell its products. One of the commissioner's experts testified about the importance of the marks: "I think the trademarks at Sherwin-Williams are very important to its business.... Their trademarks are very intertwined with the rest of their business." We agree, and conclude that the royalty payments were "'appropriate and helpful' for 'the development of [Sherwin-Williams's] business.'" Commissioner of Internal Revenue v. Tellier, supra at 689.

The payment of royalties was also an ordinary expense. "Ordinary has the connotation of normal, usual, or customary." Deputy v. DuPont, supra at 495. Although "the transaction which gives rise to [the expense] must be of common or frequent occurrence in the type of business involved... the fact that a particular expense would be an ordinary or common one in the course of one business and so deductible... does not necessarily make it such in connection with another business." Id. In finding that the expense was not "ordinary," the board credited and relied on the testimony of one of the commissioner's witnesses who testified in general terms, and without specifics, that license back arrangements between parent and subsidiary corporations are quite typically "royalty free." He also testified, however, that he was personally aware of instances where companies licensed intangible assets to affiliates and charged them royalties for their use. Puglisi testified that when Sherwin-Williams once asked him for a royalty-free license, he turned them down. Based on the particular facts of this case in all their fullness, we conclude that there was not substantial evidence before the board to support its finding that the royalty payments were not ordinary expenses.

Reasonableness of the royalty payments. Although we have concluded that the royalty payments that Sherwin-Williams made to the subsidiaries were ordinary and necessary expenses, we must also consider whether the amount of the royalty payments was reasonable. "Inherent in section 162(a)'s concept of 'ordinary and necessary' expenses is the requirement that any payment asserted to be allowable as a deduction... be reasonable in relation to its purpose. 'An expenditure may be, by its nature, ordinary and necessary, but at the same time it may be unreasonable in amount.'" Audano v. United States, 428 F.2d 251, 256 (5th Cir.1970).

The agreements under which payments are made will be given effect "if the arrangement is fair and reasonable, judged by the standards of a transaction entered into by parties dealing at arm's length." Stearns Magnetic Mfg. Co. v. Commissioner of Internal Revenue, 208 F.2d 849, 852 (7th Cir.1954). See Audano v. United States, supra at 256 (if agreement was such as "reasonable men dealing at arm's length" would have made, it should be valid for tax purposes). A common method for establishing reasonableness is the use of professional appraisers who can look broadly at related industries and practices and estimate a proper royalty rate. The AAA report appraised the value of the marks and recommended royalty rates ranging from one per cent to four and one-half per cent for each of Sherwin-Williams's product divisions. We are satisfied from our review of the record that this report established royalty rates that represented arm's-length transactions, and the commissioner's experts did not testify otherwise.

General Laws c. 63, §§ 39A. General Laws c. 63, §§ 39A, provides that the commissioner may determine the "net income of a foreign corporation which is a subsidiary of another corporation or closely affiliated therewith by stock ownership" by "eliminating all payments to the parent corporation or affiliated corporations in excess of fair value." The purpose of the statute is to give the commissioner the "authority to make adjustments to correct the effect of less than arm's length transactions," between closely affiliated companies, Commissioner of Revenue v. AMIWoodbroke, Inc., 418 Mass. 92, 97 (1994), and thereby address concerns that "tax evasion by means of intercorporate transactions... would depress the... income of corporations subject to taxation in Massachusetts." Id.

The board found that the transfer and license back of the marks in exchange for royalty payments were not arm's-length transactions because Sherwin-Williams controlled the subsidiaries and there was never a question that the marks would be licensed back to Sherwin-Williams because its existence depended on their use. It further found that the royalty payments had no economic purpose because Sherwin-Williams had itself created the obligation by transferring the marks, and the subsidiaries did nothing to add value to them which would justify such payments. Consequently, it concluded that any payments were in excess of fair market value.

Sherwin-Williams contends that §§ 39A does not apply to it because it is a parent corporation, not a subsidiary. It also contended that the royalty payments reflected fair value and arm's-length rates as evidenced by the AAA appraisal report, the testimony of its own witnesses, and the testimony of the commissioner's experts. Consequently, there were no payments to eliminate.

Although we agree with the board that the transactions were not entered into at arm's length, the relevant inquiries are whether the transfers were bona fide (which we have concluded they were) and if so, whether the royalty rates paid were in excess of fair market value (which we have concluded they were not).

Assuming that §§ 39A, construed to give effect to its broad remedial purpose, permits the commissioner to eliminate payments made by a parent to a subsidiary corporation, it does so only to the extent that those payments are in excess of fair value. Having concluded that the board was in error in concluding that the payments were in excess of fair value, we hold that the commissioner's adjustment to Sherwin-Williams's income could not have been made pursuant to Section 39A.

Interest expense. The commissioner disallowed a deduction for interest that Sherwin-Williams paid SWIMC in connection with a short-term loan of $7 million. The rationale for the disallowance was that, because the royalty payments from Sherwin-Williams to SWIMC were unnecessary, the loan back to Sherwin-Williams and the interest on that loan were also unnecessary. The board affirmed the disallowance. We reverse. Because we have concluded that the transfer and license back of the marks was not a sham and the royalty payments were necessary and ordinary expenses of Sherwin-Williams, and because there is no dispute that the loan was actually made, the interest paid to secure it was deductible.

The decision of the Appellate Tax Board is *reversed*.

Department of Taxes, State of Vermont
Ruling 2002-01
January 8, 2002

You have requested a ruling on the question of [company] status as an investment and holding company described in 32 V.S.A. §§ 5837. This ruling relies on information provided in your letters of October 12, 2001 and December 15, 2000.

Factual Background

[company], [company], [company], and [company] are affiliated corporations with [company] being the indirect parent. [company] and [company] are wholly owned subsidiaries of [company].

At all times during 2001, [company] has limited its activities to maintaining and managing its intangible investments and the collection and distribution of income from such investments. Its principal asset consists of intercompany loans to [company]. To the extent that [company] has cash that has not been loaned to [company], such cash is in checking and money market accounts with a Vermont branch of [bank] or is invested in short-term obligations through an investment account with the [bank].

A has entered into a loan agreement with [company] whereby [company] has agreed to extend credit in amounts approved from time to time for periods not to exceed sixty days. Each loan bears interest at the "CDOR Rate" plus a "market spread." The CDOR Rate is average rate for Canadian dollar denominated bankers acceptances for an equivalent term. To the extent [company] has funds not loaned to [company] the funds are invested in portfolio investments. A has one full-time employee, its president, who facilitates the intercompany loans and manages the portfolio investments. A also has one part-time employee who is responsible for these functions when the president is unavailable and one part-time clerk.

The parties contemplate a merger of [company] into [company] and the resulting company continuing the above activity. The activities may also be expanded to include holding loans of other affiliates and the acquisition of certain trademarks, tradenames and similar intellectual property from [company] or other affiliates of [company]. A would license this intellectual property in consideration for the licensees' promise to pay royalties based on sales or other indicia of the licensee's use.

Discussion

Section 5837 of title 32, titled "Investment and holding companies," provides as follows: The tax imposed by this subchapter [corporation income tax] as it applies to corporations whose activities are confined to the maintenance and management of their intangible investments and the collection and distribution of income from such investments or from tangible property physically located outside this state shall not exceed the $150.00 minimum tax provided by section 5832 of this title. For the purpose of this section "intangible investments" shall include without limitation investments in stocks, bonds, notes and other debt obligations (including obligations of affiliated corporations), patents, patent applications, copyrights, trademarks, trade names and similar types of intangible assets.

None of the activities of [company] or [company], as described above, are outside the activities allowed in §§ 5837. The statute contemplates the management of passive investments (rather than active business operations). In determining whether a corporation's activities are within the scope of §§ 5837, the Department considers the presence of an investment intent, the lack of non-investment activity (such as marketing), and whether the investment is effectively a diversion of operating income of an affiliate. In the context of the entire operation, the intercompany loans qualify as investments.

This ruling will be made public after deletion of the parties' names and any information which may identify the parties. A copy of the ruling showing the proposed deletions is attached, and you may request, within 30 days, that the Commissioner delete any further information which might tend to identify interested parties. The final discretion as to deletions, however, remains with the Commissioner.

This ruling is issued solely to your business and is limited to the facts presented as affected by current statutes and regulations. Other taxpayers may refer to this ruling to determine the Department's general approach, but the Department will not be bound by this ruling in the case of any other taxpayer or in the case of any change in the relevant statute or regulations.3 V.S.A. §§ 808 provides that this ruling will have the same status as an agency decision or order in a contested case. You have the right to appeal this ruling within thirty (30) days.

Sincerely,
George H. Phillips
Policy Analyst
Approved, this _____ day of January 2002

Janet Ancel
Commissioner of Taxes
2002 WL 660486

Harris v. Commissioner
Circuit Court of Appeals, Fifth Circuit
16 F.3d 75 (5th Cir. 1994)

E. Grady Jolly, Circuit Judge:

The taxpayer appeals from the Tax Court's denial of his deduction of his distributive share of payments made by his partnership to a corporation as a research and development expense under 26 U.S.C. § 174(a)(1). Because we find the partnership did not pay for research and development "in connection with" its own trade or business, we affirm the Tax Court.

I

In 1981, Jake Bauer and Howard Leith carried out a plan to attract capital for continued funding of their research and development of cementitious composites for use as tooling in the aerospace industry and of glass-reinforced cement for use in a substitute for wood in shipping pallets. First, Bauer and Leith formed CemCom Research Associates, Inc. ("CemCom") to own the technology and conduct research. Bauer and Leith anticipated that CemCom would license the finalized technology to other entities that would manufacture and sell the resulting cement products. Second, the two men retained an investment advisor, Mr. Townsend, to form Research One Limited Partnership (the "Partnership") to attract capital by selling limited partnership interests to the public. Third, the Partnership executed a Research and Development Agreement (the "R & D Agreement") under which the Partnership contracted out all of the research work to CemCom. The R & D Agreement provided that all property rights arising from CemCom's research would vest in the Partnership, and the Partnership would pay installments totaling $5,050,000 to CemCom for the research services. Fourth, the Partnership and CemCom executed a Technology Transfer Agreement (the "Transfer Agreement") under which CemCom received the option of obtaining a perpetual exclusive license of the resulting technology. CemCom would have to pay substantial royalties to the Partnership if it exercised the option. If it did not exercise the option, however, CemCom, Bauer, and Leith could not engage in any research, development, or business activity involving the cement technology for a period of five years.

Under the R & D Agreement, the first two installments payable to CemCom, totaling $2,250,000, would be funded with capital paid into the Partnership by the partners. The final installment of $2,800,000 would be paid over an eight-year period beginning in 1984. The investment prospectus indicated that the promoters anticipated the final installment to be offset by royalties paid by CemCom to the Partnership after the exercise of the licensing option. In the event these royalties were insufficient to provide additional research funds to CemCom, the limited partners would be personally liable for their proportionate share of the final installment. Townsend told potential limited partners that although it was not highly probable that CemCom would exercise its current option with high royalty payments, it was highly probable that CemCom would renegotiate the licensing option to provide for lower royalty payments.

When the research and development did not produce results as quickly as hoped, Mr. Townsend became involved in assisting CemCom in negotiating sublicensing agreements with third parties and in obtaining capital from outside sources. In September 1984, CemCom negotiated a new licensing agreement with the Partnership that provided for royalty payments that were lower than those projected in the original option, but were stillsufficient to avoid requiring the limited partners to fund the third installment under the R & D Agreement. Between 1984 and 1986, the Partnership, as CemCom's assignee, received six patents on the cement technology. In March 1986, CemCom granted an exclusive sublicense to a chemical company to commercialize all of CemCom's technology and products for twenty-five years. Four months later, the Partnership renegotiated its licensing agreement with CemCom to provide for lower minimum royalty payments, but higher maximum royalty payments.

In 1981, the Partnership accrued a deduction of $5,050,000 for research expenses under section 174(a)(1) of the Internal Revenue Code. As a limited partner, Mr. Harris deducted his distributive share of this amount, and the Commissioner disallowed the deduction.

II

The Tax Court agreed with the Commissioner and disallowed the deduction because it held that the Partnership did not expend the funds "in connection with [its] trade or business." Specifically, the Tax Court held that there was no "realistic prospect" that the Partnership would develop and exploit the cement technology, through manufacture of a product or licensing of technology, in a trade or business of its own. Instead, the Partnership was a passive investment vehicle. The Tax Court also found that the transfer of the cement technology to CemCom via the licensing agreement did not constitute a trade or business of the Partnership. Further, the Tax Court held that the clause in the R & D Agreement that stated that CemCom undertook the research activities "on behalf" of the Partnership did not attribute the trade or business of CemCom to the Partnership.

III
A

Before the enactment of section 174, the treatment of research expenditures depended on whether the taxpayer incurring the expenses was an ongoing business or a start-up business. Ongoing businesses could deduct research expenditures as ordinary and necessary expenses incurred in "carrying on a trade or business." *See* 26 U.S.C. § 162 (1988). Start-up companies, however, were prevented from deducting research expenses by the general rule that companies that had not yet begun business could not deduct expenses because they did not incur the expenses in "carrying on" a trade or business. Accordingly, start-up companies had to capitalize these expenditures and their future ability to recover the costs depended on the ultimate and sometimes unpredictable results of the research. If the research effort was ultimately unsuccessful, the start-up company could deduct the cost incurred as an abandonment loss.[3] If the expenditures were successful and produced a result that had a determinable useful life, such as a patent, the start-up company could amortize the cost over the relevant useful life.[4] If the successful effort produced a result without a determinable useful life, the start-up company had no means of recovering the cost of research results short of selling the project *in toto* to a third party.[5]

In designing section 174, Congress intended to: (1) eliminate the tax treatment uncertainty faced by start-up companies beginning a research project where they could not anticipate whether their efforts would result in patentable or nonpatentable results; and (2) encourage research and experimentation.[6] To this end, Congress mollified the harsh effects of section 162's beginning business requirement by drafting section 174 to allow a deduction of research expenditures incurred "in connection with," instead of in "carrying on," a trade or business language. Section 174(a)(1) provides: "A taxpayer may treat research or experimental expenditures which are paid or incurred by him during the taxable year *in connection with his trade or business* as expenses which are not chargeable to [the] capital account. The expenditures so treated shall be allowed as a deduction." (Emphasis added).

There has since been one Supreme Court case interpreting this section. In *Snow v. Commissioner*, 416 U.S. 500 (1974), the Supreme Court allowed a partnership to deduct research expenses under section 174 for the development of an incinerator even though the device had not been marketed at the end of the relevant tax year. The Court viewed section 174's "in connection with" language—unlike section 162's "carrying on" language—as allowing the partnership to deduct the research expenses even though the expenditures were connected with a future business of the partnership rather than its current business.

B

Although *Snow* settled that the temporal nexus of a research project to the start of an active trade or business was not dispositive of section 174's applicability, it left open the degree of "connection" required between the expenditures and the operation of the trade or business itself—the operational nexus—in order to trigger section 174's exception to the general rule of nondeductibility of pre-operation expenditures. In analyzing the operational nexus facet of section 174, the courts have dealt with a broad spectrum of financial arrangements. At one end of the spectrum lie arrangements in which a partnership buys stock in a corporation, which then uses the capital to fund research activities, manages the research activities itself, manufactures the resulting product, sells the product in the marketplace, and returns a portion of the profits to the partnership as dividends. In these situations, the partnership does not incur research expenses in connection with its trade or business but, instead, functions as an investment vehicle that cannot deduct the cash paid to the corporation under section 174 even if the corporation used that very cash to fund its research expenditures. At the other end of the spectrum lie financial arrangements in which a partnership uses its own funds to conduct research activities, manufactures the product itself, and sells that product in the marketplace. In this instance, the partnership incurs research and development expenditures in connection with its trade or business and can deduct them under section 174. It is between these clearly defined ends of the spectrum that the cases that guide our decision today lie.

---

3. S.Rep. No. 1622, 83d Cong., 2d Sess. 1, 33 (1954), *reprinted in* 1954 U.S.C.C.A.N. 4621, 4663.
4. *Id.* at 33, 1954 U.S.C.C.A.N. at 4663.
5. *Id.* at 33, 1954 U.S.C.C.A.N. at 4664.
6. *Id.*

In *Snow,* the partnership actually conducted research activities. The general partner was an inventor and devoted a significant amount of time to the research and development of the incinerator. The partnership also contracted out some of the research work to an engineering firm. Eventually, the research was successful, the partnership incorporated and sold the incinerators to the public. Thus, the partnership incurred the research expenditures "in connection with" its trade or business of developing, manufacturing, and selling incinerators, and the court allowed the section 174 deduction.

In *Smith v. Commissioner,* 937 F.2d 1089, 1091 (6th Cir.1991), the partnership obtained a license to use certain energy technology. In order to construct and operate an energy plant, the partnership contracted out all the research and the construction oversight to an outside research firm. After the plant was completed, however, the partnership owned, operated, and managed the plant to produce "synthetic fuel for marketing purposes." Because, the research fees paid to the outside firm were "in connection with" the partnership's trade or business of developing, owning, and operating an energy plant, and section 174 applied to allow the deduction of research expenses.

In *Zink v. United States,* 929 F.2d 1015, 1017 (5th Cir.1991), this court dealt with a financial arrangement in which individuals owned plans for component airplane parts instead of partnership interests. The taxpayers contracted out both the research work and the manufacturing and marketing activities. Under the relevant agreements, the individuals paid cash to an aircraft design company to conduct the research on the airplane parts. Although the individuals would own the resulting plans, these plans had no market value because they were only for the components of an overall design. Further, as part of the initial agreements, the individuals immediately licensed the right to use, sublicense, and otherwise exploit the results of the research. Thus, there was no "realistic prospect" that the investors who admittedly knew nothing about the airplane business would ever engage in developing or marketing airplanes or airplane parts. Accordingly, we denied the deduction under section 174.

Spellman v. Commissioner, 845 F.2d 148 (7th Cir.1988) (Posner, J.), is illustrative of cases the circuit courts have dealt with in which a partnership did not immediately grant a license to the research company to manufacture and market the results of the research, but in which the economic realities of the arrangement insured that the partnership would grant such a license instead of exploiting the research results itself.[7] In *Spellman,* a limited partnership paid a pharmaceutical company to engage in research to develop penicillins and granted the pharmaceutical company the exclusive right to "make, sell, license, etc." the new penicillins and the option to purchase any byproducts of the research for a small fee. The court found that there was no realistic prospect that the partnership would engage in the business of manufacturing or marketing the penicillins because, despite the partnership's claimed reversionary rights to the penicillins, it was not prepared to exploit the drugs itself. Furthermore, even though the partnership had the rights to the byproducts of the research, the fact that the pharmaceutical company could purchase the rights to exploit the research byproducts for a small fee

---

7. See *Kantor v. Commissioner,* 998 F.2d 1514 (9th Cir.1993) (denying section 174 deduction where partnership contracted all software research out to research corporation and, although the partnership would "own" the resulting software, the corporation had a low-cost option to market the resulting software); *Diamond v. Commissioner,* 930 F.2d 372 (4th Cir.1991) (denying section 174 deduction to partnership where the economic reality was that a research corporation would perform all robotics research and, although the partnership would "own" the results of the research, the corporation had a no-cost option to manufacture and market the results of that research).

dimmed the prospects that the partnership itself would manufacture or market the byproducts. Thus, the court affirmed the Tax Court's grant of summary judgment denying deductibility under section 174 because there was no realistic prospect the results of the expenditures would be used "in connection with" the partnership's trade or business.

C

As with the courts before us, we must sift through research and development agreements, technology transfer agreements, options, licenses, etc., in order to ascertain whether the economic realities of the financial arrangement in this case warrant allowance of the section 174 deduction.[8] All of the above cases—both those allowing and disallowing the section 174 deduction—involved a profit motive. *See, e.g., Zink*, 929 F.2d at 1021 (stating that section 174's trade or business requirement necessitates a profit motive). Consequently, the mere presence of a profit motive in the financial arrangement here is not determinative of whether the section 174 deduction will be allowed. In our view, those cases in which a section 174 deduction was upheld may be distinguished by one dispositive factor: In each of the cases allowing the deduction, the entity that incurred the research expenses actually managed and actually controlled the use or marketing of the research results. The question here is whether the Tax Court was clearly erroneous in finding the nexus of those activities was to CemCom instead of the Partnership.

IV
A

On appeal, Harris focuses his argument on the marketing of the research results.[10] He contends that the Partnership was in the trade or business of licensing—marketing the right to use—the cement technology that CemCom developed. *See Louw v. Commissioner*, 30 T.C.M. (CCH) 1421 (1971) (holding that the exploitation of inventions through royalties, sales of patents, or otherwise may constitute a business). Harris points out that the Partnership did in fact obtain patents, as CemCom's assignee. Harris argues that the Partnership had a realistic prospect of licensing those patents in either of two ways. First, because of the very high royalty expenses CemCom would incur if it exercised the option to license the patents back from the Partnership—in contrast to the small fee to license the research results that the research company was confronted with in *Spellman*—there was a significant possibility that CemCom would not license the technology and, thus, the Partnership would have to license it in the marketplace. Second, even if the Partnership did plan only to license the patents to CemCom, the licensing of those patents alone would constitute the trade or business of licensing the technology.

The Partnership did in fact license those patents to CemCom, and the Partnership's general partner, Townsend, helped CemCom in negotiating the ultimate sublicense to the chemical company. Thus, Harris contends, the monies that the Partnership paid CemCom to develop the patentable technology were in connection with the Partner-

---

8. As the Seventh Circuit noted in *Spellman*, 845 F.2d at 151, "[T]he Supreme Court's interpretation of section 174(a)(1) fairly invited the creation of R & D tax shelters, and the bar quickly took up the invitation." The financial arrangement in the instant case evidences an unusual degree of sophistication in attempting to secure the benefits of section 174 for the limited partner-investors.

10. This approach is Harris's only claim to the deduction because CemCom performed all of the research and development activities without significant oversight by the Partnership. Further, evidence showed that the Partnership was interested in "results only" and not the actual performance of research activities as it had no plans to hire any staff.

ship's trade or business of licensing that technology. The Commissioner asserts to the contrary that the Partnership was merely an investor, and that the parties always intended that CemCom would conduct all of the research and perform all of the marketing activities with third parties which, in fact, it did.

We review *de novo* the Tax Court's legal conclusions, including its interpretations of the Internal Revenue Code. We must, however, accept the Tax Court's findings of fact unless they are clearly erroneous. We must determine whether the Tax Court was clearly erroneous in finding that, in 1981, there was a realistic prospect that the Partnership, instead of CemCom, would engage in the licensing of the cement technology.

B

Harris's first contention—that there was a realistic prospect that the Partnership would market the technology because CemCom would not exercise its option—fails because the economic realities of the instant financial arrangement do not support his contention. From the face of the documents, it might appear that unlike the research company in *Spellman,* and similar cases where the section 174 deduction was denied, CemCom would *not* exercise its option because of the extraordinarily large royalty payments. Thus, the documents might suggest that the Partnership was going to license the technology in the marketplace itself. When we look beyond the face of the documents, however, we cannot characterize as clearly erroneous the Tax Court's finding that, in 1981, the parties actually intended to renegotiate the option at a lower level of royalty payments, which would allow CemCom to license the technology from the Partnership at a reasonable price. This intent was evidenced by the covenant not to compete agreement that would have put CemCom, Bauer, and Leith out of the cement business for five years if they did not license the technology back from the Partnership. Further, the partnership had no expertise in the cement industry and no remaining capital to fund any marketing efforts. Still further, Townsend told potential investors in the Partnership that the licensing agreement would probably be renegotiated to provide for lower royalty payments. The ultimate disposition of the technology reflects the intent the parties had in 1981: CemCom sublicensed the technology it developed to a third party, the chemical company, that paid royalties to CemCom, and CemCom forwarded a portion of these royalties to the Partnership under a renegotiated licensing agreement. Thus, we hold that the Tax Court was not clearly erroneous in finding that there was no realistic prospect that the Partnership would market the technology itself.[11]

---

11. The various agreements simply do not attribute CemCom's trade or business of licensing the technology to the Partnership. Although the regulations provide that another entity may perform research on behalf of the taxpayer, Treas.Reg. § 1.174-2(a)(2) (1957),they do not provide that the other entity may conduct a trade or business on behalf of the taxpayer. *See Zink,* 929 F.2d at 1022 ("[T]he mere presence of a valid business purpose at one level of a transaction does not automatically entitle passive investors distant from the day-to-day operations of the enterprise to the associated tax benefits") (internal citations omitted). As Judge Posner hypothesized in *Spellman,* 845 F.2d at 150:

[I]t does not follow that [the partnership] could deduct these expenditures under the statute if it had dealt away to [the research company] the right to [exploit] the products resulting from the research and development. Having contracted out both the research and development and the production and marketing, [the partnership's] involvement in the product cycle might be viewed as that of an investor rather than that of an entrepreneur....

Judge Posner then stated that the remote possibility that the partnership in *Spellman* would actually exploit the byproducts was insufficient to detract from the economic realities and resulting tax effects of the above hypothetical. *Id.* at 150–51.

Harris's second contention—that the intended licensing of the patents to CemCom constituted the trade or business of marketing the technology—fails because the Partnership's licensing of the patents to CemCom did not possess the indicia of continuity and regularity necessary to endow an activity with trade or business status. The Partnership's prearranged license of the inventions that resulted from CemCom's research back to CemCom was in essence a *single* prearranged deal. One prearranged deal does not evidence the continuity and regularity found in trades or businesses. *See Commissioner v. Groetzinger*, 480 U.S. 23, 35, (1987) (stating that it has long been the law that the phrase "trade or business" involves an activity conducted "with continuity and regularity"); *Green v. Commissioner*, 83 T.C. 667, 689 (1984) (holding that although the regular licensing and sale of inventions can amount to a trade or business, the intent to dispose of all the inventions in one transaction, instead of regularly licensing inventions for profit, indicates that such activity did not rise to the level of a trade or business).[12] Thus, we hold that the Partnership was not in the trade or business of marketing the technology.

In sum, the operational nexus of the trade or business in this financial arrangement was to CemCom in 1981, because the economic realities clearly show that CemCom would conduct all the research activities and would market the results of those activities to third parties. Thus, the research expenditures made by the Partnership were not "in connection with" *its* trade or business, and section 174 does not apply.

V

For the foregoing reasons, we AFFIRM the Tax Court's denial of Harris's deduction for research and development expenditures made in connection with the Partnership's trade or business.

Scoggins v. Commissioner
Circuit Court of Appeals, Ninth Circuit
46 F.3d 950 (9th Cir. 1955)

HUG, CIRCUIT JUDGE:

This case presents the question of whether research expenditures made by a partnership, that was formed in order to develop new technology, were incurred in connection with the partnership's trade or business, so as to be deductible expenses under §174. William Scoggins and Robert Christensen were the sole partners in the partnership. They also formed a corporation in which they held the majority interest. The partnership contracted with the corporation to do the research to develop the new technology, but the partnership retained ownership of any technology developed. The partnership agreed to

---

12. Further, the record fully supports the view that the Partnership and Cemcom entered into the licensing transaction to allow CemCom to obtain revenue from outside third parties from which it then would pay the Partnership royalties. Indeed, CemCom itself did not have the financial resources necessary to pay the Partnership royalties; a sale to an independent third party was a necessary prerequisite to the financial success of the arrangement. This case is not similar to those cases in which a single product sold in a prearranged deal to an independent third party constituted a trade or business. *See, e.g., S & H, Inc. v. Commissioner*, 78 T.C. 234, 244 (1982) (holding that the sale of property acquired for the purpose of selling to an independent buyer in a single transaction constituted the trade or business of selling real estate).

pay to the corporation up to $500,000 to do the research and, in addition, gave the corporation a nonexclusive license to market the technology for a 15-month period and also an option to acquire the technology for $5 million after the license expired.

The Tax Court held that the partnership was not entitled to claim the $486,000 it expended for the research during the 1985 and 1986 tax years. It upheld the deficiencies the Commissioner of Internal Revenue ("Commissioner") assessed against the two partners and the penalties assessed for substantial underpayment of tax under 26 U.S.C. §6661.

We have jurisdiction over this timely appeal pursuant to 26 U.S.C. §7482, and we reverse.

I.

William Scoggins and Robert Christensen have been in the business of designing, manufacturing, and operating epitaxial reactors since 1972. An epitaxial reactor is a machine used in the high-technology industry to apply layers of silicon on substrate silicon wafers in accordance with customer specifications. Scoggins and Christensen had formed various business entities that had researched and developed an epitaxial reactor that they invented. That product was marketed for about 1 1/2 years and then Scoggins and Christensen sold the business for about $3 million. Pursuant to a covenant not to compete in sales transactions, Scoggins and Christensen did not undertake any significant developments in reactor technology for three years.

After the expiration of the three-year period, Scoggins and Christensen began to develop technology for a new type of epitaxial reactor. In August of 1984, Scoggins and Christensen formed the B & B Research and Development Partnership ("the partnership"). The partnership agreement specified that "the purpose of the partnership is to engage in the business, research, and development of semiconductor equipment and to do all things related to, incidental to, or in furtherance of such purpose, and to engage in any other business as the general partners may deem appropriate."

About two months before, Scoggins and Christensen had formed a corporation entitled Epitaxy Systems, Inc., ("the corporation") for the purpose of providing research and experimentation services on a contract basis. Scoggins and Christensen together owned 75% of the corporation's stock. In August of 1984, the partnership executed a research and development agreement with the corporation under the terms of which the partnership engaged the corporation to perform certain research, development, and technical work toward developing the new epitaxial reactor. Under the agreement, the corporation agreed to use its best and reasonable efforts to research and develop a new epitaxial reactor. The partnership agreed to provide the corporation with up to $500,000, consisting of $43,000 to be paid upon the execution of the agreement and additional amounts to be paid at the partnership's discretion, as necessary, to complete the research. In addition to the monetary compensation, the partnership granted the corporation a 15-month nonexclusive license and thereafter an option to purchase the rights to the technology for $5 million. The nonexclusive license allowed the corporation to use and sell the technology throughout the entire world in exchange for a 20% royalty to be paid to the partnership. The option to purchase the technology provided that the corporation had one year, beginning 18 months after the technology was finally developed, in which it could purchase all the rights to the technology for $5 million. At least $1 million was to be paid in cash and the rest by a promissory note secured by the research project with interest at the rate of 110% of the applicable imputed interest rate periodically established pursuant to the Internal Revenue Code. Any licenses granted by the partnership to others were to be subject to the corporation's option.

On its partnership information returns for 1985 and 1986, the partnership reported $290,000 and $196,000, respectively, as deductible research and experimentation expenditures under 26 U.S.C. § 174(a)(1). As partners, appellants claimed their distributive share of these expenditures as pass-through deductions on their personal income tax returns for those years. Under general principles of partnership and taxation law, a partnership does not, itself, pay taxes. Instead, the partners claim a pro-rata share of the partnership's profits and losses and each pays tax on his share. *See Kantor v. Commissioner*, 998 F.2d 1514, 1517 n. 1 (9th Cir.1993).

The Commissioner disallowed appellants' deductions, determined a deficiency in their income taxes for 1985 and 1986, and added penalties for negligence and substantial understatement of tax liability. The Scogginses' combined deficiency for both years totalled $175,448. The Christensens' combined deficiency totalled $176,705. The Commissioner did not dispute that the partnership's expenditures were incurred for research and experimentation or that the enterprise was motivated by a genuine profit motive. Instead, the Commissioner determined that the partnership could not have incurred the expenditures in connection with its own trade or business, as required by section 174(a)(1).

After a consolidated trial, the Tax Court upheld the Commissioner's disallowance of appellants' deductions and the Commissioner's additions to tax for substantial underpayment, but reversed the negligence penalties. The Tax Court concluded that the partnership did not have a realistic prospect of exploiting the technology in a business of its own. Instead, the court determined that the partnership was only the investment vehicle for technology developed by the corporation which would likely be exploited, if at all, by the corporation. We conclude that the Tax Court erred in denying Scoggins and Christensen their research expenditure deductions under section 174.

II.

Section 174(a)(1) of the Internal Revenue Code allows a taxpayer to deduct from income "research or experimental expenditures which are paid or incurred by him during the taxable year in connection with his trade or business." Treasury Regulation § 1.174-2(a)(2) further provides that a taxpayer may deduct these expenses even when the research is "carried on in his behalf by another person or organization...."

In *Kantor*, we construed section 174 of the Internal Revenue Code in connection with a partnership that sought to deduct research expenditures made in connection with the development of new technology. We noted that in 1974 the Supreme Court held that section 174 deductions were available to "up-and-coming enterprises whose only 'business' at the time they incur research expenditures is the research itself." 998 F.2d at 1518 (citing *Snow v. Commissioner*, 416 U.S. 500 (1974)). We noted that the Supreme Court had concluded that section 174 was intended to modify the more restrictive provisions of section 162 "by providing new businesses, which are not yet selling goods or services, an immediate deduction for research and experimental expenditures." *Id.* However, as we held in *Kantor*, "[a]lthough a taxpayer need not be conducting a trade or business at the time it incurs the research expenditure, the taxpayer must demonstrate a 'realistic prospect' of subsequently entering its own business in connection with the fruits of the research, assuming that the research is successful." *Id.* We held that a taxpayer demonstrates such a prospect by "manifesting both the objective intent to enter such a business and the capability of doing so." *Id.*

III.

Scoggins and Christensen owned the partnership and had the controlling interest in the corporation. They had previously developed an epitaxial reactor and had successfully marketed it. They had invented a new type of "pancake-heated" epitaxial reactor and contributed to the partnership all the technology associated with the design and production of that product. They decided to contract with the corporation to do the research necessary to develop the technology into a marketable product. The corporation obviously affords limited liability to its shareholders in conducting its operations. The partnership expended $486,000 of the funds contributed by Scoggins and Christensen to pay for the corporation to do the research. That research was done under the guidance of Scoggins and Christensen with the assistance of three corporate employees. There is no question that Scoggins and Christensen had the objective intent to enter into the business of marketing the reactor if the reactor proved successful. The only question is whether they had a realistic prospect of engaging in the business as a partnership, or whether by virtue of the agreement with the corporation, they had deprived the partnership of the capability of doing so.

It is apparent that the two partners had the technical expertise to market the reactor. They were the inventors and designers of this reactor, and they had developed the business that had marketed their first reactor. They had evidenced the financial ability to conduct the business. Under the agreement, they had the right to market the product for 18 months and for an indefinite time if the corporation they controlled did not purchase the technology for $5 million within one year thereafter. It is possible that the corporation would find it economical to pay the $5 million to purchase the technology and pay the 20% royalty to the partnership if the research turned out to be successful; however, it had to be successful enough for the corporation to amortize the purchase price and pay the royalty.

It is worth noting that even the 15-month nonexclusive license given to the corporation was permissive; the corporation made no commitment to market the product. The partnership owned the technology and had the indefeasible right to market it either itself or through others for 18 months (3 months longer than the corporation). It had the indefinite right to market the product unless the corporation exercised its option to buy the technology after the first 18 months for $5 million.

We conclude that Scoggins and Christensen, through the partnership, had both the objective intent to enter the business and the capability of doing so. The possibility that the corporation could choose to buy out the technology did not vitiate either the objective intent or the capability of the partnership entering the business of marketing the reactor.

IV.

Our opinion in *Kantor* had not been published at the time of the Tax Court decision. However, the Tax Court correctly identified the relevant inquiry as being "whether the partnership had realistic prospects of engaging in a trade or business." The Tax Court concluded it did not. The historical facts relevant to this inquiry are not in dispute. The conclusion of the Tax Court is based largely upon the terms of the agreement between the partnership and the corporation, the fact that the partnership did not have office furniture, telephones, or employees, and the fact that it had made no effort during 1984 or 1985 to market the technology to other licensees.

We examine the facts relied upon by the Tax Court and the conclusions reached.

1. TERMS OF THE AGREEMENT

The focus of the Tax Court's conclusion, based on the terms of the agreement, is summarized by the following paragraph of the opinion.

> Pursuant to the R & D Agreement B & B ("the partnership") had given substantial rights to the technology to Systems ("research corporation") in exchange for a 20% royalty fee. What it had left it gave Systems an option to buy. Thus, B & B had contractually precluded itself from engaging in any trade or business.

The facts are that the agreement gave to the corporation a *nonexclusive* license to sell the technology for the limited period of 15 months. The corporation was required to pay the partnership a 20% royalty on the net sales revenue received for sales made during the 15-month period. The partnership could market the technology during this 15-month period without paying a royalty or it could engage others to market the technology.

During this 15-month period, the partnership was actually in a better financial position than the corporation to market the product because it would not have the 20% royalty taken off the top of the net sales revenue. The option to purchase the technology was not available until the end of the 15-month nonexclusive license period plus an additional three months (during which the corporation's license would have expired but before the corporation could exercise its option). After this 18-month period expired, the corporation had one year in which to decide whether to exercise the option. During that year, the corporation had no right to sell the product, while the partnership, as the owner of the technology, had the continuing right to do so.

As a practical matter, in order to remain in the business of selling the epitaxial reactor, the corporation had to exercise the option immediately after the 18-month period and pay to the partnership the $5 million purchase price for the technology. In deciding to do so, the corporation would have to be able to determine that the potential sales would justify amortizing the $5 million acquisition price plus a 20% royalty on net sales.

2. OFFICE EQUIPMENT AND TELEPHONES

The Tax Court placed some emphasis upon the fact that the partnership did not have office equipment or telephones. This certainly is not remarkable, in that until the technology had been developed into a marketable product, there was no need for office equipment or telephones. This is the very situation that was envisioned by the enactment of section 174 and the interpretation placed upon it by the Supreme Court in *Snow*. The idea behind section 174 is to encourage research and experimentation by small, new enterprises and to place them on an equal footing with established businesses, which may deduct under section 162(a) the expenses incurred while carrying on a trade or business. Consequently, taxpayers whose only "business" at the time they incur the research expenditures is the research itself are eligible for the expense deduction under section 174. *Kantor*, 998 F.2d at 1518. Thus, while new businesses must capitalize their "start-up" or "preoperational" expenses because they are not deductible under section 162, section 174 alters this requirement by permitting new, pioneering businesses, which are not yet selling goods or services, to deduct immediately expenditures incurred for research and experimentation.

3. NO EMPLOYEES

An additional justification by the Tax Court was that the partnership had no employees that could engage in the business once the technology was developed. The corporation had three employees and, in addition, had the guidance and expertise of the two partners. The partnership had the two key personnel—Scoggins and Christensen—the inventors of the epitaxial reactor and the persons most knowledgeable about the technology itself. These two partners were obviously in a position in the partnership to employ whatever marketing, manufacturing, or other personnel that would be necessary to place the product on the market. Scoggins, Christensen, and the three research employees in the corporation would be in no better position, from an employee standpoint, to market the product than would the partnership.

This partnership situation differed significantly from other frequently encountered situations where the partnership is composed entirely of investors with no expertise in the product that is to be developed. Here, this partnership was made up of the two persons who were the most intimately involved in the development of the epitaxial reactor.

4. NO EFFORT TO LICENSE THE TECHNOLOGY

The Tax Court placed some emphasis upon the fact that the partnership had not, as of 1984 or 1985, made attempts to license the technology to others as they could under their agreement. This is unremarkable, in that the technology had not, as yet, been developed and there would be serious difficulties and competitive risks in marketing an epitaxial reactor that had not been fully developed.

V.

It is important to contrast the factual situation involved in this case with that which was involved in the *Kantor* case. The partnership involved in *Kantor* was composed entirely of investors with the exception of one person who was knowledgeable about the computer software product that was sought to be developed. The research and development contract was made with a completely independent research corporation with royalty payments to be made to the partnership. In that case, although the partnership had retained ownership of a technology to be developed, it had given the independent research corporation an option to acquire exclusive licensee rights to the technology for the nominal sum of $5,000. It is clear that the $5,000-option price was nominal in comparison to the $3.15 million research expenditure that had been advanced by the partnership. In the *Kantor* case, the contractual arrangement made it unrealistic to conclude that if the $3.15 million expended in research were successful in producing a marketable product, the research corporation would not expend the $5,000 to obtain the exclusive licensing rights. In striking contrast, in this case the research expenditures by this partnership were to be $500,000 and the exclusive rights to the technology could not be obtained without paying $5 million. This was not a nominal acquisition price in comparison to the research cost, and the $5 million was a significant impediment to the corporation's ability to engage in the business of marketing the technology. In *Kantor*, on the other hand, it was virtually certain that the research firm would acquire the technology for the nominal $5,000 figure if the research was successful.

A further distinction is that in *Kantor* if the research firm paid $5,000 it was immediately entitled to market the product exclusively. The partnership had no initial 18-month period in which it could market the product as in the case now before us.

The contrast of the composition of the two entities involved in each case is also significant. In *Kantor*, the partnership contracted with a completely independent research firm. Although the general partner, Hubert, monitored the research, neither he nor the partnership had any ownership or official position in the research firm. In this case, the partnership and the corporation were both controlled and financed by Scoggins and Christensen. It was these partners who would have to be willing to raise $5 million on behalf of the corporation in order for the corporation to be able to continue to market the reactor after the 15-month nonexclusive license expired. The partnership could proceed before and after the 15-month period without raising this capital or paying any royalty.

VI.

Scoggins and Christensen were actively involved in the development of the technology as partners. Indeed, of all those working on the project, they probably had the most technical knowledge and experience with the technology. Christensen owned his own equipment which was available to the partnership should the partnership need it. On behalf of the partnership, the partners directed and guided the research of the corporation. They invented the technology, directed the research, kept their own records, expended $500,000 of their personal funds on the experimentation, and were involved on a daily basis in the progress of the technology. Scoggins and Christensen, through their partnership, are among the class of taxpayers Congress intended to encourage and reward by enacting section 174.

VII.

Based upon the undisputed facts of this case, we conclude that the partnership had a realistic prospect of subsequently entering into its own business in connection with the fruits of the research if the research was successful. The partnership's contractual arrangements and activities indicated both an objective intent and the capability to enter such business. The taxpayers' deductions under section 174 were properly taken.

Reversed.

Chapter 8

Taxation of Intellectual Property Litigation

I. Assignment for Chapter 8

Read: Internal Revenue Code: §§ 162; 212; 263

Treasury Regulations: §§ 1.263(a)-2; 1.212-1(k)

Materials: Overview
Safety Tube Corp. v. Commissioner
Urquhart v. Commissioner
Danskin, Inc. v. Commissioner
Georator Corp. v. United States
Rust-Oleum Corp. v. United States
Big Four Industries, Inc. v. Commissioner
Mathey v. Commissioner
Inco Electroenergy Corp. v. Commissioner
Illinois Tool Works v. Commissioner
Field Service Advisory 199925012

Complete the Problems.

II. Problems for Chapter 8

1. InvenCo enters into a license agreement with Licensee wherein InvenCo grants Licensee the exclusive right to use a patent for two years in connection with Licensee's manufacture and marketing of certain products covered by the patent. Licensee fails to pay royalty payments in breach of the license agreement, and InvenCo initiates a suit against Licensee. InvenCo incurs $50,000 in litigation costs. What is the tax treatment of the litigation costs?

2. InvenCo's marketing associates discover that Competitor is selling a new product that is infringing on InvenCo's patent. Upon further investigation, InvenCo initiates a suit against Competitor alleging Competitor's product is infringing on InvenCo's patent and such infringement is willful. In its complaint, InvenCo requests

the court for attorneys' fees and treble damages. Competitor asserts that InvenCo's patent is invalid. InvenCo incurs $250,000 in litigation costs associating with Competitor's invalidity defense.

    a. What is the tax treatment of InvenCo's $250,000 litigation costs?

    b. Assume that the litigation proceeds to trial and the jury enters a verdict in favor of InvenCo. The jury found that Competitor had willfully infringed InvenCo's patent and awarded InvenCo damages in the amount of $1.0 million. What is the tax treatment of the award?

    c. If InvenCo also received an award for attorneys' fees in the amount of $750,000, what is the tax treatment of the award for attorneys' fees?

3. Assume that in Problem 2, Competitor pays to InvenCo the $1.75 million judgment upon Competitor's exhaustion of all its appellate rights. In the year preceding the trial, Competitor purchased the entire business entity (BE) that was selling and marketing the infringing product. Competitor and BE negotiated the purchase price and allocated $200,000 for InvenCo's pending litigation. BE represented that InvenCo's suit was meritless, and in the worst case scenario the suit would cost $500,000. Competitor's attorneys concurred with BE's representation. Now, after paying the $1.75 million judgment to InvenCo, Competitor would like to deduct the total amount in the year it incurs. What is the tax treatment of the judgment amount?

4. Debbie has been using the trademark JDI in commerce in connection with the sale and marketing of running shoes. She applied for and received a federal trademark registration for JDI from the Patent and Trademark Office. Nike, a major shoe manufacturer and marketer, has recently filed a cancellation of the trademark registration JDI, contending that JDI is confusingly similar to Nike's "Just Do It" registered trademark. Debbie is considering defending her federal trademark registration. What is the tax consequence of the costs that Debbie will incur in the cancellation proceeding?

5. Assume that in Problem 4, Nike is vigilant in protecting its "Just Do It" trademark. Nike decides to bring an action against Debbie in a federal district court in Oregon. Nike asserts trademark infringement claim under Section 32 of the Lanham Act and unfair competition claim under Section 43(a) of the Lanham Act against Debbie. For litigation purposes, Nike commissions a consumer survey demonstrating that the "Just Do It" trademark is a known trademark. A nationwide consumer survey is rather expensive; Nike incurs $120,000 for the survey. Thereafter, Nike and Debbie decide to settle the lawsuit and the cancellation proceeding. Nike incurs $200,000 in attorneys' fees. What is the tax treatment of Nike's costs relating to the litigation, including the consumer survey?

6. MacroSoft, Inc. initiates a trademark infringement suit against a competitor for using a trademark that is similar to the MACROSOFT trademark. MacroSoft receives a settlement sum of $50,000 from the competitor. What is the tax treatment of the settlement sum?

III. Overview

A. Tax Treatment of Intellectual Property Litigation Costs

As part of intellectual property enforcement, intellectual property owners resort to litigation against infringing activities. Intellectual property infringement actions include unauthorized use of a trademark, manufacture of products based on a patent, appropriation of trade secrets, and reproduction of a registered copyright. In intellectual property litigation, the owner desires to enjoin the illegal conduct, seek compensatory or statutory damages and, in some instances, attorneys' fees and costs against willful infringers. In such litigation, the defendant often asserts affirmative defenses including that the trademark at issue is invalid because it has become generic or it is descriptive without secondary meaning established, the patent at issue is invalid because it is obvious or lacks novelty, or the work of authorship at issue contains preexisting materials available in the public domain. Consequently, the intellectual property owner will incur litigation costs, including the costs to overcome affirmative defenses that threaten to cancel or invalidate the property rights held by the owner.

In a 1999 Field Service Advisory, the Service observed that despite the existence of settled legal precedents in general intellectual property law, judicial precedents and the Service's positions pertaining to tax treatment of intellectual property litigation costs are extremely limited. *See* F.S.A. 199925012 (June 25, 1999) (citing Treas. Reg. § 1.263-2(a)). Many factors contribute to the non-uniform tax treatment of litigation costs involving different types of intellectual property. These factors include the type of intellectual property involved, the life of the property grants, whether the taxpayer is the plaintiff or defendant in the infringement action, the rationales and business reasons behind the action, as well as other factual circumstances involving the intangible intellectual property rights. There is no special tax law pertaining to intellectual property litigation costs. A taxpayer must apply the general tax principles relating to litigation costs embodied in §§ 162, 212, 263, and the regulations thereunder, as described below. Furthermore, the taxpayer must also consider the specific factual circumstances that exist in each intellectual property action.

Section 162 permits a deduction from income for all ordinary and necessary business expenses paid or incurred during the taxable year in carrying on any trade or business. Section 212 permits a deduction for all ordinary and necessary expenses paid or incurred during the taxable year for the production or collection of income. It should be noted that both § 162 and 212 are subject to certain exceptions. The most important exception is § 263, which disallows deductions for capital expenditures.

Treas. Reg. § 1.263(a)-2 states that "[t]he following paragraphs include examples of capital expenditures:...(c) The cost of defending title or perfecting title to property." *See* Treas. Reg. § 1.263(a)-2 (1960).

Treas. Reg. § 1.212-1(k) provides:

> Expenses paid or incurred in defending or perfecting title to property, in recovering property (other than investment property and amounts of income which, if and when recovered, must be included in gross income), or in developing or improving property, constitute a part of the cost of the property and

are not deductible expenses. Attorneys' fees paid in a suit to quiet title to lands are not deductible; but if the suit is also to collect accrued rents thereon, that portion of such fees is deductible which is properly allocable to the services rendered in collecting such rents.

As a result, the tax treatment of litigation costs depends on the nature of the litigation. If the litigation is about defending or perfecting title to intellectual property with a useful life greater than one year, the associated costs must be capitalized, and are not immediately deductible in the taxable year. If the litigation is related to the recovery of lost income stemming from intellectual property, the litigation costs are deductible immediately in the taxable year.

Generally, to be currently deductible, litigation costs must not have their origin in the acquisition or disposition of a capital asset. *See* Treas. Reg. § 1.212-1(k) (as amended in 1975). This is also known as the "origin of the claim" test, a factually specific inquiry wherein consideration must be given to "the issues involved, the nature and objectives of the suit in which the expenditures were made, the defenses asserted, the purpose for which the claimed deductions were expended, the background of the litigation, and all facts pertaining to the entire controversy." *See Morgan's Estate v. Commissioner*, 332 F.2d 144, 151 (5th Cir. 1964), *acq.*, 1966-2 C.B. 3. The corollary to the origin-of-the-claim principle is that the cost of defending or perfecting title to property is inherently a capital expenditure.

1. Litigation Costs in Patent and Copyright Cases

Generally, there is a distinction between (1) litigation costs incurred by a patent/copyright owner in cases relating to ownership of a patent/copyright, and (2) litigation costs in infringement suits involving patents/copyright. Litigation costs in patent/copyright ownership or title cases, such as those involving disputes over the uncontestedly valid patent or patents between two or more claimants, are capital expenditures and thus are not deductible in the year paid or incurred. *See Safety Tube v. Commissioner*, 168 F.2d 787 (6th Cir. 1948), reprinted below.

On the other hand, litigation costs in infringement suits involving patents/copyrights held in connection with a trade or business or an activity for profit are currently deductible (regardless of whether the taxpayer was successful or unsuccessful in the infringement action). The reason for the differing tax treatment is that costs of removing a cloud of title or defending ownership of property are inherently nondeductible capital expenditures, whereas costs incurred to recover lost profits that are taxable are generally deductible expenses. *See* Treas. Reg. § 1.162-1 (as amended in 1993); Treas. Reg. § 1.212-1 (as amended in 1972).

Despite the general tax treatment principles for litigation costs in patent/copyright cases, it is important to remember that different tax treatments of costs in patent/copyright litigations may arise from the factual circumstances of each litigation. As seen in *Urquhart v. Commissioner*, included in this chapter, courts generally examine the underlying claims that first give rise to the suit involving patent/copyright rights. The factual circumstances of each case are scrutinized as they affect the subsequent tax treatment of the expenses incurred in the original suit. An interesting issue arises concerning the tax treatment of the costs associated with defending the validity of a patent. Should the costs incurred in a litigation wherein patent validity is at issue be deductible? The answer is in *Urquhart*, included below.

2. Litigation Costs in Trademark Cases

Recalling trademark law discussed in Chapter 2, does the owner of a trademark really "own" the trademark? Section 43(a) of the Lanham Act prohibits unauthorized use of a trademark that is likely to cause consumer confusion as to source. Section 32 of the Lanham Act prohibits unauthorized use of registered trademarks. In the United States, a trademark right is based on the use of the trademark in commerce. The goodwill in a trademark is generated through its use in commerce. Since federal registration of a trademark provides broader protection than that provided under common law, most trademark owners obtain federal registrations for their trademarks.

Unlike litigation involving validity of patents in which the associated costs are deductible, defending a trademark in an action challenging its validity where its federal registration is subject to cancellation, the litigation costs incurred must be capitalized. This is seen in the case included in this chapter, *Georator Corp. v. United States*. Why did the court treat the litigation costs incurred in defending a federal trademark registration differently than the costs incurred in defending a patent validity?

(a) Litigation Costs Incurred in Trademark Infringement Cases

Unlike the costs associated with patent and copyright cases, the litigation costs incurred in a trademark infringement case are treated as nondeductible capital expenditures. Some courts have held that successful trademark infringement litigation increases the value of the trademark, secures the property right in the trademark, and removes threats of future infringement to the same trademark. Such benefits have a life of over one year. Therefor, the litigation expenses are "capital" in nature and not entitled to immediate deduction in the year paid or incurred. *See Danskin, Inc. v. Commissioner*, 331 F.2d 360 (2d Cir. 1964); *Medco Products Co., Inc. v. Commissioner*, 523 F.2d 137 (10th Cir. 1975). *Danskin*, reprinted below, addresses the tax treatment of litigation costs in trademark infringement cases.

However, the Tax Court in *J.R. Wood & Sons, Inc.* allowed the *deduction* of litigation costs incurred by a taxpayer who owned a trademark registration, initiated, and lost a trademark infringement suit against a defendant. *See J.R. Wood & Sons, Inc.*, 21 T.C.M. 1038 (1962). In a General Counsel Memorandum, the Service noted that the court's decision in *J.R. Wood* is "highly questionable in light of the more recent decisions in *Medco* and *Danskin*" and concluded that the decision is "incorrect." *See* Gen. Couns. Mem. 38,490 (Aug. 27, 1980); *see also* F.S.A. 199925012 (issued June 25, 1999).

(b) Litigation Costs Incurred in Unfair Competition Claims

Often in most trademark litigations, the trademark owner asserts both trademark infringement and unfair competition claims. The unfair competition claim under section 43(a) of the Lanham Act is a very broad claim that encompasses a defendant's use in commerce of a trademark or trade dress causes a likelihood of consumer confusion between its source and the plaintiff's trademark or trade dress. *See* 15 U.S.C. § 1125(a) (2000). The plaintiff who asserts such claim does not need to have a registered trademark or trade dress. On the other hand, a plaintiff pursuing a trademark infringement claim under section 32 of the Lanham Act must own a registered trademark or trade dress. *See* 15 U.S.C. §1114 (2000). However, most courts apply the likelihood-of-consumer-confusion test to both unfair competition claims and trademark infringement claims to reach its conclusions. Though damages are available for both claims under 15 U.S.C. §1117(a), only in willful infringement of registered trademark cases are treble damages and reasonable attorneys' fees available.

A question arises as to whether the tax treatment of the litigation costs incurred in the unfair competition claim is the same as in trademark infringement claim? As discussed earlier, courts have treated the litigation costs incurred in a trademark infringement claim as nondeductible capital expenditures. In the case included in this chapter, *Rust-Oleum Corp. v. United States*, the taxpayer plaintiff asserted both an unfair competition claim and a trademark infringement claim, how should the court treat the litigation costs incurred in the unfair competition claim? *See Rust-Oleum Corp. v. United States*, 280 F. Supp. 796, 797-98 (N.D. Ill. 1967). The IRS believed that the issue of tax treatment of the expenses incident to the unfair competition claim in *Rust-Oleum* was erroneously decided. The IRS, however, declined to appeal, because the case was "deemed to be an unfavorable vehicle for testing this issue." *See Rust-Oleum Corp. v. United States*, 280 F. Supp. 796 (N.D. Ill. 1967), *action on dec.*, Feb. 9, 1970, *available at* 1970 WL 22666.

B. Tax Treatment of Damage Awards and Settlement Proceeds in Intellectual Property Suits

1. *Damage Awards or Settlement Proceeds in Patent/Copyright Cases*

The general rule adopted by courts with regard to whether damage awards or out-of-court settlement proceeds are taxable to the recipient as income, or constitute a nontaxable return of capital depends upon the nature of the claim and the actual basis of recovery. Indeed, the taxability of damage awards or settlement proceeds in an intellectual property litigation is determined by examining the underlying purposes for which the patent/copyright litigation was brought. Courts analyze the origin and character of the litigated claims by reviewing the pleadings in the litigation and the terms of the settlement.

If the suit was brought to recover lost profits, the damage award proceeds are taxable as ordinary income. Damage awards or settlement proceeds for patent/copyright infringement are as much ordinary income as the royalties they replace. In patent and copyright infringement cases, the sum awarded as damages for the infringement to the patent or copyright represents the taxpayer's lost profits, and therefore it is taxable as ordinary income as seen in Field Service Advisory 199925012, included in this chapter. *See also Big Four Industries, Inc. v. Commissioner* and *Mathey v. Commissioner*, both of which are included below. Damage awards or settlement proceeds received from a patent or copyright infringer whether in a form of royalties or lump-sum payment are treated as ordinary income and taxable in the year received. *See Blake v. Commissioner*, 67 T.C. 7 (1976), *rev'd in part and remanded*, 615 F.2d 731 (6th Cir. 1980).

If the suit was brought to recover losses, injury, or damages to capital assets, the damage awards or settlement proceeds are nontaxable return of capital. The amount received is not for lost profits, but is a return of capital and, hence, is not taxable as ordinary income. In other words, the damage award or settlement proceeds will be considered a non-taxable return of capital. To the extent such damages exceed taxpayer's basis in the capital interest or goodwill, they will be taxed as capital gains and taxed at preferential rates. *Big Four*, excerpted below, addressed such a damage award.

2. Damage Awards/Settlement Proceeds in Trademark Cases

As stated above, the taxability of the damage award in a lawsuit depends upon the nature of the claim and the actual basis of recovery. The nature of the litigation recovery is determined by an examination of the origin and character of the claims that gave rise to the litigation, the nature of the harm, and the relief sought. The amounts received for damages to capital assets are taxable as capital gain. With regard to trademark cases, a trademark and its associated goodwill are capital assets in nature. The question arises as to whether the unauthorized use of a mark that is identical or similar to a protected trademark constitutes a harm in the form of lost profits or injury to a capital asset. What is the tax treatment of an award received by a taxpayer whose trademark, with its associated goodwill, is used by an infringer without authorization? Is the award to compensate for damages to the goodwill of the trademark, not lost profits, and is it therefore taxable as capital gain? How the court addressed such questions can be seen in *Inco Electroenergy Corp. v. Commissioner*, 54 T.C.M. (CCH) 359 (1987), included in this chapter. Is the tax treatment of a damage award or settlement proceeds in trademark infringement cases the same as in patent/copyright infringement cases?

Damage Awards for Goodwill-Covenant not to Compete. A damage award received by a taxpayer constituting compensation for diminution in the goodwill of the taxpayer's business or trademark is taxable as a capital gain. For example, in *State Fish Corp. v. Commissioner*, 48 T.C. 465 (1967), acq., 1968-2 C.B. 1, the taxpayer purchased an established and ongoing business from a seller who agreed not to open a similar business and compete with the taxpayer for a period of five years. The seller breached the covenant not to compete, and the taxpayer brought suit alleging damage to the goodwill of the business. The taxpayer prevailed and was awarded damages. The Tax Court examined the allegations set forth in the complaint, and concluded that the taxpayer was primarily concerned with the goodwill of the business, not lost profits. Accordingly, the judgment awarded in the suit was for damages to the goodwill of the taxpayer's business, not lost profits, and such recovery was taxable as capital gain.

3. Tax Treatment of Awards of Attorneys' Fees and Costs

Attorneys' fees are seldom awarded in intellectual property litigation. Only in exceptional cases will the court grant attorneys' fees and court costs to the prevailing party.

If the attorneys' fees and litigation costs have already been deducted by the taxpayer as ordinary business expenses in the year the taxpayer incurred them, and the taxpayer later received an award (either through jury or settlement) that included attorneys' fees and costs, the reimbursement of such fees constitutes the receipt of ordinary income and is taxable. For example, in *Big Four Industries, Inc. v. Commissioner*, the plaintiff in a patent infringement action received an award of $195,324.60 included the master's fee, attorneys' fees, accountants' fees, court reporter's fees, and all other costs pertaining to the patent infringement litigation. The taxpayer, as one of the two prevailing parties in the action, had deducted its share of the various fees and costs on its income tax returns prior to the district court's judgment. The reimbursement of such fees constituted the receipt of ordinary income and was held to be taxable. *Big Four Industries, Inc. v. Commissioner*, 40 T.C. 1055, 1060 (1963), *acq.*, 1964-2 C.B. 3.

If the taxpayer has not deducted the attorneys' fees and litigation costs in the year incurred, the taxpayer can subtract the amount (of the attorneys' fees and costs of the litigation) from the total damage award, if the award indeed includes attorney's fees and litigation costs. For example, in *Mathey v. Commissioner*, the taxpayer was the plaintiff in a patent infringement action. The plaintiff received, as part of the judgment, an amount of $30,536.63 for litigation fees and expenses. Subsequently, in the tax case, the Commissioner allowed the taxpayer to offset the litigation fees and expenses from the total judgment award.

C. Tax Treatment of Payments of Acquiring Intellectual Property Liability

The payment of an intellectual property liability of a preceding owner of the intellectual property by the entity acquiring such property, whether or not such liability was fixed or contingent at the time such property was acquired, is not an ordinary and necessary business expense. To qualify as an ordinary and necessary expense, the payment must be normal, usual, or customary in the type of business the taxpayer is involved. The payment of an intellectual property liability by the taxpayer acquiring such property is certainly not a normal, usual, or customary expense incurred in the taxpayer's business. Should such payment be capitalized and added to the cost basis of the acquired property? The case included in this chapter, *Illinois Tool Works v. Commissioner*, 117 T.C. 39 (2001), addresses this issue.

Payments to Others for Discontinuing Use of a Trademark. In some trademark litigations, the taxpayer pays a monetary sum to another party for the purpose of having that party discontinue use of a trademark. The other party's discontinued use of its mark would simplify the taxpayer's problem with trademark confusion. Namely, the taxpayer eliminates future consumer confusion between its mark and the other party's mark. This strengthens the taxpayer's trademark in the marketplace. The payments made to the other party seem to generate benefits to the taxpayer beyond the year the taxpayer paid the other party to discontinue its use of its trademark. Accordingly, tax law treats such payments as capital expenditures and not deductible in the year paid. *See Clark Thread Co. v. Commissioner*, 100 F.2d 257 (3d Cir. 1938); *J.I. Case Co. v. United States*, 32 F. Supp. 754 (Ct. Cl. 1940).

IV. Materials

Safety Tube Corp. v. Commissioner
8 T.C. 757 (1947), aff'd, 168 F.2d 787 (6th Cir. 1948)

BLACK, JUDGE:

Petitioner, a Delaware corporation, with its principal office at Nashville, Tennessee, was organized on September 8, 1939, with an authorized capital stock of 200,000 no par value shares, to take over a patent and other assets held by Garnett S. Andrews as trustee. This patent was granted in 1933 to Constantine Bradley on an improvement in puncture-healing inner tubes for pneumatic tires. Bradley died in December 1934, and thereupon Andrews took charge of the enterprise. On March 30, 1938, Andrews granted Sears, Roebuck & Co. the exclusive right to sell the tubes for replacement purposes during a period of two years, under a contract whereby a manufacturer would be licensed to produce them under the patent, pay royalties to Andrews, and sell the tubes to Sears, Roebuck & Co. or customers designated by the latter.

On August 16, 1939, Benjamin C. Seaton filed suit against Bradley's widow, Andrews, and others, alleging that in or before 1927 he had been granted three patents for improvements on inner tubes for vehicle tires, and had employed Bradley to sell interests therein under contracts.

The complainant then pray[ed] that...a decree be entered declaring:

...that complainant is the rightful owner of said Bradley patent number 1924148 and the rightful owner of all funds realized and paid to defendant, Garnett S. Andrews, by said Sears, Roebuck & Company,...and the beneficial and rightful owner of said Sears, Roebuck & Company contract.

On November 3, 1939, petitioner, which had qualified to do business in Tennessee, was joined as a party defendant after filing a petition which set forth that Andrews had assigned to it the patent, contract, and royalties upon its express agreement.... The Safety Tube Corporation demurred to the complaint upon the ground that it showed no cause of action. This demurrer was overruled on December 21, 1939. On March 21, 1940, the supreme court entered a decree in which it sustained the petitioner's demurrer to that part of Seaton's bill wherein Seaton prayed that he be declared the rightful owner of the Bradley patent. This removed from the litigation all question as to petitioner's ownership of the Bradley patent, No. 1,924,148. The supreme court sent the case back for trial on the remainder of the issues raised by the bill of complaint.

For [the year] 1940 petitioner received and reported a gross income of $14,910.96, consisting entirely of royalties. On its income tax return petitioner took a deduction of $558.81 for taxes, and miscellaneous deductions of $9,676.21, including legal expenses of $8,107.35. The Commissioner in his determination of the deficiencies allowed all the deductions except legal expenses of $8,107.35.

Petitioner, by its assignments of error, [argues] that the $8,107.35 which it paid out as legal expenses in 1940 were current operating expenses and were therefore deductible items in arriving at petitioner's net income for that year.

The Commissioner defends his disallowance of the deduction of the $8,107.35 legal expenses on the ground that the expenditures were made in defense of title or right to property and, therefore, constitute a part of the cost of such property and represent a capital investment rather than a business expense. It is well settled that legal expenditures incurred in defense or protection of title are capital in nature and nondeductible. *Bowers v. Lumpkin*, 140 Fed.(2d) 927; certiorari denied, 322 U.S. 88; *Jones' Estate v. Commissioner*, 127 Fed.(2d) 231; *Brawner v. Burnet*, 63 Fed.(2d) 129; *Murphy Oil Co. v. Burnet*, 55 Fed.(2d) 17; affirmed on another point, 287 U.S. 299.

Petitioner argues, however, that this principle is not applicable here because the litigation involved the earnings of the business, not its capital assets, and, hence, the fees and legal expenses were necessary to retain income. It relies on *Kornhauser v. United States*, 276 U.S. 145, wherein the Court upheld the deduction of attorneys' fees paid in defense of an action which the taxpayer's former partner brought for an accounting of moneys collected by the partnership.

In attempting to bring its payments within the scope of the Kornhauser case and other cases which have followed it, petitioner is at pains to stress that it was defending a claim against the income produced by its business and that Seaton's claim of title to the patent was removed in 1939 by decision of the Tennessee Supreme Court sustaining the demurer as to the ownership of the Bradley patent. As the fees covered legal services rendered in connection with the demurrer, as well as other services, we can not agree that defense of title to the patent was not involved. But, quite apart from this item of the complaint, we are of opinion that the suit involved primarily rights of a capital character and that the accounting for royalties, demanded in the complaint, was only a corollary of the determination of those rights, applicable not only to 1940, but equally to prior and subsequent years. Seaton claimed for himself and associates a participating interest in petitioner's commercial use of the patent. This claim and the expenses incurred in resisting it bore no special relation to 1940 or any other year. Seaton demanded part of all of the earnings of the business for all years, a right in or to the income-producing asset that petitioner resisted, not a claim against specific income therefrom.

We are of opinion that the facts here presented are indistinguishable from those considered in *Moynier v. Welch*, 97 Fed.(2d) 471, wherein the taxpayer's income consisted solely of royalties paid it under an oil lease. [In that case...the producing oil company sued to have settled whether it should pay the provided royalties wholly to plaintiff or divide it with others, who owned other lots in the same tract. The others claimed that the lease contemplated a division of the royalties. In defending this exclusive right to them, the taxpayer incurred and paid legal fees which he sought unsuccessfully to deduct as business expenses. The court held that:

...Attorney fees and litigation costs in such circumstances are capital expenditures and are not deductible. Such expenditures were not 'ordinary and necessary expenses paid...in carrying on any trade or business.'...]

The payment of the attorney fees and litigation expenses is...of a capital expenditure in this case as it was in *Murphy Oil Co. v. Burnet*, 9 Cir. 55 F.2d 17, 26. In conformity with these decisions, we held that the legal expenses of $8,107.35 are not deductible.

Urquhart v. Commissioner
Circuit Court of Appeals, Third Circuit
215 F.2d 17 (3d Cir. 1954)

KALODNER, CIRCUIT JUDGE:

The Tax Court determined that certain litigation expenses were capital in nature. These appeals followed, the taxpayers contending that the expenses, which were incurred by them in the course of patent litigation, were deductible from income as ordinary and necessary expenses.

The relevant facts, which are not in dispute, are as follows:

The taxable year involved is 1946. In that year, and since 1939, the taxpayers, George Gordon Urquhart, Radcliffe M. Urquhart and W. K. B. Urquhart, were participants in a joint venture engaged in the business of inventing, experimenting, developing, and exploiting patents and new processes, licensing and acting as licensor of patents and processes. In 1938 and 1940, George and Radcliffe Urquhart obtained two patents, Nos. 2,106,043 and 2,198,585, respectively, involving fire-fighting equipment. From 1942 through 1946, the sole business of the joint venture was the licensing of these two patents, and in those years the joint venture realized substantial royalties. In 1938, the title holders to patent No. 2,106,043 notified Pyrene Manufacturing Company (Pyrene) that it was infringing on their patent and threatened litigation. On April 28, 1943, they brought suit against American LaFrance Foamite Corporation, a customer of Pyrene, for infringement of both patents, seeking an injunction and recovery of profits and damages. This action was dismissed in April, 1943. On May 5, 1943, Pyrene commenced an action against the patent owners in the United States District Court for the Eastern District of Pennsylvania, seeking a declaratory judgment that both patents were invalid and that its own apparatus and methods did not infringe. A counterclaim was filed asking for an injunction against infringement, and an accounting for profits and damages. No question was raised by Pyrene in this action as to title to, or ownership of, the patents. The case came to trial in June, 1946 and later that year the District Court entered judgment in favor of Pyrene holding that the patents in question were invalid and void. The taxpayers expended $55,748.64 in 1946 for legal fees and other expenses in connection with this litigation, and it is this sum which is the subject of the instant controversy. This Court affirmed, holding the patent claims involved invalid for want of invention.

On July 22, 1949, National Foam System, Inc., the Principal non-exclusive licensee of the two patents, commenced action against the two patents, commenced action against the two patentees seeking to be relieved of its license; a counterclaim was filed for royalties. On November 29, 1949, the patent owners brought an action in the Court of Claims against the United States asserting validity of their patents and claiming compensation for unauthorized use. In this action judgment was entered for the United States.

A partnership income tax return for 1946 was filed by the taxpayers, in which return deduction in the amount of $55,748.64 was taken for legal fees and litigation expenses. Each of the taxpayers, in individual returns for 1946, showed income from the joint venture in amounts determined after deduction of the expenses on the part of the joint venture. The Commissioner disallowed the deductions the taxpayers claimed on account of the litigation expenses treating them as capital expenditures. The Tax Court sustained the Commissioner's action, holding that "the taxpayers were engaged in defending a property interest, the exclusive right to make, use and vend these inventions granted by the patents and were only incidentally engaged in seeking to collect income."

We are of the opinion that the litigation expenses here involved were ordinary and necessary expenses incurred by the taxpayers in carrying on their trade or business, and that they were incurred as normal overhead or operating costs of their business activities. As such, they are deductible.

We have no doubt that these expenses were ordinary and necessary. There is no dispute that taxpayers were engaged in the business of exploiting and licensing patents. And we have no doubt that the expenses were directly connected with and proximately resulting from the conduct of taxpayers' business. Indeed, the expenditures and the manner in which they came into being are peculiarly normal to the business in which the taxpayers were engaged. It is not of decisive significance that the taxpayers were unsuccessful, at least since *Commissioner of Internal Revenue v. Heininger, supra*. Nor is it a requirement that the expenses have been incurred in the production of income, or actually productive of income. *Bingham's Trust v. Commissioner*, 1945, 325 U.S. 365.

Nevertheless, the Commissioner characterizes the expenses as capital, i.e., incurred in the defense of perfection of the equivalent of title. He cites Regulations 111, § Sec. 29.24-

2, and the apparently settled law that expenditures for the defense or perfection of title are part of the cost of acquisition of capital assets. In this instance he brings that law into play by virtue of our determination in the Pyrene case of the issue of validity. But as we have said before 'Taxation is an intensely practical matter, and, it deals with realities not semblances; with substance and not form.... It must ever be kept in mind "that the substance of the transactions will prevail over form." And, particularly in the area of taxation with which we are concerned, we "cannot ignore the ways of conduct and forms of speech prevailing in the business world." *Commissioner of Internal Revenue v. Heininger,* supra, 320 U.S. at page 472; *Welch v. Helvering, supra*. The litigation which gave rise to the expenditures in issue was commonplace patent infringement litigation. It is conceded that no question of title was involved. The form of the action and the circumstance that it was initiated by the alleged infringer do not, at least in this instance, alter the character of the controversy. The Urquharts brought about the litigation by asserting infringement; they forced the step by threatening Pyrene's customers and instituting action against one of them; such affirmative conduct upon the part of the Urquharts was the foundation of the declaratory judgment action. Moreover, in patent infringement actions, the defense of invalidity of patent claims is normally raised, and it is normally disposed of first. In the light of the Urquharts' answer and counterclaim the situation was for general purposes the same as though they had commenced an infringement action against Pyrene. The declaratory judgment remedy merely enabled a turnabout of parties. Mere form of action is immaterial. Cf. *Rassenfoss v. Commissioner,* 7 Cir., 1946, 158 F.2d 764. Of course, it is well-settled that the Urquharts remained free to assert infringement against others in the courts, and this freedom extends to the issue of the validity of their patent claims.

Infringement litigation is a far cry from removing a cloud of title, or defending ownership of property. Here, it arose out of and related directly to the exploitation of the invention embodied in the patent. And, in our view, the purposes and intent are the same whether the Urquharts commenced the action, or maneuvered Pyrene into taking the initial litigative step. In *Mathey v. Commissioner,* 1 Cir., 1949, 177 F.2d 259, 262, which deals with the successful patentee, it was said, at pages 262–263:

"'In patent nomenclature what the infringer makes is 'profits,' what the owner of the patent loses by such infringement is 'damages.'" *Duplate Corp. v. Triplex Safety Glass Co. of North America,* 56 S.Ct. 792, 793 (1936). And usually, although not always, what a patent owner loses from infringement is the acquisition of 'a just and deserved gain' from the exploitation of the invention embodied in his patent. Therefore an award of damages in patent litigation is ordinarily an award of compensation for gains or profits lost by the patent owner and hence is taxable to him as income in the year received.

Since the Urquharts were engaged in the business of exploiting and licensing patents, we are the more clear that the litigation expenses were incurred to prevent (and recover) damage to their business, that is, to protect, conserve and maintain their business profits. There is no conflict apparent to us, as urged by the Commissioner, with the principle that expenditures which yield benefits over a period of years are not current operating expenses under Section 23(a)(1). *Commissioner of Internal Revenue v. Surface Combustion Corp.,* 6 Cir., 1950, 181 F.2d 444; cf. *Commissioner of Internal Revenue v. Heininger, supra.* If this principle were applicable here, it would also apply to successful infringement actions like *Mathey v. Commissioner,* despite the recovery of damages, if only on a proportionate basis. It may be noted, incidentally, that in the patent phase of that case one of the claims of the patent was held invalid: *United Shoe Machinery Corporation v. Mathey,* 1 Cir., 1941, 117 F.2d 331. Cases like *Safety Tube Corp. v. Commissioner,* 6 Cir., 1948, 168 F.2d 787, and *Falls v. Commissioner,* 1946, 7 T.C. 66, exemplify situations in which title to patents are involved, and the expenditures incident to such issue are deemed capital in nature.

We conclude that the expenditures in controversy are deductible as ordinary and necessary business costs. Theexpenditures were made in the course of business to protect against infringement and to recover profits and damages and they are not appropriate to be added to the cost of securing the asset, i.e., the patent.

For the reasons stated, the judgment of the Tax Court will be reversed and the cause remanded with directions to proceed in accordance with this opinion.

Danskin, Inc. v. Commissioner
Circuit Court of Appeals, Second Circuit
331 F.2d 360 (2d Cir. 1964)

WATERMAN, CIRCUIT JUDGE:

The principal question presented by this taxpayer's petition for review of a decision of the Tax Court of the United States is whether the owner of a trademark may treat legal expenses incurred in instituting and pressing to settlement an infringement action as deductible expenses under Section 162(a) of the Internal Revenue Code of 1954, or whether such charges must be regarded as a capital expenditure. We think it proper, as did the Tax Court, to classify such disbursements as a capital expenditure.

Petitioner, Danskin, Inc., is a New York corporation, engaged in manufacturing and marketing ladies' and children's leotards, tights, and related items under the federally registered trademark 'Danskin.' In 1958, a competing firm began marketing similar products under the trademark 'Gamskin,' and in 1959 in the United States District Court for the Eastern District of Pennsylvania petitioner instituted an infringement action against its competitor seeking treble damages in the amount of $75,000 and an injunction order requiring the defendant to cease and desist from using 'Gamskin' as a trademark. After a hearing the court granted petitioner's request for a temporary injunction restraining the defendant from using the trademark 'Gamskin,' and several months later a settlement agreement was negotiated under which the defendant agreed to the entry of a final decree perpetually enjoining it and its successors from using the 'Gamskin' trademark. The defendant also agreed to pay all court costs and to have a judgment entered against it in the amount of $7,000 if it ever breached any provision of the settlement agreement.

For the legal services which resulted in this favorable settlement petitioner expended the sum of $4,666, and on its 1959 corporate income tax return it sought to deduct these litigation expenses as ordinary and necessary business expenses under Section 162(a) of the 1954 Code. The Commissioner disallowed the deductions on the ground that they were a capital expenditure and asserted a deficiency against petitioner. The Commissioner's position was sustained below in the Tax Court, 40 T.C. 318, and we affirm that court.

The purpose and effect of the legal expenses, as determined by the settlement agreement eventually reached as a result of the litigation taxpayer financed, was to increase the value of taxpayer's registered trademark and to make more secure taxpayer's property in it by forever eliminating the possibility of having it impaired by the competitive use of this confusingly similar mark. Thus, though the complaint for infringement as originally drawn included a plea for damages, taxpayer's expenses did not finance legal activity which recovered for petitioner lost income or preserved its right to retain income earned. The financial gain which petitioner realized from these legal proceedings, through the enhancement of the value of its registered trademark, is an increment of a sort which will endure for many years to come; and therefore the pattern of the revenue laws of accurately matching income and expenses within annual accounting periods requires that these legal expenses be classified as capital outlays. Financing the removal of a threat to a trademark posed by an infringing mark resembles the cost of perfecting or preserving title to property, a cost well established as a capital expenditure, see *Spangler v. Commissioner*, 323 F.2d 913 (9 Cir. 1963); *Wise v. Commissioner*, 311 F.2d 743 (2 Cir. 1963); *Lewis v. Commissioner*, 253 F.2d 821 (2 Cir. 1958), much more than it resembles a current business expense.

Georator Corp. v. United States
Circuit Court of Appeals, Fourth Circuit
485 F.2d 283 (4th Cir. 1973).

Field, Circuit Judge:

This case presents the question whether for federal income tax purposes fees incurred while resisting a petition to cancel registration of a trademark may be deducted annually as an ordinary business expense or must be treated as a capital expenditure.

In 1964 Wincharger Corporation, a subsidiary of Zenith Corporation, filed a petition in the Patent Office to cancel Georator Corporation's (Georator) registration of the trademark "NOBRUSH" on the ground that the trademark had become the common descriptive name for certain types of electric generators and motors. After four years of litigation the Patent Office dismissed the proceeding because of the petitioner's failure to present any substantial evidence to refute the presumptions afforded the trademark by virtue of its registration.

In the course of defending its trademark registration, Georator incurred legal fees in excess of $18,000. These expenses were deducted annually as ordinary business expenses under Section 162(a) of the Internal Revenue Code, 26 U.S.C. § 162(a). Upon audit the Internal Revenue Service held the legal fees to be capital expenditures and determined an income tax deficiency for the years in question in the amount of $9,967.15. Georator paid the deficiency, petitioned for a refund and upon denial thereof brought suit against the government in the district court to recover the amount paid on the deficiency assessment. The district court agreed with Georator's contention that the legal fees were ordinary business expenses fully deductible in the years incurred and ordered that the deficiency, with interest, be refunded. From that judgment the government has appealed.

Our analysis of this question begins with the principle of taxation reflected in Section 162(a) of the Internal Revenue Code that an expenditure securing benefits which are realized and exhausted in the same tax period is fully deductible in that tax period. Conversely, an expenditure securing benefits beyond the taxable year must be capitalized. *Darlington-Hartsville Coca-Cola Bot. Co. v. United States*, 393 F.2d 494 (4 Cir. 1968); *Richmond Television Corporation v. United States*, 345 F.2d 901 (4 Cir. 1965).

It is clear that an expenditure need not be for a capital asset, as described in Section 1221 of the Code, 26 U.S.C. § 1221, in order to be classified as a capital expenditure. Expenditures for equipment used in a trade or business and qualifying for the depreciation allowances of Section 167 of the Code, 26 U.S.C. § 167, while specifically excluded from the provisions of Section 1221, nonetheless constitute capital expenditures. Nor is it necessary that an expenditure increase the value of an asset in order to be classified as a capital expenditure, as the district court apparently assumed. Costs of defending title to property, although adding nothing to the value of the property, have been held to be capital expenditures. *Garrett v. Crenshaw*, 196 F.2d 185 (4 Cir. 1952); *Bowers v. Lumpkin*, 140 F.2d 927 (4 Cir. 1944). It is also clear that Section 263 of the Code, 26 U.S.C. § 263, which disallows deductions for expenditures which increase the value of any property, does not provide a complete or exhaustive list of nondeductible expenditures. *Commissioner v. Lincoln Savings & Loan Assn.*, 403 U.S. 345, 358 (1971).

Registration of a trademark in the Patent Office, while not enlarging the common law rights of a trademark, does confer very real benefits upon the holder of such trademark. Those benefits include: (1) constructive notice of the registrant's claim of ownership of the trademark; (2) prima facie evidence of the validity of the registration, of the registrant's ownership of the mark, and of his exclusive right to use the mark in commerce as specified in the certificate; (3) the possibility that, after five years, registration will become incontestible and constitute conclusive evidence of the registrant's right to use the mark; (4) the right to request customs officials to bar the importation of goods bearing infringing trademarks; (5) the right to institute trademark actions in federal courts without regard to diversity of citizenship or the amount in controversy; and (6) treble damage actions against infringing trademarks and other remedies. 15 U.S.C. § 1051 et seq. Registration is effective initially for twenty years, but the possibility of renewal at the end of that time makes a determination of the effective life span impossible. Since the benefits of trademark registration are of indeterminate duration and likely to extend over several tax periods, the costs of registration have been held to be capital expenditures. Duesenberg, Inc. of Delaware, 31 B.T.A. 922 (1934), aff'd on other grounds, 84 F.2d 921 (7 Cir. 1936).

In our view, legal costs incurred resisting cancellation of a trademark registration must be treated in the same manner as the costs of the original registration. Plainly, successful opposition to a cancellation proceeding secures the benefits of registration as much as does the original registration of the trademark. The fact that dismissal of a cancellation petition is not *res judicata* does not alter the fact that the benefits of registration have been protected and preserved at least temporarily. If anything, successful opposition to a vigorous challenge will ordinarily deter all but the frivolous from future attempts at cancellation and, as appellee has noted, it is the realities rather than the formalities which must be given weight in tax litigation. Of significance here is the fact that the benefits of successful opposition to the cancellation petition were likely to extend, and in fact did extend, beyond the tax period in which they were secured.

We conclude that the Internal Revenue Service properly classified the fees incident to the cancellation proceeding as a capital expenditure and the deficiency assessed on that basis was correct. Accordingly, the judgment of the district court is reversed and the case remanded with instructions to enter judgment in favor of the plaintiff/appellee herein in the sum of $1,111.60 in taxes and $116.98 as assessed interest, or a total of $1,228.58, under the stipulations filed in the court below, in lieu of the judgment entered below for $11,278.

Rust-Oleum Corp. v. United States
U.S. District Court
280 F. Supp. 796 (N.D. Ill. 1967)

WILL, JUDGE:

Plaintiff sues for income tax refunds of deficiency assessments heretofore paid, attributable to disallowed deductions for 'professional fees' of $8,296.82 for its fiscal year 1961 and $59,008.49 for its fiscal year 1962. Theexpenditures were payments to plaintiff's attorney, Charles B. Cannon, in connection with litigation instituted on April 28, 1960, in Ohio against the Tremco Manufacturing Company, and the costs of public surveys made during the course of that litigation, which was settled, the surveys later being used in connection with plaintiff's advertising.

Subsequent to the settlement of the suit, a stipulation was filed in the Patent Office stating that: 'Whereas, Civil Action No. 36,093 in the United States District Court for the Northern District of Ohio between Applicant and Opposer has been terminated by agreement of the parties; it is hereby stipulated that the above identified opposition be and is hereby withdrawn.' On June 20, 1962, a notice from the 'Members, Trademark Trial and Appeal Board' was filed: In view of the stipulation filed June 18, 1963, the opposition is dismissed.

A stipulation and supplemental stipulation of facts have been entered into by the parties which reveal these undisputed facts: Plaintiff, an Illinois corporation, which manufactures and sells rust preventive surface coatings, reported income of $553,797.23 for the fiscal year 1961 on which it paid corporate income tax of $282,474.56. A $7,489.40 deficiency was assessed and paid, with $923.35 interest, the Government disallowing a $14,402.70 deduction for professional fees out of a claimed amount of $45,139.88. Plaintiff maintains it is entitled to a deduction of $8,296.82 of the $14,402.70 disallowed with a resulting refund of $4,314.34 and $531.96 interest.

As to 1962, plaintiff reported income of $665,183.73 on which it paid a tax of $340,395.54, and the Government assessed a deficiency of $32,619.34, which plaintiff paid with interest of $2,064.40. For that year, the Government disallowed a deduction of $68,085.57 advertising and professional fees, and plaintiff believes it is entitled to a deduction of $59,008.49 for which a refund of $30,684 and $1,942.32 interest are sought.

The Amended Complaint in the Tremco litigation in the Northern District of Ohio alleged two separate causes of action: the first for infringement of plaintiff's trademark "Stops Rust," the second, for unfair competition (realleging all the assertions as to the first cause of action) and then alleging unfair competition and aggravation of the trademark infringement, by dressing of products in a color scheme and paint motif closely resembling that of plaintiff and by employing sales displays resembling those long employed by plaintiff, thereby deceiving and tending to deceive purchasers and the consumer public into believing that, contrary to fact, defendant's products had their source in plaintiff, constituting unfair competition both at common law and under the Trademark Act. In addition to damages, an injunction against unfair competition was also sought.

The court concludes that if "taxation...is eminently practical, and a practical mind... (considers) results" (*Tyler v. United States*, 281 U.S. 497, 503, 50 S.Ct. 356, 359, 74 L.Ed.

991 (1930)), this case is a prime instance where justice can best be done by giving weight to the actualities of the situation. Since the expenditures were in substantial part utilized for purposes generally considered ordinary and necessary business expenses, i.e., litigation and advertising costs, it is necessary to ascertain, so far as possible, the extent to which they related to the protection of a capital asset, the trademark on the one hand, and the extent to which they related to the unfair competition litigation and advertising, on the other hand.

The following considerations and evidence are relevant:

(1) The Tremco litigation was settled prior to trial, with the result that the survey evidence was not used in an actual trial. Further costs of litigation were saved by plaintiff, but past costs of litigation concerned both the trademark protection and the unfair competition litigation.

(2) While the settlement of the litigation assured the dropping of the Patent Office opposition to plaintiff's trademark by Tremco, thus ensuring plaintiff the sole use of the mark, it also stopped the alleged unfair competition by Tremco apart from any trademark rights, and prescribed a permissive but restricted dress for Tremco's products in the future.

(3) The surveys were extensively used in subsequent advertising. Some 588,000 copies of the summary of the results of the Lampa-Meier survey were made and sent to over 12,000 distributors and salesmen. Plaintiff had in previous years spent large sums in advertising. It had made over a hundred surveys. It had used these surveys to guide its advertising programs.

(4) Plaintiff's business was greatly enhanced as a result of the advertising.

(5) Attorney Cannon testified that the Ohio suit was primarily to enjoin Tremco's unfair competition and recover damages and not for infringement of the trademark.

(6) Attorney Cannon further testified that the surveys, although initially prepared for the suit, were not used in the Tremco litigation, although they had been "submitted to counsel." The Ohio court suggested settlement talks. The court had not been shown the surveys nor was there discussion about them with the court. The surveys were not used in any manner in the Patent Office.

(7) The Government concedes that the surveys established confusion, an indispensable element to recovery in an unfair competition action.

The Government argues that plaintiff acquired rights which will be of benefit substantially beyond the year in which the expenditures were incurred and that the litigation against Tremco was primarily a suit to establish plaintiff's property rights to "STOPS RUST" as a trademark. The Government further urges that the principal purpose of the Tremco litigation was to establish title to the trademark and not for unfair competition and damages for lost profits. It differentiates the case of *Rassenfoss v. Commissioner of Internal Revenue*, 158 F.2d 764 (7th Cir. 1946), as being an instance where the protection of title was not the primary purpose of the suit, but merely incidental thereto, and therefore the costs of litigation could be an ordinary and necessary business expense.

It is further argued by the Government that expenditures for the protection of a trademark are notdepreciable over any period of time because no reasonably accurate estimate of the useful life of a trademark can be made. *Norwich Pharmacal Co. v. Commissioner of Internal Revenue*, 30 B.T.A. 326; 4 Mertens Law of Federal Income Taxation, Sec. 23.10, p. 35. It points out that plaintiff has the burden as to the deduction for depreciation of expenditures for capital assets and since no evidence as to the useful life of its trademark has been offered by plaintiff, no depreciation deduction is allowable, and further since plaintiff made no election under Section 177 for the five-year period of amortization of trademark expenses, none is allowable.

Finally, the Government urges that if the court concludes this is a case where a lump sum payment should be allocated between deductible and nondeductible expenditures, the burden is on the plaintiff to establish a reasonable method of allocation. Absent evidence of a reasonable method, it contends that the court has no power to make an allocation. *Colonial Ice Cream Co. v. Commissioner of Internal Revenue*, 7 B.T.A. 154. In any event, the Government asserts that the "primary purpose" for the survey expenditures was litigation, not advertising.

As to plaintiff's contention that the survey expenditures were incurred at least in part for advertising expenses, the Government answers that they were all incurred for use in litigation. Plaintiff has the burden of proving the deductible amounts and segregating them from the nondeductible amounts. *Harden M. Loan Co. v. Commissioner of Internal Revenue*, 137 F.2d 282 (10th Cir. 1943); *Nowland v. Commissioner of Internal Revenue*, 244 F.2d 450 (4th Cir. 1957); *Brinson v. Tomlinson*, 264 F.2d 30 (5th Cir. 1959). The Government cites Mr. Cannon's testimony, and the vouchers, that his charges were for preparation of the surveys for use in the litigation, as were Mr. Lampa's charges (he is in the business of trademark research). Nor were the advertising uses of the surveys discussed until after the determination to go ahead with the national survey. The court reporter's depositions of the interviewers were billed to plaintiff under the litigation heading and were evidence depositions.

While expenditures for advertising are generally ordinary and necessary business expenses, the Government points out that where the expenditures are for the acquisition or protection of a capital asset to be used in advertising they must be capitalized. *French Broad Ice Cream Co. v. United States*, 52 A.F.T.R. 1396 (involving a signboard); *Simonson v. Commissioner*, P-H Memo. T.C. P46,197. The Government contends that the survey (as well as the trademark) are capital assets to be used in advertising which definitely has a useful life of more than one year, and that the evidence indicates an original estimate of three to five years usefulness; that they have been used in all the years to plaintiff and will be so for an indefinite time in the future. The plaintiff has made no offer as to what the useful life might be but the evidence establishes that in no event could it be less than five years. *Easter v. Commissioner of Internal Revenue*, 338 F.2d 968 (4th Cir. 1964). The Government concludes therefore that all of the disallowed deductions for expenses in the Tremco litigation must be capitalized.

It is plaintiff"s position, on the other hand, that the expenditures it made were "primarily to recover lost profits and protect income and were therefore ordinary and necessary expenses' (under the unfair competition count of the Tremco litigation) and "that the survey expenses were also deductible as advertising expenses."

Plaintiff states that earlier surveys had been conducted at the dealer level to provide information for thesales structure and advertising campaign in a particular area. Later, the surveys were conducted in established markets of plaintiff to tailor sales and advertising campaigns to the specific needs of the area. Plaintiff's expansion program advertised heavily to the consumer market by means of radio and television and other forms of advertising.

Plaintiff contends that Tremco engaged in increasingly flagrant unfair practices subsequent to 1956 as to the phrase "Stops Rust" which plaintiff had extensively advertised, so plaintiff's counsel, Atty. Charles B. Cannon, on September 30, 1958, notified them of alleged trademark infringement and unfair competition, which Tremco denied. Suit was filed by plaintiff against Tremco on April 28, 1960, in the Federal Court in Ohio.

Plaintiff had theretofore on May 14, 1959, applied in the Patent Office for registration of the "Stops Rust" trademark on the principal register, alleging use since 1951 and such extensive advertising as to acquire a secondary meaning, of plaintiff, Rust-Oleum, as the source of the product. Tremco on December 11, 1959, opposed the issuance of the certificate of registration but the opposition proceeding was suspended pending the outcome of the Ohio suit.

In 1961, pilot surveys were made in Indianapolis and Pittsburgh to establish a format for further surveys. A survey of nine cities showed that 88% of the persons interviewed remembered seeing "Stops Rust" on a label and identified it as a Rust-Oleum product. As previously indicated, the Ohio suit was settled June 14, 1962, by written agreement in which no acknowledgment was made by Tremco that the trademark was valid or that Tremco had infringed or engaged in unfair competition. There was an agreement to terminate the Patent Office opposition to plaintiff's registration of "Stops Rust" and plaintiff permitted Tremco to use the text of the trademark in a non-confusing manner.

Plaintiff states that "No use was made of the survey in the litigation, but a six-page colored insert depicting the results of the survey in graphic form was drawn up for publication to dealers and distributors. Beginning in September, 1962, extensive use was made of the survey by advertising its results to dealers and distributors in house organs, trade journals, and by direct mail."

Plaintiff urges that a very substantial purpose for undertaking the surveys was its usability both as an advertising instrument and indicator to show the strength and weakness of its advertising program. *Sanitary Farms Dairy, Inc, v. Commissioner of Internal Revenue*, 25 T.C. 463 (1955).

Plaintiff maintains that the Tremco litigation was not one to establish its trademark but was to prevent future loss of revenue and to recover past losses for Tremco's unfair competition and that litigation was the normal avenue to take and the expense was an ordinary and necessary business expense.

Plaintiff especially stresses the legal principle that where an expenditure has a dual purpose its treatment for tax purposes depends on its primary purpose—if to defend of perfect title, it is capitalized under §263, but if for some other business purpose, it is deducted in the year in which incurred although perfection of title is incident. Plaintiff cites in support of its contention the decision of this Circuit'sCourt of Appeals in *Rassenfoss v. Commissioner of Internal Revenue*, 158 F.2d 764 (7th Cir. 1946), wherein it was held that legal fees paid by a partner were ordinary and necessary business expenses in the years in which paid, although the suit involved an employee's claim to a partner's interest. The suit was settled, granting the employee a 1.75% interest. The court stated, at 767:

> ....The Commissioner contends that such expenditures "were more than mere ordinary business expenses" and that they are not deductible because made in protecting and defending petitioner's title to the partnership business and property. The Tax Court sustained this view.... We reach a contrary conclusion. In the first place, the factual basis for such a contention is more fanciful than real. Laying aside the legal question as to whether petitioner had any title

to the partnership assets, it is perfectly plain...that the main and primary purpose of the suit which petitioner defended was for an accounting and any question of title was merely incidental thereto. This is borne out by the compromise which was finally effected, by which Campbell was awarded almost infinitesimal and only a limited interest in the partnership."

Plaintiff insists that the primary purpose of the Tremco litigation was the protection of income rather than the defense or perfection of title to an asset, and furthermore, since plaintiff was unsuccessful in that litigation so far as perfection of title was concerned, the expenditures were deductible since they were ordinary and necessary and resulted in neither a loss nor a gain of a capital nature.

It is plaintiff's contention that the actual use of the surveys, and counsel's fees for services in connection therewith for advertising purposes, entitles plaintiff to a deduction of the cost as an ordinary and necessary expense—despite the fact that the benefits might in some measure extend beyond the year in which the expenses were incurred, or that they were initially incurred for use in litigation pertaining to the trademark. Plaintiff negates the importance of the trademark litigation in Ohio in that it was settled prior to trial, without the results of the survey ever being utilized in any way in the suit, or in the Patent Office.

Both sides, as noted, lay emphasis on the well-established proposition that the primary purpose for which expenditures are incurred determines their tax treatment. As might be expected, they differ diametrically as to what was the principal or primary purpose of the survey expenditures. The taxpayer insists that the surveys were primarily for use in connection with the unfair competition count of the lawsuit and in its advertising program. The government equally vigorously asserts that the surveys were principally conducted to buttress the trademark infringement count and to counter the Tremco opposition to the registration of the mark by Rust-Oleum.

Omniscience, of course, is a power which every judge should possess but unfortunately few trial judges do and this court is part of the great majority. Divining the primary purpose of the surveys here is beyond our competence. Nor do we perceive that all human conduct must necessarily have one primary or principal motivation. In fact, the more "principal" purposes a venture has, the more desirable it maybe.

The evidence seems to us to demonstrate that the surveys here had two equally significant contemplated uses, Count One and Count Two of the Ohio suit. As it developed, that suit was settled as was the opposition in the Patent Office without their introduction into evidence but they clearly contributed to the negotiated disposition of those matters. Subsequently they were exploited by plaintiff for advertising purposes but this can hardly be given retroactive significance as the primary purpose for which they were secured. Similarly, the other legal expenses incurred by plaintiff in connection with the Ohio suit appear to us to be logically divisible equally between the two counts.

It is undisputed that the purpose of the first count was to secure a judicial determination that plaintiff had property rights in the mark "STOPS RUST" while the second was to secure money damages for alleged unfair competition, passing off, etc. Expenses of the former would not be deductible while those attributable to the latter clearly would.

It follows, we believe, that the proper determination of the instant controversy is to divide the expenses of the Ohio suit, including those incident to the surveys, equally between those properly deductible and those not so deductible.

We recognize that the apportionment of the expenditures between capital expenses and ordinary and necessary business expenses in the cause may not be exact or precise. But precision is not an indispensable prerequisite.

Big Four Industries, Inc. v. Commissioner
40 T.C. 1055 (1963), acq., 1964-2 C.B. 3

[The taxpayer and the IRS agreed that $876,107 of the $1,200,000 awarded by the district court in the patent infringement case represented damages for lost profits and therefore constituted taxable income, but disagreed as to the proper classification of the remaining $323,893. The IRS contended that this amount was also for lost profits or was otherwise taxable as ordinary income, whereas the petitioner argued that it was awarded for damages to its corporate capital structure and goodwill and represented a nontaxable replacement of capital. The *Big Four* court held that both parties were partly in error, and that the facts of record required a more refined treatment of the remaining $323,893]

First, it is clear from the District Court's decree that the award was intended to include the master's fee, attorneys' fees, accountants' fees, court reporter's fees, and all other costs pertaining to the proceeding. The total of all such fees was $195,324.60. The record also shows that petitioner deducted its share of the various fees and costs on its income tax returns. Plainly, the reimbursement of such fees constituted the receipt of ordinary income. *Cf. Nicholas W. Mathey*, 10 T.C. 1099, 1102, 1105, affirmed 177 F.2d 259 (C.A. 1), *certiorari denied* 339 U.S. 943; *Sager Glove Corporation*, 36 T.C. 1173, 1179, *affirmed* 311 F.2d 210 (C.A. 7).

Second, the District Court's findings explicitly state that the $1,200,000 award was intended in part to provide compensation "in some measure for damages to corporate capital structure of Big Four Industries, Inc., and to likewise compensate defendant, in some measure, for damages to good will of Big Four Industries, Inc." On this record, we could hardly conclude that the $128,568.40 remaining portion of the $1,200,000 award (after subtracting $876,107 lost profits and $195,324.60 fees), represented anything other than compensation for damages to capital structure and goodwill. To be sure, as argued by the Commissioner, petitioner nowhere specifically asked for such damages in its pleadings. But it did pray "for such other and further relief as the Court may consider proper in the premises," and we are satisfied that the District Court did intend to grant such relief. We cannot ignore the explicit language that it used.

However, having concluded that the $128,568.40 component of the award represents damages to petitioner's capital structure and goodwill, that is not the end of the matter. To the extent that such amount did not exceed the basis of the capital interest or goodwill destroyed it would be nontaxable, but it would be taxable as capital gain to the extent of any excess over basis. *Sager Glove Corp. v. Commissioner*, 36 T.C. 1173, 1179, *aff'd*, 311 F.2d 210 (7th Cir. 1962), *Freeman v. Commissioner*, 33 T.C. 323, 327 (1959); *Raytheon Production Corp. v. Commissioner*, 1 T.C. 952 (1944), *aff'd*, 144 F.2d 110 (1st Cir. 1944); *Durkee v. Commissioner*, 162 F.2d 184 (6th Cir. 1947). The report of the master shows that there was considerable damage to petitioner's goodwill. The parties have stipulated that no damage resulted to any physical assets of petitioner as a result of the infringement and that it had no cost basis for goodwill. In the circumstances, all of the $128,568.40 is taxable as capital gain.

Mathey v. Commissioner
Circuit Court of Appeals, First Circuit
177 F.2d 259 (1st Cir. 1949)

WOODBURY, CIRCUIT JUDGE:

The basic question presented by this petition for review of a decision of the Tax Court of the United States is whether the entire net amount awarded to the taxpayer in a suit for patent infringement constituted taxable income to him in the year of realization, as the Commissioner contends, or a non-taxable return of capital, as the taxpayer contends.

Following the decision of *United States v. Safety Car Heating & Lighting Co.*, 297 U.S. 88, the general rule adopted by several Courts of Appeals, including this one, apparently without a dissenting voice, is that whether the net proceeds of litigation are taxable to the recipient as income, or constitute a non-taxable return of capital, depends upon the object for which the suit was brought. If it was brought to recover lost profits, the proceeds are taxable income; if it was brought to recover for loss or damage to capital, the proceeds are non-taxable. As this court said, citing the authorities, in *Raytheon Production Corp. v. Commissioner*, 1 Cir., 144 F.2d 110, 113, certiorari denied 323 U.S. 779, "The test is not whether the action was one in tort or contract but rather the question to be asked in 'in lieu of what were the damages awarded?'". See also *Durkee v. Commissioner*, 6 Cir., 162 F.2d 184, 186, wherein, speaking of the taxability as income of a sum paid in settlement of litigation, the court said: "It is settled that since profits from business are taxable, a sum received in settlement of litigation based upon a loss of profits is likewise taxable; but where the settlement represents damages for lost capital rather than for lost profits the money received is a return of capital and not taxable."

Therefore to answer the question presented we must turn to the patent litigation in which the taxpayer was involved.

The taxpayer is a citizen of Massachusetts who during the pertinent years was on the cash-calendar year basis filing individual income tax returns with the collector of internal revenue for the district of Massachusetts. In 1931, while doing business individually as Hamlin Machine Co., he obtained a patent for a shoe machine, and later in that year gave formal notice of infringement thereof to United Shoe Machinery Corporation. In 1937 he brought suit for infringement against the latter alleging in his complaint that but for the infringement asserted he would have been "in receipt of large gains and profits", and that United Shoe Machinery Corporation had derived "great gains and profits" from its infringement. For relief he asked that United be perpetually enjoined from further infringement, that it be ordered to pay over both the profits it had made from its infringement and also the damages which the plaintiff had suffered therefrom, and that a master be appointed "to take and state an account of said profits and to assess said damages."

After hearing the district court entered judgment for the plaintiff on three of the four patent claims in issue pursuant to its memorandum opinion reported in *Mathey v. United Machinery Corp.*, D.C., 32 F.Supp. 684, and on appeal this court affirmed, except as to an item of cost. 1 Cir., 117 F.2d 331. Thereupon the court below entered a judgment on the mandate of this court awarding the plaintiff the relief for which he had asked in his complaint, and on the same date appointed a master "to take and state the amount of the damages which plaintiff has sustained, and of the gains and profits which defendant has made" by reason of its infringement of the three claims held valid.

At the hearings before the master the plaintiff abandoned his claim for profits, choosing to press only his claim for damages, which the master found amounted, with interest, to over seventh thousand dollars. To this amount the master added interest on certain items of the plaintiff's damages from a date prior to the liquidation of those damages because of "special circumstances"—those being that the defendant's infringement had been deliberate and premeditated, and that, for the purpose of destroying the plaintiff as a competitor, it had pursued a pricing policy with respect to its infringing machines which it knew would be ruinous to the plaintiff whose business was small and whose financial position was weak.

Moreover the master said at the end of his report that "The recovery allowed on the several elements of Plaintiff's 'Principal Claim' represents what has been proved to my satisfaction. As it does not represent the entire damage occasioned by Defendant's infringement and because of the 'Special Circumstances' I recommend to the Court that Plaintiff's damages be increased." And then, in conclusion the master stated: "In accordance with the order of reference, I find that Plaintiff has sustained provable damages in the amount of $63,355.00 and is also entitled to recover profits made by Defendant in the amount of $688.89. With interest on the recoveries as reported, totaling $8,118.36, the total recovery to which Plaintiff is entitled on the facts herein reported is $72,162.25. In addition, I recommend the allowance of interest on reasonable royalty recovery and for recoveries based on lost profits from lost installation fees in the sum of $15,266.70, with any other factor or multiple of items found which to the Court should seem fitting in its discretion as provided by law to make the recovery by Plaintiff more nearly adequate to compensate him for the damage to his business under his patent."

The district court confirmed the master's report in all essential respects and adopted his recommendation that because of the "special circumstances" already adverted to interest should be allowed to run on certain elements of the plaintiff's damages even from a date prior to their liquidation. In addition the district court adopted the master's recommendation that the plaintiff's award be increased because the defendant's infringement had been conscious and deliberate saying in its memorandum of decision, *Mathey v. United Shoe Machinery Corp.*, 54 F.Supp. 694, 702:

> 'As has been outlined above, this court finds the defendant did not act in good faith with respect to the infringement here. The infringement was deliberate. Enough subsidiary facts appear in the master's report and are outlined in this opinion to support this ultimate finding. However, with respect to an increase in damages, I agree with Judge Brewster of this court in increasing damages where there was a deliberate infringement. That distinguished jurist, long the senior member of this court, stated in *Muther v. United Shoe Machinery Corp.*, supra, 21 F.2d (773), 780: "While doubtless one of the purposes of the statute was to deter acts of infringement..., yet I do not conceive it to be the intent of the law to unjustly enrich the injured party at the expense of the wrongdoer." However, I believe full justice should be done to the plaintiff, the party wronged. The plaintiff has incurred considerable expense. There is little doubt that all the elements of damage done to the plaintiff are not included in

the award made. On due reflection and looking at the whole situation objectively, I believe if the award is increased fifty per cent, it will be adequate.'

A judgment for the plaintiff was thereupon entered, and United, taking no appeal, paid that judgment in full in April, 1944. It consisted of the following items:

(a) Damages for patent infringement	$ 63,355.00
(b) Interest on item (a)	$ 28,020.54
(c) Increase in award	$ 45,687.77
(d) Loss of profit on foreign sales	$ 688.89
(e) Amount of judgement	$137,752.20
(f) Interest on judgement to date of payment	$ 609.72
(g) Total	$138,361.92

The taxpayer in his income tax return for the calendar year 1944 included with respect to the proceeds of his suit for patent infringement only the amount awarded for loss of profits on foreign sales ($688.89), apparently on the ground, inter alia, that all the other items included in the judgment were awarded for injury "to my financial standing, credit reputation, good will, capital and other elements in my business." The Commissioner disagreed. In determining a deficiency in income tax in the amount of $80,746.77 for the year in question he allowed the taxpayer a deduction for litigation fees and expenses of $30,536.63 and included the balance of the judgment ($107,825.29) in the taxpayer's gross income for 1944, giving as an explanation for his action that "It is the opinion of this office the award appears to be entirely for profits, royalties, and interest." The Tax Court agreed with the Commissioner and entered its decision accordingly. 10 T.C. 1099.

"In patent nomenclature what the infringer makes is "profits," what the owner of the patent losses by such infringement is 'damages.'" *Duplate Corp. v. Triplex Safety Glass Co.*, 298 U.S. 448, 451, quoting *Diamond Stone-Sawing Machine Co. of New York v. Brown*, 2 Cir., 166 F. 306. And usually, although not always, what a patent owner loses from infringement is the acquisition of "a just and deserved gain" from the exploitation of the invention embodied in his patent. 3 Walker on Patents (Deller's Ed.) §281. Therefore an award of damages in patent litigation is ordinarily an award of compensation for gains or profits lost by the patent owner and hence is taxable to him as income in the year received. Cf. *United States v. Safety Car Heating & Lighting Co., supra; Commissioner of Internal Revenue v. S. A. Woods Mach. Co.*, 1 Cir., 57 F.2d 635.

But the plaintiff contends that this is not the ordinary case. Emphasizing the damage done to his business by United's infringement and the conclusion of the master confirmed by the district court that its infringement was deliberately undertaken for the purpose of destroying him as a competitor, he contends that the award made in the patent litigation was to compensate him for damage to his capital and that his lost profits and lost reasonable royalties were used only as a measure of that damage. He says that the distinction to be observed is between the purpose for which the damages were awarded in the patent litigation and the measure of those damages—a distinction which he asserts the Tax Court failed to perceive.

Unfortunately for the taxpayer his contention is not supported by the record in the patent litigation. In the first place the taxpayer in his complaint in the patent infringement suit did not allege any loss or damage to capital. On the contrary, as we have pointed out, he alleged that he would have been in receipt of large "gains and profits" but for the infringement, and for relief asked for an injunction against future infringement and that the infringer be ordered to pay over its profits from the infringement and the plaintiff's damages resulting therefrom. Hence it seems to us clear from an examination of the complaint that the "damages" which the plaintiff sought therein were not damages for loss or injury to capital but compensation for the profits he would have made absent the infringement complained of, and as the court said in Durkee v. Commissioner, *supra*, quoting from *Farmers' & Merchants' Bank of Catlettsburg, Ky., v. Commissioner*, 6 Cir., 59 F.2d 912, 913, "The fund involved must be considered in the light of the claim from which it was realized and which is reflected in the petition filed." Then in the second place it does not appear from the master's report that he took any evidence of damage to the plaintiff's capital assets or made any award for loss thereto. On the contrary the master's report clearly indicates that his award was wholly to compensate the taxpayer for unrealized profits from exploitation of the patented invention.

It may be that United competed unfairly with the plaintiff and thereby inflicted damage to his capital. But it seems to us clear that the damages which the taxpayer sought and which the master awarded were not for loss or injury to capital but as compensation for profits or gains which the taxpayer would have enjoyed but for United's infringement.

To be sure the master recommended that his award be increased to make the taxpayer's recovery "more nearly adequate to compensate him for the damage to his business under his patent" and that the district court, following this recommendation, increased the award by over forty-five thousand dollars. But this does not establish the taxpayer's contention that the entire award was intended as compensation for the intentional harm inflicted upon his business measured by his lost profits, or even that the amount by which the master's award was increased by the district court was designed to compensate for capital losses. The phrase "damage to his business" might in some contexts be used to describe damage to capital structure, but we do not think the master used it in that sense in his report. There is not the slightest reason to suppose that the master had tax consequences in mind when he used the phrase, and to construe it as the taxpayer urges would give it a construction at variance with the rest of the master's report. In the light of the entire report it seems to us that when the master used the phrase "damage to his business under his patent" he meant damage to the business the taxpayer would have done in the exploitation of his patent, i.e., the profits he would have made under it, absent the infringement. And the excerpt from the district court's memorandum of decision shows that it increased the award not as a penalty, but, under the remedial provisions of 35 U.S.C.A. §§ 67, 70, to do full justice to the taxpayer by adequately recompensating him for the lost profits he had sustained but was unable to prove categorically because of the "special circumstances" of the case.

. . . . .

The decision of the Tax Court is affirmed.

Inco Electroenergy Corp. v. Commissioner
T.C. Memo 1987-437

[W]hether the proceeds received by ESB Incorporated, a predecessor to both petitioners, from a settlement agreement with EXXON Corporation constituted capital gain or ordinary income.

FINDINGS OF FACT

. . . . .

Petitioner in docket No. 29491-84, Inco Electroenergy Corporation, a Pennsylvania corporation, had its principal office in New York at the time it filed its petition. Petitioner in docket No. 934-86, Inco Alloys International, Inc., a Delaware corporation had its principal office in West Virginia at the time it filed its petition. On brief both parties have indicated that all issues in docket No. 934-86 have been disposed of by agreement. Consequently, hereinafter the word petitioner in the singular shall refer only to Inco Electroenergy Corporation unless otherwise indicated.

Both petitioners are successive successors-in-interest to ESB Incorporated (ESB) and its consolidated subsidiaries. ESB was originally organized as Electric Storage Battery Company under the laws of the State of New Jersey in 1888. In 1967, Electric Storage Battery Company changed its name to ESB Incorporated. Throughout its history the company has been continuously engaged in the manufacturing business. Its products include storage batteries and related accessories.

In 1901, ESB adopted and began using the trademark 'EXIDE.' It applied the trademark, and variations thereof, to its storage batteries, related parts and accessories from 1901, through the years in issue. In 1932, ESB began to register the EXIDE trademark, and variations thereof, with the United States Patent Office when it received a certificate of registration from the Patent Office for the trademark 'EXIDE' for use with respect to its batteries, related parts and accessories. In 1935, it received a certificate of registration for the trademark 'EXIDE IRONCLA' for use with respect to storage batteries and parts. In subsequent years similar certificates of registration were obtained for the trademarks 'EXIDE ACCUMULATOR,' 'EXIDE-TYTEX,' 'EXIDOL,' and 'WHEN IT'S AN EXIDE YOU START.'

ESB intensively advertised and promoted its trademarks and they became well known nationally and internationally. Batteries and other products bearing the EXIDE trademark were consistently and conspicuously used in cars, airplanes and other vehicles and in events of historical significance including the first self-starting automobile, Admiral Byrd's first flight over the North Pole, Piccard's balloon flight to the stratosphere, and various planetary, lunar and other explorations in space, including voyages by the Mariner, Ranger, and Surveyor rockets.

EXIDE was ESB's most important trademark and over the years preceding 1967 ESB had established a policy of taking any action necessary to prevent the unauthorized use of any trademark confusingly similar to or which tended to infringe upon the EXIDE trademark. Such actions included trademark cancellation and opposition proceedings in the United States as well as foreign countries. For example, in *Electric Storage Battery Company v. Ex-Cell Battery & Equipment Company*, 537 Off. Gaz. Pat. Off. 721 (April 6, 1942) (Cancellation No. 3979), ESB obtained the cancellation of the trademark EX-CELL which had been issued to the Ex-Cell Battery & Equipment Company for use with respect to storage batteries.

Prior to January of 1968, Standard Oil Company of New Jersey ("Standard Oil"), the predecessor to EXXON Corporation, undertook to register the trademark "EXXON" in a number of foreign countries for use with respect to any product Standard Oil might wish to sell, including batteries and related products.

Upon becoming aware in January 1968 of Standard Oil's plan to adopt and use the EXXON trademark, ESB immediately instituted legal proceedings to prevent such registrations in every country in which Standard Oil had attempted to register the EXXON trademark for use with respect to batteries or any class of product that could include batteries or related products covered by the EXIDE trademark. ESB's opposition to the EXXON trademark was limited because ESB did not oppose the registration or use of the EXXON trademark with respect to products other than batteries or other products that were sold by ESB under its EXIDE trademark. Furthermore, ESB did not oppose Standard Oil's proposal to adopt "EXXON" as its corporate name.

In March 1968, ESB notified Standard Oil that it wished to protect its EXIDE trademarks "from any dilution or invalidity," and advised Standard Oil that "unless...we can arrive at a settlement whereby your Company undertakes not to use EXON or EXXON on batteries (and related items such as parts and accessories), and also to delete coverage for these goods from existing registrations and applications for EXXON and EXON, we will be compelled to take appropriate proceedings to protect our trademark." In April 1968, counsel for ESB, met with counsel for Standard Oil, to discuss the EXXON trademark. At this meeting ESB expressed concern that the EXXON trademark would be confusingly similar to the EXIDE trademark if used with respect to batteries.

Nevertheless, on April 29, 1968, Standard Oil filed with the United States Patent Office an application for registration of the EXXON trademark for use with respect to batteries. In response, ESB filed a notice of opposition to the application with the Trademark Trial and Appeal Board of the United States Patent Office. In its notice of opposition, ESB claimed that the use of EXXON asa trademark with respect to storage batteries would result in confusion, mistake, or deception as to the source of storage batteries; the use of such trademark would damage ESB; and, therefore, Standard Oil should not be permitted to register the EXXON trademark with respect to storage batteries.

In addition to the above application for registration of the EXXON trademark for use in the United States with respect to batteries, Standard Oil during the next four years applied for registrations of the EXXON trademark for various other uses in several foreign countries, as well as in the United States. The other uses included rubber tires, asphalt, and rust preventing materials. ESB continued to counter by filing notices of opposition to and petitions for cancellation of such registrations on the grounds that ESB had built up and owned valuable good will and a reputation symbolized by its EXIDE mark and that the registration of the EXXON trademark would result in confusion, mistake or deception with resulting damage to ESB, its products, and services. At no time did ESB allege, claim, refer to, or attempt to obtain "lost profits" in any of the documents filed with the United States Patent Office or any other tribunal or administrative body with respect to the EXXON trademark.

Throughout this period, ESB and Standard Oil were continuously engaged in settlement negotiations. Initially, ESB offered to settle the dispute if Standard Oil would agree not to register or use the EXXON trademark with respect to batteries in those countries, including the United States, in which ESB had a legal interest by reason of its EXIDE trademark. However, Standard Oil was unwilling to settle the dispute in this manner.

As negotiations progressed, Standard Oil raised the possibility of settling the dispute on a monetary basis with an offer in July 1971 of $300,000, which ESB rejected. Again in October 1972 Standard Oil offered "to pay to ESB the sum of one million ($1,000,000) dollars as "compensation" for the alleged detriment to ESB's goodwill in the trademark EXIDE, and to reimburse ESB for its expenses to date in challenging [Standard Oil's] trademark EXXON," provided ESB would withdraw all objections to the EXXON trademark.

This offer was followed by a series of meetings between officers of ESB and Standard Oil, and later its successor, EXXON Corporation. At these meetings Standard Oil and later EXXON Corporation made it clear that they wanted the flexibility of using the EXXON trademark with respect to any and all products. ESB indicated that it would be willing to settle for just compensation for "destruction of a valued asset."

After this series of meetings ESB made a counter offer to settle the dispute for $9,945,000, which amount ESB "calculated" by estimating "future damage to its goodwill" by projecting one-half of one percent of its estimated annual sales under the EXIDE mark "during the ten years following 1972."

On June 14, 1973, a final meeting was held, at which representatives of ESB and EXXON Corporation agreed in principle to settle the trademark dispute upon the payment by Exxon to ESB of $5,000,000.

In accordance with the [settlement] agreement, ESB withdrew its notices of objections to and petitions for cancellation of the registrations of the EXXON trademark, and EXXON Corporation paid ESB $5,000,000 during ESB's taxable year ended March 31, 1974.

On its income tax return for the year ended March 31, 1974, ESB reported the $5,000,000 received from Exxon Corporation, less the $225,000 in legal fees which ESB had incurred with respect to the various proceedings in opposition to the EXXON trademark and in negotiating the settlement, as proceeds from the sale of a capital asset, *i.e.*, as a capital gain. In his notice of deficiency respondent determined that such proceeds constituted ordinary income.

OPINION

In support of its contention that the proceeds should be taxed as capital gain, petitioner argues that the proceeds were received in settlement of a legal claim instituted by ESB to prevent damage to a capital asset. In the alternative, petitioner argues that if we find, as contended by respondent, that the proceeds were not paid and received in settlement of the trademark litigation but instead such proceeds were received by ESB as the result of a normal commercial transaction between ESB and EXXON Corporation, such transaction still constituted a sale or exchange of a capital asset. Respondent counters with several contentions but his primary argument is that the transaction between the parties amounted to a license whereby Exxon acquired the right to the EXIDE trademark and the payment was ordinary income in the nature of a license fee or royalty. For the reasons set forth below, we agree with petitioner's first argument.

We have long recognized the rule that "The taxability of the proceeds of a lawsuit, or of a sum received in settlement thereof, depends upon the nature of the claim and the actual basis of recovery." *Sager Glove Corp. v. Commissioner*, 36 T.C. 1173, 1180 (1961), affd. 311 F.2d 210 (7th Cir. 1962), cert. denied 373 U.S. 910 (1963). The nature of a litigation recovery is determined by reference to the origin and character of the claim which gave rise to the litigation. Victor E. Gidwitz Family Trust, 61 T.C. at 673. Thus, amounts received for injury or damage to capital assets are taxable as capital gain, whereas amounts received for lost profits are taxable as ordinary income. State Fish Corp., 48 T.C. at 472.

In State Fish Corp., *supra*, we concluded that a recovery received by a taxpayer constituted compensation for diminution in the goodwill of his business and, therefore, was taxable as a capital gain. 48 T.C. at 477. In that case, the taxpayer had bought an established and ongoing business, with the seller agreeing not to open a similar business and compete with the taxpayer for a period of five years. The seller, however, breached the covenant not to compete, and the taxpayer brought suit alleging damage to the goodwill of the business. After the taxpayer was awarded a judgment, the seller paid a lesser sum in settlement of the judgment. In concluding that the recovery was for damages to goodwill rather than lost profits, as contended by respondent, we relied heavily upon the allegations set forth in the complaint, a majority of which concerned goodwill. 48 T.C. at 474.

In the present case, although there was no lawsuit between ESB and the EXXON Corporation in the usual sense, it is apparent that ESB and EXXON Corporation were adversaries in the numerous proceedings before the United States Patent Office and similar tribunals in foreign countries. Furthermore, had the parties not reached a settlement, we are certain that ESB would have filed appropriate lawsuits against EXXON Corporation. Consequently, we see no reason to treat the settlement of the trademark dispute between ESB and the EXXON Corporation any differently than the settlement of claims which have proceeded to actual suit such as those involved in *Sagar Glove Corp. v. Commissioner, supra*; *Victor E. Gidwitz Family Trust v. Commissioner, supra*; and *State Fish Corp. v. Commissioner, supra*; and after carefully reviewing the entire record in the light of these decisions, we are satisfied that in this case the underlying dispute between ESB and the EXXON Corporation was in the nature of a claim for damages to the EXIDE trademark and the goodwill associated therewith.

First, all of the objections, petitions to cancel, and other documents filed by ESB in the trademark proceedings centered on the potential damage to the EXIDE trademark and goodwill. The same is also true with respect to the settlement negotiations, in which ESB consistently and repeatedly sought to protect these assets. Furthermore, ESB never alleged that it was entitled to, or attempted to obtain, lost profits. The subject of the possible impact of the EXXON trademark on ESB's sales arose only in ESB's attempt to place a value on the damage to the trademark and goodwill. Such a use of lost profits as an evidentiary factor in determining damage to goodwill has been held not to alter the true basis of the recovery. *Raytheon Production Corp. v. Commission*, 144 F.2d 110, 113 (lst Cir. 1944), cert. denied 323 U.S 779 (1944), affg. 1 T.C. 952 (1943); *Farmers' and Merchants' Bank v. Commissioner*, 59 F.2d 912, 913 (6th Cir. 1932); *State Fish Corp.*, 48 T.C. at 475–477. We see no reason not to arrive at the same conclusion with respect to the EXIDE trademark.

Having decided that ESB's claim was for damages to the EXIDE trademark and associated goodwill, we need only to characterize the nature of these assets which we find to be capital assets. With respect to a trademark, being a capital asset for Federal income tax purpose, see *Consolidated Foods Corp. v. United States*, 569 F.2d 436 (7th Cir. 1978); *United States v. Adamson*, 161 F.2d 942 (9th Cir. 194); *Avery v. Commissioner*, 47 B.T.A. 538 (1942). For similar holdings with respect to goodwill, see *Ensley Bank and Trust Co. v. United States*, 154 F.2d 968, 969 (5th Cir. 1946), cert. denied 329 U.S. 732 (1946); *VGS Corp. v. Commissioner*, 68 T.C. 563, 589 (1977); *Michaels v. Commissioner*, 12 T.C. 17, 19 (1949).

Therefore, in ultimate conclusion, we find that the actual basis of the recovery of the settlement proceeds by ESB was for damages to its trademark and the associated goodwill. Since these items are capital assets the proceeds are taxable as capital gains.

In arriving at the above conclusion, we have carefully considered respondent's primary argument that the settlement agreement constitutes a license, i.e., that ESB merely granted the EXXON Corporation a limited right to use the EXIDE trademark without interference. The argument is not persuasive, however, because the record contains no evidence from which we can find or reasonably infer that ESB and the Exxon Corporation intended to enter into a license agreement or any other type of ongoing relationship. Furthermore, the settlement agreement does not contain some important characteristics which are commonly found in license agreements.

First, under the settlement agreement, ESB had no control over the nature and quality of the products covered by the trademark which is the touchstone of the usual trademark license. 1 J. Gilson, Trademark Protection and Practice sec. 6.01 [4], at 6–8 (1984 ed.). Secondly, any rights granted by ESB under the settlement agreement to EXXON Corporation were perpetual, not of a limited duration, as is usual in the case of a license. See Armour v. Commissioner, 22 T.C. 181 (1954); *Seattle Brewing & Malting Co. v. Commissioner*, 6 T.C. 856, 869-870 (1946), affd. 165 F.2d 216 (9th Cir. 1948). Thirdly, the settlement agreement provided for a lump-sum payment rather than the usual periodic or variable production payments. See *Seattle Brewing & Malting Co. v. Commissioner*, 6 T.C. at 869. Finally, ESB had no right to terminate the agreement. See Seattle Brewing & Malting Co., *supra*, 6 T.C. at 871; *Jones v. Pepsi-Cola Co.*, 223 F. Supp. 650, 654 (D. Neb. 1963).

We have also considered but are not persuaded by respondent's other arguments, which for the most part are directed to petitioner's alternative contention, which we do not reach, that the settlement was a normal commercial transaction constituting a sale or exchange of a capital asset.

Illinois Tool Works v. Commissioner
117 T.C. 39 (2001)

Respondent determined deficiencies of $2,370,750 and $818,812, respectively, in petitioner's consolidated Federal income tax for 1992 and 1993.

After concessions, the issue for decision is whether $6,956,590 of a payment made by petitioner in satisfaction of a court judgment, based on a patent infringement claim that was brought against the acquired corporation and assumed as a contingent liability by petitioner, should be capitalized as a cost of acquisition or deducted as a business expense.

FINDINGS OF FACT

Some of the facts have been stipulated, and the stipulated facts are incorporated in our findings by this reference. Illinois Tool Works, Inc. (petitioner) is a corporation organized and existing under the laws of the State of Delaware. At the time of the filing of the petition, petitioner's principal place of business was located in Glenview, Illinois. During 1992, petitioner and its subsidiaries filed a consolidated Federal income tax return, reported income on a calendar year basis, and used the accrual method of accounting.

In 1975, the DeVilbiss Co. (DeVilbiss) was a division of Champion Spark Plug Co. (Champion). On October 9, 1975, Jerome H. Lemelson (Lemelson), an inventor and engineer, sent a letter to DeVilbiss offering to license certain patents, including a patent called the " '431 patent". In 1978, DeVilbiss secured a license, from the Trallfa Co. of Norway (Trallfa), to sell Trallfa robots in North America. Trallfa robots are computer-controlled hydraulically actuated paint spray devices that are designed to mimic human arm and wrist motions during painting operations. On September 17, 1979, attorneys for Lemelson sent a letter to DeVilbiss asserting that DeVilbiss was producing certain products in the industrial robot and manipulator field that might be infringing certain Lemelson patents including the '431 patent. On behalf of DeVilbiss, the director of robotic operations at DeVilbiss wrote a reply letter to Lemelson's attorneys that denied any infringement. On May 23, 1980, DeVilbiss and Trallfa entered into a new license agreement that gave DeVilbiss the right to manufacture, as well as to sell, Trallfa robots.

In 1981, Lemelson filed a lawsuit against the United States of America in the U.S. Court of Claims (Court of Claims lawsuit) alleging patent infringement for the Federal Government's purchase and use of certain robots including the Trallfa robot. Champion, as owner of DeVilbiss, entered the case as a third-party defendant. During one court session, the presiding judge stated that, after reviewing the merits, he did not believe that Lemelson was likely to succeed on his patent infringement claim. The parties to the Court of Claims lawsuit ultimately reached a settlement that required the Federal Government to pay $5,000 to Lemelson. The Federal Government sought indemnification from Champion.

On May 13, 1985, Lemelson filed a separate lawsuit against Champion directly, as owner of DeVilbiss, in the U.S. District Court for the District of Delaware (the Lemelson lawsuit). In his petition, Lemelson alleged that the manufacture and sale of the Trallfa robot infringed several of his patents, including the '431 patent. The Lemelson lawsuit sought damages for Trallfa robots that were sold prior to 1986. On August 16, 1989, Lemelson made an offer to settle the lawsuit for $500,000, which DeVilbiss rejected.

DeVilbiss retained Mark Curran Schaffer (Schaffer), an intellectual property attorney, to represent DeVilbiss in the Lemelson lawsuit. Schaffer reviewed the patents, studied the patent file histories, performed prior art searches, and compared Lemelson's patents with the Trallfa robot. Schaffer concluded that Lemelson's patents were not infringed by the Trallfa robot and that it was unlikely that Lemelson would succeed in proving infringement. Schaffer communicated his opinion to representatives of DeVilbiss.

Larry Becker (Becker), division counsel and secretary of DeVilbiss at the time that the Lemelson lawsuit was filed, also reviewed the Lemelson lawsuit. Although Becker believed that the Lemelson lawsuit was not worth anything, he and his staff determined that the range of exposure would be between $25,000 and $500,000.

Prior to 1990, Eagle Industries, Inc. (Eagle), a company unrelated to petitioner, purchased DeVilbiss from Champion and subsequently incorporated DeVilbiss under the laws of the State of Delaware as a wholly owned subsidiary of Eagle. In 1990, petitioner entered into a purchase agreement to acquire certain assets relating to the industrial and commercial business operations of DeVilbiss. Petitioner agreed to pay $126.5 million for the assets and an additional $12.5 million for a covenant not to compete. The purchase agreement specified that, at closing, the buyer assumed certain liabilities of the seller and, in part, states:

At the Closing, Buyer shall assume:

(a) the Liabilities associated with the Companies whose Stock is being purchased hereunder;

(b) the Liabilities to the extent of the amounts actually reserved for or that are specifically noted on the February 2, 1990 Balance Sheet and the supporting documentation thereto....

(c) those Liabilities to the extent specifically provided for in this Agreement or to the extent disclosed on the Schedules or Exhibits to this Agreement;

.....

During the due diligence period, representatives of petitioner, including Gary F. Anton (Anton), petitioner's director of audits; Thomas Buckman (Buckman), petitioner's vice president of patents and technology; and John Patrick O'Brien (O'Brien), petitioner's group technology counsel, also studied the patents and formed the conclusion that the Lemelson lawsuit would most likely result in no liability exposure. Anton was the lead on-site due diligence person for petitioner's acquisition of the DeVilbiss assets, and Buckman and O'Brien were attorneys and members of the patent bar. The representatives of petitioner estimated that legal fees of approximately $400,000 would be incurred to defend the lawsuit. The "worst case scenario" that was contemplated by petitioner's representatives was that petitioner could incur a liability of between $1 million and $3 million. However, they concluded that the likelihood of this exposure was somewhere between zero and 5 percent. They believed that there was a 98- to 99-percent chance that petitioner would prevail in the patent infringement claim.

The reserve for the Lemelson lawsuit, in the course of the acquisition, was eventually set at $350,000. At the conclusion of the due diligence review, the purchase price of the DeVilbiss assets was adjusted from $126.5 million to $125.5 million. Petitioner and DeVilbiss considered the pending Lemelson lawsuit, but the lawsuit liability did not affect the adjustment in the purchase price. The acquisition closed on April 24, 1990.

After the acquisition, petitioner assumed the defense of the Lemelson lawsuit in the District Court in 1991. On January 17, 1991, the jury returned a verdict against Champion (and, thus, against petitioner as the party in interest), finding that Champion had willfully infringed the '431 patent that was owned by Lemelson. The jury awarded damages of $4,647,905 for patent infringement and $6,295,167 for prejudgment interest. The District Court doubled the $4,647,905 damage award for patent infringement due to the jury's finding of willful infringement. The finding of willfulness was based in part on the failure of Champion (and on the failure of petitioner as the party in interest) to secure an authoritative opinion on whether the Trallfa robot violated the '431 patent until 2 months before trial.

.....

In 1992, after all appeals were exhausted, petitioner paid the judgment, including accumulated interest, of $17,067,339. The $17,067,339 judgment included the damages and prejudgment interest totaling $15,590,977 that were awarded by the District Court, postjudgment interest of $1,470,389.92, and court costs of $5,971.74.

OPINION

The portion of the $17,067,339 court judgment that is in issue is $6,956,590 because: (1) Petitioner capitalized $1 million in its tax return, (2) respondent conceded an allowance of $2,154,160 for postacquisition interest expense, and (3) respondent conceded a reduction of $6,956,589 for the disposal of acquisition assets. We must decide whether the $6,956,590 in dispute should be capitalized as a cost of acquisition or deducted as a business expense.

Section 162(a) provides a deduction for a taxpayer when an expenditure is: (1) An expense, (2) an ordinary expense, (3) a necessary expense, (4) incurred during the taxable year, and (5) made to carry on a trade or business. *Commissioner v. Lincoln Sav. & Loan Association*, 403 U.S. 345, 352-353 (1971). An expenditure is a "necessary expense" when it is appropriate or helpful to the development of a taxpayer's business. *Commissioner v. Tellier*, 383 U.S. 687, 689 (1966). An expenditure is an "ordinary expense" when it is "normal, usual, or customary" in the type of business involved. *Deputy v. Du Pont*, 308 U.S. 488, 495-496 (1940). Petitioner bears the burden of proving entitlement to the claimed deduction. Rule 142(a); *INDOPCO, Inc. v. Commissioner*, 503 U.S. 79, 84 (1992).

No current deduction is allowed for a capital expenditure. See sec. 263(a)(1). Section 1.263(a)-2(a), Income Tax Regs., includes as examples of capital expenditures "The *cost of acquisition*...of buildings, machinery and equipment, furniture and fixtures, and similar property having a useful life substantially beyond the taxable year." (Emphasis added.) Generally, the payment of a liability of a preceding owner of property by the person acquiring such property, whether or not such liability was fixed or contingent at the time such property was acquired, is not an ordinary and necessary business expense. *David R. Webb Co. v. Commissioner*, 708 F.2d 1254, 1257 (7th Cir.1983). Instead, payment of such a liability is capitalized and added to the basis of the acquired property.

Petitioner contends that the amount of the payment that was made in satisfaction of the Lemelson lawsuit should not be added to the cost basis of the property that was acquired in the asset acquisition from DeVilbiss because the payment was highly speculative and unexpected at the time of purchase. Petitioner relies on the Tax Court's decision in *Pac. Transp. Co. v. Commissioner*, T.C. Memo.1970-41, vacated and remanded 483 F.2d 209 (9th Cir.1973). Petitioner's alternative arguments are: (1) A payment in satisfaction of an assumed liability, which would have been a deductible expense if it had been paid by DeVilbiss, the acquired corporation, retains its deductible character when petitioner, the acquiring corporation, becomes the party in interest and (2) as a result of petitioner's efforts in defending the Lemelson lawsuit, the final judgment amount that petitioner paid was an ordinary and necessary business expense that was directly connected to the business operations. In support of these alternative arguments, petitioner relies on *Nahey v. Commissioner*, 196 F.3d 866 (7th Cir.1999).

Respondent maintains that the assets that petitioner received in exchange for the sales price, which included the assumed liabilities, produced a substantial benefit to petitioner in future years as the assets were used in petitioner's business. Respondent maintains that the Lemelson lawsuit was a contingent liability of DeVilbiss that was assumed, in full, by petitioner as consideration for the acquired assets of DeVilbiss. Therefore, respondent contends, regardless of whether the final amount of the liability was unexpected or remote at the time of acquisition, the total sum of the payment for the assumed contingent liability must be added to the cost basis of the property that was acquired in the asset acquisition. Respondent relies on the Court of Appeals for the Ninth Circuit's decision in *Pac. Transp. Co. v. Commissioner*, 483 F.2d 209 (9th Cir.1973), vacating and remanding T.C. Memo.1970-41.

Respondent also relies on *David R. Webb Co. v. Commissioner*, 77 T.C. 1134 (1981), affd. 708 F.2d 1254 (7th Cir.1983), in which a taxpayer expressly assumed the obligation to make pension payments to the widow of a corporate officer for her life as part of the purchase of the assets and liabilities of a corporation. Prior to the acquisition of the corporation by the taxpayer, the corporation made the pension payments and deducted the payments as ordinary and necessary business expenses. Upon acquisition, the taxpayer continued to make the pension payments to the widow and claimed a deduction for the amount of the pension payments. This Court stated:

> It is well settled that the payment of an obligation of a preceding owner of property by the person acquiring such property, whether or not such obligation was fixed, contingent, or even known at the time such property was ac-

quired, is not an ordinary and necessary business expense. Rather, when paid, such payment is a capital expenditure which becomes part of the cost basis of the acquired property. Such is the result irrespective of what would have been the tax character of the payment to the prior owner. *Id.* at 1137–1138.

On appeal, the Court of Appeals for the Seventh Circuit dismissed the taxpayer's argument that a contingent liability that was insusceptible of present valuation at the time of the acquisition could not be capitalized as a cost of acquisition. The Court of Appeals held that, when the actual amount of the contingent liability is known, the amount can be added to the cost basis of the purchased property. *David R. Webb Co. v. Commissioner,* 708 F.2d 1254, 1258 (7th Cir.1983).

We conclude that *David R. Webb Co.,* not *Nahey v. Commissioner, supra,* is applicable to the facts in this case. In *Nahey,* the issue was whether proceeds of litigation prosecuted to judgment were taxed as capital gains or ordinary income. The Court of Appeals held that the proceeds were ordinary income to the buyer of the corporation that had initially held the legal claim for lost corporate income. In that context, the Court noted that the character of income did not change as a result of the acquisition, stating that "what was transferred as part of a corporate acquisition was an asset that yields ordinary income". *Nahey v. Commissioner, supra* at 869. We are not persuaded by petitioner's attempt to extend this rationale to the present case in contravention of the consistently applied rule that payment of liabilities assumed as part of an acquisition must be capitalized.

Because we believe that *David R. Webb Co.* is the controlling authority in this case, we need not decide the dispute between the parties over the status of *Pac. Transp. Co. v. Commissioner, supra.* We note, however, that the Court of Appeals, in reversing our decision, relied on two Supreme Court cases, *Woodward v. Commissioner,* 397 U.S. 572 (1970), and *United States v. Hilton Hotels,* 397 U.S. 580 (1970), decided after our Memorandum Opinion was released.

In settling on a final price for the DeVilbiss industrial and commercial assets, the possibility of incurring a liability on the patent infringement claim in the Lemelson lawsuit was considered by both petitioner and DeVilbiss. DeVilbiss, as seller, disclosed the patent infringement claim that arose from its activities to petitioner during the due diligence period. Petitioner, as buyer, was aware of the Lemelson lawsuit and expressly assumed the contingent liability as part of the acquisition agreement. Both petitioner and DeVilbiss contemplated the possible exposure that might result from the Lemelson lawsuit and sought the opinion of their corporate officers. Although the liability did not affect the negotiations or the final established purchase price, the assumed liability of the Lemelson lawsuit transferred to petitioner pursuant to the purchase agreement.

The Lemelson lawsuit, like the contingent liability in *David R. Webb Co. v. Commissioner, supra,* was a contingent liability that petitioner was aware of prior to the acquisition of assets and liabilities from DeVilbiss and that petitioner expressly assumed in the purchase agreement. Additionally, the status of the Lemelson lawsuit was considered in determining the final purchase price, and petitioner created a reserve for the liability arising from the patent infringement claim.

Following *David R. Webb Co.,* we conclude that petitioner's payment of the court judgment, which was an obligation of DeVilbiss and acquired by petitioner, whether or not such obligation was fixed, contingent, or even known at the time such property was acquired, was not an ordinary and necessary business expense. Such payment is a capital expenditure that becomes part of the cost basis of the acquired property regardless of what would have been the tax character of the payment to the prior owner. *See David*

R. Webb Co. v. Commissioner, 77 T.C. at 1137–1138 (1981). See also Meredith Corp. & Subs. v. Commissioner, 102 T.C. 406, 454-455 (1994) (holding that the time at which a contingent liability that is assumed in an asset acquisition is to be capitalized occurs when the expense is incurred).

Field Service Advisory 199925012
(1999 WL 424839 June 25, 1999)

ISSUE:

Whether costs incurred in the pursuit and settlement of a copyright infringement action instituted by Taxpayer may be deducted as ordinary and necessary trade or business expenses or, instead, must be capitalized.

CONCLUSION:

To the extent that the litigation costs relate to the recovery of lost income, these should be deductible when accrued by Taxpayer; however, to the extent the costs are associated with a contest regarding Taxpayer's property interest itself these costs may be capital.

FACTS:

In Year 1, Taxpayer and Corp. A entered into a certain product licensing agreement (the Year 1 Agreement) whereby Corp. A would endeavor to develop certain products for use by customers in conjunction with Taxpayer's products. To that end, Taxpayer loaned various technological products to Corp. A with the express provision that title thereto would be retained by Taxpayer. This Year 1 agreement was terminated in Year 2; and eventually replaced in Year 3 with a new agreement (the Year 3 Agreement).

In the Year 3 Agreement, Corp. A acknowledged certain ***. Under that same Year 3 Agreement, Taxpayer granted Corp. A *** The Year 3 agreement, nevertheless, did not end the dispute between Taxpayer and Corp. A.

In Year 5, Taxpayer filed a federal district court action against Corp. A and Corp. B claiming copyright infringement. ***. Taxpayer asserted the infringement of X registered copyrights in all. Taxpayer also charged Corp. A with facilitating the infringement by Corp. B as well as direct infringement by Corp. A's own products. Taxpayer sought damages under the applicable copyright statutes and injunctive relief, including the destruction of all infringing products held by the defendants.

The defendants' answers included the factual assertion that the *** and the legal defenses of ***, and certain copyright defenses (including functionality, lack of originality, lack of similarity, and others). Neither defendant challenged the title or ownership, per se, of the copyrights which Taxpayer had relied upon in its action. Corp. A's answer conceded that Taxpayer had received the certificates of registration for the works in suit. Indeed, the district court noted that "the parties do not dispute [Taxpayer's] ownership of valid copyrights."

After several years of pretrial motions and rulings, summary judgment was granted in favor of defendants.

Taxpayer claimed deductions in connection with the suit for legal expenses it incurred during the Year 4 through Year 6 taxable years and for certain settlement payments made in the Year 7 taxable year. Examination disallowed all said deductions, finding these to be capital expenditures. The expenses for Year 4 and Year 5, however, were conceded by Appeals. The Year 6 through Year 7 taxable years have not been resolved and are currently in Appeals' jurisdiction.

LAW AND ANALYSIS:

Section 162 provides that a deduction from income shall be allowed for all ordinary and necessary business expenses paid or incurred during the taxable year in carrying on any trade or business. Section 263 provides that no deduction is allowed for capital expenditures. The provisions of section 263 take precedence over the business expense deduction of section 162. See section 161. Thus, the "norm" is capitalization. INDOPCO, Inc. v. Commissioner, 503 U.S. 79, 84 (1992). In determining whether litigation expenses are deductible, the origin and character of the claim with respect to which an expense was incurred is the controlling test. United States v. Gilmore, 372 U.S. 39 (1963). Gilmore dealt with the expenses of a divorce proceeding to defend against claims of community property ownership of certain closely-held corporate stock. The Supreme Court held those proceedings and the costs thereof "stemmed entirely from the marital relationship." Id. at 51. Because the costs were personal, they were also nondeductible. The origin of the claim test has also been adopted to determine whether litigation costs conceded to have been made in a trade or business context are either currently deductible ordinary expenses or capital expenditures. To be currently deductible, the legal expenses may not have their origin in the acquisition or disposition of a capital asset. See Woodward v. Commissioner, 397 U.S. 572 (1970); United States v. Hilton Hotels Corp., 397 U.S. 580 (1970). A corollary to that principle regarding asset acquisition/disposition is that "the cost of defending or perfecting title to property" is inherently a capital expenditure. Treas. Reg. § 1.263-2(a). See also California & Hawaiian Sugar Refining Co. v. United States, 311 F.2d 235 (Ct. Cl. 1962). As discussed below, however, the precise nature of the "property" itself must still be recognized and distinguished from other property rights.

Intangible intellectual property right grants in the United States chiefly take the form of patent, trademark, or copyright. Despite the long history and increasingly commonplace nature of legal actions involving such rights, the tax treatment of the costs incurred therein as yet remains less than routine. This is true as a matter of Service position as well as judicial precedent. While, from a federal income tax vantage, viewing all such intellectual property litigation generically certainly has the unarguable appeal of expediency, such treatment also ignores the actual inherent differences and purposes of the various rights and remedies involved.

Those differences, inter alia, include: the life of such property grants, the rationales and business reasons for asserting such property rights (and against which entities), the industry context, the appropriate legal and factual defenses to any claimed infringement, whether the taxpayer is the plaintiff or defendant in the action in issue, and the ultimate result of the underlying litigation and/or settlement. Thus, although analogies among the various precedents that have delved into this area may be of some help, the factual circumstances and particular intangible property rights involved in the underlying litigation must still be critically examined in each case separately. See Rev. Rul. 78-389, 1978-2 C.B. 126. With those distinguishing considerations kept in mind, we should then look to the specific cases applying the general principles set out above.

The trademark and tradename cases, specifically, are probably the better settled of this group; however, those cases are of peculiar pedigree. It has been expressly held that legal fees incurred in a trademark infringement action are not deductible as ordinary and necessary expenses. Medco Products Co., Inc. v. Commissioner, 523 F.2d 137 (10th Cir. 1975), aff'g 62 T.C. 509 (1974). The Tenth Circuit in Medco relied in part upon Danskin, Inc. v. Commissioner, 331 F.2d 360 (2d Cir. 1964), aff'g 40 T.C. 318 (1963). Danskin held that costs to prevent trademark infringement "resemble the cost of perfecting or preserving title to property, a cost well established as a capital expenditure." Id. at 361. See also Rust-Oleum Corp. v. Commissioner, 280 F.Supp. 796 (N.D. Ill. 1967) (parsing the underlying causes and the ultimate determination and settlement reached with regard to each of those counts, the opinion indicates that—although legal expenses for securing a judicial determination in rights to a specific trademark were chargeable to capital expenditure—the legal expenses for recovering lost profits as a result of infringement of a trademark by another should be currently deductible as ordinary and necessary business expenses; the court found that the taxpayer's motivation— and so too its costs—should be equally divided between capital and current expenses). Compare J.R. Wood & Sons, Inc. v. Commissioner, T.C. Memo. 1962-189, where the cost of an unsuccessful trademark infringement action was held entirely deductible.[1]

Notwithstanding Wood, another likely explanation of the more uniform treatment of costs in the trademark cases is that the trademark cases involved former section 177 (and the regulations thereunder) of the 1954 Code, which by their own terms only applied to trademark and tradename—not to patents and copyrights. Former section 177, repealed in 1986, provided that capital trademark expenditures could be amortized over five years. Those expenditures included the costs of protection and defense of trademarks. The regulations specifically stated that the section applied to "litigation expenses connected with infringement proceedings." Treas. Reg. § 1.177-1(b)(1). No analogous provision existed for patent and copyright litigation expenditures. On balance, regardless of the underpinning of their rationales, the trademark cases should not be offered as especially apposite authority for the capitalization of litigation costs in the copyright (or patent) context.

A more apt—if still inexact—comparison does exist between patents and copyrights. Patents and copyrights are intended to grant their author or inventor "the exclusive right" to their work for a limited time so as to "promote the progress of science and useful arts." U.S. Constitution, Art. I, § 8, cl. 8. Regarding patents, while it is unquestionably a property right having some value, note that simply because the United States Patent and Trademark Office (PTO) has issued the patent does not foreclose a subsequent challenge to that patent monopoly by another party in court. One reason for this is that the examination of patent claims and the granting thereof remains essentially an ex parte process. In litigating a patent infringement action, therefore, recognize that the first defense of the alleged infringer is almost invariably that no valid patent exists. In other words, the purported patent should never have issued from the PTO. It is up to the plaintiff patent-holder to rebut that assertion. In essence, while sometimes going so far as to admit using the invention (method or device) described in the patent (i.e., the purported infringement), the defendant will still almost always argue that the patent

---

1. *Wood* was expressly questioned in G.C.M. 38490 (Aug. 27, 1980), at 3, and its result was rejected. The G.C.M. asserts that protection of the trademarks involved in Wood was distinguishable from the patent litigation costs that the G.C.M. was addressing because the Wood costs were not "integrally related to the taxpayer[s'] business[es] and preservation of income [.]" Id. at 3.

should never have issued from the PTO in the first place. That there can be no infringement of an invalid patent is an inviolable tenet of patent law. See, e.g., Popeil Bros., Inc. v. Schick Electric, Inc., 494 F.2d 162 (7th Cir. 1974), aff'g 356 F.Supp. 240 (N.D. Ill. 1972). Whether the necessary litigation of the patent's validity is in essence tantamount to defending or perfecting its "title" to the grant of patent monopoly is open to debate. Although the patent itself is prima facie evidence of the invention, the federal courts can and do hold patents invalid with regularity.[2]

In certain circumstances presented to the Service, the adverse opinion in Urquhart v. Commissioner, 215 F.2d 17 (3d Cir. 1954), rev'g 20 T.C. 944 (1953), has been cited as authority for the deductibility of patent litigation expenses by the patent holder. See G.C.M. 38490, at 4; PLR 8831001; PLR 8022002. The taxpayer in *Urquhart* was found to be in the specific trade or business of securing and exploiting patent rights through licensing thereof. The taxpayer was regularly incurring legal fees to protect everyday business revenue; nevertheless, the Commissioner sought capitalization treatment arguing that the infringement action was just an attack on the validity of the patent. The Tax Court agreed. Id. at 947–48. After the Third Circuit reversed, however, there has been no further challenge of the *Urquhart* holding. Thus, an acceptance by the Service of *Urquhart* has developed.

This tacit acceptance of *Urquhart* lends support to the notion that patent litigation expenses are presumed deductible as an initial premise. The seeming inconsistency with the "norm of capitalization" in this regard, however, is not so readily explained away. See INDOPCO, supra. Yet, presumably, a uniformly recognized "title" case would involve a dispute over an uncontestedly "valid" patent or patents between two or more claimants. See, e.g., Safety Tube Corp. v. Commissioner, 168 F.2d 787 (6th Cir. 1948) (the "gist of the controversy is the right to the asset which produced the income" held capital); Falls v. Commissioner, 7 T.C. 66 (1946), acq. 1946-2 C.B. 2 (legal fees in defense of action to compel assignment of patent must be capitalized in part and may be deducted in part); Heinemann v. Commissioner, T.C. Memo. 1988-164 (costs of attempting to set aside assignment of patent to the Government by U.S. Army scientist were capital). Notwithstanding the backdrop of the foregoing, your request seeks advice on the treatment of copyright litigation expenses—not trademark or patent.[3] In this respect, we are thus facing a much easier determination. The general principle of looking to the origin and character of the claim still applies, Gilmore, supra, as does the proscription of Treas. Reg. § 1.263-2(c) against deducting the costs of defending and perfecting title to property; but, in this case, there is no need to address questions surrounding the "nature of taxpayer's business" or the sundry attempted explanations of the varying tax treatments of the patent cases.

The issue of origin and character of the claim is essentially a factual determination. Rafter v. Commissioner, 60 T.C. 1, 8 (1973), aff'd, 489 F.2d 752 (2d Cir. 1974). On the

---

2. Patent invalidity can rest on numerous legal grounds. Those include: lack of novelty; anticipation/obviousness from the prior art; prior public use; and abandonment by the inventor, among others. 35 U.S.C. §§ 102, 103.

3. In another context, the Service has ruled that since the property rights inherent in patents are similar to that of copyrights, the two should be treated similarly. See Rev. Rul. 75-202, 1975-1 C.B. 170; Rev. Rul. 60-226, 1960-1 C.B. 26 (whether certain royalty arrangements should be treated as sales). Nevertheless, the real differences between the two property rights should not be ignored for our purposes. For example, whereas a patent is issued for 17 years, a copyright (for post-1977 works) is in force for the life of the author plus 50 years or, in the case of a hired creator, 75 years from first publication. Similarly, the legal defenses and measures of damages in respective infringement actions are not simply coextensive.

basis of what we have been told of the underlying litigation, this case is akin to the example used in the section 212 regulations, i.e., "[a]ttorneys' fees paid in a suit to quiet title to lands are not deductible; but if the suit is also to collect accrued rents thereon, that portion of such fees is deductible which is properly allocable to the service rendered in collecting such rents." Treas. Reg. § 1.212-1(k).

This result is consistent with what we view as the better rule of Saltzman v. Commissioner, T.C. Memo. 1994-641. In Saltzman, a case you have also noted, in order to decide whether litigation costs were capital or ordinary under the origin of the claim rule, the court said it must "consider the issues involved, the nature and objectives of the litigation, the defenses asserted, the purposes for which the amounts claimed to be deductible were expended, the background of the litigation, and all facts pertaining to the controversy." Id. [68 T.C.M. at 1569, cites omitted, emphasis added]. See also Boagni v. Commissioner, 59 T.C. 708, 713 (1973). When litigation is conducted both to defend or perfect title (capital) and to preserve or collect income (deductible), the court may make an allocation of the costs between the two categories. Id. To the extent that the litigation costs relate to the recovery of lost income, these should be deductible when accrued by *** Taxpayer; however, to the extent the costs are associated with a contest regarding Taxpayer's property interest itself, the costs may be capital under *Saltzman*.

Chapter 9

Taxation of International IP Transactions and Cost Sharing Arrangements

I. Assignment for Chapter 9

Read: Internal Revenue Code: §§164(a); 275(a)(4); 367(d); 482; 551; 552(a)(1)–(2); 553(a)(1); 861(a)(4), (b); 862(a)(4); 864(b)–(c); 865(a), (d), (g); 871(a)–(b); 872; 873; 881; 882; 904(d); 951(a)–(b); 954(c); 957(a); 1441; 1442; 7701(a)(3)–(4), (b); 7852(d).

Treasury Regulations: §§1.551-2; 1.367(d)-1T(c)(1), (3); 1.911-2(b);1.861-8, -17(a)(4), -17(b)(1); 1.482-1(a)(1); -4(f)(3)(i)–(iv), ex. 2 & 3, -7(a)(1)–(2), -7(b)(1)–(4), -7(c)(1)–(2), -7(d)(1), -7(f)(2)–(3), -7(g), -7(j). Skim §§1.482-4(a), (c).

Materials: Overview
Excerpt from The Joint Committee on Taxation (June 28, 1999)
Boulez v. Commissioner
Revenue Ruling 68-443
Revenue Ruling 72-232
Revenue Ruling 80-362
SDI Netherlands B.V. v. Commissioner
International Multifoods Corp. v. Commissioner
Revenue Ruling 64-206
DHL v. Commissioner
Field Service Advice 200011021
Seagate Technology, Inc. v. Commissioner

Complete the Problems.

II. Problems for Chapter 9

1. McDon is a multinational fast food company with its headquarters located in Chicago. McDon decides to sell its franchising operations of McDon of Africa,

Inc., a wholly-owned subsidiary, to a competitor. The competitor will pay McDon $79.3 million in exchange for the exclusive right to use the trademark McDon, goodwill, the know-how to operate the McDon fast food franchising operations, all associated physical assets, and McDon's non-competing covenant in the North Africa region. McDon allocates $75 million of foreign source income to the sale of goodwill, $2 million of foreign source income to the covenant not to compete, and $300,000 of U.S. source income to the sale of the McDon trademark. McDon faces taxation from all the countries in Africa where McDon of Africa, Inc. has been in operations. McDon wants to receive as much foreign tax credits as possible against the sale proceeds of its foreign subsidiary. Explain what McDon should expect in light of the Tax Court's decision in *International Multifoods*.

2. Bernstein is a famous French conductor. He resides in Paris when he is not on tour. Bernstein has recorded several CDs and owns copyrights in those recordings. Bernstein is very particular about owning all copyrights in his recordings. Recently, OMD (Online Music Digital), a New York corporation, approaches Bernstein with a lucrative proposal wherein Bernstein will conduct a group of musicians and record 10 new CDs in exchange for a total $3.0 million in royalties to be paid in installments over two years. All the recording activities will occur at OMD studio located in New York City. According to the proposal, Bernstein will assign all copyrights in the new CDs to OMD. Bernstein regularly pays his taxes to the French taxing authority. Bernstein asks you to provide tax advice on his future income.

3. Briton, a foreign corporation, transfers to a U.S. corporation the exclusive right to use Briton's patented process, trademarks, and copyrights within the United States for an amount equal to a percentage of net profits the U.S. corporation earns from the process, trademarks, and copyrights. Assume there has been an actual disposition of all ownership interests in the patents, trademarks and copyrights and, hence, a sale occurred. Is the gain U.S. source or foreign source income? If the sale were not contingent on the use of the intellectual property (patents, trademarks, and copyrights), how would the gain be sourced?

4. NethSoft is a company incorporated in the Netherlands. NethSoft licensed from Bermuda corporation ("Bermuda") the worldwide rights to use Windows computer software. NethSoft in turn sublicenses those rights for use in the United States to a U.S. corporation ("Gates"). NethSoft receives royalties from Gates as well as from other sublicensees. NethSoft pays specified percentages of the royalties it receives from its sublicensees to Bermuda. NethSoft, Bermuda and Gates are members of a group of corporations under common control. What is the tax treatment of the royalties received by NethSoft from Gates and other sublicensees? What is the tax treatment of the royalties paid by NethSoft to Bermuda? Do the royalties paid to NethSoft by Gates retain their U.S. source character as part of the royalties paid by NethSoft to Bermuda?

5. Multinational Corp., a very important client, has just read a report on the *DHL* case and is concerned about §482 allocations. Multinational wants you to provide some advice on avoiding §482 related problems.

6. ItaliaCo is an Italian corporation that has its principal place of business in Florence, Italy. Italamerica is a Delaware corporation engaged in manufacturing activities. ItaliaCo and Italamerica entered into a contract wherein Italamerica would pay ItaliaCo 5% royalty for its use of ItaliaCo's patents. ItaliaCo later initiated a law suit in

Delaware against Italamerica for patent royalties. The parties settled the suit and Italamerica paid Italia an undisclosed sum. What is the tax treatment of the settlement?

7. Foreign Parent (FP) is a foreign corporation engaged in the extraction of a natural resource. FP has a U.S. subsidiary (USS) to which FP sells supplies of this resource for sale in the United States. FP enters into a cost sharing arrangement with USS to develop a new machine to extract the natural resource. The machine uses a new extraction process that will be patented in the United States and in other countries. The cost sharing arrangement provides that USS will receive the rights to use the machine in the extraction of the natural resource in the United States, and FP will receive the rights in the rest of the world.

   a. Could the arrangement between FP and USS constitute a "qualified cost sharing arrangement?" Explain the substantive and administrative requirements that must be met.

   b. Would your answer above be different if the natural resource did not exist in the United States? Why?

   c. Assume the arrangement between FP and USS is a qualified cost sharing arrangement. The parties agree to share the labor costs in connection with the development of the patent property. Labor costs include salaries and wages paid to the employees of both companies, but not the value of compensatory stock options granted to the employees of USS. Is this okay given the difficulty in determining the timing and valuation of stock options?

III. Overview

There are two broad categories of international transactions: (1) outbound transactions, which include intellectual property transfers by domestic persons out of the United States; and (2) inbound transactions, which include intellectual property transfers by foreign persons into the United States. Many of these transactions are taxed according to the usual U.S. tax rules that apply to domestic persons doing business solely in the United States because many of the themes in U.S. income tax law also appear in an international business transaction scenario. For instance, U.S. income tax rules that determine "what" is included in gross income, "when" income must be reported, and "who" is responsible for reporting income generally apply to international transactions. An additional query, however, is added in connection with international transactions: "Where," in a geographical sense, is an item income? To answer this question, source rules become very important, particularly when determining whether foreign persons are subject to U.S. income tax on international intellectual property transactions. The role of tax treaties must also be considered.

The United States has the power to tax U.S. citizens, resident aliens, and domestic corporations (collectively, U.S. persons) on their *worldwide income*, regardless of where they are or where their property is located. However, non-resident aliens and foreign corporations (those not created or organized in the United States) are generally taxed only on *U.S. source income*, not worldwide income. The Code sets forth bright line rules for determining whether a non-citizen is a resident or non-resident alien. I.R.C. § 7701(b). The test for determining whether a corporation is a domestic corporation or foreign corporation is easy because one must look only to where the corporation was created or organized. I.R.C. § 7701(a)(3)-(4).

The United States generally cedes the right to tax *foreign source income* (income derived from sources outside the United States) to the foreign country where the income is generated. The United States provides a foreign tax credit against the U.S. income tax imposed on the foreign source taxable income. Under some tax treaties, the U.S. tax assessed on *foreign source income* may be reduced or eliminated. Likewise, under some tax treaties, the U.S. tax assessed on a foreign person's *U.S. source income* may be reduced or eliminated.

A. Outbound Transactions

1. General Taxing Rules

United States persons (*e.g.*, citizens, resident aliens, domestic corporations) may derive income from a foreign jurisdiction by licensing or selling intellectual property overseas. The U.S. tax treatment of such outbound transactions depends on whether the foreign business operations are conducted directly by U.S. persons (through a foreign branch) or indirectly (thought a separate foreign corporation).

(a) Foreign Business Operations Conducted Directly by U.S. Persons

The U.S. tax treatment of U.S. persons who directly conduct their foreign business operation is relatively straightforward. United States persons engaged in activities abroad are taxed on their worldwide income under the rates specified in either § 1 (citizens and resident aliens) or § 11 (domestic corporations), with certain exceptions in the case of corporate licensors of intellectual property noted below. The computation of taxable income, which is the tax base upon which these rates apply, is the same for U.S. persons doing business abroad as for U.S. persons doing business solely in the United States. Unique in the context of outbound transactions is the availability of the foreign tax credit, discussed below.

If a domestic corporation licenses intellectual property overseas, the payments received are treated as royalty income. If that royalty income is not distributed, the domestic corporation may be subject to personal holding company rules. As discussed in Chapter 5, a domestic corporation may be subject to, in addition to other taxes, a personal holding company tax—a penalty tax that is imposed on certain closely held corporations that have a substantial amount of undistributed passive income. The tax is equal to the highest rate of tax under § 1(c) times the "undistributed personal holding company income" of every "personal holding company." I.R.C. § 541. Review Chapter 5 for a full discussion of the personal holding company tax.

(b) Foreign Business Operations Conducted Indirectly

A U.S. person that conducts foreign business operations through a foreign corporation is generally subject to U.S. tax on the foreign source income when the income is repatriated to the United States through a dividend distribution to the U.S. person. For example, InventCo, a Delaware corporation is a majority shareholder of JapanCo, a Japanese corporation. InventCo licenses its intellectual property to JapanCo, and JapanCo uses such intellectual property in the manufacturing and marketing of patented products in Japan. JapanCo distributes a dividend to InventCo. The United States imposes income tax on the dividend income. The foreign tax credit may reduce the U.S. tax levied on such income.

The United States has complex anti-deferral regimes applicable to income earned by a U.S. person through a foreign corporation. Two of the anti-deferral regimes are the the foreign personal holding company rules and the controlled foreign corporation rules of subpart F.

Foreign Personal Holding Companies. Unlike the personal holding company tax, addressed above, the foreign personal holding company rules do not impose a tax at the corporate level. Rather, if a corporation is a foreign personal holding company, the company's undistributed foreign personal holding company income must be included in the gross income of its United States shareholders (*i.e.*, the shareholders who are individual citizens or residents of the United States, domestic corporations, domestic partnerships). I.R.C. §551. For the amount of deemed dividend each U.S. shareholder must report, see Treas. Reg. §1.551-2.

A foreign personal holding company is generally any foreign corporation that meets a gross income requirement and a stock ownership requirement. The gross income requirement is met if 60% or more of the corporation's gross income for the taxable year is foreign personal holding company income as defined in §552. The stock ownership requirement is met if at sometime during the taxable year more than 50% in value of the outstanding stock of the foreign corporation was owned, directly or indirectly by or for fewer than five individuals who are citizens or residents of the United States (referred to as the U.S. group). I.R.C. §552(a)(1)-(2).

As with the personal holding company rules applicable to domestic corporations, licenses of intellectual property granted by foreign corporations generally creates royalty income, which is considered foreign personal holding company income. I.R.C. §553(a)(1). Foreign personal holding income does not include active business computer software royalties. I.R.C. §543(d).

Controlled Foreign Corporations. Like the foreign personal holding company provisions discussed above, the controlled foreign corporation provisions also may cause inclusion of foreign source income in the gross income of certain U.S. shareholders. I.R.C. §§951–964. Under the controlled foreign corporation rules, if a foreign corporation is a "controlled foreign corporation" for an uninterrupted period of thirty days or more during the taxable year, each "U.S. shareholder" who owns stock on the last day in such year shall include in his or her gross income the shareholder's pro rata share of the corporation's "subpart F income." I.R.C. §951(a). In short, U.S. shareholders are treated as receiving a current distribution out of certain income earned by certain controlled foreign corporations.

A foreign corporation is a "controlled foreign corporation" if the U.S. shareholders, in the aggregate, own more than 50% by vote or value of the foreign corporation. I.R.C. §957(a). A "U.S. shareholder" for controlled foreign corporation purposes is any U.S. person who owns 10% or more of the total combined voting power of all classes of stock entitled to vote. I.R.C. §951(b).

To identify the deemed distribution that must be included in gross income by a U.S. shareholder, the controlled foreign corporation's "subpart F income" must be determined. A major category of subpart F income is "foreign base income." I.R.C. § 954. The first category of foreign base income is "foreign personal holding company income." This category consists of passive income such as royalties from the licensing of intellectual property. It also includes net gains from the sale of intellectual property that produces royalty income. There is an important exception if these income flows are generated from an active business. In short, royalties and gains from the sale of property are not included in subpart F income if they are derived in the active conduct of a trade or business and are not received from a related person. I.R.C. § 954(c).

2. The Foreign Tax Credit

A U.S. person (*ie.*, U.S. citizen, resident alien, or domestic corporation) may earn income in a foreign country. Because U.S. persons are subject to U.S. tax on their worldwide income, that income is taxable in the U.S. That income, however, may be taxable in the foreign country as well. To provide relief from this double taxation, the United States generally allows U.S. persons to offset U.S. taxes with the income taxes paid in the foreign country. This is accomplished by applying a credit for foreign income taxes paid to any foreign country against U.S. income tax owed on the same income. I.R.C. §§ 901–908. The Code also allows a deduction for foreign income taxes. I.R.C. § 164(a). A taxpayer is not allowed to take both a deduction and a credit for the same foreign income tax and must choose between the two. I.R.C. § 275(a)(4). A taxpayer must decide to take a deduction or to take the foreign tax credit on an annual basis, and a taxpayer is permitted to flip back and forth. In most cases, U.S. persons will elect to take the foreign tax credit over the deduction because a credit offsets taxes on a dollar-for-dollar basis whereas the benefit of a deduction depends on the taxpayer's tax rate.

Subject to certain limitations, the amount of the foreign tax credit equals the amount of any income taxes paid or accrued during the taxable year to any foreign country or to any possession of the United States. I.R.C. § 901(b).

The foreign tax credit is subject to an important limitation. Generally, the amount of the foreign tax credit may not exceed the same proportion of the tax against which such credit is claimed which the taxpayer's taxable income from foreign sources bears to its entire taxable income for the same taxable year. I.R.C. § 904(a). The limitation is determined by multiplying the U.S. tax by a fraction, the numerator of which is foreign taxable income and the denominator of which is worldwide taxable income. The formula is depicted by the following equation:

$$\text{Limit} = \text{U.S. Tax} \times \frac{\text{Foreign Taxable Income}}{\text{Worldwide Taxable Income}}$$

The purpose of this limitation is to prevent foreign income taxes from reducing U.S. income taxes on U.S. source income. For example, assume that a U.S. domestic corporation earns income of $10,000 from activities in a foreign country and $20,000 of income from U.S. sources. If the U.S. tax rate is a flat 30% and the foreign tax rate is 50%, then the U.S. tax liability on the $30,000 of worldwide income would be $9,000. Without the limitation discussed above, the domestic corporation could credit the $5,000 of foreign taxes paid against the U.S. tax liability, resulting in a net U.S. tax liability of $4,000 (an effective rate of 20% rather than 30%). To prevent the foreign taxes of $5,000 from reducing U.S. income taxes on U.S. source income, the foreign tax credit is limited and cannot exceed a percentage of the U.S. tax, with the percentage being the amount which the corporation's foreign source income bears to worldwide income. In other words, applying the formula above, the maximum credit equals $3,000 [$9,000 x ($10,000/$30,000)] rather than the $5,000 paid to the foreign government. If this limitation prevents taxes from being immediately credited, the excess creditable taxes ($2,000 in the example) may be carried back two years or forward five years with an eye always on the limitation. I.R.C. § 904(c).

Because this simple formula could be manipulated, Congress further limited it by subjecting certain types of income separately to the limitation. In other words, the overall method of limiting the foreign tax credit is applied separately to different categories of income. One category or basket of income is "passive income," defined as any income received or accrued by any person which is of a kind which would be foreign personal holding company income (*e.g.*, dividends, interest, royalties, rents, and annuities). The final category is a catch-all basket of income (*e.g.*, general limitation income). Skim I.R.C. § 904(d).

B. Inbound Transactions

Non-U.S. persons (non-resident alien individuals and foreign corporations) may derive income from within the United States by licensing or selling intellectual property in the United States. The taxation of these inbound transactions is not as encompassing as the taxation of outbound transactions. This is because non-U.S. persons, unlike U.S. persons, are not subject to U.S. taxation on their worldwide income. They are generally taxed only on U.S. source income.

1. General Taxing Rules

Non-U.S. persons are taxed on most U.S. *business income* in the same manner that U.S. persons are. In other words, a non-U.S. person engaged in a trade or business in the United States is taxed under the graduated rates of either § 1 (in the case of non-resident alien individuals) or § 11 (in the case of foreign corporations) on income that is effectively connected with the conduct of a trade or business. I.R.C §§ 871(b), 882.

Non-U.S. persons are also taxed on certain types of *non-business, periodic income* at a flat tax rate if the income is derived from U.S. sources. More specifically, certain types of recurring income (such as interest, dividends, rents, and royalties) derived from sources within the United States are generally taxed on a gross basis at a flat 30% rate. If the recurring income is effectively connected with the conduct of a U.S. trade or business, then the income is taxed as business income. I.R.C. §§ 871(a), 881.

2. Taxation of Business Income
(a) In General

A non-resident alien individual engaged in a trade or business within the United States is taxed as provided in § 1 on his or her taxable income that is effectively connected with the conduct of a trade or business within the United States. I.R.C. § 871(b). A foreign corporation engaged in a trade or business within the United States during the taxable year shall be taxed as provided in § 11 on its taxable income that is effectively connected with the conduct of a trade or business within the United States. I.R.C. §882. The Code attempts to define two terms of art necessary to determine the taxation of U.S. business income derived by non-U.S. persons: (1) "engaged in a trade or business" in the United States, and (2) income "effectively connected" with the conduct of a trade or business within the United States (sometimes referred to as "effectively connected income"). *See* I.R.C. §864(b)-(c).

(b) Treaty Exceptions

The statutory concepts of "engaged in a trade or business" and "effectively connected income" that appear in the Code are replaced with thresholds much higher when there is an applicable income tax treaty. Tax treaties impose a "permanent establishment" requirement rather than an "engaged in a trade or business" requirement and an "attributable to" requirement rather than an "effectively connected" requirement. Under the treaty concepts, if a non-U.S. person lacks a permanent establishment in the United States, the business income is generally exempt from U.S. tax. If a non-U.S. person has a permanent establishment in the United States, then "business profits" that are "attributable to" the "permanent establishment" are generally subject to U.S. tax.

The term "permanent establishment" is typically defined in the relevant treaty and is usually equated with a fixed place of business, such as a factory or office through which business is conducted. The term "business profits" generally includes income derived from the active conduct of a trade or business and may include income, such as royalties, that may be exempt from U.S. tax under another treaty provision. The term "attributable to" generally refers to that income that is derived from the permanent establishment (*i.e.*, the income was generated by the assets or activities of the permanent establishment). As such, royalties, which may be included in the "business profits" article, may not be deemed "attributable to" a permanent establishment. Such royalties would retain their passive status, which causes them to be subject to the rules below (flat 30% rate or a lower treaty rate or exempt altogether).

For example, in *Simenon v. Commissioner*, 44 T.C. 820 (1965), the Tax Court held that the non-resident taxpayer had a "permanent establishment" in the United States during part of 1955, from January 1 to March 19, within the meaning of that term as used in article 7 of the tax treaty between France and the United States. The taxpayer was a novelist who lived in the United States from 1950 to March 1955. He purchased a house in Connecticut and used part of it as his office. During his stay in the United States, he wrote 46 books, novels, and short stories. His works were widely published in the United States, Canada, and Europe. He filed income tax returns for the calendar years 1951, 1952, 1953, and 1954. He claimed that the payments he received from U.S. publishing sources in 1955 should be exempted from U.S. taxation because he was a resident of France in 1955. [A treaty provision provided that royalties derived by a foreign licensor were exempt from U.S. tax.]

The Tax Court found that the taxpayer's home was his business headquarters prior to 1955 and during the period from January 1 to March 19, 1955. It was where he conducted his business activities, thus it constituted a "permanent establishment" within the meaning of article 7 of the tax treaty between France and the United States. Accordingly, the U.S. source royalties received by the taxpayer during the whole calendar and taxable year of 1955 were subject to the U.S. income tax, and no part of the amounts were exempted from the U.S income tax under the tax treaty.

3. Taxation of Non-Business Income from U.S. Sources

(a) "Fixed or Determinable, Annual or Periodical" Income

Under the Code, non-treaty, non-U.S. persons are generally subject to a flat tax of 30% (as opposed to the graduated rates of §§ 1 or 11) each taxable year on the amount of non-business income received from sources within the United States, but only to the extent the amount received is not effectively connected with the conduct of a trade or business within the United States. *See* I.R.C. §§ 871(a), 881(a). *See also* I.R.C. §§ 1441, 1442 (providing the method for collecting the 30% tax). The 30% flat tax is imposed on "fixed or determinable annual or periodical" income received, including passive income such as interest, dividends, rents, and royalties. Therefore, royalty income from the licensing of intellectual property (whether lump sum or periodic), which is not effectively connected with the conduct of a U.S. trade or business, is subject to the 30% tax, not the graduated rates of § 1 or § 11 that apply to effectively connected income. For example, in *Commissioner v. Wodehouse*, 337 U.S. 369, 395 (1949), the United States Supreme Court reversed a decision that held that a non-resident alien author not engaged in a trade or business within the United States, who did not have an office therein, owed no tax on the sums received for the sale of serial rights to his novels. The Court ruled in favor of the Commissioner that such sums constituted gross income from sources within the United States because they were royalties for the use of copyrights or other like property, regardless of whether they were paid in a lump sum or periodically. Such royalty income is taxable under the federal tax law.

Gain from the sale of intellectual property may be treated as royalty income if payments are contingent on the intellectual property's productivity, use, or disposition. I.R.C. § 871(a)(1)(D). The 30% tax on fixed or determinable income is applied on a gross basis without any deductions for costs incurred in producing the income.

(b) Treaty Exceptions

Most tax treaties impose a lower rate on non-business income, such as royalties, than the 30% statutory rate. Some treaties completely exempt royalties from tax altogether. Thus, royalties derived by a foreign licensor from the United States may either be exempt from U.S. taxation or subject to a rate lower than 30% (typically 15%). *See, e.g.,* Field Serv. Adv., 1997 WL 33314836 (July 25, 1997).

In *Boulez v. Commissioner*, included below, the Tax Court decided a case concerning the taxation of amounts received by Pierre Boulez, a resident of Germany and a world-renowned conductor, for recordings made under a contract in the United States. The court held that under the income tax treaty between Germany and the United States, the payments to Boulez were not royalties exempt from tax by the United States, but were compensation for personal services, and thus taxable by the United States. Whether the payments received by Mr. Boulez were "royalties" or "personal services" rested on whether Mr. Boulez had a copyrightable property interest in the recordings he made for CBS Records.

Under most treaties, gains from the sale of intellectual property by a non-U.S. person are not taxed by the U.S., but are taxed only in the foreign jurisdiction. However, under some treaties the United States may reserve the right to tax gains from the sale of intellectual property if payments are contingent on the productivity, use, or disposition of the intellectual property.

For a fuller discussion of the differences between U.S. taxation regime and international tax treaties see the excerpt from *The Joint Committee on Taxation, Description and Analysis of Present-Law Rules Relating to International Taxation (JCX-40-99), June 28, 1999*, included below.

C. Source Rules

For non-domestic persons, it is important to determine whether items are sourced inside or outside the United States. Sourcing is important because the Code includes in gross income those items that are effectively connected with the conduct of a trade or business within the United States. I.R.C. § 872. From business income, the Code permits a taxpayer to deduct expenses, losses, and other deductions properly apportioned or allocated thereto. I.R.C. § 861(b). The applicable rate structure imposed on non-U.S. persons depends on the sourcing rules. A tax of 30% is imposed on certain amounts received from sources within the United States by a non-U.S. person, but only to the extent amounts so received are not effectively connected with the conduct of a trade or business within the United States. I.R.C. § 871(a). If taxable income is effectively connected with the conduct of a trade or business within the United States, then taxable income is subject to the graduated rates of either § 1 or § 11. I.R.C. § 871(b).

Although the source rules with respect to U.S. persons seem irrelevant (because U.S. persons are taxed on worldwide income), they remain important, but for obscure reasons. As described above, the U.S. source rules become relevant for U.S. persons in the calculation of the foreign tax credit. Specifically, the foreign tax credit is available only for foreign taxes paid with respect to foreign source income. Review I.R.C. § 904.

The Code contains rules that determine the source of income. These source rules are broken into categories of income (*i.e.*, interest, dividends, royalties, sales of inventory property, and sales of non-inventory property). The Code also contains rules for the allocation of deductions (*i.e.*, sourcing of interest and research and development expenses).

1. Income Source Rules
(a) Personal Services

The source rule for personal services is simple. If services are performed in the United States, then the compensation is U.S. source. Therefore, if compensation is paid for services performed outside of the United States, the compensation is not subject to U.S. taxation. If compensation is paid for services performed in the United States, the foreign service provider is deemed to be engaged in a U.S. trade or business, and the compensation is treated as effectively connected income. There is a de minimis exception, under which compensation is given a foreign source if the non-U.S. service provider is only temporarily present in the United States. I.R.C. § 864(b). The time period set forth in the Code, 90 days, is typically extended by tax treaties. Review *Boulez v. Commissioner*, included below, which illustrates how the income received by Mr. Boulez was sourced.

(b) Royalties

In General. Royalties from the licensing of intellectual property are generally sourced according to where the intellectual property is used. I.R.C. § 861(a)(4). Therefore, if a licensee uses intellectual property in its U.S. trade or business, the royalties are U.S. source income even if the intellectual property was developed overseas and the royalties are paid overseas pursuant to a contract signed overseas.

Consistent with this general rule, the Service has held that the source of royalties paid with respect to the use of a trademark is the country in which the products bearing the trademark are ultimately used and where the trademark is protected. In Revenue Ruling 68-443, included below, the Service ruled that where products are ultimately used in the foreign country where their trademark is protected, a royalty received for the use of the foreign trademark is income from sources outside the United States despite the fact that the initial sale of the trademarked articles took place in the United States.

The general rule with respect to royalties has also been applied to copyrighted materials. Review Revenue Ruling 72-232, also included below, which held that royalties paid for the use of a foreign copyright for text books printed in the United States but sold solely in the foreign country were sourced outside the United States. *See also Rohmer v. Comm'r*, 14 T.C. 1467 (1950) (concluding that the source of a royalty is the place where the copyrighted material is consumed and protected by copyright law).

Cascading Royalties. The Service addressed cascading royalties for the use of intangible property in the United States in Revenue Ruling 80-362, included in the materials. In the revenue ruling, a nonresident alien individual resided in a foreign country with which the United States had no income tax treaty. He licensed his U.S. rights in a patent to an unrelated Dutch corporation. In turn, the Dutch corporation licensed the patent to a U.S. corporation. There is an income tax treaty between the United States and Holland that exempts tax on royalties received by the Dutch corporation from the U.S. corporation. The revenue ruling held that the royalties paid by the Dutch corporation to the alien individual in the non-treaty country were subject to the 30% U.S. tax and the Dutch corporation was required to withhold such tax. How did the Service reach its conclusion?

The Tax Court rejected the cascading royalty approach and refused to apply Revenue Ruling 80-362 in *SDI Netherlands B.V. v. Commissioner*, also included below. The court stated that the ruling "fails to reflect any reasoning or supporting legal authority." The Tax Court considered the proper source of royalty payments received by a foreign licensor from a foreign licensee (sublicensor) in a situation where the payments were attributable to royalties received by the sublicensor from a U.S. sublicensee that exploited the intellectual property.

(c) Sales

The source of gain from the sale of intellectual property depends on the nature of the sale. If the sale proceeds are contingent on the productivity, use, or disposition of the intellectual property by the purchaser, the proceeds are treated as royalties and, hence, sourced according to where the intellectual property is used. I.R.C. § 865(d). If the sale proceeds are not contingent, then any gain is sourced according to the seller's residence. I.R.C. § 865(a), (g). For purposes of the source rules, residency is determined by where an individual has a "tax home," which is generally the individual's regular or principal place of business. Treas. Reg. § 1.911-2(b); I.R.C. § 865(g). Thus, in the case of non-contingent sales, gain from the sale of intellectual property by an individual with a tax home in the United States is sourced in the United States, and gain from the sale of intellectual property by an individual who does not have a tax home in the United States is sourced outside the United States. I.R.C. § 865.

With regard to the sale of goodwill, the general sourcing rules above do not apply. The Code carves out a special sourcing rule for goodwill. Payments received in consideration of the sale of goodwill are treated as received from sources in the country in which the goodwill was generated. I.R.C. § 865(d)(3). *International Multifoods Corp. v. Commissioner*, included below, is a good example illustrating how goodwill should be sourced.

(d) Infringement Awards

It may be necessary to determine the proper source of settlement payments and awards for patent infringement. In Revenue Ruling 64-206, included in the materials, the Service ruled that settlement payments as a result of a patent infringement lawsuit are treated as royalties for purposes of applying the United States-Swiss income tax treaty. *See also* Rev. Rul. 80-15, 1985-1 C.B. 132 (addressing whether an amount received in a settlement agreement involving a contract suit to recover patent royalties is treated as a payment of "royalties" within the meaning of the tax treaty between United States and Italy).

2. Deduction Allocation and Apportionment Rules

(a) In General

Non-business income (fixed or determinable, annual or periodic income) of a non-U.S. person is generally taxed at a flat 30% rate (or lower treaty rate) on a gross basis with no allowance for deductions. However, business income (income that is effectively connected with the conduct of a U.S. trade or business) of a non-U.S. person is generally taxed under the graduated rates of §§ 1 or 11, with proper allowances for deductions. In other words, the Code allows deductions only where the deductions are effectively connected with a U.S. trade or business. I.R.C. §§ 873, 882.

As with income, it is important to identify the source of deductions as either U.S. source deductions or foreign source deductions. The Code and the regulations thereunder prescribe rules for the allocation and apportionment of expenses, losses, and other deductions for taxpayers. I.R.C. §§ 861; Treas. Reg. § 1.861-8. The rules are the same for both foreign and U.S. persons.

In sum, a taxpayer is required to allocate deductions to a class of gross income and then, if necessary, to make the determination required by the operative section of the Code to apportion deductions within the class of gross income between a statutory grouping of gross income and a residual grouping of gross income.

(b) Research and Development Expenditures

The allocation of research and development expenditures can be quite tricky. Assume, for example, that a taxpayer incurs $10,000 in research and development expenses in the United States to develop intellectual property, which generates $100,000 of foreign source income. How should the research and development expenses be allocated? If the research and development expenses are allocated to the foreign source income, then the foreign source taxable income is reduced, and in turn, the foreign tax credit might be reduced. If the research and development expenses are allocated to U.S. source income, then the foreign tax credit could be maximized. The Code and regulations have set forth rules for allocating research and development deductions.

First, taxpayers are required to allocate research and development expenses incurred to meet legal requirements imposed by a government to the jurisdiction of that government. Treas. Reg. § 1.861-17(a)(4). Second, taxpayers are required to allocate remaining research and development expenses using one of two methods, the sales method or the gross income method. Under the sales method, 50% of the deductions for research and development shall be apportioned exclusively to the geographic location where the activities that account for more than fifty percent of the deduction were performed, with the remainder apportioned where the sales resulting from the research and development took place. Under the gross income method, 25% of the deductions for research and development shall be apportioned exclusively to the geographic location where the activities that account for more than fifty percent of the deductions were performed, with the remainder apportioned on the basis of gross income so long as the apportionment results in 50% of the apportionment result under the sales method. Skim Treas. Reg. § 1.861-17(b)(1).

D. The Role of Treaties

1. In General

The United States has entered into numerous tax treaties with foreign countries in order to ameliorate possible double taxation and to clarify which treaty country retains the right to tax certain classes of persons and certain items of income in connection with cross-border transactions. As seen in the cases included below, there are general treaty provisions that govern the taxation of business profits. As with business income, there are also treaty provisions that govern the taxation of non-business profits. For instance, most tax treaties exempt royalties from tax or, in the alternative, impose a rate lower than the 30% statutory rate set forth in the Code. Therefore, royalties derived by a foreign licensor from the United States may be either exempt from U.S. taxation or may be subject to a lower treaty rate.

2. The Relationship Between Treaties and the Code

When the Internal Revenue Code and a particular treaty conflict, both cannot be supreme, and one must give way. Generally, when the Code and a treaty provision conflict, the latter adopted one controls. I.R.C. § 7852(d). Of course, if there is a statute and a treaty on the same subject, effect should be given to both if possible. If a treaty and a later statute relate to the same subject, courts will try to construe them in a way that is consistent with the intent of each and that results in the absence of conflict between the two. Therefore, only if it is determined that there is an actual conflict between a tax act and treaty will the later-in-time rule operate.

E. Section 367(d): Transfers to Foreign Corporations

Section 367 generally prevents § 351 non-recognition treatment, discussed in Chapter 6, on the transfer of certain types of property to a foreign corporation. I.R.C. § 367(a). The reason for taxing outbound transfers, but not domestic transfers, is the potential to avoid U.S. tax by transferring appreciated property outside the taxing jurisdiction of the United States.

Under 367(d), special rules are provided for the transfer of intellectual property (including patents, know-how, inventions, formulas, and processes) to a foreign corporation in a § 351 transaction. In such foreign outbound transfers, the transferor U.S. person is treated as receiving income (deemed payments) over the useful life of the intellectual property in an amount reflecting reasonable payments contingent upon the productivity, use, or disposition of the intellectual property. Such U.S. person must, over the useful life of the property, annually include in gross income an amount that represents an appropriate arms-length charge for the use of the property, even if payments are not actually made. For purposes of § 367, the useful life of intellectual property is the entire period during which the property has value (but not to exceed twenty years). See I.R.C. § 367(d); Treas. Reg. § 1.367(d)-1T(c)(1), (3).

F. Section 482:
International IP Transactions Between Related Parties

Transfers of intellectual property between controlled taxpayers must reflect arm's length consideration, usually in the form of a royalty payment. Otherwise, payment of consideration between the controlled parties may be required under the arm's length transfer pricing methodologies of § 482. Section 482 provides that the Service "may distribute, apportion or allocate gross income, deductions, credits or allowances" among controlled businesses where "such distribution, apportionment or allocation is necessary in order...clearly to reflect the income" of such controlled businesses. I.R.C. § 482. Section 482 ensures that taxpayers clearly reflect income attributable to controlled transactions by placing a controlled taxpayer on a tax parity with an uncontrolled taxpayer and by determining the true taxable income of the controlled taxpayer through arm's length transfer pricing adjustments. Treas. Reg. § 1.482-1(a)(1). Section 482 was amended in 1986 to require that any consideration provided for the transfer or license of intangible property be "commensurate with the income attributable to the intangible."

The regulations provide several methods for determining an arm's-length price for the transfer or use of intellectual property: (1) the comparable uncontrolled transaction method, (2) the comparable profits method, and (3) the profit split method. Treas. Reg. § 1.482-4(a) (referring to Treas. Reg. §§ 1.482-4(c), -5, -6). The comparable uncontrolled transaction method, which is perhaps the best method for determining an arm's length price, evaluates whether the amount charged for a controlled transfer of intellectual property was arm's length by reference to the amount charged in a comparable uncontrolled transaction. Treas. Reg. § 1.482-4(c)(1). For example, in *Ciba-Geigy Corp. v. Commissioner*, 85 T.C. 172 (1985), *acq.*, 1987-2 C.B. 1, the Tax Court accepted that a ten percent royalty paid by the wholly owned U.S. subsidiary to its Swiss parent did constitute an arm's length consideration for the exclusive license to manufacture, formulate, and sell certain triazine herbicides in the United States. The Tax Court upheld the royalty rate because DuPont had offered to pay a royalty between 10 (ten) and 12.5 (twelve and half) percent for a similar license.

If the owner of rights to exploit intellectual property transfers such rights to a controlled taxpayer, the owner must receive a certain amount of consideration with respect to such transfer under § 482. Treas. Reg. § 1.482-4(f)(3)(i). If a controlled taxpayer assisted the owner in developing the intellectual property, such person may also be entitled to consideration with respect to such assistance (*i.e.*, an allocation may be made under § 482 to reflect an arm's length consideration for assistance provided to the owner in connection with the development of the intellectual property). Treas. Reg. § 1.482-4(f)(3)(i), (iii). Determining the ownership of intellectual property can be tricky as the right to exploit intellectual property can be subdivided in various ways, and a single from of intellectual property could have multiple owners.

Legally protected intellectual property is considered owned by the legal owner. Legal ownership may be acquired by operation of law or by contract. Treas. Reg. § 1.482-4(f)(3)(ii)(A). Intellectual property that is not legally protected is considered owned by the developer of the intellectual property. Treas. Reg. § 1.482-4(f)(3)(ii)(B). Two members of a controlled group (parent licensor and subsidiary licensee) may attempt to argue that they jointly developed intellectual property in order to avoid royalty allocations. The regulations prevent this by providing that if two or more controlled taxpayers jointly developed intellectual property, only one of the controlled taxpayers will be regarded as the "developer" (*e.g.*, owner) of the intellectual property, and the other participating members will be regarded as "assisters" who may be deemed to have paid an arm's length royalty to the developer. The regulations provide guidance in determining which controlled taxpayer is the developer. Generally, the developer is the controlled taxpayer that bore the largest portion of the direct and indirect costs of developing the intellectual property. If it cannot be determined which controlled taxpayer bore the largest portion of the costs of development, all other facts and circumstances will be taken into consideration, including the location of the development activities, the capability of each controlled taxpayer to carry on the project independently, the extent to which each controlled taxpayer controls the project, and the conduct of the controlled taxpayers. Review *DHL v. Commissioner*, included below, which illustrates how courts have applied § 482 in complex international transactions involving trademarks between commonly controlled companies. *See also* Treas. Reg. § 1.482-4(f)(3)(iv), Examples 2 & 3.

G. Cost Sharing Arrangements

Cost sharing arrangements are tax efficient arrangements used by controlled taxpayers engaged in the co-development of intellectual property. They are alternative arrangements used to avoid the transfer pricing allocations under § 482. In general, a cost sharing arrangement is an agreement under which two or more participants, related or unrelated, agree to share the costs of developing one or more intellectual property assets in proportion to their shares of reasonably anticipated benefits from their individual exploitation of the interests in the intellectual property assigned to them under the arrangement. Treas. Reg. § 1.482-7(a)(1). One advantage of the cost sharing arrangement is that the parties can spread the costs of intellectual property development and ownership. Another advantage of the cost sharing arrangement, perhaps the most important, is that the parties may avoid the application of the arm's-length transfer pricing adjustments under § 482 (*i.e.*, cost sharing arrangements permit controlled participants to exploit the co-developed intellectual property absence a royalty payment between the controlled participants that is otherwise required under the arm's length transfer pricing rules of § 482.) All participants are considered to be the owners of any intellectual property developed under the cost sharing arrangement. As owners, the participants can exploit any intellectual property developed under the cost sharing arrangement without having to pay arm's length royalty payments to the other participants.

In 1995, the Treasury Department issued final regulations governing the use of cost-sharing arrangements. Read Treas. Reg. § 1.482-7. The regulations provide that the Service generally will not make § 482 allocations with respect to "qualified cost sharing arrangements" except to the extent necessary to make each controlled participant's share of the costs of intellectual property development equal to its share of reasonably anticipated benefits attributable to such development. Treas. Reg. § 1.482-7(a)(2). A taxpayer may claim that a cost sharing arrangement is a "qualified cost sharing arrangement" if it meets several substantive and administrative requirements.

1. Two or More Participants

Under the regulations, a qualified cost sharing arrangement must include two or more participants. Treas. Reg. § 1.482-7(b)(1). A "participant" may be either an "uncontrolled participant" or a "controlled participant." Treas. Reg. § 1.482-7(c)(1). A "controlled participant" is defined as a controlled taxpayer that meets certain requirements discussed below. A "controlled taxpayer" is defined as any one of two or more taxpayers owned or controlled directly or indirectly by the same interests. Treas. Reg. § 1.482-1(i)(5). A controlled taxpayer may be a controlled participant in a qualified cost sharing arrangement only if it (1) reasonably anticipates that it will derive benefits from the use of covered intangibles; (2) substantially complies with the accounting requirements described in § 1.482-7(i); and (3) substantially complies with the administrative requirements described in § 1.482-7(j). Treas. Reg. § 1.482-7(c)(1)(i)–(iii).

(a) Reasonably Anticipated Benefits Requirement

A controlled taxpayer may be a qualified participant only if it reasonably anticipates that it will derive benefits from the use of covered intellectual property. Treas. Reg. § 1.482-7(c)(1)(i). A controlled participant's reasonably anticipated benefits are the aggregate benefits that it reasonably anticipates that it will derive from covered intellectual property. Treas. Reg. § 1.482-7(e)(2). Benefits are additional income generated or costs saved by the use of covered intellectual property. Treas. Reg. § 1.482-7(e)(1). There is no requirement that a controlled taxpayer use the developed intellectual property in the *active* conduct of its trade or business. All that is required is that a controlled taxpayer benefit from the use of the covered intellectual property in a manner that can be reliably measured. Thus, a controlled taxpayer can qualify by either directly exploiting the developed intellectual property or from transferring or licensing the intellectual property to others (measuring the taxpayer's benefits from the developed intellectual property based on the licensee's use of the intellectual property). See Treas. Reg. §§ 1.482-7(f)(3)(ii), -7(c)(1)(iv) (providing example in which a controlled taxpayer is not a qualified participant).

If a controlled taxpayer is not a qualified participant because it will not derive a benefit from the use of intellectual property developed, but the controlled taxpayer provides assistance to the owner in relation to the intellectual property development, the taxpayer is treated as a service provider and must receive arm's length consideration for the assistance it is deemed to provide to the other parties. See Treas. Reg. § 1.482-7(c)(2) (referring to allocation rules of § 1.482-4(f)(3)(iii) with respect to assistance provided to the owner).

(b) Accounting Requirements

A controlled taxpayer may be a qualified participant in a qualified cost sharing arrangement only if the participant substantially complies with certain accounting requirements. Specifically, the controlled participants in a qualified cost sharing arrangement must use a consistent method of accounting to measure costs and benefits, and must translate foreign currencies on a consistent basis. Treas. Reg. §1.482-7(i).

(c) Administrative Requirements

To claim treatment as a qualified cost sharing arrangement, a controlled participant must substantially comply with the administrative requirements of §1.482-7(j). *See* Treas. Reg. §§1.482-7(a)(1), -7(b), -7(c)(1)(iii). These administrative requirements include both documentation requirements and reporting requirements. To satisfy the *documentation* requirements, a controlled participant must maintain sufficient documentation to establish that certain requirements under the regulations have been met. To satisfy the *reporting* requirements, a controlled participant must attach to its U.S. income tax return a statement indicating that it is a participant in a qualified cost sharing arrangement, and listing the other controlled participants in the arrangement. *See* Treas. Reg. §1.482-7(j)(1)–(3). Compliance with these requirements is critical. Failure to substantially comply with the administrative requirements (even the reporting requirement alone) may result in the Service making arm's length transfer pricing allocations in an arrangement that in substance constitutes a cost sharing arrangement. In Field Service Advisory 200011021, included in the materials, the Service concluded that a controlled taxpayer failed to substantially comply with the administrative requirements of §1.482-7(j)(3) due to its failure to attach a cost sharing statement to its U.S. income tax return or Form 5471. As a result, the controlled taxpayer could not claim treatment as a qualified cost sharing arrangement.

2. Method for Calculating Each Participant's Share of Intellectual Property Development Costs

A qualified cost sharing arrangement must provide a method of calculating each controlled participant's share of intellectual property development costs based on factors that can be reasonably expected to reflect each participant's share of anticipated benefits. Treas. Reg. §1.482-7(b)(2). As a corollary, the Service will not make allocations with respect to a qualified cost sharing arrangement except to the extent necessary to make each controlled participant's share of the costs of intangible development under the qualified cost sharing arrangement equal to its share of reasonably anticipated benefits attributable to such development. Treas. Reg. §1.482-7(a)(2). For purposes of determining whether such a cost allocation is appropriate for a taxable year, a controlled participant's share of intangible development costs for the taxable year under a qualified cost sharing arrangement must be compared to its share of reasonably anticipated benefits under the arrangement. Treas. Reg. §1.482-7(f)(1).

(a) Share of Intellectual Property Development Costs

A controlled participant's share of intangible development costs for a taxable year is equal to its intangible development costs for the taxable year divided by the sum of the intangible development costs for the taxable year of all of the controlled participants. Treas. Reg. §1.482-7(f)(2). A controlled participant's intangible development costs includes all of the costs incurred by that participant related to the intangible development area, plus all of the cost sharing payments it makes to other controlled and uncontrolled participants, minus all of the cost sharing payments it receives from other controlled and uncontrolled participants. Treas. Reg. §§1.482-7(d)(1), -7(f)(2)(ii), Example (i). Intangible development costs incurred related to intellectual property development consist of the following items: (1) operating expenses other than depreciation or amortization expense, and (2) charges for the use of any tangible property made available to the qualified cost sharing arrangement to the extent not included in operating expenses. An interesting (and controversial) issue that has arisen is whether intangible development costs include the deductions allowed for compensatory stock options. In Field Service Advisory 200003010 (Oct. 18, 1999), the Service took the position that intangible development costs include compensatory stock options granted to the employees of one of the cost sharing arrangement's participants. Accordingly, the cost of stock options must be equally shared by foreign affiliates in a cost sharing arrangement. In a recent case, the Tax Court denied a taxpayer's motion for summary judgment upholding the Service's position that employee stock option costs may be allocated in a cost sharing arrangement. Read *Seagate Technology, Inc. v. Commissioner*, included below.

(b) Share of Reasonably Anticipated Benefits

A controlled participant's share of reasonably anticipated benefits under a qualified cost sharing arrangement is equal to its reasonably anticipated benefits divided by the sum of the reasonably anticipated benefits of all the controlled (not uncontrolled) participants. Treas. Reg. §1.482-7(f)(3)(i). A controlled participant's reasonably anticipated benefits are the aggregate benefits (*i.e.*, additional income generated or costs saved by the use of covered intangibles) that it reasonably anticipates that it will derive from covered intangibles. Treas. Reg. §1.482-7(e). Reasonably anticipated benefits is determined by using the most reliable estimate of reasonably anticipated benefits. The reliability of an estimate will depend largely on the completeness and accuracy of the data, the soundness of the assumptions, and the relative effects of participant's deficiencies in data or assumptions on different estimates. Two factors particularly relevant in determining the reliability of an estimate of anticipated benefits are: (1) the reliability of the basis used for measuring benefits; and (2) the reliability of the projections used to estimate benefits. Treas. Reg. §1.482-7(f)(3)(i).

3. Periodic Adjustments

A qualified cost sharing arrangement must provide a method for adjusting each controlled participant's share of intellectual property development costs to account for changes in economic conditions, the business operations and practices of the participants, and the ongoing development of intangibles under the arrangement. Treas. Reg. §1.482-7(b)(3). If the parties do not make a self-adjustment, the Service may make an allocation if the projections used to determine anticipated benefits are off. For example, if there is a significant divergence between projected benefit shares and actual benefit shares, this may indicate that the projections were not reliable and the Service may use actual benefits as the most reliable measure of anticipated benefits. The regulations provide a safe harbor however. Projections will not be considered unreliable based on a divergence between a controlled participant's projected benefit share and actual benefit share if the amount of such divergence for every controlled participant is less than or equal to 20% of the participant's projected benefit share. Also, the Service will not make an allocation based on such divergence if the difference is due to an extraordinary event, beyond the control of the participants, that could not reasonably have been anticipated the time that costs were shared. It should be noted, however, the Service is not precluded from making an allocation if the taxpayer did not use the most reliable basis for measuring anticipated benefits. Thus, if the taxpayer measures anticipated benefits based on units sold, and the Service determines that another basis (*e.g.*, sales or operating profit) is more reliable for measuring anticipated benefits, then the fact that actual units sold were within 20% of the projected unit sales will not preclude an allocation under this section. Treas. Reg. § 1.482-7(f)(3)(iv)(B).

4. Documentation Requirements

A qualified cost sharing arrangement must be recorded in a document that is contemporaneous with the formation (and any revision) of the cost sharing arrangement. See Treas. Reg. §1.482-7(b)(4), for items to be included in the document.

5. Buy-in and Buy-out Payments for Intellectual Property Transfers

A controlled participant/owner that makes previously existing intellectual property available to a qualified cost sharing arrangement will be treated as having transferred interests in such property to the other controlled participants, and such other controlled participants must make buy-in payments to compensate the contributor/owner. The buy-in payment by each such other controlled participant is the arm's length charge for the use of the intellectual property, multiplied by the controlled participant's share of reasonably anticipated benefits (as defined above). If the other controlled participants fail to make such payments, the Service may make appropriate section 482 allocations to reflect an arm's length consideration for the transferred intellectual property. Treas. Reg. §1.482-7(g)(1)–(2).

If a group of controlled taxpayers participates in a qualified cost sharing arrangement, any change in the controlled participants' interests in covered intellectual property is a transfer of intellectual property for which the Service may make appropriate section 482 adjustments to reflect an arm's length consideration for the transfer. A change in the controlled participants' interests in covered intellectual property may occur by reason of entry of a new participant. Accordingly, if a new controlled participant enters a qualified cost sharing arrangement and acquires any interest in covered intellectual property, then the new participant must pay an arm's length consideration for such interest to each controlled participant from whom such interest was acquired. A change in the controlled participants' interest in covered intellectual property may also occur by reason of transfers of interests among existing participants. For example, a controlled participant may be deemed to have acquired an interest in one or more covered intangibles if another controlled participant transfers, abandons, or otherwise relinquishes an interest under the arrangement, to the benefit of the first participant. If such a relinquishment occurs, the participant relinquishing the interest must receive an arm's length consideration for its interest. Treas. Reg. § 1.482-7(g)(3)–(4).

IV. Materials

Excerpt from The Joint Committee on Taxation, Description and Analysis of Present-Law Rules Relating to International Taxation (JCX-40-99), June 28, 1999

C. Income Tax Treaties

1. In general

In addition to the U.S. and foreign statutory rules for the taxation of foreign income of U.S. persons and U.S. income of foreign persons, bilateral income tax treaties limit the amount of income tax that may be imposed by one treaty partner on residents of the other treaty partner. Treaties also contain provisions governing the creditability of taxes imposed by the treaty country in which income was earned in computing the amount of tax owed to the other country by its residents with respect to such income. Treaties further provide procedures under which inconsistent positions taken by the treaty countries with respect to a single item of income or deduction may be mutually resolved by the two countries.

The preferred tax treaty policies of the United States have been expressed from time to time in model treaties and agreements. The Organization for Economic Cooperation and Development (the "OECD") also has published model tax treaties. In addition, the United Nations has published a model treaty for use between developed and developing countries. The Treasury Department, which together with the State Department is responsible for negotiating tax treaties, last published a proposed model income tax treaty in September 1996 (the "U.S. model"). The OECD last published a model income tax treaty in 1992 ("the OECD model"). The United Nations last published a model income tax treaty in 1980 ("the U.N. model").

Many U.S. income tax treaties currently in effect diverge in one or more respects from the U.S. model. These divergences may reflect the age of a particular treaty or the particular balance of interests between the United States and the treaty partner. Other countries' preferred tax treaty policies may differ from those of the United States, depending on their internal tax laws and depending upon the balance of investment and trade flows between those countries and their potential treaty partners. For example, certain capital importing countries may be interested in imposing relatively high tax rates on interest, royalties, and personal property rents paid to residents of the other treaty country. Consequently, treaties with such countries may have higher withholding rates on dividends, interest, royalties, and personal property rents. As another example, the other country may demand other concessions in exchange for agreeing to requested U.S. terms. Countries that impose income tax on certain local business operations at a relatively low rate (or a zero rate) in order to attract manufacturing capital may seek to enter into "tax-sparing" treaties with capital exporting countries. In other words, the country may seek to enter into treaties under which the capital exporting country gives up its tax on the income of its residents derived from sources in the first country, regardless of the extent to which the first country has imposed tax with respect to that income. While other capital exporting countries have agreed to such treaties, the United States has rejected proposals by certain foreign countries to enter into such tax-sparing arrangements.

The OECD, the U.N., and the U.S. models reflect a standardization of terms that serves as a useful starting point in treaty negotiations. However, issues may arise between the United States and a particular country that of necessity cannot be addressed with a model provision. Because a treaty functions as a bridge between two actual tax systems, one or both of the parties to the negotiations may seek to diverge from the models to account for specific features of a particular tax system.

2. Model income tax treaty provisions

Significant features of the model income tax treaties are described briefly below.

Residence

The U.S. model generally treats as a resident of a treaty country any person who, under the laws of that country, is liable to tax therein by reason of its domicile, residence, citizenship, place of management, place of incorporation, or any other similar criterion. However, the concept of resident excludes any person who is liable to tax in a country solely in respect of income from sources in that country or of profits attributable to a permanent establishment in that country.

Business profits attributable to a permanent establishment

Under the U.S. model, one treaty country may not tax the business profits of an enterprise of a qualified resident of the other treaty country, unless the enterprise carries on business in the first country through a permanent establishment situated there. In that case, the business profits of the enterprise may be taxed in the first country on profits that are attributable to that permanent establishment. The U.S. model describes in detail the characteristics relevant to determine whether a place of business is a permanent establishment. The term includes a place of management, a branch, an office, a factory, a workshop, a mine, an oil or gas well, a quarry, or any other place of extraction of natural resources.

The U.S. model provides that the business profits to be attributed to the permanent establishment include only the profits derived from the assets or activities of the permanent establishment. The U.N. model adds a limited "force of attraction rule" which would allow the country in which the permanent establishment is located to attribute to the permanent establishment sales in that country of goods or merchandise of the same or similar kind as those sold through the permanent establishment, and to attribute to the permanent establishment other business activities carried on in that country of the same or similar kind as those effected through the permanent establishment.

The U.S., OECD, and U.N. models expressly provide for the allocation of worldwide executive and general administrative expenses in determining business profits attributable to a permanent establishment. The U.S. model also provides for the allocation of research and development expenses, interest, and other expenses incurred for the purposes of the enterprise as a whole (or the part of the enterprise that includes the permanent establishment).

Dividends

The U.S. model permits taxation of dividends by the residence country of the payor, but limits the rate of such tax in cases in which the dividends are beneficially owned by a resident of the other treaty country. In such cases, the U.S. model allows not more than a 5-percent gross-basis tax if the beneficial owner is a company that owns directly at least 10 percent of the payor's voting stock, and not more than a 15-percent gross-basis tax in any other case. Under the OECD model, the 5-percent rate is not available unless the beneficial owner of the dividends is a company other than a partnership that holds directly at least 25 percent of the capital of the dividend payor. The U.N. model expressly leaves to case-by-case bilateral negotiation the particular percentage limit to be imposed on source-country taxation of dividends.

Interest and royalties

The U.S. model generally allows no tax to be imposed by a treaty country on interest or royalties arising in that country and beneficially owned by a resident of the other treaty country. By contrast, the OECD model would permit up to 10-percent gross-basis taxation of interest by the treaty country in which the interest arises. The U.N. model expressly leaves to case-by-case bilateral negotiation the particular percentage limit to be imposed on source-country taxation of interest or royalties.

Other income

The U.S. model provides that items of income beneficially owned by a resident of a treaty country, wherever arising, that are not dealt with in the articles of the treaty are taxable only by the recipient's country of residence. By contrast, the U.N. model states that items of income of a resident of a treaty country not dealt with in the other treaty articles and arising in the other treaty country may also be taxed in that other country.

Relief from double taxation

The U.S. model obligates the United States to allow its residents and citizens as a credit against U.S. income tax: (a) income taxes paid or accrued to the treaty country by the U.S. person, and (b) in the case of a U.S. company owning at least 10 percent of the voting stock of a company resident in the treaty country, and from which the U.S. company receives dividends, the treaty country income tax paid or accrued by or on behalf of the payor company with respect to the profits out of which the dividends are paid. However, the U.S. model preserves U.S. internal law by subjecting this right to the foreign tax credit to the provisions and limitations of U.S. law as it may be amended from time to time without changing the general principle of the model provision.

A standard article in treaties specifies the U.S. and foreign taxes covered by the treaty. The U.S. model provides that such covered taxes shall be considered income taxes for purposes of the credit article, and contemplates the possibility that such a tax might be creditable solely by reason of the treaty.

Nondiscrimination

The U.S. model provides that nationals of a treaty country, wherever they may reside, shall not be subjected in the other country to any taxation (or any requirement connected therewith) that is more burdensome than the taxation and connected requirements to which nationals of that other country in the same circumstances, particularly with respect to taxation on worldwide income, are or may be subjected. Similarly, the taxation of a permanent establishment or fixed base that an enterprise or resident of a treaty country has in the other country generally shall not be less favorably levied in the source country than the taxation levied on enterprises or residents of the source country carrying on the same activities. Further, an enterprise of a source country, the capital of which is wholly or partly owned or controlled by one or more residents of the other country, shall not be subjected in the source country to any taxation (or any requirement connected therewith) that is more burdensome than the taxation and connected requirements to which other similar source-country enterprises are or may be subjected. Finally, the U.S. model generally provides (subject to certain arm's length standards) that interest, royalties, and other disbursements paid by a treaty country resident to a resident of the other country shall, for the purposes of determining the taxable profits of the payor, be deductible under the same conditions as if they had been paid to a resident of the source country.

Mutual agreement procedures

The U.S. model provides for a treaty country resident or national to obtain relief, from the competent authority of either treaty country, from actions of either or both countries that are considered to result in taxation in violation of the treaty. The U.S. model requires the competent authorities to endeavor to resolve such a case by mutual agreement where the home country authority cannot do so unilaterally.

Boulez v. Commissioner
83 T.C. 584 (1984)

KORNER, JUDGE:

The petitioner, Pierre Boulez, resided in Paris, France, at the time the petition was filed in this case. Petitioner is a citizen of France, and during the calendar year 1975 was a resident of the Federal Republic of Germany, (hereinafter 'FRG'). For the taxable year 1975, petitioner was a nonresident alien of the United States for Federal income tax purposes, and he timely filed a Federal nonresident alien income tax return for that year with the Office of International Operations of respondent.

At all times relevant to this case, petitioner was a world-renowned music director and orchestra conductor. On February 19, 1969, petitioner entered into a contract with CBS Records, a division of CBS United Kingdom, Ltd., which is a subsidiary of CBS, Inc., a United States corporation. Said contract was modified as of September 13, 1971, and March 14, 1974, and, as so modified, was in effect during the year 1975. Under date of May 1, 1972, with the consent of CBS Records, the contract was assigned by petitioner to Beacon Concerts, Ltd., of London England, which acted as petitioner's agent and undertook to provide his services to CBS Records under the terms of the basic contract, as amended.

There then followed an elaborate formula by which the petitioner was to be paid, based upon a percentage of the retail price derived by CBS Records from the sale of its phonograph records produced under the contract, with said percentage varying depending upon various factors, including, inter alia, whether the musical composition involved was in the public domain, whether the performance conducted by petitioner was made with the New York Philharmonic Orchestra, whether sales were made by direct sales or mail order through what was termed a 'Club Operation,' whether the record involved was a 're-issue,' etc., etc. In all cases, however, the payments or 'royalties' which petitioner was to be entitled to receive were dependent upon future sales of recordings by CBS Records.

Applications for the copyrights of all the master recordings, matrices and phonograph records embodying the sound recordings of the musical compositions conducted by petitioner pursuant to the contract were filed by CBS, Inc. and all registrations thereof were issued by the United States Copyright Office registered in the name of CBS, Inc.

As the result of performances conducted by petitioner under the terms of the contract, CBS, Inc. paid to Beacon Concerts, Ltd., as petitioner's agent, the sum of $39,461.47 in the year 1975. Beacon Concerts, Ltd., in turn, paid such sum to petitioner in 1976. In his 1975 United States nonresident alien income tax return, petitioner disclosed the receipt of such amount, but excluded it as not being subject to United States income taxation. Petitioner reported the identical amount in his 1976 income tax return filed with the FRG as includable income subject to the German income tax, and petitioner paid German income tax thereon.

OPINION

Petitioner contends that the payments to him in 1975 by CBS, Inc. were not taxable by the United States, because they were 'royalties' within the meaning of the applicable treaty between the United States and the FRG. Respondent, as noted above, contends that the payments in question were taxable to petitioner by the United States because they represented compensation for personal services performed in the United States by petitioner. The parties are in agreement that the outcome of this dispute is governed by the effective income tax treaty between the United States and the FRG.

Under date of July 22, 1954, there was executed a 'Convention Between the United States of America and the Federal Republic of Germany for the Avoidance of Double Taxation with Respect to Taxes on Income,' 5 U.S.T. (part 3) 2768, TIAS No. 3133. As amended by a Protocol, dated September 17, 1965, 16 U.S.T. (part 2) 1975, TIAS No. 5920, this Convention (hereinafter 'the treaty') was in effect during the year 1975, and undertook to govern, in stated respects, the income taxation of natural and juridical persons resident in either of the two nations, whose affairs might bring into play the taxing laws of both nations. Petitioner, a resident of the FRG, was a person within the coverage of the treaty. The relevant portions of the treaty provide, in part:

Article II

(2) In the application of the provisions of this Convention by one of the contracting States any term not otherwise defined shall, unless the context otherwise requires, have the meaning which the term has under its own applicable laws.

Article VIII

(1) Royalties derived by a natural person resident in the Federal Republic or by a German company shall be exempt from tax by the United States.

(3) The term 'royalties,' as used in this Article,

(a) means any royalties, rentals or other amounts paid as consideration for the use of, or the right to use, copyrights, artistic or scientific works (including motion picture films, or films or tapes for radio or television broadcasting), patents, designs, plans, secret processes or formulae, trademarks, or other like property or rights, or for industrial, commercial or scientific equipment, or for knowledge, experience or skill (know-how) and

(b) shall include gains derived from the alienation of any right or property giving rise to such royalties.

Article X

(2) Compensation for labor or personal services (including compensation derived from the practice of a liberal profession and the rendition of services as a director) performed in the United States by a natural person resident in the Federal Republic shall be exempt from tax by the United States if

Acknowledging that the provisions of the treaty take precedence over any conflicting provisions of the Internal Revenue Code of 1954, section 7852(d) see also section 894, we must decide whether the payments received by petitioner in 1975 from CBS, Inc. constituted royalties or income from personal services within the meaning of that treaty. This issue, in turn, involves two facets:

(1) Did petitioner intend and support to license or convey to CBS Records, and did the latter agree to pay for, a property interest in the recordings he was engaged to make, which would give rise to royalties?

(2) If so, did petitioner have a property interest in the recordings which he was capable of licensing or selling?

The first of the above questions is purely factual, depends upon the intention of the parties, and is to be determined by an examination of the record as a whole, including the terms of the contract entered into between petitioner and CBS Records, together with any other relevant and material evidence.

The second question—whether petitioner had a property interest which he could license or sell—is a question of law. The treaty is not explicit, and we have found no cases or other authorities which would give us an interpretation of the treaty on this point. We are therefore remitted to United States law for the purpose of determining this question. Treaty, Article II (2).

We will examine each of these questions in turn.

1. THE FACTUAL QUESTION

By the contract entered into between petitioner and CBS Records in 1969, as amended, did the parties agree that petitioner was licensing or conveying to CBS Records a property interest in the recordings which he was retained to make, and in return for which he was to receive 'royalties?'.

The contract between the parties is by no means clear. On the one hand, the contract consistently refers to the compensation which petitioner is to be entitled to receive as 'royalties,' and such payments are tied directly to the proceeds which CBS Records was to receive from sales of recordings which petitioner was to make. Both these factors suggest that the parties had a royalty arrangement, rather than a compensation arrangement, in mind in entering into the contract. We bear in mind, however, that the labels which the parties affix to a transaction are not necessarily determinative of their true nature. *Kimble Glass Co. v. Commissioner*, 9 T.C. 183, 189 (1947), and the fact that a party's remuneration under the contract is based on a percentage of future sales of the product created does not prove that a licensing or sale of property was intended, rather than compensation for services. *Karrer v. United States*, 152 F. Supp. 66 (Ct. Cl. 1957).

On the other hand, the contract between petitioner and CBS Records is replete with language indicating that what was intended here was a contract for personal services. Thus, paragraph 1. [of the contract] clearly states that CBS Records was engaging petitioner 'to render your services exclusively for us as a producer and/or performer. It is understood and agreed that such engagement by us shall include your services as a producer and/or performer.' Paragraph 3. of the contract then requires petitioner to 'perform' in the making of a certain number of recordings in each year. Most importantly, in the context of the present question, paragraph 4. of the contract makes it clear that CBS considered petitioner's services to be the essence of the contract: petitioner agreed not to perform for others with respect to similar recordings during the term of the contract, and for a period of five years thereafter, and he was required to 'acknowledge that your services are unique and extraordinary and that we shall be entitled to equitable relief to enforce the provision of this paragraph 4.'

Under paragraph 5. of the contract, it was agreed that the recordings, once made, should be entirely the property of CBS Records, 'free from any claims whatsoever by you or any person deriving any rights or interests from you.' Significantly, nowhere in the contract is there any language of conveyance of any alleged property right in the recordings by petitioner to CBS Records, nor any language indicating a licensing of any such purported right, other than the designation of petitioner's remuneration as being 'royalties.' The word 'copyright' itself is never mentioned. Finally, under paragraph 13. of the contract, CBS Records was entitled to suspend or terminate its payments to petitioner 'if, by reason of illness, injury, accident or refusal to work, you fail to perform for us in accordance with the provisions of this agreement.'

Considered as a whole, therefore, and acknowledging that the contract is not perfectly clear on this point, we conclude that the weight of the evidence is that the parties intended a contract for personal services, rather than one involving the sale or licensing of any property rights which petitioner might have in the recordings which were to be made in the future.

2. THE LEGAL QUESTION

Before a person can derive income from royalties, it is fundamental that he must have an ownership interest in the property whose licensing or sale gives rise to the income. Thus, in *Patterson v. Texas Co.*, 131 F.2d 998, 1001 (5th Cir. 1942), the Court of Appeals adopted the definition of a 'royalty' as "a share of the product or profit reserved by the owner for permitting another to use the property." Likewise, in *Hopag S.A. Holding De Participation v. Commissioner*, 14 T.C. 38 (1950), this Court held that in order for a payment to constitute a 'royalty,' the payee must have an ownership interest in the property whose use generates the payment, *citing* the definition of royalties in section 119(a)(4) of the Internal Revenue Code of 1939 (section 861(a)(4) in the 1954 Code is the same), which states:

> Rentals or royalties from property located in the United States or from any interest in such property, including rentals or royalties for the use of or for the privilege of using in the United States patents, copyrights, secret processes and formulas, good will, trademarks, trade brands, franchises, and other like property.

In its definition of royalties, the treaty embodies the same fundamental concept of ownership. Thus, in Article VIII (3) (a) 'royalties' are defined to mean "amounts paid as consideration for the use of, or THE RIGHT TO USE, copyrights, artistic or scientific works or other like property or rights," and Article VIII (3) (b) also states that the term 'royalties' "shall include gains derived from the alienation of any right for property giving rise to such royalties."

It is clear, then, that the existence of a property right in the payee is fundamental for the purpose of determining whether royalty income exists, and this is equally true under our domestic law as well as under the treaty.

Did the petitioner have any property rights in the recordings which he made for CBS Records, which he could either license or sell and which would give rise to royalty income here? We think not.

As noted in our findings, the basic contract between petitioner and CBS Records was executed in 1969. At that time, petitioner had no copyrightable property interest in the recordings which he made for CBS Records under the Copyright Act of 1909, as amended, 17 U.S.C. sec. 1 et seq., and petitioner concedes that this was so.

Petitioner contends, however, that the Copyright Act of 1909 was amended by the Sound Recording Amendment of 1971, and by virtue of this amendment, petitioner then acquired copyrightable property interests in the recordings which he thereafter made for CBS Records.

We think that petitioner is correct, in that the Sound Recording Amendment of 1971, supra, did amend the Copyright Act of 1909 so as to create, for the first time, copyrightable property interests in a musical director or performer such as petitioner who was making sound recordings of musical works, a property right which had not existed theretofore. 17 U.S.C. secs. 1(f), 5(n), 26. In discussing the changes made by the Sound Recording Amendment of 1971, and the new property rights therein created in both record producers such as CBS Records and performers such as petitioner, the legislative history contains the following significant statement: "As in the case of motion pictures, the bill does not fix the authorship, or the resulting ownership, of sound recordings, but leaves these matters to the employment relationship and bargaining among the interests involved.'" H. Rept. 92-487 (1971), 1971 U.S. Code Cong. & Adm. News 1566, 1570.

In spite of this change in the law in 1971, however, petitioner's contractual relationship with CBS Records went on as before. Neither the amendment to that contract of 1971, nor the further amendment in 1974, made any reference to the change of the copyright laws, nor modified the basic contract in any respect which would be pertinent to the instant question. We conclude, therefore, that the parties saw no need to modify their contract because they understood that even after the Sound Recording Amendment of 1971, petitioner still had no licensable or transferable property rights in the recordings which he made for CBS Records, and we think this was correct.

The Copyright Act of 1909, even after its amendment by the Sound Recording Amendment of 1971, describes the person having a copyrightable interest in property as the "author or proprietor," 17 U.S.C. sec. 9, and further provides that "the word 'author' shall include an employer in the case of works made for hire." 17 U.S.C. sec. 26. The above is a statutory enactment of the long-recognized rule that where a person is employed for the specific purpose of creating a work, including a copyrightable item, the fruits of his labor, carried out in accordance with the employment, are the property of his employer. The rule creates a rebuttable presumption to this effect, which can be overcome by express contractual provisions between the employee and the employer, reserving to the former the copyrightable interest.

Here, the petitioner, a musical conductor of world-wide reputation, was employed to make recordings for CBS Records, and in doing so, was to exercise his peculiar and unique skills in accordance with his experience, talent, and best judgment. In these circumstances, we do not think that petitioner was an 'employee' in the common law sense, but rather was an independent contractor, with the same relationship to CBS Records as a lawyer, an engineer, or an architect would have to his client, or a doctor to his patient, see Eicher v. Commissioner, T.C. Memo. 1984-468. This, however, provides no grounds for distinction, since the 'works for hire' rule applies to independent contractors just as it does to conventional employees.

In the instant case, the application of the works for hire rule means that petitioner had no copyrightable property interest in the recordings which he created for CBS Records, even after 1971. Petitioner was engaged for the specific purpose of making the recordings in question; his contract with CBS Records reserved no property rights in the recordings to him, and indeed made it specific that all such rights, whatever they were, were to reside in CBS Records. Under these circumstances, we do not think that petitioner has overcome the statutory presumption of the works for hire rule, nor that he has shown that he had any property interest in the recordings, either before 1971 or thereafter, which he could either license or sell to CBS Records so as to produce royalty income within the meaning of the treaty. This conclusion, in turn, reinforces our belief, which we have found as a fact, that the contract between petitioner and CBS Records was one for the performance of personal services. It follows that respondent was correct in taxing this income to petitioner under the provisions of article X of the treaty.

Revenue Ruling 68-443
1968-2 C.B. 304

Royalties for the use of a foreign trademark on products that are ultimately used in foreign countries are income from sources without the United States even though the initial sale of the articles took place in the United States.

Advice has been requested whether the place of initial sale of a product that bears a trademark is the controlling factor in the determination of the source of the royalties paid for the use of the trademark under the circumstances described.

X, a resident foreign corporation, owns a trademark for certain products in many foreign countries. X corporation entered into a license agreement with Y, a domestic corporation, pursuant to which Y was given the right to place the foreign trademark owned by X on Y's products and sell the trademarked products. The United States trademark for these products is owned by Z, an unrelated party. The license agreement between X and Y is a conventional trademark license agreement for a limited period of time and includes customary provisions to identify and protect the licensor's proprietorship of this mark. Under the terms of the license, Y corporation pays X corporation a royalty measured by a percentage of the initial sales price of the trademarked products.

Y manufactures the trademarked products in the United States and sells them to foreign buyers in the United States for resale and consumption in foreign countries; all rights, title, and interest of Y in the products pass to the foreign buyers within the United States. Thus, the initial sale of the trademarked products is regarded as having taken place in the United States.

The specific question presented is whether, by reason of the initial sale of the products to the foreign buyers in the United States, Y corporation has 'used' the foreign trademark in the United States and the royalties paid by Y to X are income from sources within the United States.

Section 861(a)(4) of the Internal Revenue Code of 1954 states, in part, that royalties for the use of or for the privilege of using in the United States trademarks and other like property shall be treated as income from sources within the United States.

Section 862(a)(4) of the Code states, in part, that royalties for the use of or for the privilege of using without the United States trademarks and other like properties shall be treated as income from sources without the United States.

The gist of a trademark is its association in the public mind with the product, it being the identifying mark of the trade. Ambrosia Chocolate Co. v. Ambrosia Cake Bakery, Inc., 165 F.2d 693, at 697 (1947).

The function of a trademark is to designate the goods as the product of a particular trader and to protect his goodwill against the sale of another's product as his. J. S. Tyree Chemist, Inc. v. Thomo Borine Laboratory, 151 F.2d 621, at 623 (1945).

In the instant case the character of X corporation's income is royalty income measured by a percentage of the sales of the foreign trademarked products. The initial sale of the trademarked products to foreign shippers is a means of placing the products in the avenues of commerce with a view towards their ultimate consumption outside the United States. Although the amount of the royalty income is measured by the sales of the trademarked products, the place of sale does not necessarily determine the source of such royalty income.

Since Z owns the United States trademark to these products, the products manufactured by Y and identified by the trademark under the license from X cannot be sold in the United States for consumption in the United States. Moreover, the foreign countries do not protect the foreign trademarks in the United States. It is concluded, therefore, that the royalties paid by Y to X are paid for the use of the trademarks in the foreign countries and that the place of initial sale of the trademarked products is not the controlling factor in the determination of the source of income.

Accordingly, in the instant case, where products are ultimately used in the foreign country where their trademark is protected, a royalty, received by X for the use of the foreign trademark, is income from sources outside the United States despite the fact that the initial sale of the trademarked articles took place in the United States.

Revenue Ruling 72-232
1972-1 C.B. 276

Royalties paid to a nonresident alien by a domestic corporation for books printed in the U.S. and sold exclusively in a foreign country under that country's copyright are income from sources without the U.S. and are not subject to withholding; I.T. 3296 superseded.

The purpose of this Revenue Ruling is to update and restate, under the current statute and regulations, the position set forth in I.T. 3296, C.B. 1939-2, 133.

The question presented is whether a domestic corporation is required to withhold income tax at the source with respect to royalties paid to a nonresident alien individual under the circumstances described below:

A, a nonresident alien individual, residing in a foreign country with which the United States has not entered into an income tax treaty, prepared the manuscript, as an independent contractor, for certain textbooks to be used in the public schools of that country. The books were printed in the United States by M, a domestic corporation, and were copyrighted in the United States and the foreign country. The books were not designed for use in the United States and are sold exclusively in the foreign country. A received the royalties from M for the books sold in that foreign country.

Section 1441 of the Internal Revenue Code of 1954 provides, in part, that all persons, in whatever capacity acting, having the control, receipt, custody, disposal, or payment of any of the items of income specified in section 1441(b) of the Code, to the extent that any of such items constitutes gross income from sources within the United States, or any nonresident alien shall deduct and withhold from such items a tax equal to 30 percent thereof.

Section 1.1441-2 of the Income Tax Regulations provides that other kinds of income are included in section 1441(b) of the Code such as, for instance, royalties.

Section 861(a)(4) of the Code provides, in pertinent part, that royalties shall be treated as income from sources within the United States where they are received from property located in the United States or from any interest in such property, including royalties for the use of, or for the privilege of using copyrights in the United States.

Section 862(a)(4) of the Code provides, in pertinent part, that royalty income from property located without the United States or from any interest in such property, including royalties for the use of or for the privilege of using copyrights without the United States shall be treated as income from sources without the United States.

In the instant case there is no commercial publication of the textbooks within the United States in that the textbooks are not sold within the United States. Without such commercial publication M is engaged solely in printing or manufacturing books within the United States, which books are later sold in the foreign country. In the vending of such books in the foreign country, the foreign country copyrights are used and not the United States copyright.

Accordingly, the royalties paid by M in the instant case are not taxable to A, a nonresident alien individual, as income from sources within the United States, and are not subject to the withholding of Federal income tax under the provisions of section 1441 of the Code.

Revenue Ruling 80-362
1980-2 C.B. 208

ISSUE

Are royalties paid for the use of a patent in the United States, under the circumstances described below, subject to United States tax?

FACTS

A, a citizen and resident of a country other than the United States or the Netherlands, licenses the United States rights on a patent to X, a Netherlands corporation. X is a bona fide corporation unrelated to A. X agrees to pay A a fixed royalty each year in return for the patent license. X relicenses the patent to Y, a United States corporation, for use in the United States. Y agrees to pay X royalties based on the number of units produced by Y each year under the patent. X's fixed royalty to A is not contingent upon the receipt of royalties from Y. A's royalty income is not effectively connected with the conduct of a trade or business within the United States within the meaning of section 871(b) of the Internal Revenue Code.

Article IX(1) of the United States-Netherlands Income Tax Convention, T.D. 5778, 1950-1 C.B. 92, as amended by the United States-Netherlands Supplementary Income Tax Convention, 1967-2 C.B. 472, provides that royalties paid to a resident or corporation of the Netherlands shall be exempt from tax by the United States. There is no income tax convention between A's country of residence and the United States.

LAWS AND ANALYSIS

Section 861(a)(4) of the Code provides that royalties for the privilege of using a patent in the United States are treated as income from sources within the United States.

Section 871(a)(1)(A) of the Code imposes a tax of 30 percent of the amount received from sources within the United States by a nonresident alien individual as interest, dividends, rents, salaries, wages, premiums, annuities, compensations, remunerations, emoluments, and other fixed or determinable annual or periodical gains, profits, and income.

Section 1.871-7(b) of the Income Tax Regulations provides that royalties, including royalties for the use of a patent, constitute fixed or determinable annual or periodical income to which the 30-percent tax rate imposed by section 871(a)(1)(A) applies.

Section 1441(a) of the Code provides that all persons, in whatever capacity acting, having the control, receipt, custody, disposal or payment of any of the items of income specified in section 1441(b) (to the extent that any of such items constitute gross income from sources within the United States), of any nonresident individual shall deduct and withhold from such items a tax equal to 30 percent thereof.

Section 1.1441-2(a) of the regulations provides that royalties are included in the items of income enumerated under section 1441(b) of the Code.

In the present factual situation, the royalties from Y to X are exempt from United States tax under Article IX(1) of the Convention. However, the royalties from X to A are not exempt from taxation by the United States because there is no income tax convention between A's country of residence and the United States providing for such an exemption. Since the royalties from X to A are paid in consideration for the privilege of using a patent in the United States, they are treated as income from sources within the United States under section 861(a)(4) of the Code and are subject to United States income taxation under section 871(a)(1)(A).

HOLDING

Royalties paid by X to A are subject to United States tax at the 30-percent rate pursuant to section 871(a)(1)(A) of the Code. X, under section 1441(a), is required to withhold from the royalties paid to A a tax equal to 30 percent of such royalties.

SDI Netherlands B.V. v. Commissioner
107 T.C. 161 (1996)

P was the licensee of a Bermuda corporation (SDI Bermuda) of worldwide rights to use computer software. P in turn licensed those rights for use in the United States to a U.S. corporation (SDI USA). P received royalties from SDI USA as well as from other licensees. P paid specified percentages of the royalties it received from its licensees to SDI

Bermuda. P, SDI USA, and SDI Bermuda were members of a group of corporations under common control.

OPINION
Background

Petitioner's Corporate Structure

Petitioner is a foreign corporation organized in 1974 under the laws of the Kingdom of The Netherlands. Petitioner was formerly known as SDI International B.V. At the time of filing the petition, petitioner maintained its principal office in Rotterdam, The Netherlands.

During the years in issue, petitioner was a member of an affiliated group of companies (the SDI Group) whose members designed, manufactured, marketed, and serviced commercial systems software for use on IBM mainframe computers worldwide.

SDI Ltd., a corporation organized under the laws of Bermuda, is the parent company of the SDI Group. During the years in issue, petitioner was a wholly owned subsidiary of SDI Antilles, a Netherlands Antilles corporation, which was a wholly owned subsidiary of SDI Ltd. The SDI Group also included SDI Bermuda Ltd. (SDI Bermuda), a corporation organized under the laws of Bermuda which, during the years in issue was a wholly owned subsidiary of SDI Ltd.

SDI USA, Inc. (SDI USA), a corporation organized under the laws of the State of California was, during the years at issue, a wholly owned subsidiary of petitioner. Petitioner also had subsidiary corporations in Germany, France, and the United Kingdom.

A brochure used by the SDI Group for the years in issue describes SDI Ltd. as the "Corporate Office" of the SDI Group, and petitioner, SDI USA and other members of the SDI Group as "Marketing" offices of the SDI Group.

SDI Ltd. provided management services to certain of its direct and indirect subsidiaries for which such subsidiaries paid it management fees.

Royalty Payments Made By Petitioner

During the years in issue, petitioner licensed from SDI Bermuda, pursuant to a license agreement dated November 28, 1986 (Bermuda license agreement), the worldwide rights to certain commercial systems software for use on IBM mainframe computers (the software). The Bermuda license agreement granted petitioner a nonexclusive license to use or to market the use of, on a worldwide basis, all of the software and any and all industrial and intellectual property rights SDI Ltd. had or would acquire from the effective date of the agreement, in exchange for certain royalty payments. The agreement further provided that petitioner "shall specifically have the right to grant sublicenses and Agents for the right to use and to market the use of any and all marketing rights granted to [petitioner] under the terms" of the agreement. The agreement was valid for an indefinite period and could be unilaterally terminated by either party on 3 months' written notice.

The Bermuda license agreement contained no express reference to the United States. With respect to royalties, the Bermuda license agreement provided:

> 8.1 The royalties payable to [SDI Bermuda] by [petitioner] under this Agreement are fixed at 93% of the net amount of all of the royalties due to [petitioner] by all persons, entities and institutions which [petitioner] subli-

censed any of the rights licensed to [petitioner] under this Agreement ("Sublicensees"). The aforementioned net amount is the amount that remains after the deduction of the withholding tax on royalties to be withheld when the Sublicensees of [petitioner] or Agents of [petitioner] pay the royalties due to the [petitioner]. 8.2 The aforementioned percentage of 93% will be increased if the net amount of royalties received by [petitioner] exceeds in a specific accounting period [the following amounts in Dutch florins]:

Petitioner made royalty payments to SDI Bermuda, pursuant to the Bermuda license agreement, during the years in issue, in the following amounts: 1987 ($3,583,983); 1988 ($5,104,781); 1989 ($5,146,862);1990 ($4,768,349).

Royalty Payments Received by Petitioner from SDI USA

During the years in issue, petitioner was a party to an exclusive license agreement with SDI USA, dated October 1, 1972, and as modified from time to time, regarding the use and licensing of the software in the United States (the U.S. license agreement). SDI USA was responsible for the direct marketing and sales of the software in the United States.

Until February 1987, the agreement provided that SDI USA would pay to petitioner "an annual royalty equal to fifty percent (50%) of the annual gross revenues of [SDI USA] from leasing and sublicensing of [the software], without any deductions therefrom except rebates, discounts and sales or value added taxes."

The U.S. license agreement was modified in February 1987 to provide that SDI USA would pay petitioner "a royalty equal to (50%) fifty percent of the gross billable or invoiced revenues of [SDI USA] with regard to all products licensed herein or further licensed in the future, without any deductions therefrom except rebates, or, sales or value added taxes."

Petitioner received royalty payments pursuant to the U.S. license agreement from SDI USA, during the years in issue, in the following amounts:1987 ($2,663,401); 1988 (2,936,889); 1989 ($3,092,710); 1990 ($2,139,458). Respondent mailed notices of deficiency to petitioner, one for 1987, 1988, and 1989, and one for 1990, on July 29, 1994.

Discussion

Liability for Withholding

Section 881(a) provides that a 30-percent tax shall be imposed on "the amount received from sources within the United States by a foreign corporation" falling within certain categories of income. Section 1442 provides a method for collecting that tax. *Central de Gas de Chihuahua, S.A. v. Commissioner*, 102 T.C. at 519.

Royalties are among the types of income included in section 1441(b). Sec. 1.1441-2(a), Income Tax Regs.; see also sec. 1.881-2(b), Income Tax Regs. In addition, section 861(a)(4) provides that U.S. source income includes:

> (4) Rentals and Royalties.—Rentals or royalties from property located in the United States or from any interest in such property, including rentals or royalties for the use of or for the privilege of using in the United States patents, copyrights, secret processes and formulas, good will, trade-marks, trade brands, franchises, and other like property.

Section 1441(a) completes the picture of the statutory provisions involved herein. It provides:

> all persons having the control, receipt, custody, disposal, or payment of any of the items of income specified in subsection (b) [which includes "royalties"] (to the extent that any of such items constitutes gross income from sources within the United States), of any nonresident alien individual or of any foreign partnership shall deduct and withhold from such items a tax equal to 30 percent thereof.

There can be no dispute that the royalty payments received by petitioner from SDI USA constitute U.S. source income and were received by petitioner as such within the meaning of section 1442(a). See *Commissioner v. Wodehouse*, 337 U.S. 369 (1949); see also *Estate of Marton v. Commissioner*, 47 B.T.A. 184 (1942). However, royalties paid by SDI USA to petitioner are exempt from taxation by virtue of section 894 and article IX of the United States-Netherlands Income Tax Convention, April 29, 1948, 62 Stat. 1757, 1762, 1950-1 C.B. 92, as amended by the Supplementary Protocol, June 15, 1955, 6 U.S.T. 3696, 1956-2 C.B. 1116, and as further amended by the United States-Netherlands Supplementary Income Tax Convention, Dec. 30, 1965, 17 U.S.T. 896, 1967-2 C.B. 472 (U.S.-Netherlands treaty); see also sec. 894. There is no comparable U.S. treaty exemption that would apply to royalty payments from petitioner to SDI Bermuda.

The parties have locked horns on several aspects of the application of the statutory provisions in light of the impact of the U.S.-Netherlands treaty exemption: (1) Whether the royalties paid by petitioner to SDI Bermuda constitute income "received from sources within the United States by" SDI Bermuda and are thus subject to withholding under section 1441(a); (2) whether petitioner can be considered a "withholding agent;" (3) whether there is a limitations period that has expired in respect of respondent's right to assess a deficiency in withholding tax against petitioner; and (4) whether petitioner is liable for additions to tax under section 6651(a)(1) for failure to file withholding tax returns.

For reasons hereinafter set forth, we resolve the first issue in petitioner's favor with the result that it is unnecessary for us to address the remaining issues. Before proceeding with our analysis of the first issue, however, it is important to note that respondent does not question the existence of petitioner as a valid Netherlands corporation or the application of the treaty exemption insofar as the payments by SDI USA to petitioner are concerned. Similarly, respondent does not attack the arrangements under which petitioner had a license of the worldwide rights and SDI USA had a license of the U.S. rights, although respondent does ask us to take into account the close relationship of the various corporations involved. *Compare Gaw v. Commissioner*, T.C.Memo. 1995-531, on appeal (D.C.Cir., May 20, 1996).

Rather, respondent focuses her argument solely on the proposition that, since the royalties paid by SDI USA to petitioner were U.S. source income, they retained that character as part of the royalties paid by petitioner to SDI Bermuda and, *as a matter of law*, constitute income "received from sources within the United States by" SDI Bermuda under section 881(a). Respondent contends that the fact that such royalties were combined with non-U.S. source royalties received by petitioner to determine the amount of royalties payable by petitioner to SDI Bermuda does not preclude the tracing of the royalties received by petitioner from SDI USA to U.S. sources. To implement such tracing, respondent simply applies the percentage specified in the worldwide license agreement between petitioner and SDI Bermuda and utilized in computing the amount of the required payment by petitioner to SDI Bermuda. To support her contention that such an allocation is permissible, respondent cites *Wodehouse v. Commissioner*, 15 T.C. 799 (1950); *Rohmer v. Commissioner*, 14 T.C. 1467 (1950); *Rohmer v. Commissioner*, 5 T.C. 183 (1945), affd. 153 F.2d 61 (2d Cir.1946); *Estate of Marton v. Commissioner*, 47 B.T.A. 184 (1942); *Molnar v. Commissioner*, 156 F.2d 924 (2d Cir.1946), affg. a Memorandum Opinion of this Court. In all of these cases, however, the payments, upon which a withholding tax was imposed, were directly from a U.S. payor and the U.S. withholding tax was imposed on that payor. None of them address the situation involved herein, where there is a second licensing step under which royalties are being paid and upon which the U.S. withholding tax is sought to be imposed. Thus, these cases provide no guidance in respect of whether the U.S. source characterization of the royalties paid by SDI USA to petitioner flows through to the royalties paid by petitioner to SDI Bermuda.

Petitioner argues that the royalties paid by SDI USA to petitioner and exempt from tax under the Netherlands treaty became merged with the other royalties received by petitioner from non-U.S. sources and consequently lost their character as U.S. source income. Petitioner submits that, while the royalty payments from SDI USA may be U.S. source income, its royalty payments to SDI Bermuda were made on a separate and independent basis. With respect to the payments to SDI Bermuda, petitioner contends that they were made pursuant to a worldwide licensing agreement between two foreign corporations, and as such do not constitute income "received from sources within the United States" so that no withholding is required under section 1442(a).

Pertinent authority on the issue before us is sparse. Indeed respondent relies solely on Rev.Rul. 80-362, 1980-2 C.B. 208, for her "flow-through" position. In Rev.Rul. 80-362, A, a resident of a country other than the United States and The Netherlands, licensed the rights to a U.S. patent to X, a Netherlands corporation. X agreed to pay a fixed royalty each year to A. X relicenses those rights to Y, a U.S. corporation, for use in the United States. In ruling that X was liable for a withholding tax under section 1441, the ruling states:

> In the present factual situation, the royalties from Y to X are exempt from United States tax under Article IX(1) of the Convention. However, the royalties from X to A are not exempt from taxation by the United States because there is no income tax convention between A's country of residence and the United States providing for such an exemption. Since the royalties from X to A are paid in consideration for the privilege of using a patent in the United States, they are treated as income from sources within the United States under section 861(a)(4) of the Code and are subject to United States income taxation under section 871(a)(1)(A). [Rev.Rul. 80-362, 1980-2 C.B. at 208–209.]

We are not persuaded that Rev.Rul. 80-362, *supra*, provides any significant support for respondent's position herein. It fails to reflect any reasoning or supporting legal authority. This circumstance is particularly relevant in applying the usual rule that, in any event, revenue rulings are not entitled to any special deference.

At this point, we note that respondent has not argued that petitioner was a mere conduit or agent of SDI USA in paying royalties to SDI Bermuda or that SDI Bermuda was the beneficial owner of the royalties petitioner received from SDI USA so that the U.S.-Netherlands treaty exemption should not apply. Compare *Aiken Industries, Inc. v. Commissioner*, 56 T.C. 925 (1971), with *Northern Indiana Public Service Co. v. Commissioner, supra*; cf. *Estate of Petschek v. Commissioner*, 81 T.C. 260 (1983), affd. 738 F.2d 67 (2d Cir.1984). Presumably such an argument would have produced a situation where

SDI USA rather than petitioner would have been targeted by respondent as the taxpayer liable for the withholding tax under section 1442(a). See *Northern Indiana Public Service Co. v. Commissioner*, 105 T.C. at 347.

In the instant case, there was a close relationship between the parties. However, although respondent asks us, in passing, to take that relationship into account, she does not pursue the matter to the point where she contends that it is a significant factor. Given the fact that respondent recognizes the existence of all of the parties as valid corporate entities and does not attack the bona fides of the license agreements between SDI USA and petitioner, on the one hand, or petitioner and SDI Bermuda, on the other, we are not disposed to allow the close relationship element to control our decision.

The facts of the matter are that the two license agreements had separate and distinct terms and that petitioner had an independent role as the licensee from SDI Bermuda and the licensor of the other entities, including but not limited to SDI USA. Under the circumstances herein, we think these arrangements should be accorded separate status with the result that, although the royalties paid by petitioner to SDI Bermuda were derived from the royalties received by petitioner from SDI USA, they were separate payments.

We find support for our conclusion herein in that respondent's view of the law could cause a cascading royalty problem, whereby multiple withholding taxes could be paid on the same royalty payment as it is transferred up a chain of licensors. But for the U.S.-Netherlands treaty, the royalty payments from SDI USA could be subject to withholding tax twice under respondent's reasoning herein.

Respondent argues that only one withholding tax is being sought herein. However, this ignores the fact that, by treaty, the U.S. agreed to forgo taxing royalties and to allow them to be taxed by The Netherlands. Whether or not The Netherlands actually taxed the royalties is irrelevant.

Respondent also infers that she would use her discretion not to apply more than one level of withholding tax on multiple transfers of income that originated as U.S. source income. We think this places an improper exercise of discretion in respondent's hands. To avoid the imposition of interest and additions to tax as determined by respondent herein, each payor in the chain might well feel compelled to file returns and pay withholding taxes. See Glicklich, Final Regulations on Conduit Financing Arrangements Empower the IRS, 84 J.Taxn. 5, 12 (1996). We are not disposed to conclude, in the absence of any legislative expression on the subject, that Congress intended the statutory provisions to permit "cascading" with the question of relief left to the mercy of respondent.

We hold that the payments by petitioner with respect to which respondent seeks to impose liability for the 30 percent withholding tax herein were not "received from sources within the United States by" SDI Bermuda under sections 881(a), 1441(a), and 1442(a).

Decision will be entered for petitioner.

International Multifoods Corp. v. Commissioner
108 T.C. 25 (1997)

RUWE, JUDGE:

We must decide what portion, if any, of the gain realized by petitioner on the sale of Asian and Pacific operations of Mister Donut of America, Inc. (Mister Donut), petitioner's wholly owned subsidiary, to Duskin Co. (Duskin) on January 31, 1989, constitutes foreign source income for purposes of computing petitioner's foreign tax credit limitation pursuant to section 904(a).

FINDINGS OF FACT

At the time its petition was filed, petitioner maintained its principal place of business in Minneapolis, Minnesota. Petitioner is a Delaware corporation which filed consolidated Federal income tax returns for itself and its affiliated subsidiaries for the relevant taxable years. During these years, petitioner and its subsidiaries were involved primarily in the manufacture, processing, and distribution of food products.

Mister Donut franchised Mister Donut pastry shops in the United States and abroad. As of January 1989, there were approximately 500 Mister Donut shops in the United States, 78 shops in Asia and the Pacific, and approximately 35 to 40 shops in Europe, the Middle East, and Latin America. Mister Donut joined in the filing of petitioner's consolidated returns. Hereinafter, we will generally refer to Mister Donut's transactions as petitioner's, since Mister Donut was petitioner's wholly owned subsidiary.

Petitioner's Asian and Pacific Mister Donut Operations

As of January 1989, petitioner had registered Mister Donut trademarks in the following countries: Indonesia, the Philippines, Taiwan, Thailand, Australia, the People's Republic of China, Hong Kong, Malaysia, New Zealand, Singapore, and South Korea.

Petitioner, as franchisor, had entered into Mister Donut franchise agreements in Indonesia, the Philippines, Thailand, and Taiwan (the operating countries).

These agreements contained substantially similar requirements except for provisions dealing with franchise fees, royalties, development schedules, and the length of the agreement. As of January 31, 1989, petitioner did not have franchise agreements in any of the other countries in which it had registered trademarks; i.e., Australia, Hong Kong, Malaysia, New Zealand, the People's Republic of China, Singapore, and South Korea (the nonoperating countries).

Mister Donut had perfected a system that utilized franchisees to prepare and merchandise distinctive quality doughnuts, pastries, and other food products.

Petitioner's Sale of Its Asian and Pacific Mister Donut Operations to Duskin

Duskin is a Japanese corporation which markets a variety of goods and services, primarily through franchise operations. On January 31, 1989, following 2 years of negotiations, petitioner and Duskin entered into an agreement for the sale of petitioner's entire interest in Mister Donut in designated Asian and Pacific nations for $2,050,000. Pursuant to the agreement, petitioner sold its existing franchise agreements, trademarks, Mister Donut System, and goodwill for each of the operating countries, and its trademarks and Mister Donut System in the nonoperating countries.

The purchase agreement also contained a covenant by petitioner not to compete in the operating and nonoperating countries for a period of 20 years.

Petitioner's Allocation and Reporting of the Proceeds From the Sale

In reporting its foreign and domestic source income for its taxable year ended February 28, 1989, petitioner followed the allocation contained in article IV of the purchase agreement. After allocating its selling expenses among the goodwill and trademarks sold to Duskin, petitioner reported $1,016,643 of foreign source income from the sale of goodwill, $820,000 of foreign source income from the covenant not to compete, and $109,907 of U.S. source income from the sale of the trademarks. Petitioner did not allocate any of its selling expenses to the sale of the covenant not to compete.

OPINION

We begin with the sourcing of income rules under section 865. Section 865(a)(1) provides that income from the sale of personal property by a U.S. resident is generally sourced in the United States. Section 865(d) provides that in the case of any sale of an intangible, the general rule applies only to the extent that the payments in consideration of such sale are not contingent on the productivity, use, or disposition of the intangible. Sec. 865(d)(1)(A). Section 865(d)(2) defines "intangible" to mean any patent, copyright, secret process or formula, goodwill, trademark, trade brand, franchise, or other like property. Section 865(d)(3) carves out a special sourcing rule for goodwill. Payments received in consideration of the sale of goodwill are treated as received from sources in the country in which the goodwill was generated.

1. *Goodwill*

Petitioner allocated $1,110,000 of the sale price to goodwill. On brief, petitioner maintains that the franchisor's interest it conveyed to Duskin consisted exclusively of intangible assets in the nature of goodwill; i.e., franchises, trademarks, and the Mister Donut System. Petitioner contends that the income attributable to the sale of this goodwill constitutes foreign source income pursuant to section 865(d)(3).

This argument mistakes goodwill for the intangible assets which embody it. Goodwill represents an expectancy that "old customers will resort to the old place" of business. The essence of goodwill exists in a preexisting business relationship founded upon a continuous course of dealing that can be expected to continue indefinitely. The Supreme Court has explained that "The value of every intangible asset is related, to a greater or lesser degree, to the expectation that customers will continue their patronage [i.e., to goodwill]." *Newark Morning Ledger Co. v. United States*, 507 U.S. 546, 556 (1993). An asset does not constitute goodwill, however, simply because it contributes to this expectancy of continued patronage.

Section 865(d)(1) provides that income from the sale of an intangible asset by a U.S. resident will generally be sourced in the United States. Section 865(d)(2) defines "intangible" to include, among other things, secret processes or formulas, goodwill, trademarks, and franchises. Section 865(d)(3) then provides a special rule for goodwill, sourcing it in the country in which it was generated.

Petitioner's argument equates goodwill with the other assets listed in the definition of "intangible" in section 865(d)(2). This Court has recognized that intangible assets such as trademarks and franchises are "inextricably related" to goodwill. However, we believe that Congress' enumeration of goodwill in section 865(d)(2) as a separate intangible asset necessarily indicates that the special sourcing rule contained in section 865(d)(3) is applicable only where goodwill is separate from the other intangible assets that are specifically listed in section 865(d)(2). If the sourcing provision contained in section 865(d)(3) also extended to the goodwill element embodied in the other intangible assets enumerated in section 865(d)(2), the exception would swallow the rule. Such an interpretation would nullify the general rule that income from the sale of an intangible asset by a U.S. resident is to be sourced in the United States.

Respondent contends that, although not denominated as such, what Duskin acquired from petitioner was a territorial franchise for the operating and nonoperating countries. Petitioner, on the other hand, argues that it did not sell Duskin a franchise, but, rather, the entire Mister Donut franchising business in Asia and the Pacific. Petitioner maintains that the sale of a franchise requires the franchisor to retain an interest in the business and that petitioner failed to retain the requisite interest in this case following the sale to Duskin. Petitioner contends that section 1253(a) and our opinion in *Jefferson-Pilot Corp. v. Commissioner,* 98 T.C. 435 (1992), affd. 995 F.2d 530 (4th Cir. 1993), support its interpretation of "franchise."

Although section 865 does not provide a definition of franchise, section 1253(b)(1) defines it for purposes of section 1253(a) to include "an agreement which gives one of the parties to the agreement the right to distribute, sell, or provide goods, services, or facilities, within a specified area." We have found this definition to be consistent with the common understanding of the term. *Jefferson-Pilot Corp. v. Commissioner, supra* at 440–441. When Congress uses a term that has accumulated a settled meaning under equity or the common law, courts must infer that Congress intended to incorporate the established meaning of the term, unless the statute otherwise dictates. *NLRB v. Amax Coal Co.,* 453 U.S. 322, 329 (1981); see also *Jefferson-Pilot Corp. v. Commissioner, supra* at 442 n.8. Since we find no indication that Congress intended "franchise" to carry a different meaning in the context of section 865, we adopt this definition for purposes of this section.

Pursuant to section 1253(a), the transfer of a franchise, trademark, or trade name shall not be treated as the sale or exchange of a capital asset if the transferor retains a significant power, right, or continuing interest with respect to the subject matter of the franchise, trademark, or trade name. Prior to its amendment in the Omnibus Budget Reconciliation Act of 1993 (OBRA), section 1253(d)(2)(A) provided that if a transfer of a franchise, trademark, or trade name is not treated as the sale or exchange of a capital asset, then any single payment in discharge of a principal sum agreed upon in the transfer agreement shall be deducted ratably by the payor over a period of 10 years or the period of the transfer agreement, whichever is shorter.

Neither the language of section 1253(a) nor our opinion in *Jefferson-Pilot* supports petitioner's position. Section 1253(a) provides that the transfer of a franchise will not be treated as the sale or exchange of a capital asset so long as the transferor retains a significant power, right, or continuing interest with respect to the subject matter of the franchise. The necessary implication is that a franchise can be transferred without the retention by the transferor of any significant degree of control. In such a case, the transfer will be treated as the sale or exchange of a capital asset, and the transferee will not be permitted to amortize any portion of the purchase price. See sec. 1253(d)(2) (prior to amendment by OBRA sec. 13261(c)). Indeed, if petitioner's argument were correct, section 1253(a) would have been altogether unnecessary, as the sale of a franchise would only occur where the transferor retained a significant interest in the franchise. However, as we explained in *Jefferson-Pilot Corp. v. Commissioner,* 98 T.C. at 441–442 n.7:

> Sec[tion] 1253 requires a two-step analysis. First, we must determine if the interest transferred was a "franchise" as defined in sec[tion] 1253(b)(1); then we determine whether a significant power was retained. Limiting the definition of "franchise" based on inferences from the retained powers requirement begs the

question of whether the interest transferred is a "franchise" in the first place. (citation omitted)

Petitioner's sale of its Mister Donut operations to Duskin constituted the sale of a "franchise" for purposes of section 865(d)(2). Petitioner transferred to Duskin its existing franchise agreements, trademarks, and Mister Donut System in each of the operating countries, as well as its trademarks and Mister Donut System in the nonoperating countries. Petitioner's Mister Donut operation utilized franchisees to prepare and merchandise distinctive quality doughnuts. This system included methods of preparation, serving, and merchandising doughnuts. In the purchase agreement, petitioner not only sold Duskin petitioner's rights as franchisor in the existing franchise agreements in the operating countries, but also all its rights to exclusive use in the designated Asian and Pacific territories of its secret formulas, processes, trademarks, and supplier agreements; *i.e.*, its entire Mister Donut System. Duskin received petitioner's existing rights as franchisor, as well as the right to enter franchise agreements in the nonoperating countries.

While there are no cases on point under section 865, case law interpreting other provisions of the Code supports respondent's position. In *Canterbury v. Commissioner*, 99 T.C. 223 (1992), we considered whether the excess of a franchisee's purchase price of an existing McDonald's franchise over the value of the franchise's tangible assets was allocable to the franchise or to goodwill for purposes of amortization pursuant to section 1253(d)(2)(A). We recognized that McDonald's franchises encompass attributes that have traditionally been viewed as goodwill. The issue, therefore, was whether these attributes were embodied in the McDonald's franchise, trademarks, and trade name, which would make their cost amortizable pursuant to section 1253(d)(2)(A), or whether the franchisee acquired intangible assets, such as goodwill, which were not encompassed by, or otherwise attributable to, the franchise and which were nonamortizable.

We found that the expectancy of continued patronage which McDonald's enjoys "is created by and flows from the implementation of the McDonald's system and association with the McDonald's name and trademark." *Id.* at 248. In addition, we stated:

> The right to use the McDonald's system, trade name, and trademarks is the essence of the McDonald's franchise. Respondent did not identify, and we cannot discern, any quantifiable goodwill that is not attributable to the franchise. We find that petitioners acquired no goodwill that was separate and apart from the goodwill inherent in the McDonald's franchise.

We concluded that the goodwill produced by the McDonald's system was embodied in, and inseverable from, the McDonald's franchise that the taxpayer received.

Similarly, in *Montgomery Coca-Cola Bottling Co. v. United States*, 615 F.2d 1318, 1331-1332 (1980), the Court of Claims, in valuing a Coca-Cola franchise, explained:

> Defendant's expert has testified that there is no goodwill in a Coca-Cola bottling operation. Anything resembling goodwill attaches solely to the national company and the name of the product. Customers buy Coca-Cola because of the product, not because of who bottles it. Since goodwill is considered to be the value of the habit of customers to return to purchase a product at the same location, the absence of the product would destroy the value of the habit; and since only one entity has the perpetual right to distribute Coca-Cola in a territory, *the value of goodwill, and the franchise are so interrelated as to be indistinguishable, all the value should then be assigned to the franchise.*

In *Zorniger v. Commissioner*, 62 T.C. 435 (1974), we addressed the issue of whether the taxpayer's shares of stock in a Chevrolet dealership possessed goodwill that should have been reflected in the valuation of the stock for purposes of the gift tax. We held that no goodwill existed in the stock, since the dealership agreement required Chevrolet's prior approval of any transfer of the taxpayer's interest therein. *Id.* at 444–445. We relied principally on our decision in *Akers v. Commissioner*, 6 T.C. 693, 700 (1946), where we determined that no goodwill existed in a General Motors' dealership upon liquidation, as the taxpayer had a nontransferable, personal services contract, which could have been divested from the taxpayer under circumstances outside his control. In *Zorniger v. Commissioner, supra* at 444–445 (quoting *Akers v. Commissioner, supra* at 700), we stated:

> "The franchises were not assignable and by their terms were made personal contracts between the parties. Such good will or going-concern value as the corporation might have created during its existence was subject at all times to be divested by termination of the franchises without action by the corporation. The good will, if any, continued to be embodied in the franchises and they, under the circumstances, were not property subject to transfer or other disposition by the corporation."

It is also well established that trademarks embody goodwill. Consumers associate the Mister Donut trademark with their pleasurable experience at Mister Donut shops. As a result, goodwill is also embodied in the trademarks, which Duskin acquired and which cause customers to return to Mister Donut shops in the future and patronize them.

Petitioner's business in the operating countries was conducted by granting Mister Donut franchises. Under the purchase agreement, Duskin received petitioner's rights as franchisor under the existing franchise agreements in the operating countries. The franchisees in the operating countries possessed the exclusive right to open stores pursuant to established conditions and at locations approved by the franchisor. In order to ensure that the distinguishing characteristics of Mister Donut were uniformly maintained, the franchise agreements had established standards for furnishings, equipment, product mixes, and supplies, which the franchisees were required to meet. The franchise agreements also required that franchisees operate their shops in accordance with uniform standards of quality, preparation, appearance, cleanliness, and service. The agreements provided that the franchisor could not open, or authorize others to open, any Mister Donut shops in the franchisee's country until the franchise agreement expired, or was terminated, or unless the franchisee did not meet its development schedule by failing to open the requisite number of Mister Donut shops.

Mister Donut's success resulted from the Mister Donut System and the high standards for quality and service, which the franchisees were required to meet. Although these characteristics produced goodwill in the operating countries, that goodwill was embodied in the franchises and trademarks conveyed to Duskin.

Petitioner also transferred its Mister Donut System and trademarks for each of the nonoperating countries. Duskin received the right to exploit—either by entering franchise agreements in these territories or by opening shops itself—the Mister Donut System along with the accompanying trademarks, formulas, and other intangible assets. In the nonoperating countries, there were no Mister Donut shops for customers to patronize at the time the purchase agreement was executed. Goodwill is founded upon a continuous course of dealing that can be expected to continue indefinitely.

We find that petitioner did not establish that it transferred any goodwill separate and apart from the goodwill inherent in the franchisor's interest and trademarks that petitioner conveyed to Duskin. Pursuant to section 865(d)(1), income attributable to the sale of a franchise or a trademark is sourced in the residence of the seller. The income petitioner received upon the sale of these assets must, therefore, be sourced in the United States.

2. Covenant Not To Compete

The only remaining asset transferred to Duskin that could produce foreign source income is petitioner's covenant not to compete. Respondent concedes that any amount allocated to the covenant constitutes foreign source income to petitioner.

Respondent argues that the covenant (like goodwill) was inseverable from the franchisor's interest that petitioner conveyed to Duskin. Respondent alleges that the franchise rights Duskin acquired provided it with the exclusive right to use the know-how, trade secrets, trademarks, and other components of the Mister Donut System in the operating and nonoperating countries. Any competition or disclosure of the Mister Donut System by petitioner in these countries, respondent contends, would have deprived Duskin of the beneficial enjoyment of the rights it had acquired. Thus, respondent maintains that petitioner's covenant should be viewed as an inseverable element of the franchisor's interest acquired by Duskin. We disagree.

The covenant granted Duskin benefits in addition to those necessarily conveyed by petitioner's transfer of its franchisor's interests and trademarks. The covenant prohibited petitioner from conducting any business similar to the Mister Donut business in the operating or nonoperating countries or from otherwise selling doughnuts in any of these countries. Since petitioner possessed expertise, knowledge, and contacts regarding the donut business, it was reasonable for Duskin to preclude petitioner from reentering the donut business in Asia and the Pacific under a different name. We conclude that the covenant not to compete possessed independent economic significance, as it did more than simply preclude petitioner from depriving Duskin of rights which it had acquired in purchasing petitioner's franchise rights and trademarks.

It is necessary, therefore, to determine what portion of the $2,050,000 sale price must be allocated to the covenant not to compete. Petitioner urges us to uphold the allocation in the purchase agreement of $820,000.

Based on our review of the record, we conclude that $300,000 of the sale price should be allocated to the covenant not to compete. Respondent concedes that the amount allocable to the covenant not to compete constitutes foreign source income for purposes of computing petitioner's foreign tax credit limitation pursuant to section 904(a).

Revenue Ruling 64-206
1964-2 C.B. 591 (1964)

A citizen and a resident of Switzerland who does not maintain a place of business in the United States or conduct any business through a "permanent establishment" situated in the United States owns a United States patent. He was awarded a judgment for damages and interest for the infringement of this patent within the United States. Held, the damages constitute amounts received as consideration for the right to use the patent. Accordingly, the damages are exempt from the tax under Article VIII of the United States-Swiss Confederation Income Tax Convention, T.D. 6149, C.B. 1955-2,

814. Held further, the interest received constitutes interest income from sources within the United States under section 871(a)(1) of the Internal Revenue Code of 1954, and is taxable at the reduced rate of five percent under Article VII of the convention.

Advice has been requested as to the tax status, under the United States-Swiss Confederation Income Tax Convention, T.D. 6149, C.B. 1955-2, 814, of a judgment for damages and interest awarded under the circumstances described below.

A is a citizen and a resident of Switzerland who does not maintain a place of business in the United States or conduct any business through a "permanent establishment" situated in the United States.

A is the owner of a United States patent and he and his licensee, the N company, sued the O company, in a United States District Court, for infringement of the patent. The court found that an award to the plaintiffs based only upon a reasonable royalty would be in conformity with the law; that upon the basis of the testimony a fair royalty payment would be x cents for each of the infringing devices sold by defendant; and that an award to the plaintiffs based upon such reasonable royalty "would, together with attorneys' fees, be adequate compensation for defendant's infringement." The judgment amounting to 182x dollars which was entered for the plaintiffs by the court represented 126x dollars for damages and 56x dollars for attorneys' fees and disbursements, and for costs.

The plaintiffs appealed from the judgment of the court contending that the damages awarded were inadequate. Subsequently, the appellate court entered its opinion finding for the plaintiffs in the sum of 636x dollars, without costs but with interest from the date of entry of judgment. The appellate court's judgment for damages was based upon the profits realized by the defendant through the production and sale of infringing products.

The infringement of the United States patent occurred solely within the United States.

The statute governing damages in patent infringement cases, 35 U. S.C.A. section 284, provides in pertinent part:

Upon finding for the claimant the court shall award the claimant damages adequate to compensate for the infringement, but in no event less than a reasonable royalty for the use made of the invention by the infringer, together with interest and costs as fixed by the court.

Compensatory damages for patent infringement, based upon reasonable royalties for the use made of the invention by the infringer or the amount of profits realized by him, are gross income. The W.W. Sly Manufacturing Company v. Commissioner, 24 B.T.A. 65 (1931); Mathey v. Commissioner, 177 F.(2d) 259 (1949), certiorari denied, 339 U.S. 943 (1950); Commissioner v. Glenshaw Glass Co., 348 U.S. 426 (1955). This rule is based on the fact that these damages constitute compensation for loss of royalties or profits, and are amounts received in lieu thereof. Such damages would also constitute fixed or determinable annual or periodical income within the meaning of section 871(a) of the Internal Revenue Code of 1954 and sections 1.871-7(b)(2)(I) and 1.1441-2(a) of the Income Tax Regulations, except where a specific treaty provision provides otherwise.

Article VIII of the convention provides:

Royalties and other amounts derived, as consideration for the right to use copyrights, artistic and scientific works, patents, designs, plans, secret processes and formulae, trade-marks, and other like property and rights (including rentals and like payments in respect to motion picture films or for the use of industrial, commercial, or scientific equipment), from sources within one of the contracting States by a resident or corporation or other entity of the other contracting State not having a permanent establishment in the former State shall be exempt from taxation in such former State.

Based on the foregoing, it is concluded that the amount received as damages under the judgment awarded to A for infringement of his patent constitutes an amount received as consideration for the right to use a patent by a resident of Switzerland not having a "permanent establishment" in the United States. Accordingly, such damages are exempt from United States income tax under Article VIII of the convention. However, the amount received by A from the O company representing interest on the judgment is interest income from sources within the United States and is subject to the tax under section 871(a)(1) of the Code. G.C.M. 21963, C.B. 1940-1, 67. Under Article VII of the convention this interest is taxed at the reduced rate of 5 percent.

DHL v. Commissioner
Circuit Court of Appeals, Ninth Circuit
285 F.3d 1210 (9th Cir. 2002)

FLETCHER, CIRCUIT JUDGE:

A. The DHL Network

Adrian Dalsey, Larry Hillblom, and Robert Lynn formed DHL Corporation (DHL), a package delivery company, in California in 1969. Document Handling Limited, International (DHLI), was incorporated in Hong Kong in 1972. Generally, independent local agents conducted the international operations and paid a network fee to DHLI. Middleston, N.V. (MNV), incorporated in 1979, owned most of the overseas local operating companies. At trial before the tax court, DHL conceded that, because of overlapping stock ownership, common control existed among DHL, DHLI, and MNV for all relevant times up to December 7, 1990.

From 1972 to 1992, DHL and DHLI/MNV were part of a global network in which DHL handled United States operations exclusively and DHLI/MNV handled foreign operations. DHL delivered DHLI's America-bound shipments, and DHLI delivered DHL's foreign-bound shipments. Until 1987, each company kept for itself the full amount paid by the local customer, and the companies did not exchange fees. Each company also paid for its own advertising expenses in its respective markets. A network steering committee, a specially formed corporation, and other mechanisms coordinated the worldwide DHL network. In 1988, a Worldwide Coordination Center was established in Belgium, with the world operations of the DHL network divided into three regions, each with its own CEO. DHL struggled in the competitive American market, sustaining losses during the 1980s, but DHLI/MNV expanded rapidly and profitably.

B. The DHL Trademark

In 1974, DHL and DHLI entered into a Memorandum of Oral Agreement ("MOA"), under which DHL licensed the name "DHL" to DHLI for five years, terminable by DHL on 90 days notice. Under the MOA, DHLI would be prohibited from using the DHL name for five years after termination. The MOA did not include any provision for the payment of royalties by DHLI to DHL for use of the DHL trademark. Through a series of amendments, the MOA was extended through 1990.

In 1977, DHL began the process of registering the DHL trademark in the United States. DHLI commissioned the first DHL logo, which was then used worldwide. Beginning in 1983, DHLI incurred the expenses of registering the DHL trademark under DHLI's name in various foreign countries.

On December 7, 1990, DHL and DHLI entered into a new agreement. Under its terms, DHL had the exclusive right to use and sublicense the DHL trademark in the United States, and DHLI had corresponding rights overseas. The agreement included reciprocal performance standards, and DHL and DHLI agreed to compensate each other, at cost plus 2%, for any shipment imbalances between the two entities. The agreement was terminable only for cause and had a 15-year term, with an automatic 10-year renewal if both parties were satisfied. If the agreement was terminated, DHLI would be prohibited from using the DHL trademark for 5 years. The agreement contained no provision for payment of royalties for DHLI's use of the trademark.

C. Sale of DHLI/MNV[3] and the DHL Trademark

From late 1986 to early 1988, DHL and DHLI negotiated with United Parcel Service ("UPS") concerning merger possibilities, but these negotiations broke down over price. UPS expressed little or no interest in the DHL trademark during these negotiations.

On December 21, 1988, Japan Airlines Co., Ltd. ("JAL") and Nissho Iwai Corp. ("NI") made an offer to purchase [certain percentage of] the combined DHL network. This offer was not well received. A second offer was made on June 14, 1989. In December 1989, the parties reached a memorandum of understanding for the sale based on the $450 million value for DHLI/MNV and the $50 million price, "subject to confirmation of the tax effect," for the trademark.

During the course of the negotiations, different parties provided a number of valuations of the DHL network and the DHL trademark. In February 1989, Robert Fleming Co. valued DHLI/MNV in a range of $392.2 to $680.4 million, and found that the DHL name, while intangible, was of some value that should be reflected in the final price. Peers and Co. produced a report on June 8, 1989, valuing DHLI/MNV at $522 to $580.9 million. In a revised report of September 14, 1989, it placed the value at $625 to $700 million. In June 1989, Nicholas Miller of Coopers & Lybrand valued the DHL trademark, outside the United States, at $25 million. This valuation was based in part on the view that DHL's trademark rights were diluted by its agreements with DHLI. On February 23, 1990, First Boston, retained by Lufthansa (JAL and NI's new partner), valued DHLI/MNV at $400 to $600 million and the trademark at $100 to $200 million. The First Boston trademark valuation, however, appears to have been done without knowledge of any ownership problems in the trademark.

On May 31, 1989, a Coopers & Lybrand report, commissioned by the foreign investors, raised the following concerns relevant to a possible purchase of DHLI/MNV: (1) DHL should receive an injection of capital via sale of the trademark; (2) DHL might be charged with imputed income based on prior uncharged royalties; and (3) DHL, in a trademark sale, should not have to pay royalties given its difficult financial position. DHL representatives also began to express concern about the tax conse-

---

3. Hereinafter, DHLI is sometimes used to refer to both DHLI and MNV collectively, as together they constitute the international component of the DHL network.

quences of the sale of the trademark, and they therefore sought a lower value for the trademark. As a result of these concerns, in July 1990, DHL sought a comfort letter from Bain & Co. on a $20 million trademark valuation. Bain supported the $20 million valuation after taking into account DHLI's possible ownership of the trademark and encumbrances in the form of royalty-free licenses to both DHLI (for the non-U.S. trademark interest) and DHL (for the U.S. trademark interest). On July 9, 1990, DHL and DHLI executed an agreement granting DHLI an option to purchase the "DHL" trademark for $20 million.

In late 1989, Lufthansa joined JAL and NI (collectively, the "Consortium"). On December 7, 1990, the Consortium and DHL/DHLI reached a final agreement under which the Consortium acquired (1) a 12.5% stock interest in DHLI/MNV, with an option to purchase an additional 45% interest based on a $450 million valuation of DHLI/MNV; (2) a 2.5% interest in DHL; and (3) an option to purchase the DHL trademark for $20 million, conditional upon the Consortium having first exercised its option to purchase the additional 45% interest.

The trademark option provided that DHL could use the DHL trademark in the United States royalty-free for 15 years. After 15 years, DHL would have the exclusive U.S. rights to the trademark for 10 years, but would have to pay a royalty fee of 0.75%. The final trademark purchase and sale agreement allocated the $20 million for the trademark in the following way: $17 million for the transfer of U.S. trademark rights, and $3 million for a quitclaim in the non-U.S. trademark rights. These two interests were to be transferred to separate entities.

The two-step acquisition process was designed to give the Consortium an opportunity to learn more about the DHL network prior to making a control commitment. During the interim period, the Consortium had the power to appoint 7 of the 13 directors of DHLI/MNV. The Consortium exercised this power, but the employees at the management level of DHLI/MNV remained the same. The Consortium did not exercise control over day-to-day management.

On June 7, 1992, the Consortium exercised its stock option, purchasing a majority stake in DHLI/MNV. The Consortium subsequently reorganized the entity into DHL International Ltd., incorporated in Bermuda. On September 17, 1992, the Consortium caused this new entity to exercise its option to purchase the DHL trademark rights for $20 million.

The Tax Court's Decision

After an extended trial, the tax court upheld deficiencies and penalties totaling $59,427,093. Although the amount of the deficiencies and penalties was much less than had been contained in the original notice of deficiency, the tax court held that the Commissioner had not abandoned his valuation. Accordingly, the tax court held that the burden of proof did not shift from the taxpayer.

The tax court accepted the Commissioner's contention that DHL and DHLI were commonly controlled until 1992. The tax court upheld an income allocation to DHL under 26 U.S.C. § 482 based on a $100 million valuation of the trademark. Of this $100 million figure, $50 million was for the domestic trademark rights and $50 million was for the overseas trademark rights.

In addition, the tax court upheld an allocation to DHL based on imputed income from uncharged royalties for DHLI's prior use of the DHL trademark. It also upheld an allocation based on imputed income from uncharged transfer fees between DHL and

DHLI. The transfer fees represented amounts to compensate DHL for the excess of packages that it delivered on DHLI's behalf as against those that DHLI delivered on DHL's behalf.

The tax court's decision was entered on August 17, 1999. DHL timely appealed.

III

Section 482 gives the Commissioner authority to allocate income between two or more businesses "owned or controlled directly or indirectly by the same interests...if he determines that such...allocation is necessary in order to prevent evasion of taxes." 26 U.S.C. §482. The purpose of §482 is "to place a controlled taxpayer on a tax parity with an uncontrolled taxpayer." Treas. Reg. §1.482-1(b)(1) (1968). We first decide whether the tax court erred in finding sufficient common control between DHL and DHLI to justify application of §482 to the sale of the DHL trademark rights.

A. Timing of the Analysis

We agree with the tax court that the relevant time period for determining whether common control existed for purposes of §482, given the particular business context here, is the period of negotiation and completion of the trademark option agreement between DHL, DHLI, and the Consortium. That is, the endpoint for the period over which there needed to be common control within the meaning of §482 was the completion of the binding option agreement. The economic reality of the transaction was that the price of the trademark was established at the time the Consortium obtained the option to buy it at the specified price. The ultimate purchase of the trademark at that price merely ratified the price that had been established at the earlier time. Because both parties concede there was common control between DHL and DHLI during all relevant times up to December 7, 1990, and because DHL and DHLI—largely without objection by the Consortium, *see infra* Part III. B—set the price term of the Consortium's option to purchase the DHL trademark in July 1990, we find that §482 applies here. Thus, we need not determine whether there was sufficient common control for §482 purposes at the time the trademark option was exercised.

This transactional approach for determining common control under §482 comports with common sense, and the regulations, which state that "[i]t is the reality of the control which is decisive, not its form or the mode of its exercise." Treas. Reg. 1.482-1(a)(3) (1968); *accord Waterman S.S. Corp. v. Comm'r,* 430 F.2d 1185, 1192 (5th Cir.1970). The transactional analysis also finds support in *Rooney v. United States,* 305 F.2d 681 (9th Cir.1962). Applying *Rooney* to this case, we conclude that the time when the taxpayers (DHL and DHLI) were dealing with each other was when they set the terms of the option agreement.

IV

Under Treasury Regulation §1.482-2(d)(1)(I), where intangible property is transferred between commonly controlled entities, "the district director may make appropriate allocations to reflect arm's length consideration for such property or its use." The tax court found that $100 million ($50 million for the U.S. rights, $50 million for the foreign rights), rather than $20 million, was the arm's length value of the DHL trademark. We do not find the tax court's valuation, a factual determination, to be clearly erroneous; thus we uphold the $100 million value.

DHL argues that the tax court's valuation is arbitrary and unreasonable and that the tax court failed to articulate its reasoning as required by *Leonard Pipeline Contractors*

Ltd. v. Comm'r, 142 F.3d 1133 (9th Cir.1998). Under *Leonard Pipeline* the tax court is required

> "to spell out its reasoning and to do more than enumerate factors and leap to a figure intermediate between petitioner's and the Commissioner's.... A reasoned decision... must bring together the disparate elements and give some account of how the judge has reached his conclusion."

Id. at 1135.

The tax court has complied with this standard by giving a step-by-step account of its reasoning. First, following the Commissioner's approach, the tax court reached a $300 million value for all unbooked intangibles, measuring the equity value of DHL and DHLI's intangibles based on what the Consortium paid for the company in excess of its book value. Although not without problems,[4] this is a systematic, defensible approach. Second, the tax court determined that one-half of the total intangibles, or $150 million, was attributable specifically to the DHL trademark. The tax court, at several points, explained its belief that the trademark was worth at least as much as the other intangibles. Third, the tax court determined that two-thirds of the value of the trademark, or $100 million, was attributable to the non-U.S. rights to the trademark. Fourth, the tax court discounted the non-U.S. rights by 50% to reflect a marketability discount, based on potential problems with DHL's ownership of the foreign trademarks. The tax court therefore concluded that the foreign and domestictrademarks were each worth $50 million, for a combined value of $100 million.

We therefore affirm the tax court's valuation of the trademark at $100 million, based on a $50 million figure for the domestic rights and a $50 million figure for the overseas rights.

V

Having affirmed the application of § 482 to the trademark sale and the $100 million valuation for the trademark, we must next ask whether the tax court properly allocated the full $100 million to DHL. DHL does not appeal the tax court's finding that it was the legal owner of both the domestic and foreign trademark rights. Rather, DHL asserts that the tax court erred in applying the § 482 developer-assister regulations, which preclude the allocation to DHL of the $50 million value of the foreign trademark rights.[5] We agree and reverse the tax court accordingly.

The 1968 Treasury Regulations[6] for § 482 state

---

4. DHL points out the following two problems. First, the approach was not used by any of the experts, all of whom measured the value of the trademark based on an "income" approach, where the value of the trademark is based on the present value of the trademark's future stream of income. Second, the book value of a company is often understated, so it may be misleading to assume that the value of the company in excess of its book value consists entirely of intangibles. Nonetheless, these shortcomings are debatable and certainly do not warrant reversal in this case.

5. Because DHL's "developer" defense only applies to the overseas rights in the DHL trademark, we affirm the tax court's allocation to DHL of $50 million for the sale of the domestic trademark rights. Because the tax court's $50 million valuation fully captures the value of the domestic rights, we need not consider respondent's *Alstores* argument for imputing additional income to DHL for its 15 year royalty-free license to use the DHL trademark in the United States. *See Alstores Realty Corp. v. Comm'r*, 46 T.C. 363, 1966 WL 1162 (1966).

6. The 1968 regulations were the governing regulations during the tax years at issue (1990–1992) and, as the tax court correctly observed, apply in this case. Superceding regulations were adopted in 1994.

> [W]here one member of a group of related entities undertakes the development of intangible property as a developer...no allocation with respect to such development activity shall be made...until such time as any property developed...is sold, assigned, loaned or otherwise made available in any manner by the developer to a related entity in a transfer subject to the rules of this paragraph.

Treas. Reg. § 1.482-2(d)(1)(ii)(a). DHL contends that DHLI was the developer of the overseas trademarks. If this is true, DHL argues, the tax court's allocation for the foreign trademark value was erroneous under § 1.482-2(d)(1)(ii)(a) because the transfer in this case was not "*by* the developer *to* a related entity," but rather *from* a related entity (DHL) *to* the developer (DHLI).

Alternatively, should the court find DHL to be the developer, DHL argues that DHLI should be allowed a set-off under § 1.482-2(d)(1)(ii)(b) for the amount of assistance that it provided to DHL in developing the foreign trademarks:

> Where one member of a group renders assistance in the form of loans, services, or the use of tangible or intangible property to a developer in connection with an attempt to develop intangible property...the value of such assistance shall be allowed as a set-off against any allocation that the district director may make under this paragraph as a result of the transfer of the intangible property to the entity rendering the assistance.

Id. § 1.482-2(d)(1)(ii)(b). DHLI would be entitled to the setoff because the transfer under this scenario was from DHL (developer) to DHLI (assister).

Under the 1968 regulations governing this case, the tax court's determination of whether an entity is a developer or an assister in the development of an intangible asset requires a case-by-case approach:

> The determination as to which member of a group of related entities is the developer and which members of the group are rendering assistance to the developer in connection with its development activities shall be based on all the facts and circumstances of the individual case. Of all the facts and circumstances to be taken into account in making this determination, the greatest weight shall be given to the relative amounts of all the direct and indirect costs of development and the corresponding risks of development borne by the various members of the group.... Other factors that may be relevant in determining which member of the group is the developer include the location of the development activity, the capabilities of the various members to carry on the project independently, and the degree of control over the project exercised by the various members.

Id. § 1.482-2(d)(1)(ii)(c).

The tax court found that DHLI was neither a developer nor an assister. However, we hold that the tax court applied the wrong legal tests under the developer-assister regulations in reaching its conclusions.

A. Legal Ownership / Licensor-Licensee Standard

For the tax court, the fact that in its view DHL was the legal owner of the "worldwide"[7] trademark rights was decisive, in spite of the unusual circumstances of the li-

---

7. Strictly speaking, there is no such thing as a single worldwide trademark: a company must register and maintain a trademark in each separate country. *See* 4 J. Thomas McCarthy, *McCarthy on Trademarks and Unfair Competition* § 29:1 (4th ed. 2001) ("[A] trademark is recognized as hav-

censing arrangement. The tax court stated, "[t]he related parties' relationship regarding the use of the DHL trademark was not a textbook example of a licensing agreement, but it was sufficient to bind these related parties and to effectuate control over the use of the trademark." Based on its resolution of the ownership question, the court then required DHL to demonstrate that DHLI's expenditures as either a developer or assister were more than the promotional expenses that a similarly situated licensee would expend at arm's length.

There are two problems with the tax court's approach. First, the tax court's ownership analysis and licensee-expenditure tests are in conflict with the plain language of the governing 1968 regulation, which lists four factors that the tax court should consider: (1) the relative costs and risks borne by each controlled entity; (2) the location of the development activity; (3) the capabilities of members to conduct the activity independently; and (4) the degree of control exercised by each entity. Treas. Reg. § 1.482-2(d)(1)(ii)(c). On a plain reading of the regulation, the principal focus appears to be not on legal ownership, but on equitable ownership based on economic expenditure. Legal ownership is not even listed among the factors.

Additional evidence that legal ownership is not the proper test under the 1968 regulations comes from the process of drafting the superceding 1994 regulations. The 1994 regulations appear designed to correct for the fact that the old regulations ignored legal ownership in favor of an economic approach. The critical language from the preamble to the 1994 regulations is as follows:

> The 1993 regulations provided that...intangible property generally would be treated as owned by the controlled taxpayer that bore the greatest share of the costs of development. This rule was criticized by many commenters, principally *because it disregarded legal ownership*.... For instance, a controlled taxpayer that was treated as the owner of an intangible for section 482 purposes might not be the legal owner. At arm's length, the legal owner could transfer the rights to the intangible to another person irrespective of the developer's contribution to the development of the intangible.

Intercompany Transfer Pricing Regulations Under Section 482, 59 Fed.Reg. 34,971, 34,984 (July 8, 1994) (emphasis added).

Although the preamble refers to the 1993 temporary regulations rather than the 1968 regulations, the relevant provisions in the 1993 temporary regulations were the same as those in the 1968 regulations. The 1994 regulations are completely different from both the 1968 and 1993 proposed regulations, explicitly stating that legal ownership is the test for identifying the intangible. See Treas. Reg. § 1.482-4(f)(3)(ii)(A) (1994) ("The legal owner of a right to exploit an intangible ordinarily will be considered the owner for purposes of this section."). The 1994 revision of the 1968 regulations thus strongly reinforces a plain-meaning reading of the 1968 regulations, with the result that legal ownership is not the analytical touchstone for those regulations.

Second, the tax court erroneously required DHL to demonstrate that DHLI's expenditures as either a developer or assister were more than the promotional expenses that a similarly situated licensee would expend at arm's length. The tax court appears to have found this requirement in the 1994 regulations. See id. § 1.482-4(f)(3)(iii) ("Assistance does not, however, include expenditures of a routine nature that an unrelated party

---

ing a separate existence in each sovereign territory in which it is registered or legally recognized as a mark.").

dealing at arm's length would be expected to incur under circumstances similar to those of the controlled taxpayer."). However, the applicable 1968 regulations impose no such burden and simply turn on the relative amounts spent and risks borne by the related entities in developing the intangible.

Even if "arm's length" licensee expenditures were the correct standard, it does not fit the facts of the present case. Such a standard may work where there is a clear line between development and exploitation. For example, the development of a drug (the basic fact-pattern employed in the examples for the 1968 regulations) can be distinguished from the marketing of that drug. Or, even in the trademark context, if a company with a product already recognized in the target market incorporated a local subsidiary, the subsidiary's expenditures might be presumed to be exploiting this trademark rather than developing its value.

The tax court treated this case as one in which a well-established product or service is licensed to a licensee. This is a mistake, however, because the value of the DHL trademark was created only by virtue of the sustained and combined efforts of both DHL and DHLI. Although DHL began with domestic delivery, the ultimate value of the DHL trademark was dependent on demonstrating the company's ability to deliver internationally. DHLI was formed shortly after DHL began operations. The only entity that moved packages out of the United States, and between all foreign points, was DHLI. DHLI therefore both developed the trademark in foreign countries and developed the service network that was the foundation for the trademark. Given the growth and profitability of DHL's international operations, the history looks much more like an equal partnership than a subsidiary incurring advertising expenses to exploit the trademark of a parent company.

B. Four Factors under the 1968 Regulation

The tax court failed to apply the relevant factors mandated by the 1968 regulation for determining who is a developer or assister. First and foremost, the regulation provided that "greatest weight shall be given to the relative amounts of all the direct and indirect costs of development and the corresponding risks of development borne by the various members of the group." Treas. Reg. § 1.482-2(d)(1)(ii)(c). Here, the relevant intangible is the foreign trademark rights. Trademark rights are created by registration and/or use in a given country and have a separate legal existence under each country's laws. *See* 4 McCarthy, *supra*, § 29:1._ Trademark rights are further developed and strengthened by advertising and promotional activities. *Nestle Holdings, Inc. v. Comm'r*, 70 T.C.M. (CCH) 682, 716-17 (1995), *rev'd on other grounds*, 152 F.3d 83 (2d Cir.1998).

DHLI undertook the registration of the DHL trademark in numerous foreign countries and bore essentially all related costs. Furthermore, DHLI paid for all of the overseas marketing campaigns with the DHL trademark, an expense that exceeded $340 million. Since developing a trademark includes advertising that mark, it does not make sense to distinguish between typical marketing activity and development.[8] *See* Marc M. Levey, *Tax Court Sends Messages to Taxpayers in* DHL, 482 PLI/Tax 775, 786 (2000) ("For

---

8. The tax court, in finding that DHL did not meet its burden of proof, relied in part on what it deemed a "paradox" in DHLI's claim that $340 million was spent on development of a trademark worth, in DHLI's view, only $20 million. However, the $20 million figure represented the sale of DHL's rights in the DHL trademark, not the total value of the foreign trademark rights, which may have a considerably greater value. Moreover, a trademark requires ongoing development activity. Advertising is ephemeral, and trademarks require continued promotion. *See Nestle Holdings*, 70 T.C.M. (CCH) at 716–17.

trademarks connoting brand image, which is highly company and market specific, this test may be an impossible benchmark to quantify."). In addition, DHLI bore the costs of protecting the foreign trademarks against infringement and handled all disputes relating to trademark usage abroad. Conversely, it was undisputed at trial that DHL bore none of the costs and risks in developing the foreign trademark rights. Thus, the first and most important factor clearly favors DHLI as the developer of the foreign trademark rights.

The other three factors, less important but nonetheless relevant, further support DHLI's status as the developer. The location of the development activity was in the foreign countries which DHLI, not DHL, served. DHLI was better suited to carry on the advertising and marketing independently given its connections to the foreign countries. Finally, DHLI exercised greater, if not exclusive, control over the advertising and development of the foreign trademarks.

Even if we accepted the tax court's conclusion that DHL was the developer, DHLI would at least qualify as an assister under the aforementioned regulations. The tax court therefore clearly erred in saying that the Commissioner may not be compelled to set off the value of the assistance against any allocation. The 1968 regulation provides that "the value of the assistance *shall* be allowed as a set-off against any allocation." Treas. Reg. § 1.482-2(d)(1)(ii)(b) (emphasis added). Thus, the set-off is mandatory. Moreover, the petitioner need not show the precise amount of its development expenditures here, since presumably at least $50 million (the amount the tax court allocated to DHL for the foreign trademark rights) of the $340 million spent by DHLI in overseas advertising constitute development expenditures for the DHL trademark.

In summary, we hold that DHLI was the developer of the international trademark, in which case no allocation to DHL for the value of the foreign trademark rights was appropriate, or, alternatively, that DHLI provided assistance to DHL's development, thereby entitling DHL to a complete setoff against the $50 million allocation.

VI

The tax court upheld deficiencies based on allocated imputed income for the tax years 1990–1992 from uncharged royalties. The royalties were those the tax court held that DHL should have charged to DHLI for use of the DHL trademark from 1982 through 1992. [FN11] Applying the same developer-assister regulations as in Part V, *supra*, we reverse the allocation of unpaid royalties to DHL.[9]

The concept of the developer-assister regulations is that the party that incurred the costs and risks of developing the intangible should not be required to pay a royalty to use that intangible. Levey, *supra*, at 786; James P. Fuller, *Jim Fuller's U.S. Tax Review*, 18 Tax Notes Int'l 391 (1999). As we held in Part V, DHLI was the developer of the overseas component of the DHL trademark, and thus no royalty income should be allocated to DHL for DHLI's use of those rights. Since the trademark license was *from* a related en-

---

9. Because we decide that the developer-assister regulations preclude any allocation to DHL assuming § 482 applies, we need not address DHL's argument that § 482 is inapplicable because DHL and DHLI lacked common control from 1990–1992. Nor do we need to decide whether evidence that DHLI entered into similar royalty-free licensing agreements with local operating agents establishes that there was arm's length consideration between DHL and DHLI under § 1.482-2(d)(2)(ii).

tity (DHL) *to* the developer (DHLI) rather than a transfer by the developer, no allocation is permitted under § 1.482-2(d)(1)(ii)(a).[10]

VII

The tax court upheld two types of penalties under 26 U.S.C. § 6662 against petitioner: 1) a substantial understatement penalty for the unpaid royalties, and (2) a gross valuation misstatement penalty on the additional $80 million that the tax court allocated to DHL for the sale of the "DHL" trademark to DHLI. Because we reverse the allocation of imputed income from the unpaid royalties in Part VI, we reverse the first penalty in its entirety without further discussion.

As to the second penalty, we turn to the statute. Substantial valuation misstatements, which incur a 20% penalty on underpaid tax, include determinations under § 482 where the reported price is 50% or less of the arm's length price. *See* 26 U.S.C. § 6662(e)(1)(B) (1994). Gross valuation misstatements, which incur a 40% penalty on underpaid tax, include determinations under § 482 where the reported price is 25% or less of the arm's length price. *See id.* § 6662(h). If a § 6662 penalty is assessed, the question of which penalty (substantial or gross) applies is purely a question of computation.

No valuation misstatement penalty is warranted, however, if "there was a reasonable cause" for the underpayment and "the taxpayer acted in good faith" with respect to the underpayment. *Id.* § 6664(c). The key issue before the tax court was whether DHL showed good faith by obtaining a comfort letter from Bain & Co. regarding the $20 million valuation for the DHL trademark, or whether the comfort letter was an instrument in DHL's allegedly evasive scheme. The tax court rejected Bain's appraisal as a basis for demonstrating good faith reliance on an expert. The tax court stated that it was not reasonable for DHL to have relied on the comfort letter because DHL sought the letter only after choosing an artificially depressed price, which it then communicated to Bain. The tax court observed that "parties can find experts who will advance and support values that favor the position of the person or entity that hired them."

We are less inclined than the tax court to condemn a taxpayer who seeks a comfort letter from a respected financial firm in order to ensure compliance with IRS standards. There is no evidence that DHL manipulated Bain's appraisal or that Bain blindly affirmed DHL's desired figure. Indeed, the $17 million valuation of the domestic trademark rights which Bain supported was much closer to the tax court's valuation of $50 million than the IRS's own original valuation of over $350 million for the domestic rights. Accordingly, the tax court clearly erred in rejecting DHL's reliance on the Bain comfort letter as an indication of DHL's good faith, and we reverse its penalty assessment under § 6662.

Conclusion

For the fore going reasons, we AFFIRM in part and REVERSE in part, and REMAND for further proceedings consistent with this opinion.

---

10. Again, had we deemed DHL the developer of the overseas trademark rights, assessing additional taxes from imputed royalty income would still be inappropriate because DHL would be entitled to set off the assistance DHLI provided in promoting the mark against the royalty allocation.

Field Service Advice 200011021
2000 WL 1183611 (Mar. 17, 2000)

ISSUE:

For Taxable Year 1, whether a controlled taxpayer may claim that a cost sharing arrangement is a qualified cost sharing arrangement under Treas. Reg. § 1.482-7(a)(1) despite its failure to substantially comply with Treas. Reg. § 1.482-7(c)(1)(iii) and the administrative requirements of Treas. Reg. § 1.482-7(j) due to its failure to attach a cost sharing statement to its U.S. income tax return or Forms 5471.

CONCLUSION:

No. A controlled taxpayer may not claim that a cost sharing arrangement is a qualified cost sharing arrangement where it did not substantially comply with the administrative requirements for qualified cost sharing arrangements because it did not attach a cost sharing statement to its Taxable Year 1 U.S. income tax return and related Forms 5471 as required by Treas. Reg. §§ 1.482-7(c)(1)(iii) and 1.482-7(j).

FACTS:

USCorp, a U.S. corporation organized under State A law on Date C with its principal place of business in State B, is engaged in the manufacture of Product A. USCorp is not a Coordinated Examination Program taxpayer, and therefore is subject to random audit as opposed to continuous audit on a three-year cycle. USCorp and its subsidiaries filed a consolidated U.S. income tax return (Form 1120) for Taxable Year 1, which began subsequent to January 1, 1996. USCorp also filed Forms 5471 (Information Return of U.S. Persons With Respect to Certain Foreign Corporations) for nine controlled foreign corporations located in several countries, including Country A, Country B and Country C.

A. Taxable Year 1

The beginning of USCorp's Taxable Year 1 was Date B, a date subsequent to January 1, 1996. For Taxable Year 1, USCorp did not attach a cost sharing statement to its Form 1120 or Forms 5471 filed on behalf of its nine controlled foreign corporations. Furthermore, USCorp did not file Forms 5472 (Information Return of a 25% Foreign-Owned U.S. Corporation or a Foreign Corporation Engaged in a U.S. Trade or Business).

With reference to its Taxable Year 1 Form 1120 filed by USCorp and its subsidiaries, USCorp listed a Cost 1 payment received totaling $ Amount A. USSub, a domestic subsidiary of USCorp organized under State A law, listed a Cost 1 payment received totaling $ Amount B. No information was provided on, or attached to, the Form 1120 to explain why USCorp or USSub received the Cost 1 payments and specifically, whether they were received pursuant to a cost sharing arrangement.

As regards the Taxable Year 1 Forms 5471 filed by USCorp and its subsidiaries, two of the Forms 5471 related to transactions with two of USCorp's wholly-owned foreign subsidiaries, Holding Company1 and Holding Company2. On both Forms 5471, Holding Company1 and Holding Company2 listed "partnership income" which Examination believes includes income and expenses relating to transactions between USCorp and CFC1. CFC1 is a Country A "Type X Corporation" which is jointly owned by Holding Company1 and Holding Company2, which have elected to treat CFC1 as a partnership for U.S. tax purposes.

During audit, USCorp provided Examination with a copy of a Date A cost sharing agreement between USCorp and CFC1.

B. Overview of the Cost Sharing Arrangement between USCorp and CFC1

As of Date A, a date prior to January 1, 1996, USCorp and CFC1 entered into a "Technology Cost and Risk Sharing Agreement" ("CSA") with the intent to "establish a structure whereby each party will share in the research and development costs incurred...in order to further develop the Existing Technology, and whereby each party will be a joint owner of any technology developed on or after [Date A]." CSA, Recitals. "Existing Technology" was defined to mean,

> any proprietary designs, plans, processes, instruments, machines, materials, compositions, test procedures, manufacturing procedures, techniques, formulations, methodologies, software, data and information which is owned, discovered or developed by [USCorp], other than in cooperation with [CFC1], and which is involved in the manufacture, use or sale of the Products.

CSA, Sec. 1. We note that "Products," which is apparently the focus of the research and development performed pursuant to the CSA, is not defined in the agreement. Additionally, the CSA does not clarify or describe the scope of the research and development to be undertaken, or the intangible or class of intangibles intended to be developed. No further information is provided in the CSA regarding the role of each party in the research, design, manufacture, distribution or geographic exploitation of the covered intangible(s).

The CSA provides that it will remain in force until terminated by either party giving thirty days written notice during the thirty-day period following the close of a fiscal quarter. CSA, Sec. 12.

In accordance with the terms of the CSA, USCorp and CFC1 agreed to jointly own "all right, title and interest" in new technology developed by either party. CSA, Sec. 2. "New Technology" refers to technology developed by either USCorp or CFC1 on or after the Date A effective date of the CSA. CSA, Sec. 1(c). USCorp technology is deemed to include technology of USCorp subsidiaries that are included in USCorp's consolidated Federal income tax return. Id. It is not clear whether one or both parties retained legal title to the new technology, nor whether exploitation was divided between the participants geographically. USCorp retained responsibility for obtaining worldwide legal protection for new technology. CSA, Sec. 10. CFC1 retained the right to obtain protection for new technology where USCorp elected not to do so, provided that such legal protection remained in USCorp's name so long as USCorp took steps reasonably requested by CFC1 to facilitate registration of the new technology. CSA, Sec. 10.

LAW AND ANALYSIS:

A. Cost Sharing Arrangements Generally

Pursuant to Code section 482, transfers of intangible property between controlled taxpayers must reflect arm's length consideration, typically in the form of a royalty payment. Treas. Reg. §§ 1.482-1, 1.482-4 through 1.482-6. A cost sharing arrangement is an alternative available to controlled taxpayers engaged in the codevelopment of intangible property, and permits exploitation of the developed intangible property absent payment of consideration (i.e., a royalty) between the controlled participants as is otherwise required under the transfer pricing rules. Pursuant to the terms of the cost sharing arrangement, the parties agree to share the costs of development of the intangible in proportion to their shares of reasonably anticipated benefits from their individual exploitation of their interests in the intangible. Treas. Reg. § 1.482-7(a)(1).

B. Development of the Cost Sharing Regulations

Section 482 provides that the Service "may distribute, apportion or allocate gross income, deductions, credits or allowances" among controlled businesses where "... such distribution, apportionment or allocation is necessary in order...clearly to reflect the income..." of such controlled businesses. I.R.C. § 482. The intent of section 482 is,

> [T]o place a controlled taxpayer on a tax parity with an uncontrolled taxpayer, by determining according to the standard of an uncontrolled taxpayer, the true taxable income from the property and business of a controlled taxpayer....The standard to be applied in every case is that of an uncontrolled taxpayer dealing at arm's length with another uncontrolled taxpayer.

Treas. Reg. § 1.482-1(b)(1) (1968). See also Treas. Reg. § 1.482-1(a)(1) (1994), effective for USCorp's Taxable Year 1.

1. Pre-1995 Final Cost Sharing Regulations

In 1968, specific guidance on the application of the arm's length standard regarding transfers of intangible property was added to the section 482 regulations. 33 Fed. Reg. 5848 (April 16, 1968). These intangible property regulations included a provision on cost sharing arrangements, which provided:

> A bona fide cost sharing arrangement is an agreement, in writing, between two or more members of a group of controlled entities providing for the sharing of the costs and risks of developing intangible property in return for a specified interest in the intangible property that may be produced. In order for the arrangement to qualify as a bona fide arrangement, it must reflect an effort in good faith by the participating members to bear their respective shares of all the costs and risks of development on an arm's length basis. In order for the sharing of costs and risks to be considered on an arm's length basis, the terms and conditions must be comparable to those which would have been adopted by unrelated parties similarly situated had they entered into such an arrangement.

Treas. Reg. § 1.482-2(d)(4) (1968).

Under the 1968 cost sharing regulations, a cost sharing arrangement was "bona fide" if the agreement was written and reflected a good faith effort of the participants to share costs and risks associated with the development of covered intangibles on an arm's length basis. Id. Additional administrative requirements for participants of a bona fide cost sharing arrangement were not imposed until the issuance of the 1995 cost sharing regulations.

In 1986, concerned about income tax deferral and effective tax exemptions resulting from U.S. corporations transferring intangible property to related foreign corporations in low tax jurisdictions while retaining the value of the earnings in the related group, Congress amended section 482 by adding an additional sentence. Joint Committee on Taxation Staff, General Explanation of the Tax Reform Act of 1986, 99th Cong. 2d Sess., 1013–1014 ["JCT Explanation"]. Section 1231(e) of the Tax Reform Act of 1986 added the requirement to section 482 that where there is a transfer or license of intangible property between controlled parties, "the income with respect to such transfer or license shall be commensurate with the income attributable to the intangible." Tax Reform Act of 1986, Pub. L. 99-514, 100 Stat. 2085, 2561, et. seq., 1986-3 C.B. (Vol. 1) 1, 478–81. Congress intended that this "commensurate with income" standard meet the objective that the allocation of income between related parties reasonably reflect the economic activity and risks undertaken respectively. See H.R. Rep. No. 426, 99th Cong., 1st Sess. (1985), 1986-3 C.B. 424–26; JCT Explanation at 1015. A related concern was the Service's ability to administer section 482 regulations due to difficulties in obtaining pricing and valuation information for transferred intangibles. See JCT Explanation at 1015 (stating "There are extreme difficulties in determining whether the arm's length transfers between unrelated parties are comparable. Congress thus concluded that it is appropriate to assure that the division of income between related parties reasonably reflect the relative economic activities undertaken by each"). Congress explicitly noted that amendments to section 482 were not intended to preclude the use of [c]ertain bona-fide research and development cost-sharing arrangements as an appropriate method of allocating income attributable to intangibles among related parties, if and to the extent such agreements are consistent with the purposes of this provision that the income allocated among the parties reasonably reflect the economic activity undertaken by each. H.R. Conf. Rep. No. 841, 99th Cong., 2d Sess. 638 (1986), 1986-4 C.B. 638.

In 1988, following a Congressional recommendation, the Treasury Department and the Service conducted and published for comment a study of intercompany transfer pricing, which included among other things, the Service's proposed administrative requirements for taxpayers seeking to participate in a cost sharing arrangement. Notice 88-123, 1988-2 C.B. 458 ("White Paper"). The White Paper proposed that taxpayers seeking to enter into cost sharing arrangements make a formal election and contemporaneously document the specifics of the cost sharing arrangement. White Paper, 1988-2 C.B. 458, 498. Furthermore, any U.S. participant in a cost sharing arrangement was to include a copy of the agreement with its first return filed after the effective date of the agreement. Id. Additionally, within 60 days of the Service's request, participants were to agree to produce, in English, the records of foreign participants to verify computation and appropriateness of cost shares. Id.

Following review of public comments, the Service issued proposed regulations on the transfer of intangible property and cost sharing arrangements. 57 Fed. Reg. 3571 (Jan. 30, 1992), 1992-1 C.B. 1164. The proposed cost sharing regulations required that taxpayers substantially comply with each administrative requirement to be deemed a participant in the cost sharing arrangement. Prop. Treas. Reg. § 1.482-2(g)(6)(ii) (1992). The proposed administrative requirements for participants were as follows:

(A) The material provisions of the arrangement are summarized in (or a copy of the agreement is attached to) the income tax return filed by the participant, if any, or they are summarized in any attachment to Schedule M of Form 5471 or any attachment to Form 5472 filed with respect to that participant in each year that the arrangement is in effect;

(B) The participant maintains records that are sufficient to verify the material provisions of the arrangement, the amount of the costs borne under the arrangement by each participant during the taxable year, and the computation of each participant's operating income resulting from the arrangement; and

(C) The records described [in paragraph (B) above] are produced within 60 days of a request by the district director for such records....

Prop. Treas. Reg. §§ 1.482-2(g)(6)(ii) (A)–(C) (1992).

In 1993, the Service issued temporary section 482 regulations, which incorporated verbatim the 1968 regulation on cost sharing. 58 Fed. Reg. 5263 (Jan. 21, 1993), 1993-1 C.B. 90; Temp. Treas. Reg. § 1.482-7T (1993). Thus, the administrative requirements suggested in the White Paper and 1992 proposed cost sharing regulations were not incorporated in the 1993 temporary cost sharing regulations, which were effective for taxable years beginning after April 21, 1993. Temp. Treas. Reg. § 1.482-1A (1993).

On July 8, 1994, the Service published final section 482 regulations, which included general transfer pricing rules relating to intangible property, but did not include final cost sharing regulations. T.D. 8552, 1994-2 C.B. 93. Thus, the 1993 temporary cost sharing regulations, which incorporated the text of the 1968 regulations, continued to apply. Id. at 112.

2. 1995 Final Cost Sharing Regulations

On December 20, 1995, the Service published final cost sharing regulations. 60 Fed. Reg. 65553 (Dec. 20, 1995), 1996-1 C.B. 85. These final regulations replaced the 1993 temporary cost sharing regulations for taxable years beginning on or after January 1, 1996. Treas. Reg. § 1.482-7(k) (1995).

Section 1.482-7(a)(1) defines a cost sharing arrangement as

> [A]n agreement under which the parties agree to share the costs of development of one or more intangibles in proportion to their shares of reasonably anticipated benefits from their individual exploitation of the interests in the intangibles assigned to them under the arrangement.

Treas. Reg. § 1.482-7(a)(1) (1995).

Under the final cost sharing regulations, a taxpayer may claim that a cost sharing arrangement is a "qualified cost sharing arrangement," provided it meets the requirements of Treas. Reg. § 1.482-7(b). Treas. Reg. § 1.482-7(a)(1). In general, the district director shall not make section 482 allocations with respect to a qualified cost sharing arrangement except to the extent necessary to make each controlled participant's share of the costs of intangible development under the qualified arrangement equal to its share of reasonably anticipated benefits attributable to such development. Treas. Reg. § 1.482-7(a)(2). Among the requirements set forth in Treas. Reg. § 1.482-7(b), a qualified cost sharing arrangement must include two or more participants and be recorded in a document contemporaneous with the formation of the cost sharing arrangement. Treas. Reg. §§ 1.482-7(b)(1), (4). A "participant" in a cost sharing arrangement may be either a "controlled participant," defined as a controlled taxpayer meeting the requirements of Treas. Reg. § 1.482-7(c)(1), or an "uncontrolled participant," defined as an uncontrolled taxpayer that is a party to the cost sharing arrangement. Treas. Reg. § 1.482-7(c)(1).

A "controlled taxpayer" is defined as any one of two or more taxpayers owned or controlled directly or indirectly by the same interests; whereas an "uncontrolled taxpayer" is defined as any one of two or more taxpayers not owned or controlled directly or indirectly by the same interests. Treas. Reg. § 1.482-1(i)(5).

A controlled taxpayer may be a controlled participant in a qualified cost sharing arrangement only if it:

> (i) Reasonably anticipates that it will derive benefits from the use of covered intangibles;

(ii) Substantially complies with the accounting requirements described in paragraph (i) of this section; and

(iii) Substantially complies with the administrative requirements described in paragraph (j) of this section.

Treas. Reg. § 1.482-7(c)(1)(i)–(iii) (emphasis added). Thus, to qualify as a "controlled participant" in a qualified cost sharing arrangement under the final cost sharing regulations, the taxpayer must "substantially compl[y] with the administrative requirements described in paragraph (j)..." Treas. Reg. § 1.482-7(c)(1)(iii) (1995).

Pursuant to section 1.482-7(j), the administrative requirements are divided into two categories, the documentation requirements of Treas. Reg. § 1.482-7(j)(2) and the reporting requirements of Treas. Reg. § 1.482-7(j)(3). The documentation prong of the administrative requirements requires a controlled participant to maintain sufficient documentation to establish that the requirements of Treas. Reg. §§ 1.482-7(b)(4) and 1.482-7(c)(1) have been met, as well as additional documentation specified in Treas. Reg. § 1.482-7(j)(2). Treas. Reg. § 1.482-7(j)(2)(i). A controlled participant is not required to attach this documentation to its income tax return, rather such documentation must be provided to the Service within thirty days of a request. Treas. Reg. § 1.482-7(j)(2)(i).

The reporting prong requires:

> A controlled participant must attach to its U.S. income tax return a statement indicating that it is a participant in a qualified cost sharing arrangement, and listing the other controlled participants in the arrangement. A controlled participant that is not required to file a U.S. income tax return must ensure that such a statement is attached to Schedule M of any Form 5471 or to any Form 5472 filed with respect to that participant.

Treas. Reg. § 1.482-7(j)(3) (emphasis added).

In sum, a controlled participant must substantially comply with the administrative requirements of Treas. Reg. § 1.482-7(j) to claim qualified cost sharing arrangement treatment. Treas. Reg. §§ 1.482-7(a)(1), 1.482-7(b) and 1.482-7(c)(1)(iii). Furthermore, the district director may apply the cost sharing regulations to any arrangement that in substance constitutes a cost sharing arrangement, notwithstanding a failure to comply with any of the qualified cost sharing arrangement requirements. Treas. Reg. § 1.482-7(a)(1). Finally, where a controlled taxpayer acquires an interest in intangible property (other than in consideration for bearing a share of the costs of the intangible's development), the district director may make appropriate allocations to reflect an arm's length consideration for the acquisition of the interest in such intangible under the rules of Treas. Reg. §§ 1.482-1 and 1.482-4 through 1.482-6. Treas. Reg. § 1.482-7(a)(2).

If, after any cost allocations the district director may make pursuant to Treas. Reg. § 1.482-7(a)(2), a controlled participant bears costs of intangible development that over a period of years are consistently and materially greater or lesser than its share of reasonably anticipated benefits, then the district director may conclude that the economic substance of the arrangement between the controlled participants is inconsistent with the terms of the cost sharing arrangement. In such case, the district director may make an allocation by which the participant that bore a disproportionately greater share of costs must receive an arm's length payment (under Treas. Reg. §§ 1.482-1 and 1.482-4 through 1.482-6) from the controlled participant whose share of the intangible development costs is less than its share of reasonably anticipated benefits over time in consideration for the effective receipt of additional interests in the covered intangibles. Treas. Reg. § 1.482-7(g)(5).

C. Substantial Compliance under Treas. Reg. § 1.482-7(j)(3)

Initially, we note that "substantial compliance" is defined neither in Code section 482, nor the 1995 final cost sharing regulations, nor the general definitions of Code section 7701. See I.R.C. §§ 482, 7701, and Treas. Reg. § 1.482-7.

In the absence of a definition of "substantial compliance," we rely on case law to interpret the meaning within the context of Federal tax law. While Federal Circuit A case law would control this issue because USCorp's principal place of business is in State B, the leading cases on substantial compliance for federal tax purposes are decisions by the 7th Circuit Court of Appeals and the United States Tax Court, see infra.

Case law has established two constructs for evaluating "substantial compliance," a plain-language test and a Federal common law doctrine. The Federal common law doctrine of substantial compliance generally does not control in instances where, as here, the plain-language of a statute or regulation specifically includes the language of substantial compliance. Therefore, our analysis focuses on the plain-language test.

The leading case which analyzes the plain-language test of substantial compliance is Prussner v. United States, 896 F.2d 218 (7th Cir. 1990), aff'g 87-2 USTC ¶ 13, 739 (C.D. Ill. 1987). In Prussner, the Seventh Circuit concluded that failure to attach a recapture agreement to a timely filed estate tax return meant that the taxpayer had not substantially complied with the special use valuation requirements of Treas. Reg. § 20.2032A-8(c) as required by Code section 2032A(d)(3).

The Prussner court analyzed the case under the Federal common law doctrine of substantial compliance and applied the American Air Filter five factor test to distinguish between essential and procedural regulatory requirements. The Seventh Circuit noted that multifactored tests, like the American Air Filter test, are difficult to apply, and criticized the "incomplete dichotomy [between essential and procedural requirements] that the Tax Court commonly uses to frame the issue of substantial compliance." Nevertheless, the Prussner court applied the essential-procedural distinction embodied in the American Air Filter five factor test, because in several other cases, the Tax Court had concluded previously that there was no defense of substantial compliance for failure to comply with an "essential requirement"—a requirement which harms or prejudices the Service when not complied with.

Before reviewing the Prussner court's application of the five factor test, review of American Air Filter, Co., Inc. v. Commissioner, 81 T.C. 709, 711 (1983), is instructive. In American Air Filter, the petitioner was a U.S. shareholder of 22 foreign subsidiaries, and claimed that it intended to exclude Subpart F income of two of its foreign subsidiaries pursuant to Code section 963 ("Receipt of Minimum Distributions by Domestic Corporations") minimum distribution rules (repealed in 1975 for taxable years beginning after December 31, 1975). See Sec. 602(a) Tax Reduction Act of 1975, P.L. 94-12, 89 Stat. 26). Due to a clerical error, the petitioner failed to file an election statement with its timely filed 1974 income tax return as required by the statute and regulations under section 963. No amount was included on the petitioner's 1974 income tax return as Subpart F income from the two controlled foreign corporations at issue. Additionally, on the Forms 3646 ("Income from Controlled Foreign Corporation") filed for the two foreign subsidiaries for the which petitioner sought to exclude Subpart F income, the petitioner represented that no 963 election had been made. Other portions of the Forms 3646 were completed in a manner contradictory to the representation that no 963 election was made. The petitioner later provided the Service with an election statement when notified during audit in that no such election statement had been filed. In Tax Court, petitioner contended that it substantially complied with the election requirements of Code section 963; whereas the Commissioner claimed that the failure to include the election statement with the income tax return prejudiced the conduct of the audit, that the Service was unable to determine from the return the petitioner's method for computing the minimum distribution, the corporations involved in the elections and the correct amounts of the distributions.

In evaluating the petitioner's substantial compliance argument, the American Air Filter court noted that full compliance with regulations may be required when the requirements relate to the substance or essence of a statute, but that substantial compliance suffices where requirements are procedural and the essential regulatory purpose of the requirements was fulfilled. The American Air Filter court cited the following five factor test to determine whether substantial compliance is appropriate when weighed against the harm to the Service resulting from the lack of taxpayer's full compliance with certain regulatory requirements. The American Air Filter court considered whether:

1) the taxpayer's failure to comply fully defeats the purpose of the statute;

2) the Commissioner is prejudiced by the untimely election;

3) the regulation provided with detailed specificity the manner in which an election was to be made;

4) the sanction imposed on the taxpayer for the failure is excessive and out of proportion to the default; and

5) the taxpayer attempts to benefit from hindsight by adopting a position inconsistent with his original action or omission.

Despite the failure to timely file an election statement for section 963 treatment, the American Air Filter court concluded that the petitioner had substantially complied with the requirements for the following reasons. First, filing the election statement merely would have confirmed that the petitioner had made the election in substance. Second, the petitioner did not adopt a position inconsistent with its earlier treatment of the minimum distributions as non-Subpart F income, nor did it attempt to "whipsaw" the Commissioner based on hindsight since the treatment of payments as minimum distributions on its 1974 income tax return were consistent with the minimum distribution election. Third, the Commissioner was not prejudiced by the petitioner's omission of the election statement because the petitioner's income tax return alone provided most of the information required by the regulations although it was not included in a timely filed election statement. Fourth, the court believed that precluding the petitioner's use of section 963 treatment due to its delay in filing the election statement would disproportionately punish the petitioner for a clerical omission. Fifth, the court concluded that the information returns filed by the petitioner (Forms 3646) were ambiguous and contradictory, and did not clearly indicate that a 963 election was not made.

Returning to Prussner, in applying the five factor American Air Filter substantial compliance test, the Prussner court concluded that the estate had not substantially complied with the special use valuation requirements of section 2032A(d)(3). The Seventh Circuit stated that the common law doctrine of substantial compliance should be applied narrowly, and courts should not use it to "nullify valid regulations." Prussner, 896 F.2d 218, 224–25 (7th Cir. 1990). The court noted that the special use valuation regulation "unequivocally required the filing of a recapture agreement with the return," and that the estate's attorney made no attempt to either attach the recapture agreement nor to seek an extension of time to file the agreement. In conclusion, the court stated that although the requirement to attach a recapture agreement to a timely filed estate tax return may not be essential, it is also not unimportant because the Service cannot permit qualified-use valuation until the recapture agreement is filed, which is a condition of a valid election.

Several judicial doctrine cases unrelated to special use valuation are in accord with Prussner, holding that failure to file a form required for a valid election is not a procedural requirement for which substantial compliance is permissible. See Dunavant v. Commissioner, 63 T.C. 316 (1974) (holding petitioners were not qualified electing shareholders under Code section 333 where they failed to file an election on Form 964, although the same information was supplied on Form 966; and petitioners failed to comply with a substantive requirement for specific, contemporaneous and incontrovertible evidence of a binding election); Penn-Dixie Steel Corp. v. Commissioner, 69 T.C. 837 (1978) (stating election for rapid amortization of pollution control facility was invalid under Treas. Reg. § 1.169-4(a)(1) where the taxpayer did not comply with an essential regulatory requirement due to its failure to attach to its income tax return a statement of certification for the pollution control facility). But see Columbia Iron & Metal Co. v. Commissioner, 61 T.C. 5 (1973) (holding that petitioner had substantially complied with the procedural requirements for charitable deductions where all underlying requirements were met pursuant to I.R.C. § 170(a)(2) and Treas. Reg. § 1.170-3(b) despite its failure to attach to its income tax return a copy of the corporate minutes authorizing the contribution and a verified written declaration of an officer of the corporation, and where the regulations failed to delineate the consequences of noncompliance with the requirements), acq. 1979-2 C.B. 1.

We note also that in several cases, Federal courts have required complete compliance with reporting requirements where taxpayers have sought to avail themselves of a benefit afforded by regulation or election. See Credit Life Ins. Co. v. United States, 948 F.2d 723 (Fed. Cir. 1991) (requiring strict compliance with reporting requirements for section 166 "bad debt" deduction and noting that doctrine of substantial compliance should be narrowly applied); Fischer Indus., Inc. v. Commissioner, 843 F.2d 224 (6th Cir. 1998) (holding that taxpayer did not substantially comply with inventory accounting election requirements due to failure to file a Form 970 ("Application to Use LIFO Inventory Method") although information required on the form was provided subsequently during the audit). Of particular relevance to the present situation is a statement by the Federal Circuit in Credit Life regarding the purpose of the reporting requirements,

> [T]he purpose of the reporting requirement is obvious: [it] places the Service on notice of the taxpayer's position and gives [the Service] an opportunity to investigate and verify.... Thus, to apply the doctrine of substantial compliance here would not only be inconsistent with our own cases limiting its application, but even with the Tax Court's application of it as well.

Credit Life Ins. Co. v. United States, 948 F.2d at 727–28.

In sum, a controlled participant must substantially comply with the administrative requirements of Treas. Reg. § 1.482-7(j), including both the documentation and reporting requirements, to claim qualified cost sharing arrangement treatment. Treas.

Reg. §§ 1.482-7(a)(1), 1.482-7(b) and 1.482-7(c)(1)(iii). Due to the importance of attaching the cost sharing statement to Forms 1120, 5471 and 5472, as discussed infra, the failure to comply with the reporting requirement alone leads to the conclusion that the taxpayer failed to substantially comply with the administrative requirements in toto.

DISCUSSION:

USCorp may not claim treatment as a qualified cost sharing arrangement for Taxable Year 1 due to its failure to substantially comply with the administrative requirements of Treas. Reg. § 1.482-7(j)

Treas. Reg. § 1.482-7 applies to USCorp's Taxable Year 1, which began on Date B, a date subsequent to the January 1, 1996 effective date of the final cost sharing regulations. Here, the issue is whether USCorp failed to substantially comply with the administrative requirements of Treas. Reg. § 1.482-7(j) due to its failure to attach a cost sharing statement to its U.S. income tax return and Forms 5471.

A. The Plain-Language Test of Substantial Compliance

In determining whether USCorp substantially complied with the reporting requirements for controlled participants in a qualified cost sharing arrangement, we believe the plain-language test governs this case based on the "substantial compliance" language in Treas. Reg. § 1.482-7(c)(1)(iii). Accordingly, we begin our analysis with the plain-language review of the cost sharing regulations and follow with an application of the American Air Filter five factor test, as did the Seventh Circuit in Prussner.

The flush language of Treas. Reg. § 1.482-7(j)(3) explicitly requires a controlled participant, i.e., USCorp, to attach a cost sharing statement to its U.S. income tax return. USCorp failed to do so. USCorp cannot claim that it did not have notice of this requirement since the 1995 final cost sharing regulations were published in December 1995 and became effective on January 1, 1996, prior to the commencement of USCorp's taxable year under examination. Therefore, USCorp had at least 14½ months notice of the requirement prior to the due date of its tax return.

Applying the Tax Court's analysis in Prussner, we believe that failure to file a cost sharing statement altogether cannot be deemed substantial compliance, as "no compliance" cannot constitute substantial compliance. The fact that there is a separate documentation requirement under Treas. Reg. § 1.482-7(j)(2) does not alter this conclusion given the importance of compliance with the reporting requirement. (See discussion infra regarding import). Therefore, pursuant to the plain-language test of substantial compliance, USCorp did not substantially comply with the administrative requirements of Treas. Reg. § 1.482-7(j) due to its failure to attach a cost sharing statement to its Taxable Year 1 income tax return.

B. The Federal Common Law Doctrine of Substantial Compliance

Additionally, we believe that the Federal common law doctrine of substantial compliance supports the above conclusion that USCorp's failure to attach a cost sharing statement to its U.S. income tax return does not constitute substantial compliance. In applying the five factor American Air Filter test to the present situation to determine whether the requirement to attach a cost sharing statement to a timely filed income tax return is either essential or procedural, we conclude that it is an essential requirement with which taxpayers must comply. Otherwise, failure to comply circumvents the purpose of the requirement and results in prejudice to the Service.

First, USCorp's failure to substantially comply with the reporting requirement of Treas. Reg. § 1.482-7(j)(3) defeats the purpose of the cost sharing regulations. The purpose of attaching the cost sharing statement to an income tax return or Forms 5471/5472 is to provide timely notice to the Service that the taxpayer claims a qualified cost sharing arrangement and provides the identities of the participants. As in Credit Life Ins. Co., the cost sharing statement alerts the Service of the possible need to investigate and verify the special requirements associated with a qualified cost sharing arrangement, including issues that may arise such as a buy-in or a buy-out.

Second, the Commissioner is prejudiced by USCorp's failure to attach cost sharing statements to its Forms 1120 and 5471. USCorp may argue that the Commissioner has not been harmed because Examination was able to discern the existence of a cost sharing arrangement during the audit and thus request additional supporting documentation pursuant to Treas. Reg. § 1.482-7(j)(2). Nevertheless, effective tax administration is harmed or prejudiced to the extent that Examination may not be able to discern the existence of a cost sharing arrangement from the tax return or Forms 5471/5472 in order to timely and effectively audit such arrangements. Taxable years do not remain subject to audit for an indefinite duration. Specifically, situations may arise where there should have been a cost sharing-related adjustment in a year of the cost sharing arrangement, but such year is closed to audit when, owing to lack of notice via the cost sharing statement, Examination discerns the existence of the cost sharing arrangement and identifies the participants.

Third, the cost sharing regulations articulate the reporting requirement with detailed specificity. Applying the 9th Circuit's reasoning in Sawyer, USCorp could not prevail here by relying on the doctrine of substantial compliance because it had knowledge of the prerequisites for qualified cost sharing arrangement treatment since the 1995 final cost sharing regulations were published and effective prior to the beginning of Taxable Year 1. Support for this conclusion can also be found from the Tax Court's analysis in Columbia Iron & Metal Co. because here, the cost sharing regulations clearly make the attachment of a cost sharing statement to a Form 1120 or 5471 a sine qua non for qualified cost sharing treatment. See generally Treas. Reg. § 1.482-7(c)(1)(iii). Furthermore, the requirement to attach a cost sharing statement to a timely filed income tax return cannot be deemed a burdensome requirement that is difficult with which to comply given that the only information required is a statement that the taxpayer is a participant in the arrangement and the identification of other participants.

Fourth, the sanction imposed on USCorp for the failure to substantially comply with the administrative requirements of Treas. Reg. § 1.482-7(j) is neither excessive nor disproportionate compared with its default. Specifically, USCorp is precluded from claiming qualified cost sharing arrangement treatment due to its failure to alert the Service that it was a controlled participant in a cost sharing arrangement. The situation here is not like that in Columbia Iron & Metal Co. where the applicable Code section and regulations failed to specify the consequences of a failure to comply with the requirements for charitable deductions. Here, the cost sharing regulations plainly state that the taxpayer may not claim treatment as a qualified cost sharing arrangement in the absence of meeting certain requirements, including substantial compliance with the administrative requirements.

Finally, whereas it is not clear that USCorp attempts to benefit from hindsight by adopting a position inconsistent with its original action or omission, it is possible that taxpayers in similar situations could do so. Since the essence of a cost sharing arrangement is to share the risks and benefits of the exploitation of intangibles, taxpayers may be tempted not to reveal their cost sharing arrangements by timely and properly notifying the Service as required in Treas. Reg. §1.482-7(j)(3) in order to use hindsight to gain significant tax benefits.

Seagate Technology, Inc. v. Commissioner
T.C. Memo. 2000-388

GERBER, J.

Petitioner moved for partial summary judgment concerning what has been denominated the "section 482 stock option cost-sharing issue". In particular, petitioner questions whether respondent may employ section 482 to make an allocation to include petitioner's cost, if any, of employee stock options in the cost-sharing pool for purposes of a cost-sharing agreement between petitioner and its foreign subsidiaries.

In support of its motion, petitioner argues that, as a matter of law, respondent is prohibited from making an allocation with respect to the cost-sharing arrangement for the following reasons: (1) Respondent is not aware of specific arm's-length dealings where stock option costs were shared; (2) respondent relies on opinion as opposed to factual support for inclusion of the "at-the-money" stock options in the pool of costs; (3) section 1.482-2(b)(5)(ii), Income Tax Regs., excludes "expenses associated with the issuance of stock"; and (4) petitioner allocated and apportioned the costs of nonintegral support services consistently using a reasonable method in keeping with sound accounting practices within the meaning of section 1.482-2(b)(6)(i), Income Tax Regs.

Respondent counters that: (1) Section 1.482-2(d)(4) and (b)(4), Income Tax Regs., requires that "all costs" be included in cost-sharing arrangements, and "all costs" include employee stock options; and (2) there are disputed material facts concerning whether arm's-length parties would share the cost of stock options granted to employees who performed the research and development for the transferred intangible.

Background

Petitioner is the successor in interest to Conner Peripherals, Inc. (Conner Domestic), which developed and manufactured hard disk drives for sale to personal computer manufacturers and others. Effective January 1, 1988, Conner Domestic and its wholly owned foreign manufacturing subsidiary, Conner Peripherals Singapore, Ltd. (Conner Foreign 1), entered into a cost-sharing agreement. Effective July 1, 1990, Conner Domestic, Conner Foreign 1, and Conner Domestic's wholly owned Singapore corporation, Conner Peripherals Pte., Ltd., entered into a new cost-sharing agreement for sharing research and development (R & D) costs, and the 1988 cost-sharing agreement was terminated. Pursuant to the new agreement, the three corporations shared $62.9 million, $85 million, and $94.7 million of R & D costs for the development of a new generation of disk drives for 1990, 1991, and 1992, respectively.

In connection with an audit, respondent challenged certain of the allocations under the cost-sharing agreement. Agreement was reached with respect to all determined allocations with the exception of respondent's determination that the value or cost of stock options granted to Conner Domestic's employees had to be included in the cost-sharing pool. Petitioner contended that arm's-length parties would not share the cost, if any, of employee stock options, and respondent was not aware of any arm's-length cost-sharing arrangement where the parties shared the cost incurred with respect to the grant of an at-the-money stock option to the employees of one of the parties.

Discussion

Summary judgment is an appropriate means by which to decide a legal issue if the pleadings, admissions, and other materials, including affidavits, demonstrate that no genuine issue exists as to any material fact and a decision may be rendered as a matter of law. Summary judgment is a device used to expedite litigation, but it is not a substitute for a trial in that disputes over factual issues are not to be resolved in such proceedings. The party moving for summary judgment has the burden of showing the absence of a genuine issue as to any material fact.

The dispute here concerns a cross-border transfer of intangibles by a domestic parent to its foreign subsidiaries. Under the regulations in effect for the years under consideration, if a group of controlled entities participated in a "bona fide cost-sharing arrangement" as to the development of intangibles, then the district director is limited in his approach to reallocation. Sec. 1. 482-2(d)(4), Income Tax Regs. In particular, the regulation provides that if there is a "bona fide cost-sharing arrangement", then "the district director shall not make allocations with respect to such acquisition [of intangibles] except as may be appropriate to reflect each participant's arm's length share of the costs and risks of developing the property." Id.

The regulation goes on to direct that cost-sharing arrangements will be considered "arm's length" where the "terms and conditions * * * [are] comparable to those which would have been adopted by unrelated parties similarly situated had they entered into such an arrangement." Id. There is no disagreement about the bona fides of the cost-sharing agreements between the controlled entities in this case. Respondent and petitioner have also resolved their differences regarding several other reallocations determined by respondent. The only question presented is whether the controlled entities must share the cost, if any, of the domestic parent's stock options given to the parent's employees who performed research and development regarding particular intangibles.

Petitioner argues that where a bona fide cost-sharing arrangement exists, section 1.482-2(d)(4), Income Tax Regs., requires respondent to have a factual predicate in order to make any allocations. Petitioner also points out that respondent has admitted that he does not have evidence or knowledge of an actual arm's-length transaction where stock option costs were shared. Respondent, instead, relies on an affidavit containing an expert's opinion that options are part of the costs that would be shared between arm's-length parties. Where a bona fide cost-sharing arrangement exists, petitioner contends that respondent may not rely solely on an expert's opinion as a basis for a stock option cost-sharing allocation. Petitioner also argues that respondent's expert's opinion is unreliable under the standard set forth in Daubert v. Merrell Dow Pharms., Inc., 509 U.S. 579 (1993), and related cases. Additionally, petitioner contends that even if the expert's opinion was acceptable and/or admissible, it is "opinion" and not "fact" and, therefore, could not be the basis for a genuine issue as to a material fact so as to preclude the use of summary judgment.

Petitioner contends that it has shown that stock option costs would not be shared in an arm's-length transaction. Petitioner's proof on this point consists of the experiences of its officers and employees, some of whom have worked for or with unrelated third parties. Petitioner also relies on the fact that the Federal Acquisition Regulations System (FARS) classifies qualifying employee stock purchase plans as "noncompensatory." That classification precludes payment by the Federal Government for costs of qualified employee stock options in connection with contracts governed by FARS. Because FARS governs all civil and military Federal executive branch contracts with private business for goods and services, petitioner reasons that a large number of "arm's-length transactions" do not include the cost-sharing of employee stock options.

Respondent counters that the regulations provide that all costs should be included and that stock option costs are "costs" that may be allocated. In addition, respondent relies on an expert's opinion that stock option costs would be accounted for in an arm's-length business relationship. Respondent also relies on what he believes are analogous court opinions in which the stock options have been treated as compensation or as part of the consideration for a transaction. Finally, respondent contends that the FARS contracts are not comparable to the circumstances in this case.

The parties' disagreement raises several questions about the regulations. Firstly, we must consider whether the Commissioner must be aware of an actual arm's-length transaction before allocating costs between controlled entities that have a bona fide cost-sharing arrangement. Secondly, if an actual arm's-length example is not required, then we must decide whether the Commissioner must possess facts and/or admissible evidence before making such an allocation.

We do not agree with petitioner's perception that respondent would have to be aware of an actual arm's-length transaction as a prerequisite to making any allocations. Section 1.482-2(d)(4), Income Tax Regs., limits the Commissioner's ability to make an allocation, in the case of a bona fide cost-sharing arrangement, to the appropriate reflection of each participant's arm's-length share of the costs and risks of developing the property. The regulation goes on to direct that cost-sharing arrangements will be considered "arm's length" where the "terms and conditions [are] comparable to those *which would have been adopted by unrelated parties similarly situated had they entered into such an arrangement."* (Emphasis added.) Accordingly, there is no requirement that the Commissioner have actual knowledge of an arm's-length situation as a prerequisite to the determination of an allocation in the case of a cost-sharing arrangement.

In addition, the regulatory standard does not require that the Commissioner rely on fact, as opposed to opinion, before making an allocation where there is a bona fide cost-sharing arrangement. There is no specific minimum standard prerequisite to the Commissioner's determination that an allocation should be made. Such a determination, however, may ultimately be found to be arbitrary, capricious, or unreasonable, but that standard is not the threshold enabling the Commissioner's determination that an allocation should be made.

We do not conclude that respondent's determination is or is not well founded. Likewise, we do not, in the context of this opinion, accept, agree with, or disagree with respondent's expert's opinion. We must however, observe that for better or for worse, expert witnesses have become the prognosticators and the bane of transfer pricing cases. Both parties may rely on expert advice/opinions in reaching their conclusions and/or defending their positions.

Here we will be engaged in deciding whether the sharing of stock option costs is a circumstance "comparable to those which would have been adopted by unrelated parties". Sec. 1.482-2(d)(4), Income Tax Regs. Petitioner, from a limited universe of information, has attempted to show that it is not aware of an arm's-length transaction where the costs of stock options were shared; i.e., that its officers and employees are not aware of any circumstances where costs of stock options have been shared in petitioner's experiences and in those of employees who have experience with other companies. Through Government FARS contract standards, petitioner has attempted to show that some portion of the potential universe of unrelated (arm's-length) research and development transactions did not involve the sharing of the cost of employee stock options.

In the context of a partial summary judgment motion, we should not undertake the role of a fact finder. In such a setting, a judge should not engage in credibility determinations, weighing the evidence, or drawing inferences from the "facts" that the moving and nonmoving parties present. As significantly, the evidence of the non-movant is to be believed, and all justifiable inferences are to be drawn in his favor.

Neither party has advanced evidence or affidavits completely resolving, as a factual matter, the question of whether arm's-length parties to a similar transaction would share the cost of employee stock options. There are also questions about whether the options had any cost to petitioner at the time of issuance and/or the appropriate time to measure the cost of the stock options. Under these circumstances, we are compelled to hold that there is a genuine dispute about material facts. We cannot say that either party has presented or had the opportunity to fully present facts or other evidence adequately addressing, for the benefit of a fact finder, whether the regulatory standard has been met. Accordingly, this matter is not ripe for summary adjudication, and further development and/or a trial may be necessary to resolve the disputed factual aspects of this case.

As to petitioner's argument that there is no genuine dispute about a material fact because respondent relies solely on opinion evidence, we disagree with petitioner's perspective. Petitioner chooses to focus on the means by which respondent may attempt to convince the Court that his determination is well founded and/or that his determination is based on conditions that are comparable to those that would have been adopted by unrelated parties similarly situated had they entered into such an arrangement. Even though an expert's opinion may be hearsay (i.e., not based on the expert's personal knowledge but on his perception of the operative facts of a case), courts may rely on the expert's affidavits in denying motions for summary judgment.

As explained above, under the regulations, respondent is not required to present an actual example of an arm's-length transaction where the costs of employee stock options were shared. Petitioner, if it follows its present approach, will try to show that such costs are not shared by proving a negative; i.e., no transactions where there was cost sharing. Respondent, on the other hand, if he follows his present approach, will attempt to show by means of expert opinion that such costs would or should be shared within the meaning of the regulations. Obviously, an expert's opinion and/or testimony is generally not admissible as fact because he or she generally renders opinions after the fact. Nevertheless, experts' opinions are received for the purpose of assisting the trier of fact in reaching a factual conclusion.

Our conclusion that there remains a genuine dispute about a material fact does not presume that respondent's expert(s) is qualified or that the opinion(s) is necessarily helpful or admissible, but that such questions cannot be decided in the context of this summary judgment motion. Likewise, petitioner's proposed evidence of the nonexistence of such an arm's-length sharing of stock option costs is not being "judged" at this time.

To reflect the foregoing,

An order will be issued denying petitioner's motion for partial summary judgment regarding the "section 482 stock-option cost-sharing issue".

Chapter 10

Internet/E-Commerce Taxation

I. Assignment for Chapter 10

Read:

    Materials: Overview
                    Internet Tax Freedom Act
                    Quill v. North Dakota
                    NEW YORK ADVISORY OPINION TSB-A-02(7)(S)(2002)
                    Wal-Mart Stores, Inc. v. City of Mobile
                    Andersen Consulting, LLP v. Comm'r of Revenue Services
                    NEW YORK ADVISORY OPINION TSB-A-02(13)(S)(2002)
                    NEW YORK ADVISORY OPINION TSB-A-02(3)(C)(2002)
                    NEW YORK ADVISORY OPINION PETITION NO. 5000510A (2001)
                    Chart of 50 States

Complete the Problems.

II. Problems for Chapter 10

1. Citrus.com is a Texas corporation selling gift boxes of Texas grown citrus fruits over the Internet from a Dallas-based computer server owned by Citrus.com. Citrus.com is accessible by Internet users worldwide. Should the ability to access Citrus.com's site in a state outside of Texas be considered a factor in determining whether Citrus.com must collect sale taxes and remit them to those states?

2. If Citrus.com, the company in Problem 1, is hosted on a computer server located in Oklahoma City, may the State of Oklahoma establish nexus based on the location of the computer server and require Citrus.com to collect and remit sale taxes to Oklahoma? Citrus.com refuses to comply with the State of Oklahoma's requirement of collecting and remitting sale taxes on goods sold over the Internet to Oklahomans. How would you defend Citrus.com?

3. Further to Problem 1, a group of French citizens who reside in Paris want to purchase 120 boxes of Texas grown citrus fruits from Citrus.com. Would France be entitled to any sales tax collected by Citrus.com? At the end of the calendar year, Citrus.com estimates that it has sold about 30% of its fruits to the same French

citizens. Must Citrus.com report its taxable income to France and pay tax on such income to France?

4. In 1996, assume that California began to impose a 3% sales tax on all online transactions of goods purchased by Californians in general. In the same year, the City of San Francisco also imposed a similar tax on online transactions of goods purchased by San Franciscans. Are the taxes legal?

5. To encourage more consumers to engage in e-commerce, the State of Walla Walla (the 51st state) decides to impose a sales tax of 5% on all online sale transactions of goods and 7% on all off-line sale transactions of goods. Is the tax lawful? What changes should be made so the tax is permissible?

6. Technology Solutions, Inc. ("TSI") is a full service multi-media company. TSI designs, produces, implements, and maintains websites, intranets, online advertising, and e-commerce and network-based software applications. TSI wants to know whether its website development services (such as consulting, designing, and the actual creation of websites) are subject to New York state and local sales and compensating use taxes? Will the answer change if TSI uploads electronically to the World Wide Web or delivered to a client in the form of a CD-ROM? If TSI uses both pre-written software and custom software (developed by others to TSI's specifications) in performing its website development services, is TSI's purchase of the pre-written software taxable? Custom software taxable?

7. E-Info.com provides financial information services over the Internet. Clients, under fee-paid license agreements with E-Info.com, gain access to the financial information databases. Clients are from all fifty states. Applying the New York advisory opinions, included in the materials, how should the fees received by E-info.com be sourced?

8. NapsterBros is an online music distribution company with its corporate office located in New York City. NapsterBros wants to know whether the sales of music delivered electronically over the Internet are subject to New York sales or compensating use taxes?

III. Overview

The global and electronic nature of the Internet has brought numerous opportunities and challenges to online companies. To develop a presence on the Internet, an online company must obtain a domain name, preferably a memorable one, build a structure for the website, and create contents for it. The goal in the creation of the online company's Internet presence is to attract unique visitors to the website for the contents (goods and services) offered by the online company. Online companies face many issues related to Internet taxation.

This chapter explores Internet taxation issues. The federal government enacted two statutes relating to a moratorium of Internet taxation. This chapter provides an analysis of the Internet Tax Freedom Act, particularly its impact on Internet companies. The text of the statute on Internet taxation is included below. To fully understand the complexity of Internet taxation issues, a reading of a seminal Supreme Court case, *Quill v. North Dakota*, though decided before the Internet age, is essential. This case is excerpted below. Also, state supreme court cases on the sales and use tax of canned software and customized software, though in non-Internet context, are important to the discussion of Internet taxation of software sales. *Wal-Mart Stores, Inc. v. City of Mobile* and *Andersen Consulting, LLP v. Commissioner* are included in the materials.

Taxing Internet sales of goods or services is governed at the state level. New York, for example, has issued a number of advisory opinions relating to sales of software, goods, digitized music, digitized photographic images, database licenses, information, and other web contents over the Internet. Excerpts of such advisory opinions are included in this chapter.

Further, a detailed summary of all fifty states Internet sales taxes and charts for such taxes is included at the end of this chapter.

A. The Internet Nondiscrimination Act and The Internet Tax Freedom Act

On November 28, 2001, President Bush signed into law the Internet Tax Nondiscrimination Act ("ITNA"). Pub. L. No. 105-277, 112 Stat. 2681 (1998) (codified at 47 U.S.C. § 151 (1999)). The ITNA extends until November 1, 2003 the Internet Tax Freedom Act ("ITFA"), which expired on October 21, 2001. The new federal legislation continues to impose a moratorium on *new* taxes imposed by states and local government entities on Internet access services, multiple taxes, and discriminatory taxes on electronic commerce transactions.

1. No New Tax on Internet Service Access

Under the ITFA, "Internet access service" means a service that enables users to access content, information, electronic mail, or other services offered over the Internet. *See* Internet Tax Freedom Act § 1101(e)(3)(D). Though states and local government entities are prohibited from imposing new taxes on Internet access services, they are allowed to collect taxes on Internet access services that were generally imposed and actually enforced prior to October 1, 1998. *Id.* § 1101(a)(1).

Specifically, before October 1, 1998, if a tax was authorized by a statute and an Internet Service Provider ("ISP") had a reasonable opportunity to know by virtue of a rule or other public proclamation that such tax would be imposed on Internet access, the taxing state or local government may continue to collect the tax from the ISP. *Id.* § 1101(d)(1). Also, if a state or local government generally collected such tax on charges for Internet access before that date, the taxing entity may continue to collect the tax from the ISP. *Id.* § 1101(d)(2).

This means Internet access service providers cannot be subjected to any new taxes, but the taxes previously authorized by statutes and levied prior to October 1, 1998, will continue to be imposed on ISPs. *Id.* § 1101.

2. No Multiple Taxes on Electronic Commerce Transactions

The ITFA prohibits state and local government entities from collecting multiple taxes and discriminatory taxes on transactions conducted over the Internet or through Internet access. *Id.* § 1101. Such transactions include the sale, lease, license, offer, or delivery of property, goods, services, or information. *Id.* § 1104(3).

Under the ITFA, "multiple tax" means a tax imposed by more than one state on the same electronic commerce transaction where the taxpayer did not receive credit for the tax paid in the other jurisdictions. *Id.* § 1104(6)(A). The term "multiple tax," however, does not extend to sales or use taxes imposed by a state and its political subdivisions on the same electronic commerce transaction. For example, state A and state B are prohibited from imposing a tax on the same electronic commerce transaction, unless state A or state B provides a tax credit for the transaction. *Id.* § 1104(6)(B). However, state A and its political subdivisions are allowed to collect sales or use taxes on the same electronic commerce transaction.

A sales or use tax is a tax that is imposed on or incident to the sale, purchase, storage, consumption, distribution, or other use of tangible personal property or services as may be defined by the specific tax law. Such tax is measured by the amount of the sales price or other charges for the property or service at issue. *Id.* § 1104(6)(C).

3. No Discriminatory Taxes on Electronic Commerce Transactions

The ITFA prohibits discriminatory taxes on electronic commerce transactions. *Id.* § 1104(2). Examples of discriminatory taxes on electronic commerce transactions are taxes not generally imposed on transactions involving similar property, goods, services, or information accomplished through other means. For example, if a state does not impose a tax on food sold at supermarkets, then the state cannot levy a tax against food sold on the Internet.

Also, discriminatory taxes on electronic commerce transactions include taxes imposed at different rates for online transactions compared to offline transactions. *Id.* § 1104(2)(A). For example, if a state imposes only a 6% tax on book sales offline, the state cannot impose a different tax rate for book sales online. Otherwise, the state would violate the ITFA's prohibition against discriminatory taxes on electronic commerce transactions.

Under the ITFA, "discriminatory tax" also includes any tax imposed by a state or local government on an out-of-state vendor if "the sole ability to access a site on a remote seller's out-of-state computer server is considered a factor in determining a remote seller's tax collection obligation." *Id.* § 1104(2)(B). This provision reflects the well established law that a state cannot require an out-of-state vendor to collect sale taxes unless the vendor has a physical presence such as agents or stores located in the state. *See Quill Corp. v. North Dakota*, 504 U.S. 298 (1992). Essentially, a state may collect taxes from a vendor if the state can establish that the vendor has a nexus with the state. Under the ITFA, no nexus exists if the vendor's Internet site is hosted on an out-of-state computer server. In other words, the nexus is determined on the basis of the computer server location. Where the computer server is located in a state, does it mean that under the ITFA a nexus exists between the state and the vendor whose Internet site is hosted on the computer server? The future of Internet taxation remains unclear at the present time. Presently, the ITFA is scheduled to expire on November 1, 2003.

B. State Taxation on Internet Sales

The ITFA prohibits a discriminatory tax that is imposed by a state or local government on an out-of-state vendor that does not have a nexus with the state. As long as a state can establish that an online company has a substantial nexus or physical presence in the state, the state can require the online company to collect a sales or use tax on goods purchased online from customers in the state.

1. *Substantial Nexus Standard — Offline Environment*

In 1992, the United States Supreme Court in *Quill v. North Dakota*, 504 U.S. 298 (1992), considered a tax case in which the state of North Dakota attempted to require Quill, an out-of-state mail-order company that had neither outlets nor sales representatives in North Dakota, to collect taxes on goods purchased by consumers in North Dakota. The Court agreed with the state court's conclusion that the Due Process Clause does not bar enforcement of the state's use tax against Quill because Quill had purposefully directed its activities at North Dakota residents and the use tax was related to the benefits Quill received from access to North Dakota. Under the Commerce Clause, however, the Court held that North Dakota's tax liability was unconstitutional because it unduly burdened interstate commerce.[1]

Under *Quill v. North Dakota*, a state or local tax survives a Commerce Clause challenge when the tax (1) is applied to an activity with a substantial nexus with the taxing state, (2) is fairly apportioned, (3) does not discriminate against interstate commerce, and (4) is fairly related to the services provided by the states. The second and third prongs of the analysis prohibit taxes that pass an unfair share of the tax burden onto interstate commerce. The first and fourth prongs require a substantial nexus between the vendor and the taxing state and a relationship between the tax and the state-provided goods or services. The first and fourth prongs limit the reach of the taxing state that may cause undue burdens on interstate commerce. Accordingly, the "substantial nexus" requirement is not identical to due process's "minimum contacts" requirement. A company may have the "minimum contacts" with a taxing state required under the Due Process Clause, yet lack the "substantial nexus" with the State under the Commerce Clause. No substantial nexus exists in cases where a vendor's "only connection with customers in the taxing state is by common carrier or the United States mail." Such vendors are free from state-imposed duties to collect sales and use taxes. This bright-line rule in the area of sales and use taxes, according to the *Quill* court, encourages settled expectations and fosters investment by businesses and individuals. Further, the *Quill* court credited the bright-line rule of exempting mail-order sales from state taxation for the dramatic growth of the industry.

Essentially, under *Quill v. North Dakota*, a vendor has a substantial nexus with a taxing state if the vendor has a physical presence in the taxing state, such as an office, warehouse, or retail store located in the taxing state.

2. *Substantial Nexus — Internet Implications*

Applying *Quill v. North Dakota* to the online environment, Internet companies may avoid having a substantial nexus with a state and thus avoid having to collect

---

1. 504 U.S. at 312. The Supreme Court explained that the nexus analysis under the Due Process Clause concerns "notice" or "fair warning" for the defendant whereas the nexus analysis under the Commerce Clause focuses on the effects of state regulation on the national economy. *Id.* The Commerce Clause prohibits discrimination against interstate commerce and state regulations that unduly burden interstate commerce. *Id.*

sales taxes from customers of that state. States and local taxing authorities, however, will attempt to establish a substantial nexus over companies that sell goods or services online in their states. A pertinent question for both online companies and taxing states is how much online activity is sufficient to create a substantial nexus under *Quill v. North Dakota*?

If a California-based Internet company (*i.e.*, the company as a physical presence in California) builds an active website that is accessible by residents of all fifty taxing states, forty-nine states outside California cannot establish a substantial nexus to require the company to collect use or sales taxes. Congress carved out a substantial nexus provision in the ITFA wherein a state may require an Internet company to collect a use or sales taxes if the company stores its website on an in-state server or owns an in-state server. Where the California-based Internet company has its website hosted by a computer server located in Ohio, under ITFA, Ohio may require the Internet company to collect sale taxes from the electronic transactions the company has with Ohio residents and remit such taxes to Ohio.

Where an Internet company has offices or agents to market, solicit, bill, or conduct business activities directly related to sales of goods or services offered online in a state, a substantial nexus is created in the state, and the Internet company is required under state law to collect sales tax. Similarly, if the Internet company stores its inventory in warehouses located in the state, a substantial nexus exists between the company and the taxing state. A question arises, however, concerning whether there is a substantial nexus if the Internet company's inventory is held by a third party for delivery.

Other difficult questions concerning whether a substantial nexus exist in cases when the online company has offline affiliate stores located in a state. It is fairly common that potential customers go to an offline affiliate store to examine the merchandise and then purchase the item online to avoid sales tax. A taxing state would probably argue that a substantial nexus exists through affiliate presence in the state. If the online company and offline store are completely isolated from each other, despite corporate relation between the two companies, no substantial nexus exists.

3. States' Sales Taxes on Electronic Commerce Transactions

All states, except Alaska, Delaware, Montana, New Hampshire and Oregon, require an online company with a substantial nexus in a state to collect taxes from sales of goods over the Internet from in-state consumers.

Some states include software and information sold online in the definition of sales of goods or personal property over the Internet and collect taxes on such sales. Other states exempt from sales and use tax for software and information purchased via downloading from the Internet. Currently, the tax-exempt states include Arkansas, California, Florida, Georgia, Iowa, Kentucky, Maryland, Massachusetts, Missouri, Nevada, New Jersey, North Carolina, Rhode Island, South Carolina, Vermont, and Virginia.

States such as Illinois, Indiana, Kansas, Michigan, Minnesota, Nebraska, Pennsylvania, Tennessee, Wisconsin and Wyoming exempt information, but collect sales and use taxes on software purchased via downloading from the Internet. Ohio collects sales and use taxes for on-line information and software purchased for commercial use. Oklahoma exempts online information and software purchases unless the purchaser receives a backup copy or manual in addition to the downloaded software.

Detailed tax information for each state is described in the charts included at the end of the Chapter. The charts summarize states' treatment of the Internet sales of goods, software, customized software, information, and Information services.

IV. Materials

INTERNET TAX FREEDOM ACT
47 U.S.C. § 151 (2000)

§ 1100. Short title

This title [Pub.L. 105-277, Div. C, Title XI, Oct. 21, 1998, 112 Stat. 2681-719, which enacted this note] may be cited as the 'Internet Tax Freedom Act.'

§ 1101. Moratorium

(A) **Moratorium.** No State or political subdivision thereof shall impose any of the following taxes during the period beginning on October 1, 1998, and ending on November 1, 2003—

(1) taxes on Internet access, unless such tax was generally imposed and actually enforced prior to October 1, 1998; and

(2) multiple or discriminatory taxes on electronic commerce.

(B) **Preservation of state and local taxing authority.** Except as provided in this section, nothing in this title [this note] shall be construed to modify, impair, or supersede, or authorize the modification, impairment, or superseding of, any State or local law pertaining to taxation that is otherwise permissible by or under the Constitution of the United States or other Federal law and in effect on the date of enactment of this Act [Oct. 21, 1998].

(C) **Liabilities and pending cases.** Nothing in this title [this note] affects liability for taxes accrued and enforced before the date of enactment of this Act [Oct. 21, 1998], nor does this title [this note] affect ongoing litigation relating to such taxes.

(D) **Definition of generally imposed and actually enforced.** For purposes of this section, a tax has been generally imposed and actually enforced prior to October 1, 1998, if, before that date, the tax was authorized by statute and either :

(1) a provider of Internet access services had a reasonable opportunity to know by virtue of a rule or other public proclamation made by the appropriate administrative agency of the State or political subdivision thereof, that such agency has interpreted and applied such tax to Internet access services; or

(2) a State or political subdivision thereof generally collected such tax on charges for Internet access.

(E) **Exception to moratorium.**

(1) **In general.** Subsection (a) shall also not apply in the case of any person or entity who knowingly and with knowledge of the character of the material, in interstate or foreign commerce by means of the World Wide Web, makes any communication for commercial purposes that is available to any minor and that includes any material that

is harmful to minors unless such person or entity has restricted access by minors to material that is harmful to minors:

(a) by requiring use of a credit card, debit account, adult access code, or adult personal identification number;

(b) by accepting a digital certificate that verifies age; or

(c) by any other reasonable measures that are feasible under available technology.

(2) **Scope of exception.** For purposes of paragraph (1), a person shall not be considered to making a communication for commercial purposes of material to the extent that the person is:

(a) a telecommunications carrier engaged in the provision of a telecommunications service;

(b) a person engaged in the business of providing an Internet access service;

(c) a person engaged in the business of providing an Internet information location tool; or;

(d) similarly engaged in the transmission, storage, retrieval, hosting, formatting, or translation (or any combination thereof) of a communication made by another person, without selection or alteration of the communication.

(F) **Additional exception to moratorium.**

(1) **In general.** Subsection (a) shall also not apply with respect to an Internet access provider, unless, at the time of entering into an agreement with a customer for the provision of Internet access services, such provider offers such customer (either for a fee or at no charge) screening software that is designed to permit the customer to limit access to material on the Internet that is harmful to minors.

§ 1102. Advisory Commission on Electronic Commerce

(A) **Establishment of commission.** There is established a commission to be known as the Advisory Commission on Electronic Commerce (in this title [this note] referred to as the 'Commission'). The Commission shall:

(1) be composed of 19 members appointed in accordance with subsection (b), including the chairperson who shall be selected by the members of the Commission from among themselves; and

(2) conduct its business in accordance with the provisions of this title [this note].

(B) **Sunset.** The Commission shall terminate 18 months after the date of the enactment of this Act [Oct. 21, 1998].

(C) **National Tax Association Communications and Electronic Commerce Tax Project.** The Commission shall, to the extent possible, ensure that its work does not undermine the efforts of the National Tax Association Communications and Electronic Commerce Tax Project.

§ 1103. Report

Not later than 18 months after the date of the enactment of this Act [Oct. 21, 1998], the Commission shall transmit to Congress for its consideration a report reflecting the results, including such legislative recommendations as required to address the findings of the Commission's study under this title. Any recommendation agreed to by the Commission shall be tax and technologically neutral and apply to all forms of remote commerce. No finding or recommendation shall be included in the report unless agreed to by at least two-thirds of the members of the Commission serving at the time the finding or recommendation is made.

§ 1104. Definitions

For the purposes of this title [this note]:

(A) **Bit tax.** The term 'bit tax' means any tax on electronic commerce expressly imposed on or measured by the volume of digital information transmitted electronically, or the volume of digital information per unit of time transmitted electronically, but does not include taxes imposed on the provision of telecommunications services.

(B) **Discriminatory tax.** The term 'discriminatory tax' means:

(1) any tax imposed by a State or political subdivision thereof on electronic commerce that:

(a) is not generally imposed and legally collectible by such State or such political subdivision on transactions involving similar property, goods, services, or information accomplished through other means;

(b) is not generally imposed and legally collectible at the same rate by such State or such political subdivision on transactions involving similar property, goods, services, or information accomplished through other means, unless the rate is lower as part of a phase-out of the tax over not more than a 5-year period;

(c) imposes an obligation to collect or pay the tax on a different person or entity than in the case of transactions involving similar property, goods, services, or information accomplished through other means;

(d) establishes a classification of Internet access service providers or online service providers for purposes of establishing a higher tax rate to be imposed on such providers than the tax rate generally applied to providers of similar information services delivered through other means; or

(i) any tax imposed by a State or political subdivision thereof, if:

(ii) except with respect to a tax (on Internet access) that was generally imposed and actually enforced prior to October 1, 1998, the sole ability to access a site on a remote seller's out-of-State computer server is considered a factor in determining a remote seller's tax collection obligation; or

(iii) a provider of Internet access service or online services is deemed to be the agent of a remote seller for determining tax collection obligations solely as a result of:

a) the display of a remote seller's information or content on the out-of-State computer server of a provider of Internet access service or online services; or

b) the processing of orders through the out-of-State computer server of a provider of Internet access service or online services.

(C) **Electronic commerce.** The term 'electronic commerce' means any transaction conducted over the Internet or through Internet access, comprising the sale, lease, license, offer, or delivery of property, goods, services, or information, whether or not for consideration, and includes the provision of Internet access.

(D) **Internet.** The term 'Internet' means collectively the myriad of computer and telecommunications facilities, including equipment and operating software, which comprise the interconnected world-wide network of networks that employ the Transmission Control Protocol/Internet Protocol, or any predecessor or successor protocols to such protocol, to communicate information of all kinds by wire or radio.

(E) **Internet access.** The term 'Internet access' means a service that enables users to access content, information, electronic mail, or other services offered over the Internet, and may also include access to proprietary content, information, and other services as part of a package of services offered to users. Such term does not include telecommunications services.

(F) **Multiple tax.**

(1) **In general.** The term 'multiple tax' means any tax that is imposed by one State or political subdivision thereof on the same or essentially the same electronic commerce that is also subject to another tax imposed by another State or political subdivision thereof (whether or not at the same rate or on the same basis), without a credit (for example, a resale exemption certificate) for taxes paid in other jurisdictions.

(2) **Exception.** Such term shall not include a sales or use tax imposed by a State and 1 or more political subdivisions thereof on the same electronic commerce or a tax on persons engaged in electronic commerce which also may have been subject to a sales or use tax thereon.

(3) **Sales or use tax.** For purposes of subparagraph (B), the term 'sales or use tax' means a tax that is imposed on or incident to the sale, purchase, storage, consumption, distribution, or other use of tangible personal property or services as may be defined by laws imposing such tax and which is measured by the amount of the sales price or other charge for such property or service.

(G) **State.** The term 'State' means any of the several States, the District of Columbia, or any commonwealth, territory, or possession of the United States.

(H) **Tax.**

(1) **In general.** The term 'tax' means:

(a) any charge imposed by any governmental entity for the purpose of generating revenues for governmental purposes, and is not a fee imposed for a specific privilege, service, or benefit conferred; or

(b) the imposition on a seller of an obligation to collect and to remit to a governmental entity any sales or use tax imposed on a buyer by a governmental entity.

(2) **Exception.** Such term does not include any franchise fee or similar fee imposed by a State or local franchising authority, pursuant to section 622 or 653 of the Communications Act of 1934 (47 U.S.C. 542, 573), or any other fee related to obligations or telecommunications carriers under the Communications Act of 1934 (47 U.S.C. 151 et seq.).

(I) **Telecommunications service.** The term 'telecommunications service' has the meaning given such term in section 3(46) of the Communications Act of 1934 (47 U.S.C. 153(46)) and includes communications services (as defined in section 4251 of the Internal Revenue Code of 1986) [26 U.S.C.A. § 4251].

(J) **Tax on Internet access.** The term 'tax on Internet access' means a tax on Internet access, including the enforcement or application of any new or preexisting tax on the sale or use of Internet services unless such tax was generally imposed and actually enforced prior to October 1, 1998.

Quill v. North Dakota
Supreme Court of the United States
504 U.S. 298 (1992)

Justice STEVENS delivered the opinion of the Court.

This case, like *National Bellas Hess, Inc. v. Department of Revenue of Ill.*, 386 U.S. 753 (1967), involves a State's attempt to require an out-of-state mail-order house that has neither outlets nor sales representatives in the State to collect and pay a use tax on goods purchased for use within the State. In *Bellas Hess* we held that a similar Illinois statute violated the Due Process Clause of the Fourteenth Amendment and created an unconstitutional burden on interstate commerce. In particular, we ruled that a "seller whose only connection with customers in the State is by common carrier or the United States mail" lacked the requisite minimum contacts with the State. *Id.,* at 758.

In this case, the Supreme Court of North Dakota declined to follow *Bellas Hess* because "the tremendous social, economic, commercial, and legal innovations" of the past quarter-century have rendered its holding "obsole[te]." 470 N.W.2d 203, 208 (1991). Having granted certiorari, 502 U.S. 808, we must either reverse the State Supreme Court or overrule *Bellas Hess.* While we agree with much of the state court's reasoning, we take the former course.

I

Quill is a Delaware corporation with offices and warehouses in Illinois, California, and Georgia. None of its employees work or reside in North Dakota, and its ownership of tangible property in that State is either insignificant or nonexistent. Quill sells office equipment and supplies; it solicits business through catalogs and flyers, advertisements in national periodicals, and telephone calls. Its annual national sales exceed $200 million, of which almost $1 million are made to about 3,000 customers in North Dakota. It is the sixth largest vendor of office supplies in the State. It delivers all of its merchandise to its North Dakota customers by mail or common carrier from out-of-state locations.

As a corollary to its sales tax, North Dakota imposes a use tax upon property purchased for storage, use, or consumption within the State. North Dakota requires every "retailer maintaining a place of business in" the State to collect the tax from the consumer and remit it to the State. N.D.Cent.Code §57-40.2-07 (Supp.1991). In 1987, North Dakota amended the statutory definition of the term "retailer" to include "every person who engages in regular or systematic solicitation of a consumer market in th[e] state." §57-40.2-01(6). State regulations in turn define "regular or systematic solicitation" to mean three or more advertisements within a 12-month period. N.D.Admin.Code §81-04.1-01-03.1 (1988). Thus, since 1987, mail-order companies that engage in such solicitation have been subject to the tax even if they maintain no property or personnel in North Dakota.

Quill has taken the position that North Dakota does not have the power to compel it to collect a use tax from its North Dakota customers. Consequently, the State, through its Tax Commissioner, filed this action to require Quill to pay taxes (as well as interest and penalties) on all such sales made after July 1, 1987. The trial court ruled in Quill's favor, finding the case indistinguishable from *Bellas Hess;* specifically, it found that because the State had not shown that it had spent tax revenues for the benefit of the mail-order business, there was no "nexus to allow the state to define retailer in the manner it chose." App. to Pet. for Cert. A41.

The North Dakota Supreme Court reversed, concluding that "wholesale changes" in both the economy and the law made it inappropriate to follow *Bellas Hess* today. 470 N.W.2d, at 213. The principal economic change noted by the court was the remarkable growth of the mail-order business "from a relatively inconsequential market niche" in 1967 to a "goliath" with annual sales that reached "the staggering figure of $183.3 billion in 1989." *Id.*, at 208, 209. Moreover, the court observed, advances in computer technology greatly eased the burden of compliance with a "'welter of complicated obligations'" imposed by state and local taxing authorities. *Id.*, at 215 (quoting *Bellas Hess*, 386 U.S. at 759–760).

Equally important, in the court's view, were the changes in the "legal landscape." With respect to the Commerce Clause, the court emphasized that *Complete Auto Transit, Inc. v. Brady*, 430 U.S. 274 (1977), rejected the line of cases holding that the direct taxation of interstate commerce was impermissible and adopted instead a "consistent and rational method of inquiry [that focused on] the practical effect of [the] challenged tax." *Mobil Oil Corp. v. Commissioner of Taxes of Vt.*, 445 U.S. 425, 443 (1980). This and subsequent rulings, the court maintained, indicated that the Commerce Clause no longer mandated the sort of physical-presence nexus suggested in *Bellas Hess*.

Similarly, with respect to the Due Process Clause, the North Dakota court observed that cases following *Bellas Hess* had not construed "minimum contacts" to require physical presence within a State as a prerequisite to the legitimate exercise of state power. The state court then concluded that "the Due Process requirement of a 'minimal connection' to establish nexus is encompassed within the *Complete Auto* test" and that the relevant inquiry under the latter test was whether "the state has provided some protection, opportunities, or benefit for which it can expect a return." 470 N.W.2d, at 216.

Turning to the case at hand, the state court emphasized that North Dakota had created "an economic climate that fosters demand for" Quill's products, maintained a legal infrastructure that protected that market, and disposed of 24 tons of catalogs and flyers mailed by Quill into the State every year. *Id.*, at 218–219. Based on these facts, the court concluded that Quill's "economic presence" in North Dakota depended on services and benefits provided by the State and therefore generated "a constitutionally sufficient nexus to justify imposition of the purely administrative duty of collecting and remitting the use tax." *Id.*, at 219.

II

As in a number of other cases involving the application of state taxing statutes to out-of-state sellers, our holding in *Bellas Hess* relied on both the Due Process Clause and the Commerce Clause. Although the "two claims are closely related," *Bellas Hess*, 386 U.S., at 756, 87 S.Ct., at 1391, the Clauses pose distinct limits on the taxing powers of the States. Accordingly, while a State may, consistent with the Due Process Clause, have the authority to tax a particular taxpayer, imposition of the tax may nonetheless violate the Commerce Clause. See, *e.g., Tyler Pipe Industries, Inc. v. Washington State Dept. of Revenue*, 483 U.S. 232 (1987).

The two constitutional requirements differ fundamentally, in several ways. As discussed at greater length below, see Part IV, *infra*, the Due Process Clause and the Commerce Clause reflect different constitutional concerns. Moreover, while Congress has plenary power to regulate commerce among the States and thus may authorize state actions that burden interstate commerce, see *International Shoe Co. v. Washington*, 326 U.S. 310, 315 (1945), it does not similarly have the power to authorize violations of the Due Process Clause.

Thus, although we have not always been precise in distinguishing between the two, the Due Process Clause and the Commerce Clause are analytically distinct.

> 'Due process' and 'commerce clause' conceptions are not always sharply separable in dealing with these problems.... To some extent they overlap. If there is a want of due process to sustain the tax, by that fact alone any burden the tax imposes on the commerce among the states becomes 'undue.' But, though overlapping, the two conceptions are not identical. There may be more than sufficient factual connections, with economic and legal effects, between the transaction and the taxing state to sustain the tax as against due process objections. Yet it may fall because of its burdening effect upon the commerce. And, although the two notions cannot always be separated, clarity of consideration and of decision would be promoted if the two issues are approached, where they are presented, at least tentatively as if they were separate and distinct, not intermingled ones. *International Harvester Co. v. Department of Treasury*, 322 U.S. 340, 353 (1944).

Heeding Justice Rutledge's counsel, we consider each constitutional limit in turn.

III

The Due Process Clause "requires some definite link, some minimum connection, between a state and the person, property or transaction it seeks to tax," *Miller Brothers Co. v. Maryland*, 347 U.S. 340 (1954), and that the "income attributed to the State for tax purposes must be rationally related to 'values connected with the taxing State,'" *Moorman Mfg. Co. v. Bair*, 437 U.S. 267, 273 (1978). Here, we are concerned primarily with the first of these requirements. Prior to *Bellas Hess*, we had held that that requirement was satisfied in a variety of circumstances involving use taxes. For example, the presence of sales personnel in the State or the maintenance of local retail stores in the State justified the exercise of that power because the seller's local activities were "plainly accorded the protection and services of the taxing State." *Bellas Hess*, 386 U.S., at 757. The furthest extension of that power was recognized in *Scripto, Inc. v. Carson*, 362 U.S. 207 (1960), in which the Court upheld a use tax despite the fact that all of the seller's in-state solicitation was performed by independent contractors. These cases all involved some sort of physical presence within the State, and in *Bellas Hess* the Court suggested that such presence was not only sufficient for jurisdiction under the Due Process Clause, but also necessary. We expressly declined to obliterate the "sharp distinction..... between mail-order sellers with retail outlets, solicitors, or property within a State, and those who do no more than communicate with customers in the State by mail or common carrier as a part of a general interstate business." 386 U.S., at 758.

Our due process jurisprudence has evolved substantially in the 25 years since *Bellas Hess*, particularly in the area of judicial jurisdiction. Building on the seminal case of *International Shoe Co. v. Washington*, 326 U.S. 310 (1945), we have framed the relevant inquiry as whether a defendant had minimum contacts with the jurisdiction "such that the maintenance of the suit does not offend 'traditional notions of fair play and substantial justice.'" *Id.,* at 316 (quoting *Milliken v. Meyer,* 311 U.S. 457, 463 (1940)). In that spirit, we have abandoned more formalistic tests that focused on a defendant's "presence" within a State in favor of a more flexible inquiry into whether a defendant's contacts with the forum made it reasonable, in the context of our federal system of Government, to require it to defend the suit in that State. In *Shaffer v. Heitner,* 433 U.S. 186, 212 (1977), the Court extended the flexible approach that *International Shoe* had prescribed for purposes of *in personam* jurisdiction to *in rem* jurisdiction, concluding that "all assertions of state-court jurisdiction must be evaluated according to the standards set forth in *International Shoe* and its progeny."

Applying these principles, we have held that if a foreign corporation purposefully avails itself of the benefits of an economic market in the forum State, it may subject itself to the State's *in personam* jurisdiction even if it has no physical presence in the State. As we explained in *Burger King Corp. v. Rudzewicz,* 471 U.S. 462 (1985):

> Jurisdiction in these circumstances may not be avoided merely because the defendant did not *physically enter the forum State. Although territorial presence frequently will enhance a potential defendant's affiliation with a State and reinforce the reasonable foreseeability of suit there, it is an inescapable fact of modern commercial life that a substantial amount of business is transacted solely by mail and wire communications across state lines, thus obviating the need for physical presence within a State in which business is conducted. So long as a commercial actor's efforts are 'purposefully directed' toward residents of another State, we have consistently rejected the notion that an absence of physical contacts can defeat personal jurisdiction there.* Id., at 476 (emphasis in original).

Comparable reasoning justifies the imposition of the collection duty on a mail-order house that is engaged in continuous and widespread solicitation of business within a State. Such a corporation clearly has "fair warning that [its] activity may subject [it] to the jurisdiction of a foreign sovereign." *Shaffer v. Heitner,* 433 U.S., at 218. In "modern commercial life" it matters little that such solicitation is accomplished by a deluge of catalogs rather than a phalanx of drummers: The requirements of due process are met irrespective of a corporation's lack of physical presence in the taxing State. Thus, to the extent that our decisions have indicated that the Due Process Clause requires physical presence in a State for the imposition of duty to collect a use tax, we overrule those holdings as superseded by developments in the law of due process.

In this case, there is no question that Quill has purposefully directed its activities at North Dakota residents, that the magnitude of those contacts is more than sufficient for due process purposes, and that the use tax is related to the benefits Quill receives from access to the State. We therefore agree with the North Dakota Supreme Court's conclusion that the Due Process Clause does not bar enforcement of that State's use tax against Quill.

IV

Article I, §8, cl. 3, of the Constitution expressly authorizes Congress to "regulate Commerce with foreign Nations, and among the several States." It says nothing about the protection of interstate commerce in the absence of any action by Congress. Nevertheless, as Justice Johnson suggested in his concurring opinion in *Gibbons v. Ogden,* 9 Wheat. 1, 231-232, 239 (1824), the Commerce Clause is more than an affirmative grant of power; it has a negative sweep as well. The Clause, in Justice Stone's phrasing, "by its own force" prohibits certain state actions that interfere with interstate commerce. *South Carolina State Highway Dept. v. Barnwell Brothers, Inc.,* 303 U.S. 177, 185 (1938).

Our interpretation of the "negative" or "dormant" Commerce Clause has evolved substantially over the years, particularly as that Clause concerns limitations on state taxation powers. See generally P. Hartman, Federal Limitations on State and Local Taxation §§ 2:9–2:17 (1981). Our early cases, beginning with *Brown v. Maryland,* 12 Wheat. 419 (1827), swept broadly, and in *Leloup v. Port of Mobile,* 127 U.S. 640, 648 (1888), we declared that "no State has the right to lay a tax on interstate commerce in any form." We later narrowed that rule and distinguished between direct burdens on interstate commerce, which were prohibited, and indirect burdens, which generally were not. See, *e.g., Sanford v. Poe,* 69 F. 546 (CA6 1895), aff'd *sub nom. Adams Express Co. v. Ohio State Auditor,* 165 U.S. 194, 220 (1897). *Western Live Stock v. Bureau of Revenue,* 303 U.S. 250, 256-258 (1938), and subsequent decisions rejected this formal, categorical analysis and adopted a "multiple-taxation doctrine" that focused not on whether a tax was "direct" or "indirect" but rather on whether a tax subjected interstate commerce to a risk of multiple taxation. However, in *Freeman v. Hewit,* 329 U.S. 249, 256 (1946), we embraced again the formal distinction between direct and indirect taxation, invalidating Indiana's imposition of a gross receipts tax on a particular transaction because that application would "impos[e] a direct tax on interstate sales." Most recently, in *Complete Auto Transit, Inc. v. Brady,* 430 U.S., at 285 we renounced the *Freeman* approach as "attaching constitutional significance to a semantic difference." We expressly overruled one of *Freeman's* progeny, *Spector Motor Service, Inc. v. O'Connor,* 340 U.S. 602 (1951), which held that a tax on "the privilege of doing interstate business" was unconstitutional, while recognizing that a differently denominated tax with the same economic effect would not be unconstitutional. *Spector,* as we observed in *Railway Express Agency, Inc. v. Virginia,* 358 U.S. 434, 441 (1959), created a situation in which "magic words or labels" could "disable an otherwise constitutional levy." *Complete Auto* emphasized the importance of looking past "the formal language of the tax statute [to] its practical effect," 430 U.S., at 279 and set forth a four-part test that continues to govern the validity of state taxes under the Commerce Clause

Bellas Hess was decided in 1967, in the middle of this latest rally between formalism and pragmatism. Contrary to the suggestion of the North Dakota Supreme Court, this timing does not mean that *Complete Auto* rendered *Bellas Hess* "obsolete." *Complete Auto* rejected *Freeman* and *Spector's* formal distinction between "direct" and "indirect" taxes on interstate commerce because that formalism allowed the validity of statutes to hinge on "legal terminology," "draftsmanship and phraseology." 430 U.S., at 281. *Bellas Hess* did not rely on any such labeling of taxes and therefore did not automatically fall with *Freeman* and its progeny.

While contemporary Commerce Clause jurisprudence might not dictate the same result were the issue to arise for the first time today, *Bellas Hess* is not inconsistent with *Complete Auto* and our recent cases. Under *Complete Auto* 's four-part test, we will sustain a tax against a Commerce Clause challenge so long as the "tax [1] is applied to an activity with a substantial nexus with the taxing State, [2] is fairly apportioned, [3] does not discriminate against interstate commerce, and [4] is fairly related to the services provided by the State." 430 U.S., at 279. *Bellas Hess* concerns the first of these tests and stands for the proposition that a vendor whose only contacts with the taxing State are by mail or common carrier lacks the "substantial nexus" required by the Commerce Clause.

Thus, three weeks after *Complete Auto* was handed down, we cited *Bellas Hess* for this proposition and discussed the case at some length. In *National Geographic Society v. California Bd. of Equalization,* 430 U.S. 551, 559 (1977), we affirmed the continuing vitality of *Bellas Hess*' "sharp distinction...between mail-order sellers with [a physical presence in the taxing] State and those...who do no more than communicate with customers in the State by mail or common carrier as part of a general interstate business." We have continued to cite *Bellas Hess* with approval ever since. For example, in *Goldberg v. Sweet*, 488 U.S. 252, 263 (1989), we expressed "doubt that termination of an interstate telephone call, by itself, provides a substantial enough nexus for a State to tax a call. See *National Bellas Hess*...(receipt of mail provides insufficient nexus)." See also *D.H. Holmes Co. v. McNamara*, 486 U.S. 24, 33 (1988); *Commonwealth Edison Co. v. Montana*, 453 U.S. 609, 626 (1981); *Mobil Oil Corp. v. Commissioner of Taxes*, 445 U.S. at 437;*National Geographic Society*, 430 U.S., at 559. For these reasons, we disagree with the State Supreme Court's conclusion that our decision in *Complete Auto* undercut the *Bellas Hess* rule.

The State of North Dakota relies less on *Complete Auto* and more on the evolution of our due process jurisprudence. The State contends that the nexus requirements imposed by the Due Process and Commerce Clauses are equivalent and that if, as we concluded above, a mail-order house that lacks a physical presence in the taxing State nonetheless satisfies the due process "minimum contacts" test, then that corporation also meets the Commerce Clause "substantial nexus" test. We disagree. Despite the similarity in phrasing, the nexus requirements of the Due Process and Commerce Clauses are not identical. The two standards are animated by different constitutional concerns and policies.

Due process centrally concerns the fundamental fairness of governmental activity. Thus, at the most general level, the due process nexus analysis requires that we ask whether an individual's connections with a State are substantial enough to legitimate the State's exercise of power over him. We have, therefore, often identified "notice" or "fair warning" as the analytic touchstone of due process nexus analysis. In contrast, the Commerce Clause and its nexus requirement are informed not so much by concerns about fairness for the individual defendant as by structural concerns about the effects of state regulation on the national economy. Under the Articles of Confederation, state taxes and duties hindered and suppressed interstate commerce; the Framers intended the Commerce Clause as a cure for these structural ills. See generally The Federalist Nos. 7, 11 (A. Hamilton). It is in this light that we have interpreted the negative implication of the Commerce Clause. Accordingly, we have ruled that that Clause prohibits discrimination against interstate commerce, see, *e.g., Philadelphia v. New Jersey*, 437 U.S. 617 (1978), and bars state regulations that unduly burden interstate commerce, see, *e.g., Kassel v. Consolidated Freightways Corp. of Del.*, 450 U.S. 662 (1981).

The *Complete Auto* analysis reflects these concerns about the national economy. The second and third parts of that analysis, which require fair apportionment and non-discrimination, prohibit taxes that pass an unfair share of the tax burden onto interstate commerce. The first and fourth prongs, which require a substantial nexus and a relationship between the tax and state-provided services, limit the reach of state taxing authority so as to ensure that state taxation does not unduly burden interstate commerce. Thus, the "substantial nexus" requirement is not, like due process' "minimum contacts" requirement, a proxy for notice, but rather a means for limiting state burdens on interstate commerce. Accordingly, contrary to the State's suggestion, a corporation may have the "minimum contacts" with a taxing State as required by the Due Process Clause, and yet lack the "substantial nexus" with that State as required by the Commerce Clause.

The State Supreme Court reviewed our recent Commerce Clause decisions and concluded that those rulings signaled a "retreat from the formalistic constrictions of a stringent physical presence test in favor of a more flexible substantive approach" and thus supported its decision not to apply *Bellas Hess*. 470 N.W.2d, at 214 (citing *Standard Pressed Steel Co. v. Department of Revenue of Wash.*, 419 U.S. 560 (1975), and *Tyler Pipe Industries, Inc. v. Washington State Dept. of Revenue*, 483 U.S. 232 (1987)). Although we agree with the state court's assessment of the evolution of our cases, we do not share its conclusion that this evolution indicates that the Commerce Clause ruling of *Bellas Hess* is no longer good law.

First, as the state court itself noted, 470 N.W.2d, at 214, all of these cases involved taxpayers who had a physical presence in the taxing State and therefore do not directly conflict with the rule of *Bellas Hess* or compel that it be overruled. Second, and more importantly, although our Commerce Clause jurisprudence now favors more flexible balancing analyses, we have never intimated a desire to reject all established "bright-line" tests. Although we have not, in our review of other types of taxes, articulated the same physical-presence requirement that *Bellas Hess* established for sales and use taxes, that silence does not imply repudiation of the *Bellas Hess* rule.

Complete Auto, it is true, renounced *Freeman* and its progeny as "formalistic." But not all formalism is alike. *Spector* 's formal distinction between taxes on the "privilege of doing business" and all other taxes served no purpose within our Commerce Clause jurisprudence, but stood "only as a trap for the unwary draftsman." *Complete Auto*, 430 U.S., at 279, 97 S.Ct. at 1079. In contrast, the bright-line rule of *Bellas Hess* furthers the ends of the dormant Commerce Clause. Undueburdens on interstate commerce may be avoided not only by a case-by-case evaluation of the actual burdens imposed by particular regulations or taxes, but also, in some situations, by the demarcation of a discrete realm of commercial activity that is free from interstate taxation. *Bellas Hess* followed the latter approach and created a safe harbor for vendors "whose only connection with customers in the [taxing] State is by common carrier or the United States mail." Under *Bellas Hess*, such vendors are free from state-imposed duties to collect sales and use taxes.

Like other bright-line tests, the *Bellas Hess* rule appears artificial at its edges: Whether or not a State may compel a vendor to collect a sales or use tax may turn on the presence in the taxing State of a small sales force, plant, or office. Cf.*National Geographic Society v. California Bd. of Equalization*, 430 U.S. 551 (1977); *Scripto, Inc. v. Carson*, 362 U.S. 207 (1960). This artificiality, however, is more than offset by the benefits of a clear rule. Such a rule firmly establishes the boundaries of legitimate state authority to impose a duty to collect sales and use taxes and reduces litigation concerning those taxes. This benefit is important, for as we have so frequently noted, our law in this area is something of a "quagmire"" and the "application of constitutional principles to specific state statutes leaves much room for controversy and confusion and little in the way of precise guides to the States in the exercise of their indispensable power of taxation." *Northwestern States Portland Cement Co. v. Minnesota*, 358 U.S. 450, 457-458 (1959).

Moreover, a bright-line rule in the area of sales and use taxes also encourages settled expectations and, in doing so, fosters investment by businesses and individuals. Indeed, it is not unlikely that the mail-order industry's dramatic growth over the last quarter century is due in part to the bright-line exemption from state taxation created in *Bellas Hess*.

Notwithstanding the benefits of bright-line tests, we have, in some situations, decided to replace such tests with more contextual balancing inquiries. For example, in *Arkansas Electric Cooperative Corp. v. Arkansas Pub. Serv. Comm'n*, 461 U.S. 375

(1983), we reconsidered a bright-line test set forth in *Public Util. Comm'n of R.I. v. Attleboro Steam & Electric Co.,* 273 U.S. 83 (1927). *Attleboro* distinguished between state regulation of *wholesale* sales of electricity, which was constitutional as an "indirect" regulation of interstate commerce, and state regulation of *retail* sales of electricity, which was unconstitutional as a "direct regulation" of commerce. In *Arkansas Electric,* we considered whether to "follow the mechanical test set out in *Attleboro,* or the balance-of-interests test applied in our Commerce Clause cases." 461 U.S., at 390–391. We first observed that "the principle of *stare decisis* counsels us, here as elsewhere, not lightly to set aside specific guidance of the sort we find in *Attleboro.*" *Id.* at 391. In deciding to reject the *Attleboro* analysis, we were influenced by the fact that the "mechanical test" was "anachronistic," that the Court had rarely relied on the test, and that we could "see no strong reliance interests" that would be upset by the rejection of that test. 461 U.S. at 391–392. None of those factors obtains in this case. First, the *Attleboro* rule was "anachronistic" because it relied on formal distinctions between "direct" and "indirect" regulation (and on the regulatory counterparts of our *Freeman* line of cases); as discussed above, *Bellas Hess* turned on a different logic and thus remained sound after the Court repudiated an analogous distinction in *Complete Auto.* Second, unlike the *Attleboro* rule, we have, in our decisions, frequently relied on the *Bellas Hess* rule in the last 25 years, see *supra,* at 1912, and we have never intimated in our review of sales or use taxes that *Bellas Hess* was unsound. Finally, again unlike the *Attleboro* rule, the *Bellas Hess* rule has engendered substantial reliance and has become part of the basic framework of a sizable industry. The "interest in stability and orderly development of the law" that undergirds the doctrine of *stare decisis,* see *Runyon v. McCrary,* 427 U.S. 160, 190-191 (1976), therefore counsels adherence to settled precedent.

In sum, although in our cases subsequent to *Bellas Hess* and concerning other types of taxes we have not adopted a similar bright-line, physical-presence requirement, our reasoning in those cases does not compel that we now reject the rule that *Bellas Hess* established in the area of sales and use taxes. To the contrary, the continuing value of a bright-line rule in this area and the doctrine and principles of *stare decisis* indicate that the *Bellas Hess* rule remains good law. For these reasons, we disagree with the North Dakota Supreme Court's conclusion that the time has come to renounce the bright-line test of *Bellas Hess.*

This aspect of our decision is made easier by the fact that the underlying issue is not only one that Congress may be better qualified to resolve, but also one that Congress has the ultimate power to resolve. No matter how we evaluate the burdens that use taxes impose on interstate commerce, Congress remains free to disagree with our conclusions. See *Prudential Insurance Co. v. Benjamin,* 328 U.S. 408 (1946). Indeed, in recent years Congress has considered legislation that would "overrule" the *Bellas Hess* rule. Its decision not to take action in this direction may, of course, have been dictated by respect for our holding in *Bellas Hess* that the Due Process Clause prohibits States from imposing such taxes, but today we have put that problem to rest. Accordingly, Congress is now free to decide whether, when, and to what extent the States may burden interstate mail-order concerns with a duty to collect use taxes.

Indeed, even if we were convinced that *Bellas Hess* was inconsistent with our Commerce Clause jurisprudence, "this very fact [might] giv[e us] pause and counse[l] withholding our hand, at least for now. Congress has the power to protect interstate commerce from intolerable or even undesirable burdens." *Commonwealth Edison Co. v. Montana,* 453 U.S. at 637. In this situation, it may be that "the better part of both wisdom and valor is to respect the judgment of the other branches of the Government." *Id.* at 638.

The judgment of the Supreme Court of North Dakota is REVERSED, and the case is REMANDED for further proceedings not inconsistent with this opinion.

It is so ordered.

NEW YORK ADVISORY OPINION
TSB-A-02(7)(S), PETITION NO. 5991221A
May 30, 2002

On, December 21, 1999, the Department of Taxation and Finance received a Petition for Advisory Opinion from Liquid Digital Information Systems Inc., 180 Varick Street 12th floor, New York, New York 10014.

The issue raised by Petitioner, Liquid Digital Information Systems Inc., is whether any of its services described below involving (A) Web site development, design, implementation and maintenance, or (B) Web site consulting, is subject to sales and use tax.

Petitioner submits the following facts as the basis for this Advisory Opinion.

Petitioner is a full service new media company providing technology solutions for corporate clients. Petitioner will design, produce, implement, and maintain interactive media solutions, including commercial and corporate Web sites, intranets, kiosks, on-line advertising, and e-commerce and network-based software applications. Web sites may be furnished to clients in the form of a CD-ROM.

Prior to the design phase, Petitioner will learn about its client's business; what the market is, how the client got started, and where it hopes to go in the future. Petitioner will try to understand specifically what the client hopes to accomplish by using interactive media to enhance its marketing and sales efforts. Once Petitioner has reached an understanding of a client's goals, Petitioner suggests particular solutions based on the scope of the project and starts designing those solutions.

The design phase of a project involves conceiving the actual structure of a Web site, intranet, etc., to determine how many parts it is going to have, how a user will move from one part to another, what kind of content it will have, and what it will look like. Before moving to the production stage of a project, Petitioner estimates the scope of the work necessary to make the design a reality. This outline details software and staff needs, as well as time and budgetary limits.

During the production stage, programmers code software and applications. Designers format the look and feel of a Web site, including how it will be navigated and how a user will interact with it. As work progresses, the project is tested to make sure it is functioning as planned.

Implementation can be as simple as posting a banner ad on a Web site or as complicated as setting up an e-commerce Web site that allows for products to be purchased on-line. E-commerce involves on-line credit card transactions and requires customers to fill out forms. Each piece of data on a form may be stored in a different data base.

Maintenance agreements vary from project to project. Petitioner sometimes provides ongoing service to clients after the project is completed, such as updating portions of a Web site, or adding a new element to a database system when needed.

Applicable Law

Section 1101(b) of the Tax Law provides, in part:

When used in this article for the purposes of the taxes imposed by subdivisions (a), (b), (c) and (d) of § 1185 and by § 1110, the following terms shall mean:

(6) Tangible personal property. Corporeal personal property of any nature. Such term shall also include pre-written computer software, whether sold as part of a package, as a separate component, or otherwise, and regardless of the medium by means of which such software is conveyed to a purchaser.

(14) Pre-written computer software. Computer software (including pre-written upgrades thereof) which is not software designed and developed by the author or other creator to the specifications of a specific purchaser. The combining of two or more pre-written computer software programs or pre-written portions thereof does not cause the combination to be other than pre-written computer software. Pre-written software also includes software designed and developed by the author or other creator to the specifications of a specific purchaser when it is sold to a person other than such purchaser. Where a person modifies or enhances computer software of which such person is not the author or creator, such person shall be deemed to be the author or creator only of such person's modifications or enhancements. Pre-written software or a pre-written portion thereof that is modified or enhanced to any degree, where such modification or enhancement is designed and developed to the specifications of a specific purchaser, remains pre-written software; provided however, that where there is a reasonable, separately stated charge or an invoice or other statement of the price given to the purchaser for such modification or enhancement, such modification or enhancement shall not constitute pre-written computer software.

Section 1105 of the Tax Law provides, in part:

On and after June first, nineteen hundred seventy-one, there is hereby imposed and there shall be paid a tax of four percent upon:

(a) The receipts from every retail sale of tangible personal property, except as otherwise provided in this article.

(c) The receipts from every sale, except for resale, of the following services:

(3) Installing tangible personal property.....or maintaining, servicing or repairing tangible personal property.....not held for sale in the regular course of business.....whether or not any tangible personal property is transferred in conjunction therewith.

(5) Maintaining, servicing or repairing real property, property or land, as such terms are defined in the real property tax law, whether the services are performed in or outside of a building.

Section 1115(o) of the Tax Law provides:

Services otherwise taxable under subdivision (c) of section eleven hundred five or under section eleven hundred ten shall be exempt from tax under this article where performed on computer software of any nature; provided, however, that where such services are provided to a customer in conjunction with the sale of tangible personal property any charge for such services shall be exempt only when such charge is reasonable and separately stated on an invoice or other statement of the price given to the purchaser.

Technical Services Bureau Memorandum, TSB-M-93(3)S, March 1, 1993, pertaining to the taxability of computer software and certain related services provides, in part:

Effective September 1, 1991, State and local sales and compensating use taxes are imposed on the sale or use of pre-written computer software and certain related services.

The effect of this change in the Tax Law is to broaden the types of computer software that are subject to sales and use taxes.....certain software previously considered "custom" may now be considered *pre-written computer software* and subject to such taxes.....The only software that is exempt from sales and use taxes under the new law is software designed and developed to the specifications of a specific purchaser.

Pre-written computer software is any computer software that is not designed and developed by the author or other creator to the specifications of a specific purchaser.

Software that was originally designed and developed to the specifications of a specific purchaser (*i.e.*, "custom" software) loses its identity as such and becomes pre-written software, subject to tax, if and when it is sold to someone other than the person for whom it was specifically designed and developed.

Pre-written software is subject to tax whether sold as part of a package or separately. Software created by combining two or more pre-written programs or portions of pre-written programs is still pre-written software subject to tax. The medium by which the software is transferred to the purchaser has no effect on the software's taxability. Thus, pre-written software is taxable whether sold, for example, on a disk, tape or by electronic transmission over telephone lines.

Pre-written software, even though modified or enhanced to the specifications of a specific purchaser, remains pre-written software subject to tax. However, if a charge for the custom modification or enhancement is reasonable and separately stated on the invoice or billing statement, then the separately stated charge for the custom modification or enhancement is not subject to tax.

The incidental use of a development language (e.g., COBOL, BASIC, C, etc.) or of libraries of "pre-written" functions or routines in designing and developing a "custom" software program to the specifications of a specific purchaser will not, in and of itself make the sale of an otherwise custom program taxable. The "custom" program must be examined as a whole to determine whether it is exempt from tax. If the pre-written components of a custom program are sold separately, their sale is subject to tax.

Use tax generally applies to taxable uses of pre-written computer software in the same manner that the use tax applies to uses of other tangible personal property, except that: (1) no use tax is imposed on software used by its author if the author does not offer similar software for sale in the regular course of business, and (2) where software is used by its author and the author does sell the same or similar software in the regular course of business, use tax applies and is computed on the cost of the medium (floppy disk, magnetic tape, etc.) that contains or is used in conjunction with the program.

Opinion

The Web site development services provided by Petitioner to its clients, which involve consulting, designing, and the actual creation of Web sites, do not constitute the sale of tangible personal property and are not included among the enumerated services that are subject to New York State and local sales and compensating use taxes. *See Alan J. Goldstein/The Computer Studio*, Adv Op Comm T & F, July 31, 2001, TSB-A-01(21)S. This is so, regardless of whether the Web sites are created for purposes of advertising or promotion, Internet commerce, intranets or other communications and support functions (*see David H. Posmantier*, Adv Op Comm T&F, June 7, 1999, TSB-A-99(31)S; *K2 Desi2n Incorporated*, Adv Op Comm T&F, July 23, 1997, TSB-A-97(43)S; *Pat Rolland*, Adv Op Comm T&F, July23, 1997, TSB-A-97(41)S; *Ski Soft Inc. d/b/a Ski Areas of New York Internet Publishing Services*, Adv Op Comm T&F, June 25, 1997, *TSB-A-97(35)S)*. Accordingly, Petitioner's charges to its clients for such services are not subject to sales or compensating use tax. Petitioner's charges for Web site development are not taxable whether the Web site is uploaded electronically to the World Wide Web or delivered to a client in the form of a CD-ROM or other media. When a client purchases Web site development from Petitioner and receives the Web site in the form of a CD-ROM or other media, the transfer of the medium such as a disk or tape to the client as an incident to the Web site development is not subject to tax under Section 1105(a) of the Tax Law. *See EMCON*, Adv Op Comm T&F, December 16, 1996, TSB-A-96(79)S respecting the transfer of items as an incident to nontaxable engineering services.

Petitioner's purchase of pre-written software for use in performing its Web site development services is subject to tax under Section 1105(a) of the Tax Law as a purchase at retail of tangible personal property. See Section 1 l0l(b)(6) of the Tax Law. The purchase by Petitioner of custom software designed and developed to Petitioner's specifications is not taxable. Pre-written software, even though modified or enhanced to the specifications of a specific purchaser, remains pre-written software subject to tax. However, if a charge for the customization or enhancement is reasonable and separately stated on the invoice or billing statement, then the separately stated charge for the customization or enhancement is not subject to tax. See TSB-M-93(3)S, *supra*.

Petitioner's use in its Web site development service of software that it develops in-house is not subject to compensating use tax if similar software is not offered for sale by Petitioner in the regular course of business. If Petitioner offers similar software for sale in the regular course of business, then Petitioner's use of the software would be subject to tax based on the cost of the medium that contains or is used in conjunction with the program. See TSB-M-93(3)S, *supra*.

It is noted that Web site maintenance services generally are not subject to sales tax. See *Salomon & Leitgeb CPA's. LLP*, Adv Op Comm T&F, July 23, 1997, TSB-A-97(44)S. If a nontaxable service, however, is performed in conjunction with the sale of tangible personal property, the entire receipts from the sale are subject to tax unless the charges for the service and tangible personal property are separately stated and reasonable, and the service and property may be separately purchased. *See Salomon & Leitueb CPA's LLP, supra*. Section 1105(c) of the Tax Law imposes tax on the services of maintaining, servicing or repairing tangible personal property or real property. Maintenance services performed by Petitioner on computer hardware or kiosks, therefore, are subject to sales tax unless otherwise exempt.

Jonathan Pessen
Tax Regulations Specialist IV
Technical Services Division

NOTE: The opinions expressed in Advisory Opinions are limited to the facts set forth therein.

Wal-Mart Stores, Inc. v. City of Mobile
Supreme Court of Alabama
696 So.2d 290 (1997)

KENNEDY, JUSTICE.

The plaintiff, Wal-Mart Stores, Inc. ("Wal-Mart"), appeals from a summary judgment entered in favor of the defendants, the City of Mobile, Mobile County, and others (collectively "Mobile"). At issue is whether computer software is intangible personal property. If it is, then Mobile is forbidden from collecting gross receipts taxes on computer software. The parties agree that Mobile has the authority to collect gross receipts taxes on sales of tangible personal property and that if computer software is tangible personal property, then it is properly included in the gross receipts calculations on which Wal-Mart is taxed.

Wal-Mart sued Mobile, seeking to enjoin it from collecting gross receipts taxes on sales of computer software by Wal-Mart. The trial court held that computer software was tangible personal property and entered a summary judgment in favor of Mobile. On appeal, Wal-Mart relies on *State v. Central Computer Servs., Inc.*, 349 So.2d 1160 (Ala.1977), arguing that it stands for the general proposition that computer software is *intangible* personal property, and, thus, cannot be included in a gross receipts tax formulation.

In many jurisdictions, early cases held that computer software was intangible property. See, e.g., *South Cent. Bell Tel. Co. v. Barthelemy*, 643 So.2d 1240, 1244–45 (La.1994). Often, courts based their reasoning in part on "the idea that the information contained on the software is the product being sold" and that the choice of a tangible medium for conveying it was incidental to this fact—"that this information can be transmitted in many forms, including over the telephone." *Matter of Protest of Strayer*, 239 Kan. 136, 716 P.2d 588, 591 (1986).

This reasoning appears to underlie this Court's 1977 decision in *Central Computer Servs., Inc.*, where the Court held that computer software was intangible property for purposes of a use tax on tangible personal property. The Court suggested that the buyer seeks the information, rather than the medium by which it is conveyed, and emphasized that the information is not dependent on a software-type medium to be conveyed—that it can be conveyed by several means, for example, by telephone. Also, the Court discussed then common software mediums and concluded that there was only an "incidental physical commingling of the intangible information sought...and the tangible magnetic tapes and punched cards themselves." *Id.* at 1162. Finally, the Court quoted *District of Columbia v. Universal Computer Assocs., Inc.* 151 U.S.App. D.C.

30, 465 F.2d 615 (D.C.Cir.1972): "'What rests in the machine [from the software] is an intangible—"knowledge"—which can hardly be thought to be subject to a personal property tax.'" *Central Computer Servs., Inc.*, 349 So.2d at 1163.

Since the time of the *Central Computer Servs.* case, there has been a shift in the view of many courts:

> "[A]s computer software became more prevalent in society, and as courts' knowledge and understanding of computer software grew, later cases saw a shift in courts' attitudes towards the taxability of computer software, and courts began holding computer software to be tangible for sales, use and property tax purposes."

Barthelemy, 643 So.2d at 1245.

One of the changes that has occurred in this state and elsewhere, which was perhaps not reasonably to be anticipated in 1977, is the proliferation of "canned" computer software, such as is sold by stores like Wal-Mart. As a practical matter, the marketing of such "canned" software *presumes* that the information sought *will* be conveyed by way of a tangible medium. In this sense, the merchandiser is making a sale of tangible property, like the sale of a book.

Similarly, we observe:

> "The software itself, i.e, the physical copy, is not merely a right or an idea to be comprehended by the understanding. The purchaser of the computer software neither desires nor receives mere knowledge, but rather receives a certain arrangement of matter that will make his or her computer perform a desired function. This arrangement of matter, physically recorded on some tangible medium, constitutes a corporeal body."

Barthelemy, 643 So.2d at 1246.

Based on the foregoing, we hold that the trial court properly entered the summary judgment in favor of the defendants. To the extent that *Central Computer Servs.* would dictate a different holding, it is overruled. However, we note that the Mobile ordinance taxing sales of computer software was adopted in 1993 and that until we issued our original opinion in this case on September 13, 1996, the ordinance conflicted with the law as it had been set out in *Central Computer Servs.* For this reason, we hold that our ruling in this case should have prospective application only, i.e., that Mobile cannot collect gross receipts taxes on sales of computer software that occurred before September 13, 1996.

ALMON, SHORES, COOK, and BUTTS, JJ., concur.

MADDOX, Justice (concurring specially).

I simply would note that I wrote a lengthy dissent in *State v. Central Computer Services, Inc.*, 349 So.2d 1160 (Ala.1977), advocating that computer software be defined as tangible personal property for tax purposes. The holding here is consistent with that position.

HOOPER, Chief Justice (dissenting).

Computer software is intangible personal property. This Court has previously so held. *State v. Central Computer Servs., Inc.*, 349 So.2d 1160 (Ala.1977). The majority today states that the marketing of "canned" computer software "*presumes* that the information sought *will* be conveyed by way of a tangible medium." However, whether the software is "canned" or not, the purchaser is primarily buying the intangible knowledge on the software, and the software is incidental to the purchase. The fact that it is presumed that the information will be "conveyed by way of a tangible medium" does not make the purchase primarily one of tangible personal property. Alabama caselaw precedent has been based on whether the personal property is *primarily* tangible or is primarily intangible. Under Alabama case precedent, personal property does not have to be entirely intangible in order to be considered intangible. *State Department of Revenue v. Kennington*, 679 So.2d 1059 (Ala.Civ.App.1995).

The majority cites *South Central Bell Tel. Co. v. Barthelemy*, 643 So.2d 1240 (La.1994). However, the holding of the Louisiana Supreme Court in *Barthelemy* was based on the civil law viewpoint of that State regarding property. The basis of the holding was §461 of the Louisiana Civil Code, which stated:

> "Corporeals are things that have a body, whether animate or inanimate, and can be felt or touched.
>
> "Incorporeals are things that have no body, but are comprehended by the understanding, such as the rights of inheritance, servitudes, obligations, and right of intellectual property." Quoted at 643 So.2d at 1244. The *Barthelemy* court said:
>
> "The term 'tangible personal property' set forth in the City Code, and its synonymous Civil Code concept 'corporeal movable,' must be given their properly intended meaning. Physical recordings of computer software are not incorporeal rights to be comprehended by the understanding. Rather, they are part of the physical world. For the reasons set out below, we hold the computer software at issue in this case constitutes corporeal property under our *civilian concept of that term*, and thus, is tangible personal property...."

643 So.2d at 1244.

The civil law does not determine whether a thing purchased is primarily tangible or primarily intangible. The civil law considers anything "tangible" that has any property. Adopting the logic of the Civil Code of Louisiana could potentially cause serious problems with the caselaw of Alabama on the question whether particular property is tangible or intangible.

I would reaffirm the Alabama caselaw and hold that computer software is intangible property. However, if the majority of the Court wishes to hold that computer software is "tangible," it should do so through the application of common law concepts of what is tangible property and what is intangible property. Alabama is a common law state. I am concerned that the majority today changes Alabama caselaw as to what is tangible property and what is intangible property and in doing so relies on the civil law precedent of Louisiana. The civil law precedent of Louisiana is inapplicable to the common law precedent of Alabama. Therefore, I must dissent.

Andersen Consulting, LLP v. Comm'r of Revenue Services

Supreme Court of Connecticut
767 A.2d 692 (2001)

BORDEN, J.

The issue in this appeal is whether payments made pursuant to certain contracts entered into by the plaintiff, Andersen Consulting, LLP (Andersen), with Connecticut Natural Gas (gas company) and with Northeast Utilities (electric company), were subject to sales and use taxes as sales of computer and data processing services pursuant to General Statutes (Rev. to 1993) § 12-407(2)(i)(A). The defendant, Gene Gavin, the commissioner of revenue services (commissioner), appeals from the judgment of the trial court, in favor of Andersen, determining that the payments were not subject to the tax. The commissioner claims that the payments at issue were subject to sales and use taxes as sales of computer services pursuant to General Statutes (Rev. to 1993) §§ 12-408(2) and 12-407(2)(i)(A) and § 12-426-27 [FN5] of the Regulations of Connecticut State Agencies, and that such an interpretation has recently been ratified by the legislature. We reverse the judgment of the trial court.

The trial court found the following facts. Andersen, an Illinois limited liability partnership with an office in Connecticut, has extensive experience in developing information computer programs for utility companies. The gas company is a Connecticut public utility that provides local gas distribution to various areas of the state. Finding that its information system, which it developed in 1972 and which was performed manually, was old and outdated, the gas company decided, in 1991, to acquire new computer information systems to manage its financial, accounting and cost control functions. Specifically, it decided that it needed two systems to update its informational systems, the first of which was a customer information system (customer system), which would manage billing, accounts receivable, customer service, credit and collection, marketing and the dispatching of customer service personnel. The second system was a distribution and construction information system (distribution system), which would manage planning, cost estimating and cost analysis relating to the installation of gas mains in the streets served by the gas company. The gas company's main purpose was to obtain computer software systems that would meet the business requirements of the company. It had assembled a team to search for a system that would meet these requirements of the company. The team considered off-the-shelf, or canned, software, but found that such software could not be modified by the user, and that it would become very expensive to tie into an existing system. Thus, the team decided that it needed a customized information system.

After reviewing various proposals, the gas company selected Andersen to develop the customer and the distribution systems. In developing the customer system, Andersen modified its Customer 1 software to meet the gas company's requirements. Approximately 60 percent of its requirements could be met through the use of the Customer 1 software in developing the customer system; the remaining 40 percent was custom developed by Andersen. The custom work included the development of a meter inventory system, the creation of a marketing system to keep track of marketing and sales efforts and to target prospective customers, and the development of a means to integrate an existing computer aided dispatching system with the customer system. In developing the distribution system, Andersen used its core package of software known as Work 1. Work 1 met approximately 85 percent of the gas company's requirements for the distribution system; the remaining 15 percent was custom developed by Andersen. The custom work included the development of a system that would automatically schedule maintenance for equipment used in the field, and a means to integrate the distribution system with the customer system. Andersen and the gas company entered into two contracts (gas company contracts), one for each system. Both contracts were fixed fee contracts with the fees contingent on the delivery by Andersen of a fully functioning software system in accordance with the agreed upon specifications. The product that resulted from the development of the systems remained the property of Andersen after the fulfillment of the contracts. The gas company received, however, a perpetual, nonexclusive license to use and modify the software. Andersen's fees under the gas company contracts were $12,979,000. Andersen collected a sales and use tax from the gas company with respect to the two contracts and remitted the payments to the commissioner.

In 1988, the electric company had no unified system for accounting, budgeting and work management functions, and had eleven informational systems in operation, which were inadequate. The electric company explored the use of canned software. Some software was developed in-house where commercial software was not available. The electric company established a task force to conduct a feasibility study to evaluate its systems and make recommendations for improvement. The goal of the task force was to develop a system that would permit the electric company to monitor and budget for costs on a detailed level so that costs could be controlled more effectively. The task force recommended replacing existing systems with a management information and budgeting system (management system), which could only be done with the use of custom software because the canned software met only 20 to 25 percent of the electric company's requirements.

Andersen and the electric company entered into a contract (electric company contract), and used a team approach to create the software for the management system. The electric company provided the space and 50 percent of the staffing for the project. Andersen provided consulting services for architecture and engineering in the development and construction of the software. The management system began with a core package of canned software known as the Dunn and Bradstreet (McCormack and Dodge) Series M General Ledger software package, which provided for 20 to 25 percent of the management system's functional requirements. The remaining 75 to 80 percent was custom developed by a joint team of Andersen's and the electric company's personnel. Andersen's fees under the electric company contract were $15,826,601. Upon delivery, Andersen transferred to the electric company all intangible rights to the management system software, but retained rights to certain tools used in the development of the software.

From June 1, 1990, to October 31, 1993, the gas company and the electric company made payments to Andersen pursuant to the contracts previously described. Andersen collected sales and use taxes from both companies with respect to those payments. After remitting the sales and use taxes imposed on the contracts in question, Andersen requested a refund from the commissioner in the amount of $1,438,828—$525,522 attributable to the gas company contracts and $913,306 attributable to the electric company contract—based upon amounts charged in connection with the development, license and sale of the custom software. The commissioner granted Andersen a refund of $76,500 for payments that Andersen had received from the gas company for license fees. The commissioner denied Andersen's claim for the balance of the refund claimed with respect to the gas company contracts and for the entire refund claim with respect to the electric company contract.

Andersen appealed from the denials of the commissioner to the trial court pursuant to General Statutes (Rev. to 1993) § 12-422. After a trial, the trial court found that the true object of the contracts was "to provide computer software programs that would meet [the] business needs [of the gas company and the electric company]." The court also stated that the true object was "the creation of informational systems for both [companies], not the creation of the various elements necessary to reach the final product." The court concluded that "these software programs, and the labor used to produce these programs, are not taxable under the sales or use tax statutes." The trial court reasoned, on the basis of its understanding of this court's decision in *Northeast Datacom, Inc. v. Wallingford*, 212 Conn. 639, 644–46, 563 A.2d 688 (1989), that "all computer software is nontaxable as intangible property regardless [of] whether the software is 'off the shelf' or custom designed." Accordingly, the court rendered judgment for Andersen, ordering the commissioner to refund to Andersen $1,362,328, with interest. This appeal followed.

The commissioner claims that the trial court improperly concluded that the payments at issue, made to Andersen pursuant to the gas company and the electric company contracts, were not subject to sales and use taxes. Specifically, the commissioner claims that the payments at issue were taxable as computer services pursuant to §§ 12-408(2) and 12-407(2)(i)(A), and § 12-426-27 of the Regulations of Connecticut State Agencies. The commissioner also contends that the trial court: (1) failed to apply the definition of "computer services" pursuant to § 12-426-27 of the regulations; and (2) misinterpreted and misapplied this court's decision in *Northeast Datacom, Inc. v. Wallingford*, supra, 212 Conn. 639, 563 A.2d 688. The commissioner further contends that his decision that the services at issue are taxable computer services has been ratified by recent legislation, namely, Public Acts 2000, No. 00-174, §§ 71, 74 (P.A. 00-174). We agree.

Andersen, as did the trial court, also improperly relies on *Northeast Datacom, Inc. v. Wallingford*, supra, 212 Conn. 639, 563 A.2d 688, and misapplies the principles represented therein. Instead, we conclude that the holding in *Northeast Datacom, Inc.*, is not so broad as to apply to the issue in the present case. In *Northeast Datacom, Inc.*, software owned by the named plaintiff, which included canned software that it had purchased, software customized by outside contractors, and custom software that it had developed, had been assessed as tangible personal property for municipal taxation purposes. *Id.*, at 641–42, 563 A.2d 688. We concluded that the "physical devices are only the most tangential incidents of a computer program and the fact that tangible property is used to store or transmit the software's binary instructions does not change the character of what is fundamentally a classic form of intellectual property." *Id.*, at 644, 563 A.2d 688. We further concluded that the taxation of the software at issue, which was primarily custom software, as tangible personal property was improper because it impermissibly linked the incidents of the intellectual, intangible component of the software, namely, "the right to produce and sell more copies, the right to change the underlying work, the right to license its use to others and the right to transfer the copyright itself," to "the tangible medium in which the software is stored and transmitted." *Id.*, at 646, 563 A.2d 688. Simply put, what is at issue in the present case, namely, whether the services provided to develop, create or produce software are taxable as computer services, was not at issue in *Northeast Datacom, Inc.*

Therefore, in view of our conclusion that computer and data processing services encompasses the development, creation or production of software, the parties shall have an opportunity to present evidence as to the proper allocation, if any, of fees charged by Andersen between the transfer of intangible rights and the services involved in developing, creating or producing the software. The judgment is reversed and the case is remanded for a new trial.

NEW YORK ADVISORY OPINION
TSB-A-02(13)(S), PETITION NO. 5000406A
June 25, 2002

On April 6, 2000, the Department of Taxation and Finance received a Petition for Advisory Opinion from Pegasus Internet, Inc., 333 Seventh Avenue, New York, NY 10001.

The issue raised by Petitioner, Pegasus Internet, Inc., is whether its charges for Web site design and development services are subject to New York State sales tax.

Petitioner submitted the following facts as the basis for this Advisory Opinion.

Petitioner is located in New York and provides Web site design and development services to customers located both within and outside New York. Delivery of the finished Web site is accomplished by placing the site on a hosted server. On occasion, Petitioner will send its customer a copy of the Web site on a Compact Disk.

Applicable Law and Regulations

Section 1105(a) of the Tax Law imposes sales tax on the "receipts from every retail sale of tangible personal property, except as otherwise provided in this article."

Section 1105(c) of the Tax Law imposes sales tax upon receipts from the sales, except sales for resale, of certain enumerated services.

Section 1115 of the Tax Law provides, in part:

> (a) Receipts from the following shall be exempt from the tax on retail sales imposed under subdivision (a) of section eleven hundred five and the compensating use tax imposed under section eleven hundred ten:
>
> (35) Computer system hardware used or consumed directly and predominantly in designing and developing computer software for sale or in providing the service, for sale, of designing and developing Internet websites.

Section *526.6(c)(7)* of the Sales and Use Tax Regulations provides:

Tangible personal property purchased for use in performing a service not subject to tax is not purchased for resale.

Opinion

Petitioner designs and develops Web sites which are placed on a hosted server. On occasion, Petitioner will send its customer a copy of the Web site on a compact disk. The Web site development provided by Petitioner to its clients, which involves designing and the actual creation of a Web site, does not constitute the sale of tangible personal property and is not included among the enumerated services that are subject to New York State and local sales and compensating use taxes. *See Alan J. Goldstein/The Computer Studio,* Adv Op Comm T & F, July 31, 2001, TSB-A-01(21)S. This is so, regardless of whether the Web sites are created for purposes of advertising or promotion, Internet commerce, intranets or other communications and support functions (*see David H. Posmantier,* Adv Op Comm T&F, June 7, 1999, TSB-A-99(3 l)S; *K2 Design Incorporated,* Adv Op Comm T&F, July 23, 1997, TSB-A-97(43)S; Pat Rolland, Adv Op Comm T&F, July 23, 1997, TSB-A-97(41)S; *Ski Soft. Inc. d/bIa Ski Areas of New York Internet Publishing Services,* Adv Op Comm T&F, June 25, 1997, TSB-A-97(35)S). Accordingly, Petitioner's charges to its clients for such services are not subject to sales or compensating use tax. Petitioner's charges for Web site development are not taxable whether the Web site is uploaded electronically to the World Wide Web or delivered to a client in the form of a CD-ROM or other media. When a client purchases Web site development from Petitioner and receives the Web site in the form of a CD-ROM or other media, the transfer of the medium such as a disk or tape to the client as an incident to the Web site development is not subject to tax under Section *1105(a)* of the Tax Law. *See EMCON,* Adv Op Comm T&F, December 16, 1996, TSB-A-96(79)S respecting the transfer of items as an incident to nontaxable engineering services. CD-ROMs or other media such as disks or tapes purchased by Petitioner for use in delivering the non-taxable Web site development services to customers are not eligible for the resale exemption and are subject to sales and compensating use tax if purchased or used by Petitioner in New York. See Section *526.6(c)(7)* of the Sales and Use Tax Regulations.

In the event Petitioner supplies its client with a CD-ROM pursuant to a separate contract or agreement apart from the contract or agreement for the sale of the Web site design and development service, then the charge for the CD-ROM would be taxable under Section 1105(a) of the Tax Law. *See EMCON, supra.*

The purchase by Petitioner of pre-written software for use in performing its Web site development services is subject to tax under Section 1105(a) of the Tax Law as a purchase at retail of tangible personal property. See Section 1 10l(b)(6) of the Tax Law. The purchase by Petitioner of custom software designed and developed to Petitioner's specifications is not taxable. Pre-written software, even though modified or enhanced to the specifications of a specific purchaser, remains pre-written software subject to tax. However, if a charge for the customization or enhancement is reasonable and separately stated on the invoice or billing statement, then the separately stated charge for the customization or enhancement is not subject to tax. *See* Technical Services Bureau Memorandum TSB-M-93(3)S, dated March 1, 1993, entitled "State and Local Sales and Compensating Use Taxes Imposed on Certain Sales of Computer Software."

Also, it should be noted that Section 1115(a)(35) of the Tax Law was amended, effective March 1, 2001 to provide an exemption for hardware used directly and predominantly in providing the service, for sale, of designing and developing Internet Web sites.

Jonathan Pessen
Tax Regulations Specialist IV
Technical Services Division

NOTE: The opinions expressed in Advisory Opinions are limited to the facts set forth therein.

NEW YORK ADVISORY OPINION
TSB-A-02(3)(C), PETITION NO. C010110A
April 18, 2002

On January 10, 2001, a Petition for Advisory Opinion was received from Deloitte & Touche LLP, 1633 Broadway, 38th Floor, New York, New York 10019.

The issue raised by Petitioner, Deloitte & Touche LLP, is how to determine the source of receipts from Internet sales of Merchant Certificates, Taxpayer X Certificates, and Gift Checks for purposes of determining the numerator of the receipts factor of the business allocation percentage computed under section 210.3(a)(2) of Article 9-A of the Tax Law.

Petitioner submits the following facts as the basis for this Advisory Opinion.

Taxpayer X is an online marketer and transaction processor of gift certificates, gift cards and other related products. Taxpayer X markets products over the Internet. Taxpayer X's product line includes various types of proprietary gift certificates ("Taxpayer X Certificates"), gift certificates of unrelated retailers, restaurants and providers of travel related services ("Merchant Certificates"), and Gift Checks issued by a certain financial services institution. Gift certificates may be either physical, represented by a physical certificate or card, or digital, where value is presented solely by a digital code that is delivered electronically via Taxpayer X's Web site, an online service that is open 24 hours a day, seven days a week.

The core of Taxpayer X's business involves the sale of Merchant Certificates. Taxpayer X purchases these certificates from participating merchants at a discount. An inventory sufficient to meet two to three weeks' worth of sales is maintained by Taxpayer X. In a typical transaction involving these certificates, a customer accesses Taxpayer X's Web site to place an order for a Merchant Certificate. The Merchant Certificate is then shipped via common carrier or other expedited courier service to the destination selected by the customer. The Merchant Certificate is attractively packaged and is usually sent with a personalized card and message. For an additional fee, the Merchant Certificate may be packaged with an elegant box and a satin ribbon. The Merchant Certificate is then presented by the recipient, who is usually a person other than Taxpayer X's customer, to the merchant for redemption.

Where a physical Merchant Certificate is purchased and physically shipped, Taxpayer X has a record of the credit card information, including the address, for the purchaser. All transactions subsequent to the shipping of the Certificate are between the merchant and the recipient. Taxpayer X has no control over the redemption policies, refunds and exchanges of Merchant Certificates. In short, once purchased, the Merchant Certificates generally cannot be returned to Taxpayer X for exchange or refund.

Taxpayer X's merchant product line also includes digital (e-mailable) Merchant Certificates ("Digital Merchant Certificates") that are redeemable at the merchant's Web site and/or the merchant's brick and mortar retail location. Taxpayer X maintains an inventory of digital codes purchased from the merchant which represent Digital Merchant Certificates. When an order for a digital certificate is received, Taxpayer X sends, via e-mail, a digital code representing the gift certificate to the recipient. Taxpayer X has a record of the purchaser's e-mail address, street address and credit card information, and the e-mail address of the recipient (if different from the purchaser).

Taxpayer X also sells its own Taxpayer X Certificates that may be either physical or digital and may only be redeemed at Taxpayer X's Web site, or by phone, for the Merchant Certificates described above. As with Merchant Certificates, physical Taxpayer X Certificates are attractively packaged and usually include a personalized card and message. Each physical and digital certificate is controlled and tracked by an identifying code that is unique for each certificate and contains all the relevant information relative to that particular certificate.

To date, physical gift certificates, both Merchant Certificates and Taxpayer X Certificates, comprise the majority of Taxpayer X's sales.

In addition to the above, Taxpayer X sells Gift Checks of a certain financial services institution. Taxpayer X purchases and maintains an inventory of Gift Checks, then resells the Gift Checks on its Web site. As with Merchant Certificates, Taxpayer X has no control over the contractual terms of Gift Checks.

Petitioner states that Taxpayer X has a record of the credit card billing address of all customers.

Discussion

Section 208.11 of the Tax Law provides that the term "tangible personal property" means corporeal personal property, such as machinery, tools, implements, goods, wares and merchandise, and does not mean money, deposits in banks, shares of stock, bonds, notes, credits or evidences of an interest in property and evidences of debt.

The term "gift certificate" means a certified statement entitling the recipient to select merchandise in the amount stated thereon. (Webster's Third New International Dictionary 956 (unabridged 1961)). In this case, the underlying value of a Merchant Certificate, Taxpayer X Certificate or Gift Check represents the intangible right to redeem it for property or services at some future time. As such, a Merchant Certificate, Taxpayer X Certificate or Gift Check is not considered to be tangible personal property under section 208.11 of the Tax Law.

Section 210.3(a)(2) of the Tax Law provides that the receipts factor of the business allocation percentage is determined by ascertaining the percentage which the receipts of the taxpayer, arising during such period from sales of its tangible personal property where shipments are made to points within New York State, services performed within New York State, rentals from property situated, and royalties from the use of patents or copyrights, within New York State, receipts from the sales of rights for closed-circuit and cable television transmissions of an event taking place within New York State as a result of the rendition of services by employees of the corporation, as athletes, entertainers or performing artists, and all other business receipts earned within New York State, bear to the total amount of the taxpayer's receipts, arising during such period from all sales of its tangible personal property, services, rentals, royalties, receipts from the sales of rights for closed-circuit and cable television transmissions and all other business transactions, whether within or without New York State.

In *New York Mercantile Exchange*, Adv Op Comm T&F, April 7, 1999, TSB-A-99(16)C *(NYMEX)*, the petitioner's Market Data was its exclusive property, and petitioner entered into license agreements with direct and indirect Vendors for worldwide distribution of the Market Data. The Vendors generally did not use the Market Data other than to provide it to Subscribers via electronic transmission. The Subscribers were only permitted to use the Market Data internally and could not distribute it to any third parties. The petitioner placed its own modems and other transmission equipment at a direct Vendor's place of business for the Vendor's telecommunications link with the petitioner's network. At all times, such equipment remained the property of the petitioner. The indirect Vendors obtained access to the Market data through a direct Vendor. A Vendor paid the petitioner a monthly subscription fee based on the number of terminals at Subscriber locations that provided access to the petitioner's Market Data. The advisory opinion held that the monthly subscription fees that the petitioner received from the Vendors constituted "other business receipts" for purposes of the receipts factor, and were earned at the location where the petitioner delivered the Market Data to the Vendors. That is, they were earned at the location of the modems and other transmission equipment that the Vendor used to draw upon the Market Data. When the location of such modems and other transmission equipment was in New York State the subscription fees were earned in New York.

The conclusion in *NYMEX, supra* was instructive, in reaching the conclusion in *Insurance Services Office Inc.*, Adv Op Comm T&F, September 6, 2000, TSB-A-00(15)C. In *Insurance Services*, the petitioner's customers subscribed to its Internet service to access petitioner's databases. The customers were paying the petitioner for the intangible right to access and obtain copyrighted data. Customers that subscribed to the databases signed a license agreement to that effect. Similar to *NYMEX, supra* it was held that the revenues for access to the petitioner's copyrighted material constituted "other business receipts" for purposes of the receipts factor. It was concluded that the fees that the petitioner received from its customers for access to the copyrighted databases were properly sourced within and without New York on the basis of the location of modems and other transmission equipment that the customer used to draw upon the material obtained under the licensing agreement with the petitioner. That is, the petitioner's fees from a customer under the licensing agreement were earned in New York when the location of the modems and other transmission equipment that the customer or its agent used to draw upon the petitioner's copyrighted databases was in New York State. In instances where information was not available to determine the location of the modems and other transmission equipment that the customer used to draw upon the petitioner's databases, such location was presumed to be at the customer's mailing address, as indicated in the records of the petitioner.

In this case, Taxpayer X's sale of the Merchant Certificates, Taxpayer X Certificates and the Gift Checks, whether delivered physically or electronically, does not constitute the sale of tangible personal property. The underlying value of a Merchant Certificate, Taxpayer X Certificate or Gift Check represents the intangible right to redeem it for property or services at some future time. Further, the receipts from such sales do not represent receipts from services, rentals, royalties, sales of rights for closed-circuit and cable television transmissions. Therefore, the receipts from Taxpayer X's sale of the gift certificates and Gift Checks are characterized as "other business receipts" under section 210.3(a)(2) of the Tax Law.

Pursuant to section 21 0.3(a)(2) of the Tax Law and section 4-4.6 of the Business Corporation Franchise Tax Regulations (Article 9-A Regulations) all business receipts earned by the taxpayer in New York State are allocated to New York State. Section 4-4.6 of the Article 9-A Regulations provides that "[r]eceipts from the sale of intangible personal property included in business capital, held by the taxpayer as a dealer for sale to customers in the regular course of its business, are business receipts and are allocated to New York State if the sales were made in New York State or through a New York office of the taxpayer."

The term "dealer" means, in a popular sense, one who buys to sell; not one who buys to keep, or makes to sell. (Black's Law Dictionary 359, (5th Edition 1978))

In this case, Taxpayer X's sale of Merchant Certificates, Taxpayer X Certificates and Gift Checks are made through its Web site on the Internet. Such sales are not made through a New York office of Taxpayer X. Therefore, pursuant to section 210.3(a)(2) of the Tax Law and section 4-4.6 of the Article 9-A Regulations, the receipts from such sales are earned in New York State when the sales are made in New York State.

Taxpayer X's business activities are substantially similar to *NYMEX, supra,* and *Insurance Services, supra,* in that the receipts from the sale of the Merchant Certificates, Taxpayer X Certificates and Gift Checks are derived from the activity of the customer that accesses the Internet to purchase Taxpayer X's products from its Web site.

Accordingly, for purposes of determining the numerator of the receipts factor, Taxpayer X's sales of such gift certificates and Gift Checks are made in New York State when the location where the customer accesses Taxpayer X's Web site is located in New York State. However, from the facts submitted, it appears that Taxpayer X may not always know where its customers access the Web site. In those instances where information is not available for Taxpayer X to determine the location where the customer accesses the Web site, such location may be presumed to be at the customer's billing address, as indicated in the records of Taxpayer X.

Note, this Advisory Opinion does not address the treatment of Taxpayer X's receipts representing the additional fees paid by customers for special packaging of

Merchant Certificates, Taxpayer X Certificates and Gift Checks that are physically shipped.

> Jonathan Pessen
> Tax Regulations Specialist IV
> Technical Services Division

NOTE: The opinions expressed in Advisory Opinions are limited to the facts set forth therein.

NEW YORK ADVISORY OPINION
PETITION NO. 5000510A
April 18, 2001

On May 10, 2000, the Department of Taxation and Finance received a Petition for Advisory Opinion from Universal Music Group, 800 Third Avenue, New York, New York, 10022.

The issues raised by Petitioner, Universal Music Group, are whether:

1) Petitioner's sale of music delivered electronically over the Internet is a sale of tangible personal property subject to sales or compensating use tax.

2) Petitioner's sale of music delivered electronically over the Internet is an information service subject to sales or compensating use tax under Section 1105(c)(1) or 1105(c)(9) of the Tax Law.

3) Petitioner's sale of music delivered electronically over the Internet is an entertainment service subject to sales tax under Section 1105(c)(9) of the Tax Law.

Petitioner submitted the following facts as the basis for this Advisory Opinion.

Petitioner is a unit of Vivendi Universal, a global media and communications company. Petitioner's worldwide operations encompass the development, manufacture, marketing, sales and distribution of recorded music through a network of subsidiaries, joint ventures and licensees in 63 countries around the world.

Petitioner has established headquarters in New York for the digital distribution of music over the Internet. Through subsidiaries and joint ventures, Petitioner's business will include the development of new methods of digital distribution of music through a variety of channels such as the Internet, cable, satellite, wireless and other platforms, as well as other related functions.

Through subsidiaries and joint ventures, Petitioner plans to sell digitized music over the Internet to customers located throughout the United States, including customers located in New York. Petitioner will digitize its copyrighted catalog of music and store the digitized catalog with a third party for distribution over the Internet. Customers, using their personal computers, will order music over the Internet. Payment will be made using a credit card serviced by a third party financial institution. The music will be delivered electronically in digital form and stored on the customers' computer hard drives. Customers will then be able to play the music on their computer. In order to have the capability to download music, customers will be required to download and install software on their computer hard drives. The software is available from third party vendors over the Internet at no cost to the customer. Petitioner does not furnish any such software to its customers.

The downloaded music will remain on the customers' personal computers and is not capable of being copied to a compact disc ("CD"). It is anticipated that future technology will permit limited copying of digitized music to CDs or to a chip for play on handheld electronic devices. Under current technology, Petitioner will know whether customers are located within the United States; however, the location of a customer within a particular state or local jurisdiction is not determinable.

Applicable Law and Regulations

Section 1101(b) of the Tax Law provides, in part:

> When used in this article for purposes of the taxes imposed by subdivisions (a), (b), (c) and (d) of section eleven hundred five and by section eleven hundred ten, the following terms shall mean:
>
> (4) Retail sale. (i) A sale of tangible personal property to any person for any purpose, other than (A) for resale as such.
>
> (5) Sale, selling or purchase. Any transfer of title or possession or both, exchange or barter, rental, lease or license to use or consume (including, with respect to computer software, merely the right to reproduce), conditional or otherwise, in any manner or by any means whatsoever for a consideration, or any agreement therefor, including the rendering of any service, taxable under this article, for a consideration or any agreement therefor.
>
> (6) Tangible personal property. Corporeal personal property of any nature.

Section 1105 of the Tax Law provides, in part:

On and after June first, nineteen hundred seventy-one, there is hereby imposed and there shall be paid a tax of four percent upon:

> (a) The receipts from every retail sale of tangible personal property, except as otherwise provided in this article.
>
> (c) The receipts from every sale, except for resale, of the following services:
>
> > (1) The furnishing of information by printed, mimeographed or multigraphed matter or by duplicating written or printed matter in any other manner, including the services of collecting, compiling or analyzing information of any kind or nature and furnishing reports thereof to other persons, but excluding the furnishing of information which is personal or individual in nature and which is not or may not be substantially incorporated in reports furnished to other persons, and excluding the services of advertising or other agents, or other persons acting in a representative capacity, and information services used by newspapers, radio broadcasters and television broadcasters in the collection and dissemination of news, and excluding meteorological services.
> >
> > (9)(i) The furnishing or provision of an entertainment service or of an information service (but not an information service subject to tax under paragraph one of this subdivision), which is furnished, provided, or delivered by means of telephony or telegraphy or telephone or telegraph service (whether intrastate or interstate) of whatever nature, such as entertainment or information services provided

through 800 or 900 numbers or mass announcement services or interactive information network services. Provided, however, that in no event (i) shall the furnishing or provision of an information service be taxed under this paragraph unless it would otherwise be subject to taxation under paragraph one of this subdivision if it were furnished by printed, mimeographed or multigraphed matter or by duplicating written or printed matter in any other manner nor (ii) shall the provision of cable television service to customers be taxed under this paragraph.

Section 1110(a) of the Tax Law provides, in part:

> Except to the extent that property or services have already been or will be subject to the sales tax under this article, there is hereby imposed on every person a use tax for the use within this state on and after June first, nineteen hundred seventy-one except as otherwise exempted under this article, (A) of any tangible personal property purchased at retail...(C) of any of the services described in paragraphs (1), (7) and (8) of subdivision (c) of section eleven hundred five.

Section 526.7 of the Sales and Use Tax Regulations provides, in part:

Sale, selling or purchase. (Tax Law Sec. 1101(b)(5))

> (a) Definition. (1) The words sale, selling or purchase mean any transaction in which there is a transfer of title or possession, or both, of tangible personal property for a consideration.

> (2) Among the transactions included in the words sale, selling or purchase are exchanges, barters, rentals, leases or licenses to use or consume tangible personal property.

Opinion

Petitioner's copyrighted catalog of digitized musical recordings will be stored with a third party for distribution to Petitioner's customers over the Internet. Petitioner, through subsidiaries and joint ventures, will sell its digitized music recordings in electronic form, over the Internet to customers located within and outside of New York State. *The Stock Market Photo Agency Inc.*, Adv Op Comm T&F, November 12, 1999, TSB-A-99(48)S, concluded that "receipts from the electronic transfer of digital photographic images over the Internet represent receipts from the sale of an intangible and are not subject to sales tax." *See also New York Society of Renderers*, Adv Op Comm T&F, July 1, 1998, TSB-A-98(43)S. Based on the foregoing, Petitioner's sale of digitized music recordings over the Internet constitutes the sale of intangible property and is not subject to sales or compensating use tax under Section 1105(a) or 1110(a)(A) of the Tax Law.

Additionally, Petitioner's sale of digitized music recordings delivered electronically over the Internet does not constitute the provision of a taxable information service or an entertainment service within the meaning and intent of Section 1105(c)(1) or 1105(c)(9) of the Tax Law.

Jonathan Pessen
Tax Regulations Specialist III
Technical Services Division

NOTE: The opinions expressed in Advisory Opinions are limited to the facts set forth therein.

State	Sale of Goods	Information/Information Services	Miscellaneous Comments
Alabama	Taxable if online retail sellers are located in Alabama. Ala. Dept. of Revenue, Sales, Use & Bus. Tax Division, Frequently Asked Questions, *available at* http://www.ador.state.al.us/salestax/faq.html (last modified at Mar. 1, 2002).	"Computer exchange service" does not include the storage or retrieval of information or access to the Internet. Ala. Code § 40-21-80.	"Wholesale sales" is defined as sale of tangible personal property to licensed retail merchants, jobbers, dealers, or other wholesalers. It does not include sales to users or consumers that are not for resale. Ala. Dept. of Revenue, Sales, Use & Bus. Tax Division, Frequently Asked Questions, *available at* http://www.ador.state.al.us/salestax/faq.html (last modified at Mar. 1,2002).
Alaska	Not applicable.	Not applicable.	No statewide sales tax levied and no personal state income tax. Office of the State Assessor (AK). Sales tax ranges from 1-7% though a "typical" sales tax is 3-5%. Municipalities have the right to levy a general sales tax. Alaska Dept. of Cmty. and Econ. Dev., Office of the State Assessor, Ala. Tax Facts *available at* http://www.dced.state.ak.us/cbd/osa/taxfacts.htm.
Arizona	Considered tangible personal property within the definition of "sale" and subject to tax. Ariz. Rev. Stat. § 42-1310.01.	Information downloaded from the Internet is not subject to the Arizona Privilege/Compensating Use Tax. Ariz. State & Local Taxes Explanations, Transaction Privilege and Use Tax 22,040.	Section 42-5001-(13) of the Arizona Revised Statutes defines "sale" as any transfer of title or possession or both, exchange, barter, lease or rental, conditional or otherwise, in any manner or by any means whatever including consignment transactions and auctions of tangible property.
Arkansas	Taxable and considered tangible property. Ark. Code Ann. § 26-52-301.	Information downloaded via the Internet is not subject to tax. Ark. Code Ann. § 26-52-301.	Under Act 922 of 2001 which became effective January 1, 2002, out of state vendors are subject to the compensating use tax on orders

	processed via the Internet if the vendor holds a substantial interest, directly or through a subsidiary, in retailer maintaining locations in Arkansas and the vendor sells the same or substantially similar line of products as the Arkansas retailer under the same or substantially similar business name, or the facilities or employees of Arkansas retailer are used to promote sales or advertise to Arkansas purchasers.	Out of state vendors subject to nexus requirement to determine if they are subject to CA tax. Cal. Rev. & Tax Code section 65002(f) states that new taxes on transactions via the Internet can be imposed. Software downloaded via the Internet is exempt from tax.
California	Considered tangible property and subject to tax. The presence of a website in the state does not create nexus. Cal. Code Regs. tit. 18, § 1684.	Information downloaded via the Internet and online computer services are exempt from tax. Cal. Rev. & Tax Code, Division 2, Part 32, § 65004.
Colorado	Subject to tax. Colo. Rev. Stat. § 29-2-105.	Information downloaded from the Internet is subject to sales tax if the purchaser retains a right to maintain a copy of the information in any printed, digital or other format. The transmission is exempt if access to the information ends when the transmission is terminated. Colo. Rev. Bull. 99-26.	Colo. Dept. of Revenue compares sales of goods over the Internet to catalog sales. Therefore, if the vendor is in Colorado and the purchaser is a resident of Colorado, then sales tax applies. If the vendor is out of state, the consumer is responsible for the consumer use tax. The vendor is subject to the nexus requirement. Forty-nine Colorado municipalities collect, administer their own sales tax, and under the grandfather exception impose sales tax on Internet access. Luanne Kadlub, *Confusion Reigns Over Internet Sales Taxes*, N. Colo. Bus. Rep. (July 27, 2001).

Connecticut	Subject to tax from a computer in state. Conn. Gen. Stat. § 12-407.	Information downloaded from the Internet to computers in Connecticut exempt from tax as of July 1, 2002. Conn. Gen. Stat. § 12-408.	Sales and computer and data processing services taxes have been phased out and as of July 2, 2002 will be exempt. Canned software is considered tangible property and subject to tax. Conn. Gen. Stat. § 12-407; Conn. Gen. Stat. § 12-408.
Delaware	Not applicable.	Not specifically addressed.	No general sales tax.
District of Columbia	Taxable as tangible property. D.C. Code Ann. § 47-2001.	Information services are taxable. D.C. Code Ann. § 47-001(n)(1)(N); § 47-2201(a)(1)(K). Downloaded information from the Internet is taxable. D.C. Code Ann. § 47-2001.	Sales of goods over the Internet fall within the definition of "retail sales" or "sales at retail" and are subject to tax. D.C. Code Ann. § 47-2001.
Florida	Considered tangible property and subject to tax. Fla. Stat. § 212.02(12).	Downloading information from the Internet is excluded from the definition of "tangible property" and not subject to tax. *Florida Dep't of Revenue v. Quotron Sys., Inc.*, 615 So.2d 774 (Fla. Dist. Ct. App. 1993).	The nexus requirements must be met for out of state vendors to be subject to tax. The definition of "tangible personal property" means and includes any personal property that may be seen, weighed, touched, or in any manner perceptible to the senses. Fla. Stat. § 212.02(12).
Georgia	Subject to 4% state sales tax local jurisdictions may impose additional tax. Ga. Code Ann. § 48-8-30.	Information downloaded from the Internet is not taxable. Ga. Sales & Use Tax (Exp) 22,040 and 22,040.15.	In order for out of state vendors to be subject to the sales tax in GA, vendors must meet the nexus requirements.
Hawaii	Has a general excise tax on all business activities. Hawaii Dept. of Taxation, Tax Facts No. 96-1.	Downloaded information purchased via the Internet is taxable. Haw. Admin. Rul. § 18-237-13-06.16.	For more information on general excise tax see Tax Facts 96-1. "General Excise Tax" is imposed on the business, not the customer, and is levied on gross income from, almost all types of businesses. Dept. of Taxation, Tax Facts No. 96-1.

INTERNET/E-COMMERCE TAXATION 455

Idaho	Subject to 5% sales tax. Idaho Code § 63-3624.	Downloading information via the Internet is subject to tax. Idaho Reg. Rule 35.01.02.027.04.	A resident of Idaho not charged a sales tax, but is subject to and responsible for a 5% use tax. Idaho Code § 63-3621.
Illinois	Subject to tax. ILL. Admin. Code tit. 86, § 130.935.	Transfer of information is not taxable; however, the transfer of canned computer software via the Internet is taxable. Ill. Reg. 130.1935.	
Indiana	Treated as a sale of tangible personal property and subject to tax. Ind. Code § 6-4.1-1-13.	Transfer of canned computer software is taxable. Other information downloaded via the Internet is not taxable. Ind. Sales & Use Tax (Official Materials) (issued 01/09/1990).	The definition of "telecommunications services" which includes the transmission of message or information by or using wire cable, fiber optics, laser, microwave, radio, satellite or similar facilities. The terms do not include value added services in which computer processing applications are used to act on the form, content, code, or protocol of the information for purposes other than transmission. Ind. Code 6-2.5-4.6 §6(a).
Iowa	Considered tangible property. 23 Iowa Admin. Bull. 523.	All online contracted information services are exempt from tax. Iowa Admin. Code r. 701-18.20(5). For the period beginning March 15, 1995 until December 31,2002, information transmitted via the Internet was not taxable. Iowa Code § 422.43.	The 2000 session of the legislature excluded from the definition of taxable "sale" of tangible property any transactions delivered over the Internet. But the definition has been repealed and since December 31, 2002, canned software has been subject to tax. The exclusion amendment does not allow goods that are ordered on the Internet and then delivered by conventional means to be exempt from tax. Amendment to Ch. 18, "Taxable and Exempt Sales Determined by Method of Transaction or Usage." Iowa Administration Code; 23 Iowa Admin. Bull. 523.

INTERNET/E-COMMERCE TAXATION

Kansas	Taxable if tangible personal property. Priv. Ltr. Rul.: P-1998-76; P-1999-64; P-1999-230 Opinion Ltr. O-1999-05.	Information transmitted via the Internet is not taxable. Kan. Stat. Ann. §79-3603b.	Definition of tangible personal property includes canned computer software, and excludes custom computer software. Kan. Stat. Ann. §79-3603.
Kentucky	Taxable if tangible personal property. Ky. Rev. Stat. Ann. §139.100(3).	Information services are not taxable because they are specifically excluded from the definition of "Communications Services." Ky. Rev. Stat. Ann. §139.100(3).	
Louisiana	Taxable. La. Rev. Stat. Ann. §47:304.	Information and data services are excluded from the definition of Telecommunications Services. La. Rev. Stat. Ann. §47:301.	
Maine	Taxable. Me. Rev. Stat. Ann. tit. 36, §1861.	Charges for information downloaded from Internet are subject to sales tax—if the exchange of database or textual information is involved. Me. Rev. Stat. Ann. tit. 36, §1752.	Corporations can receive a credit if engaged primarily in high technology. Me. Rev. Stat. Ann. tit. 36, §5219-M(1-A) and 5219-M(1)(C).
Maryland	Taxable. Md. Code Ann., Tax-Gen. §11-101.	Products delivered over the Internet via download into a computer are not taxed. Such digitized products are not tangible personal property or taxable services. Md. Code Ann., Tax-Gen §11-102(a).	Sales tax does not apply to computer maintenance contracts. In *Quotron Systems*, the court held that information services provided to subscribers were not subject to tax. *Quotron Sys., Inc. v. Comptroller of the Treasury*, 411 A.2d 439 (Md. 1980).
Massachusetts	Taxable if tangible personal property. Mass. Regs. Code tit. 830, §64H.2.	Information services—sale of information to two or more purchasers—are taxable, but if it is a sale of individual information it is exempt, unless it can be incorporated into reports furnished to others. Mass. Regs. Code tit. 830, §64H.1.3(8).	Sales of custom modified canned software are exempt if the sales price of the canned software is an inconsequential element of the cost of the transaction and is separately stated. Mass. Regs. Code tit. 830, §64H.1.3(6)(b).

Michigan	Taxable if tangible personal property. Mich. Comp. Laws § 205.52.	Information delivered electronically is not taxable. Mich. Revenue Admin. Bull. 1999-5.
Minnesota	Taxable regardless of how it was obtained. Minn. Sales & Use Tax (Annotations) 21,150.10.	Information services are not taxable. Minn. Stat. § 297A.61.
Mississippi	Taxable if tangible personal property. Miss. Code. Ann. § 27-67-11.	Information services and data processing services are not subject to taxation. Minn. Sales & Use Tax (Exp.) 22,060.
Missouri	Taxable if tangible personal property. Mo. Rev. Stat. § 144.010.	Interactive computer services and electronic publishing services do not fall under telecommunications services as long as charges are separately stated on the customer's bill and on the seller's records. Mo. Rev. Stat. § 144.010(13)(a). Purchasing online financial services are not taxable because they are not specifically enumerated in the statute. Mo. Ltr. Rul. 2702.
Montana	No state sales tax.	The Retail Telecommunications Tax Act" applies to transmission of information over wire, cable, fiber optics, microwave, radio or similar facilities. No definition of information.
Nebraska	Taxable. Neb. Rev. Stat. §77-2703.	Initial connection to information service is taxable but charges for accessing online service are not taxable. Neb. Rev. Rul. 1-96-1 (May 14, 1996). Charges applied for training are non-taxable, but must be separately stated and not used as a means of avoiding tax. Neb. Rev. Stat. §77-2702.07(3). Sales of data files—including music, books and other publications—are not subject to tax when delivered electronically. Neb. Admin. R. & Regs. § 1-080.
Nevada	Taxable if tangible personal property. Nev. Admin. Code § 372.050.	No tax on Internet access if tangible personal property is an inconsequential element of the sale. Nev. Rev. Stat. § 372.105; 372.185; 374.110 and 374.190.

New Hampshire	No sales tax.	Communications service tax applies to services for transmitting or receiving signals of any nature by any electromagnetic system capable of two-way communication and includes the transmission of information by electronic or similar means. N.H. Rev. Stat. Ann. § 82-A:2.	No sales tax, but has communications service tax. This does not include automated data storage, data retrieval and processing services, use of computer time, and use of other equipment. N.H. Rev. Stat. Ann. § 1602.04(c).
New Jersey	Taxable if tangible personal property. N.J. Rev. Stat. § 54:32B-3.	Sales of Internet or online information services are not subject to the New Jersey sales and use tax. N.J. Division of Taxation. N.J. Rev. Stat. § 54:32B-3.	Data processing services are exempt. N.J. Rev. Stat. § 54:32B-6 and N.J. Admin. Code § 18:24-25.2(b)(1).
New Mexico	Taxable if tangible personal property. N.M. Stat. Ann. § 7-9-2; § 7-9-4; § 7-9-7.	When information is used in New Mexico, the fees received are taxable. N.M. Admin. Code § 2.1.18.27.	Definition of property includes licenses, thus the sale of a license to use prepackaged software is a sale subject to tax. N.M. Admin. Code § 2.1.27(B).
New York	Taxable if tangible personal property. N.Y. Tax Law § 1101.	Information services transferred electronically are subject to tax, however, it is not the information is personal or individual in nature and cannot be incorporated into reports furnished to others. N.Y. Comp. Codes R. & Regs. Tit. 20, § 527.3(b)(2).	
North Carolina	Taxable if tangible personal property. N.C. Gen. Stat. § 105-164-3(20).	Information services are specifically excluded from sales and use tax. N.C. Gen. Stat. § 105-164-4B(c)(12).	Specifically excluded from gross receipts: Internet access service, electronic mail service, electronic bulletin service and web hosting service. N.C. Gen. Stat. § 105-164-4B(c)(13).
North Dakota	Taxable if tangible personal property. N.D. Cent. Code	Sale of digitized products is taxable even if transferred by remote telecommunications	Tax includes present and future license fees, royalty fees, or program design fees included

INTERNET/E-COMMERCE TAXATION 459

Ohio	$57-39.2-01.7. Taxable if tangible personal property. Ohio Rev. Code Ann. §5741.01.	to the purchaser's computer terminal. N.D. Admin. Code §81.-04. 1-03-11-3(a)(3). Information services are taxable unless exempt under the true object test. If true object of the transaction is the receipt of exempt personal or professional services and provides no significant benefit to consumer, then not subject to tax. Ohio Rev. Code Ann. §5739.01(B)(3) and 5739.01(Y).	in purchase price. N.D. Admin. Code §81.-04. 1-03-11-3(a)(2). Ohio Department of Taxation stated that website creation charges for an Internet provider is a personal service and not subject to sale or use tax. Ohio Sales & Use Tax (Exp.) 21,540.
Oklahoma	Taxable if tangible personal property. Okla. Admin. Code §710:65-19-156(a).	Designing, creating, or storing information for a website or homepage and sales of advertising space on electronic media are exempt transactions. Okla. Admin. Code §710:65-19-156(b).	Electronic data processing services are tax exempt. Okla. Admin. Code §710:65-19-86.
Oregon	No sales tax.	Provides a tax credit for investing in electronic commerce.	
Pennsylvania	Taxable if tangible personal property. Pa. Stat. Ann. tit. 72, §7202.	Website design is subject to tax. Selling advertising space on the Internet website is not taxable. Pa. Sales & Use Tax 00-039; Pa. Sales & Use Tax 98-081.	
Rhode Island	Taxable if tangible personal property. R.I. Gen. Laws §44-18-15.	Information services provided over the Internet are not subject to taxation. R.I. Sales & Use Tax (Exp.) 22,040.	
South Carolina	Taxable if tangible personal property. S.C. Information Ltr 02-3.	Data processing services are not taxable. S.C. Code Ann. §12-36-910.	
South Dakota	Taxable personal property. S. D. Codified Laws §10-45-1.	Electronic transmission of information services via the Internet is subject to sales and use tax. S. D. Codified Laws §10-45-5.	

Tennessee	Taxable if tangible personal property. Tenn. Ltr. Rul. 00-29.	Information services are not taxable because not a sale of telecommunication services, but the charges must be listed separately. Dept. Rev.Notice 11/96.	Virtually all Internet services are taxable. Tenn. Ltr. Rul.: 97-54, 96-13, and 96-09.
Texas	Taxable if tangible personal property. Tex. Ltr. Opinion 9908618L.	Information services are taxable, however, 20% of the value of the information service is exempt from tax. Tex. Tax Code Ann. §151.0101(a)(10) and 151.351; Tex. Admin. Code §3.342(b).	Data processing services — 20% of the value of the service is exempt from tax. Tex. Tax Code Ann. §151.351; Tex. Admin. Code §3.330(b).
Utah	Taxable if tangible personal property. Utah State Tax Commission Press Release 2-99.	Information is taxable if the primary object of the sale is the sale and not the services that go into the compiling of information. Utah Admin. R. §R865-19S-92(A)(3).	
Vermont	Taxable if tangible personal property. Vt. Stat. Ann. §9701; §9771.	Information services are not taxable as long as their charges are separate from taxable charges. Vt. Stat. Ann. §9741.	Vermont Supreme Court held that pre-written software transferred on tape was tangible property subject to tax. *Chittenden Trust Co. v. King*, 465 A.2d 1100 (Vt. 1983). Repairs and services exempt if separately stated. Vt. Stat. Ann. §9701(4).
Virginia	Taxable if tangible personal property. Va. Code Ann. §58.1-602.	Charges for access to electronic information services are not taxable. Va. Public Document Rul. 98-15 and 95-30.	Charges for designing and creating an Internet website are tax exempt. Va. Public Document Rul. 00-161.
Washington	Taxable if tangible personal property. Wash. Rev. Code §82.12.020.	Information services are not taxable if they do not involve the sale or transfer of tangible personal property. Wash. Rev. Code §82.04.055.	
West Virginia	Taxable if tangible personal property. W. Va. Code §11-13B-3.	Electronic data processing services and related software are not subject to tax. W. VA. CODE §11-15-9(a)(22); W. Va. Code St. R.	

Wisconsin	Taxable if tangible personal property. Wis. Stat. §77-51.	Electronic information transmission is taxable if the transmission originates in Wisconsin and the service is charged to a Wisconsin address. Wis. Admin. Reg. 11.66.	Data processing services are not subject to tax. Wis. Admin. Code §11.71(3)(a)-(e).
Wyoming	Taxable if tangible personal property. Wyo. Stat. Ann. §39-16-101; Wyo. Stat. Ann. §39-15-103; Wyo. Stat. Ann. §39-15-101.		

§110-15-9.3.11; W. Va. Code St. R. §110-15-76.1.

462   INTERNET/E-COMMERCE TAXATION

State	Pre-packaged Software	Custom Software	Miscellaneous Comments
Alabama	Considered canned software and falls within definition of tangible property. It does not matter if the software was purchased at a retailer or downloaded, it is taxable. Ala. Reg. 810-6-1-.37(3),(4); *Wal-Mart Stores, Inc. v. City of Mobile*, 696 So.2d 290 (Ala. 1996).	Custom software programming is subject to tax. The cost of tangible media used to transfer the custom software is taxable. Ala. Reg. 810-6-1-.37(5),(6).	The Alabama Supreme Court held that canned software is taxable in *Wal-Mart Stores, Inc. v. City of Mobile*, 696 So.2d 290 (Ala. 1996). Prior to *Wal-Mart Stores*, canned software was not taxable.
Alaska	Not specifically addressed.	Not specifically addressed.	
Arizona	Considered sale of tangible personal property subject to tax under retail classification. Ariz. Reg. 15-5-154(C); *IBM Corp. v. Arizona Dep't of Revenue*, Ariz. B.T.A., Div. 2, No. 812-91-S (Jan. 28, 1992).	Considered to be sale of professional service and not subject to tax. Ariz. Reg. 15-5-154(D). Ariz. Dept. of Revenue. Ariz. Transaction Privilege Tax Rul. TPR 093.48.P.	Section 42-5001(13) of the Arizona Revised Statutes defines of "sale" as any transfer of title or possession or both, exchange, barter, lease or rental, conditional or otherwise, in any manner or by any means whatever including consignment transactions and auctions of tangible property.
Arkansas	Not specifically addressed.	Not specifically addressed.	The sale of computer software is taxable. Software is defined as "tapes, disks, cards or other devices or materials which contain instructions for a computer." Ark. Code Ann. § 26-52-304; Ark. Code Ann. § 26-53-109. The code does not distinguish between pre-packaged and custom software.
California	Sales of canned programs are taxable. Canned software is not taxable if it is transferred by remote telecommunications. Fees paid to obtain a copyright right to the program, even if a tangible copy of	Tax does not apply to the sale or lease of custom computer program, regardless of the form in which the program is transferred. Cal. Code Regs. Tit. 18, § 1502.	

	the program is transferred with the right is not taxed. Cal. Code Regs. Tit. 18, §1502 (f).	
Colorado	Prewritten software is taxable. Colo. Code Regs. §201-5.	Custom software is not taxable. Colo. Code Regs. §201-5.
Connecticut	Prepackaged software is considered tangible property subject to tax even if downloaded from a computer. Conn. Gen. Stat. §12-407; Conn. Gen. Stat. §12-408; Dep't of Rev. Serv., Announcement 94(10.1), 94(10.2), Dep't of Revenue Servs. (March 24, 1995), Dep't of Revenue Serv. (Jan 6, 1995).	Exempt as of July 1, 2002 because custom software falls under the definition of "sales and computer and data processing services." Conn. Gen. Stat. §12-408.
Delaware	Not specifically addressed.	Not specifically addressed.
District of Columbia	Taxable as a retail sale or sale at retail. D.C. Code Ann. §47-2001.	Taxable as a retail sale or sale at retail. D.C. Code Ann. §47-2001.
Florida	Pre-packaged program fully useable without modification at time of sale is considered the sale of tangible property and is taxable. Fla. Rule 12A-1.032.	Customized software is considered a service and is not taxable. Fla. Rule 12A-1.032.	If a vendor modifies prepackaged software it is considered custom software and is exempt from tax. Fla. Rule 12A-1.032. The definition of "tangible personal property" means and includes any personal property that may be seen, weighed, or touched or in any manner perceptible to the senses. Fla. Stat. §212.02(12). Electronically downloaded software does not constitute a sale of tangible personal property and is exempt from tax. *Florida Dep't of Revenue v. Quotron Sys., Inc.*, 615 So.2d 774 (Fla. Dist. Ct. App. 1993).

Georgia	Not specifically addressed.	Not specifically addressed.
Hawaii	Prepackaged software and downloaded information purchased via the Internet is taxable. Haw. Rev. Stat. § 237-29.6. Haw. Sales & Use Tax (Rul.), issued 02/12/1988.	Software transmitted out of state for use out of state is exempt from taxation. Haw. Tax Information Release No. 88-2, Haw. Dep't of Tax'n (Feb. 12, 1988).
Idaho	Subject to tax as tangible personal property. Idaho Code § 63-3616(b).	Tangible personal property is defined as "any computer program which is not custom computer software." Idaho Code § 63-3616(b). Downloaded software or information via the Internet is subject to tax. Idaho Reg. 35.01.02.027.04.
Illinois	Prepackaged software subject to tax. Ill. Admin. Code tit. 86, § 495; Ill. Admin. Code tit. 86, § 130.1935(a).	Custom software is not subject to tax. 86 Ill. Admin. Code tit. 86, 130.935	Prepackaged software is subject to tax even if it is downloaded or transmitted electronically. Ill. Admin. Code tit. 86, 130.1935(a).
Indiana	Downloaded information and prepackaged software is subject to tax. Ind. Informational Bull. No. 8, Dep't of Revenue (Feb. 9, 1990).	Indian Informational bulletin suggests custom software would not be subject to tax. Ind. Informational Bull. No. 8, Dep't of Revenue (Feb. 9, 1990).
Iowa	Considered taxable tangible property. Iowa Admin. Code § 701-18.34. Prepackaged software delivered to the person via the Internet is not taxable until December 31, 2002. 23 Iowa Admin. Bull. 523.	Considered a service not subject to tax. The charge for modification of canned software must be separately stated. Iowa Admin. Code r. 701-18.34.
Kansas	Considered tangible property subject to tax regardless of being obtained over the Internet or over the counter.	Not subject to tax, but has to be developed for a single user and charge for modification of canned software must be separately stated.	Definition of tangible personal property includes canned computer software, and excludes custom computer software.

Kentucky	Kan. Stat. Ann. §79-3602; Opinion Ltr. 0-1998-17.	Kan. Stat. Ann. §79-3602; PLR P-1999-46.	Kan. Stat. Ann. §79-3602.
Kentucky	Subject to tax. Ky. Rev. Cabinet Tax Policy 51-P170.	Not subject to tax as long as developed for an individual customer. Ky. Rev. Cabinet Tax Policy 51-P171.	
Louisiana	Taxable regardless of how obtained. La. Admin. Code § 47:301. La. Admin. Code § 361:I.4301.	Taxable as tangible property. La. Admin. Code § 361:I.4301.	Both pre-written and custom software are considered tangible property subject to taxation even if the software is transferred. *South Cent. Bell Tel. Co. v. Barthelemy*, 643 So.2d 1240 (La. Ct. App., 4th Cir. 1994).
Maine	Taxable regardless of how obtained, considered tangible personal property. Me. Rev. Stat. Ann. tit. 36, § 1752(17).	Not subject to taxation. Me. Rev. Stat. Ann. tit. 36, § 1752(17).	Corporations are entitled to receive a credit if engaged primarily in high technology, more than 50% of the time. Me. Rev. Stat. Ann. tit. 36, § 5219-M.
Maryland	Not subject to taxation, if intended for sale or to be incorporated into another program. Md. Code Ann., Tax-Gen § 11-225	Not subject to taxation. Md. Code Ann., Tax-Gen § 11-219(b)	Sales tax does not apply to computer maintenance contracts. Md. Code Ann., Tax-Gen § 11-219(c).
Massachusetts	Taxable, but not if downloaded. Mass DOR Directive 01-3 and Mass. Ltr. Rul. 00-14.	Not subject to taxation. Mass. Regs. Code tit. 830, § 64H.I.3(3).	Sale of copyright right in software is not taxable unless a master copy of the program transferred with the right. Mass. Regs. Code tit. 830, § 64H.I.3(5). Electronically transferred software is not taxable. Mass. Regs. Code tit. 830, § 64H.1.3(7).
Michigan	Considered tangible property and is taxable regardless of how it obtained. Mich. Comp. Laws § 205.51; Mich. Comp. Laws § 205.92(k).	Not subject to taxation. Mich. Comp. Laws § 205.92(k).	

Minnesota	Considered tangible property that is taxable regardless of how it obtained. Minn. Reg. 8130.9910.	Not subject to taxation. Minn. Reg. 8130.9910.
Mississippi	Taxable regardless of how it obtained. Miss. Code Ann. § 27-67-3(i); Miss. Rule Ann. 75.	Taxable as tangible property. Miss. Code Ann. § 27-67-3(i); Miss. Rule Ann. 75.
Missouri	Taxable if received in a tangible medium. Mo. Code Regs. Ann. § 144.010(13)(a). Mo. Code Regs. Ann. § 10-109.050(3)(A).	Custom made software is not taxable. Mo. Code Regs. Ann. § 10-109.050(3)(A); Mo. Code Regs. Ann. tit. 12, § 10-3.588.	Not specifically addressed, however, modifying canned programs to a customer's equipment are considered part of the sale and are taxable. Mo. Code Regs § 10-109.050(3)(C).
Montana	No sales tax.	No state sales tax.
Nebraska	Taxable regardless of how obtained. Neb. Rev. Stat. § 77-2702.07(3)(a); § 77-2703(1), Neb. Admin. R. & Regs. § 1-088.	Taxable. Neb. Rev. Stat. § 77-2702.07(3)(a); § 77-2703(1), Neb. Admin. R. & Regs. § 1-088.	Gross receipts include the gross income derived from supplying computer software, including coding, punching or otherwise producing software and charges for tapes, discs, punch cards and other items supplied by seller. Neb. Rev. Stat. § 77-2702.07(3).
Nevada	Subject to tax, applies to sale, lease, rental or license for use. Nev. Admin. Code § 372.880.	Not subject to tax; considered non-taxable professional service. Nev. Admin. Code § 372.875.	Charges for modifications to canned programs are excluded if separately stated. Nev. Admin. Code § 372.885.
New Hampshire	No sales tax.	No state sales tax.
New Jersey	If bought off the shelf, taxable, if downloaded from Internet, non-taxable. N.J. Admin. Code § 18:24-25.2(b)(2)(iv) and N.J. Rev. Stat. § 54:32B-3(a).	Not subject to tax. N.J. Admin. Code § 18:24-25.2(b)(2)(iii).	Pre-packaged software is taxed when bought from a retailer because considered tangible personal property. However, when downloaded not taxable because considered intangible personal property. N.J. Rev. Stat. § 54:32B-3.
New Mexico	Subject to tax. N.M. Admin. Code	Considered sale of a service subject to tax.	Receipts from hosting web sites can be

INTERNET/E-COMMERCE TAXATION

	§ 2.1.15(J)(1).	N.M. Admin. Code § 2.1.15(J)(1); N.M. Stat. Ann. 7-9-3, 7-9-4.	deducted from gross receipts. N.M. Stat. Ann. § 7-9-56-2 (1978).
New York	Taxable regardless of how obtained. N.Y. Tax Law § 1101(b)(6).	Not subject to tax. N.Y. Tax Law § 1101(b)(6).	Embedded software is treated as part of computer hardware. N.Y. Tech. Serv. Bureau Memo TSB-M-98(5)S.
North Carolina	Taxable if delivered on a storage medium. N.C. Gen. Stat. § 105-164.3(20).	Not subject to tax. N.C. Gen Stat. N.C. Gen. Stat. § 105-164.13(43).	Definition of tangible personal property includes software delivered on a storage medium. N.C. Gen. Stat. § 105-164.3(20).
North Dakota	Taxable regardless of how obtained. N.D. Admin. Code §§ 81-04.1-03-11(2)(b) and § 81-04.1-03-11(3)(a)(3).	Not subject to tax. N.D. Admin. Code § 81-04.1-03-11(3)(d)(1).	Designing and placing custom web pages on Internet are nontaxable services, reasoning is not tangible personal property. Sales Tax Ltr. Vol. 24, No. 4, Dec 1997.
Ohio	Taxable. Ohio Admin. Code § 5739.01(B)(3) and § 5739.01(Y) § 5703-9-46(A)(7).	Canned software modified or customized for a particular customer, is taxable if modification is no more than one-half of the sales price. Ohio Admin. Code § 5703-9-46(A)(7).	Custom applications software is not taxable. Ohio Admin. Code § 5703-9-46(A)(5).
Oklahoma	Taxable if not obtained solely via the Internet. Okla. Admin. Code § 710:65-19-156(c)(2).	Not subject to tax. Okla. Admin. Code § 710:65-19-52(g).	Advertising sales proceeds through the Internet are exempt. Okla. Admin. Code § 710:65-13-1.
Oregon	No state sales tax. Or. Rev. Stat. § 307.020.	No state sales tax. Or. Rev. Stat. § 307.020.	Provides a state tax credit for investing in electronic commerce. L.2001 § 8.
Pennsylvania	Downloaded via the Internet not taxable, taxable when tangible personal property. Pa. Sales & Use Tax 99-024.	Not addressed.	Website design is subject to tax. Pa. Sales & Use Tax 00-039 Selling advertising space on an Internet website is not taxable. Pa. Sales & Use Tax 98-081.
Rhode Island	Taxable as tangible personal property. When downloaded via Internet, not taxable. RI Reg SU 94-25.	Not subject to tax. RI Reg SU 94-25.	Licensing of canned software and any related services are taxable. RI Reg SU 94-25.

South Carolina	Taxable if tangible personal property, S.C. Code Ann. Regs. § 117-174.262, not taxable if downloaded via the Internet, S.C. Rev. RuL. 96-3.	Taxable. S.C. Code Ann. Regs. § 117-174.262.	South Carolina has a sales tax holiday effective for the year 2000 and after, applicable to the purchases of computers, printers and computer software, no sales tax. S.C. Code Ann. § 12-36-2120(57).
South Dakota	Taxable even if downloaded if would have paid tax if sold in tangible form. S. D. Codified Laws § 10-54-2.	Taxable. S.D. Admin. R. § 64:06:02:80.	All technical service transactions are subject to sales tax. S.D. Admin. R. § 64:06:02:78.
Tennessee	Taxable as tangible personal property, even if downloaded via the Internet. Tenn. Code Ann. § 67-6-102(24)(B).	Taxable. Tenn. Code Ann. § 67-6-102(24)(B).	Repair, maintenance and installation services and warranty and service contracts are taxable. Training and support services are exempt if separately stated. Dept. Rev. Notice 3/98.
Texas	Taxable as tangible personal property. Tex. Tax Code Ann. § 151.009 and Tex. Admin. Code § 3.308(b)(4).	Taxable as tangible personal property. Tex. Tax Code Ann. § 151.009 and Tex. Admin. Code § 3.308(b)(4).	Installation, repairing, maintaining, or restoring computer hardware and programs are taxable. Tex. Admin. Code § 3.308(a)(3)-(5)&(b)(2).
Utah	Considered tangible property subject to tax even if transferred electronically. Utah Admin. R. § 865-19S-92(B).	Considered a service and not subject to tax. Utah Admin. R § 865-19S-92(C).	Computer generated output is taxable if primary object of transaction is the sale and not the service of producing the output. Utah Admin. R. § 865-19S-92(A)(3).
Vermont	Taxable as tangible personal property, but if downloaded via the Internet it is nontaxable. Vermont Formal Rul. 93-08 (July 12, 1993).	Not subject to tax. Vermont Formal Ruling 93-08 and Vt. Stat. Ann. § 9701(6).	Vermont Supreme Court held that pre-written software transferred on tape was tangible property subject to tax. *Chittenden Trust Co. v. King*, 465 A.2d 1100 (Vt. 1983). Repairs and services exempt if separately stated. Vt. Stat. Ann. § 9701(4).
Virginia	Taxable as tangible personal property, Va. Code Ann. § 58.1-602, but if downloaded via the Internet it is	Not subject to tax. Va. Code Ann. § 58.1-609.5(7).	Tangible personal property used directly and exclusively in computer software research and development is exempt from tax. Va. Code

	nontaxable, Va. Rul. PD 97-405 (Oct. 3, 1997).	Ann. § 10-210-765(A). Software downloaded by modem is not taxable. Va. Rul. PD 96-72 (May 1, 1996).
Washington	Taxable as tangible personal property. Wash. St. Reg. 458-20-155. Software downloaded electronically is taxable. Wash. Rev. Code § 82.04.055.	Considered a service and not subject to sales tax. Wash. St. Reg. 458-20-155.	Custom programs are subject to the business and occupations tax. Wash. St. Reg. 458-20-155.
West Virginia	Taxable unless used to process data for others. W. Va. Code St. R. § 110-15-9.3.11.1.	Taxable unless used to process data for others. W. Va. Code St. R. § 110-15-9.3.11.1.	Electronic data processing services and related software are not subject to tax. W. Va. Code § 11-15-9(a)(22); W. Va. Code St. R. § 110-15-9.3.11.
Wisconsin	Taxable as tangible personal property even if transmitted to purchaser electronically. Wis. Stat. § 77.51(20), 11.71(2) and Wis Dept. Rev. Tax Bull. 122.	Not taxable. Wis. Admin. Code § 11.71(1)(e)(1)–(7).	There is a rebuttable presumption that any program that costs less than $10,000 is not a custom program. WIS. Admin. Code § 11.71(1)(e)(1)–(7).
Wyoming	Prewritten software is taxable as tangible personal property. Wyo. Rules Dept. Rev. § 3(d)(i).	Service of creating custom software is not subject to tax. Wyo. Rules Dept. Rev. § 14(d)(i).	

Table of Cases

A.E. Staley Manufacturing Co. v. Commissioner, 112
AAMCO Transmissions, Inc. v. Taxation and Revenue Dep't, 262–263
Abercrombie & Fitch Co. v. Hunting World, Inc., 17, 40, 44
ACME Royalty Co. v. Director of Revenue, 243, 248, 264
Adams Express Co. v. Ohio State Auditor, 429
Agro Science Co. v. Commissioner, 140
Aiken Industries, Inc. v. Commissioner, 379
Akers v. Commissioner, 385
Alabama Coca-Cola Bottling Co. v. Commissioner, 114, 116
Allied Chemical Corp. v. United States, 191, 225, 230
Allied-Signal v. Comm'r of Finance, 263
American Air Filter, Co., Inc. v. Commissioner, 404
American Dairy Queen Corp. v. Taxation and Revenue Dep't, 262, 264
American Fruit Growers, Inc. v. Brogdex Co., 21
AMF Inc. v. Sleekcraft Boats, 43–44, 46–47, 49
Andersen Consulting, LLP v. Comm'r of Revenue Services, 415, 417, 439–442
Apple Computer, Inc. v. Franklin Computer Corp., 33
Arkansas Electric Cooperative Corp. v. Arkansas Pub. Serv. Comm'n, 431–432
Arthur N. Blum, 215–216
Associated Patentees, Inc. v. Commissioner, 151, 160, 171–173, 175, 194, 231, 234
AT&T Corp. v. Excel Communications, Inc., 9
Audano v. United States, 289

Avco Financial Services Consumer Discount Co. v. Director, Division of Taxation, 263
Avery v. Commissioner, 102, 147, 333
Bailey v. Commissioner, 98
Beausoleil v. Commissioner, 190
Bell Intercontinental Corp. v. United States, 226, 230
Besser Co. v. Bureau of Revenue, 263
Best Lock Corp. v. Commissioner, 113
Best Universal Lock Co. v. Commissioner, 145
Big Four Industries, Inc. v. Commissioner, 305, 310–312, 325
Bingham's Trust v. Commissioner, 315
Blake v. Commissioner, 192, 223, 310
Bloom & Hamlin v. Nixon, 207
Bobbs-Merrill v. Straus, 207
Boulez v. Commissioner, 345, 353–354, 367–372
Bowers v. Lumpkin, 313, 319
Brawner v. Burnet, 313
Brinson v. Tomlinson, 322
Broderick v. Neale, 184
Brookfield, 43–47, 49
Brown v. Maryland, 429
Burger King Corp. v. Rudzewicz, 428
Burnet v. Logan, 51, 56, 85
Burrow-Giles Lithographic Co. v. Sarony, 22–23
Busse v. Comm'r, 197
C.R. Bard Inc. v. M3 Sys., Inc., 9
California & Hawaiian Sugar Refining Co. v. United States, 340
Canterbury v. Commissioner, 384
Cascade Designs, Inc. v. Commissioner, 193
Casebeer v. Commissioner of Internal Revenue, 277

Central de Gas de Chihuahua, S.A. v. Commissioner, 377
Central Texas Savings & Loan Assn. v. United States, 82
Champayne v. Commissioner, 203
Chappell & Co. v. Fields, 207
Checkpoint Sys., Inc. v. Check Point Software Techs., Inc., 43
Chesapeake Industries, Inc. v. Comptroller, 275
Chilton v. Commissioner, 181, 190, 210
Chittenden Trust Co. v. King, 460, 468
Ciba-Geigy Corp. v. Commissioner, 358
City Bank Farmers Trust Co. v. Helvering, 70–71
Clark Thread Co. v. Commissioner, 312
Cleveland Electric Illuminating Co. v. United States, 116
Cleveland v. Commissioner, 9, 116, 143, 145, 148, 279
Cohan v. Commissioner, 134–135
Cohen v. Commissioner, 146
Colonial Ice Cream Co. v. Commissioner of Internal Revenue, 322
Columbia Iron & Metal Co. v. Commissioner, 406
Commissioner of Internal Revenue v. Heininger, 288, 315–316
Commissioner of Internal Revenue v. Lincoln Sav. & Loan Ass'n, 288
Commissioner of Internal Revenue v. Surface Combustion Corp., 316
Commissioner of Internal Revenue v. Tellier, 289
Commissioner of Revenue v. AMIWoodbroke, Inc., 289
Commissioner v. Celanese Corp., 184, 192, 220
Commissioner v. Glenshaw Glass Co., 54, 387
Commissioner v. Groetzinger, 51, 59, 68–69, 71–72, 98, 102, 130, 298
Commissioner v. Hopkinson, 220
Commissioner v. Idaho Power Co., 81, 168
Commissioner v. Lincoln Savings & Loan Ass'n, 51, 58, 74, 81–82, 111, 319, 336
Commissioner v. Shapiro, 88
Commissioner v. Tellier, 76–77, 81, 289, 336
Commissioner v. Wodehouse, 353, 378–379
Commonwealth Edison Co. v. Montana, 430, 432
Community for Creative Non-Violence v. Reid, 7, 15, 24
Complete Auto Transit, Inc. v. Brady, 263, 273, 426, 429–431
Comptroller of the Treasury v. Armco Export Sales Corp., 272–274
Comptroller of the Treasury v. Atlantic Supply Co., 272–274
Computer Assoc. Int'l, Inc. v. Altai, Inc., 34
Consolidated Foods Corp. v. United States, 333
Coplan v. Commissioner, 203
Cory v. Commissioner, 205
Crane v. Commissioner, 55
Credit Life Ins. Co. v. United States, 406
Cripto, Inc. v. Carson, 427, 431
Crouch v. Commissioner, 140
Crown Cork & Seal, Inc. v. Comptroller of the Treasury, 247, 249
Curry v. McCanless, 263–264
D.H. Holmes Co. v. McNamara, 430
Dalzell v. Dueber Watch Case Mfg. Co., 217
Danskin, Inc. v. Commissioner, 305, 309, 317, 341
Darlington-Hartsville Coca-Cola Bot. Co. v. United States, 318
Data General Corp. v. Grumman Systems Support Corp., 7, 20, 32
Daubert v. Merrell Dow Pharms., Inc., 410
David R. Webb Co. v. Commissioner, 337–338
Deputy v. Du Pont, 70–71, 76–77, 81, 97, 145, 181, 191, 224, 337
Design Options, Inc. v. Bellepointe, Inc., 30
DHL v. Commissioner, 345, 359, 388
Diamond v. Commissioner, 254, 295
Diamond Stone-Sawing Machine Co. of New York v. Brown, 328
Diamond v. Chakrabarty, 7–8, 20
Diamond v. Diehr, 19

Dickie v. Commissioner, 98
Dickson v. Commissioner, 132
Diodes, Inc. v. Franzen, 37
District of Columbia v. Universal Computer Assocs., Inc., 437
Doyle v. Commissioner, 88
Doyle v. Mitchell Bros. Co., 87
Dreymann v. Commissioner, 220
Duesenberg, Inc. of Delaware, 92, 319
Dunavant v. Commissioner, 406
Duplate Corp. v. Triplex Safety Glass co. of North America, 316
Durkee v. Commissioner, 325–326, 329
Dymow v. Bolton, 207
Dynamic Solutions, Inc. v. Planning & Control, Inc., 35
E.H. Sheldon & Co. v. Commissioner, 114
E.I. du Pont de Nemours & Co. v. United States, 181, 191, 198, 224, 246
E.W. Bliss Co. v. United States, 227
Easter v. Commissioner of Internal Revenue, 322
Eckes v. Card Prices Update, 34–35
Eicher v. Commissioner, 371
Ekman v. Commissioner, 138
Ensley Bank and Trust Co. v. United States, 333
Enzo Biochem Inc. v. Calgene, Inc., 10
Estate of Klein v. Commissioner, 218–220, 223
Estate of Laurent v. Commissioner, 227, 231
Estate of Marton v. Commissioner, 378–379
Evans Cooling Systems, Inc. v. General Motors Corp., 9
Express, Inc. v. State of New York, 249
Falls v. Commissioner, 316, 342
Farmers Union Corp. v. Commissioner, 83
Farmers' & Merchants' Bank v. Commissioner, 90, 329, 333
Farmers' & Merchants' Bank of Catlettsburg, Ky. v. Commissioner, 329
Fawick v. Commissioner, 191, 219, 221–222, 227, 229
Feist Publications, Inc. v. Rural Telephone Service Co., 7, 22
First Nat'l Bank of Princeton v. United States, 187, 192, 227

Fischer Indus., Inc. v. Commissioner, 406
Flint v. Stone Tracy Co., 69–71
Florida Dep't of Revenue v. Quotron Sys., Inc., 454, 463
Francis v. McNeal, 89
Frank Lyon Company v. U.S., 281–282
Fred W. Amend Co. v. Commissioner, 134
Freeman v. Commissioner, 325
Freeman v. Hewit, 429, 431–432
French Broad Ice Cream Co. v. United States, 322
Gamble v. Commissioner, 206
Garrett v. Crenshaw, 319
Gaw v. Commissioner, 378
General Aniline & Film Corp. v. Commissioner, 225
General Bancshares Corp. v. Commissioner, 82–83
Genetech, Inc. v. Novo Nordisk, A/S, 10
Geoffrey, Inc. v. South Carolina Tax Commission, 243, 248, 260, 269–270, 274–275
Georator Corp. v. United States, 305, 318
Gestrich v. Commissioner, 98
Gibbons v. Ogden, 428
Goldberg v. Sweet, 430
Golsen v. Commissioner, 68, 219
Graham v. John Deere Co., 10
Green v. Commissioner, 91, 102, 143, 253–254
Greene v. Commissioner, 151, 159, 167
Gregory v. Helvering, 277, 284, 286
Haberle Crystal Springs Brewing Company v. Clarke, 89
Hapgood v. Hewitt, 11, 217
Harden M. Loan Co. v. Commissioner of Internal Revenue, 322
Harper & Row, 22–23
Harris v. Commissioner, 243, 254, 292–293, 296–298
Hartranft v. Wiegmann, 21
Hasbro Inc. v. Clue Computing, Inc., 45–46
Helvering v. Smith, 88
Helvering v. Gregory, 277, 284, 286
Higgins v. Commissioner, 70–72, 145
Holcomb v. Commissioner, 224
Holt v. Winpisinger, 26

Holtzbrinck Publishing Holdings v. Vyne Communications, 26
Hopag S.A. Holding De Participation v. Commissioner, 370
Horn v. Commissioner of Internal Revenue, 277
I.A.E., Inc. v. Shaver, 30
Illinois Tool Works v. Commissioner, 305, 312, 334
In re Alappat, 19
In re Burnham Corporation, 249
In re Karl Ziegler, 10
In re Sherwin-Williams Co., 243, 250, 279
In re Swartz, 10
In re Vaeck 10
In re Wands, 10
Inco Electroenergy Corp v. Commissioner, 305, 311, 329–330
INDOPCO, Inc. v. Commissioner, 51, 57–58, 79–80, 94–95, 112–113, 134, 337, 340, 342
Int'l Harvester Co. v. Wisconsin Dep't of Taxation, 264, 270
Inter-City Television Film Corp. v. Commissioner, 169
International Harvester Co. v. Department of Treasury, 427
International Multifoods Corp. v. Commissioner, 345, 356, 380
International Shoe Co. v. Washington, 427
Interstellar Starship Services, Ltd. v. Tchou, 7, 18, 41, 42–43, 46
Inwood Laboratories, Inc. v. Ives Laboratories, Inc., 39
J.I. Case Co. v. United States, 312
J.R. Wood & Sons, Inc. v. Commissioner, 309, 341
James v. Commissioner of Internal Revenue, 277
Jefferson-Pilot Corp. v. Commissioner, 383
Jet Spray Cooler, Inc. v. Crampton, 37
Jones v. Pepsi-Cola Co., 334
Jones' Estate v. Commissioner, 313
Kantor v. Commissioner, 102, 254, 295, 300–303
Karrer v. United States, 369
Karsten Mfg. Corp. v. Cleveland Golf Co., 9

Kassel v. Consolidated Freightways Corp. of Del., 430
Kellogg Co. v. National Biscuit Co., 40
Kewanee Oil Co. v. Bicron Corp., 20
Kimble Glass Co. v. Commissioner, 220, 369
King Instrument Corp. v. Otari Corp., 11
KIRO, Inc. v. Commissioner, 166
Klein v. Commissioner, 191, 218, 220
Kmart Properties, Inc. v. Taxation and Revenue Department, 248
Koch v. Commissioner of Revenue, 277, 284
Kollsman Instrument Corp. v. Commissioner, 140
Koons v. Commissioner, 145
Kornhauser v. United States, 313
Kronner v. United States, 220
Kueneman v. Commissioner, 181, 191, 217, 229
Lamar v. Granger, 220
Lamont v. United States, 99
LDL Research & Development II, Ltd. v. Commissioner, 254
Leloup v. Port of Mobile, 429
Leonard Pipeline Contractors Ltd. v. Comm'r, 391–292
Levy v. Commissioner, 181, 188, 208
Lewis v. Commissioner, 318
Lockhart v. Commissioner, 187, 225
Louw v. Commissioner, 102, 296
MacDonald v. Commissioner, 229
Mahurkar v. C.R. Bard, Inc., 11
MAI Sys. Corp. v. Peak Computer, Inc., 36
Marco v. Commissioner, 185, 220, 223
Marshall v. Colgate-Palmolive-Peet Co., 216
Massey Motors, Inc. v. United States, 168
Mathey v. Commissioner, 305, 310, 312, 316, 326, 387
Matter of Protest of Strayer, 437
Matter of Silver King Broadcasting of N.J., 280
Maximoff v. Commissioner, 98
Mayrath v. Commissioner, 140
McClain v. Commissioner, 190
McClellan v. Commissioner, 88
MCIIT v. Comptroller, 271–275

Medco Products Co., Inc. v. Commissioner, 309, 341
Merck & Co., Inc. v. Smith, 225, 227
Michaels v. Commissioner, 333
Micro Consulting, Inc. v. Zubeldia, 14
Midway Mfg. Co. v. Arctic Int'l, Inc., 33
Miller Brothers Co. v. Maryland, 427
Milliken v. Meyer, 428
Mills Estate, Inc. v. Commissioner, 83
Mitchell v. Commissioner, 146
Mobil Oil Corp. v. Commissioner of Taxes, 426, 430
Mobil Oil Corp. v. Pegasus Petroleum Corp., 43
Mobil Oil Corp. v. Commissioner of Taxes of Vt., 262, 426, 430
Moline Props. v. Commissioner of Internal Revenue, 286–287
Montgomery Coca-Cola Bottling Co. v. United States, 384
Moorman Mfg. Co. v. Bair, 427
Morgan's Estate v. Commissioner, 308
Motta v. Weiser, Inc., 32
Moynier v. Welch, 314
Mros v. Commissioner, 191, 219, 222
Murphy Oil Co. v. Burnet, 313–314
Muther v. United Shoe Machinery Corp., 327
Myers v. Commissioner, 184, 192, 203, 220
N. Light Tech., Inc. v. N. Lights Club, 49
Nabisco, Inc. v. Commissioner, 67, 91, 94, 110, 116
Nahey v. Commissioner, 337
National Bellas Hess, Inc. v. Department of Revenue, 263, 274, 425–427, 429–432
National Bread Wrapping Mach. Co. v. Commissioner, 184
National Geographic Society v. California Bd. of Equalization, 429
National Starch & Chemical Corp. v. Commissioner, 80–81
Nestle Holdings, Inc. v. Comm'r, 395
Newark Morning Ledger Co. v. United States, 112, 382
Newton Insert Co. v. Commissioner, 181, 194, 229
Nicholas W. Mathey, 325

Nichols v. Universal Pictures Corp., 207
NLRB v. Amax Coal Co., 25, 383
Northeast Datacom, Inc. v. Wallingford, 441–442
Northern Ind. Pub. Serv. Co. v. Commissioner of Internal Revenue, 285–286
Northern Indiana Public Service Co. v. Commissioner, 379–380
Northwestern States Portland Cement Co. v. Minnesota, 431
Norwich Pharmacal Co. v. Commissioner of Internal Revenue, 321
Nowland v. Commissioner of Internal Revenue, 322
Oak Mfg. Co. v. United States, 184, 230
Olympic & York State St. Co. v. Assessors of Boston, 284
Outten v. Commissioner, 98
Pac. Transp. Co. v. Commissioner, 337–338
Panavision Int'l L.P. v. Toeppen, 48
Parke, Davis & Co. v. Commissioner, 220
Park'N Fly, Inc. v. Dollar Park & Fly, Inc., 40
Patterson v. Texas Co., 370
Penn-Dixie Steel Corp. v. Commissioner, 406
Philadelphia v. New Jersey, 430
Philip Morris, Inc. v. Star Tobacco Corp., 115
Pickren v. United States, 184
Poole v. Commissioner, 193, 232–233
Pope Manufacturing Co. v. Gormully & Jeffery Manufacturing Co., 227
Prudential Insurance Co. v. Benjamin, 432
Prussner v. United States, 404
Public Util. Comm'n of R.I. v. Attleboro Steam & Electric Co., 432
Quill v. North Dakota, 261, 263, 273–275, 415–416, 418–420, 425–426, 428
Quotron Sys., Inc. v. Comptroller of the Treasury, 456
Rafter v. Commissioner, 342
Railway Express Agency, Inc. v. Virginia, 429
Rassenfoss v. Commissioner, 316, 321, 323
Raytheon Production Corp. v. Commissioner, 51, 57, 89, 325–326, 333

Raytheon Production Corp. v. Commissioner, 51, 57, 89, 325–326
Redler Conveyor Co. v. Commissioner, 221
Reid v. Commissioner, 220
Rice's Toyota World, Inc. v. Commissioner of Internal Revenue, 281, 285
Richmond Television Corporation v. United States, 318
Rodgers v. Commissioner, 218–223, 229
Rohmer v. Comm'r, 355
Rollman v. Commissioner, 184, 187, 226
Rooney v. United States, 391
Rouverol v. Commissioner, 185, 219, 227
Ruge v. Commissioner, 220
Rust-Oleum Corp. v. United States, 305, 310, 320
S & H, Inc. v. Commissioner, 298
Safety Tube Corp. v. Commissioner, 305, 312, 316, 342
Sager Glove Corp. v. Commissioner, 325, 332
Sanford v. Commissioner, 135
Sanford v. Poe, 429
Sanitary Farms Dairy, Inc. v. Commissioner of Internal Revenue, 323
Savage v. Hoffmann, 207
Schmitt v. Commissioner, 225
Schneider v. Commissioner, 169
Scoggins v. Commissioner, 243, 254, 298–301, 303–304
Scott v. Finney, 11
SDI Netherlands B.V. v. Commissioner, 345, 355, 375
Seagate Technology, Inc. v. Commissioner, 345, 362, 409
Seattle Brewing & Malting Co. v. Commissioner, 334
Secretary of Revenue of North Carolina v. A & F Trademark, Inc., 248
Shaffer v. Heitner, 428
Sheldon v. Metro-Goldwyn Pictures Corp., 22
Shell Development Co. v. Watson, 21
Sherwin-Williams Co. v. Commissioner of Revenue, 243, 251, 283
Sicilia Di R. Biebow & Co. v. Cox, 41
Siegel v. Commissioner, 121, 169–170
Simenon v. Commissioner, 352

Simonson v. Commissioner, 322
Smith v. Commissioner, 206, 225, 295
Smith v. Dunn, 206
Snow v. Commissioner, 71, 91, 102, 141, 145–146, 148, 253, 294–295, 300
Snyder v. Commissioner, 69–71
Sochin v. Commissioner of Internal Revenue, 285
South Carolina State Highway Dept. v. Barnwell Brothers, Inc., 428
South Central Bell Tel. Co. v. Barthelemy, 437, 439, 465
Southern Express Co. v. Spigener, 262
Spangler v. Commissioner, 318
Spector Motor Service, Inc. v. O'Connor, 429, 431
Spellman v. Commissioner, 254, 295–297
Sporty's Farm LLC v. Sportsman's Market, Inc., 48–49
Standard Parts Co. v. Peck, 217
Standard Pressed Steel Co. v. Department of Revenue of Wash., 431
State Department of Revenue v. Kennington, 439
State v. Central Computer Servs., Inc., 437–438
State Fish Corp. v. Commissioner, 311, 332–333
State Street Bank & Trust Co. v. Signature Fin. Group, Inc., 9
Stearns Magnetic Mfg. Co. v. Commissioner of Internal Revenue, 288–289
Stern v. United States, 181, 188, 203
Stilgenbaur v. United States, 88
Stokely USA, Inc. v. Commissioner, 181, 195, 236
SYL v. Comptroller of the Treasury, 243, 248–249, 271
Syms Corp. v. Commissioner of Revenue, 243, 250, 275
Taylor v. Commissioner, 220
TCPIP Holding Co. v. Haar Communications, Inc., 44, 49
Tomerlin Trust v. Commissioner, 195
The Trade-Mark Cases, 22
Trandes Corp. v. Guy F. Atkinson Co., 37
Tribune Publishing Co. v. Commissioner, 169

TSR, Inc. v. Commissioner, 140
Two Pesos, Inc. v. Taco Cabana, Inc., 7, 17, 39
Tyler Pipe Industries, Inc. v. Washington State Dept. of. Revenue, 426, 431
Tyler v. United States, 320
United Shoe Machinery Corporation v. Mathey, 316
United States v. Carruthers, 185, 227
United States v. Dubilier Condenser Corp., 216
United States v. Estate Preservation Servs., 278
United States v. Hilton Hotels, 338, 340
United States v. Mississippi Chemical Corp., 82
United States v. Pyne, 70–71
United States v. Safety Car Heating & Lighting Co., 326, 328
Universal Analytics, Inc. v. MacNeal-Schwendler Corp., 37
Universal Oil Co. v. Globe Co., 20
Universal Pictures Co. v. Harold Lloyd Corp., 207
Urquhart v. Commissioner, 305, 308, 314, 342
Vanicek v. Commissioner, 134
VGS Corp. v. Commissioner, 333
Virginia v. Imperial Coal Sales Co., Inc., 262
Virtual Works, Inc. v. Volkswagen of America Inc., 47–49
Vitale v. Commissioner, 91, 98, 126
W.W. Sly Manufacturing Company v. Commissioner, 387
Wal-Mart Stores, Inc. v. City of Mobile, 415, 417, 437, 462
Warner Bros. Pictures v. Columbia Broadcasting System, 207
Waterman S.S. Corp. v. Comm'r, 391
Waterman v. Mackenzie, 51, 54, 84–85, 184, 201–202, 219–220, 222–223, 227, 230, 317, 391
Watson v. Commissioner, 181, 184–185, 200, 220
Watson v. United States, 181, 220
Wedgwood Homes, Inc. v. Lund, 48
Welch v. Helvering, 51, 57, 72–73, 76, 81, 97, 314, 316
Western Live Stock v. Bureau of Revenue, 429
Wheeling Steel Corp. v. Fox, 262
Whelan Associates, Inc. v. Jaslow Dental Laboratory, Inc., 209–210
Whipple v. Commissioner, 70, 147
Wildman v. Commissioner, 169–171
Williams v. McGowan, 51, 56, 63, 87
Williams v. United States, 134
Wise v. Commissioner, 318
Wodehouse v. Commissioner, 353, 378–379
Woodward v. Commissioner, 338, 340
Yosha v. Commissioner of Internal Revenue, 284
Zink v. United States, 295–297
Zorniger v. Commissioner, 385

Table of Statutes, Regulations, and Rulings

Internal Revenue Code (Title 26, U.S.C.)

1, 51, 60, 181, 186, 348, 351, 353, 354
1(a), 51
1(b), 51, 186
1(c), 51, 162, 186, 348
1(d), 51, 186
1(e), 51
1(f), 51
1(h), 51, 61, 181, 186
1(i), 51, 181, 186
1(i)(2), 51
11, 51, 60, 162, 348, 351, 353, 354
11(a), 51
11(b), 51
41, 64, 93, 106-110
41(a)(1), 106
41(a)(2), 106
41(b), 106
41(c), 106
41(d), 65, 91, 106-110
41(d)(1)(B)(i), 106
41(d)(1)(C), 107-108
41(d)(4), 108
41(d)(4)(A), 108
41(d)(4)(E), 109
55(b)(2), 104
56(b)(2), 91, 104, 243, 254
56(b)(2)(D), 105
59(e), 105
59(e)(1), 91, 105
59(e)(2), 105
59(e)(2)(B), 91
59(e)(6), 91, 105
61(a), 51, 54
61(a)(3), 54
61(a)(6), 54, 161
61(a)(7), 162, 181, 197, 248
63, 57
102, 54, 342
104, 54
108, 54
132, 167, 356
162, 52, 57, 93-94, 97-99, 101-102, 105, 126, 130, 134, 145, 156, 161, 249, 287-288, 293-294, 300, 305, 307, 340
162(a), 51, 57, 59, 68-69, 71, 73-74, 76-77, 79-83, 91, 93-94, 97-98, 110-113, 130, 133, 142, 151, 249, 289, 302, 317-318, 336
162(a)(3), 230
164(a), 345, 350
165, 51, 57
165(a), 51
165(b), 51
165(c), 51, 57, 59
167, 51-52, 55, 59, 61, 101, 104-106, 121, 138-139, 151-152, 157-160, 163, 175, 181, 189-190, 193-194, 228, 234, 236, 319
167(a), 51, 59, 91, 144, 151, 157, 164-165, 168, 174-175, 181, 229
167(b), 59, 163, 165, 168
167(c), 51, 91, 151, 181
167(c)(1), 51
167(f), 51, 91, 149, 151, 158
167(f)(1), 51, 59, 96, 149
167(g), 51, 59, 65, 91, 151, 158-159

167(g)(1)(C), 159
167(h)(2), 51, 59, 91
168, 59, 155
168(a), 59
168(b)(1), 59, 151, 155
168(c), 59, 151, 155
168(e)(3)(B)(iv), 59, 151, 155
168(i)(2), 59, 151, 155
170, 181, 199
170(a), 181, 199
170(a)(2), 406
170(b), 199
170(c), 199
170(e)(1)(A), 181, 199
170(e)(1)(B), 199
174, 66, 71, 91, 93, 99-106, 135, 137-146, 148-149, 181, 194, 253-257, 293-298, 300, 302, 304
174(a), 92, 99, 101, 103-105, 138-139, 143, 149, 188, 253
174(a)(1), 71, 99, 141-142, 144-145, 292-294, 296, 300
174(a)(2)(A), 103
174(a)(3), 103
174(b), 92, 103-105, 149, 188
174(b)(1), 99, 103-105
174(b)(2), 104
174(c), 101, 137
174(e), 99, 103
179, 111
183, 51, 59, 91, 98, 102, 130
183(a), 51, 59, 98, 102
183(b), 59, 98, 102
183(c), 51
183(d), 51, 98
197, 51-52, 59, 61, 65, 91, 96, 104-106, 149, 151-152, 154-158, 160-161, 176-178, 183, 186-190, 194, 199
197(a), 51, 59, 91, 105, 151, 154-156, 177
197(b), 91, 151, 154
197(c), 149, 177
197(c)(1), 151, 154, 156
197(c)(1)(A), 65
197(c)(2), 105
197(d)(1), 151
197(d)(1)(C), 154
197(d)(1)(F), 105, 154
197(e), 157

197(e)(1), 151, 155
197(e)(3), 91, 105, 151
197(e)(3)(B), 154
197(e)(4), 91, 105, 151, 154
197(e)(4)(D), 155, 161
197(f)(1), 181, 186
197(f)(2), 181
197(f)(2)(A), 199
197(f)(4)(C), 151
197(f)(7), 51, 61, 181, 188, 190, 194
212, 59, 91, 151, 156, 305, 307, 343
243, 243, 252
243(a)(1), 252
243(a)(3), 252
246, 252
246A, 252
262, 134
262(a), 51
263, 58, 79, 81-82, 94-96, 124, 154, 159, 305, 307, 319, 323, 340
263(a), 51, 57, 91, 94, 99, 111
263(a)(1), 81-82, 337
263(a)(1)(B), 99
263A, 94, 96-97, 101, 117-125
263A(a), 51, 57, 91, 96, 118
263A(a)(2)(A), 96
263A(b), 96, 118-121, 123
263A(b)(1), 91, 118
263A(c)(2), 91, 99
263A(f), 121
263A(h), 91, 97, 101, 105, 117-120
263A(h)(1), 118
263A(h)(2), 97, 118-120
263A(h)(3), 97, 118-120
263A(h)(3)(A), 118-120
263A(h)(3)(C), 118
267(a), 185-186
267(a)(1), 181
267(b), 181, 193
267(b)(1), 186
267(b)(2), 186
267(b)(3), 186
267(b)(10), 186
267(b)(11), 186
267(b)(12), 186
267(c), 181
267(c)(4), 125, 186
267(f), 186
274(d), 59, 126, 130, 135

275(a)(4), 345, 350
280A, 134
331, 243, 252
332, 252
332(b), 229, 243
332(b)(1), 252
332(b)(2), 252
332(b)(3), 252
334(b), 236, 243, 252
334(b)(1), 252
334(b)(2), 230
336, 252
337, 243, 252
338, 151, 155, 157
351, 55, 80, 185, 197-199, 246-247, 357-358
351(a), 181, 197, 243, 246
351(b), 246
357(a), 246
357(c), 246
358, 199
358(a), 181
358(a)(1), 243, 247
362(a), 243, 247
367, 357-358
367(a), 357
367(d), 345, 358
368(c), 197, 247
446, 150
446(b), 165-166
446(e), 149
453, 51, 56, 181, 196
453(a), 51, 56, 181, 196
453(b), 51, 181
453(b)(1), 51, 56, 181, 196
453(c), 51, 56, 181, 196
453(d), 51, 56, 181, 196
453(i), 181, 196
461(a), 165
465, 243
469, 243, 254-255
469(a)(2), 255
469(b), 255
469(c)(5), 255
469(h)(1), 255
469(h)(2), 255
469(g), 255
481, 150

482, 243, 250-251, 345-346, 358-360, 363, 390-392, 394-397, 399-402, 404, 409
483, 181, 196-197
483(a), 181
483(b), 181
483(c)(1), 181, 197
483(d)(4), 181, 197
541, 151, 162
542(a)(1), 151, 162
542(a)(2), 151, 162
543(a)(1), 151, 162
543(a)(4), 151, 162
543(d), 151, 162, 349
545(a), 151, 162
547, 151, 162
551, 345, 349
552, 345, 349
552(a)(1), 345, 349
552(a)(2), 345, 349
553(a)(1), 345, 349
561(a), 151, 162
701, 243, 256
704(a), 243, 256
704(b), 243, 257
704(c)(1)(B), 257
704(d), 243, 257
705, 256
705(a), 243, 257
707(b), 181, 186, 193-194
707(b)(2), 194
707(b)(3), 194
721, 181, 185, 197, 199, 243, 256
722, 181, 199, 243, 256-257
723, 243, 256
731(a), 257-258
731(a)(1), 243, 257-258
731(b), 257
732(a)(1), 243, 257-258
733, 243, 257
736, 258
737, 257
741, 243, 257-258
742, 243, 258
751, 243, 257-258
752, 257
752(a), 243, 257
752(d), 243, 258
761, 146

761(d), 258
861, 356
861(a)(4), 345, 354, 370, 372, 374-375, 377, 379
861(b), 345, 354
862(a)(4), 345, 373-374
864(b), 345, 352, 354
864(c), 345, 352
865, 355, 382-384
865(a), 345, 355
865(a)(1), 382
865(d), 345, 355, 382
865(d)(1), 382, 386
865(d)(1)(A), 382
865(d)(2), 382, 384
865(d)(3), 356, 382
865(g), 345, 355
871(a), 345, 351, 353-354, 387
871(a)(1), 387-388
871(a)(1)(A), 375, 379
871(a)(1)(D), 353
871(b), 345, 351, 354, 374
872, 345, 354
873, 345, 356
881, 345, 351
881(a), 353, 377-378, 380
882, 345, 351-352, 356
894, 369, 378
901(b), 350
904, 386
904(a), 350, 381, 386
904(c), 351
904(d), 345, 351
951, 349
951(a), 345, 349
951(b), 345, 349
954, 350
954(c), 345, 350
957(a), 345, 349
963, 404-405
1001, 54
1001(a), 51, 55, 181, 185, 187, 197
1001(b), 51, 55, 181, 185
1001(c), 51, 181, 185
1001(d), 51, 181
1011(a), 51
1012, 51, 55, 151, 181, 185
1016, 55, 185
1016(a)(1), 51

1016(a)(2), 51, 59, 181
1031, 185
1032, 243
1041, 185
1059, 252
1060, 56, 63, 156
1060(a), 51
1060(b), 51
1060(c), 51, 151, 156
1211, 51, 57, 181, 186
1212, 186
1212(a)(1), 51, 181
1212(b), 181
1212(b)(1), 51
1221, 61, 63, 65, 88, 187-188, 194, 203, 208, 229, 319
1221(a)(1), 51, 61, 181, 187, 219
1221(a)(2), 51, 61, 63, 181, 187, 189
1221(a)(3), 51, 62, 181, 188, 199, 208-210
1222, 51, 61, 63, 181, 187, 194, 224
1222(3), 61-62, 187, 189
1222(11), 61, 187
1223, 62, 189
1223(1), 199, 243, 247, 256
1223(2), 62, 181, 189, 243, 247, 256
1231, 62-63, 187-190, 194, 199, 224, 228-229, 247
1231(a), 181, 228-229
1231(a)(1), 51, 62
1231(a)(2), 51, 62
1231(a)(3), 51
1231(a)(3)(A)(i), 62, 189
1231(a)(3)(A)(ii), 62
1231(a)(4)(C), 62
1231(b), 228
1231(b)(1), 51
1231(b)(1)(A), 62, 181, 189
1231(b)(1)(B), 62, 181, 189
1231(b)(1)(C), 62, 181, 189, 199
1235, 61, 65, 161, 176-178, 181, 185, 189-194, 197, 199, 203, 215-224, 228-229, 231-234
1235(a), 177, 190, 218, 221, 224, 231-234
1235(a)(1), 151
1235(b), 191
1235(d), 193, 232
1235(d)(2), 193

1239, 181, 189, 193
1239(a), 193
1239(b), 193
1239(c), 193
1239(e), 193
1245, 63, 183, 189, 194, 196, 229-230, 234-236
1245(a), 63, 194
1245(a)(1), 51, 181
1245(a)(2), 181
1245(a)(3), 51, 63, 181, 194
1253, 61, 161, 189, 195, 199, 237-242
1253(a), 181, 195, 237-242, 383
1253(b), 181
1253(b)(1), 383
1253(b)(2), 195, 238-242
1253(b)(2)(A), 238-242
1253(b)(2)(C), 238
1253(c), 181, 195
1253(d), 151, 237, 242, 383-384
1253(d)(1), 156, 161
1274, 196-197
1274(a), 181

1274(b), 181, 197
1274(c)(1), 181
1274(c)(1)(B), 197
1274(c)(3)(C), 181, 197
1274(c)(3)(E), 181, 197
1274(d), 181, 197
1441, 345, 353, 374, 379
1441(a), 375, 378, 389
1441(b), 374-375, 377
1442, 345, 353, 377
1442(a), 378-380
6110(k)(3), 179
6651(a)(1), 378
6662, 397
6662(e)(1)(B), 397
6662(h), 397
6664(c), 397
7701(a)(2), 146
7701(a)(3), 345, 348
7701(a)(4), 345, 348
7701(b), 345, 347
7805(a), 65
7852(d), 345, 357, 369

Treasury Regulations

1.41-4, 91, 106-110
1.41-4(a)(3), 91, 106-107
1.41-4(a)(4), 91, 107
1.41-4(a)(3)(i), 106
1.41-4(a)(3)(iv), 107
1.41-4(a)(5), 107-108
1.41-4(a)(6), 91, 108, 110
1.41-4(c)(2), 108
1.41-4(c)(6), 108-110
1.41-4(c)(6)(vi), 109-110
1.61-6(a), 51, 54
1.162-1, 112-114, 116, 308
1.167(a)-1, 51, 91, 151, 158, 181
1.167(a)-1(b), 51, 91, 151, 158
1.167(a)-3, 51, 59, 91, 96, 151, 157, 165, 175, 181, 188
1.167(a)-6, 165, 228-229
1.167(a)-10(b), 165
1.167(a)-14, 51, 151, 157, 161
1.167(a)-14(c)(2), 51, 151, 161
1.167(a)-14(c)(3), 51, 151, 161
1.167(b)-1, 51, 91, 151, 158

1.167(b)-1(a), 51, 91, 151, 158
1.170A-1(c)(1), 181, 199
1.170A-1(c)(2), 181
1.174-1, 91
1.174-2, 66, 99-101, 103, 107, 137-142, 145, 148, 297, 300
1.174-2(a), 66, 99-101, 107, 137-142, 145, 148, 297, 300
1.174-2(a)(1), 66, 99-100, 107, 137, 140
1.174-2(a)(2), 99, 101, 137, 140, 142, 145, 148, 297, 300
1.174-2(a)(3), 100-101, 137-138, 140-141
1.174-2(a)(3)(i), 100, 138
1.174-2(a)(3)(ii), 100
1.174-2(a)(3)(iii), 100
1.174-2(a)(3)(iv), 100
1.174-2(a)(3)(v), 100, 141
1.174-2(a)(3)(vii), 101
1.174-2(a)(4), 100-101, 138-140
1.174-2(a)(8), 101
1.174-2(a)(9), 101

1.174-2(b)(1), 101, 103, 138-139
1.174-2(b)(2), 101, 138-139
1.174-2(b)(3), 101, 138-139
1.174-2(b)(4), 101, 138-139
1.174-3, 103-104
1.174-3(a), 103-104
1.174-3(b), 103-104
1.174-3(b)(1), 103
1.174-4, 103-105
1.174-4(a)(1), 103
1.174-4(a)(2), 104-105
1.174-4(a)(3), 104
1.174-4(a)(4), 104
1.174-4(a)(5), 104
1.174-4(b)(1), 103-104
1.174-4(b)(2), 104-105
1.183-1(b), 51, 59
1.183-2(a), 91, 98, 102
1.183-2(b), 59, 91, 98, 102, 131-133
1.183-2(b)(6), 132
1.183-2(b)(7), 133
1.183-2(b)(9), 133
1.197-2(a), 91, 105, 151, 155-157, 160-161, 177, 194, 199
1.197-2(a)(1), 105, 151, 155-156
1.197-2(a)(3), 91, 105, 160-161, 177
1.197-2(b)(1), 105, 151, 154-155, 161
1.197-2(b)(4), 149, 151, 154
1.197-2(b)(5), 151, 154
1.197-2(b)(10), 91, 105, 151, 154
1.197-2(b)(11), 151, 160, 177
1.197-2(c), 91, 105, 151, 154-157
1.197-2(c)(4), 105, 151, 154-155
1.197-2(c)(4)(iv), 154
1.197-2(c)(5), 151, 154
1.197-2(c)(7), 91, 105, 151
1.197-2(d)(2), 91, 105
1.197-2(e)(1), 154-155
1.197-2(e)(2), 155
1.197-2(e)(2)(i), 155
1.197-2(e)(2)(ii)(A), 155
1.197-2(e)(2)(ii)(B), 155
1.197-2(e)(2)(ii)(C), 155
1.197-2(e)(5), 154-155
1.197-2(f), 105, 154, 156-157, 160-161, 177-178, 194, 199
1.197-2(f)(1), 105, 154, 156, 161
1.197-2(f)(1)(i), 156
1.197-2(f)(1)(ii), 156, 161

1.197-2(f)(2), 157
1.197-2(f)(2)(i), 157
1.197-2(f)(2)(ii), 157
1.197-2(f)(3), 160-161, 177-178
1.197-2(f)(3)(ii), 160-161
1.197-2(f)(3)(ii)(A), 160
1.197-2(f)(3)(ii)(B), 161
1.197-2(f)(3)(iii), 161, 177-178
1.197-2(g)(2)(ii), 194, 199
1.197-2(g)(7), 155
1.212-1, 305, 307-308, 343
1.212-1(k), 305, 307-308, 343
1.263(a)-1(b), 51, 57, 91, 94
1.263-2, 307, 340, 342
1.263(a)-2(a), 51, 57, 91, 94, 151, 154, 305, 307, 337
1.263-2(c), 342
1.263A-1(c)(3), 118
1.263A-1(e)(2), 91, 96
1.263A-1(e)(3), 91, 96
1.263A-2(a), 96, 118-119
1.263A-2(a)(1)(i), 118
1.263A-2(a)(2), 96, 118-119
1.263A-2(a)(2)(i), 118
1.263A-2(a)(2)(ii), 96, 118-119
1.263A-2(a)(2)(ii)(A)(2), 96, 118-119
1.263A-2(a)(2)(ii)(B)(2), 96
1.274-5T(a), 135
1.274-5T(c)(1), 59, 135
1.332-3, 243, 252
1.132-4, 243, 252
1.351-1(a)(1), 243, 247
1.367(d)-1T(c)(1), 345, 358
1.367(d)-1T(c)(3), 345, 358
1.446-1(e), 149-150
1.446-1(e)(2)(ii)(b), 150
1.446-1(e)(3)(ii), 149
15A.453-1(c)(1), 51, 56, 181
15A.453-1(c)(2), 51, 56, 181, 196
15A.453-1(c)(2)(i), 51, 56, 181, 196
15A.453-1(c)(2)(i)(A), 51, 56, 181, 196
15A.453-1(c)(3), 51, 56, 181, 196
15A.453-1(c)(3)(i), 51, 56, 181, 196
15A.453-1(c)(4), 51, 56, 181, 196
15A.453-1(d)(2)(i), 56, 196
15A.453-1(d)(2)(iii), 56, 196
1.469-5T(a), 255
1.469-5T(a)(1), 255
1.469-5T(a)(5), 255

1.469-5T(a)(6), 255
1.469-5T(e)(2), 255
1.482-1, 243, 250, 345, 358, 360, 391, 399-400, 402-403
1.482-1(a)(1), 243, 250, 345, 358, 391, 400
1.482-1(b)(1), 243, 250, 345, 391, 400
1.482-1(i)(5), 360, 402
1.482-2(b)(4), 409
1.482-2(b)(5)(ii), 409
1.482-2(b)(6)(i), 409
1.482-2(d)(4), 400, 409-412
1.482-4, 251, 345, 358-360, 394, 399, 403
1.482-4(a), 251, 345, 358-359, 394, 399, 403
1.482-4(b), 251, 359
1.482-4(c), 251, 345, 358, 360
1.482-4(c)(1), 251, 358
1.482-4(f)(3)(i), 359
1.482-4(f)(3)(ii)(A), 359, 394
1.482-4(f)(3)(ii)(B), 359
1.482-4(f)(3)(iii), 359-360, 394
1.482-4(f)(3)(iv), 359
1.482-5, 251
1.482-5(a), 251
1.482-6, 403
1.482-7, 359-363, 398, 400, 402-404, 406-409
1.482-7(a)(1), 359-361, 363, 398, 400, 402-403, 407-408
1.482-7(a)(2), 360-363, 402-403, 407
1.482-7(b), 360-363, 402-403, 407
1.482-7(b)(1), 360-361, 402-403, 407
1.482-7(b)(2), 361, 402
1.482-7(b)(3), 362-363
1.482-7(b)(4), 363, 402-403
1.482-7(c)(1), 360-361, 398, 402-403, 407-408
1.482-7(c)(1)(i), 360, 403
1.482-7(c)(1)(ii), 360, 403
1.482-7(c)(1)(iii), 360-361, 398, 403, 407-408
1.482-7(c)(1)(iv), 360
1.482-7(c)(2), 360
1.482-7(d)(1), 362
1.482-7(e), 362
1.482-7(f), 360-363
1.482-7(f)(1), 360-362
1.482-7(f)(2), 360, 362
1.482-7(f)(2)(ii), 362
1.482-7(f)(3)(i), 362
1.482-7(f)(3)(ii), 360
1.482-7(f)(3)(iv)(B), 363
1.482-7(g), 363, 404
1.482-7(g)(1), 363
1.482-7(g)(2), 363
1.482-7(g)(3), 363, 404
1.482-7(g)(4), 363
1.482-7(g)(5), 404
1.482-7(i), 360-362, 403
1.482-7(j), 360-361, 398, 403-404, 406-409
1.482-7(j)(1), 360-361, 398, 403, 407
1.482-7(j)(2), 403, 407-408
1.482-7(j)(2)(i), 403
1.482-7(j)(3), 360-361, 403-404, 407-409
1.482-7(k), 402
1.483-1(a)(2)(ii), 181, 197
1.551-2, 345
1.704-1(b)(2), 243, 257
1.751-1(a), 258
1.752-2, 243, 257
1.752-3, 243, 257
1.861-8, 345
1.861-17(a)(4), 357
1.861-17(b)(1), 357
1.871-7(b)(2)(I), 387
1.881-2(b), 377
1.911-2(b), 345, 355
1.1001-2, 51, 181
1.1001-2(a)(1), 51, 181
1.1060-1(b)(1), 51, 151, 156
1.1060-1(b)(2), 51, 151, 155-156
1.1060-1(b)(2)(i)(A), 155
1.1060-1(b)(2)(i)(B), 155
1.1060-1(c), 51, 56, 63, 151, 156
1.1221-1(c)(1), 51, 62, 181, 188, 209-210
1.1221-1(c)(3), 62, 181, 188
1.1235-1(b), 181, 193, 224
1.1235-1(c)(2), 181, 190, 215
1.1235-2(a), 178, 191-192
1.1235-2(b), 178, 191-192, 218, 224, 229
1.1235-2(b)(1), 178, 191-192, 218, 224
1.1235-2(b)(1)(i), 224
1.1235-2(b)(2), 178, 192
1.1235-2(b)(2)(i), 192
1.1235-2(b)(2)(ii), 192

1.1235-2(b)(3), 178, 192
1.1235-2(b)(4), 178, 192
1.1235-2(d), 191
1.1235-2(d)(2), 191
1.1239-1(b), 181

1.1239-1(c)(5), 181
1.1441-2(a), 374-375, 377, 387
1.1245-3(b), 51, 63, 181, 194, 230, 235
1.1245-3(b)(2), 181, 235
301.7701-3, 146

Proposed Treasury Regulations

1.41-4, 91, 106-110
1.41-4(a)(3), 107
1.41-4(a)(3)(iii), 107
1.41-4(a)(4), 107
1.41-4(a)(5), 107-108
1.41-4(a)(5)(ii), 108
1.41-4(a)(5)(iv), 108
1.41-4(a)(6), 108
1.41-4(c)(2), 108
1.41-4(c)(6), 109-110
1.41-4(c)(6)(vi), 109-110
1.167(a)-3, 51, 91, 96
1.167(a)-3(b), 96
1.167(n)-1, 151, 159
1.167(n)-3, 151, 159
1.167(n)-4, 151, 159
1.167(n)-7, 151, 159
1.167(n)-3(c), 159
1.167(n)-4(b)(1), 159

1.167(n)-4(b)(2), 159
1.167(n)-4(d)(1)(i), 159
1.167(n)-4(d)(2), 159
1.167(n)-4(d)(3), 159
1.167(n)-4(d)(4), 159
1.263(a)-4, 51, 91, 95-96, 154
1.263(a)-4(b), 58
1.263(a)-4(b)(2), 95
1.263(a)-4(b)(3), 95
1.263(a)-4(b)(2)(i)(D), 95
1.263(a)-4(b)(2)(ii), 95
1.263(a)-4(c), 151
1.263(a)-4(c)(1), 154
1.263(a)-4(d)(1), 95
1.263(a)-4(d)(5), 95
1.263(a)-4(e)(1)(i), 96
1.263(a)-4(e)(3), 96
1.263(a)-4(f)(1)(i), 96
1.263(a)-4(f)(5), 96

Revenue Rulings

54-56, 193
54-409, 202-203
55-58, 202-203
55-706, 188
58-74, 103
58-353, 203, 206
58-356, 103
59-210, 193
60-226, 181, 184, 202, 342
60-358, 121, 151, 158, 163, 165-166, 168-170
62-141, 188
64-56, 13, 184, 198
64-206, 345, 356, 386
64-273, 165, 169
67-136, 151, 160, 175
68-443, 345, 355, 372

69-156, 198
69-482, 193, 197, 224, 228
71-177, 151, 155, 158, 162
71-564, 13, 184, 198
72-232, 345, 355, 373
73-275, 139
75-202, 342
76-324, 103
78-28, 166
78-328, 181, 192, 228
78-389, 340
79-285, 151, 157-158, 164
80-15, 356
80-362, 345, 355, 374, 379
85-186, 188, 194
89-23, 116
92-80, 58, 94, 100, 113-114, 116

Revenue Procedures

69-21, 95, 149
97-50, 67, 94
98-39, 116

99-49, 103-104, 150
2000-50, 91, 95, 100, 148

Miscellaneous

G.C.M. 36,922, 246
G.C.M. 38490, 341-342
P.L.R. 8022002, 342
Notice 88-62, 91, 97, 101, 105, 121
Notice 88-123, 401
P.L.R. 8831001, 342
Notice 89-67, 120
T.A.M. 9643003, 91, 97, 117

A.O.D. 1999-012, 67, 116
F.S.A. 199925012, 305, 307, 309-310, 339
F.S.A. 200003010, 362
F.S.A. 200011021, 345, 361, 398
Notice 2001-19, 106
F.S.A. 200125019, 91, 100, 135
P.L.R. 200137013, 151, 161, 176

Index

Acquiring intellectual property liability 312, 334–339
Acquisitions
   asset acquisitions (see asset acquisitions)
   stock acquisitions 155–157
Advertising costs
   deductibility of 58, 94, 100
Alternative minimum tax considerations 63–64, 104–105
Amortization
   adjustments to basis 55, 185
   computer software 96, 105, 154–155, 157–158
   contingent payments 157, 160
   contingent serial payments 156
   copyrights 96–97, 105, 154, 157
   creation costs 105
   domain names 152
   generally 105, 154–160
   income-forecast method 105, 157–160
   intellectual property contributed to a business 199
   methods 105, 154–160
   patents 96, 105, 154, 157
   purchase costs 154–160
   recapture 63, 194
   straight–line method 157–158
   trademarks 96, 105, 154–157
   trade names 96, 105, 154–157
   trade secrets 96, 105, 154
Asset acquisitions
   amortization of purchase costs 154–160
   capitalization of purchase costs 154
   computer software 154–155, 157
   copyrights 154, 157
   domain names 152
   generally 153
   licenses of 160–161
   patents 154, 157
   trademarks 154–156
   trade names 154–156
   trade secrets 154
Awards of attorneys' fees and costs 311
Basis 55, 58–59, 156–157, 159, 185
Capital assets
   defined 187–188
   Gains and losses of (see Capital gains and losses)
   quasi-capital assets 188, 189–190
Capital gains and losses
   capital asset 61, 187–188
   charitable contributions of capital assets 199
   generally 61–63, 186–195
   holding period 62, 189
   limitation of capital loss deductions 57, 186
   preferential rate treatment for long-term capital gains 60–61, 186
   recapture 63, 194
   sale or exchange requirement 61, 187
   section 1231 property 62–63, 189–190
Capitalization
   computer software 94–95
   copyrights 95–97
   domain names 52, 152
   generally 57–58, 94–97, 153–154
   inapplicability to research and experimental expenditures 99
   patents 99
   qualified creative expenses 97
   trademarks 95
   trade names 95
   trade secrets 96
   uniform capitalization rules 57, 94, 96–97, 99

Cascading royalties 855
Character of gains and losses
    (see Capital gains and losses)
Charitable contributions of intellectual
    property 199
Computer software
    acquired computer software 154–155,
        157
    amortization 96, 105, 154–155,
        157–158
    bundled software 155, 158
    capital gains and losses (see Capital
        gains and losses)
    capitalization 94–95
    chart of states' sales and use taxation
        462–469
    contributions to charity 199
    copyright infringement 32–36
    development costs 94–95, 100
    internal use software, credit for
        109–110
    international transactions 375–380
    legal protection 19
    licenses of 160–161, 197
    misappropriation of trade secret 32,
        36–39
    pre-written computer software
        434–435
    purchase costs 154–155, 157
    readily available software 155
    research credit for 106–110
    sales of computer and data processing
        services 440–442
    sales of computer software 185–197,
        438
    self-created computer software 94–96,
        100
    Uniform Computer Information
        Transactions Act 19
    web applications 19
    website development 433–437,
        443–444
Contingent payments 157, 160, 195–197
Contributions of intellectual property to
    charities 199
    corporations 197–199, 246–247
    partnerships 197–199, 255–256
Controlled Foreign Corporations 349
Copyrights
    acquisition costs 154, 157
    amortization 96–97, 105, 154, 157
    authorship 15
    capital gains and losses (see Capital
        gains and losses)
    capitalization 94–97, 99
    creation costs 95–97, 100–101
    contributions to charity 199
    damages 16
    exclusive rights 15–16
    fair use 16
    fixed in a tangible medium 15
    infringement 15, 31, 32
    international transactions 367–374
    licenses of 29–31, 160–161, 197
    litigation costs 308, 339–343
    originality 22–24
    ownership 15–16, 24, 26
    sales of 185–197
    registration 35
    work made for hire 24–26, 32
Cost sharing arrangements
    accounting requirement 361
    administrative requirements 361,
        398–409
    buy-in and buy-out payments 363
    co-development of intellectual prop-
        erty 359
    controlled participants 360
    documentation requirements 363
    OECD 364–366
    periodic adjustments 362
    reasonably anticipated benefits
        360–361
    share of intellectual property develop-
        ment costs 361
    share of reasonably anticipated bene-
        fits 361
    stock option cost sharing 409–413
    uncontrolled participants 360
Creation costs
    amortization of 105
    computer software 94–96, 100
    copyrights 95–97, 100–101
    domain names 52
    generally 93–104
    patents 95–96, 100
    trademarks 95–96
    trade names 95–96

trade secrets 96
websites 52, 93
web content 52, 93
Damages
  copyright cases 16
  patent cases 12
  tax treatment of damage awards 56–57, 310–311
  tax treatment of damage awards for goodwill-covenant not to compete 311
  trade secret cases 14
  trademark cases 18
Deductions
  advertising costs 58, 94, 100
  amortization 59, 154–160
  capital expenditures 94–97
  charitable contributions 199
  hobby losses 59, 98, 102
  legal expenses (see Intellectual property litigation costs)
  license payments 160–162
  losses 57, 59, 185–186
  personal expenses, nondeductibility of 59
  research and experimental expenditures 99–104
  substantiation of 59
  trade or business expenses 57, 59, 93–99
Deferred payment sales 55–56, 195–197
Depreciation
  intellectual property (see Amortization)
  tangible property 59, 155
Depreciation recapture 194
Dispositions of intellectual property (see Transfers of intellectual property)
Domain names
  Anticybersquatting Consumer Protection Act 42, 47–48
  acquisitions 152
  ICANN 17
  initial interest confusion 43–47
  Internet Protocol 18
  registration costs 52
  top-level domain 18
  second-level domain 18
  metatags 18

web pages 42
Foreign personal holding companies 349
Foreign source income and deductions 354–356
Foreign tax credit 350
Foreign transactions (see International intellectual property transactions)
Hobby losses 59, 98, 102
Imputed interest 196–197
Inbound international transactions 347, 351–354
Income forecast method of depreciation 158–160
Installment sales 55–56, 195–197
Intellectual Property Holding Company
  "business purpose" test 281
  combined corporation franchise tax report 283
  combined reports 279
  disallowance of deduction 249
  dividends received deduction 252
  economic substance 281, 286–287
  formation of IP holding companies 246
  investment companies 259
  investment and holding companies 259, 291
  non-recognition 246, 252
  non-taxable liquidation 252
  ordinary and necessary business expenses 249, 278, 287–290
  passive investments 251
  passive management of intellectual property 245
  phantom 248, 272–275
  sham transaction 249–250 259, 275, 277–278, 283–287
  "solely in exchange for stock" 246
  stock basis and holding period 247
  substantial economic substance 272, 277
  substantial nexus 263–264, 274–75
  transfer-license back 247, 249. 277
  transfer-pricing adjustments 250–251
  tax avoidance 268
Intellectual property litigation costs
  copyright cases 308, 339–343
  defending title 307, 313, 342

origin of the claim 308, 342
patent cases 308, 313–317, 325–329, 334–339, 341
perfecting title 307, 342
trademark cases 309, 317–325, 329–334, 341
unfair competition 309, 320–325
International intellectual property transactions
    assisters-developers 359, 388–397
    cascading royalties 855
    comparable profits method 358
    comparable uncontrolled transaction method 358
    controlled foreign corporation 349
    copyright cases 367–374
    cost sharing arrangements (see Cost sharing arrangements)
    deduction allocation and apportionment rules 356–357
    foreign personal holding companies 349
    foreign tax credit 350
    inbound transactions 347, 351–354
    Joint Committee on Taxation, Description and Analysis of Present-Law Rules Relating to International Taxation 364–367
    legal owner 359, 393–395
    outbound transactions 347–351
    patent cases 374–375, 386–388
    permanent establishment 352, 365, 386–388
    personal holding company 348
    profit split method 358
    section 482 358
    software transactions 375–380
    source rules 354–356
    trademark cases 372–373, 380–386
    transfers to foreign corporation 357–358
    treaties 357
    treaty exceptions 352–353
Internet/E–commerce taxation
    digital Merchant Certificates 445
    digitized music 448–450
    discriminatory taxes 418, 423
    Internet Nondiscrimination Act 417
    Internet Tax Freedom Act 416–417, 421–424
    multiple taxes 417–418, 424
    pre-written computer software 434–435
    sales of computer and data processing services 440–442
    sales of computer software 438
    sales of music delivered electronically over the Internet 448–450
    states' Sales Taxes on Electronic Commerce Transactions 420–421, 452–469
    substantial nexus 419–420, 429–430
    website design and development services 443–444
    website development services 433, 436–437
Know-how
    (see Trade secrets)
Licenses
    contingent serial payments 161
    generally 54, 160–161, 197
    international transactions (see International intellectual property transactions)
Litigation costs
    (see Intellectual property litigation costs)
Loss disallowance rules 57, 185–186
Non-recognition transactions
    transfers to corporations 55, 185, 197–199, 246–247
    transfers to partnerships 55, 185, 197–199, 255–256
    transfers to spouses 185
Outboud international transactions 347–351
Package designs 116, 154
Partnerships
    (see Research and development limited partnerships)
Patents
    actual reduction to practice 11
    acquisitions costs 154, 157
    amortization 96, 105, 154, 157
    business method patents 12
    capitalization of development and acquisition costs 99, 153–154

design patents 12
development costs 95–96, 100
enablement 10
international transactions 374–375, 386–388
internet patents 12
licenses of 160–161, 197
litigation costs 308, 313–317, 325–329, 334–339, 341
nonobviousness 9
novelty 9
patent applications 193
patentable subject matter 20–21
provisional application 11
research credit 106–110
sales of 185–197
transfers to business entities 197–199
transfers to charities 199
utility 9
utility patents 12
Personal holding companies 162
Qualified creative expenses 97
Recapture of depreciation 63, 194
Related party transactions
cost sharing arrangements (see Cost sharing arrangements)
international transactions (see International intellectual property transactions)
loss disallowance under section 267 185–186
section 1239 ordinary income 193–194
Research and development credit
generally 64, 106–110
internal–use computer software 109–110
qualified research defined 106–108
research after commercial production 108
Research and development limited partnerships
at-risk limitations 254
formation of 255–256
generally 253–258
liquidation of 258
operation of 256–257
passive loss limitations 254–255
Research and experimental expenditures
current expense method 103
deferred expense method 102–104
defined 99–100
disqualified expenditures 100–101
generally 99–104
reasonableness of 103
trade or business requirement 101–102
Sales
amount realized 54, 185
amount recognized 55, 185
character of gain or loss (see Capital gains and losses)
contingent payments 54–55, 195–197
generally 54, 185–197
installment sales 54–55, 195–197
international transactions (see International intellectual property transactions)
loss disallowance rules 57, 185–186
nonrecognition provisions 55, 185
recapture of depreciation 63, 194
sale versus license distinction 54, 183–185
trade or business, of 56, 63
Section 197 intangibles
defined 105, 154–156
treated as depreciable property 61, 188, 190, 194
Settlement Proceeds
copyright cases 310
patent cases 310
trademark cases 311
Software
(see Computer software)
Source rules 354–356
Straight-line method of depreciation 157–158
Tax credits 64, 106–110
Tax rates
corporations 60, 162
individuals 60, 162, 186
international transactions (see International intellectual property transactions)
long-term capital gains 60–61, 186
Tax treaties 352–353, 357
Trademarks
acquisitions of 154–156
advertising, building goodwill of 58, 94, 100

amortization 96, 105, 154–157
arbitrary 17, 19, 40, 44
capital gain and loss (see Capital gains and losses)
capitalization 95, 153–154
contingent serial payments 156
damages 18
descriptive 17, 19, 40, 44
development costs 95–96
distinctiveness 16–17, 40, 44
fanciful 17, 19, 40, 44
Federal Trademark Dilution Act 17
generic 17–19, 40
ICANN 17
international transactions 372–373, 380–386
licenses of 156, 160–161, 197
litigation costs 309, 317–325, 329–334, 341
registration costs 95–96
sales of 185–197
secondary meaning 17, 19, 40–41
suggestive 17, 19, 40, 44
trade dress 17
trade names 17
transfers to business entities 197–199
unfair competition 17–18, 39

Trade names
acquired trade names 154–156
amortization 96, 105, 154–157
capital gains and losses (see Capital gains and losses)
capitalization 95, 153–154
contingent serial payments 156
contributions to charity 199
development costs 95–96
international transactions (see International intellectual property transactions)
licenses of 160–161, 197
purchase costs 154–156
sales of 185–197
transfers to business entities 197–199

Trade or business requirement
creation costs, deductibility of 97–99
defined 97–98
hobby, distinguished from 98, 102
ordinary and necessary expenses, deductibility of 97–99
research and experimental expenditures, deductibility of 101–102
research tax credit
section 197 property 154–155

Trade secrets
acquisitions of 154
amortization 96, 105, 154
capitalization 96
capital gain and loss (see Capital gains and losses)
damages 14
development costs 96
injunctive relief 14
licenses of 160–161, 197
misappropriation 13–14, 36–39
sales of 185–197
secrecy 13–14, 37–38
transfers to business entities 197–199
transfers to charities 199
Uniform Trade Secrets Act 13

Transfers of intellectual property
by license 54, 197
by sale 54, 185–197
characterization of gain or loss (see Capital gains and losses)
contingent payment sales 55–56, 195–197
generally 54, 183–199
international transfers (see International intellectual property transactions)
license versus sale distinction 54, 183–185
loss disallowance rules 185–186
nonrecognition provisions 185
recapture of depreciation 194
to charities 199
to corporations 55, 185, 197–199, 246–247
to partnerships 55, 185, 197–199, 255–256
to spouses 185

Uniform capitalization rules 57, 94, 96–97, 99